DATE DUE

			PRINTED IN U.S.A.

JAN 16 2013

THE ASHGATE RESEARCH COMPANION TO HENRY PURCELL

'Dr Herissone has assembled a team of distinguished scholars to produce a companion to Purcell's music for the twenty-first century. The strength of *The Ashgate Research Companion to Henry Purcell* is not just its encyclopaedic summary of Purcell scholarship to date, but the suggestions for potentially rewarding areas for future research. Time and again we read that a topic or an area has "potential as a field for further investigation": this is a strength not a fault of the book. Scholars and students of Purcell and his contemporaries will find this Companion an invaluable reference tool and source of information for years to come.'

– Jonathan Wainwright, University of York, UK

'The fact that so much has been written about Purcell and his music during the last two decades makes *The Ashgate Research Companion to Henry Purcell* a timely publication. But it is much more than timely: it dovetails deft and in-depth syntheses of recent research about Purcell with considerable new insights provided by the authors of the individual chapters. This clever integration brings our early twenty-first-century picture of Purcell into high-definition. Simply put, the Companion expands the list of important writings about Purcell it seeks to chronicle.'

– Robert Shay, University of Missouri, USA

ASHGATE
RESEARCH
COMPANION

The *Ashgate Research Companions* are designed to offer scholars and graduate students a comprehensive and authoritative state-of-the-art review of current research in a particular area. The companions' editors bring together a team of respected and experienced experts to write chapters on the key issues in their speciality, providing a comprehensive reference to the field.

The Ashgate Research Companion to Henry Purcell

Edited by

REBECCA HERISSONE

University of Manchester, UK

ASHGATE

Published by
Ashgate Publishing Limited
Wey Court East
Union Road
Farnham
Surrey GU9 7PT
England

Ashgate Publishing Company
Suite 420
101 Cherry Street
Burlington,
VT 05401–4405
USA

www.ashgate.com

British Library Cataloguing in Publication Data
The Ashgate research companion to Henry Purcell.
    1. Purcell, Henry, 1659–1695 – Criticism and interpretation.
    I. Research companion to Henry Purcell II. Herissone, Rebecca.
    780.9'2–dc23

Library of Congress Cataloging-in-Publication Data
The Ashgate research companion to Henry Purcell / edited by Rebecca Herissone.
    p. cm.
    Includes bibliographical references and index.
    ISBN 978–0–7546–6645–5 (hardcover : alk. paper) – ISBN 978–1–4094–4161–8
    (ebook) 1. Purcell, Henry, 1659–1695 – Criticism and interpretation.
    I. Herissone, Rebecca.
    ML410.P93A83 2011
    780.92–dc23   2011033459

ISBN 9780754666455 (hbk)
ISBN 9781409441618 (ebk)

MIX
Paper from
responsible sources
FSC
www.fsc.org FSC® C018575

Printed and bound in Great Britain by
MPG Books Group, UK

Contents

List of Figures		*vii*
List of Music Examples		*ix*
List of Tables		*xi*
Notes on Contributors		*xiii*
Acknowledgements		*xv*
Abbreviations		*xvii*
1	Introduction *Rebecca Herissone*	1
2	Sources and Transmission *Robert Thompson*	13
3	Understanding Creativity *Alan Howard*	65
4	Performance Practices *Stephen Rose*	115
5	Theatre Culture *Andrew Pinnock*	165
6	Politics, Occasions and Texts *Andrew R. Walkling*	201
7	Society and Disorder *Amanda Eubanks Winkler*	269
8	Performance History and Reception *Rebecca Herissone*	303
Bibliography		353
Index of Purcell's Works		403
General Index		407

List of Figures

3.1   Purcell's alterations in his autograph score of *My Beloved Spake*,   80
        Lbl Add. 30932, fol. 88v. Reproduced by permission of the British
        Library. © The British Library Board; all rights reserved.

List of Music Examples

3.1   *My Beloved Spake,* three problematic variants from Cfm 117:   87
      (a) b. 19; (b) b. 301; (c) b. 307.
3.2   *My Beloved Spake,* three further variants found in both Cfm 117   88
      and KNt MR 2–5.4: (a) b. 41 (bracketed note does not occur in
      Lbl Add. 30932 or Ob T 1031); (b) b. 102 (small staves represent
      readings in Cfm 117 and KNt MR 2–5.4); (c) b. 122 (bracketed
      notes are not found in Lbl Add. 30932 or Ob T 1031).
3.3   *My Beloved Spake,* bb. 135–55.   106
3.4   Imitative materials in *My Beloved Spake,* bb. 146–55: (a) two-part   108
      interlocks; (b) 'skeleton' score showing disposition of these
      materials.

4.1   Henry Purcell, 'Ah me! To many Deaths decreed' (from John   135
      Crowne, *Regulus,* as printed in *Orpheus Britannicus* (1698),
      p. 179), bb. 1–5.
4.2   'Plain Note and Shake': (a) as defined by Purcell; (b) as   142
      emended by Howard Ferguson.
4.3   'Beat': (a) as defined by Purcell; (b) as emended by Howard   142
      Ferguson.
4.4   Purcell, Voluntary for Double Organ, bb. 1–2, with H. Diack   143
      Johnstone's realization of the ornaments.
4.5   Purcell, *A New Ground,* b. 6: (a) ornaments notated in *The Second* 143
      Part of Musick's Hand-maid (1689); (b) ornaments given by Charles
      Babell (Lbl Add. 39569, p. 35).
4.6   Purcell, Keyboard jig transcribed from *Abdelazer,* bb. 1–2:   144
      (a) ornaments notated in *A Choice Collection of Lessons* (1696),
      p. 60; (b) ornaments given by Charles Babell (Lbl Add. 39569, p. 61).
4.7   Plain and ornamented cadences from Pietro Reggio, *The Art of*   146
      Singing or a Treatise, Wherein is Shown How to Sing Well any
      Song Whatsoever (Oxford, 1677), p. 31. 'L' and 'S' denote 'Loud'
      and 'Soft'.
4.8   Purcell, 'Lucinda is Bewitching Fair' (from *Abdelazer*), bb. 1–2   147
      and 16–17. Plain version as published in *Thesaurus Musicus:*
      Being, a Collection of the Newest Songs Performed at His Majesties

Theatres … The Fourth Book (1695), pp. 6–7; ossia ornaments
from the Gresham autograph, Lg Safe 3, fols 66v–67r.

4.9   Purcell, 'Thus the Gloomy World' (from *The Fairy Queen*),   148
bb. 63–4 and 88–91. Plain version as in Lam 3, fol. 87r; ossia
ornaments from the Gresham autograph, Lg Safe 3, fols 4r–5v
(transposed to facilitate comparison).

4.10   Purcell, 'From Silent Shades' (Bess of Bedlam), bb. 1–3 and   149
23–6: (a) ornaments from Lbl Add. 29397, fol. 71r; (b) ornaments
from Elizabeth Segar Songbook, US-NH Osborn 9, fol. 7r.

4.11   Purcell, 'Fairest Isle', bb. 1–4: (a) rhythms as notated in *Orpheus*   152
Britannicus (1698), p. 83; (b) rhythms given in *Apollo's Banquet …*
The Second Book (1691), sig. F1v.

4.12   Purcell, Second Act Tune from *Distress'd Innocence*, bb. 3–5:   153
(a) rhythms as notated in Ob Tenbury 785; (b) rhythms given in
A Collection of Ayres (1697).

4.13   Purcell, *My Heart is Inditing*, bb. 128–9. Violin 1 and Treble 1   154
parts from Purcell's autograph manuscript, Lbl R.M. 20.h.8,
fols 56v–57r.

4.14   Purcell, Sonata 12 in D major, bb. 15–19, from *Sonnata's of III*   161
Parts (1683).

4.15   Purcell, Sonata 7 in E minor, bb. 107–10, from *Sonnata's of III*   163
Parts (1683). Shading denotes melodic dissonance not indicated by the
continuo figuring.

6.1   Comparison of opening note-sequences of Purcell's catch 'Since   238
the Duke is Return'd' and the ballad tune 'Hey Boys, up go We'.

6.2   Comparison of passages from 'To Urania and Caesar Delights   248
without Measure' and 'How Great are the Blessings of
Government Made'.

List of Tables

2.1   Categories of paper used in music manuscripts.   23
2.2   Collation of Henry Purcell, *Sonnata's of III Parts* (London, 1683).   57
2.3   Paper types and watermarks in Pepys 1987–90 copy of Purcell,   59
      Sonnata's of III Parts.
2.4   Position of IHS countermark in three representative folios.   59

6.1   Political catches by or attributed to Purcell.   232
6.2   Purcell's reuse of musical material in *The Gordian Knot Unty'd*   260
      (1690).

Notes on Contributors

Rebecca Herissone is Senior Lecturer in Musicology and Head of Music at the University of Manchester, and a co-editor of *Music & Letters*. She is the author of *Music Theory in Seventeenth-Century England* (Oxford University Press, 2000) and *'To Fill, Forbear, or Adorne': The Organ Accompaniment of Restoration Sacred Music* (Ashgate, 2006). Her article on the scoring of Purcell's *Come ye Sons of Art* won the Westrup Prize for 2007, and she has also written extensively on approaches to composition in late seventeenth-century English music. She has recently completed a four-year research project funded by the Arts and Humanities Research Council; her monograph resulting from the project Musical Creativity in Restoration England is due to be published shortly by Cambridge University Press alongside an interdisciplinary collection of essays, *Concepts of Creativity in Seventeenth-Century England*, which will be published by Boydell and Brewer.

Alan Howard is Lecturer in Musicology at the University of East Anglia, Norwich; he is also reviews editor for *Eighteenth-Century Music*, and one of the General Editors of the Collected Works of John Eccles. His edition of Odes on the Death of Henry Purcell will be published by Stainer & Bell as vol. 5 of the Purcell Society Edition Companion Series, and his book *Contrapuntal Artifice in the Music of Henry Purcell* is in preparation for publication by Cambridge University Press.

Andrew Pinnock is Reader in Musicology, Arts Management and Cultural Policy at the University of Southampton, and Head of Music there. He worked in the Arts Council's Music Department for thirteen years, making public policy before taking a university job and starting to research it. He is a prize-winning cultural economist, a much-published Purcell scholar particularly interested in Purcell's operas, a Purcell production adviser to (among others) the York Early Music Festival and Glyndebourne Productions, and current Honorary Secretary to the Purcell Society.

Stephen Rose is Senior Lecturer in Music at Royal Holloway, University of London. His research focuses on German music between 1550 and 1750, in particular its social contexts, performance practices, and the printing and publishing of music. His book *The Musician in Literature in the Age of Bach* was published by Cambridge University Press in 2011. He is reviews editor of the journal *Early Music*, and he is also active as an organist and harpsichordist. He directs Early Music Online, a project to digitize early printed music from the British Library.

Robert Thompson is Head of English and Assistant Head of Sixth Form at Colfe's School, Lee, South London. He is the author of several articles on seventeenth-century music and its sources, and is one of the compilers of *The Viola da Gamba Society Index of Music for Viols*. In 1995 he was external curator of the British Library's Purcell Tercentenary exhibition 'The Glory of the Temple and the Stage' and subsequently co-authored (with Robert Shay) *Purcell Manuscripts: The Principal Musical Sources*, published by Cambridge University Press in 2000. His Purcell Society edition of the composer's later continuo anthems was published in 2011.

Andrew R. Walkling is Dean's Assistant Professor of Early Modern Studies at Binghamton University (State University of New York). His work incorporates the study of Restoration art, history, literature, music and theatre. He has published a number of articles on Henry Purcell and the political contexts of late seventeenth-century musical drama, and is currently completing a book entitled *Masque and Opera in Restoration England*.

Amanda Eubanks Winkler is Associate Professor and Chair in the Department of Art and Music Histories at Syracuse University. She is the author of *O Let Us Howle Some Heavy Note: Music for Witches, Melancholics and the Mad on the Seventeenth-Century English Stage* (Indiana University Press, 2006), which was a finalist for the American Musicological Society's Lewis Lockwood Award, and *Music for Macbeth* (A-R Editions, 2004). Her articles on English theatre music have appeared in essay collections and journals, including the *Cambridge Opera Journal*, *The Journal of Musicology* and *Musical Quarterly*. She was the recipient of a long-term fellowship at the Folger Shakespeare Library (funded by the National Endowment for the Humanities) and was awarded an Enitiative grant from the Kauffman Foundation to support her teaching initiatives. She is currently one of the General Editors of the Collected Works of John Eccles, a multi-volume set forthcoming with A-R Editions.

Acknowledgements

The editor and contributors would like to thank staff at the following libraries for their assistance in research carried out in the preparation of this book: the Bodleian Library; the British Library; Cambridge University Library; the John Rylands University Library at the University of Manchester; and the Pepys Library, Magdalen College, Cambridge. We would also like to thank Heidi Bishop and the editorial staff at Ashgate for their support and patience during the preparation of this volume.

Abbreviations

Pitch

Pitch is denoted using the Helmholtz pitch system, in which c' denotes middle C.

Manuscript Shelfmarks

Manuscripts are identified using RISM sigla (see below) followed by the library shelfmark; the term 'MS' is omitted.

RISM Sigla

Belgium

B-Bc   Brussels, Conservatoire Royal, Bibliothèque, Koninklijk Conservatorium, Bibliotheek

France

F-Pn   Paris, Bibliothèque Nationale de France

Great Britain ('GB' is omitted)

Bu   Birmingham, Birmingham University
CA   Canterbury, Cathedral Library
Cfm   Cambridge, Fitzwilliam Museum
Cjc   Cambridge, St John's College
Ckc   Cambridge, King's College, Rowe Music Library
Cmc   Cambridge, Magdalene College, Pepys Library
Ctc   Cambridge, Trinity College, Library
Cu   Cambridge, University Library
DRc   Durham, Cathedral Church, Dean and Chapter Library
En   Edinburgh, National Library of Scotland, Music Department
H   Hereford, Cathedral Library
KNt   Knutsford, Tatton Park

Lam	London, Royal Academy of Music, Library
Lbl	London, British Library
Lcm	London, Royal College of Music, Library
Lg	London, Guildhall Library
Ll	Lincoln, Cathedral Library
Mp	Manchester, Central Library, Henry Watson Music Library
Ob	Oxford, Bodleian Library
Och	Oxford, Christ Church Library
Ooc	Oxford, Oriel College Library
WO	Worcester, Cathedral Library
Y	York, Minster Library

Japan

J-Tn	Tokyo, Nanki Ongaku Bunko

United States of America

US-AUS	Austin, University of Texas at Austin, The Harry Ransom Humanities Research Center
US-LAuc	Los Angeles, University of California, William Andrews Clark Memorial Library
US-NH	New Haven (CT), Yale University, Irving S. Gilmore Music Library
US-NHub	New Haven (CT), Yale University, Beinecke Rare Book and Manuscript Library
US-NYp	New York, Public Library at Lincoln Center, Music Division
US-R	Rochester, Eastman School of Music, Sibley Music Library
US-Ws	Washington, Folger Shakespeare Library

Introduction

Rebecca Herissone

If there was one thing about the tercentenary of Purcell's death on which reviewers were agreed, it was that the 1995 anniversary spawned an abundance of publications on the composer.[1] While these were very broad-ranging – both in terms of their intended readership and of their quality – they included a substantial amount of genuinely new research, which not only significantly changed our understanding of Purcell and his music, but has also shaped much of the subsequent work carried out in the field. The tercentenary understandably provoked a good deal of reflection on the state of Purcell scholarship, which was largely optimistic in tone, but nevertheless showed an awareness that the field had not been especially well served in previous decades and that much remained to be done. Writing in the Introduction to *Performing the Music of Henry Purcell*, for example, Nicholas Kenyon recalled the words of Vaughan Williams, penned in 1951 – 'We all pay lip service to Henry Purcell, but what do we really know of him?' – and lamented 'More than forty years on, are we much the wiser?';[2] and Peter Holman was able to note enthusiastically that Purcell scholarship was 'on the move after a fallow period', but nevertheless cautioned that there was 'a pressing need at the moment for informed and up-to-date writing on his music'.[3]

---

1   See, for example, Robert Shay's review of Michael Burden (ed.), *The Purcell Companion* (London: Faber, 1995; Portland, OR: Amadeus Press, 1995), in *Notes* Series 2/54 (1997–98): 69; Mark Radice's review of Peter Holman, *Henry Purcell*, Oxford Studies of Composers (Oxford: Oxford University Press, 1994), Michael Burden, *Purcell Remembered* (London and Boston: Faber, 1995), and Curtis Price (ed.), *Purcell Studies* (Cambridge: Cambridge University Press, 1995), in *Notes* Series 2/53 (1996–97): 791; Richard Semmens's review of Curtis Price (ed.), *Purcell Studies* (Cambridge: Cambridge University Press, 1995), in *Music & Letters* 78 (1997): 107–8; and my own review of Martin Adams, *Henry Purcell: The Origins and Development of his Musical Style* (Cambridge: Cambridge University Press, 1995), in *Early Music History* 15 (1996): 270.

2   Nicholas Kenyon, 'Henry Purcell: Towards a Tercentenary', in Michael Burden (ed.), *Performing the Music of Henry Purcell* (Oxford: Clarendon, 1996), p. 1.

3   Peter Holman, *Henry Purcell*, Oxford Studies of Composers (Oxford: Oxford University Press, 1994), pp. vii–viii.

The scholarly books, compendia, journal issues[4] and articles that were published around the year of the anniversary were significant in two different ways: they addressed some glaring omissions in the existing literature, and in some cases they also helped firmly to move Purcell scholarship beyond the narrow frame of reference on which it had often concentrated – a traditional approach that had already begun to look seriously dated by the mid-1990s in the light of the major shifts occurring in musicology as a whole at the time. Curtis Price saw *Purcell Studies* particularly in terms of the former function, as an opportunity to fill 'a perceived gap' in aspects of Purcell research he felt 'lag[ged] behind that into the music of other Baroque composers of similar stature'.[5] The book was important for bringing into the public domain ongoing research by Robert Thompson and Robert Shay into the codicology of Purcell's autograph manuscripts, the changing nature of Purcell's handwriting, and relationships between his autographs and other major primary sources of Restoration music – work that was published in full in their groundbreaking book published in 2000, *Purcell Manuscripts: The Principal Musical Sources*, and that has transformed our knowledge both of the dating of many of his works and of the transmission of music in the circles in which he moved.[6] Several chapters also revealed emerging approaches to understanding Purcell's creative processes: alongside my own preliminary account of the evidence of his revision techniques preserved in his autographs were three notable contributions – Shay's essay and Bruce Wood's '"Only Purcell e're shall equal Blow"' both began to consider in depth Purcell's use of compositional models, and Katherine Rohrer's important essay on relationships between poetic and musical metre opened up a new way of thinking about preliminary creative choices Purcell made when composing his vocal music.[7] Ellen Harris's chapter on eighteenth-century performances of

---

4   Issue 4 of *Early Music* vol. 23, and vol. 5 of the French journal *Ostinato rigore: revue internationale d'études musicale*, both published in 1995, were special issues devoted wholly or primarily to Purcell.

5   Curtis Price, 'Preface', in Curtis Price (ed.), *Purcell Studies* (Cambridge: Cambridge University Press, 1995), p. xi.

6   Robert Thompson, 'Purcell's Great Autographs', in Curtis Price (ed.), *Purcell Studies* (Cambridge: Cambridge University Press, 1995), pp. 6–34; Robert Shay, 'Purcell as Collector of "Ancient" Music: Fitzwilliam MS 88', in Curtis Price (ed.), *Purcell Studies* (Cambridge: Cambridge University Press, 1995), pp. 35–50; Robert Shay and Robert Thompson, *Purcell Manuscripts: The Principal Musical Sources* (Cambridge: Cambridge University Press, 2000). Thompson's 'The Sources of Purcell's Fantasias', *Chelys* 25 (1996–97): 88–96 was another early article demonstrating the importance of viewing sources of Restoration pieces not just from the perspective of filiation and critical editing, but also as a source of information on paths of transmission and the nature of scribal communities in the period.

7   Rebecca Herissone, 'Purcell's Revisions of his Own Works', in Curtis Price (ed.), *Purcell Studies* (Cambridge: Cambridge University Press, 1995), pp. 51–86; Bruce Wood, 'Only Purcell e're shall equal Blow', in Curtis Price (ed.), *Purcell Studies* (Cambridge: Cambridge University Press, 1995), pp. 106–44; Katherine T. Rohrer, 'Poetic Metre, Musical Metre, and the Dance in Purcell's Songs', in Curtis Price (ed.), *Purcell Studies*

King Arthur, meanwhile, became only the second substantial investigation of the reception of Purcell's works;[8] and Margaret Laurie's investigation of the possibility that Purcell intended proportional or quasi-proportional relationships between metres in many of his multi-section works was one of the first pieces of research to address issues of performance practice specific to the composer.[9]

Laurie's chapter in fact appeared almost contemporaneously with Andrew Parrott's thoughtful overview of the subject in *The Purcell Companion,*[10] and the much more substantial contribution to this area of research, *Performing the Music of Henry Purcell,* which grew out of a 1993 conference in Oxford. The latter book included systematic and detailed investigations of the instrumental and vocal performing resources that would have been available to Purcell, of technical issues affecting particular instruments and repertories, and of interpretative challenges in specific pieces; in addition, it brought into the realm of Purcell scholarship research on multimedia elements of the dramatick operas – dance, costume and staging – that had previously been considered only rarely by musicologists working in the field. As Stephen Rose and Andrew Pinnock note in Chapters 4 and 5 below, these studies collectively revolutionized our understanding of historically informed performance of Purcell's music, and of the context of his theatre music.

Some of the new contributions were additions to traditional areas of research for Purcell scholars: the fortuitous discovery of a major new autograph manuscript of the composer's keyboard music in the early 1990s, for example, led to a series of articles describing the source and its music,[11] in some respects very similar to those by scholars such as Watkins Shaw and Bruce Wood that had grown up from the time of an earlier anniversary – the tercentenary of Purcell's birth in 1959 – onwards, although with clear hints of the more forensic approach associated with Shay and Thompson, which was already proving influential. But other publications

---

(Cambridge: Cambridge University Press, 1995), pp. 207–42.

8   Ellen T. Harris, '*King Arthur*'s Journey into the Eighteenth Century', in Curtis Price (ed.), *Purcell Studies* (Cambridge: Cambridge University Press, 1995), pp. 257–89. It was preceded by Richard Luckett's 1983 essay, '"Or Rather Our Musical Shakspeare": Charles Burney's Purcell', in Christopher Hogwood and Richard Luckett (eds), *Music in Eighteenth-Century England: Essays in Memory of Charles Cudworth* (Cambridge: Cambridge University Press, 1983), pp. 59–77. During the tercentenary period Michael Burden also produced an essay and an article that helped to open up the performance history of Purcell's operas. See Michael Burden, '"Gallimaufry at Covent Garden": Purcell's *The Fairy Queen* in 1946', *Early Music* 23 (1995): 268–84; and Burden, 'Purcell Debauch'd: The Dramatick Operas in Performance', in Michael Burden (ed.) *Performing the Music of Henry Purcell* (Oxford: Clarendon, 1996), pp. 145–62. All these publications are considered in detail in Chapter 8 below.

9   A. Margaret Laurie, 'Continuity and Tempo in Purcell's Vocal Works', in Curtis Price (ed.), *Purcell Studies* (Cambridge: Cambridge University Press, 1995), pp. 192–206.

10   Andrew Parrott, 'Performing Purcell', in Michael Burden (ed.), *The Purcell Companion* (London: Faber, 1995; Portland, OR: Amadeus Press, 1995), pp. 387–444.

11   For a list of the articles reporting the discovery and assessing the manuscript, see Chapter 2, n. 36 below.

established methodologies that more explicitly helped Purcell scholarship move into new areas, and particularly to develop more closely contextualized interpretations that took into account a host of extra-musical factors and that were less inclined to treat the composer in isolation from his contemporaries. Alongside the essays in *Purcell Studies* and *Performing the Music of Henry Purcell* highlighted above, Peter Holman's new overview of the composer, *Henry Purcell*, was especially significant in this latter respect: it was the first general study of the composer's works to provide a perspective on Purcell that did not just grow out of a detailed knowledge of his own music, but that also interpreted these materials within the wider perspective of the cosmopolitan musical communities in which he worked and lived. Holman's stated principal aim, indeed, was 'to establish a credible context for the various genres to which Purcell contributed',[12] which included consideration of political, economic, social and musical factors that affected the composer's output, leading Holman to identify numerous composers and works that acted as Purcell's models throughout his career and that helped to shape his own compositional style. Like other volumes in the series Oxford Studies of Composers, the book was aimed at a general readership, but for scholars of Restoration music it laid the foundation for the more strongly contextualized interpretation that has characterized Purcell scholarship since that time. To a lesser extent the opening chapters of *The Purcell Companion* – which Robert Shay interpreted as having tried 'to place Purcell within the musical scene that was Restoration England, in a real sense to take him off his pedestal' – achieved some of the same ideals.[13] Even the famous debate that had grown up around the likely date of the premier of *Dido and Aeneas* following Wood and Pinnock's article of 1992,[14] led to a more thorough contemplation of the nature of hidden meanings in contemporary texts used in Restoration music than had previously existed.[15]

In the years since 1995 – a period that has in fact seen another anniversary in 2009, although (perhaps because of its proximity to the tercentenary) this did not result in a major outpouring of new publications – Purcell scholarship has

---

12   Holman, *Henry Purcell*, p. viii.

13   Shay, review of Burden (ed.), *The Purcell Companion*: 70.

14   Bruce Wood and Andrew Pinnock, '"Unscarr'd by Turning Times"? The Dating of Purcell's *Dido and Aeneas*', *Early Music* 20 (1992): 372–90; John Buttrey, 'The Dating of *Dido*' (Correspondence), *Early Music* 20 (1992): 703; Martin Adams, 'More on Dating *Dido*' (Correspondence), *Early Music* 21 (1993): 510; Curtis Price, '*Dido and Aeneas*: Questions of Style and Evidence', *Early Music* 22 (1994): 115–25; Bruce Wood and Andrew Pinnock, '"Singin' in the Rain": Yet More on Dating *Dido*' (Correspondence), *Early Music* 22 (1994): 365–7; Andrew Walkling, '"The Dating of Purcell's *Dido and Aeneas*"?: a reply to Bruce Wood and Andrew Pinnock', *Early Music* 22 (1994): 469–81; Bruce Wood and Andrew Pinnock, 'Not Known at this Address: More on the Dating of *Dido*' (Correspondence), *Early Music* 23 (1995): 188–9.

15   For example in Andrew R. Walkling, 'Political Allegory in Purcell's "Dido and Aeneas"', *Music & Letters* 76 (1995): 540–71; and Walkling, 'Performance and Political Allegory in Restoration England: What to Interpret and When', in Michael Burden (ed.), *Performing the Music of Henry Purcell* (Oxford: Clarendon, 1996), pp. 163–79.

profited greatly from this broadening of approaches, and has also begun to move in new directions, many of them interdisciplinary. The aim of *The Ashgate Research Companion to Henry Purcell* is to provide a comprehensive review of current research in the field, together with reflection on both the state of existing research and areas that remain largely overlooked but that have the potential to contribute significantly to our understanding of the composer and his music. Because of the transformative nature of the tercentenary publications, several chapters take the mid-1990s as their starting point, but a much fuller body of Purcell scholarship is encompassed within the book as a whole, the intention being to place the current state of research in the field in context as far as possible.

In a titular sense, this research companion relates both to Faber's *Purcell Companion* of 1995, and to Franklin B. Zimmerman's 1989 Garland resource manual, *Henry Purcell: A Guide to Research*.[16] Its contents, however, bear little comparison to either volume. Zimmerman's research guide – despite the promise of having been compiled by one of the foremost figures in the vanguard of Purcell scholarship, whose 1967 *Analytical Catalogue* remains an indispensable, if dated, reference tool – was generally regarded as 'a missed opportunity'.[17] Its contents were a curious mixture, comprising two lists of works (one organized by genre like the *Analytical Catalogue*, the other incorporated within a 'Selective List of Editions'); a short biography of the composer; reproductions of the prefatory material in seventeenth-century printed editions that included Purcell's music; a short list of works 'modelled after Purcell's compositions'; and a selective bibliography of secondary literature on the composer with brief annotations. As with the other Garland guides, the bibliography and its commentary formed the most substantial part of the book, but its relatively incomplete nature – one reviewer identified more than fifty important items that had been excluded or overlooked[18] – and at times the rather personal and cursory style of the annotations rendered this resource less useful than might have been hoped. Obviously Zimmerman's guide is also now seriously outdated, but the present volume has not been designed in order merely to reflect its aims for more recent research: instead of commenting systematically on individual items in the secondary literature, it concentrates on analysis of seven over-arching themes detectable in research involving or pertinent to Purcell, with the intention of assessing the impact of the scholarship on current understanding of the composer, and the potential application of such research in future projects.

Similarities with *The Purcell Companion* are even more slight, since Burden's collection was aimed at a student or general readership and – apart from the opening

---

16   Franklin B. Zimmerman, *Henry Purcell: A Guide to Research*, Garland Composer Resource Manuals, vol. 18 (New York and London: Garland, 1989).

17   Curtis Price, Review of Franklin B. Zimmerman, *Henry Purcell: A Guide to Research*, Garland Composer Resource Manuals, vol. 18 (New York and London: Garland, 1989), in *Early Music* 17 (1989): 577; see also the similar comments in Robert Manning's review in *Music & Letters* 71 (1990): 552–4; and in Robert Ford's review in *Journal of Musicological Research*, 10 (1991): 283–5.

18   Manning, Review of Zimmerman, *Henry Purcell: A Guide to Research*: 553.

section mentioned above – was designed to give an overview of Purcell's works in a similar way to Holman's book, although with less consistency of purpose.[19] Nevertheless, the two *Companions* do share a focus on Purcell as a single composer, a concept that has arguably become contentious for musicologists working on early music in the years since Burden's compendium was published. In today's scholarly climate, the idea of devoting a volume such as this to an individual – one who may have gained canonical status since his death, but who was writing at a time when there was no developed concept of the composer as artist, individual or genius – might seem old-fashioned or inappropriate. Yet precisely because it remains the case that the music of the Restoration period is still accessed primarily through the activities of its most famous exponent, a composer companion focusing on Purcell is a crucial tool through which we can try to develop a more rounded view of the environment in which Purcell lived, the people with whom he worked, the social conditions that influenced his activities, and the ways in which our modern perception of him has been affected by reception of his music after his death. In this sense it does not privilege the individual over the environment: rather it uses the modern reader's familiarity with Purcell's music as a gateway into the broader Restoration world. Consequently, the book does not comprise a traditional series of chapters focusing on genres, or periods of the composer's life. Rather it takes as its starting point a variety of approaches to understanding Purcell and his music that have developed for the most part since the early 1990s, and that seem likely to be influential to the direction of future research in the field. The emphasis is therefore on the impact or potential impact of methodologies that can be applied to late seventeenth-century English music generally, rather than to Purcell's music in particular.

The seven themes into which the book has been divided are intended to incorporate within them commentary on the significance of as much as possible of the recent research on Purcell and his contemporaries, as well as to reflect on approaches to understanding their music that have thus far been explored to only a limited extent. Naturally, this material could have been considered in any number of different ways, and no doubt some might disagree with the emphases brought out by the structure as it has been devised. Nevertheless, I believe that the topics are representative of the directions in which research on Restoration music has been moving in recent years, something that is supported by the broad correlation between many of the themes covered here and those adopted by Peter Holman in the recent Ashgate volume on Purcell in the series The Baroque Composers,[20] which reprints a cross-section of the most important articles and essays published

---

19   In reviewing the volume, Martin Adams commented that it had an 'insouciant mix of methods and emphases', and noted that, although the book did not claim to be comprehensive, it was 'strange' that there was no chapter on Purcell's vocal music. See Martin Adams, Review of Michael Burden (ed.), *The Purcell Companion* (London: Faber, 1995; Portland, OR: Amadeus Press, 1995), in *Music & Letters* 77 (1996): 264–5.

20   Peter Holman (ed.), *Purcell*, The Baroque Composers (Farnham: Ashgate, 2010).

on the composer in recent decades – virtually all of which are examined within the *Ashgate Research Companion*.

The chapters that follow begin with three that investigate different approaches to understanding Purcell's music: how forensic analysis of the contemporary manuscripts and printed sources in which his music was notated informs us both about the music itself and about the musical community in which he worked; how both these sources and newly developing analytical techniques can give us insights into creative practices in the period; and how our knowledge of the sources together with a host of other written and pictorial evidence has begun to influence historically informed performance practices in modern times. Chapters 5–7 take as their points of departure primarily extra-musical perspectives: how the multimedia culture of the theatre in Purcell's day influences our understanding of his theatre music; how the political climate and pervasive literary habit of incorporating hidden meaning into texts leads us to need to reassess the contexts in which much of his music was composed; and how the themes and characterization of his vocal music reflects the social undercurrents of his day. The final chapter serves to highlight some of the contrasts between these heavily contextualized ways of understanding Purcell's music through the times in which he lived and many of the pervasive views of the composer still prevalent today, by identifying how modern perceptions have been influenced by the reception of Purcell and his music in the centuries after his death.

Robert Thompson begins by assessing the major changes that have occurred in our understanding of sources of Purcell's music, based on research in which he himself has played a substantial part and that has advanced our knowledge of the dating of Purcell's works and of the contexts in which Restoration sources were produced and used. Since interest in Purcell's autographs began in the eighteenth century, the history of research in this field is closely allied with the growth of musical antiquarianism, and Thompson therefore outlines a history for source studies of Purcell's music that dates back beyond even the bicentenary of 1895. What has changed in more recent times, however, is the gradual increase in contextualization, and in particular the incorporation of codicological studies among the techniques use to assess the sources. Thompson outlines and assesses the related methodologies that are being applied to manuscripts of this period – including detailed information on techniques used for analysing paper types, watermarks, rastrology, collation, binding and handwriting – investigates their continuing significance to research on Restoration music manuscripts and understanding of their contents, and considers prospects for future research, such as the creation of databases to enhance the value of this sort of technique. He then assesses in detail the way in which his and Robert Shay's codicological research into Purcell's sources has stimulated new perspectives on the purposes for which manuscripts were created, which, in turn, leads him to consider the role codicology can play in enhancing understanding of creative activity and the working lives of musicians in Purcell's day. Finally, he considers for the first time the application of codicology to research into printed music in the period, revealing some surprisingly significant results from his own preliminary investigations on this topic that suggest there is much to be learned from this kind of research.

In Chapter 3, Alan Howard assesses how our conception of Purcell's approaches to composition has changed in the last decade, partly in response to the technical and perceptual developments outlined in Chapter 2, and partly due to enhanced understanding of the theoretical contexts in which his music was being produced. He begins by considering how what he terms 'palaeographical' methods of researching approaches to creativity in the period through study of the primary sources have changed focus in recent years. In moving from what were arguably problematical origins – in the methodology of 'sketch studies' first developed for much later music – towards an approach much more heavily embedded in the creative contexts of the time, such research now focuses on techniques that take into account the purposes for which sources were copied, the relationships between autograph and non-autograph sources, and the often flexible approach to notation, which frequently renders traditional notions of progression towards a final 'definitive' version of a piece inappropriate. In the latter part of the chapter he turns to recent analytical research on Purcell's music that has used historically sensitive methodologies in order to uncover some of the preliminary creative decisions that must have been made by composers, even though they cannot be rediscovered directly in notation; in turn these help us to understand Purcell's music more clearly in terms of the aesthetic priorities and theoretical principles of his day.

Chapter 4 focuses on the more familiar area of performance practice, taking as its point of departure the important work published in the mid-1990s mentioned above. Probably the most significant message of the explosion of literature on the topic in that period was that a wide variation in practices not only separated interpretations appropriate to Purcell's England from those that might be adopted for later Baroque music or other locations, but also distinguished approaches taken when playing music for different instruments or in different genres or that was written for different locations within Restoration repertory itself. Stephen Rose gives an overview of ways in which recent research highlighting these sorts of distinctions has begun to inform interpretation of the music of Purcell and his contemporaries, and also assesses their application in a wide range of historically informed recordings. In the process, he identifies a number of areas where knowledge remains markedly incomplete – including issues of vocal technique and vocal ornamentation – and reveals the importance of considering both the multicultural influences on the professional musical communities working in and around London and the prevailing culture of adaptability, equally detectable in the attitudes to creativity outlined in Chapter 3, when seeking to understand such performance practices.

Chapter 5 provides an introduction to research on the theatre environment in which Purcell worked in the latter part of his career, and how this milieu can inform us about the composer and his music. Concentrating particularly on the multimedia extravaganzas – in this book referred to by the term coined by John Dryden for *King Arthur* in 1691, 'dramatick operas'[21] – it takes as its starting point the daunting

---

21   There is as yet no complete consensus among Purcell scholars about terminology for Purcell's part-sung, part-spoken public operas. In Purcell's own day, as well as

range of reference materials on the London stage that began to be produced in the early part of the nineteenth century, cataloguing a vast array of documents on theatre productions, plays, actors, managers, publicity and comment relevant to the Restoration. Andrew Pinnock then moves on to consider three specific aspects of the theatre world: its commercial foundation, the theatre as a physical space, and the theatre as a centre for musical production. While knowledge of the last of these is founded on research and editions that will be familiar to musicologists working on the seventeenth century, Pinnock demonstrates the profound significance to the development of music in the theatre – and in particular the dramatick-opera form – of the financial circumstances of the London theatre companies; he also illustrates how research on the physical construction of the theatres can inform our understanding of how musicians participated in dramatic productions in the period. Finally he considers how current research trends have begun to move attention away from a Purcell-centred approach to one in which the composer is seen as a full participant in the rich and complex multimedia environment of the London stage.

The focus shifts in Chapter 6 to interpretations that embed Purcell's music even more deeply within its cultural surroundings, here by considering the composer's output from a political perspective, within the prevailing ethos of propaganda and allegory that governed the expectations and interpretations of audiences throughout the period. Scholarship on Purcell's music has hitherto considered such issues almost exclusively in terms of his dramatic music, and Andrew Walkling

---

'dramatick opera', the genre was sometimes referred to simply as 'opera' (as in Matthew Locke's provocative title for his publication of the vocal music from *Psyche* in 1675, '*The English Opera*'). It was only later, in his first *Musicall Grammarian* of *c.*1726, that Roger North – writing from the perspective of one enamoured by the Italian all-sung opera that had since flooded the English stage – described English operas with the pejorative terms 'ambigue entertainments' and 'semi-operas' (see John Wilson (ed.), *Roger North on Music: Being a Selection from his Essays Written during the Years c.1695–1728* (London: Novello, 1959), pp. 306–7 and, for the 1728 version, ibid., pp. 353–4, and Mary Chan and Jamie C. Kassler (eds), *Roger North's The Musicall Grammarian 1728*, Cambridge Studies in Music (Cambridge: Cambridge University Press, 1990), pp. 215 and 266–7). In opting for the use of 'dramatick opera', I follow the argument first articulated by Richard Luckett that North's 'critical rather than descriptive' terms are best avoided in favour of terminology that existed when the genre was still active, and extremely popular. See Richard Luckett, 'Exotick but Rational Entertainments: The English Dramatick Operas', in Marie Axton and Raymond Williams (eds), *English Drama: Forms and Development – Essays in Honour of Muriel Clara Bradbrook* (Cambridge, London and New York: Cambridge University Press, 1977), p. 125. Michael Burden has since put forward a similar defence in 'Aspects of Purcell's Operas', in Michael Burden (ed.), *Henry Purcell's Operas: The Complete Texts* (Oxford and New York: Oxford University Press, 2000), p. 3, n. 1. Roger Savage raises a different, but equally notable, objection to North's terms by pointing out that North's extreme sensitivity to music may account for his objection to the spoken parts of dramatick opera; see Roger Savage, 'Calling Up Genius: Purcell, Roger North, and Charlotte Butler', in Michael Burden (ed.), *Performing the Music of Henry Purcell* (Oxford: Clarendon, 1996), pp. 216–17.

gives a comprehensive assessment of what the long-running debates about possible symbolic meaning in *Dido and Aeneas* and the interpretations that have been attached to several of the dramatick operas and plays produced in the public theatres have revealed. But he also investigates the potential for research that takes seriously the political contexts of other parts of Purcell's output, both in the public domain – such as in some of his catches – and in his court music – including his odes and welcome songs, much of his sacred music and a small number of songs that appear to have had courtly origins. In arguing for a more complete assessment of symbolism in the texts of Purcell's music for voices, Walkling highlights the way in which Purcell's music was enmeshed within the turbulent and highly politicized times in which he lived. While it is clearly important to consider carefully the extent to which Purcell's own contribution could have been politicized, Walkling also notes the potential significance of Purcell's re-use of his own musical material in a number of politically sensitive contexts, and even the character of some of his more personal compositions, which suggests that it might be misleading to suggest that Purcell himself stood entirely apart from the political contexts in which he worked.

Paired with Walkling's chapter, Amanda Eubanks Winkler's contribution to the *Companion* explores interdisciplinary research in a different way, by focusing on the impact studying some of the social conditions in which Purcell lived and worked can have on our understanding of his music and the contexts in which it was created and performed. She considers first the complex and changing perspectives on gender in the period and how the incorporation of women onto the public stage at the Restoration brought to the fore prevailing conceptions relating to their sexual and moral identities. She then turns to consider how Purcell's theatrical music and songs – most notably his mad songs and laments – reflect prevailing views of the physical afflictions of 'love melancholy' (or 'erotomania') and various forms of madness in the period, including those caused by love itself and by religious enthusiasm. Beliefs about such disorders were again heavily conditioned by gendered modes of behaviour that can be detected in the approaches of both dramatists and composers such as Purcell. Distinctions were also made between male and female practitioners of witchcraft in the period – Winkler's third main focus in the chapter – but she argues that the figure of the witch in Restoration theatre was in fact influenced by a multiplicity of factors, including not only gender and domesticity, but also religion and politics. While such interdisciplinary approaches have been explored in depth in many studies of *Dido and Aeneas*, Winkler highlights the relative paucity of similar scholarly investigations of other parts of Purcell's output, suggesting that much work remains to be done if we are to be able to view his music as a whole within the context of larger cultural discourse in the period.

The final chapter of the *Companion* concentrates on performance history and posthumous reception of Purcell and his music, an aspect of research on the composer that has not previously been considered in a comprehensive way, despite its significant impact on the ways in which interest in and knowledge of Purcell has been shaped over time. I begin by considering a number of mostly extra-musical factors that appear to have contributed to the emergence of Purcell as the dominant figure of Restoration music in the period following his death. Most relate to the way in which his career developed in the last five years or so of his life, which led to a developing posthumous view of the composer that was not fully representative of his output as a whole – being dominated by his theatre music and songs – but that was ripe for cultivation by eighteenth-century commentators for particular musical-political purposes. The second part of the chapter assesses the complex and developing image of Purcell towards the end of the eighteenth century, when tensions emerged between a growing antiquarian appreciation for the composer as a canonical figure and prevailing views of the importance of progress in music, resulting in contradictions that can be detected both in performances of his works and in writings about his music, most famously the accounts of Burney and Hawkins. In the last sections of the chapter, I investigate a range of attempts to elevate Purcell to the status of national representative of English music, particularly by figures central to the so-called English Musical Renaissance of the late nineteenth and early twentieth centuries. Ultimately these efforts were mostly made by a small number of enthusiasts involved in multiple activities – including editing music, arranging performances and mounting anniversary commemorations – and they were designed primarily to promote the cause of modern music. Yet the image of Purcell that began to be cultivated during this period has had a lasting legacy for the composer's reception today – one that continues to be highly influential to popular perceptions of the composer's importance, but on which research remains in its infancy.

Taken as a whole, *The Research Companion to Henry Purcell* aims to provide a thorough analysis of a wide range of methodologies that inform current research on late seventeenth-century English music, or that have the potential to do so; while these approaches are seen from the perspective of scholarship on Purcell, they are intended to reach far beyond the composer as an isolated figure to encompass many aspects of his wider environment. Such reflection on the ways in which we can and do approach study of Purcell and his contemporaries has never previously been carried out in such a comprehensive way. It reveals a field ripe for new discoveries. I hope, therefore, that this book will stimulate both existing Purcell scholars, and those newly entering the field, to investigate some of the many unexplored areas of research revealed by the contributors to the *Companion*, and that the result will provide us with a whole range of new perspectives on the composer and his world.

Sources and Transmission

Robert Thompson

After Purcell's death in 1695 his autograph manuscripts began their slow transformation from everyday working material to precious cultural artefacts, an evolution that naturally made them objects of acquisitive antiquarian interest and, in due course, of critical scholarship. Recognition of the autographs' intrinsic value appears to have been almost immediate and, paradoxically, to have been sustained throughout a period when their textual readings were sometimes adapted to conform to eighteenth-century musical taste. Of the three major autograph scores to have survived into modern times, Cfm 88 belonged in 1728 to Bernard Gates, who became Master of the Children at the Chapel Royal in 1727, Lbl R.M. 20.h.8 clearly remained in the Purcell family, and – while the provenance of the third large manuscript, Lbl Add. 30930, cannot be traced back further than Philip Hayes's ownership in the mid-eighteenth century – it is likely that any significant excisions from it were made in Purcell's lifetime and that thereafter it too was carefully preserved.[1]

In addition, a number of originally separate, unbound scores of Purcell's music survived into the eighteenth century and came to be of interest to later musicians and antiquarians. Only one, the autograph of *Of Old, when Heroes thought it Base*, now forms a discrete volume, Lbl Egerton 2956, the others being incorporated in guard-books such as Ob Mus.c.26, Lbl Add. 30934 and Bu 5001. The last of these belonged in the eighteenth century to John Barker, who was trained as a chorister in the Chapel Royal and became organist of Holy Trinity Church, Coventry, in 1731;[2] in that year he signed and dated the back cover of Bu 5001, which must therefore have been bound as one volume by then but in fact mainly consists of a collection of

---

1   For a detailed account of the known provenance and early history of these three manuscripts see Robert Shay and Robert Thompson, *Purcell Manuscripts: The Principal Musical Sources* (Cambridge: Cambridge University Press, 2000), pp. 33–47 (Cfm 88), 84–100 (Lbl Add. 30930) and 126–35 (Lbl R.M. 20.h.8).

2   Ibid., p. 143. A possible connection between Bu 5001 and Stanford Hall, Stanford-on-Avon, is explored in Nigel Fortune with Iain Fenlon, 'Music Manuscripts of John Browne (1608–91) and from Stanford Hall, Leicestershire', in Ian Bent (ed.), *Source Materials and the Interpretation of Music: a Memorial Volume to Thurston Dart* (London: Stainer and Bell, 1981), p. 163, n. 167.

originally separate autograph scores by Chapel Royal composers including Cooke, Humfrey and Blow as well as Purcell.[3] As the volume contains no earlier evidence of ownership it is a reasonable inference that Barker had the separate manuscripts bound together, as Shaw suggested,[4] although of course they may previously have been formed into a discrete collection by a senior member of the Chapel Royal; in either case, Bu 5001 provides evidence of selective, purposeful collecting, as do the organ parts now incorporated in Cfm 152, which were extracted from one or more Chapel Royal organ-books and include autograph copies by Humphrey, Blow, Purcell and Croft (discussed below).

Perhaps the most important eighteenth-century collector, however, was William Flackton (1709–98), who assembled the material now in Lbl Add. 30931–3.[5] Flackton was ideally equipped to contribute to what might be considered the first steps in the critical evaluation of source material. In his professional life he became a highly distinguished bookseller in Canterbury, with recognized expertise in antiquarian collections; from 1718 to 1726, however, he had been a choirboy at Canterbury Cathedral, later serving for some years as organist of the major parish church in nearby Faversham and establishing a considerable reputation as a composer. He assembled a wide variety of manuscripts, many clearly acquired from his Canterbury musical circle,[6] and his annotations identifying Purcell's copying from different periods of his career have stood the test of time. Towards the end of the eighteenth century Flackton collaborated with Philip Hayes, who transcribed a number of anthems from his collection; consequently, it is impossible to be certain how much the latter contributed to the correct attribution of Purcell's hand, but it is clear that both Hayes and Flackton were scrupulous and methodical in their identification of autographs. At the end of *Out of the Deep*, for example (Lbl Add. 30931 fols 67r–70v), Flackton first wrote 'This is an Original of Mr Purcells own hand writing' but then corrected his comment to express an element of doubt, while acknowledging that 'two different papers & also different pens & wrote at divers times may make a seeming difference in any mans hand writeing'. The final annotation on the page was by Hayes, who reassured Flackton that Purcell's 'hand writing differ'd a little at different Periods of his life'. The sound judgement and scholarly integrity of these two men lends authority to two transcriptions of lost Purcell autographs: Flackton's copy in Lbl Add. 30931 of a distinctive version of *The*

---

3   Iain Fenlon, *Catalogue of the Printed Music and Music Manuscripts before 1801 in the Music Library of the University of Birmingham, Barber Institute of Fine Arts* (London: Mansell, 1976), pp. 113–14; as published, this volume contains a microfiche of Bu 5001.

4   H. Watkins Shaw, 'A Collection of Musical Manuscripts in the Autograph of Henry Purcell and Other English Composers, c.1665–85', *The Library: The Transactions of the Bibliographical Society*, Series 5/14 (1959): 129.

5   H. Watkins Shaw and Robert Ford, 'Flackton, William', in *Grove Music Online*, http://www.oxfordmusiconline.com (last accessed 29 July 2010).

6   Ian Spink, *Restoration Cathedral Music, 1660–1714*, Oxford Studies in British Church Music (Oxford: Clarendon, 1995), p. 208.

Lord is King;[7] and Hayes's transcription in KNt MR 2–5.4 of a version of *My Beloved Spake* resembling the extant copy in Cfm 117.[8]

While it would be perverse to characterize Flackton's and Hayes's work with Purcell sources as anything other than 'scholarly', the first steps towards a modern approach to source studies of his music, with evidence presented in printed form to a wide readership, appear to have been associated with the British Museum's exhibition in 1895 marking the bicentenary of Purcell's death. A contemporary summary of the material exhibited reflects not only the range of material put on view for the general public at that time but also the state of current scholarship, with a number of sources marked 'Autograph?' and two manifestly faulty unqualified attributions (see below);[9] nevertheless, the exhibition clearly acknowledged the role of other copyists, among whom Henry Bowman, William Croft and William Davis were identified.

An article subsequently published by Augustus Hughes-Hughes,[10] who was, of course, an employee of the British Museum, reflects the state of Purcell source scholarship at the end of the nineteenth century. Hughes-Hughes was often self-contradictory, admitting sources to his own list of probable or possible autographs when his comments and facsimiles clearly proved otherwise, and his unequivocal identifications of autographs were rarely original, generally drawing on the authority of Hayes or Flackton. His conclusions appear at times to have been influenced by consideration either for the collectors who made privately owned manuscripts available for the 1895 exhibition, or for the reputation of the Museum itself; a score of Purcell's Te Deum and Jubilate belonging to Sir Frederick Bridge,[11] for example, was presented in the exhibition as an autograph and described in Hughes-Hughes's 1896 article in terms that could suggest it might indeed be one,[12] but elsewhere he left no doubt that the manuscript is in fact the work of the two copyists now recognized as John Walter and William Isaack.[13] In addition, his facsimile of the clef and key signature of another 1895 exhibit – an alleged autograph of 'Cease Anxious World' belonging to Julian Marshall – bears no resemblance to

7   Lbl Add. 30931, fols 75r–78r; on fol. 78v are some attempts by Flackton to imitate Purcell's text hand.

8   KNt MR 2–5.4 pp. 118–37; see Shay and Thompson, *Purcell Manuscripts*, p. 139 and Chapter 3, pp. 70–72 in this volume.

9   Augustus Hughes-Hughes, William Barclay Squire and F.M. O'Donoghue, 'The Purcell Exhibits at the British Museum', *Musical Times and Singing Class Circular* 36 (1895): 797–9.

10   Augustus Hughes-Hughes, 'Henry Purcell's Handwriting', *Musical Times and Singing Class Circular* 37 (1896): 81–3.

11   This was later located by Zimmerman in the Music Memorial Library, University of Stanford, Palo Alto, California; see Franklin B. Zimmerman, *Henry Purcell, 1659–1695: An Analytical Catalogue of his Music* (London: Macmillan; New York: St Martin's Press, 1963), p. 471.

12   'If the main body of this MS. is not in Purcell's hand it must have been dictated by him, or written under his supervision'; Hughes-Hughes, 'Henry Purcell's Handwriting', p. 83.

13   He described Ob Mus.c.27 (i.e. fols 27–32, now Ob Mus.c.27*) as 'in the same two hands as Dr. Bridge's Te Deum'; ibid.

any genuine example of Purcell's hand. In spite of such equivocations, however, Hughes-Hughes acknowledged the potential importance of non-autograph sources, as the exhibition had done, and also dismissed a number of incorrect attributions, including not only the extraordinary assertion that the manuscript now Lcm 2011 is an autograph (a claim that had been made by Richard Clark, who sometimes 'allowed his zeal to get the better of his discretion'),[14] but also Cummings's suggestion that US-R M2040/A628/Folio was an autograph, presumably on the grounds that it featured the hand of Purcell's main assistant in Lbl R.M. 20.h.8. He introduced the possibility of Purcell working closely with an assistant and named Daniel Henstridge as a copyist, identifying him, rather than Purcell, as the copyist of Lbl Add. 33240, fols 1–5.[15] In addition Hughes-Hughes suspected long before other scholars that Cfm 117 (then 30. G. 10) was not in the hand of John Blow,[16] took some tentative steps towards using watermarks as an aid to musical bibliography – including the correct observation that the paper types of Lbl Add. 30930 and Lbl R.M. 20.h.8 are the same – and made some important observations about Purcell's literary and musical handwriting.

At this point, sadly, matters remained essentially fixed until and beyond the next major anniversary, the tercentenary of Purcell's birth in 1959, and even then source-related studies played only a minor part in scholarly activity. In the interim, G.E.P. Arkwright made good use of Hughes-Hughes's suggestions in seeking to establish a chronology for Purcell's church music,[17] and two major manuscripts came to light: the partial autograph of *The Fairy Queen*, Lam 3, which had been lost after Purcell's death, was rediscovered in the library of the Royal Academy of Music in about 1900 by J.S. Shedlock,[18] and the Gresham song-book, Lg Safe 3, was brought to public attention as an autograph by William Barclay Squire in

---

14 Ibid., 81.

15 Although Hughes-Hughes identified the hand correctly in 1896, the manuscript was exhibited as a possible autograph in 1895 and later described as such by Hughes-Hughes himself in the British Museum catalogue; see Augustus Hughes-Hughes, *Catalogue of Manuscript Music in the British Museum* (3 vols, London: British Museum, 1906–09; repr. 1966), vol. 2, p. 211.

16 Hughes-Hughes commented about the hand now recognized as Isaack's that it is 'found also in a very large volume of anthems and songs in the Fitzwilliam Museum, dated 1683 (30 G-10 [now Cfm 117]), where it is attributed to Dr. Blow; it appears also in Additl. 31453, bearing the date January, 1699; but none of them are at all like Blow's autograph (dated November, 1695) in Additl. 31457'; Hughes-Hughes, 'Henry Purcell's Handwriting', p. 83.

17 Godfrey E.P. Arkwright, 'Purcell's Church Music', *Musical Antiquary* 1 (1909–10): 63–72, 234–48. The chronological discussion is entirely in the latter section.

18 For an early account of this rediscovery and its significance, see Henry Purcell, *The Fairy Queen*, ed. John South Shedlock, The Works of Henry Purcell, vol. 12 (London: Novello; New York: Novello and Ewer, 1903), pp. ii–iii; see also Henry Purcell, *The Fairy Queen*, eds Bruce Wood and Andrew Pinnock, The Works of Henry Purcell, vol. 12 (new edn, London: Stainer and Bell, 2009), pp. xiii–xiv.

1911.[19] Around the 1959 tercentenary, however, increasing interest in 'early music' led, among other things, to the beginning of a steady stream of publications about sources of works by Purcell and his contemporaries, ranging from the monumental, in the form of Franklin B. Zimmerman's *Analytical Catalogue* of 1963, to articles tightly focused on a single library or a single manuscript.[20] This new research did much to contextualize Purcell's music, drawing attention not only to the extent of the study of earlier composers apparent in his copying,[21] but also to his personal involvement in performances,[22] his working relationships with other musicians and the reception and dissemination of his music.[23] Studies of important secondary copyists also added to our knowledge of Purcell's musical circle.[24]

---

19   William Barclay Squire, 'An Unknown Autograph of Henry Purcell', *Musical Antiquary* 3 (1911–12): 5–17.

20   Franklin B. Zimmerman, 'Purcell's Handwriting', in Imogen Holst (ed.), *Henry Purcell (1659–1695): Essays on his Music* (London: Oxford University Press, 1959), pp. 103–5 makes no advances on Hughes-Hughes's work; the essay by Nigel Fortune and Franklin B. Zimmerman, 'Purcell's Autographs', in Holst (ed.), *Henry Purcell (1659–1695)*, pp. 106–21, usefully lists the known autograph copies and reinforces the conclusions about handwriting drawn by Hughes-Hughes and amplified by Arkwright. Other examples include: H. Watkins Shaw, 'A Contemporary Source of English Music of the Purcellian Period', *Acta Musicologica* 31 (1959): 38–44 (on Lbl R.M. 27.a.1–3, 5, 6 and 8, *olim* 23.m.1–6); Shaw, 'A Collection of Musical Manuscripts' (on Bu 5001); Shaw, 'A Cambridge Music Manuscript from the English Chapel Royal', *Music & Letters* 42 (1961): 263–7 (on Cfm 152); Gwilym Beechey, 'A New Source of Seventeenth-Century Keyboard Music', *Music & Letters* 50 (1969): 278–89 (on En Inglis 94 MS 3343); Franklin B. Zimmerman, 'Anthems of Purcell and Contemporaries in a Newly Rediscovered "Gostling Manuscript"', *Acta Musicologica* 41 (1969): 55–70; Gloria Rose, 'A New Purcell Source', *Journal of the American Musicological Society* 25 (1972): 230–36 (on US-NHub 9); Richard Charteris, 'Some Manuscript Discoveries of Henry Purcell and his Contemporaries in the Newberry Library, Chicago', *Notes* 37 (1980–81): 7–13; and Charteris, 'A Checklist of the Manuscript Sources of Henry Purcell's Music in the University of California, William Andrews Clark Memorial Library, Los Angeles', *Notes* Series 2/52 (1995–96): 407–21.

21   Notably in Franklin B. Zimmerman, 'Purcell and Monteverdi', *Musical Times* 99 (1958): 368–9 (on Purcell's transcription of an extract from *Cruda Amarilli* in Ob Mus.a.1); Thurston Dart, 'Purcell and Bull', *Musical Times* 104 (1963): 30–31 (includes an illustration of a now inaccessible copy in Purcell's hand of a canon by Bull).

22   See Hugh McLean, 'Purcell, and Blow in Japan', *Musical Times* 104 (1963): 702–5 (on J-Tn N5/10: a Chapel Royal bass part-book including an autograph copy of the chorus of *Sing unto God*); and Bruce Wood, 'A Newly Identified Purcell Autograph', *Music & Letters* 59 (1978): 329–32 (on Och Mus. 1188–9, partial autograph string parts to Purcell's *My Song shall be Alway*).

23   See, for example, Peter Holman, 'Purcell and Roseingrave: a New Autograph' in Curtis Price (ed.), *Purcell Studies* (Cambridge: Cambridge University Press, 1995), pp. 94–105 (announcing the discovery of a transmission copy by Purcell of a Roseingrave anthem).

24   Bruce Wood, 'A Note on Two Cambridge Manuscripts and their Copyists', *Music & Letters* 56 (1975): 308–12 (on Cfm 117 and Ckc Rowe 22); and Peter Holman, 'Bartholomew Isaack and "Mr Isaack" of Eton: a Confusing Tale of Restoration Musicians', *Musical Times* 128 (1987): 381–5.

Although the physical aspects of manuscripts generally played no more than a minor part in this research, increasing emphasis was placed upon source function. Overall, the direction of scholarly activity gradually shifted away from seeking a hypothetical 'best' or 'definitive' text of a work, with its concomitant if possibly misplaced preference for autographs, and towards an enquiry into the function of musical texts that acknowledged their inherent instability, to some extent analogous to that of playscripts. In due course, it began to interact with the entirely separate discipline of codicology – in essence, the study of books as artefacts – to inspire a more searching approach to the purpose of musical documents, their relationship with each other and with the social contexts in which they were produced, and the evidence their material attributes could provide about the music they contain.

The concept of codicology as a distinct discipline developed among medievalists,[25] and it is by no means clear whether the codicological approaches devised by musicologists represented a conscious adaptation of existing methods or an independent invention to which an appropriate term was retrospectively applied. In either case the special circumstances of music, with its extensive reliance on manuscript material well into the early modern era and beyond, mean that an approach parallel to that of medieval codicology is relevant to musicology of a more recent period, as the following definitions of the term make abundantly clear:

> The study or science of manuscripts and their interrelationships.[26]

> [T]he study of manuscripts as cultural artefacts for historical purposes.[27]

> [T]he archaeology of the book (the codex); the study of the material and physical history of books and, in more directly practical terms, the identification of similarities between particular volumes with a view towards identifying the scriptoria that produced them.[28]

In particular, 'the archaeology of the book' is a useful metaphor, since in musicology a primary concern is often to distinguish between 'layers' that may or may not coincide with changes of hand or content, or to establish the order in which significant events took place, such as the copying or binding of different sections.

One significant difference between medieval and musicological codicology is the obvious fact that whereas the former is more likely to involve parchment documents, the majority of musical sources are made of paper. The potential

---

25 See James Marchand, 'What Every Medievalist Should Know', 20, http://www.the-orb. net/wemsk/codicologywemsk.html (last accessed 15 May 2010).

26 'Codicology', *Oxford English Dictionary*, http://dictionary.oed.com (last accessed 2 August 2010).

27 'Codicology', *Merriam-Webster's Online Dictionary*, http://www.merriam-webster.com/ dictionary/ codicology (last accessed 30 July 2010).

28 Stephen R. Reimer, 'Manuscript Studies: Medieval and Early Modern', http://www. ualberta.ca/~sreimer/ms-course/course/defintn.htm (last accessed 31 July 2010).

value of paper evidence was recognized by musicologists at an early stage,[29] not least by Philipp Spitta who believed that in Bach studies watermarks in paper were 'almost the most important means of establishing the chronology' among the vast quantity of undated works.[30] A full appreciation of the information contained in paper did not, however, begin to develop until the mid twentieth century, when the work of Allan Stevenson progressively demonstrated the value to bibliography of systematic and detailed paper study[31] and some long-standing assumptions about the chronology of Bach's cantatas were called into question, in part on the basis of codicological evidence.[32] The validity of comparable methods in studying musical sources of the later eighteenth and early nineteenth centuries was subsequently established by Alan Tyson and others,[33] and from the 1980s onwards an increasing number of musicologists have used paper-type analysis in work on earlier material;[34] the most recent extended publication in this field

29   For an overview and bibliography, see Stanley Boorman, 'Watermarks', in *Grove Music Online*, http://www.oxfordmusiconline.com (last accessed 29 July 2010).

30   Philipp Spitta, *Johann Sebastian Bach* (2 vols, Leipzig: Breitkopf, 1873–80), vol. 2, p. 776.

31   Most significantly in Allan Stevenson, *The Problem of the Missale Speciale* (London: Bibliographical Society, and Pittsburg: Thomas C. Pears, 1967); Stevenson, 'Watermarks are Twins', *Studies in Bibliography* 4 (1951–52): 57–91. See also Paul Needham, 'Allan H. Stevenson and the Bibliographical Uses of Paper', *Studies in Bibliography* 47 (1994): 24–65.

32   Georg von Dadelsen, *Beiträge zur Chronologie der Werke Johann Sebastian Bachs*, Tübinger Bach-Studien, vol. 4/5 (Trossingen: Hohner, 1958); Alfred Dürr, 'Zur Chronologie der Leipziger Vokalwerke J.S. Bachs', *Bach-Jahrbuch* 44 (1957): 5–162; repr. as book of the same title, Musikwissenschaftliche Arbeiten, vol. 26 (Kassel and London: Bärenreiter, 1976). See also Arthur Mendel, 'Recent Developments in Bach Chronology', *Musical Quarterly* 46 (1960): 283–300.

33   For example, in Eugene K. Wolf and Jean K. Wolf, 'A Newly Identified Complex of Manuscripts from Mannheim', *Journal of the American Musicological Society* 27 (1974): 379–437; Alan Tyson, 'The Problem of Beethoven's "First" *Leonore* Overture', *Journal of the American Musicological Society* 28 (1975): 292–334; Tyson, 'Mozart's "Haydn" Quartets: the Contribution of Paper Studies', in Christoph Wolff and Robert Riggs (eds), *The String Quartets of Haydn, Mozart and Beethoven: Studies of the Autograph Manuscripts – A Conference at Isham Memorial Library, March 15–17, 1979*, Isham Library Papers, vol. 3 (Cambridge, MA.: Harvard University Press, 1980), pp. 179–90; Douglas Johnson, Alan Tyson and Robert Winter, *The Beethoven Sketchbooks: History, Reconstruction, Inventory* (Oxford: Clarendon, 1985) and Alan Tyson, *Mozart: Studies of the Autograph Scores* (Cambridge, MA and London: Harvard University Press, 1987).

34   For example, Wisso Weiss and Yoshitake Kobayashi, *Katalog der Wasserzeichen in Bachs Originalhandschriften*, Neue Ausgabe sämtlicher Werke, Johann Sebastian Bach, Serie 9, vol. 1 Addenda (2 vols, Kassel, Basel and London: Bärenreiter, 1985); Gary Towne, 'Music and Liturgy in Sixteenth-Century Italy: The Bergamo Organ Book and its Liturgical Implications', *Journal of Musicology* 6 (1988): 471–509; Robert Thompson, 'George Jeffreys and the "Stile Nuovo" in English Sacred Music: a New Date for his Autograph Score, British Library Add. MS 10338', *Music & Letters* 70 (1989): 317–41; Suparmi Elizabeth Saunders, *The Dating of the Trent Codices from their Watermarks: With a Study of the Local Liturgy of Trent in the Fifteenth Century*, Outstanding Dissertations

is currently Christine Jeanneret's study of Roman keyboard music.[35] The Purcell keyboard manuscript Lbl Mus. 1 – probably the most significant of a number of autograph sources brought to light towards the end of the twentieth century – was discussed from the outset in codicological as well as musicological terms,[36] while, on a larger scale, Jonathan Wainwright's *Musical Patronage in Seventeenth-Century England* (1997) combined musicological, codicological and archival information to create a persuasive account of one of the major English music collections of mid seventeenth-century England;[37] similar methods have been adopted in the ongoing *Viola da Gamba Society Index of Manuscripts Containing Music for Viols*.[38] In connection with Purcell sources, the approach followed in two chapters of the 1995 volume *Purcell Studies* – 'Purcell's Great Autographs' by Robert Thompson and 'Purcell

---

in Music from British Universities (New York and London: Garland, 1989); Peter A. Wright, *The Related Parts of Trent, Museo Provinciale d'Arte MSS 87 (1374) and 92 (1379): a Paleographical and Text-Critical Study*, Outstanding Dissertations in Music from British Universities (New York and London: Garland, 1989); Tsutomu Sasaki, 'The Dating of the Aosta Manuscript from Watermarks', *Acta Musicologica* 64 (1992): 1–16; Donald Burrows and Martha J. Ronish, *A Catalogue of Handel's Musical Autographs* (Oxford: Clarendon, 1994); Henry Purcell, *The Gresham Autograph*, introduction by Margaret Laurie and Robert Thompson (facsimile edition, London: Novello, 1995); Peter A. Wright, 'Paper Evidence and the Dating of Trent 91', *Music & Letters* 76 (1995): 487–508; Wright, 'Johannes Wiser's Paper and the Copying of his Manuscripts', in Peter A. Wright (ed.), *I codici musicali trentini: nuove scoperte e nuovi orientamenti della ricerca*, Biblioteca musicale Laurence K.J. Feininger (Trent: Provincia autonoma di Trento, 1996), pp. 31–53. In addition, four articles about musical sources appeared in Daniel W. Mosser, Michael Saffle and Ernest W. Sullivan (eds), *Puzzles in Paper: Concepts in Historical Watermarks* (New Castle, DE: Oak Knoll Press; London: British Library, 2000): Jeremy L. Smith, 'Watermark Evidence and the Hidden Editions of Thomas East' (pp. 67–80); Ulrich Konrad, 'Use of Watermarks in Musicology' (pp. 93–106); Stephen Shearon, 'Watermarks and Rastra in Neapolitan Music Manuscripts, 1700–1815' (pp. 107–24); and Steven Zohn, 'Music Paper at the Dresden Court and the Chronology of Telemann's Instrumental Music' (pp. 125–68).

35   Christine Jeanneret, *L'oeuvre en filigrane: une étude philologique des manuscrits de musique pour clavier à Rome au XVIIe siècle*, Historiae musicae cultores, vol. 116 (Florence: Olschki, 2009).

36   Curtis Price, 'New Light on Purcell's Keyboard Music', in Price (ed.), *Purcell Studies* (Cambridge: Cambridge University Press, 1995), pp. 87–93; Price, 'Newly Discovered Autograph Keyboard Music of Purcell and Draghi', *Journal of the Royal Musical Association* 120 (1995): 77–111. See also Robert Klakowich, 'Seventeenth-Century English Keyboard Autographs', *Journal of the Royal Musical Association* 121 (1996): 132–5; Chris Banks, 'British Library MS Mus. 1: a Recently Discovered Manuscript of Keyboard Music by Henry Purcell and Giovanni Battista Draghi', *Brio* 32 (1995): 87–93; Christopher Hogwood, 'A New English Keyboard Manuscript of the Seventeenth Century: Autograph Music by Draghi and Purcell', *British Library Journal* 21 (1995): 161–75.

37   Jonathan Wainwright, *Musical Patronage in Seventeenth-Century England: Christopher, First Baron Hatton (1605–1670)* (Aldershot: Scolar Press; Brookfield: Ashgate, 1997).

38   Andrew Ashbee, Robert Thompson and Jonathan Wainwright (eds), *The Viola da Gamba Society Index of Manuscripts Containing Consort Music* (2 vols, Aldershot and Burlington: Ashgate, 2001, 2008).

as Collector of "Ancient" Music' by Robert Shay[39] – was applied more widely in the same authors' *Purcell Manuscripts* of 2000, which proposed a more detailed chronology for Purcell's handwriting than any previously suggested, attempted a comprehensive evaluation of important copyists' sources and went some way towards establishing 'families' of manuscripts in which extant autographs are not necessarily the exemplars for all the others.

While codicological methodologies achieve nothing on their own, their usefulness in conjunction with other approaches is now beyond doubt, and certainly has not been exhausted in the studies of Purcell manuscripts and printed material so far carried out. The purpose of this chapter is to provide an 'interim report' on the progress of codicology in connection with Purcell and his period, to summarize current perceptions of the most significant Purcell sources, and to suggest possible lines of future enquiry. The first section outlines the methodologies that might be applied to manuscript sources; the second considers a number of manuscripts in relation to their musical function; and the third explores the way in which approaches initially developed for the study of manuscripts might usefully be adapted for printed music, an aspect of Purcell research that has until recently been relatively neglected.

Codicological Methodologies: Manuscripts

A comprehensive codicological study of a manuscript source covers all of its material features: the paper type and its provenance; the stave ruling or 'rastrology'; the way the separate folios have (or have not) been assembled into a book and whether there was any form of binding; and any features of the handwriting which might be significant. A broadly similar approach can be taken towards printed music, with due adaptation for the different way in which it was produced, but because printed material differs from manuscripts in terms of function and transmission as well as in some aspects of codicology, it is dealt with in a separate section at the end of the chapter.

In some rare circumstances, such as the documented establishment in business of a named papermaker who used an identifiable personal mark, paper evidence can provide a definitive *terminus post quem* for the production of a manuscript or book; far more often, dated occurrences of a particular paper type offer a probability rather than certainty of an earliest possible date, while the *terminus ante quem* is even less precise, as it is clearly impossible to prove beyond any possible doubt that paper had not been stored for some time before it was used. Rather than offering absolute chronological proof, paper type and rastrology are more often valuable in

---

39   Robert Thompson, 'Purcell's Great Autographs' in Curtis Price (ed.), *Purcell Studies* (Cambridge: Cambridge University Press, 1995); Robert Shay, 'Purcell as Collector of "Ancient" Music: Fitzwilliam MS 88', in Curtis Price (ed.), *Purcell Studies* (Cambridge: Cambridge University Press, 1995), pp. 6–34 and 35–50.

providing relative evidence of a source's history; as an expensive and to an extent perishable commodity, paper was usually purchased in relatively small quantities for short-term use, so that the presence of a single paper type and stave ruling throughout a large volume is a clear sign either that a bound book was planned from the outset or – particularly when associated with regular quiring – that the book was bound before copying, which generally indicates that it was bought as a bound manuscript book for pedagogical or archival use. For the same reason, coincidences of paper type and ruling in different sources may suggest that they are roughly contemporary, while the presence of different paper types in a single volume might not only imply that binding took place later in its history but also cast possible light on the order of its production.[40] Composers' and copyists' handwriting varied over time and according to whether they were writing on flat sheets or, somewhat awkwardly, in a large bound book. In printed material, where much larger stocks of paper are involved, a change in paper type might also mark a significant event in a book's evolution. All of these features provide potential evidence of a source's history, and, although it is unusual for codicology to clinch an argument, it often provides a useful pointer towards the most fruitful lines of enquiry.

Paper Type

Hand-made paper in Purcell's period was available in a variety of weights and qualities, although the range regarded as suitable for manuscript music was limited.[41] Contemporary terminology recognized four broad categories of paper likely to be found in music books, outlined in Table 2.1.[42] As supplied from the paper mill, each sheet of paper faithfully reflected the properties of the oblong mould on which it had been formed, not only in its size but also in the pattern of its wires, which appear in the paper as heavy 'chain lines', usually between 18 mm and 28 mm apart, running up and down the sheet parallel to the shorter side, and finer, much more closely spaced 'laid lines' running horizontally. The term 'identical paper' should be used only of leaves which correspond in measurable details of the watermark, chain and laid-line patterns, and as papermakers traditionally worked in pairs using two moulds, an 'identical paper type' exists only when correspondence of both members of the mould pair can be established.[43] The occasional occurrence of a 'quartet' of similar marks in related sources is evidence

---

40   See, for example, Eugene K. Wolf, 'The Rediscovered Autograph of Mozart's Fantasy and Sonata in C Minor, K. 475/457', *Journal of Musicology* 10 (1992): 3–47.

41   For a comprehensive general discussion of the subject see Jan LaRue 'Watermarks and Musicology', *Journal of Musicology* 18 (2001): 313–43 (first published in *Acta Musicologica* 33 (1961): 120–46); see also Shay and Thompson, *Purcell Manuscripts*, pp. 8–20.

42   For a contemporary list of available paper types see Robert William Chapman, 'An Inventory of Paper, 1674', *The Library* Series 4/7 (1927): 402–8.

43   Stevenson, 'Watermarks are Twins'.

Table 2.1   Categories of paper used in music manuscripts.

Contemporary terminology	Approximate dimensions of sheet (mm)	Characteristic watermarks
Royal	440 x 580	Bend on shield
Medium	405 x 540	Fleur-de-lys on shield
Demy	370 x 480	Fleur-de-lys on shield
Foolscap	320 x 420	Foolscap, Arms of Amsterdam, Dutch Lion

that the paper containing them was produced in a two-vat mill with a double pair of moulds, although the paper produced by each pair sometimes appears in separate volumes, leaving open the possibility that it was made in nearby mills served by the same mould-maker rather than in the same establishment.[44]

The focus of attention in paper is naturally the watermark, which is in fact an inessential addition to the mould serving as a maker's trademark and an indicator of quality and area of origin. In the late seventeenth century watermarks were almost always positioned in the middle of one half of the oblong sheet, a 'countermark' identifying the individual maker sometimes appearing in the corresponding position in the other half; the watermark or countermark therefore appears in the centre of the page in a folio book, in which the original sheet was folded once along its vertical centre line. In paper from the Angoumois area of south-western France, the origin of most of the paper used in Purcell sources copied up to c.1690, any initials associated with the watermark itself were normally those of the wholesale merchant or 'factor' who had commissioned the production of the paper and then exported it through the port of La Rochelle.[45]

---

44   See, for example, Robert Thompson, 'A further look at the Consort Music Manuscripts in Archbishop Marsh's Library, Dublin', *Chelys* 24 (1995): 3–18; Ashbee, Thompson and Wainwright (eds), *The Viola da Gamba Society Index*, vol. 1, pp. 305–6; vol. 2, p. 305. In 1672 one Jean Delafont 'l'aisné' was identified as a 'maître faiseur de formes à papier' at La Couronne in the Angoumois, suggesting that mould-making was recognized as a distinct craft at that period and that several mills might have been supplied with similar moulds; see Gustave Babinet de Rencogne, 'Recueil de documents pour servir à l'histoire de commerce et de l'industrie en Angoumois: Recherches sur l'origine des moulins à papier de l'Angoumois', *Bulletin de la société archéologique et historique de la Charente* Série 5/2 (1878–79), p. 96.

45   For a detailed history of the Angoumois paper industry see Babinet de Rencogne, 'Recueil de documents'.

Many of these merchants were Dutch, leading to the use of the term 'Dutch paper' for the product of this area and the appearance of characteristic Dutch emblems as watermarks, such as the Arms of Amsterdam and the patriotic 'Dutch Lion' motif.

As with the chain- and laid-line patterns, claiming 'identity' between watermarks requires a high standard of proof; complex late seventeenth-century marks were made on patterns,[46] and bibliographically purposeful description therefore involves detailed measurement of several features of the mark itself as well as of its position in the sheet and relationship with the chain lines. Nor is paper evidence always easy to obtain; in some cases the format of source material causes all or part of a watermark to be removed or concealed, which makes it difficult to establish proof of identity, as might the fragility of source material. Like other features of the mould, marks and countermarks were naturally subject to distortion through repeated use, a fact that on the one hand offers a potential method of sequencing the production of a large stock of paper from the same mill, but on the other poses a further obstacle to establishing identity; in high-quality papers of Purcell's period, however, movement visible to the eye is generally confined to outlying parts of marks such as the stem and 'WR' lettering characteristically found beneath a fleur-de-lys.

The domination of the English music-paper market by the Playfords meant that their preferences and personal decisions further narrowed an already quite restricted field of suitable material.[47] Although a native Dutch white-paper industry had existed since the mid-1670s, and its products appeared in printed music as early as the *Sonnata's of III Parts* of 1683 (see below), paper made in Holland was not the usual choice for use in English music manuscripts until circumstances changed in its favour: during the Nine Years' War of 1688–97, unlike in previous conflicts, the Dutch and English governments actively sought to undermine French trade,[48] including the trade in paper, while, aided by exiled Huguenot craftsmen, the indigenous Dutch paper industry made rapid advances that enabled it to match the quality of paper that had been available from the Angoumois, where the industry had in any case been substantially funded by Dutch capital.[49] The war led to a shift in the source

---

46 Stevenson, *The Problem of the Missa Speciale*, pp. 245–7, referring to M.J. Brusse, *Hoe het bosch papier wordt* (Rotterdam: W.L. and J. Brusse, 1917), which describes the use of traditional methods of making watermarks long into the period of mechanized industrial papermaking.

47 For this and other aspects of the English commercial trade in music paper in the later seventeenth century, see Robert Thompson, 'Manuscript Music in Purcell's London', *Early Music* 23 (1995): 605–18.

48 David Ogg, *Europe in the Seventeenth Century* (9th edn, London: A. and C. Black, 1971), p. 259.

49 For the relationship between the Angoumois paper industry and Dutch capital, and the commercial impact of national and international politics in the late seventeenth century see Warren C. Scoville, *The Persecution of Huguenots and French Economic Development, 1680–1720* (Berkeley and Los Angeles: University of California Press, 1960), p. 185 and nn. 230–31; Willem E.J. Berg, *De réfugiés in de Nederlanden na de herroeping van het Edict van Nantes* (Amsterdam: Müller, 1845), pp. 141–2, quoting *Hollandse Mercurius* (1671): 164–7 and ibid., (1672): 30–31.

of supply of high-quality paper used in English manuscripts from the Angoumois to Holland and other areas, a change reflected in the paper of some later Purcell manuscripts: the outer sections of *Hail, bright Cecilia* in Ob Mus.c.26, for example, consist mainly of paper made in Holland by Jacob and Adriaan Corneliszoon Honigh;[50] Lam 3 has a monogram countermark of the van der Ley family;[51] and some folios of *Who can from Joy Refrain?* are formed of paper marked with the Arms of Berne and the initials of the Bernese papermaker Niklaus Malacrida.[52]

While the change in the preferred source of supply from the Angoumois to more northerly parts of Europe provides a useful rule of thumb in distinguishing between sources dating from before and after *c.*1690, paper analysis of Purcell's manuscripts has had limited significance for establishing their overall chronology. Most of his major works can be dated on straightforward historical or contextual grounds with more precision than watermark evidence alone would make possible, and where there are genuine uncertainties, as in the case of *Dido and Aeneas* or the anthem *O Consider my Adversity*, no contemporary source exists. Nevertheless, particularly when supported by rastrology (see below), paper evidence has much to offer in the interpretation of individual sources; in the case of Lbl Add. 30930, identification of the watermark and countermark of each mould of the pair not only confirms that the paper is from the same stock as that of a number of other manuscripts, and therefore could have been available before 1680, but also proves critically important in establishing the volume's current collation and reconstructing its organization at different points in its history, thus providing evidence for a probable order of copying and an earlier starting date than was previously accepted.[53] In the important secondary source Lbl Add. 47845, apparently bound in the early eighteenth century, paper evidence confirms that the book was brought together some time after its earliest contents were copied and that the sections are not arranged chronologically.[54] Conversely, identity of paper type along with continuity of pagination show that Cfm 683 and Ob Tenbury 785 once formed part of a much larger, and potentially important, bound manuscript.[55]

Some of the reservations about paper evidence expressed above might of course be eliminated by the establishment of a comprehensive database of relevant paper types and the wider application of technical means of imaging and reproducing watermarks.[56] Specialized photographic methods offer a range of possibilities for

---

50   Ob Mus.c.26 fols 21–69; see Shay and Thompson, *Purcell Manuscripts*, p. 162.
51   Ibid., p. 240.
52   Ibid., pp. 161–3.
53   Ibid., pp. 88–100.
54   Ibid., pp. 144–50.
55   Margaret Laurie, 'The "Cambury" Purcell Manuscript', in Patrick F. Devine and Harry M. White (eds), *The Maynooth International Musicological Conference 1995: Selected Proceedings, II*, Irish Musical Studies, vol. 5 (Dublin: Four Courts, 1996), pp. 262–71.
56   See, for example, the following articles in Mosser, Saffle and Sullivan (eds), *Puzzles in Paper*: Carol Ann Small, 'Phosphorescence Watermark Imaging' (pp. 169–81); Rolf Dessauer, 'DYLUX, Thomas L. Gravell, and Watermarks of Stamps and Papers' (pp. 183–5); Daniela Moschini (trans. Conor Fahy), 'La Marqua d'Acqua: a System for

creating accurate images, although the measurement-based approach adopted in *The Viola da Gamba Society Index of Manuscripts* and many other studies is also practicable when the sources concerned contain a limited range of watermark types. In principle there is no reason, other than time and expense, to prevent the recording and classification in one form or another of every extant type of paper in English music manuscripts of Purcell's period; while it has been calculated that the sum total of different watermarks produced in Europe before 1800 exceeded a million,[57] the range used in the English music-paper trade was much more limited, thereby making an impossible task merely difficult. Any such survey should not, of course, confine itself to musical materials; the papers selected for manuscript music were also those appropriate for official records of different kinds, and thus far little systematic use has been made of official English legal and administrative archives to provide points of reference. Standard protocols have been proposed for the recording of watermarks,[58] and in conjunction with modern technology these might offer ways of both subdividing the overall project and making its findings available to the widest possible audience.

Rastrology

By the late seventeenth century, paper ruled for music was available for sale from stationers in England[59] and it is highly unlikely that any professional musician would have spent time ruling his own, not least because most of the value of the ruled paper lay in the paper itself rather than the stave ruling; in 1703 Henry Playford paid no more than a shilling for the ruling of four quires of paper, which would have been enough for a 192-page folio book.[60] English music paper at this time was almost always ruled with a multi-stave rastrum drawing between two and six staves at a time, and it is probable that most of the ruled paper used by Purcell

---

the Digital recording of Watermarks' (pp. 187–92); and Daniel W. Mosser and Ernest W. Sullivan II, 'The Thomas L. Gravell Watermark Archive on the Internet' (pp. 211–28).

57   Alfred Schulte, 'Papiermuhlen- and Wasserzeichenforschung', *Gutenberg Jahrbuch* 9 (1934): 9–27.

58   For the International Association of Paper Historians' proposal, *International Standard for the Registration of Papers*, see http://www.paperhistory.org/standard.htm (last accessed 20 July 2009); for examples of technology being used both to illustrate and disseminate watermarks see Daniel W. Mosser and Ernest W. Sullivan II, *The Thomas L. Gravell Watermark Archive*, http://www.gravell.org/ (last accessed 30 July 2010) and David L. Gants, *A Digital Catalogue of Watermarks and Type Ornaments Used by William Stansby in the Printing of The Workes of Beniamin Jonson (London: 1616)*, http://www2.iath. virginia.edu/gants/ (last accessed 30 July 2010).

59   Thompson, 'Manuscript Music in Purcell's London': 606–8.

60   Cyrus Lawrence Day and Eleanore Boswell Murrie, 'Playford *versus* Pearson', *The Library* Series 4/17 (1937): 427–47.

and his copyists came directly or indirectly from the Playfords or their occasional partner John Carr, all of whom regularly advertised it in their publications.[61]

The rastrum more or less fixes the spacing and width of staves within the block ruled in one stroke, although small variations are to be expected because of irregularity in ink flow or the flexibility of the rastrum. Any substantial difference in rastrology points towards a change in paper stock, implying that the paper was purchased on a different occasion and, in turn, possibly reflecting a significant aspect of the source's history;[62] conversely, while English manuscripts generally present a broadly standardized appearance, the range of differences between them in detailed rastral measurements suggests that the life of a rastrum was short, so that a comprehensive database of rastral measurements might in due course allow us to identify specific rastra and the periods over which they were used. Together with paper evidence, rastrology can also contribute to the structural analysis of a source: in Lbl Add. 30930, for example, where the 16 staves on each page were drawn in two blocks of six and one of four, the position of the four-stave block combined with watermark evidence helps to establish the manuscript's collation.[63]

Collation and Binding

For a printed book the collation of sheets clearly reflects the way the book was created, since each side of two, four, eight or more pages was produced in a single impression; consequently details of collation not only help inform the modern scholar about the format in which the book was produced, but also highlight the mechanisms by which last-minute, stop-press changes were made (see below). In contrast, the collation of manuscripts was more a matter of convenience unless, as not infrequently happened, pages which had already been copied had to be assembled in the right order; the presence of original pagination, or of a binder's scheme showing the relationship between quires, is sometimes an indication that a book was bound after copying.[64] The distinction between manuscripts sold as bound

---

61   Thompson, 'Manuscript Music in Purcell's London': 612–13.

62   This is an approach explored with reference to different historical periods in Owen Hughes Jander, 'Staff-Liner Identification: a Technique for the Age of Microfilm', *Journal of the American Musicological Society* 20 (1967): 112–16; Jean K. Wolf and Eugene K. Wolf, 'Rastrology and its Use in Eighteenth-Century Manuscript Studies' in Eugene K. Wolf and Edward H. Roesner (eds), *Studies in Musical Sources and Style: Essays in Honour of Jan LaRue* (Madison: A-R Editions, 1990), pp. 237–92; and Cathie Miserandino-Gaherty, 'The Codicology and Rastrology of GB-Ob Mus. Sch. MSS c. 64–9: Manuscripts in Support of Transmission Theory', *Chelys* 25 (1996–97): 78–87.

63   Shay and Thompson, *Purcell Manuscripts*, pp. 88–97.

64   Notable examples of manuscripts with binders' schemes are George Jeffreys's autograph score Lbl Add. 10338 and Charles Morgan's song-book Lbl Add. 33234; see Robert Thompson, 'George Jeffreys and the "Stile Nuovo" in English Sacred Music', and Thompson, 'English Music Manuscripts and the Fine Paper Trade, 1660–1688' (2 vols, PhD dissertation, University of London, 1988), pp. 292–4.

volumes, those bound within a short time of copying and those assembled only by later collectors or modern conservators has proved significant to recent studies of Purcell's sources, primarily because such information can aid our understanding of the purposes for which books were created as well as shedding light on the way in which pieces were composed.

As far as we can tell from surviving evidence, only a minority of musical sources in this period were assembled as bound volumes with board or limp vellum covers. Music books with substantial original bindings were generally produced for a specific purpose requiring a high level of durability, most of the bound manuscript books available from the Playfords probably being purchased by amateur musicians or their teachers for vocal or keyboard music.[65] With very few exceptions, the sheep- or calf-covered boards of late seventeenth-century music sources are standard bookbinders' work, handsome and distinctive in their own way but adding little of significance to our understanding of the music they contain.[66] Other bound volumes include cathedral choir and organ-books, which are likely to have been at least partly copied before they were bound, and file copies in parts or in score. Among Purcell's larger autographs, the regular structure of Cfm 88 and Lbl R.M. 20.h.8 implies that both were purchased as bound volumes from a stationer, probably as special commissions, and both appear to have acted as file copies either for the composer personally or for the court musical establishment.[67] The full score of *The Fairy Queen*, Lam 3, apparently served a similar function for the Theatre Royal; here, consistency of paper type suggests that the book was prepared from a discrete, dedicated paper stock unusually containing a 'PVL' countermark without a corresponding watermark, but irregularity in the distribution of these marks indicates that binding took place after most of the copying had been completed. The original quiring was evidently regular in both of the smaller bound Purcell autographs, Lbl Mus. 1, the original boards of which survive,[68] and the Gresham song-book Lg Safe 3.[69]

Any music book bound after partial or complete copying, such as Lam 3 or Lbl Add. 30930, is highly likely to reveal some irregularities as a result of the way sheets were grouped together during copying as well as the removal or insertion of folios

---

65 Some examples form items 103–8 in Henry Playford's sale catalogue of 1690, Lbl Harleian 5936 nos. 419–20; see Thompson, 'Manuscript Music in Purcell's London': 614.

66 One of the exceptions is the Durham bass part-book DRc Mus. C34, which appears to be one of the volumes recorded in the cathedral account books for the year ending Michaelmas 1693 as having been bound for the personal use of the Dean; see Brian Crosby, *A Catalogue of Durham Cathedral Music Manuscripts* (Oxford: Oxford University Press, 1986), p. 51. In this case, however, it is the not the binding itself but its relationship to a dated archival reference which is of importance, helping to fix the date of Purcell's anthem *Be Merciful*.

67 Thompson, 'Purcell's Great Autographs'; Shay and Thompson, *Purcell Manuscripts*, pp. 33–46 and 126–43.

68 Price, 'Newly Discovered Autograph Keyboard Music': 81–2.

69 See Laurie and Thompson's Preface to Purcell, *The Gresham Autograph*, p. iv.

due to corrections and alterations, and the bibliographical formats found in music manuscripts in this period often allow easy identification of such inconsistencies. Many are folios, in which the original sheet of paper is folded once, along the spine; most others are oblong quartos, in which the sheet is folded twice, usually first horizontally and then along the spine, making a quire of four folios in which the upper or lower sections of the watermarks can be found either at the top or the bottom edge. The only other format to appear at all frequently in musical sources is upright quarto, in which the first fold is made along the shorter mid-line of the sheet and the spine follows the horizontal mid-line. Whereas the oblong quarto format was essentially produced for musical convenience, as it allowed the use of fewer but longer staves and gave rise to fewer line-ends, the purpose of the upright quarto format was to enable much larger, heavier paper to be formed into a book of folio proportions generally of the size of a cropped foolscap volume; such volumes are often catalogued as 'small folios', a term which accurately reflects their size but not their make-up. In this format, the watermark sections can be found at the inner edge of the page and are inevitably partly concealed in the binding, so that an upright quarto is the most difficult type of book to deal with in terms of watermark study. In all three formats watermarked folios should be balanced by their countermarked or unmarked conjuncts, and in quartos each upper section of a mark should be matched by a lower one, although heavy trimming of oblong quarto books can completely remove sections of small countermarks. The removal of a folio will, nevertheless, always be reflected by an interruption to the expected sequence of marks, as, in most cases, will the replacement of a folio by a tipped-in manuscript substitute or a cancellans in a printed volume.

Many important Purcell sources were not bound in the seventeenth century and survive in modern guard-books, where their original structure is sometimes obscured. Indications of a 'separate' original existence, where this is not immediately obvious, include the darkening and discolouration of the outer pages, contrasts in paper type or rastrology with adjacent material and independent schemes of pagination or foliation. In some examples, such as *Blessed are They that Fear the Lord* in Lbl Add. 30931, the back page is discoloured but not the front, suggesting that the score was folded in half for storage; and other Flackton scores appear to have been folded several times, presumably to save postage costs. There is no evidence, however, that they were actually used at Canterbury as transmission copies, and they are more likely to have been sent through the post for essentially antiquarian reasons, as seems to have happened in the early eighteenth century to *In the Midst of Life* when James Hawkins of Ely copied it into Cu EDC 10/7/6.[70] The most extreme form of unbound source, which includes John Blow's organ-book Mp BRm 370 Bp35, is copied 'stratigraphically' across the whole of each side of unbound sheets, a format more suitable for archiving or transmission than for use in performance.

While the unbound sources may seem to offer little in terms of conventional bibliographical evidence, they lend themselves well to a wider codicological approach. Paper type and rastrology link Purcell's autographs of *In Thee O Lord do*

---

70   Shay and Thompson, *Purcell Manuscripts*, p. 228.

I put my Trust and *Let mine Eyes Run Down with Tears* in Ob Mus.c.26 with *The Lord is my Light* in Bu 5001,[71] suggesting that all three are more or less contemporary. In other cases the extant source evidence suggests a complex internal history: the autograph of *Who can from Joy Refrain?* in Lbl Add. 30934 fols 80–93, for example, contains three different paper types probably arranged in five original quires, the first and last of which respectively contained the complete overture and final chorus.[72] Although steps must have been taken to keep the different sections of the work together, there may also have been some practical purpose in the separation of different quires, which may have been kept unbound in a paper wrapper. In this case there is clear evidence that the score could have been divided up for copying and rehearsal, perhaps overlapping with the later phases of composition, but it is quite possible that further investigation of the collation of sources bound at an earlier stage and consisting of a single paper type will show that they also could have been treated in the same way.

Handwriting

Both text and music handwriting can provide useful codicological evidence. Hughes-Hughes had already identified distinct changes in the characteristics of Purcell's text and musical hands when he published his 1896 article,[73] and more detailed work presented in *Purcell Manuscripts* has enabled these features to be associated with specific periods of the composer's career:[74] in his early autographs he used a distinctive hook-shaped bass clef, similar to Pelham Humfrey's, which makes a final isolated appearance in Cfm 88; in his text hand he changed from a secretary-hand form of the lower-case 'e' to an italic one, probably around 1678, and then progressively replaced the secretary-hand lower-case 'r' with the italic version between about 1681 and 1685. The latter change can be charted in the datable welcome songs and other court works in Lbl R.M. 20.h.8, and the implied chronology applied to other sources; most significantly, the dating of *Out of the Deep* in or later than 1685 substantially depends on handwriting evidence.[75] Further systematic study of Purcell's handwriting might yield useful results; the statistical decline in Purcell's use of the secretary-form lower-case 'r' between 1680 and 1685,[76] which now seems so obvious, was measured as a result of a chance observation about tempo directions in the Lbl Add. 30930 sonatas, and it is quite possible that other characteristics as yet unnoticed will seem equally obvious once pointed out.

Apart from these qualities unique to Purcell, other handwriting features sometimes prove revealing. Contrasts in ink colour possibly reflect the order in

---

71 Ibid., pp. 142–3, 216–17.
72 Ibid., p. 164.
73 Hughes-Hughes, 'Henry Purcell's Handwriting': 83.
74 Shay and Thompson, *Purcell Manuscripts*, pp. 23–32.
75 Ibid., p. 217.
76 Ibid., pp. 30–32 and 130–33.

which parts were copied, and there is likely to be a difference in appearance between pages written before binding and those added later, another factor in assessing the likely history of Lbl Add. 30930. Purcell was not, of course, the only musician whose handwriting changed during the course of his career, and characteristics of several other scribes' hands have proved relevant in dating copies of his music. Daniel Henstridge's long career provides a good example, with a major and apparently conscious change in the form of his G clef made *c.*1682, which in turn provides evidence that his score of Purcell's Funeral Sentences in US-LAuc fC6966/M4/A627/1700 precedes that date.[77] There may also be more to be discovered about the small number of musicians who appear to have collaborated directly with Purcell on manuscript scores and parts. These include 'London A', who was possibly Francis Pigott,[78] 'London B' and 'London C',[79] John Blow,[80] 'Oxford B'[81] and the first three of the *Fairy Queen* contributors, 'FQ1', 'FQ2' and 'FQ3',[82] of whom FQ1 also wrote out the final repeated section in the last movement of *Hail, bright Cecilia* in Ob Mus.c.26.[83]

Codicology and Musicology

Codicological assessment of Purcell's manuscripts has enhanced understanding of the composer's music in a number of ways, allowing more precise dating of some pieces and sources, and providing fresh perspectives on the professional and cultural milieu in which he worked. In addition, it has given rise to new approaches to studying Purcell's music that had previously been hampered both by the incomplete nature of the codicological data, and by the fact that most interest in Purcell's sources prior to the publication of *Purcell Manuscripts* had centred on the composer's autographs. In an important article published in 2006,[84] Rebecca Herissone used the codicological material in *Purcell Manuscripts* as a starting point for an examination of the purposes for which sources were produced in the Restoration period. Drawing attention to contemporary definitions that demonstrate that the modern terms 'rough draft' and 'fair copy' cannot be equated

---

77 Ibid., p. 221–5.
78 Ibid., pp. 131–5.
79 Ibid., pp. 131, 133, 135, 308–9 and 316.
80 The song 'O Solitude' in Lbl R.M. 20.h.8 fols 173v–174r inv. was copied by 'London A' and John Blow; the second hand in the song, which I assumed in *Purcell Manuscripts* was Purcell's, was recently recognized by Bruce Wood as that of Blow.
81 Shay and Thompson, *Purcell Manuscripts*, pp. 157, 255 and 317.
82 Ibid., pp. 234–40 and 316.
83 I am grateful to Rebecca Herissone for pointing this connection out to me as well as the fact that FQ1 takes over on fol. 67 in Ob Mus.c.26 rather than at the start of fol. 68, as I stated in Table 4.18 of *Purcell Manuscripts* (p. 162).
84 Rebecca Herissone, '"Fowle Originalls" and "Fayre Writeing": Reconsidering Purcell's Compositional Process', *Journal of Musicology* 23 (2006): 569–619.

with the late seventeenth-century descriptions 'fowle originall' and 'fayre writing', she categorized Purcell's autograph manuscripts into five 'functional types': 'fowle originalls' ('the composer's first, original copies, inelegantly written but nevertheless used by other copyists as exemplars'),[85] performance materials, file copies, transmission copies and teaching materials. To cover the complete spectrum of late seventeenth-century sources it would be necessary to add a sixth category not represented in Purcell's own production, that of manuscripts produced as collectors' items. Two important overall reservations must also be recognized: first, many sources served more than one purpose, most of the functions being implicit in at least one of the others; second, codicology not infrequently adds little or nothing to the understanding that could be gained from a detailed comparison of musical texts.[86] Nevertheless, it is always worth considering whether the physical characteristics of a musical source cast any light on the reason it was produced or the way it was used.

These questions are explored in the following section using the classification suggested by Herissone, adapted very slightly to place the emphasis more strongly on musical functions rather than specific sources. Shifting the focus in this way allows the discussion of cases in which a single source seems to have served more than one musical function, and produces the following categories: composition (which could take place at different stages), performance, archiving, transmission, education, and collecting and antiquarianism. In the field of keyboard music, a broadly similar approach based upon overlapping function is taken in Andrew Woolley's recent thesis.[87]

Composition

Purcell's autograph manuscripts of all types offer direct and indirect evidence of compositional process,[88] but there is sometimes a surprising lack of correlation between the amount of compositional activity reflected in a source, its format and its apparent wider purpose. The unbound Purcell autographs traditionally referred to as 'rough drafts' or 'preliminary copies' do not appear to be 'rough drafts' in the sense of being copies primarily or exclusively intended for the composer's private use before he released a work for a wider audience, while the bound score-books, which we might expect to contain the composer's definitive versions of existing works, frequently reveal instances of substantial recomposition as well as blank bars corresponding with passages Purcell presumably wished to reconsider at a

85   Ibid., 586.
86   As, for example, in Martin Adams, *Henry Purcell: The Origins and Development of his Musical Style* (Cambridge: Cambridge University Press, 1995).
87   Andrew Woolley, 'English Keyboard Sources and their Contexts, *c*.1660–1720' (PhD dissertation, University of Leeds, 2008).
88   For full lists of Purcell's autographs, see Shay and Thompson, *Purcell Manuscripts*, pp. 22–3 and Herissone, '"Fowle originals"': 574–6.

later date. The lack of a clear relationship between source function and creative activity in Purcell's manuscripts was discussed by Herissone in her 2006 article, and its implications are considered in detail in Alan Howard's chapter in this volume.

Assessment of creative activity of this sort generally entails detailed analysis of the notation itself, but codicological methods can be of value, since they can help establish the chronology and dating of revised workings as well as revealing the physical methods used by the composer to incorporate them, which in turn can imply something of their intended status. A good example is the score of the continuo anthem *Let mine Eyes Run Down with Tears*, in Ob Mus.c.26, fols 4–9, which is one of a small number of extant Purcell scores to contain internal evidence of extensive revision and the only source to provide evidence of a composing sketch, on the reverse of a revision slip.[89] The paper type and stave ruling are identical to those of the symphony anthems *In Thee O Lord do I put my Trust* in Ob Mus.c.26 and *The Lord is my Light* in Bu 5001, both datable to *c*.1682 from the position of Purcell's second autograph copies in Lbl R.M. 20.h.8, and Purcell's handwriting in all three works is closely similar.

Although Purcell copied the score of *Let mine Eyes Run Down with Tears* in Ob Mus.c.26 stratigraphically, he did not use the recto and verso sides of complete sheets, as was the normal procedure in stratigraphic copies intended primarily for archiving or transmission, but formed the sheets into three bifolia so that they could be read normally in folio format. His reason for copying across complete openings cannot, therefore, have been to save time, as he gave himself the extra problem of aligning separate pieces of paper; presumably, then, his intention was to set out as much of the score as possible without line ends or page turns, but in a format that could be used for rehearsal and performance. The score underwent a high level of revision, and Purcell incorporated several revision slips, of which two (foliated 7b and 8b) cover the whole lower system of the opening fols 7v–8r. These pieces of paper are clearly not 'correction slips' rectifying errors but replace readings initially considered satisfactory with later ones, and they appear to have been attached to the main body of the score by stitching, through holes that are still visible, in the same way as a large revision slip in Ob Mus.a.1, where the thread itself is still present.

Revision slip fol. 8c perhaps holds the clue to Purcell's procedure in this anthem. Unlike the other slips, it did not simply cover existing material but also hinged outwards from the edge of fol. 8v, an arrangement required by the fact that Purcell replaced two half-bars of common time at this point with three and a half bars; the change must have been made after the next section of the anthem had been copied, as otherwise the outward hinge would have been unnecessary even if Purcell had decided that his alterations required a revision slip for clarity. Fol. 8c in fact contains the conclusion of Purcell's most extensive revision in the anthem, the rewriting of the verse 'Do not abhor us for thy name's sake', mainly on fols

---

89   See Rebecca Herissone, 'Purcell's Revisions of his Own Works', in Curtis Price (ed.), *Purcell Studies* (Cambridge: Cambridge University Press, 1995), pp. 63–5, and also Alan Howard's chapter in this volume, p. 74.

7b and 8b, which increases its overall length from 12½ common-time bars to 17. The revision slips fol. 8b and the much smaller fol. 7a bear sketches for sections of the anthem on their reverse. That on the back of fol. 8b is an outline for the revised version on the recto, implying that having found the key to a satisfactory solution Purcell retained it in his memory for completion without reference to the written notation; while subsequent changes were made in the complete text of fol. 8b, the sketch on the reverse corresponds closely to the final outcome. The same is not true of the sketch on fol. 7a, which apparently gives a version of bb. 13–16 somewhat different from the one incorporated in Ob Mus.c.26, which it presumably pre-dates; whereas, therefore, the notation on the face of each slip represents a post-copying revision, the verso of fol. 7a provides evidence of some form of revision or development at an earlier stage, before the original text of Ob Mus.c.26 was copied. Herissone inferred from the omission of text and the fact that only the first treble and countertenor parts are included in the fragment that it represents a preliminary stage in the process of composition,[90] but it could well be a reworking of existing material: if Purcell wished to try out the relationship between the upper part and one of the inner parts, he would not necessarily have needed to include the complete score nor, indeed, to be exact about pitches, which on the reverse of the slip have some possible variants with the final version of the countertenor part.[91]

Close examination of the paper types in the revision slips indicates that by the time Purcell made his changes he was no longer using a single consistent paper stock initially allocated for his work on this anthem. While three of the revision slips appear to have been ruled identically with the main paper of the score, two were definitely ruled with a different rastrum: fol. 7a, where the two staves are separated by a 14.5 mm gap, wider than any in the main stave ruling, and the large revision slip fol. 8b, where the rastrum span is about 3 mm less than elsewhere. A partial Amsterdam watermark visible in fol. 8b seems to be different from the main watermark, and the reverse of fols 7b and 8c contain treble parts of unidentified instrumental movements copied in a different hand, implying that for his later alterations Purcell may have used a stock of 'spoilt paper' set aside for use in this way. Little musicological significance, however, should be attached either to differences in paper or to variant stave-rulings in this case, as Purcell's handwriting in the corrections is indistinguishable from that in the main body of the work, strongly suggesting that all the post-copying changes in the piece were made very soon after the initial copy.

There may, of course, have been many more autographs with similar characteristics to *Let mine Eyes Run Down with Tears*, but in many cases compositional process has to be inferred from the distinctive readings of different sources, and we have no way of knowing what had happened in earlier autograph versions. The

---

90   Ibid., p. 64; an illustration of the sketch is given on this page.
91   As Howard indicates in Chapter 3, n. 37 below, two of the three variants are probably more apparent than real, resulting from Purcell's lack of care in writing down his sketch.

only other extant source to reflect internally a level of revision comparable to *Let mine Eyes Run Down with Tears* is the score of the B♭ Benedicite in Ob Mus.a.1, which can be dated to *c.*1679–81 on the evidence of Purcell's handwriting. Opportunities to evaluate Purcell's compositional processes on the basis of significant revisions are therefore likely to be limited to the works already known to exist in more than one form, but there are more of these than might at first be assumed and in some cases codicological issues may prove relevant to their assessment.[92]

Performance

Individual performing parts for instruments, voices or the organ copied by Purcell or his close collaborators are relatively rare, partly, no doubt, because regular use wore them out, but also perhaps because they were considered by later collectors to be less worthy of preservation than copies containing the complete text of a work. Nevertheless, performing material often casts interesting light on the working life of musicians of Purcell's time and on his own professional career, not least because its function is unambiguous, and may well repay closer enquiry into its significance and function than it has so far received.

One surprising aspect of Purcell's activities that is illuminated by considering performing parts is the extent to which he was involved in the practicalities of music-making at a time when his own status in the court musical establishment was very high. A fragmentary autograph solo bass part of the symphony anthem *I was Glad*, offered for auction at Bonhams, New Bond Street, London, in June 2003 but apparently not sold,[93] is a case in point. The fragment appears to be a partial sheet representing the lower half of a twelve-stave page, which has been mounted on plain paper so that whatever was on the verso is concealed; the visible staves contain the work up to b. 182, so if in fact they represent a recto the remaining 62

---

92   Examples of revised works include the Funeral Sentences (see Robert Ford, 'Purcell as his Own Editor: the Funeral Sentences', *Journal of Musicological Research* 7 (1986): 47–67; Robert Shay, 'Purcell's Revisions to the Funeral Sentences Revisited', *Early Music* 26 (1998): 457–67; and Chapter 3 below); *My Beloved Spake* (see Adams, *Henry Purcell*, pp. 168–9 and Chapter 3 below); *Hear me, O Lord* (discussed in Adams, *Henry Purcell*, pp. 172–3); *I Will Give Thanks unto Thee O Lord* (see Shay and Thompson, *Purcell Manuscripts*, p. 145); 'What a Sad Fate' (Adams, *Henry Purcell*, pp. 217–18); the symphony of *Swifter Isis, Swifter Flow* (Adams, *Henry Purcell*, pp. 118–19); Sonata 7 of the *Sonatas of Four Parts* (see Adams, *Henry Purcell*, pp. 112–13 and Chapter 3 below); and various instrumental movements (Adams, *Henry Purcell*, p. 139). See also Peter Holman, *Henry Purcell*, Oxford Studies of Composers (Oxford: Oxford University Press, 1994), p. 67.

93   The fragment formed Lot 8 in Bonhams's sale 10339, 24 June 2003, and had a guide price of £30,000–£40,000; see Bonhams's sale catalogue for this date *Printed Books, Maps & Manuscripts*, Part 1, pp. 8–10 and the online catalogue, http://www.bonhams. com/cgi-bin/public.sh/pubweb/publicSite.r?sContinent=EUR&screen=catalogue&isale No=10399 (last accessed 19 July 2009).

bars could have been on the verso of the missing upper half of the page, and might have been mounted in a similar way in order to display the part in its entirety. Rubrics indicating 'Symph[ony]' and 'Ritor[nello]' seem to imply that performance with strings was envisaged, and therefore that the copy was intended for the Chapel Royal either in Charles II's reign or in the period after 1685 when string players had to attend the Chapel Royal whenever Princess Anne was present.

Whereas the work itself can firmly be dated to 1682–83, Purcell's handwriting in this fragment features a looped italic 'r', suggesting a date in or after 1685.[94] The source therefore raises two questions: why was a new solo part needed at that stage and why was a musician of Purcell's standing copying out the parts himself? In all probability the leaf was removed from a Chapel Royal symphony-anthem part-book, possibly compiled after 1685; presumably the music on the upper half of the page was not in Purcell's hand and therefore was not preserved as a collector's item. In this case, the reason for Purcell copying the anthem is unclear – it may simply have been that it was his work and he wanted to do so – but in the other two extant autograph performing sources of sacred music there appears to have been a degree of urgency. Purcell copied the brief chorus bass part of *Sing unto God* into J-Tn N5/10 in such haste that he mistitled the work 'Sing unto the Lord', possibly because he did not complete the choruses until the last minute, and further evidence of haste is to be found in Och Mus. 1188–9 fols 42–5, which were identified as partly autograph by Bruce Wood in 1978.[95] These folios comprise four string parts for *My Song shall be Alway*, which in most sources appears as a continuo anthem accompanied by organ only. The three lower parts are completed in Purcell's hand; it seems that he had already given the symphony to a copyist, but decided himself to write out the *petite reprise* and then added string parts to the choruses.

The two remaining performing sources entirely or partly in Purcell's hand are a set of instrumental bass parts in US-NHub Osborn 515 and the organ part to *O Give Thanks* in Cfm 152, both of which survive in guard-books that to some extent obscure the origin of the music but reveal different uses for performing parts in the period. The autograph bass parts clearly date from the earliest years of Purcell's career, and were apparently brought together with other material by a compiler active towards the end of the seventeenth century.[96] The inclusion of an autograph work by Robert Wren, organist of Canterbury Cathedral from 1671 to 1691, and the fact that the set was included in William Gostling's sale in 1777, is strong evidence of a local Kentish provenance,[97] and the contents could be the performing part-books of a provincial music club. The Cfm 152 organ part, in contrast, clearly belonged to the Chapel Royal, where it must have been in use around or after 1700

---

94   For an illustration of this letter formation in the birthday ode *Who can from Joy Refrain?* (1695), see Shay and Thompson, *Purcell Manuscripts*, p. 29.

95   Wood, 'A Newly Identified Purcell Autograph'.

96   Described in Robert Ford, 'Osborn MS 515, A Guardbook of Restoration Instrumental Music', *Fontes Artis Musicae* 30 (1983): 174–84.

97   As outlined in Shay and Thompson, *Purcell Manuscripts*, p. 293.

because the last page was recopied by John Church.[98] In its surviving form, Cfm 152 probably represents an attempt by an eighteenth-century collector to salvage pages containing composers' autographs, which include, apart from Purcell, works by Humfrey, Croft and Blow, as mentioned above;[99] the Humfrey source is particularly important, since this represents the only known example of his autograph apart from an anthem in Bu 5001. The number of composer autographs perhaps reflects an expectation that composers would play the organ in performances of their own work, a suggestion reinforced by the relative simplicity of much of Purcell's copying in *O Give Thanks*, in which many passages consisted only of the bass line.

Non-autograph organ parts, while posing a number of textual difficulties, are often of considerable interest in reflecting musicians' perception of the music they were to perform, and were used by Rebecca Herissone as a major source of information on performance practices in thoroughbass playing in the period.[100] Other books not included by Herissone in her study (which was confined largely to London sources) provide further insight into practices in individual institutions, exemplified by the Canterbury Cathedral organ-books CA Mus. 10 and 11, copied by Daniel Henstridge. In his copy of Purcell's *Sing unto God* (CA Mus. 10, pp. 1–4) Henstridge not only transcribed the bass solo vocal line in full but later carefully added a great deal of articulation, suggesting that this sort of detail was important to the accompanist. Other than organ-books, surviving performing materials mainly consist of choir part-books, which have been little studied outside the major centres of the Chapel Royal, Windsor and the great London churches.[101] Such sources need to be approached with some caution, as it seems likely that works were sometimes added to the Chapel Royal part-books only after they had been accepted as part of the repertory and were well known to the singers, for whom the copied text therefore acted as an *aide-memoire* rather than an indispensible script; familiarity with the music must explain why, for example, in Purcell's *O Give Thanks* the omission of b. 66 from the countertenor part apparently went unnoticed for a considerable time in both Chapel Royal countertenor books (Lbl R.M. 27.a.1 and 27.a.5), as well as in related sources such as the Worcester Cathedral part WO A.3.4. Similarly, the approach to accidentals in cathedral part-books is sometimes casual in the extreme, and serves as a reminder that the relationship between aural and visual approaches to music was not the same in the seventeenth century as it is today. In spite of occasional deficiencies, however, cathedral and other part-books clearly represent an important link between composer and performance,

---

98   Described in Shaw, 'A Cambridge Music Manuscript'.

99   Shay and Thompson, *Purcell Manuscripts*, p. 190.

100 See Rebecca Herissone, *'To Fill, Forbear, or Adorne': The Organ Accompaniment of Restoration Sacred Music*, RMA Monographs, vol. 14 (Aldershot: Ashgate, 2006).

101 See Margaret Laurie, 'The Chapel Royal Part-books', in Oliver Neighbour (ed.), *Music and Bibliography: Essays in Honour of Alec Hyatt King* (New York: Saur; London: Bingley, 1980), pp. 28–50; Shay and Thompson, *Purcell Manuscripts*, pp. 177–230; and Keri Dexter, *'A Good Quire of Voices': The Provision of Choral Music at St George's Chapel, Windsor Castle, and Eton College, c.1640–1733* (Aldershot and Burlington: Ashgate, 2002).

and it may be that a systematic study of their variants will cast light both on source relationships and on performing practice.

Archiving

The function of archiving is not, of course, necessarily separate from other musical functions, and any material ever filed away for future reference or performance would have become 'archival' even if its initial purpose had been entirely different. Conversely, since the whole point of an archival copy was to serve as an exemplar for new parts if required, every such copy was, in a sense, intended for transmission. If absence offers any kind of proof, we might reasonably conclude that most of Purcell's separate autographs of his court odes and anthems were archived at Whitehall and destroyed in the disastrous fire of 1698, along with any performing material that existed. Nevertheless, some important extant sources must have had an archival function, including the composer's major autographs Lbl Add. 30930, Lbl R.M. 20.h.8 and Cfm 88.

The distinctive characteristics of these three file copies are explored in detail in *Purcell Manuscripts*, and taken together they demonstrate vividly the wide range of reasons for which such archival sources might be made. The most personal of the three is Lbl Add. 30930, which, as noted above, was demonstrably used by Purcell as unbound sheets before it was finally assembled as a book in the early 1680s; straightforward proof of this statement is provided by John Walter's copy of the sacred partsongs in Ob Mus.c.28, which presents all the works contained entirely within gatherings of Lbl Add. 30930 before those copied from one gathering to the next, which were presumably composed later.[102] With only a few exceptions, the contents of Lbl Add. 30930 consist of music Purcell did not have to write in connection with his court employment and, in the case of the fantazias, had more to do with his own development as a composer than with the immediate advancement of his career.

Lbl R.M. 20.h.8 consists of the same type of paper as Lbl Add. 30930, but its regular quiring and the absence of any assertion of ownership suggest that it was issued to Purcell as a bound volume in which he chose, or was required, to make a copy of each work he wrote for the court between 1681 and Charles II's death in 1685. In this way the score would provide a formal record of music composed for public court ceremony, which would include the odes and symphony anthems, as well as symphony songs and other vocal pieces written for less formal occasions. The 'official' character of the volume as a court document is underlined by the fact that 'O Solitude' (fols 173v–174r inv.) was copied by Purcell's assistant 'London A' and John Blow,[103] rather than Purcell. This could be because one of them had to play the harpsichord when it was performed, but more extensive later additions by 'London

---

102 Thompson, 'Purcell's Great Autographs', p. 12.
103 See above, n. 80.

A' and other hands were made after 1685, when the book's distinctive character as a repository for music dedicated to the King had to an extent been lost.[104]

While the manuscript's overall function as an archive of music for the court is not in doubt, its combination of different repertories is harder to explain, not least because it contains court odes, which were unlikely to be repeated, interspersed with solo songs that were presumably performed quite frequently. The presence of symphony anthems at one end and odes at the other makes perfect sense, as does the inclusion of symphony songs in the ode sequence; all these works involve solo voices and an instrumental group, and are to that extent repertorially connected. The solo songs, however, are generically quite distinct and must have been archived in this volume because they belonged to the repertory of the same singers as the other works. The manuscript's apparent role as an accessory of court ritual and ceremony also makes it surprising that some of the works it contains are incomplete; unlike other autographs, this incompleteness cannot necessarily be explained as part of the process of initial composition, or as the result of Purcell as performer omitting detail he did not need.

Purcell's priority in Lbl R.M. 20.h.8, although one not invariably achieved, appears to have been to preserve the essential framework of every piece even if inner parts are sometimes missing. There is good evidence, for example in the anthem *Rejoice in the Lord Alway*, that Purcell sometimes made the transcription from his separate autograph into Lbl R.M. 20.h.8 at an intermediate point in the process of composition, so that it might represent the 'state' of a separate autograph in which the vocal parts and the outline of instrumental sections were complete but the inner string parts had yet to be finished, a procedure reminiscent of some sections of the *Fairy Queen* autograph, Lam 3. Herissone has argued that there are strong reasons for believing that Purcell sometimes completed the vocal parts of his odes first in a separate score and then copied them into Lbl R.M. 20.h.8 before adding the instrumental parts.[105] There would be many practical reasons for following a two-stage procedure, which need not, of course, have been exactly the same in every case; apart from security, the existence of two scores would enable the copying of parts to begin before the work was finished, while Lbl R.M. 20.h.8 could also have been used as a rehearsal score for working with solo singers. This would explain both its strange repertorial combination and the fact that the solo vocal parts are almost always complete whatever else is missing.

The earliest of the three autograph scores, Cfm 88, may also have been the most varied in function. Its initial custodian was John Blow, who copied a number of symphony anthems by himself, Pelham Humfrey and Matthew Locke, possibly as an official Chapel Royal file but more probably, in view of the limited selection contained, either out of personal interest or for use in rehearsal. Purcell's first contribution to the score, which he seems to have begun in 1677, was an extensive series of full and continuo anthems by other composers, which in due course

104 Shay and Thompson, *Purcell Manuscripts*, pp. 131–5.
105 Herissone, '"Fowle Originalls"': 611–16.

incorporated similar works of his own.[106] Shay's extensive research on the sources Purcell used to make his copies in Cfm 88 has demonstrated that the initial purpose of this partly retrospective sequence may well have been both archival and educational for the composer.[107] Yet the manuscript does not seem to have served as an exemplar for the majority of extant copies of Purcell's own works; on the contrary, it seems to have been used as a retrospective, personal file in which he transcribed existing full and verse anthems, making alterations both before and after transcription, with the result that in several cases the readings of Cfm 88 are different from those of the majority of other sources.[108] For Purcell's latest works in this volume there are in fact few or no concordances, those that exist being based either on Cfm 88 itself or a closely related copy which may well have been Purcell's unbound autograph.

The three autograph score-books all to some extent reflect 'work in progress', with blank bars sometimes left in problematic areas, significant variants from concordances based on earlier autographs and internal evidence of post-copying revision. Paradoxically, the most 'definitive' file copies are not those in the composer's hand but those made by his colleagues for practical purposes of their own, which would of course require a text that was 'final', if only provisionally so or in a particular context. The disaster of the Whitehall fire in 1698 makes it doubly fortunate that two highly reliable copyists, William Isaack and John Walter, were active at Windsor throughout Purcell's working lifetime, their extensive output including a large number of Purcell's major works.

Isaack and Walter between them produced two important secondary sources of *Who can from Joy Refrain?* in a format easily usable only in file or transmission copies. Both Ob Mus.c.27*,[109] in which they worked in partnership, and Cfm 684, copied by Isaack alone, are laid out 'stratigraphically', using the whole of each side of foolscap-sized sheets with the separate blocks of staves intended for each page joined together. Either side of each sheet was copied in sequence, so that the score can only be read by opening out the full sheets as they are now conserved, although both copies were clearly stored in the late seventeenth century by being folded together vertically into a folio format; a patterned paper wrapper to surround the folded sheets survives in Cfm 684. The fact that the score was copied on loose sheets might of course have had considerable advantages when parts had to be copied, as it would be possible for a team of copyists to work simultaneously on different sections, and the duplicate scores may well have been produced to speed up this process; another purpose may have been to file one copy at Windsor and the other elsewhere.

---

106 Shay and Thompson, *Purcell Manuscripts*, pp. 33–46; Shay, 'Purcell as Collector of "Ancient" Music'.

107 Shay, 'Purcell as Collector of "Ancient" Music', pp. 44–8.

108 See Ford, 'Purcell as his Own Editor' and Herissone, '"Fowle Originalls"': 593–604.

109 These folios were extracted in 1939 from Ob Mus.c.27 and retain their previous folio numbers, 27–32.

A perhaps more surprising use of this 'file copy' format, with whole sheets folded together for shelving, occurs in John Blow's collection of 13 organ parts now Mp BRm 370 Bp35. This source, probably intended for use at St Paul's Cathedral after the opening of the rebuilt choir in December 1697, consists of 12 foolscap-sized sheets and at first sight appears to be a performing organ-book in an unusually large format. The sheets were clearly folded to normal folio size, however, and discoloration of fol. 12v suggests that it formed the outside of the collection for a considerable time; moreover, the sheets are so large that turning one from front to back would be awkward in any circumstances and there are a number of highly inconvenient page turns. This collection may therefore have formed part of a file of parts from which organists were expected to copy their own performing material.

Some vocal part-books also served an archival function. Performing part-books were generally large volumes with heavy, easily legible notation, and copyists sometimes made smaller versions from which they could draw up performing parts as required. File-copy part-books therefore served the same purpose as scores, but had the advantage both of presenting the music in the format in which it was to be reproduced and of saving considerable amounts of space. The most famous example, the 'Bing-Gostling' set Y M1 (1–8) S, was described and indexed in 1986 by Harold Watkins Shaw, who clearly demonstrated its archival purpose on the grounds of the small format of the books, the way parts of different works are sometimes crammed into any space left available and the general inclusion of parts duplicated between decani and cantoris sides in one volume only.[110] In other cases, a smaller repertory and more user-friendly layout means that part-book sets that probably were primarily archival might also have doubled as rehearsal copies for use in surroundings more intimate than a cathedral choir; examples in this category include Lcm 1061 and Ob Tenbury 1505. Finally, John Gostling's major collection in Ob Tenbury 1176–82, compiled c.1705–15, appears from its later ownership history and pristine condition to have been a private set of file copies, even though its large format and clarity would have made it usable in a cathedral.[111] A close relationship with the repertory of St Paul's Cathedral is reflected both in the fact that Tenbury 1176–82 do not duplicate the 'A2' set of St Paul's part-books, copied by Gostling in

110 H. Watkins Shaw, *A Study of the Bing-Gostling Part Books in the Library of York Minster together with a Systematic Catalogue* (Oxford: Oxford University Press, 1994), pp. 11–12. See also Spink, *Restoration Cathedral Music*, p. 78 and Shay and Thompson, *Purcell Manuscripts*, p. 202.

111 Shaw argues on the grounds of format and dimensions that Ob Tenbury 1176–82 were performance copies, file copies of some of their repertory being contained in another, smaller Gostling set, Ob Tenbury 797–803. The fact remains that both sets were Gostling's personal property; Ob Tenbury 1176–82 and 797–803 appear respectively to have formed lots 2 and 83 in *A Catalogue of the Scarce, Valuable and Curious Collection of Music, Manuscript and Printed, of the Reverend and Learned William Gostling* ([London], 1777), p. 5 and the larger set appears never to have been used in performance. See Shay and Thompson, *Purcell Manuscripts*, p. 209.

the 1690s, and by the close relationship of some of the organ parts to Blow's in Mp BRm 370 Bp35.[112]

Between the extremes of unquestionable cathedral performance material, typically showing signs of considerable damage and extensive repair, and the kind of file copy represented by Y M1 1–8 (S) lie a number of sources whose purpose is uncertain. Further research into the relationship between file copies and their derivatives and into the rehearsal arrangements of seventeenth- and eighteenth-century cathedral singers may well lead to a greater understanding of many sources which, although laid out as if for performance, do not appear to have been used in the choir stalls or organ loft.

Transmission

The concept of 'transmission' lies at the heart of attempts to understand the wider musical culture of any period in history, as it seeks to explain how music was disseminated from its creator to a wider audience. The function of transmission was, of course, carried out whenever a document was used to transfer a work from one place to another, whatever its primary purpose, but transmission copies were sometimes produced especially to be sent elsewhere, particularly by cathedral musicians who tended to develop a network of acquaintances in distant places. In this context, a score of two anthems by William King sent from Edward Jackson at Gloucester[113] to Daniel Henstridge in Rochester merits careful attention (Lbl Add. 30932 fols 70v–71r).[114] This is a single sheet of paper on which the anthems are written stratigraphically with enough space left at the bottom for a letter from Jackson, the contents suggesting the manuscript was copied shortly after Henstridge's move to Gloucester in 1673.[115] Jackson's letter contains significant information about the process of transmission:

> I have here sent ye 2 full Anthems of Mr King's (wch you desired in yo[u]r
> Letter dated Feb. 2^d.) I put y^m in a Score; because thus they take up lesse roome,
> & so will aske ye lesse postage; I suppose they are altogether as fit for your use

---

112 Shay and Thompson, *Purcell Manuscripts*, p. 208.

113 Jackson (d. 3 January 1677) was a minor canon at Gloucester from 1664 and precentor from 1667; see Suzanne Eward (ed.), *Gloucester Cathedral Chapter Act Book, 1616–1687*, Gloucester Record Series, vol. 21 (Bristol: Bristol and Gloucestershire Archaeological Society, 2007), p. 165.

114 The bifolio fols 70–71 has been opened out and bound in to the guard-book sideways, so that it looks like a single large folio.

115 Apart from the musical requests in the letter, which imply that both cathedrals had recently changed their organist, personal comments in the letter, such as 'I am glad Mrs Henstridge got safe to Rochest[e]r w[i]th yo[u]r little ones' also suggest a date in 1673. The letter is transcribed in full in H. Watkins Shaw, *The Succession of Organists of the Chapel Royal and the Cathedrals of England and Wales from c.1538*, Oxford Studies in British Church Music (Oxford: Clarendon, 1991), pp. 235–6.

in a Score. What words of the Psalms are repeated you are not unacquainted with: Notwithstanding I have marked the repetitions so y^t any body may understand y^m with ease.

Henstridge had specifically asked for a copy of two particular anthems, which he presumably wished to introduce to the repertory at Rochester;[116] Jackson made a copy of them to send by post, which apparently involved not only scoring up the separate parts but also ruling most of one side of a sheet of paper, using a straight edge and drawing one stave line at a time; Jackson presumably went to this trouble in order to produce a more compact score than it would have been possible to produce with normal manuscript paper. As Jackson explained, he provided only text incipits, but in enough detail to enable a scribe to draw up parts directly from the score.

The copy was sent through the post by folding the sheet down to one-eighteenth of its original size, making a little packet measuring 110 mm by 73 mm, with the address 'For Mr Daniel Henstridge Organist of Rochester at his house on Bulley hill' in the centre of fol. 71v; the same panel also tells us that the packet was sent via London and cost 3d to send to that city and a further 2d for its transportation onwards to Rochester. Jackson appears to have been concerned about the cost of this correspondence, which he clearly regarded as a normal form of exchange between cathedrals and expected to continue:

> I pray, send us ye Organ p[ar]t of <u>Behold thou hast made my dayes</u>. & Mr <u>Wren</u>'s full Anthem wch is prickt in ye bookes: or any thing else that you know wee have not here: & I shall bee ready to repay you in any Services or Anthems o[u]r Church affords: if you will lett me know in yo[u]r next, where your Rochester Carrier lyes I might send papers or any thing else to you, at an easier rate, yn now I doe by ye post. Send ye Organ p[ar]t assoon [sic] as you can; if it bee large, direct it to bee left at ye Bull and Mouth… [sic] for ye Glouc[este]r carrier to convey it to mee.[117]

This brief note not only provides concrete evidence of a mode of transmission we might have assumed took place anyway but also reflects practical consideration of ways in which such exchanges could most economically be carried out.[118] It is interesting, if hardly surprising, to find Purcell himself engaged in similar

---

116 These are William King's *O Lord our Governor* and *The Lord is King*. A note by Philip Hayes on fol. 70r mistakenly ascribes both works to George King, William King's father.

117 The Bull and Mouth was a coaching inn in Aldersgate; see Henry A. Harben, *A Dictionary of London: being Notes Topographical and Historical relating to the Streets and Principal Buildings in the City of London* (London: Jenkins, 1918); electronic version in British History Online, http://www.british-history.ac.uk/Default.aspx (last accessed 2 June 2009).

118 This kind of informal exchange between musicians is a different process from the official purchase of copies recorded in Spink, *Restoration Cathedral Music*, p. 77, for which payment is recorded in cathedral accounts; in such cases, the copyist was probably expected to provide usable performance material.

activities, although probably at a relatively early stage of his career. One of the items in the guard-book Och Mus. 1215 is a single stratigraphically copied sheet containing Daniel Roseingrave's anthem *Lord Thou art become Gracious*, in which, as Peter Holman revealed in 1995, the music was copied by Purcell and most or all of the somewhat sparse text, mainly confined to incipits, apparently by Roseingrave himself.[119] Edward Jackson's letter shows that, as musicians moved around the country, they could indeed find themselves without a copy of their own earlier works; the 'Mr Wren' whose full anthem was available at Rochester but not at Gloucester was presumably Charles Wren who moved from Rochester to Gloucester in late 1673 or 1674. It seems, therefore, that in writing out a score of Roseingrave's anthem, Purcell was performing a favour that certainly was not unprecedented and may have been quite common. The sheet was folded into four, implying that it was sent by post either to Gloucester or Winchester, where Roseingrave successively served as organist from 1678 to 1681 and 1681 to 1692; paper evidence, and the limited evidence of a rubric 'vers 4 voc' that might be in Purcell's hand, suggest that the manuscript belongs to the beginning of this period and may in turn mean that the anthem was composed while Roseingrave was a chorister at the Chapel Royal, where Purcell had access to a score or parts after Roseingrave had left, presumably, as Holman suggests, without taking with him his own copy.[120]

While the two sources just described are clear examples of one possible mechanism of transmission – by means of a score – they give little indication of either the full extent or the overall nature of the transmission activity that must have taken place. In cathedral manuscripts, related readings of anthems in geographically distant locations bear indirect witness to a process of dissemination sometimes carried out through performing parts rather than through transmission scores; in Purcell's *O Give Thanks*, for example, the error of omitting b. 66 from the countertenor part mentioned above is easy to understand in a part-book but would have been noticed at once if transmission had been effected through a score. At times, however, it seems that transmission was associated with deliberate changes to the original musical text not necessarily sanctioned by its creator, and in this context as well as others transmission is an area much in need of further investigation.

For practical reasons, symphony anthems composed for the Chapel Royal were often adapted for accompaniment by organ alone, a practice investigated in depth by Keri Dexter,[121] but by the time Purcell's symphony anthems began

---

119 Holman, 'Purcell and Roseingrave'.
120 Ibid., p. 105.
121 Keri Dexter, 'The Restoration "Symphony" Anthem in Organ Transcription: Contemporary Techniques and Transmission' (MMus dissertation, University of Reading, 1996). See also Lionel Pike, 'Alternative Versions of Purcell's Praise the Lord, O my Soul: O Lord my God', in Patrick F. Devine and Harry M. White (eds), *The Maynooth International Musicological Conference 1995: Selected Proceedings, II*, Irish Musical Studies, vol. 5 (Dublin: Four Courts, 1996), pp. 272–80; Pike, 'Purcell's "Rejoice in the Lord",

to circulate widely, the regular use of strings in the Chapel Royal had ceased, so such arrangements were not necessarily confined to the provinces and some appear in John Blow's organ-book Mp BRm 370 Bp35. Other alterations are less readily identifiable, a major example occurring in the case of *Blessed is the Man that Feareth the Lord*, which Gostling copied in US-AUS HRC [formerly pre-1700] 85 as an anthem for two soloists, countertenor and bass, without a chorus. An attractive and evidently popular work composed for the Charterhouse in London, it was adapted for use in cathedrals and comparable establishments in different ways; in the eighteenth century, the most widespread version was one with an extra solo part for tenor and an effective final chorus that begins with the melodic outline of the start of the final verse but soon pursues a direction of its own. The earliest sources of this version complete with its chorus appear to be Ctc RISM 2 and 4 (tenor and bass), Cjc T.2–4 and T.6–8 (cantoris and decani parts of all voices except the treble) and Cu EDC 10/7/6, a score from Ely copied by James Hawkins. Since the two part-book sets have always belonged to their Cambridge colleges, and the earliest source of the three-voice setting without the chorus is Lbl Add. 31445, also in the hand of James Hawkins, it is reasonable to suggest that this particular version emanated from East Anglia and that Hawkins himself, who was no inconsiderable composer,[122] might have been responsible for it.

A different adaptation was made in sources associated with John Gostling or Canterbury Cathedral, which retain the two-voice setting and provide a final chorus based very closely on the final solo verse; Gostling added this chorus to his score of the anthem in US-AUS HRC 85 and Daniel Henstridge's organ-book CA Mus. 11 contains two copies of this setting, the first with the original organ passages from the Gostling score-book and the second with two of these passages adapted as they were in a later Gostling source, Ob Tenbury 1180.[123] Source evidence suggests that all of these alterations date from after Purcell's death; the same cannot be true, however, of an adaptation made at Lincoln, where the tenor and bass chorus part-books LI Mus. 2–4 contain not only a concluding chorus different from either of those mentioned above but also an intermediate one based upon the 3/2-time verse section. Since the Lincoln books were periodically dated for accounting purposes we can be sure these choruses were added before 7 December 1693, but they are stylistically most unlikely to be Purcell's own work.

Something similar may well have happened to the beautiful two-treble anthem *O Lord, Rebuke me Not*, the chorus of which again appears, incomplete, in the Lincoln part-books and in contemporary part-books at Durham; the complete anthem exists only in Ob Tenbury 789, an early eighteenth-century score from Peterborough. The work's form could be expressed as A B (b) C B (b), where A and C are declamatory

---

All Ways', *Music & Letters* 82 (2001): 391–420; and Pike, 'The Ferial Version of Purcell's "I Was Glad"', *Royal Musical Association Research Chronicle* 35 (2002): 41–59.

122 Spink, *Restoration Cathedral Music*, pp. 243–53.

123 A further copy by Henstridge, of the chorus alone, appears in US-LAuc fC6966/M4/A627/1700. In Ob Tenbury 1178, a tenor part-book, Gostling left space for the added tenor solo part but did not copy it.

common-time verse sections and B a more lyrical triple-time verse which is adapted to form the chorus (b). The addition of a further level of modified repetition to a work that already contains the major structural repeat of B is uncharacteristic of Purcell and, although in this case the style of the chorus is much more convincing, it is at least possible that the extant 'anthem' is a work analogous to *Blessed is the Man*, again adapted for use as a conventional cathedral work with a chorus. Another verse-only continuo anthem, *Blessed is He that Considereth the Poor*, displays a reasonably conventional pattern of sources, appearing in unquestionably liturgical contexts in Mp BRm 370 Bp35, the Hereford Cathedral organ-book H 30.b.10 and in Ob Tenbury 1505. Yet in Ob Tenbury 1176–80 Gostling added a chorus to it which, with the possible exception of the incomplete additions in Lincoln, is much the least satisfactory of the apparently inauthentic accretions acquired by the works mentioned here.

In complete contrast, 'transmission' might also involve the despatch of a new work for scribal copying, which would require conscious attention to detail by the compiler of the transmission copy and in turn demand meticulous observation of the composer's directions by the copyists of the performing parts. Transmission may, therefore, have been the initial purpose of some sources that appear to be file copies; it is highly probable, for example, that *Who can from Joy Refrain?* was performed at Windsor,[124] so that the duplicate stratigraphic copies in Ob Mus. c. 27* and Cfm 684 might well have been drawn up from Purcell's score at Whitehall for Isaack and Walter to take with them to Windsor and produce the performing parts for the work to be rehearsed against a tight deadline. Incomplete transmission copies, conversely, could sometimes lead to unsuccessful outcomes: Isaack's Cfm 117 copy of *My Beloved Spake* uncharacteristically has major problems of underlay, which appear to stem from his initially copying from a score containing incipits only and perhaps reflect a transmission copy of the revised version of this work made by Purcell himself or a London copyist.[125]

Purcell's major score-books seem themselves to have acted at times as transmission copies. Several anthems in Cfm 117 and US-AUS HRC 85, not all by Purcell, were copied directly from Cfm 88, and certainly in the case of Cfm 117 the transcription is most likely to have taken place at Windsor, where Purcell must have taken the score during one or more of the court's regular visits.[126] The fact that Isaack's two sections of direct copying from Cfm 88 are separated by more than 100 folios strongly suggests that he had access to the score on different occasions some considerable time apart. In its early unbound state, Lbl Add. 30930 could also

---

124 Ian Spink, 'Purcell's Odes: Propaganda and Panegyric', in Curtis Price (ed.), *Purcell Studies* (Cambridge: Cambridge University Press, 1995), p. 159; Olive Baldwin and Thelma Wilson, '"Who can from Joy Refraine?": Purcell's Birthday Song for the Duke of Gloucester', *Musical Times* 122 (1981): 596–9.
125 For an illustration see Shay and Thompson, *Purcell Manuscripts*, p. 63. Isaack's copy is discussed further in Alan Howard's chapter in this volume, pp. 85–90.
126 Shay and Thompson, *Purcell Manuscripts*, pp. 50–60; Herissone, '"Fowle Originalls"': 603–4.

have been used quite conveniently as a transmission manuscript, as appears to have happened when Richard Goodson, then Oxford Professor of Music, copied Sonatas 9, 7 and 8 from the set published in 1697 as *Sonatas of Four Parts*, in the same order as they occur in the autograph, into Och Mus. 3 and the Fantazia on One Note into Och Mus. 620. Before the autograph score was bound, the three sonatas would have been contained in a single separate gathering and the fantazia on a separate bifolio.[127]

Education

Purcell is known to have taught a number of individual pupils, some young men training for professional careers, such as the organist Robert Hodge, others the daughters of wealthy families, for whom skill as a singer or at the harpsichord was a valuable social accomplishment. Both categories of pupil had some discernible impact on extant source material, but while many Restoration teaching sources record the names of their pupil owners, none is attached to Purcell's manuscripts, so any relationship between surviving manuscripts and specific individuals can be no more than speculative.[128] Manuscript material explicitly dedicated to musical education is generally confined to keyboard- and song-books, and amongst Purcell's autographs only the keyboard-book Lbl Mus. 1 and the Gresham song-book Lg Safe 3 could be considered 'teaching material'. While the pedagogical function of Lbl Mus. 1 was recognized at once in accounts published after its discovery in 1993,[129] the purpose of the Gresham autograph is more problematical; in 1911 Squire suggested the possibility that the manuscript was intended for a pupil,[130] but its challenging repertory and frequently missing continuo parts may instead indicate that it was used for private performances at court with Purcell himself playing the harpsichord.[131] Given the importance of musical accomplishment for upper-class women of the time, the two interpretations may not be exclusive, and new information explored below could imply a different, though related, context for the manuscript.

There is sound documentary evidence to show that in the 1690s Purcell taught two upper-class girls: Michael Burden demonstrated that Rhoda Cartwright – to whom as Rhoda Cavendish the 1697 sonatas were dedicated – had lessons with him from no later than November 1691 until November 1693;[132] and Maureen Duffy uncovered evidence that Diana Howard, the granddaughter of Sir Robert Howard, studied with him between late 1693, when she would have been aged about seven, and early

---

127 Thompson, 'Purcell's Great Autographs', pp. 12 and 14–15.

128 Some of the subordinate hands in Lbl R.M. 20.h.8 may be those of Purcell's professional pupils; see *Purcell Manuscripts*, pp. 128–35.

129 See n. 36 above, and Woolley, 'English Keyboard Sources and their Contexts', pp. 53–60.

130 Squire, 'An Unknown Autograph of Henry Purcell': 7.

131 See Laurie and Thompson's Preface to Purcell, *The Gresham Autograph*, pp. viii–ix.

132 Michael Burden, '"He Had the Honour to be Your Master": Lady Rhoda Cavendish's Music Lessons with Henry Purcell', *Music & Letters* 76 (1995): 532–9.

1695.[133] A pupil of much greater significance who has generally been overlooked, however, was Sir Robert's fourth wife Annabella Dyve, whom he married in 1693.[134] In this case her relationship with Purcell is established by the dedication to her of *Orpheus Britannicus* and by circumstantial evidence, including her donation of the memorial tablet to Purcell in Westminster Abbey. The dedication ascribed to Frances Purcell in *Orpheus Britannicus* refers to Lady Howard's 'extraordinary skill in music' and states that 'as several of [Purcell's] best Compositions were originally design'd for Your Ladiship's Entertainment, so the Pains he bestowed in fitting them for Your Ear, were abundantly rewarded by the Satisfaction he has received from Your Approbation, and admirable performance of them'.

As the wife (and soon to be widow) of Sir Robert Howard, Annabella must have been one of the wealthiest women in England,[135] and was therefore a natural patron for Frances Purcell to cultivate. However, strong evidence that the dedication is more than empty flattery survives in a series of letters preserved amongst the Marlborough correspondence,[136] which suggests that she and Sir Robert spent much of their time at Bell Barr, a location close to the Marlboroughs' home at St Albans that gives its name to the title or subtitle of the song 'I Love and I Must' in the Gresham manuscript and the D minor keyboard Almand Z668/i. Bell Barr, an area of North Mimms close to Hatfield, at that time lay on the Great North Road.[137] The place is named only in a letter dated 'Thursday the 24th of September' [1696] addressed from 'Bellbarr' and another undated letter, in which Annabella asks Lady Marlborough to 'be so kind as to let me see you at Bell barr'.[138] Nevertheless, on 'April 29. Satterday' – which must have been in 1693 – Annabella wrote 'I am in such raptures with yᵉ hopes of being deare Lady Marlborough['s] nei[gh]bour this sum[m]er' and shortly afterwards 'I have quite left yᵉ thoughts of Uxbridge, and 'tis Mr Cookes house I have taken … 'tis but five mile from St Talbans, and I think itt is

---

133 Records of Diana's lessons with Purcell appear in the accounts of Ashtead Manor, which Sir Robert Howard settled on his son Thomas before his marriage to Annabella Dyve; see Jean-Pierre Vander Motten, 'Howard, Sir Robert (1626–1698)', in *Oxford Dictionary of National Biography*, http://www.oxforddnb.com (last accessed 30 July 2010) and Maureen Duffy, *Henry Purcell* (London: Fourth Estate, 1994), p. 214. Duffy points out that the extant Ashtead accounts are those of Thomas Howard and his wife Diana (ibid., p. 217).

134 See H.J. Oliver, *Sir Robert Howard (1626–1698): A Critical Biography* (Durham, NC: Duke University Press, 1963), pp. 281–3. According to Narcissus Luttrell, *A Brief Historical Relation of State Affairs from September 1678 to April 1714* (6 vols, Oxford: Oxford University Press, 1857) vol. 3, p. 45, Annabella was 'a maid of honour to the princess [Anne], aged about 18'.

135 Luttrell states that she inherited £40,000; *A Brief Historical Relation*, vol. 4, pp. 423–4.

136 Lbl Add. 61455, fols 138r–177v.

137 The Great North Road was diverted to a more direct route as late as 1851; for this and other information about Bell Barr see Peter Kingsford, *Victorian Lives in North Mymms* Ch. 9, 'Change in Bell Barr', http://www.brookmans.com/history/kingsford4/ch9.shtml (last accessed 26 May 2009).

138 Lbl Add. 61455, fols 157r and 168r.

as pretty a place as ever I saw'.[139] Since Bell Barr is indeed roughly five miles from St Albans, and several other letters imply that both Lady Marlborough's home and Hatfield House were close by,[140] it is reasonable to infer that the house at Bell Barr was the Howards' summer retreat from the time of their marriage in 1693 until Sir Robert's death in 1698.

The 'Bell Barr' keyboard movement does not appear in Lbl Mus. 1, but the song with that subtitle in the Gresham autograph may indicate a closer connection between Purcell and Annabella Howard than has previously been recognized; Frances Purcell referred to 'several' of her husband's compositions being written for Annabella, and perhaps these included some of the other songs in the Gresham autograph that were not taken from longer works. Lg Safe 3 has a number of striking features which point towards a distinctive and special purpose: a high proportion of the songs it contains are extracts from major works adapted if necessary to bring the vocal line within the soprano range, often achieved by transposing the whole piece downwards and then raising the vocal line by an octave. Seven of the songs by Purcell are incomplete, generally through the absence of all or part of the continuo line, which he could of course have supplied himself either from memory or as an improvisation. Yet if, as Frances Purcell wrote in *Orpheus Britannicus*, Annabella Howard's skill in music was 'beyond most of either Sex', she might well have been able to accompany herself on the harpsichord or another instrument without the help of bass or figures.

The keyboard manuscript Lbl Mus. 1 also contains an interesting and quite challenging repertory. While the book contains a limited amount of simple didactic material, the music by Giovanni Battista Draghi copied at one end of the book, probably in his own hand,[141] is of considerable difficulty, and the latter part of the sequence copied by Purcell also consists of quite complex suite movements. Paper type unfortunately provides no evidence to help resolve one of the manuscript's main mysteries, which is whether Draghi or Purcell copied his music in it first; the source's most striking codicological feature is that it is a finely bound manuscript book consisting of paper likely to have been made no later than 1682, whereas Purcell's contribution to the copying appears from his handwriting style as well as concordances with stage works to date from the 1690s. The complete absence of any form of personal identification inside or outside the binding, and the lack of flyleaves, strongly suggest that Lbl Mus. 1 was an off-the-shelf, though high-quality, manuscript book produced speculatively by a stationer, possibly not sold for some time and then not necessarily used straight away by its new owner.

While it is not possible from the physical evidence of the book to confirm or challenge Price's hypothesis, made partly on the basis of the relative difficulty of the

---

139 Ibid., fols 140r and 142r.
140 Lady Marlborough visited Annabella Howard for dinner (fol. 152r); Lady Salebury [i.e. Salisbury] 'sent her chares' for Annabella, presumably to take her to Hatfield (fol. 168r).
141 Woolley, 'English Keyboard Sources and their Contexts', pp. 54–8, presents this argument most persuasively.

material copied by each composer, that copying passed from Purcell to Draghi,[142] there is more to be said on the contents themselves. When the manuscript came to public attention in 1994, interest naturally focused on the autograph material by Purcell, but in many ways the 'Draghi end' is more remarkable; Draghi was a virtuoso harpsichordist whose *Six Select Sutes of Lessons for the Harpsichord* were published only in 1707, the year before he died, and the relatively limited circulation of his music in manuscript form suggests that he guarded his repertory with some care until age and infirmity meant that he could no longer perform it in person.[143] Moreover, no. 15 of the Draghi works is a toccata which has all the appearance of professional performing material and, indeed, of written-down improvisation, analogous with a contemporary organ voluntary. All this would tend to support the argument that his contribution to the manuscript was later than Purcell's, but a few Draghi works do appear in earlier manuscripts such as Och Mus. 1177, and it would be difficult to prove conclusively on this basis which composer was the earlier copyist. The pieces at the 'Purcell end' are, as Price indicated, much more varied in level of difficulty, style and authorship than Draghi's, and at the start juxtapose simple and challenging pieces in a manner that cannot easily be reconciled with the progression of an individual pupil. A number of explanations could be offered for this anomaly, such as the presence in a household of two or more pupils at different levels of ability,[144] the possibility that Purcell was in fact collecting material to be organized later into a progressive didactic publication,[145] or the fact that a teacher might well prescribe apparently very basic exercises for a pupil in order to focus on hand position, fingering, legato and so on.

One of the most interesting aspects of Purcell's section of the manuscript, which has yet to be investigated in detail, is the inclusion of unattributed copies of several pieces by other composers, which perhaps offer evidence of the imprecise boundaries of authorship in the field of keyboard music. The Orlando Gibbons Prelude in G from *Parthenia* is a well-known work that hardly needed an attribution, but the little prelude included in the Lbl Mus. 1 version of Purcell's C major suite also seems to be the work of another musician, as it is a metrical version of a presumably French *prélude non mesuré* found anonymously in F-Pn Rés. Vmd. 18, Lbl Add. 39569 and Ob Mus. Sch.e.426.[146] The jig concluding the Suite in A minor

---

142 Price, 'New Light on Purcell's Keyboard Music', pp. 92–3. Price's perceived need to apologize for the proposal that the book belonged to a pupil rather than the composer ('although it might sound preposterous') highlights the extent to which general understanding of source function and of musicians' working lives has changed since the mid-1990s.

143 Draghi appears to have been seriously incapacitated from early 1698; see Robert Thompson, 'Draghi, Giovanni Battista (1640–1708)', in *Oxford Dictionary of National Biography*, http://www.oxforddnb.com (last accessed 31 July 2010). If so, his copying in Lbl Mus. 1 may well have been completed by 1697.

144 As suggested in Price, 'New Light on Purcell's Keyboard Music', p. 93.

145 As suggested by Hogwood, 'A New English Keyboard Manuscript': 164.

146 Shay and Thompson, *Purcell Manuscripts*, p. 277, n. 24, and Woolley, 'English Keyboard Sources and their Contexts', p. 54. For F-Pn Rés. Vmd. 18 see *Manuscrit de Mademoiselle*

appears anonymously in Ob Mus.Sch.e.399 and Cfm 653, the former manuscript, copied by Francis Forcer, bearing dates in 1681 and 1682.[147] Other movements in Lbl Mus. 1 probably not by Purcell are the Air Z661/xi, which circulated on the continent under the title 'La Furstenberg' and in England apparently formed part of the incidental music for *The Virtuous Wife* but, significantly, was omitted from the published *Ayres* of 1697,[148] and a Hornpipe in A which elsewhere is attributed to John Eccles.

A possible reason for the exclusion of the Jig in A minor from *A Choice Collection*, as also of the manuscript's C major Prelude, may therefore have been its authorship; perhaps it was regarded as acceptable to include another composer's work in a performing sequence, or to use it for teaching, but not deliberately to imply a misattribution in print. There is some circumstantial evidence, however, that a piece might come to be associated with a performer rather than its original composer: the impressive, and probably German, Toccata in A (ZD229) is highly unlikely on stylistic grounds to be by Purcell, but is unequivocally ascribed to him in two otherwise authoritative sources from the north-east, Lbl Add. 31446 and 34695. A plausible explanation for this attribution is that the work was taken to Durham by Purcell's pupil Robert Hodge, and that music from Purcell's repertoire came to be regarded by others as his composition.[149] The whole issue of authorship in keyboard music may be one that merits future research, but in an area where, as performers, the leading practitioners would generally have improvised, it may well prove impossible to arrive at any more definite conclusion than we have already.

Collecting and Antiquarianism

The concept of collecting music manuscripts, or musical texts themselves, as desirable possessions in their own right has a relatively limited impact on primary sources of Purcell, the great majority of his works being represented in authoritative working documents compiled before the composer had acquired a classical status. There are, nevertheless, a handful of sources that deserve comment. Two scores at Christ Church, Oxford, likely to have formed part of the bequest of Henry Aldrich,[150] appear from their content or presentation to have been intended in some

La Pierre: pièces de clavecin c.1680 – facsimilé du ms. de la Bibliothèque nationale, Paris, Rés. Vmd.ms.18, Introduction by Pierre Féruselle (facsimile edition, Geneva: Minkoff, 1983).

147 Woolley, 'English Keyboard Sources and their Contexts', pp. 17 and 29.

148 Henry Purcell, *A Collection of Ayres, Compos'd for the Theatre* (London, 1697). The 'Furstenberg' movement is clearly associated with *The Virtuous Wife* and attributed to Purcell on fol. 3v of Lcm 1172; see *Instrumental Music for London Theatres, 1690–1699: Royal College of Music, London, MS 1172*, Introduction by Curtis Price, Music for London Entertainment, Series A/3 (facsimile edition, Withyham: Richard Macnutt, 1987).

149 Shay and Thompson, *Purcell Manuscripts*, p. 290.

150 For Aldrich's status as a collector see John Milsom, *Christ Church Library Music Catalogue*, http://library.chch.ox.ac.uk/music/ (last accessed 29 July 2010) and Robert Shay, '"Naturalizing" Palestrina and Carissimi in Late Seventeenth-Century Oxford:

way as collectors' items. The less musically significant of these is Och Mus. 39, a score of Purcell's 1683 sonatas calligraphically copied, apparently from the printed parts, by the singing man Edward Hull.[151] The second probable Aldrich score is Och Mus. 628, copied by John Blow c.1678 and containing some of his own anthems alongside anthems by Pelham Humfrey, sacred part-songs by Purcell and his own symphony song *Go Perjured Man*.[152] The appearance and repertory of this score, with its unusual combination of genres, strongly convey the impression that the music by Humfrey, Blow and Purcell was meant to represent the finest achievements of the past, present and future of serious English music and Blow's copies of early works by Purcell, sometimes in versions slightly different from the autograph score, provide not only an interesting insight into Purcell's development as a composer but also a remarkably prescient recognition of the young composer's promise.

Some finely copied scores of theatre works and odes produced soon after Purcell's death by the copyist identified as 'London E', such as Ooc Ua 34–7, Lam 21 and Lam 24 have the appearance of collector's items but present Purcell's music in isolation.[153] In contrast, the six-volume anthology of church music assembled by Thomas Tudway between 1715 and 1720 for Edward Harley (Lbl Harleian 7337–42) involves an element of conscious antiquarianism, and although the later volumes contain progressively more recent music the intention was to represent modern English music as part of a tradition.[154] Hogwood's account of Tudway's work focuses primarily on the historical introductions he appended to most of the volumes, and the collection is in fact more significant for our understanding of the reception of Purcell's music in the early eighteenth century than as a textual source, since all the anthems exist in earlier copies elsewhere and Tudway adopted, or introduced himself, some readings which adapt Purcell's music to eighteenth-century taste.[155]

Henry Aldrich and His Recompositions', *Music & Letters* 77 (1996): 368–400. Apart from the calligraphic sources mentioned here, Aldrich owned a score of the B flat service copied by John Walter (Och Mus. 38) and one of the symphony-anthem versions of *My Song shall be Alway* (Och Mus. 766). Printed music included a copy of the 1683 St Cecilia ode and the 1694 Te Deum (both lost), *The Vocal and Instrumental Musick of The Prophetess* (Och Mus. 787), the 1697 sonatas (Och Mus. 824–7) and *A Collection of Ayres, Compos'd for the Theatre* (Och Mus. 828–31).

151 Shay and Thompson, *Purcell Manuscripts*, pp. 124 and 309; see also the entry for Och Mus. 39 in Milsom, *Christ Church Library Music Catalogue*.

152 See the entry for Och Mus. 628 in Milsom, *Christ Church Library Music Catalogue* and Shay and Thompson, *Purcell Manuscripts*, pp. 100–104.

153 See Shay and Thompson, *Purcell Manuscripts*, pp. 241–7.

154 Spink, *Restoration Cathedral Music*, pp. 87–8 and 434–49; see also Christopher Hogwood, 'Thomas Tudway's History of Music', in Christopher Hogwood and Richard Luckett (eds), *Music in Eighteenth-Century England: Essays in Memory of Charles Cudworth* (Cambridge: Cambridge University Press, 1983), pp. 19–48.

155 For example, in *Be Merciful*, b. 9, the word 'merciful' is set by Purcell in the rhythm semiquaver–semiquaver–quaver, followed by a quaver rest, but Tudway gives dotted-quaver–semiquaver–dotted-quaver (Lbl Harleian 7340, fol. 162).

As Rebecca Herissone demonstrates in Chapter 8 of this volume, scholars such as Ellen Harris have begun to explore eighteenth-century sources of Purcell's music from the perspective of reception,[156] concentrating particularly on the common practice of updating the music in the way Tudway did. It is also important to acknowledge, however, that at least two of Purcell's compositions – *Dido and Aeneas* and *Come ye Sons of Art* – would be unknown as complete works without such antiquarian copies. While the earliest surviving complete source for *Come ye Sons of Art*, Lcm 993, is an extreme example of an eighteenth-century adaptation,[157] the main sources of *Dido and Aeneas*, Ob Tenbury 1266 and KNt MR 2–5.3, pp. 1–72, both dating from *c.*1785, appear to be accurate copies of a much earlier exemplar.[158] In the latter Philip Hayes modernized the notation,[159] but the unknown copyist of Ob Tenbury 1266 preserved the old-fashioned features of the original, including the C2 tenor violin clef, 'incomplete' key signatures and the absence of natural signs. These characteristics would preclude a date for the exemplar much later than 1710, and the surviving text, omitting the prologue, probably derives from a performance in 1704.

Codicological Methodology and Printed Sources

The codicology of printed sources differs sufficiently from that of manuscripts to need to be considered separately, not least because the potential overlap between different musical functions already present in manuscripts is even more significant in a printed book: material from the same impression could well be used for any of the functions listed above for manuscripts except composition. There are also important physical differences between manuscript and printed sources: the paper in printed material is rarely of the kinds favoured for manuscripts, and collation is not only replicated in all copies of the same impression, but also, as mentioned above, is a direct reflection of the way the sheets were printed rather than, as in the case of a manuscript, a description of the book's physical construction that may or may not be intimately related to its contents. The printing process itself opens up a rich field of evidence, and while the purpose of printing was to produce multiple copies of the same text, in practice individual copies often display distinctive and potentially revealing characteristics.

---

156 See the section 'Purcell in Later Eighteenth-Century Public Performance Culture' in Chapter 8 below.

157 See Henry Purcell, *Birthday Odes for Queen Mary, Part II*, ed. Bruce Wood, The Works of Henry Purcell, vol. 24 (new edn, London: Novello, 1998), especially pp. xvi–xvii; and Rebecca Herissone, 'Robert Pindar, Thomas Busby, and the Mysterious Scoring of Henry Purcell's "Come ye Sons of Art"', *Music & Letters* 88 (2007): 1–48.

158 Shay and Thompson, *Purcell Manuscripts*, pp. 232–4.

159 Evidence that Hayes was copying from an exemplar that used the C2 tenor violin clef is given by the first system of the overture, where a C2 clef is mistakenly written.

The technical, social and commercial aspects of English music printing and publication before 1700 were comprehensively outlined by Donald Krummel in 1975.[160] Two different technologies for printing music were available in Purcell's lifetime; most music was produced in the same way as books, using movable type assembled into a forme to impress two or more pages, but a minority of publications were printed from engraved plates, a process which was to become general in the eighteenth century. Printing music from type, which had been made commercially successful in England by John Playford, involved the considerable initial expense of purchasing a fount of type, but then offered flexibility because the type could be reused indefinitely for different works; a corresponding disadvantage however, was the fact that each forme had to be dismantled in order to assemble the next one, so that reprinting all or part of an edition was a costly and protracted process. As a consequence there was an incentive for overproduction, since any loss caused by unsold sheets would be mainly limited to the cost of the paper. Engraving, conversely, had the advantages and disadvantages of a more permanent means of origination; a unique plate had to be produced for each page, but thereafter the production of prints could respond closely to actual demand, not only in quantity but also in timing.

The greatest advantage of engraving for musical purposes, however, was the facility it offered to reproduce accurately all the features of a well-written manuscript, such as the beaming of quavers and shorter notes. In contrast, most of John Playford's typeset publications used the well-established Granjon typeface, in which the notes had diamond-shaped heads and could not be beamed together; Purcell's decision to have his 1683 *Sonnata's of III Parts* engraved would be explicable on these grounds alone, apart from wider considerations of appearance and prestige. Nevertheless, English printers and publishers clearly saw an economic case for printing from type until the final years of the seventeenth century and beyond; both volumes of *Harmonia Sacra* (1688 and 1693) were printed by Edward Jones in the Granjon face, but from the late 1680s improved round-note typefaces permitting proper grouping of short notes became available, the most significant being Heptinstall's 'new tied note', introduced in 1687 and used for *The Vocal and Instrumental Musick of the Prophetess* in 1691, and then, at the end of the century, William Pearson's 'new London character'.

As well as Krummel, other scholars – including Mary Chan, Richard Luckett, Nicholas Temperley and Stacey Houck – have thoroughly explored the technical, economic and social aspects of seventeenth-century music publication.[161] What has

---

160 Donald W. Krummel, *English Music Printing, 1553–1700* (London: Bibliographical Society, 1975).

161 See Frank Kidson, *British Music Publishers, Printers and Engravers: London, Provincial, Scottish, and Irish. From Queen Elizabeth's Reign to George the Fourth's* (London: W.E. Hill, 1900; repr. Benjamin Blom, 1967); Day and Murrie, 'Playford versus Pearson'; Nicholas Temperley, 'John Playford and the Metrical Psalms', *Journal of the American Musicological Society* 25 (1972): 331–78; Temperley, 'John Playford and the Stationers' Company', *Music & Letters* 54 (1973): 203–12; Mary Chan, 'A Mid-Seventeenth-Century

until recently been missing, however, is a recognition that printed material is capable of offering codicological and historical evidence in the same way as manuscripts, although research in this area has recently been carried out by Alon Schab and Stephanie Carter.[162] Neither movable type nor engraved publications are necessarily identical throughout a print run or, for that matter, any more accurate than handwritten copies; once type had been committed to a forme, it was unavailable for anything else and, as a result, there was considerable pressure to work quickly. Detailed preliminary proofreading appears to have been impossible, so that even in prestigious editions corrections might be made progressively as errors were noticed. Contrary to expectation, therefore, printed pages can in their way be as individual as manuscripts, with variants in type as well as manuscript alterations made either for the publisher or by the book's user. Purcell's printed score of *The Vocal and Instrumental Musick of the Prophetess*, for example, although clearly a high-quality piece of work, contains manuscript additions and corrections in a number of copies and a stop-press correction of a mispagination at pp. 166–7, which are misnumbered 165–6 in some copies but altered in print in others (an earlier pagination error is corrected in manuscript).[163] More seriously, there are further errors affecting the musical text, not necessarily blatantly obvious, which can be identified and corrected through an appreciation of the printing technology of the time.[164]

Engraved music could similarly be altered in manuscript, or the plates themselves could be corrected or emended; unlike typeset editions, however, engravings could economically be printed in small numbers in response to demand, and in this respect the history of Purcell's *Sonnata's of III Parts* could well be rather more complex than at first appears.[165] Two distinct impressions of this work were issued

Music Meeting and Playford's Publishing' in Edward D. Olleson, Susan Wollenberg and John Caldwell (eds), *The Well Enchanting Skill: Music, Poetry and Drama in the Culture of the Renaissance – Essays in Honour of F.W. Sternfeld* (Oxford: Clarendon, 1990), pp. 231–44; Stacey Houck, 'John Playford and the English Musical Market', in Jessie Ann Owens (ed.), *'Noyses, Sounds and Sweet Aires': Music in Early Modern England* (Seattle and London: Folger Shakespeare Library, 2006), pp. 48–61; and Richard Luckett, 'The Playfords and the Purcells', in Robin Myers, Michael Harris and Giles Mandelbrote (eds), *Music and the Book Trade: From the Sixteenth to the Twentieth Century* (New Castle, DE: Oak Knoll Press and London: The British Library, 2008), pp. 45–67.

162 Alon Schab, 'Revisiting the Known and Unknown Misprints in Purcell's "Dioclesian"', *Music & Letters* 91 (2010): 343–56; Stephanie Carter, 'Published Variants and Creativity: An Overview of John Playford's Role as Editor', in Rebecca Herissone (ed.), *Concepts of Creativity in Seventeenth-Century England* (Woodbridge: Boydell and Brewer, forthcoming).

163 For details of the manuscript changes, see Henry Purcell, *Dioclesian*, ed. Margaret Laurie, The Works of Henry Purcell, vol. 9 (rev. edn, London: Novello, 1961), p. xiii. In the four British Library copies the stop-press pagination correction appears in Lbl K.4.i.21 and Lbl Mad. Soc. 27 but not in Lbl Hirsch II. 754 or Lbl R.M. 12.e.10.

164 Schab, 'Revisiting the Known and Unknown Misprints'.

165 Comments on the watermarks and paper are based on inspection of the following copies: Cu MR320.b.65.301–4 (first edition, first impression); Cmc 1987–90 (first edition, second impression); Lbl K.11.e.10 (second edition).

in 1683, the second incorporating some corrections of the first as well as a slightly altered dedication to the King.[166] As the two surviving sets of this second impression bear the royal arms on their bindings, it is reasonable to suppose that Purcell had the changes and corrections made primarily for presentation to his patron, Charles II. The incomplete British Library set Lbl K.11.e.10, however, has the words 'The Second Eddition' added to the extant title-pages and the date altered to 1684 as well as a small number of further corrections to the music. A number of references attest to the existence of other 'second edition' sets: the eighteenth-century manuscript score B-Bc V.14.981 refers to parts 'reprinted in 1684'; the *British Union Catalogue of Early Music* identifies a now lost 1684 'second edition' at the Royal Academy of Music in London and John Playford advertised the sonatas in the fifth book of *Choice Ayres, Songs and Dialogues* in the same year.[167]

The codicology of the *Sonnata's* is complicated by the fact that Purcell's engraver, Thomas Cross, apparently did not understand printers' signature marks, so that he or one of his assistants incorrectly marked some of the plates in ways that could be as unhelpful to contemporary printers and binders as they are to modern scholars. The part-books are upright quartos measuring approximately 270 x 205 mm,[168] the watermark distribution confirming that the music pages consist of three complete sheets plus a single quarter-sheet, actually collated A–C4 D1. The first recto of signature A is the title-page, necessitating the addition of an extra folio printed on one side only at the end of each part-book, a bibliographically awkward arrangement but one that enables every sonata to be played without page turns. The first violin part-book has four additional folios containing Purcell's portrait, a duplicate title-page, the dedication to the King and the address 'To the Reader'. The collation of the set with the exclusion of these preliminary pages is set out in Table 2.2.

Two features of this collation are immediately noteworthy. The first is that the final singleton was clearly produced in a different way from the rest of each part-book, perhaps by printing all four parts simultaneously. Second, the printed signature marks in all parts except the basso continuo (added, according to Purcell, as an afterthought) give the incorrect impression that the title-page and the music on its verso are not part of signature A, and therefore that it might have been possible to reprint a singleton page to be issued as a 'new edition' with material already in existence. In reality, as described above, the title-page is integral to the first signature, and could not have been reprinted without the subsequent seven pages as well.

---

166 See Henry Purcell, *Twelve Sonatas of Three Parts*, ed. Michael Tilmouth, The Works of Henry Purcell, vol. 5 (new edn, Borough Green: Novello, 1976), pp. x and xv.

167 Ibid., pp. xi and xv. A privately owned microfilm of the lost Royal Academy set includes an unaltered title-page of 1683; possibly the set was a composite made up of parts from different sets, or perhaps one or more of the title- pages missing from Lbl K.11.e.10 was never altered.

168 It should be noted that whereas the format of a movable-type printed book is a function of the forme, engraved plates do not in themselves dictate a format; in the case of the 1683 *Sonnata's* the same plates could have been used to produce folio volumes on smaller paper.

Table 2.2   Collation of Henry Purcell, *Sonnata's of III Parts* (London, 1683).

Actual collation	Signature marks (Vn I)	Signature marks (Vn II)	Signature marks (Basso)	Signature marks (Thoroughbass)
A1	–	–	–	–
A2	A	AA	AAA	AAAA2
A3	A2	AA2	AAA2	AAAA3
A4	A3	AA3	AAA3	AAAA4
B1	B	BB	BBB	BBBB
B2	B2	BB2	BBB2	BBBB2
B3	B3	AA3	AAA3	BBBB3
B4	B4	BB4	BBB4	BBBB4
C1	D	CC	CCC	CCCC
C2	C2	CC4	CCC2	–
C3	–	CC3	–	CCCC3
C4	C4	CC2	–	–
D	–	–	–	–

While the plates were altered only slightly to produce the second impression, the physical characteristics of the Pepys Library copy, Cmc Pepys 1987–90, suggest that this impression was indeed produced for a special purpose.[169] In the first impression, the music pages consist of two paper types, one with no visible watermark (possibly paper with a corner mark that has been trimmed away), but the other with a conventional Bend mark countermarked with a monogram identifying the Honigh family.[170] This is an early, though not unparalleled, use of

169   For a facsimile of this set see Henry Purcell, *Sonnata's of III Parts … First Published 1683*, Introduction by Richard Luckett (facsimile edition, London: Paradine, 1975).

170   For similar countermarks see Henk Voorn, *De papiermolens in de provincie Noord-Holland*, *De geschiedenis der Nederlandse papier-industrie*, vol. 1 (Haarlem: Papierwereld,

Dutch paper in an English music source, and the marks reveal the expected pattern of upper and lower segments of watermark and countermark that confirm the upright quarto format and the normal four-folio quiring. In Cmc Pepys 1987–90, however, both the paper type and the watermark distribution are entirely different, as set out in Table 2.3. All visible marks are 'IHS' countermarks of two distinct kinds ('1' and '2'); the 'IHS 1' countermark is divided as one would expect into upper and lower sections, but appears well below the middle of the page; the 'IHS 2' mark appears in quarters at the top corner of the inner edge of each page in which it occurs. The segments of the countermark are identified in the table as i and ii for the left and right sides of the upper part and iii and iv for the corresponding sides of the lower part.

The pattern of watermarks here is puzzling in many ways. Both members of the 'IHS 1' countermark pair are exceptionally large, with an overall width of about 79 mm or 83 mm, and the countermark's position is unusual, being much closer to the lower edge than the top. Variations of the exact level of the mark on the page, however, do not appear to be related to differences between the two moulds (see folios CC and CCCC in Table 2.4, which both contain the 83 mm countermark). In upright quarto format the height of a page made from an entire quarter of the original sheet would be half that sheet's overall width, equivalent to the width of a folio page made from the same material. If the 'IHS 1' countermark was conventionally positioned, we would expect an approximately equivalent distance to the edges above and below it, so that for the wider of the two marks (83 mm) the distance from the mark to the lower edge would be at least 147 mm, as revealed in folio CCCC, and possibly (if we assume 13 mm were trimmed from the top edge) 160 mm. In that case, the mid-line of the sheet used for folio CCCC might be expected to lie 403 mm (160 + 83 + 160) from the from the top edge, and therefore 132 mm (403 – 271) from the bottom of the fold between CCCC and CCCC2. If, like the countermark, the watermark lay a further 160 mm or more from the mid-line, it would therefore have been completely removed from a page no more than 270 mm high; a similar calculation shows that even where the impression was made a little more centrally on the sheet, as on folio CC, a watermark narrower than the very wide countermark would still be removed completely.

This suggestion explains the absence of corresponding watermarks for the 'IHS 1' countermark, but, more importantly, emphasizes the very special nature of the Pepys Library part-books through their use of paper with the exceptional sheet width of about 800 mm, or 32 inches. Larger papers, as a rule, tended to be of higher quality than smaller ones, and in this case it seems that exceptional paper has been employed with extravagant wastage and no regard for expense. The 'IHS 2' paper, in which the countermark is quartered at the top of the inside edge of each folio, is even more remarkable, as here the plates of the signature have been printed either on a normally dimensioned sheet marked only with a centrally positioned countermark, or on a half-sheet of double-sized paper in which, most unusually, the chain lines ran parallel to the longer side of the mould with the countermark

---

1960), marks 38, 46 and 88.

Table 2.3   Paper types and watermarks in Pepys 1987–90 copy of Purcell, *Sonnata's of III Parts.*

Actual collation	Cmc Pepys 1987 Vn 1	Cmc Pepys 1988 Vn 2	Cmc Pepys 1989 Basso	Cmc Pepys 1990 Thoroughbass
A1	–	–	IHS 1: iii, iv	IHS 1: i, ii
A2	IHS 1: i, ii	IHS 1: i, ii	–	–
A3	IHS 1: iii, iv	IHS 1: iii, iv	–	–
A4	–	–	IHS 1: i, ii	IHS 1: iii, iv
B1	IHS 2: iv	IHS 1: iii, iv	IHS 2: ii	IHS 2: ii
B2	IHS 2: iii	–	IHS 2: i	IHS 2: i
B3	IHS 2: i	–	IHS 2: iii	IHS 2: iii
B4	IHS 2: ii	IHS 1: i, ii	IHS 2: iv	IHS 2: iv
C1	IHS 2: iii	IHS 1: iii, iv	–	IHS 1: i, ii
C2	IHS 2: iv	–	IHS 1: i, ii	–
C3	IHS 2: ii	–	IHS 1: iii, iv	–
C4	IHS 2: i	IHS 1: i, ii	–	IHS 1: iii, iv
D	–	IHS 1: iii, iv	IHS1: i, ii	IHS 1: iii, iv

Table 2.4   Position of IHS countermark in three representative folios.

	[A2][a]	CC	CCCC
Top edge to mark (mm)	140	125	147
Width of mark (mm)	79	83	83
Mark to lower edge (mm)	50	63	42
Total	**269**	**271**	**272**

[a] Actually marked 'A'

(and presumably the watermark) on its side in relation to the normal orientation. The Pepys Library set of part-books therefore seems highly likely to have been a special commission, consisting of unusually large paper used at times in an apparently uneconomical way, a feature which strongly supports the suggestion made by Tilmouth that they were made especially to be presented to Charles II, whose arms are stamped on the covers.[171]

For 'The Second Eddition' of 1684 the title-page plate was altered, thus usefully confirming that all known copies except Lbl K.11.e.10 date from no later than 1684. In the second-violin part of Lbl K.11.e.10 Sonatas 9 and 11 have exchanged position, a mistake probably made because of the incorrect signature marks on the plates (see Table 2.2) which reverse CC4 and CC2, but there is no reason to assume that all copies with the 'second edition' title-page were printed at the same time and necessarily shared this fault; one of the advantages of engraving over movable type was that the composer could retain ownership of the plates to use them as required to produce copies for pupils or patrons,[172] and the paper type of most of Lbl K.11.e.10 (all apart from the final folio of each book) raises a distinct possibility that this individual print was in fact produced some time after 1684. The part-books are made of Dutch paper of very fine quality, marked with the Arms of Strasbourg and identifiable from its countermark as the work of the Huisduijnen family at the De Walvis mill.[173] While the Huisduijnens began the production of white paper there in 1682, Heawood identified a very similar combination of mark and countermark in the 1693 edition of Richard Blome's *Cosmography and Geography*,[174] a work published in 1682 and reissued in 1683 and 1693 using the same map plates.[175] In fact the Huisduijnen watermark appears only in five of the engraved maps in the second part,[176] which has its own title-page dated 1680 in all editions of the

---

171 See Purcell, *Twelve Sonatas of Three Parts*, ed. Tilmouth, p. xv.

172 See Harold Love, *The Culture and Commerce of Texts: Scribal Publication in Seventeenth-Century England* (Amherst: University of Massachusetts Press, 1998; originally published as *Scribal Publication in Seventeenth-Century England* (Oxford: Clarendon, 1993)), pp. 64–5.

173 Voorn, *De papiermolens in de provincie Noord-Holland*, p. 278, and watermarks 39, 48 and 50.

174 Edward Heawood, *Watermarks, Mainly of the 17th and 18th Centuries*, Monumenta chartae papyraceae historian illustrantia, vol. 1 (2nd rev. edn, Hilversum: Paper Publications Society, 1969), mark 152. His source was Richard Blome, *Cosmography and Geography: in Two Parts* (London, 1693).

175 The plates were engraved in 1667 and first published in Richard Blome, *A Geographical Description of the Four Parts of the World* (London, 1670). See Ashley Baynton-Williams, *Richard Blome*, http://www.mapforum.com/09/9blome.htm (last accessed 5 August 2010).

176 'A Generall Mapp of Asia' (between pp. 216 and 217); 'A General Mapp of the Coast of Barbarie' (between pp. 340 and 341); 'A New Mappe of Africa' (between pp. 334 and 335); 'A New Mapp of America Septentrionale' (between pp. 422 and 423); and 'A New Mapp of America Meridionale' (between pp. 422 and 423). Copy consulted: Cu Adams 3.69.2.

complete work, but if anything the occurrence of the mark in engraved rather than typeset pages adds to its evidential significance: the maps printed on Huisduijnen paper in 1693 were produced on Norman paper made by the Durand family in the previous edition,[177] and there is no reason to suspect that they were reprinted long before the 1693 edition was published.

There are difficulties in undertaking detailed comparison between the Huisduijnen papers in the sonata print and in *Cosmography and Geography*: in the former the marks are substantially concealed and in the latter the paper in question is in delicate fold-out maps in a large and fragile volume. Nevertheless, the marks appear to coincide in significant respects and, tellingly, the map between pp. 340 and 341 of *Cosmography and Geography* consists of two sheets with countermark but no watermark, a feature shared with some folios of Lbl K.11.e.10. While the evidence is limited, it therefore suggests that the paper stock of Lbl K.11.e.10 may have been available to a printer who worked with engravings shortly before 1693, and so reinforces the possibility that the 'second edition' of the *Sonnata's of III Parts* was not a single print-run produced in 1684 but a succession of printings which took place over a number of years. If so, the judgement of the reception of Purcell's sonatas implied by Roger North's famous references to their being 'unworthily despised' may need substantial re-evaluation;[178] the fact that Frances Purcell had copies of both sonata sets available in 1699, and, indeed, that John Walsh advertised copies as late as 1707, has been held to imply commercial failure,[179] but may indicate no more than a determination to get the most out of the engraved plates and, in fact, reflect the work's continued popularity. Indeed, the absence of the 1683 sonatas from the advertisement of 'Other Pieces of the Late Mr Henry Purcell's, Printed for the Widow' in the 1706 edition of *Orpheus Britannicus* may mean that those offered for sale at a later date were newly printed in response to demand, in contrast to the movable-type editions for which economic considerations had strongly encouraged initial over-production.

The nature of the printer's paper stock might be equally revealing in the case of movable-type editions. Each of the British Library copies of *The Vocal and Instrumental Musick of the Prophetess* consists of two principal paper stocks: one is Norman, marked with a shield typical of the area bearing two fleurs-de-lys, and the other is Dutch, marked with a single fleur-de-lys on a shield and the 'PVL' monogram of Peter van der Ley. In each case the change to Dutch paper occurs at signature R (p. 61), and is largely maintained until signature Oo (p. 144), after which

---

177 Copy consulted: Lbl 1481.f.14.

178 John Wilson (ed.), *Roger North on Music: Being a Selection from his Essays Written during the Years c.1695–1728* (London: Novello, 1959), p. 310 n. 65, from 'An Essay of Musicall Ayre', Lbl Add. 32536, fols 78v–79.

179 For example, in Holman, *Henry Purcell*, pp. 92–3 and Michael Tilmouth, 'The Technique and Forms of Purcell's Sonatas', *Music & Letters* 40 (1959): 121; Walsh's advertisement in *The Daily Courant* (28 April 1707, repeated on 1 May) does not imply a general attempt to clear 'old stock' but simply lists the 'first and second Sets of Sonatas' after other works including the new second edition of the Te Deum and Jubilate as well as *Orpheus Britannicus* and *A Collection of Ayres, Compos'd for the Theatre*.

a much wider variety of papers was used for the last eight signatures, including some definitely of Norman origin. One possible interpretation of the change in the running mark at p. 61, of course, is the altered pattern of trade that followed the outbreak of the Nine Years' War (see pp. 24–5 above), but in a postscript to the edition Purcell referred to his employment of 'two severall printers', one of whom ran into difficulties. It is possible, then, that the two main paper stocks were used in different workshops; both printers, if this suggestion is correct, used Heptinstall's 'new tied note', but once Heptinstall had invested in the punches and matrices to make the type there is no reason why several sets should not have been cast and used by others under his general supervision.

These assessments of Purcell's *Sonnata's of III Parts* and *The Vocal and Instrumental Musick of the Prophetess*, while on a relatively small scale, reflect the potential of codicological analysis of printed musical sources from the Restoration period, and suggest that systematic and detailed study of the physical aspects of such publications is a promising area for future research. If, for example, more than one fount of Heptinstall's type was in use, each might have minor but significant idiosyncrasies, and it would also be possible to establish whether all sources of the two publications conform to the paper-type patterns identified above. Such investigations might also be linked to a thorough search for stop-press corrections and unnoticed but explicable errors, again a time-consuming task, but one that would increase our understanding of the printed source material of the period.

Conclusions

This chapter has outlined some of the ways in which an appreciation of the sources themselves, and of the modes of transmission of musical texts, has already been shown to contribute to our understanding of late seventeenth-century music and the contexts in which it was performed, as well as indicating some potentially rewarding areas for future research. Codicology clearly has much to offer in establishing potential links between different sources and in helping to clarify the internal history of manuscripts and printed music books, but also – through its intrinsic links with the industries of papermaking and typefounding – serves to ground cultural artefacts in the societies and economies to which they belonged, an aspect of musical history explored by Margaret Murata in connection with source function as long ago as 1987.[180] At the same time, a certain tension exists between the pursuit of codicology in its own right – without question a worthy endeavour – and its practical application to the understanding and interpretation of music, an issue brought to the foreground in Stanley Boorman's 1988 review of Stephen Spector

---

180 Margaret Murata, 'Roman Cantata Scores as Traces of Musical Culture and Signs of its Place in Society', in Angelo Pompilio (ed.), *Atti del XIV congresso della Società internazionale di musicologia, Bologna, 1987: trasmissione e recezione delle forme di cultura musicale* (3 vols, Turin: Edizioni di Torino, 1990), vol. 3, pp. 272–84.

(ed.), *Essays in Paper Analysis*;[181] in some quarters at least there remains a suspicion that paper analysis and other scientific approaches to musicology lead away from, rather than towards, a true appreciation of the music itself.[182] An observation made by Jan LaRue near the start of the 'modern' period of musical codicology perhaps puts matters in perspective: 'The main service of watermarks is as a direction-finder; they suggest promising avenues of search and research, saving much floundering in the open sea of possibilities.'[183] In other words, codicology supports, but in no sense replaces, traditional musicological research.

---

181 Stanley Boorman, Review of Stephen Spector (ed.) *Essays in Paper Analysis* (Washington: Folger Shakespeare Library, 1987), in *Music & Letters* 69 (1988): 495–6; see also the subsequent correspondence, 'Essays in Paper Analysis', *Music & Letters* 70 (1989): 599–601.

182 A suspicion explored, though with qualification, in Basil Lam, Review of Alfred Dürr, *Studien über die frühen Kantaten Johann Sebastian Bachs* (rev. edn, Wiesbaden: Breitkopf & Härtel, 1977) and *Zur Chronologie der Leipziger Vokalwerke J.S. Bachs* (2nd impression, Kassel and London: Bärenreiter, 1976), in *Music & Letters* 60 (1979): 325–8.

183 Jan LaRue, 'Classification of Watermarks for Musicological Purposes' *Fontes Artis Musicae* 13 (1966): 59–63.

Understanding Creativity

Alan Howard

This chapter is concerned with what we can know about the genesis of Purcell's music: what evidence survives concerning his creative strategies, how we can recover and interpret this evidence, and indeed why we might be interested in so doing. Scholarly interest in such matters relates closely to the branches of musicological study usually referred to as 'sketch studies' and the investigation of 'compositional process'; the broader term 'creativity' reflects more recent thinking which has called into question a number of the basic assumptions of these sub-disciplines – particularly concerning the nature of musical texts and the functions of their sources – such that it is beginning to be acknowledged that the study of the creation of a seventeenth-century musical work cannot simply seek to account for a putative process of 'composition'. It must equally consider the work's various notated guises, how they relate to one another and to the music as it may have been performed, how and why its sources were originally produced, and, above all, what impact all of these factors may have had upon the music as it is known today.[1] Thus to stress the term 'creativity' in this connection is to reject the caricature of the composer spending his days writing music for others to distribute and perform (a caricature which is in any case far from the reality for virtually any composer, for all that this is sometimes forgotten), and instead to approach Purcell's music as the product of a musician active in musical performance, improvisation, notation, criticism, teaching, editing, arranging, distribution and any number of other activities alongside his composing.

I would like to thank Rebecca Herissone, Peter Holman and Stephen Rose for their comments on the first draft of this chapter.

1   This is part of the background behind the use of the word 'creativity' for the project Musical Creativity in Restoration England, which was sponsored by the UK Arts and Humanities Research Council, and was based at the University of Manchester under the direction of Rebecca Herissone from 2006–10 and led to a monograph by Herissone under the same title, currently in preparation; the present author was employed as postdoctoral research assistant on the project until August 2009. An interdisciplinary conference, Concepts of Creativity in Seventeenth-Century England, was held under the auspices of the project at Manchester in September 2008; a volume of essays selected from among the contributions is also in preparation.

The study of Purcell's creativity embraces two principal methodologies, both of which draw additionally on seventeenth-century music theory in order to facilitate and evaluate their interpretations, and as a means of contextualizing their findings.[2] The first might broadly be described as a palaeographical approach: that is, one that involves the analysis and comparative study of the sources and texts in which the music is preserved. The second, meanwhile, seeks to recover the composer's creative strategies by identifying and interpreting their traces in the music preserved within these texts.

What I am calling the 'palaeographical' approach to Purcell's creativity takes its precedent from numerous studies of the compositional habits of other composers, most of which trace their roots to Gustav Nottebohm's pioneering studies of Beethoven's sketchbooks beginning in the 1860s.[3] Even prior to this, in fact, authors referred to autograph music manuscripts and multiple versions of works for didactic purposes: as early as 1800, William Shield, for example, published a lengthy extract from the (now lost) 'Author's foul score' of Arne's *Artaxerxes*, complete with his own annotations designed to show how Arne's various crossings-out and other changes improved the composition.[4] Interest in compositional process as an academic topic in its own right, however, really began with Nottebohm, whose legacy was taken up in the 1960s by scholars such as Douglas Johnson, Joseph Kerman, Lewis Lockwood and Alan Tyson. Among the composers to have attracted this kind of attention since that time are (for example) Mozart, Schubert, Schumann and Wagner, Mahler, Debussy, Stravinsky and Tippett.[5]

The motivation behind such studies has been varied, but tends to include (in differing proportions for different scholars and at different times) the clarification of work chronology and other biographical details concerning the composer, the attempted completion of unfinished works, the examination of successive 'stages' in the composition of a given work together with the extrapolation from this information to produce more general statements about the composer's working methods, and the derivation of analytical insight into the finished work.[6] This latter goal has not been without controversy, with purists arguing that any analytical

2   For a comprehensive introduction to and analysis of English music theory in Purcell's lifetime, see Rebecca Herissone, *Music Theory in Seventeenth-Century England* (Oxford: Oxford University Press, 2000).

3   For a summary, see Douglas Johnson, 'Beethoven Scholars and Beethoven's Sketches', *19th-Century Music* 2 (1978): 3–17.

4   William Shield, *An Introduction to Harmony* (London, 1800), pp. 120–21. On Shield's wider interest in eighteenth-century autograph manuscripts, see Clare Brown and Peter Holman, 'Thomas Busby and his "Fac Similes of Celebrated Composers"', *Early Music Performer* 12 (2003): 3–12. I am grateful to Peter Holman for alerting me to Shield's interest in such matters.

5   For a good basic bibliography, see Nicholas Marston, 'Sketch', in *Grove Music Online,* http://www.oxfordmusiconline.com (last accessed 27 November 2009).

6   Ibid.; or for a more detailed examination of the usual aims of so-called 'sketch studies', see Joseph Kerman, 'Sketch Studies', in D. Kern Holoman and Claude V. Palisca (eds), *Musicology in the 1980s: Methods, Goals, Opportunities* (New York: Da Capo, 1982), pp. 53–65.

observation arrived at through the study of superseded 'early versions' ought in any case to be detectable in the work as heard by audiences of the final version (and that if it is not, it is irrelevant).[7] Such a hard line has had little impact upon studies of Purcell's working manuscripts, which have not in any case been of great interest to the institutionalized discipline of music theory that is more prevalent in the United States; rather, this aspect of Purcellian research is well placed to benefit from the brand of richly contextualized 'criticism', incorporating study of early versions and working methods alongside insights arrived at through varied analytical, biographical and historiographical approaches, envisaged by Joseph Kerman.[8]

What is most notable about those composers whose sketches generally attract interest is their overwhelming concentration in the nineteenth and twentieth centuries; indeed, Kerman went as far as to suggest that the increasing trend in 1970s' American musicology towards work in these time periods was itself a major factor in the 'upsurge of sketch studies' he observed in 1982.[9] By way of explanation of the good fit between 'sketch studies' and these comparatively recent repertoires, Nicholas Marston observes that 'research along these lines will necessarily be partly dependent upon the survival of a critical mass of material' and 'tends to proceed from a particular understanding of the composer as original creative artist and of the musical work as an organic and teleological whole'.[10]

Both of these factors, needless to say, conspire against the successful 'palaeographic' examination of music from earlier periods. Nevertheless, a number of studies have assessed the autograph documents of early composers for evidence of compositional activity: Robert Marshall published his important book *The Compositional Process of J.S. Bach* in 1972, and more recently David Hurley has considered Handel's creative habits in his later oratorios and dramatic works.[11] An important precedent for recent developments in the understanding of Purcell's creativity is Jessie Ann Owens's systematic study of evidence of compositional activity in Renaissance composer autographs, which offers a potential methodological model for future studies of compositional process in the music of Purcell and his contemporaries: it tackles the dearth of surviving sources by presenting a systematic overview alongside discussion of individual works, and it attempts to consider the working methods of composers inasmuch as they can be discerned from the individual sources and their intended functions, rather than reading the sources in the light of creative paradigms originally designed to elucidate nineteenth-century compositional habits.[12] Rebecca Herissone's

7 Johnson, 'Beethoven Scholars': 15.
8 Kerman, 'Sketch Studies', p. 65.
9 Ibid., p. 64.
10 Marston, 'Sketch'.
11 Robert Lewis Marshall, *The Compositional Process of J.S. Bach* (2 vols, Princeton: Princeton University Press, 1972); David Ross Hurley, *Handel's Muse: Patterns of Creation in his Oratorios and Musical Dramas, 1743–1751* (Oxford: Oxford University Press, 2000).
12 Jessie Ann Owens, *Composers at Work: The Craft of Musical Composition, 1450–1600* (New York and Oxford: Oxford University Press, 1997).

forthcoming monograph *Musical Creativity in Restoration England* will be the first full-length study of this type concentrating on seventeenth-century English composers, but there is already a growing body of literature on the creative process as it relates to Purcell's near contemporaries. The sources of consort music by William Lawes and Matthew Locke have been examined extensively, for example,[13] while Herissone's work on creative process in the music of composers other than Purcell has included, apart from her PhD thesis, articles on Richard Goodson, William Turner, Edward Lowe and Henry Aldrich.[14]

The second methodological approach to Purcell's creativity has similarly strong connections with work on other composers. In a penetrating recent essay, Nicholas Cook points out that most musical literature written under the broad heading of 'analysis' makes implicit use of what he calls the 'language of creative intention', citing not just the obvious ways in which analytical observations are commonly expressed as compositional acts ('*N* delays the cadence …'), but also how apparently more systematized approaches such as Schenkerian analysis remain firmly tied to Romantic notions of genius on the part of the few 'great' composers.[15] For all his healthy scepticism about the extent to which this might genuinely express the creative agency of the composer, and his entreaties to seek a more pluralistic theory of music that is less reliant on an idea of musical creation that he identifies as 'historically and ideologically specific', Cook nevertheless acknowledges that this kind of discourse about music has become an important facet of the Western tradition since the nineteenth century, and is likely to remain so.[16]

Indeed, a growing body of analytical work on several earlier composers has explicitly appealed to the language of creative intention: John Milsom has recently

---

13   See, for example, Michael Tilmouth, 'Revisions in the Chamber Music of Matthew Locke', *Proceedings of the Royal Musical Association* 98 (1971–72): 89–100; Robert Thompson, 'The Sources of Locke's Consort "For Seaverall Friends"', *Chelys* 19 (1990): 16–44; David Pinto, 'New Lamps for Old: the Versions of the Royall Consort', in Andrew Ashbee (ed.), *William Lawes (1602–1645): Essays on his Life, Times and Work* (Aldershot: Ashgate, 1998), pp. 251–81; and John Cunningham, *The Consort Music of William Lawes, 1602–1645* (Woodbridge: Boydell and Brewer, 2010).

14   See Rebecca Herissone, 'The Theory and Practice of Composition in the English Restoration Period' (PhD dissertation, University of Cambridge, 1996); Herissone, 'Richard Goodson the Elder's Ode "Janus did ever to thy sight": Evidence of Compositional Procedures in the Early Eighteenth Century', *Music & Letters* 79 (1998): 167–91; Herissone, 'The Revision Process in William Turner's Anthem "O Praise the Lord"', *Journal of the Royal Musical Association* 123 (1998): 1–38; and Herissone, '"To entitle himself to ye Composition": Investigating Concepts of Authorship and Originality in Seventeenth-Century English Ceremonial Music' (Unpublished paper presented at the Annual Meeting of the Society for Seventeenth-Century Music, Huntington Library, San Marino, 17–19 April 2008).

15   Nicholas Cook, 'Playing God: Creativity, Analysis, and Aesthetic Inclusion', in Irène Deliège and Geraint A. Wiggins (eds), *Musical Creativity: Multidisciplinary Research in Theory and Practice* (Hove: Psychology Press, 2006), p. 18. Note the parallel here with Marston's observation about the theoretical basis of 'sketch studies' cited above.

16   Ibid., pp. 18–19.

illuminated the methods of sixteenth-century polyphonists including Josquin, Clemens non Papa and Crecquillon by seeking to reveal 'the composer's conceptual starting-points' through analysis; Christopher Wintle observed the 'workbench methods of the composer' in Corelli's transformations of 'tonal models' in his sonatas, and Laurence Dreyfus has approached the music of J.S. Bach through the 'historical modus operandi that informs the practice of [his] daily craft'.[17] Each of these at some level acknowledges the inadequacy of standard analytical tools when it comes to accounting for the characteristics of early music, and of course it is no coincidence that these same imperfect tools are closely tied to the historically specific idea of creativity described by Cook. Rather than addressing this problem by abandoning the notion of creative intention, however, the approaches taken by Milsom, Wintle and Dreyfus – different as they are in many ways – all effectively exploit the familiarity and ubiquity of this concept as an opportunity to discover more historically sensitive methods of analysis.[18] By positing the attempted recovery of creative decisions and the contexts in which these were made by the composer as the goal of an analysis, scholars have been successful in presenting analytical insights that, while they cannot be proved to represent the composer's conception of the music, are at least informed by theoretical and even aesthetic principles that would have been familiar to contemporary musicians.

That a large amount of this kind of work is directed particularly towards composers' handling of strict contrapuntal idioms is a function of the fact that it was these techniques that required the most effort on the part of the composer, who had to devise and manipulate his material successfully within the constraints of idiomatic handling of consonance and dissonance (as determined by chronological and local consensus), rather than relying simply on tasteful invention. The challenges of this kind of composition provide opportunities for the analyst who can identify and attempt to resolve once more the technical difficulties and creative decisions that the composer may have faced, and it is exactly for this reason that certain parts of Purcell's repertoire have proved similarly suited to such an analytical approach.

In order to examine how these two methods of investigating musical creativity have contributed to our understanding of Purcell's music, and indeed how the approaches themselves have developed more recently, the remainder of this chapter is divided into three sections: the first two deal with 'palaeographical'

---

17 John Milsom, 'Crecquillon, Clemens, and Four-Vice "Fuga"', in Eric Jas (ed.), *Beyond Contemporary Fame: Reassessing the Art of Clemens non Papa and Thomas Crecquillon* (Turnhout: Brepols, 2005), p. 300; Christopher Wintle, 'Corelli's Tonal Models: The Trio Sonata Op. III, n.1', in Sergio Durante and Pierluigi Petrobelli (eds), *Nuovissimi studi Corelliani: atti del terzo congresso internazionale, Fusignano, 4–7 settembre, 1980*, Quaderni della Rivista italiana di musicologia, vol. 7 (Florence: Olschki, 1982), p. 31; and Laurence Dreyfus, *Bach and the Patterns of Invention* (Cambridge, MA: Harvard University Press, 1996), p. 30.

18 This concern has been prominent in recent studies of pre-1750 musical repertoire; for the main arguments, see Margaret Bent, 'The Grammar of Early Music: Preconditions for Analysis', in Cristle Collins Judd (ed.), *Tonal Structures in Early Music* (New York: Garland, 1996), pp. 15–59.

studies of creativity, initially in their more conventional manifestations and then through some of the recent challenges that have arisen; the third concentrates on analytical approaches to Purcell's creative strategies, and their potential to increase still further our understanding of how he and his contemporaries may have worked. This critical review of Purcellian and related literature aims to provide an overview of past and present understandings of Purcell's creative habits, while pointing up methodological problems and likely areas of future research along the way. At the same time, the chapter adopts a single case study, the symphony anthem *My Beloved Spake*, in order to illustrate and test the ideas explored; as well as providing a point of entry for the questions raised by this kind of research, the case study draws together and builds upon some of the many tangential references in other studies to what is one of Purcell's most interesting works from the perspective of creativity.

Exploring Creativity: Conventional Source-based Approaches

As Robert Thompson explains in Chapter 2 above, interest in the autograph sources of Purcell's music stretches back to the eighteenth century, and can often be detected where manuscripts have passed through the hands of collectors. This is indeed the case with the only surviving autograph of *My Beloved Spake*, which is preserved in the second volume of the important collection of Canterbury stationer William Flackton, compiled in the late eighteenth century (now Lbl Add. 30931–3).[19] Two particular annotations made to this score are typical: one attests to the presence of Purcell's hand ('[by Hen. Purcell] in his own hand writing, the original score | P Hayes | 1785'); while the other draws attention to concordances ('see a fair copy of this in catalogue No 72').[20] Although Flackton seems to have acquired most of his documents from the manuscripts of Canterbury musicians, and may not therefore deliberately have collected Purcell's autographs, inscriptions like these nevertheless demonstrate the value conferred upon such documents because of their autograph status, to the extent

---

19   On Flackton see Robert Shay and Robert Thompson, *Purcell Manuscripts: The Principal Musical Sources* (Cambridge: Cambridge University Press, 2000), p. 306, and also Chapter 2, pp. 14–15 above. His collection also includes several other Purcell autographs, as well as a large amount of material (mainly sacred music) copied by the Canterbury Cathedral musicians Daniel Henstridge and William Raylton.

20   The two remarks occur respectively on fols 87 and 93v of Lbl Add. 30932. That on f. 93v is in Flackton's own hand, and refers to a copy that is apparently no longer extant; see the discussion below. On Philip Hayes, Heather Professor of Music at Oxford University from 1777, see Simon Heighes and Peter Ward Jones, 'Hayes: (2) Philip Hayes', in *Grove Music Online*, http://www.oxfordmusiconline.com (last accessed 27 November 2009); and Shay and Thompson, *Purcell Manuscripts*, p. 308.

of ensuring their survival despite duplication in more legible form elsewhere in the same collection.[21]

The antiquarian interests of Hayes, Flackton and other collectors of 'ancient musick' fed directly into the presentation of Purcell's music in modern printed editions, which began as early as the eighteenth century with William Boyce's *Cathedral Music* and Benjamin Goodison's proposed complete edition of Purcell's works.[22] The task of determining which sources of Purcell's music should be considered definitive, however – traditionally a key tenet of 'monumental' editions like that of the Purcell Society – has proved problematic.

For *My Beloved Spake*, as G.E.P. Arkwright explained in the Purcell Society's first volume of Purcell's sacred music (1921):

> we have Purcell's early autograph copy, with emendations and excisions marked on it; but that [the work] underwent further revision still is evident from there being yet more emendations and a new slow movement of the Symphony printed in Novello's edition (supported by Blow's [*recte* William Isaack's] MS., Fitzwilliam, 117), which was derived from a second Purcell autograph now missing.[23]

Arkwright chose to base his edition on the Lbl Add. 30932 autograph, but a second part of Volume 13 (never published) was additionally to include the later version published by Novello and concordant with that in Cfm 117. When Peter Dennison later revised Volume 13 in 1988, however, he chose the slightly different form of the latter version copied by Charles Badham in Ob Tenbury 1031 (fols 3–13) as his copy text for *My Beloved Spake*, considering that some of the variants in Cfm 117 'could not possibly represent Purcell's intentions'.[24] More recently, Shay and Thompson

---

21   Shay and Thompson, *Purcell Manuscripts*, p. 139.

22   See the section 'Editions of Purcell's Music' in Chapter 8 below; H. Diack Johnstone, 'The Genesis of Boyce's "Cathedral Music"', *Music & Letters*, 56 (1975): 26–40; and A. Hyatt King, 'Benjamin Goodison and the first "Complete Edition" of Purcell', in Richard Baum and Wolfgang Rehm (eds), *Musik und Verlag: Karl Vötterle zum 65. Geburtstag am 12. April 1968* (Kassel: Bärenreiter, 1968), pp. 391–6.

23   Henry Purcell, *Sacred Music, Part I*, ed. G.E.P. Arkwright, The Works of Henry Purcell, vol. 13a (London: Novello, 1921), p. vii. Arkwright refers here to Henry Purcell, *My Beloved Spake*, ed. Vincent Novello, Purcell's Sacred Music, no. 13 (London: Novello, *c*.1829), a version of the work that Novello asserts to have been made 'From an unpublished M.S. formerly in the possession of Mr Bartleman'. (James Bartleman (1769–1821) was an English bass; see Robert Toft, 'Bartleman, James', in *Grove Music Online*, http://www.oxfordmusiconline.com (last accessed 27 November 2009).) Arkwright repeats the common nineteenth-century attribution of Cfm 117 to John Blow, though it was in fact copied by William Isaack of St George's Chapel, Windsor; for literature on this attribution, see Shay and Thompson, *Purcell Manuscripts*, pp. 40 and 311; see also Chapter 2, p. 16 above.

24   Henry Purcell, *Sacred Music, Part I: Nine Anthems with Orchestral Accompaniment*, ed. Peter Dennison, The Works of Henry Purcell, vol. 13 (rev. edn, London: Novello, 1988), p. 162.

have argued that the Fitzwilliam version may well have been preferable, given its similarity to a copy made by Philip Hayes in 1785 (KNt MR 2–5.4, pp. 118–38),[25] which apparently derives from the second copy that once formed part of Flackton's collection;[26] this in turn is almost certainly to be identified with the lost autograph mentioned by Arkwright.[27]

What all this shows is that many of the questions asked by scholars interested in Purcell's creative habits have long been posed by editors of his music; further evidence, if it is needed, is apparent in the detailed stemmatic diagrams, and appendices containing 'earlier versions', found in several of the Purcell Society volumes.[28] Consideration of source priority, and the apparent replacement of one version of a given passage with another, provide many of what Kerman described as the 'hard facts' that are the first findings of all 'sketch studies'.[29] Notwithstanding the desire to include transcriptions of significant superseded or alternative readings in such editions, however, the traditional concerns of editors with the establishment of clear hierarchies among sources, and the determination of a 'best text' (or even an idealized reconstruction of 'the composer's intentions') as the basis for the edition, tend to relegate evidence for more localized variants and creative decisions on the part of the composer to critical commentaries, which, even when complete and accurate, can make their recovery laborious. Perhaps it was for this reason that Michael Tilmouth chose to publish his thoughts on Locke's

---

25 Shay and Thompson, *Purcell Manuscripts*, pp. 62–4 (note that the page range for Hayes's copy of *My Beloved Spake* in KNt MR 2–5.4 is given incorrectly on p. 62, where it should read 'pp. 118–37', not 108–37).

26 At the end of his copy of *My Beloved Spake* on p. 138 of KNt MR 2–5.4, Hayes writes: 'This and the following Anthem were transcrib'd from Purcell's Original Scores in the possession of Mr W: Flacton at Canterbury who favor'd me with the loan of them | 1785. | Phil. Hayes'. See also Chapter 2, pp. 14–15 in this volume.

27 That these two sources are one and the same is evident from Novello's statement quoted above that his text derived from Hayes's score via a copy once owned by Bartleman. However, the footnote on the first page of Novello's edition complicates the issue by stating that Hayes later deposited his source in the King's Library; since Hayes's note in KNt MR 2–5.4 indicates that he had borrowed his source from Flackton, this seems unlikely. The autograph described by Novello as owned by the Rev. Joshua Dix of Faversham (d. 1832; see *Jackson's Oxford Journal*, no. 4139 (25 August 1832): 3) is probably the copy in Lbl Add. 30932, providing additional information on the whereabouts of Flackton's collection between his death and the time it was owned by Julian Marshall (who sold the manuscripts to the British Museum). See Robert Ford, 'A Sacred Song Not by Purcell', *Musical Times* 125 (1984): 45, n. 4; and Arthur Searle, 'Marshall, Julian', in *Grove Music Online*, http://www.oxfordmusiconline.com (last accessed 21 August 2009).

28 See, for example, Henry Purcell, *Ten Sonatas of Four Parts*, ed. Michael Tilmouth, The Works of Henry Purcell, vol. 7 (rev. edn, London: Novello, 1981), pp. xii and 132–44. Note, however, that Christopher Hogwood's interpretation of the source relationships in the *Sonatas of Four Parts* differs considerably from Tilmouth's; see Henry Purcell, *Ten Sonatas of Four Parts*, ed. Christopher Hogwood (2 vols, London: Eulenberg, 1978), vol. 1, p. vi, and below.

29 Kerman, 'Sketch Studies', pp. 57–8.

revisions to his consort music separately from his editions for *Musica Britannica,* in what was one of the earliest studies of creative process in the music of Purcell's contemporaries.[30] Study of alternative versions in Purcell's music with the aim of critical insight apart from (or as well as) the creation of modern editions began a decade later, with the appearance of a survey of 'Revisions and Reworkings in Purcell's Anthems' by Robert Manning, and a detailed investigation by Robert Ford of the Funeral Sentences, prompted in part by Manning's article.[31]

At this point some clarification of the relationship between Purcellian studies and the wider discipline of 'sketch studies' as described by Kerman is necessary, since the surviving sources that preserve evidence of Purcell's creative activities present one considerable methodological obstacle in this respect: the conspicuous absence of almost anything among them that could even loosely be described as a 'sketch'. The Lbl Add. 30932 copy of *My Beloved Spake* is a good example of the kinds of autograph manuscripts we do possess from near the beginning of Purcell's creative process: there are alterations and deletions in several places, but the score is continuous from beginning to end, all the necessary parts are present, the layout is planned, and sufficient verbal cues are provided that a competent musician could complete the underlay with few problems.[32] While not particularly neat, the music is entirely legible and there is nothing to suggest that this is anything but a finished version of the piece. In other words, any attempt to approach this (or, for that matter, any other piece by Purcell) from the methodological angle of 'sketch studies' in the strict sense inevitably stretches the term 'sketch' almost to breaking point.[33]

This may seem no more than terminological pedantry, but the point is worth making since it draws attention to the fact that, unlike scholars of some other composers, those working on Purcell's music have very little opportunity to penetrate the earliest stages of the creative process – stages that can in consequence take on something of an occult status. Yet while Purcell may indeed have been, as Manning put it, 'a composer who was able to write down his musical ideas clearly and spontaneously',[34] it does not follow from this that we should understand Purcell as a sort of seventeenth-century Mozart, a romantic genius working in a fervour of divine inspiration.[35] Indeed, it is worth considering briefly what other explanations there could be for Purcell's apparent compositional facility.

---

30   Tilmouth, 'Revisions in the Chamber Music of Matthew Locke': 89–100.

31   Robert Manning, 'Revisions and Reworkings in Purcell's Anthems', *Soundings* 9 (1982): 29–37; Robert Ford, 'Purcell as his Own Editor: the Funeral Sentences', *Journal of Musicological Research* 7 (1986): 47–67.

32   Nevertheless, Isaack's evident difficulty with this task in his Cfm 117 score of *My Beloved Spake* (copied not from Lbl Add. 30932, but from another source with only incipits underlaid) suggests that he found this more troublesome than might be expected; see Shay and Thompson, *Purcell Manuscripts*, p. 64.

33   This possibility was indeed acknowledged by Kerman; see 'Sketch Studies', pp. 54–5.

34   Manning, 'Revisions and Reworkings in Purcell's Anthems': 29.

35   Even for Mozart, of course, this popular image has been largely discredited in the scholarly literature; see, for example, Maynard Solomon, 'The Rochlitz Anecdotes: Issues of Authenticity in Early Mozart Biography', in Cliff Eisen (ed.) *Mozart Studies*

It should not be thought that Purcell was unusual among his peers in this respect: there are equally few surviving true 'sketches' in the hands of Matthew Locke, John Blow or Pelham Humfrey, or for that matter of Jeremiah Clarke, William Croft or John Eccles.[36] One reason for this might be that the higher costs of writing materials encouraged composers to reuse paper for other purposes; this would explain the presence of the only known sketch fragment in Purcell's hand on the underside of a correction slip pasted into fol. 7 of Ob Mus.c.26, an autograph copy of the anthem *Let mine Eyes Run Down with Tears*.[37] It may also be relevant that this fragment is contrapuntal, since the greater technical demands of such passages might understandably have demanded notated trials more often than did more homophonic writing.[38] It is possible, of course, that rather more sketches were made than have survived: we have several fragmentary jottings in the hand of Henry Aldrich, for example, and it may be that his academic training and antiquarian interests encouraged him to hold onto materials of a kind that were not so valued by professional composers.[39] Equally, it may be that some material was sketched using erasable tablets, though as Herissone observes, there is no evidence for such a practice in Restoration England.[40]

These considerations aside, however, it is clear that Purcell made much less use of what we would consider 'sketches' than did some later composers, not because he was more talented or inspired than they were, but simply because that was the norm at the time. One reason for this could be stylistic: it seems obvious that even the most ambitious music of the seventeenth century is simpler both in texture and structure than, say, a Beethoven symphony or Verdi opera, and might therefore

---

(Oxford: Clarendon, 1991), pp. 1–59.

36 Fragmentary sketch-like material by James Hawkins and John Blow is discussed and reproduced in Herissone, 'The Theory and Practice of Composition in the English Restoration Period', pp. 136, 137 and 144.

37 See Rebecca Herissone, 'Purcell's Revisions of his Own Works', in Curtis Price (ed.), *Purcell Studies* (Cambridge: Cambridge University Press, 1995), pp. 63–4. As I read it, the fourth and fifth notes after the first bar line on the lower stave of this 'sketch' were intended to be e♭' and f' respectively, not d' and e' as transcribed in Herissone's article; thus there is very little difference between the part as sketched and as in the final version of the piece.

38 See Rebecca Herissone, '"Fowle Originalls" and "Fayre Writeing": Reconsidering Purcell's Compositional Process', *Journal of Musicology* 23 (2006): 591. Some similar sketch-like material survives in the hand of Daniel Henstridge, on either side of fol. 127 of Lbl Add. 30933 (vol. 3 of Flackton's collection), although here the sketching (of canonic voices from a larger, four-part texture) is laid out in the context of whole systems, suggesting that these are aborted drafts rather than sketches as such.

39 For a list of sketch-like materials in Aldrich's hand at Christ Church, Oxford, see John Milsom, 'Henry Aldrich: The Autograph Manuscripts', in Milson, *Christ Church Library Music Catalogue*, http://library.chch.ox.ac.uk/music/ (last accessed 18 August 2009). Another reason that more sketches survive in Aldrich's hand could simply be that, as an amateur composer, he required them more often to martial his thoughts.

40 Herissone, '"Fowle Originalls"': 585. For a discussion of this phenomenon in earlier Italian music, see Owens, *Composers at Work*, p. 97.

require less written experimentation. On the other hand, the argument of scale and complexity is not entirely persuasive, since Beethoven and his contemporaries also left sketches for much simpler works than operas and symphonies.[41] There is considerable research to be done, therefore, into why musicians in the seventeenth and early eighteenth centuries seem not to have needed extensive sketches, and how we can gain an insight into other methods composers may have used to invent their materials. One possibility, as discussed in the third part of this chapter below, is to examine some of the specific musical techniques that we know Purcell used (such as imitative counterpoint) to see how these might have affected his invention of materials. Another important line of inquiry, as Herissone points out, is the significance of musical memory, which was far more central to the skills of musical performers during the seventeenth century than it is today, and is thus likely to have influenced the activities of composers as well.[42]

It is in the techniques of improvisation, at the boundaries of composition and performance, that most information might be forthcoming. Two particular accounts of Restoration creative processes are instructive in this respect: Thomas Mace's extraordinary description of his composition of the lesson 'My Mistress' in *Musick's Monument*,[43] and the inscription by Edward Lowe in Ob Mus.Sch.c.138, fol. 146, that records Matthew Locke's composition of the Prelude and Gloria on fols 146v–7 'at ye musick schoole betweene ye Houers of 12, & 3 afternoone the 9th of November [1665]'. From Mace, we learn that his 'Secret Genius, or Fancy, prompted [his] Fingers, (do what [he] could) into This very Humour; So that every Time [he] walk'd, and took up [his] Lute, (in the Interim, betwixt Writing, and Studying) This Ayre would needs offer It self unto [him], Continually', and only after some time '(liking it Well, (and lest It should be Lost,) [he] took Paper, and set It down[)]'.[44] In other words, the composition of the work itself was largely intuitive: Mace perceived it as almost involuntary, coming to him unbidden as he procrastinated over letters to his sweetheart and her mother (as we learn elsewhere in his account); the notation of the music was a separate event, linked to its preservation rather than its composition. Mace is somewhat notorious for his over-romanticized view of his own youth, and since he was an amateur musician

---

41 See, for example, Lewis Lockwood, 'Beethoven's Sketches for *Sehnsucht* (WoO 146)', in Alan Tyson (ed.), *Beethoven Studies* (New York: Norton, 1974), pp. 97–122. Peter Holman has suggested that the presence of sketches even for comparatively simple pieces during the nineteenth century may to some extent be explained by the need to produce legible copy for printers once the ubiquity of later print culture made it common for composers to sell their autographs to publishers: autographs preserving evidence of multiple versions would obviously be ambiguous, hence the need for separate notated records of the earlier stages of the creative process (private communication, 20 November 2009).

42 Herissone, '"Fowle Originalls"': 585; see also Stephen Rose, 'Memory and the Early Musician', *Early Music Performer* 13 (2004): 3–8.

43 Thomas Mace, *Musick's Monument, or a Remembrancer of the Best Practical Musick* (London, 1676), pp. 122–3.

44 Ibid., p. 122.

we should be careful about applying this account too widely, but it does at least provide an indication of one way of working.

The Locke example is somewhat different. From Lowe's inscription we know that the piece was 'made, prickt, & Sunge' in the three hours Locke spent at the Oxford Music School. In this case, 'prickt' probably referred simply to the copying of the performing parts, since the Gloria and its Prelude on fols 146v–7 are clearly the composing manuscript: there are several obvious alterations and aborted lines, and even despite these there remain numerous problems with the voice-leading that Locke would not usually have allowed to stand given the leisure of more time. Although the compositional process did involve notation in this instance, Locke still seems to have relied on techniques closely related to improvisational practice, such as the long falling bass line that underpins the prelude, and the heavy use of writing in parallel thirds in the violin parts.[45]

In the absence of 'sketches' in the strictest sense of the word, then, the 'palaeographical' study of creative process in Purcell's music concerns itself instead with the broader range of documents – drafts, working autographs, paste-overs and so on – admitted by Kerman into the more pragmatically defined field of 'sketch studies' on the basis of their fulfilment of two criteria which he considered essential: '(1) it has survived, and (2) it was in the composer's mind superseded'.[46] On this basis, he argued, one might proceed logically to study the successive forms and early versions of particular works, and from there to 'questions about composers' criticism of their own music'.[47] The attraction of such a model in terms of understanding the formation and development of a composer's style over the course of a career is obvious, and it was from this methodological starting point, derived directly from the conventional discipline of 'sketch studies', that several articles of the 1980s and 1990s provided important insights into Purcell's own music. Although much of this literature has since been superseded, it provides a crucial background to the more recent reassessment of Purcell's creative activities explored in the subsequent sections of this chapter.

Manning's groundbreaking article of 1982 is a particularly good example of the direction in which 'questions about composers' criticism of their own music' tend to lead: in the course of his discussion of Purcell's autographs of four well-known anthems, he described the revisions made by the composer, evaluating their success according to the largely unspecified criteria that for him constituted Purcell's 'sensitive musical discrimination'.[48] His comments on the Funeral Sentences, which initiated a series of perceptive studies of these heavily revised works, provide a case in point: Manning accounted for the composer's revisions in terms of the 'extra harmonic and melodic interest', 'slightly firmer feeling of continuity' and

---

45   See, for example, the similar techniques Locke recommends in his thoroughbass 'rules': *Melothesia, or, Certain General Rules for playing upon a Continued-Bass* (London, 1673), pp. 5–[11].

46   Kerman, 'Sketch Studies', p. 54.

47   Ibid., pp. 54–5.

48   Manning, 'Revisions and Reworkings in Purcell's Anthems': 35.

'greater affective and melodic unity' that they achieved and, towards the end of *Thou knowest, Lord*, the 'better command of tonality' shown in the later version.[49]

If Manning's observations seem fundamentally persuasive, this is perhaps because most readers who share a twentieth-century Western musical education will recognize their origins in the values of musicality and taste inculcated by such a background. On the other hand, more recent developments have shown that the picture presented by Manning is at the very least oversimplified, and perhaps even misleading in places.

One problem is the selectivity of his account: it may be true that the revisions Manning discussed provide ample evidence of Purcell's refined musicality, but what of all those revisions he omitted to mention, which in some cases, at least to modern ears, seem detrimental to the effectiveness of the music? By ignoring these, he presented a coherent account of the kind of consistent improvement we would expect from the 'great' composer, when in reality the situation is much more problematic. This was one of the criticisms implied by Robert Ford's response to Manning's article: by drawing attention to a number of other changes made by the composer, many apparently in the name of consistency (including one that introduced particularly flagrant consecutive perfect fifths), Ford was able to show that Purcell's revisions were rather more hit-and-miss than the unerring sense of self-criticism implied by Manning would suggest.[50] Despite Ford's greater awareness of variation in the quality of Purcell's revisions, however, the methodology of the two articles is basically similar: both evaluated the revisions according to what might be called criteria of general musicality, and both assumed that changes made by the composer represented putative improvements in Purcell's estimation, and were therefore evidence of his musical judgement according to those same criteria. Hence Ford's attempt to excuse Purcell's fallibility on the grounds that he 'may well have been a far better composer than editor'.[51]

For all that he remains within this paradigm, though, Robert Ford made one particularly important contribution in his article that has been borne out by more recent work: his insistence on the importance of non-autograph sources as records of compositional reworkings.[52] Ford observed that a large group of sources of the Funeral Sentences commonly regarded as preserving corrupted or inauthentic texts in fact agreed sufficiently with one another to suggest that their variants all derived from a common source.[53] Particular features of the handwriting of Daniel Henstridge in one of these manuscripts, US-LAuc fC6966/M4/A627/1700, allowed him to date this

---

49   Ibid.: 30–31.
50   Ford, 'Purcell as his Own Editor': 54–62.
51   Ibid.: 66.
52   Ibid., *passim*, but see especially p. 47. As Herissone observes in pointing out this aspect of Ford's article, the importance of non-autograph sources in this respect has been more widely recognized in studies of Locke's music: see Tilmouth, 'Revisions in the Chamber Music of Matthew Locke': 89–100; and Thompson, 'The Sources of Locke's Consort "For Seaverall Friends"': 16–44.
53   Ford, 'Purcell as his Own Editor': 51–2.

version to around 1681–82, meaning that it almost certainly predated the autograph score of the first two Sentences in Cfm 88, and therefore seemed most likely to represent an intermediate stage of revision by Purcell between the earliest extant autograph in Lbl Add. 30931 and the version in the Fitzwilliam collection.[54] Although he was concerned only with the Funeral Sentences, the case of *My Beloved Spake* demonstrates the wider applicability of Ford's observation about copyist sources: as we have seen already, even a source as late as Philip Hayes's score of the work from the 1780s can prove pivotal to the comparative evaluation of surviving versions.

Comparatively little of Purcell's music will admit such detailed investigation of earlier versions; there are simply no sources preserving significant variant texts for the vast majority of his works. Nevertheless, an overview of those works that are susceptible to such treatment was provided by Herissone's early *Purcell Studies* article, which also showed two notable developments on earlier approaches to Purcell's creativity: the attempt to present a more general overview, and the linking of the implicit criteria of general musicality found in earlier studies with more explicit observations about stylistic change.[55]

In attempting a global description of Purcell's working methods drawn from the broad corpus of surviving sources, rather than concentrating on a given work, Herissone's 1995 article offered a number of invaluable starting points for the analysis of individual sources. One such insight was Purcell's care in planning his copying, although like most Restoration copyists he occasionally seems to have lost his place in his source text, prepared systems for the wrong numbers of parts, or entered the music for a given voice or instrument on the wrong stave.[56] When such mistakes occurred, or indeed when revising a score, Purcell would use one of a number of methods of amendment: he might enlarge or otherwise modify notated symbols such that their pitch or rhythm (or both) were altered, cross out individual notes or whole passages, or scrape away the surface of the paper in order to remove the notation and write over the top of it; each of these methods can be seen in the Lbl Add. 30932 score of *My Beloved Spake*. More extensive revisions might be notated elsewhere in the manuscript, their intended use being indicated by some sort of written rubric, or they might be added on separate sheets and secured into the manuscript using glue or pins.

Of even greater interest in terms of compositional process was Herissone's observation that Purcell tended to notate outer parts first, before going back to complete the texture.[57] This can be seen in certain autograph works where the inner

54   Ibid.: 52–3. For the most recent discussion of the relevant qualities of Henstridge's handwriting, see Shay and Thompson, *Purcell Manuscripts*, pp. 223–4.

55   Herissone, 'Purcell's Revisions of his Own Works', *passim*; this article actually derived from Herissone's MMus dissertation, 'The Compositional Techniques of Henry Purcell as Revealed through Autograph Revisions Made to His Works' (MMus dissertation, King's College, London, 1993).

56   Herissone, 'Purcell's Revisions of his Own Works', p. 56.

57   In fact, there is considerable precedent for this kind of compositional process in comparable repertoires: Peter Holman makes reference to its use in homophonic dance music as early as the 1550s (see *Four and Twenty Fiddlers: The Violin at the English Court 1540–1690*, Oxford

parts were never filled in, such as the Suite in G and the symphony anthem *Rejoice in the Lord Alway*, and where changes in ink colour show that the parts were notated at different times, as in anthems like *Bow Down thine Ear* and *My Heart is Fixed*, and in the *Chacony* in G minor.[58] In other works, such as the symphony anthem *I was Glad*, the number of revisions to the inner parts seems to indicate that they were being composed directly into the manuscript despite the fact that there is no change of ink; it may be that, rather than having composed the treble and bass and later returning to the same manuscript in order to complete the remaining parts, Purcell was here actually copying from another source containing outer parts only, and composing the inner parts in the process.[59]

Once again, *My Beloved Spake* provides a convenient testing ground, and there are indeed passages in the Lbl Add. 30932 score that seem to confirm that Purcell began by notating outer parts alone: on the second system of the opening symphony on fol. 87, for example, the alignment of the inner string parts is clearly different from that of the first violin and thoroughbass, and the same is true of the start of the middle system of fol. 90v (the end of the ritornello following the first 'alleluia'). There is, however, one passage in which Purcell's revisions to the score defy explanation in these terms – a passage that thus helps both to refine the theory and to pin down the function of this source. At the top of fol. 88v (see Figure 3.1), before he made a significant cut at the words 'the rain is over and gone', Purcell altered the text underlay and the notes of the tenor part. Two aspects of these revisions are crucial. First, they show that Purcell was copying, rather than composing: as he wrote out the text beneath the first empty stave (using the text to determine the spacing before any music was copied was another common working method), he made the classic copying error of jumping ahead to a similar passage later in the music, with the result that all the text from the first 'the' on this line was effectively copied three bars early.[60] Second, the revisions to the notes in the tenor part show that he was copying both the alto and tenor simultaneously, or at least a few notes at a time: we can see that he had copied four notes in the tenor before realizing his mistake and attempting to remedy it, but he cannot by this point have copied the whole of the alto line for this system, since there are no corrections to the notes in the top part. Instead, it seems he had completed just the first three notes of the alto – the three notes, indeed, that were the same at the beginning of this phrase and the next, and hence that contributed to the mistake in the first place. Perhaps at this point Purcell added the start of the first bass part to the alto and tenor already

---

Monographs on Music (Oxford: Clarendon, 1993), p. 90), and the practice of *remplissage* in Lully's operas, whereby the inner parts were apparently supplied by the performers and transcribers of the works rather than by Lully himself, is well known (see Ronald Broude, 'Le Cerf, Lully, and the Workshop Tradition', in Ronald Broude (ed.), *Studies in the History of Music 3: The Creative Process* (New York: Broude Brothers, 1992), pp. 17–30).

58   Herissone, 'Purcell's Revisions of his Own Works', p. 57.
59   Ibid.
60   All references to barring and bar numbers refer to the edition of *My Beloved Spake* in Purcell, *Sacred Music, Part I*, ed. Dennison, pp. 103–32.

Figure 3.1 Purcell's alterations in his autograph score of *My Beloved Spake*, Lbl
Add. 30932, fol. 88v. Reproduced by permission of the British Library.
© The British Library Board; all rights reserved.

notated, since doing so would immediately have alerted him to the error in his copying and prompted him to revise the text and tenor part before going on to complete the alto line without need for any alterations.

Thus, despite Hayes's annotation to the effect that the Lbl Add. 30932 autograph is Purcell's 'original score', and its rough appearance, it is clear that this source is in itself a copy of an earlier source of some sort; indeed, this would explain how what has always been thought of as a composing score found its way into Flackton's collection: perhaps after all it is a transmission copy that was sent to Henstridge at Rochester, as has been suggested for the other autographs in Lbl Add. 30931–3.[61] The implications for Purcell's copying habits, meanwhile, are that, while it may be true that he completed outer parts first for passages in which the inner parts were yet to be composed (perhaps, in other words, his copy text had only outer parts for the symphony and ritornelli), at least on fol. 88v he copied in descending order from the highest part. The evidence is far from conclusive, since the second bass is silent for the crucial notes, but given that Ford observed a similar pattern in the sources of the Funeral Sentences, it is worth considering that, at least when copying textures that were already complete, Purcell may have followed such an order. Apart from anything else, there are good practical reasons for doing so, giving the danger of smudging an already notated bass part if the inner parts are added immediately.

In addition to describing Purcell's general working methods, the other main focus of Herissone's *Purcell Studies* chapter was the analysis of the actual revisions he made in the works under discussion, and their interpretation as indicators of stylistic change in Purcell's music. Given least attention were the expected corrections of errant voice-leading, as well as some seemingly less important revisions of detail that involve the handling of dotted rhythms in any part, and of octave displacements and rhythmic simplification in thoroughbass lines, and the kind of neutral reworkings of melodic details, especially in the approaches to cadences, characterized by both Manning and Ford as 'tinkering'.[62] Examples of such details in *My Beloved Spake* might include the handling of the second repeat in the overture (a literal repeat from the anacrusis to the last four bars in Lbl Add. 30932 and Badham's Ob T 1031, but with the bass altered to crotchet F – minim f immediately prior to the *petite reprise* in Cfm 117, Lbl Add. 17820, KNt MR 2–5.4 and Novello's edition), or the sixth note of the first bass part in the verse 'For lo the winter is gone' (b♭ in the autograph and Ob T 1031, c' in the other sources).

Three kinds of more extensive revision were treated at greater length by Herissone in this chapter: modifications to harmonic language and tonal content (particularly in the Funeral Sentences and the anthems *Hear me, O Lord* and *Let mine Eyes Run Down with Tears*), to imitative textures (in *Let mine Eyes Run Down with Tears* and the Benedicite from the Service in B Flat), and to large-scale structural organization, particularly towards the ends of pieces (in the 'Golden' Sonata,

---

61   Ford, 'Purcell as his Own Editor': 48–9.
62   Herissone, 'Purcell's Revisions of his Own Works', pp. 82–6; Manning, 'Revisions and Reworkings in Purcell's Anthems': 35; Ford, 'Purcell as his Own Editor': 66.

no. 9 from the 1697 *Sonatas of Four Parts*, and in Fantazia 2).[63] Included in this latter bracket are the two more significant structural revisions made to *My Beloved Spake* in the Lbl Add. 30932 autograph: the removal of the last nine bars and anacrusis from the end of 'For lo the winter is gone' – the last two of which are reinstated in all sources of the later version – and the cutting of five bars from 'My beloved is mine'. As Herissone observed, these greatly improve the sense of climax of their respective verses,[64] although in this case as a result of removing harmonically redundant phrases rather than due to improvements in part-writing.

Herissone's analysis of the revisions in the works covered by her essay aimed to present a clear picture of the stylistic background to Purcell's 'criticism of his own music', to return to Kerman's idea about the class of questions probed by 'sketch studies' in the broad sense: drawing on common observations about the stylistic trajectory of Purcell's career, she observed harmony becoming more tonally directed and less locally idiosyncratic, imitative textures tighter and more motivically concentrated, and structures more balanced, with clearly driven climaxes.[65] Such arguments have their own potential problems, however, and Herissone's penultimate sentence is revealing: 'Even where change seems to have resulted in significant improvement, one can only speculate about Purcell's intentions as a reviser of his own music.' In other words, given the ultimate inaccessibility of Purcell's actual reasons for reworking a given passage, stylistic arguments like those advanced here may prove little more than a thin veneer covering an analysis that is still essentially subjective.

This is not to say that such arguments are inherently less persuasive. The relative merits of the versions of Sonatas 7 and 8 from the 1697 *Sonatas of Four Parts* preserved in the print and in the autograph manuscript, Lbl Add. 30930, for example, are a matter of individual taste; in theory one might agree with Michael Tilmouth that the printed version of Sonata 7 is 'a clear advance' on the Add. 30930 text, or with Herissone that certain passages of this sonata sound 'weak and uninspired' in the print, but are 'considerably stronger and more vital' in Lbl Add. 30930.[66] As observations about Purcell's revisions, however, Herissone's comments gain more weight from the fact that material from the printed version of Sonata 8 appears on the reverse of correction slips used in the Lbl Add. 30930 copy of Sonata 9, suggesting

---

63   Herissone, 'Purcell's Revisions of his Own Works', pp. 66–73, 73–80 and 80–82 respectively.

64   Ibid., p. 82.

65   On the increasingly Italianate style of Purcell's music see (for example) Jack A. Westrup, *Purcell*, The Master Musicians (rev. edn, Oxford: Oxford University Press, 1995; originally published London: Dent, 1937), pp. 240–47; Kenneth R. Long, *The Music of the English Church* (London: Hodder and Stoughton, 1972), p. 272; or for a more subtle account incorporating recent emphasis on the importance of 'ancient' contrapuntal methods even in Purcell's later music, Martin Adams, *Henry Purcell: The Origins and Development of his Musical Style* (Cambridge: Cambridge University Press, 1995), *passim* (see the statement of Adams's main thesis in his preface, pp. ix–x).

66   Purcell, *Ten Sonatas of Four Parts*, ed. Tilmouth, p. xv; Herissone, 'Purcell's Revisions of his Own Works', pp. 60–61.

that the version of Sonata 8 that was later to be printed had already by this time been altered. The existence of such physical evidence for the chronological order of the different versions suggests that Herissone's opinion might indeed have been closer to Purcell's own, and also allowed her to add the more Italianate and violinistic style of the manuscript versions to the list of likely reasons for his revisions.

Nevertheless, it is important to understand the limitations of this kind of evidence, since in other contexts it can prove unreliable or even downright misleading. Manning, for example, based his entire argument concerning the relative chronology of the versions of *My Beloved Spake* on criteria of taste, resulting in an idiosyncratic view of the piece that has apparently no grounds in the surviving evidence. Manning's interpretation rested on the qualities of the two versions of the first strain of the opening symphony, a third important variant among the sources that we are yet to consider. He observed that the Cfm 117 version of these opening bars 'modulates rather more freely' than the autograph text, and contains 'more passing harmonic and melodic quirks'; the autograph, he suggested, 'seems to be the more assured of the two passages musically; on stylistic grounds we might therefore date it slightly later' than the Fitzwilliam version.[67] The argument here was essentially that, since Manning believed the autograph version to be better, it must necessarily have been later. Yet as Robert Ford was later to show, it is unwise to assume Purcell's infallibility of judgement when editing his own music. Manning's belief in the legitimacy of this kind of stylistic evidence was sufficient that it even outweighed the evidence presented by the cuts to 'For lo the winter is past' and 'My beloved is mine' in Lbl Add. 30932, which are followed in every other source of the anthem; his attempt to explain this away as an exceptional instance of indecision in the process of revision was extremely unconvincing and, to my knowledge, his theory has never gained currency.

Apart from the danger of using stylistic arguments in the absence of secure chronological evidence, this view of *My Beloved Spake* also hints at further methodological problems with the explanation of revisions in terms of stylistic development. First, it is far from clear that a gradual change of style over a whole career (even a short one like Purcell's) can always be used to explain revisions made within a short period of time of the original composition. There are very few works that are known to have been composed near the beginning of Purcell's career and revised towards the end of his life. Most, like *My Beloved Spake*, were probably composed and revised within a rather shorter space of time – perhaps months, or a few years at most – such that it may be safer to view the revisions as reflections of increasing competence rather than long-term stylistic change (although the two are admittedly difficult to disentangle). It would be more convincing to compare revisions made, say, between the late 1670s and the 1690s, but such a project would be hampered by the fact that the overwhelming majority of works containing significant revisions

---

67   Manning, 'Revisions and Reworkings in Purcell's Anthems': 32–3. The Lbl Add. 30932 autograph of *My Beloved Spake* is in fact the only source to preserve its version of the opening of the symphony; all other sources contain readings similar to that in Cfm 117.

date from the late 1670s and early 1680s, while those works from the 1690s that do display some textual fluidity have variants for very different reasons.[68]

Second, and perhaps more importantly, the association of a given set of revisions with a particular stylistic trend risks underplaying other, perhaps equally important motivating factors. At its extreme, this can lead to apparently contradictory accounts of the same music. Consider, for example, Herissone's account of the Funeral Sentences, which attributes Purcell's revisions of *In the Midst of Life* and *Thou knowest, Lord* to his desire to 'clarif[y] the harmonic content', 'simplify the chromaticism', 'remove pungent harmonies' and '[reorganize] the tonal plan', all of which are discussed in the context of the stylistic trajectory towards a more Italianate, tonal harmonic style.[69] By contrast, Robert Shay, in a 1998 article that is the most recent contribution to the extensive literature on these works, associates Purcell's revisions with the lessons he learnt from studying the polyphony of older English composers including Tallis, Byrd and Gibbons.[70] One of the most significant aspects of Purcell's revisions in this regard is his tendency to introduce greater elision of imitative entries.[71] In this context, the very increase in harmonic control and balance associated by Herissone with an emerging tonal style is attributed by Shay to a better understanding of Renaissance imitative procedures.[72] To complete the reversal, whereas Herissone observes the removal of 'pungent harmonies', Shay points out the introduction of unconventional dissonances for specific affective purposes, noting their frequent citation as 'the most conspicuous (*and modern*) feature of [Purcell's] polyphonic works' (my emphasis).[73]

---

68   Isolated instances from the works of other composers might help here, such as the case, suggested to me by Peter Holman (private communication, 20 November 2009), of a symphony song by Blow, which occurs as 'Whilst on Septimnius's panting Breast' in *The Theater of Music: Or a Choice Collection of the Newest and Best Songs Sung at the Court, and Public Theaters … The First Book* (London, 1685), p. 68 in a version that includes three singers in the chorus sections, with a French-style overture and ritornelli; the version that appears with the text 'As on Septimius' panting Breast' in Blow's *Amphion Anglicus: A Work of Many Compositions, for One, Two, Three and Four Voices* (London, 1700), p. 171, however, is a vocal duet with imitative, Italianate instrumental parts. The issue of whether or not these clear stylistic changes constituted the original motivation behind the revision requires further investigation, as does the actual date of the revisions themselves: were they carried out expressly for the publication (and thus at least 15 years after the original composition), or might they be somewhat earlier?

69   Herissone, 'Purcell's Revisions of his Own Works', pp. 66–8.

70   Robert Shay, 'Purcell's Revisions to the Funeral Sentences Revisited', *Early Music* 26 (1998): 460. Shay's article draws on material originally included in his unpublished doctoral thesis, 'Henry Purcell and "Ancient" Music in Restoration England' (PhD dissertation, University of North Carolina at Chapel Hill, 1991), in which he explores a similar thesis with respect to a wider selection of Purcell's music, through a detailed examination of contemporary theoretical texts and Purcell's contribution to Cfm 88.

71   Shay, 'Purcell's Revisions to the Funeral Sentences Revisited': 463–4.

72   Ibid.: 463–5.

73   Ibid.: 465.

The point of contrasting these views of Purcell's revisions of the Funeral Sentences is not that one or the other is less persuasive or even 'wrong', but that by associating the revisions with a particular stylistic trait or trend each author has excluded other interpretations that are equally plausible. It seems far more likely that the impulses behind any given alteration were multiple and varied, and some of them perhaps unconscious; the search for multiple interpretations, then, might yield both explanatory power and a greatly increased richness of discourse within future discussions of Purcell's compositional revisions and reworkings.

Sources, Versions and Revisions: The Example of *My Beloved Spake*

Over little more than a decade since Robert Shay's article on the Funeral Sentences, the 'palaeographical' study of Purcell's creativity has begun to change in a number of ways, partly in response to the kinds of methodological debates outlined above, and perhaps even more so as a result of increasing realization that the models of creative activity on which most studies of the 1980s and 1990s were based are in many respects unsuited to Restoration music. At this point we might look in more detail at *My Beloved Spake* in order to bring out some of these problems with the traditional approach, and in the process provide a more comprehensive account of Purcell's anthem itself.

One of the casualties of recent thinking has been the assumption, irrespective of variation in creative habits caused by genre or performance circumstances, that we can understand Purcell's creative process as an orderly succession of compositional stages from initial inspiration through the working out of a composition to its arrival in a definitive version, and that these stages will be preserved in an equally orderly series of documents from sketches through rough drafts to the final fair copy. It is these kinds of assumptions that underpin the criteria applied by Kerman for the admission of materials into his broadly defined discipline of 'sketch studies' cited above: '(1) it has survived, and (2) it was in the composer's mind superseded'.[74] It does not take much study of the sources of *My Beloved Spake* to arrive at the conclusion that these criteria are deeply problematical when applied rigidly to Purcell's music.

As we have already seen, it has been widely assumed that the surviving sources preserve evidence of two versions of *My Beloved Spake*: one in the Lbl Add. 30932 autograph, and one represented by a group of sources including both Cfm 117 and Ob T 1031. The minor controversy over the relationship between these latter two, however, may derive ultimately from a multi-stage revision process similar to that observed by Robert Ford in the Funeral Sentences: both the Fitzwilliam and Tenbury texts, I would suggest, can be traced to different exemplars likely to have come from Purcell's own hand. The study of Purcell's creative process in this piece

---

74   Kerman, 'Sketch Studies', p. 54.

thus inevitably involves the conceptual reconstruction of at least one source that has not survived.

Dennison's assertion that some of the Cfm 117 variants 'could not possibly represent Purcell's intentions' is a good place to start.[75] In fact, many of the variants in Isaack's copy are relatively easy to explain. As Shay and Thompson note, it is clear that Isaack copied very little text at the time he notated the music;[76] thus we may safely attribute the often faulty underlay to him, noting in passing that this is a common problem throughout Cfm 117, and that several other passages also seem likely to represent simple misreadings on Isaack's part.[77]

Such infelicities aside, three features of Isaack's text are likely to have aroused Dennison's suspicions (see Example 3.1): a viola part that creates particularly ugly consecutive fifths in the second strain of the symphony (b. 19), and a tenor line in the closing chorus that makes two unconventional minor seconds with the bass (b. 301) and consecutive fifths with the alto (b. 307). These three readings are distinct from the obvious inaccuracies of Cfm 117 since each is shared with Hayes's KNt MR 2–5.4 score, which as we have seen is likely to derive independently from the later Purcell autograph, now lost.[78] What Dennison does not make clear, however, is that these two scores also share other readings that are not found either in the Lbl Add. 30932 autograph or in the Ob T 1031 score by Badham that was his copy text (see Example 3.2).

Such a level of agreement between Isaack's and Hayes's scores seems unlikely to have arisen by chance, so we need to consider what reasons there could be for the three problematic readings. In fact the first can be explained rather simply: as Novello evidently realized, there is a sharp missing from the third note of b. 19 in the viola part, which when restored creates perfectly acceptable counterpoint.[79] As for the two problems with the tenor line in the final chorus, it may simply be necessary to recall Robert Ford's observation that Purcell sometimes made

---

75 Unfortunately, Dennison's conviction that these readings were simply spurious led him to ignore most of them in his critical report, with the result that the relationships between them and two additional sources he did not collate (Hayes's KNt MR 2–5.4 and Novello's edition of the work largely derived from it) are difficult to spot – an object lesson in the necessity of listing every variant, even if only to attribute them to apparent corruption. If patterns do not occur to the editor during collation, they may well appear to the reader in considering additional sources or simply approaching the data with a fresh eye.

76 Shay and Thompson, *Purcell Manuscripts*, p. 64.

77 See, for example: faulty accidentals at bb. 13 (thoroughbass), 41 (bass) and 78 (thoroughbass); two vocal bass parts in parallel unison at bb. 103–7; rhythmically nonsensical second bass part at bb. 170–72; and a missing note in the thoroughbass, first beat of b. 146.

78 The same readings are also found in an early eighteenth-century source, Lbl Add. 17820 fols 96–102, although this source also contains many of the obvious errors found in Cfm 117 and for this reason seems likely to have been copied directly from Isaack's score.

79 There is even a clear technical reason why Purcell might have preferred this reading in his later revision: it avoids the accented passing note in the first violin sounding against its note of resolution as it had in Lbl Add. 30932.

Example 3.1   *My Beloved Spake,* three problematic variants from Cfm 117: (a) b. 19; (b) b. 301; (c) b. 307.

Example 3.2   *My Beloved Spake*, three further variants found in both Cfm 117 and KNt MR 2–5.4: (a) b. 41 (bracketed note does not occur in Lbl Add. 30932 or Ob T 1031); (b) b. 102 (small staves represent readings in Cfm 117 and KNt MR 2–5.4); (c) b. 122 (bracketed notes are not found in Lbl Add. 30932 or Ob T 1031).

ill-advised revisions on the spur of the moment. In this case there are attractive incentives for both changes: the first smooths out a rather angular moment from an otherwise pleasingly intuitive line, and the second strengthens the final cadence by introducing a seventh to the penultimate chord; the resulting contrapuntal transgressions are probably no more than unfortunate by-products.

If the version of *My Beloved Spake* in Cfm 117 and KNt MR 2–5.4 itself derives from Purcell's revised 'fair copy', then Ob T 1031 is left in something of a state of limbo: Badham's score has all the major revisions, including the new first strain in the symphony and the two cuts shown by the crossings-out on fols 88v and 92 of the surviving autograph, yet contains none of the smaller variants found in the Isaack and Hayes scores. Any explanation of how this came about necessarily relies on a degree of speculation, but it is nevertheless possible to arrive at a convincing reconstruction of events. We have already seen that the Lbl Add. 30932 autograph is itself a copy from an earlier source, which for the present purposes we will call Source A. Given that the cuts on fols 88v and 92 of Lbl Add. 30932 were made after the notation of the music, it seems likely that Source A also originally contained those bars that were later removed: the alternative – that Purcell added the material as he copied Lbl Add. 30932 only to delete it later – is less probable, although his revision practices elsewhere indicate that he may well have introduced other, smaller variants as he copied. Thus we have evidence so far of at least two 'states' of the work: first as written in Source A, and originally copied (although perhaps with some revision) in Lbl Add. 30932, then as amended with the two significant cuts in Lbl Add. 30932.

Exactly when these cuts were made is difficult to establish, but the unusual system braces found in the Lbl Add. 30932 autograph of *My Beloved Spake* suggest that they were introduced at some remove from its original notation. In his mature hand, beginning probably as early as the late 1670s with the autographs in Cfm 88 and Lbl Add. 30930, Purcell tended not to use system braces at all; the inverted form originally used in *My Beloved Spake*, similar to that used by Blow in Och Mus. 628, is a particular feature of Purcell's earliest autographs, such as the copy of Pelham Humfrey's *By the Waters of Babylon* in Lbl Add. 30932, fols 52–55v, and the two Funeral Sentences in Lbl Add. 30931, fols 81v–84v.[80] But *My Beloved Spake* also contains a second layer of braces that have a more conventional shape which is also found in the Lbl Add. 30932 autograph of *Behold now, Praise the Lord*, from c.1678–79, and which is strikingly similar in formation to those used by the scribe referred to by Shay and Thompson as 'London A' in Lbl R.M. 20.h.8 and US-R M2040/A628/Folio.[81] Purcell seems to have added these braces at the same time that the cuts were made, since on the second system of fol. 88v the newer style of brace is drawn not at the left-hand extreme of the page – which would have been its conventional position, but occurs in the middle of the cut passage – but at the beginning of the ritornello

---

80   An accessible reproduction of a page of the Humfrey score can be found in Shay and Thompson, *Purcell Manuscripts*, p. 3.

81   On London A, see ibid., pp. 78–83, 131–5, 312; images of his copying in US–R M2040/A628/Folio and Lbl R.M. 20.h.8 can be seen on pp. 82 and 132 respectively.

that follows three bars later. I suspect that the alterations were made in the Lbl Add. 30932 autograph of *My Beloved Spake* some time after it was originally notated, in order to make it conform to Source A which had already been amended, and that the new braces were inserted deliberately to show that the manuscript had been checked against the revised Source A, either by Purcell or perhaps by London A (although the style of the system braces alone is insufficient to prove it).[82] If this is indeed the case, it may even be that the last two bars of the first cut (setting 'is over and gone'), rather than being reinstated in the later versions, were never intended to have been cut at all, but rather were crossed out as a result of carelessness.

Thus far, then, we have established that the Lbl Add. 30932 autograph was copied from Source A, and that both sources may have been amended with the cuts described. We can date these cuts to before 1677, since they are followed in a bass part of *My Beloved Spake* in the hand of William Tucker at fols 7–7v of Lbl Add. 50860, in between items attributed to 'Mr' John Blow.[83] It was at this point in the creative process that the Lbl Add. 30932 score left Purcell's possession, presumably passing to Henstridge at Rochester (such an intention may even suggest the reason for its revision), since this source does not record the next stage in the revision process, which was the replacement of the first strain of the symphony. If this was done in Source A using a paste-down slip or similar means of inserting the 11 new bars, the resulting text would have been more or less exactly that of Badham's score in Ob T 1031 – incorporating the two cuts and the new symphony, but without the variant details from Cfm 117 and KNt MR 2–5.4 described above. Only after the changes to the symphony, and perhaps prompted by concerns about the legibility of Source A, which was by now heavily revised, did Purcell copy out the whole piece for a third time, giving rise to what we shall call Source B, from which Isaack and Hayes both copied their scores.[84] Thus Kerman's criterion of survival seems almost irrelevant: at least three autograph scores (containing in total four states of the work) can be inferred from the surviving sources of *My Beloved Spake*, even though only one autograph is extant.

If this comes at all close to an accurate description of Purcell's work on *My Beloved Spake*, then it also starts to make Kerman's other condition – that original materials are superseded by later sources – look increasingly problematic. By the early 1680s there were evidently at least two forms of the anthem in circulation: the Lbl Add. 30932 version (which was probably known by Henstridge at Rochester), containing

---

82 Only one of the other autographs in Lbl Add. 30932 has both styles of braces written one over the other as in *My Beloved Spake – Who hath Believed our Report?* – and there is no obvious evidence of revision in this case.

83 See Shay and Thompson, *Purcell Manuscripts*, pp. 144–6.

84 Novello's text perhaps requires further explanation: in his edition of the revised version only the variant given in Example 3.1(a) is followed, with the addition of a sharp as already described. Given that Novello seems to have taken Hayes's score as his copy text, we might expect it to follow more of the Isaack/Hayes variants, but Novello also notes that he collated his text with that in the second volume of Tudway's *Services and Anthems* (Lbl Harleian 7338, dated 1716). Tudway's text is all but identical to Badham's, and thus could easily have provided Novello with these readings.

the cuts but not the new symphony, and the version derived from Source B copied by Isaack at Windsor; in addition, the revised Source A cannot by this stage have been destroyed, since it was still available to Charles Badham at St Paul's Cathedral when he copied Ob T 1031 in the first decade of the eighteenth century. Had Purcell truly considered each set of revisions to supersede all previous versions, he would surely have taken steps to ensure that earlier texts were removed from circulation; that he did not suggests that, as Ford observed in the case of the Funeral Sentences, he was content that the music should be known and performed in multiple versions.

The evidence for the persistence of earlier versions alongside revisions of Purcell's music is not limited to works found in the Lbl Add. 30931–3 autographs like the Funeral Sentences and *My Beloved Spake*. Indeed, the classic example – which has been widely quoted since 1995 when it was first expressed in print – is that of the revisions in Lbl Add. 30930 to what would become Sonatas 7 and 8 of the 1697 *Sonatas of Four Parts*. Robert Thompson pointed out these were made using correction slips originally pinned, rather than glued, in place.[85] The suggestion is that this method was used deliberately in order to permit selection between the different versions, and that neither was to be considered definitive; here, then, is an alternative interpretation that offers a way out of the impasse we encountered on pp. 83–5 above. No doubt some revisions were intended to replace earlier readings: it is difficult to imagine that Purcell himself continued to perform *My Beloved Spake* in its original form as notated in Source A after the cuts found in Lbl Add. 30932 were made, for example. Yet examples like those given here contribute to a growing body of evidence that challenges the idea that Restoration musical works ultimately existed in some definitive form arrived at through an organic and teleological process of creation and revision on the part of a composer.

This is not intended as a criticism of Kerman's assumptions, since he did not really consider much music before the middle of the eighteenth century and in any case quite calculatedly avoided the additional complication of notions of finality even in his core nineteenth-century repertoire.[86] However, recent work on Purcell's compositional process by Rebecca Herissone has shown that studies of Restoration music can ill afford to skirt this issue if they are to provide useful insight into the ways in which the music was created, notated and even perhaps performed.[87]

Rethinking Purcell's Compositional Process

Herissone's reframing of the question of Purcell's creativity as evident from the sources begins with a problem that lurked not far beneath the surface of her 1995 *Purcell Studies* article: the terminology used to describe manuscript sources of

85   Robert Thompson, 'Purcell's Great Autographs', in Curtis Price (ed.), *Purcell Studies* (Cambridge: Cambridge University Press, 1995), pp. 15–16.

86   Kerman, 'Sketch Studies', p. 55.

87   Herissone, '"Fowle Originalls"': 569–619.

Restoration music. Discomfort with the term 'fair copy' is already evident in the earlier article, perhaps most notably in its apparent synonymity with 'neat copy' despite the disclaimer in note 1 stating that the term 'fair copy' is intended not to reflect attention to presentation but simply the fact of post-compositional notation.[88] As we have seen, almost all Purcell's autograph sources seem to meet this second criterion; furthermore, even if 'fair' is open to interpretation, 'neat' is surely an unambiguous reference to the appearance of the notation, with the result that the article's use of these terms as largely interchangeable often seems to contradict the earlier footnote.

Further reflection on the use of the term 'fair copy' along with another common label, 'rough draft', led Herissone to arrive at two significant objections to the use of such terminology in conjunction with Purcell's manuscripts: one ontological, the other etymological. The latter argument in particular brings the problem into focus. It seems that the apparent similarities between the modern terms 'rough draft' and 'fair copy' on the one hand, and seventeenth-century labels such as 'fowle originall' and 'fayre writing' on the other, can by no means be taken for granted. Most obvious is the problem with assuming equivalence between 'originall' and 'draft': these terms did indeed carry similar meanings in the late seventeenth century, but denoted an authentic original or exemplar, without the connotations of preliminary status or fragmentary nature usually implied by modern definitions of the term 'draft'.[89]

In effect, this confirms the observation made above about the problem with the rough draft/fair copy distinction in Herissone's earlier article, and it demands a significant change in the way we think about the relationship between Purcell's creativity and the documents in which his music is preserved. In the nineteenth-century traditions at the heart of Kerman's discipline of 'sketch-studies' it was possible to observe a number of largely discrete stages in the compositional process, their notated corollaries each differing in terms of visual appearance and even technology: from initial sketches through successive drafts to a fair copy and, ultimately, a printed edition that represented a form of authorized definitive version. By contrast, Restoration manuscript culture can now be seen as one in which even the earliest surviving sources preserve little detailed evidence of the initial creative act, and in which notational characteristics are at best a poor guide to the compositional status of a given source.

In such a context issues like the chronological sequence of revisions and the problem of whether or not one version is to be considered definitive start to appear less and less relevant. According to the nineteenth-century model, the creation of each source of a given work is a direct outcome of a given stage in the compositional process; thus if one can arrange the sources in the right order, one can be fairly sure of reconstructing a more or less coherent process leading up to the composer's 'final thoughts' on that piece. In Restoration music, by contrast, sources seem to

---

88 Herissone, 'Purcell's Revisions of his Own Works', p. 51; see, for example, pp. 54–5 where Cfm 88 is described as containing 'fair copies', and pp. 66–7 where the same manuscript has 'neat copies'.

89 Herissone, '"Fowle Originalls"': 578–80.

have been created in response to particular functional demands rather than as part of a systematic 'creative process'. In such a context, Herissone suggests, music is constantly changing in response to the demands of differing performance contexts and resources, a situation she likens to Philip Bohlman's formulation of 'music as process' as against the more familiar (if equally flawed) nineteenth-century model of 'music as object'.[90] We have arrived, in other words, at the ontological problem with the conventional manuscript terminology: the written preservation of music in such a culture invariably reflects the intended use of the source, and the variation of musical details that goes with this use, much more than it does any teleological progress towards a definitive version of the work in question.

From this starting point, Herissone was able to outline a fresh approach to Purcell's creative processes based on the interpretation of sources in the context of their practical functions, rather than relying principally upon the relationship between their texts and any putative ideal forms of the works they contain. This is a task that has been largely facilitated by the appearance of Shay and Thompson's *Purcell Manuscripts* in 2000, with its detailed codicological study of all the principal autograph sources and many more copyist manuscripts containing Purcell's music.[91] Shay and Thompson's volume presents a wealth of information derived from the study of handwriting, paper types, bindings and collation, and textual comparison, which permits a much more detailed understanding of individual manuscripts, the circumstances of their creation and the complicated relationships among them than has hitherto been possible. Purcell's creative habits are greatly illuminated by this kind of information alone, but the book's authors also offer numerous intriguing nuggets that suggest further lines of enquiry, of which the various comments on *My Beloved Spake* taken up in this essay are just one example. Perhaps even more suggestive in the context of Herissone's work, however, was the organization of *Purcell Manuscripts* into chapters focusing on Purcell's most important score-books, and on the sources of music in particular genres. As Herissone points out, this kind of structure reflects Purcell's own categorization by genre of large score-books like Cfm 88, Lbl Add. 30930 and Lbl R.M. 20.h.8, both within volumes (by copying different repertoires from alternate ends of the same book) and between them.[92] The question that arises, then, is to what extent these differences in genre are discernible in the surviving sources, and how far they reflect Purcell's different creative habits when working in different contexts.

---

90   Ibid.: 572; see also Philip V. Bohlman, 'Ontologies of Music', in Nicholas Cook and Mark Everist (eds), *Rethinking Music* (Oxford and New York: Oxford University Press, 1999), p. 18.

91   Related material also appeared earlier in Robert Shay, 'Purcell as Collector of "Ancient" Music: Fitzwilliam MS 88', in Curtis Price (ed.), *Purcell Studies* (Cambridge: Cambridge University Press, 1995), pp. 35–50, and Thompson, 'Purcell's Great Autographs', pp. 6–34. For a recent reappraisal, see Robert Thompson's chapter in this volume.

92   See Herissone, '"Fowle Originalls"': 572–6.

A key preliminary stage in this project is the establishment of a working vocabulary to replace the conventional references to source types as 'rough drafts' and 'fair copies'. For Purcell's manuscripts, Herissone suggests a five-fold division of document types, four of which can be illustrated with reference to the sources of *My Beloved Spake* discussed above.[93] The appearance of the surviving autograph, Lbl Add. 30932, might suggest that we designate it a 'fowle originall' – that is, what might be called a primary exemplar: the first complete text of the work, usable by copyists and, in some instances, performers (perhaps in the case of the composer playing continuo), defined as such by its untidy appearance and not by any preliminary or incomplete status.[94] However, we have seen that the Lbl Add. 30932 source of *My Beloved Spake* is in fact a copy from an earlier manuscript; thus it may be that the work's true 'fowle originall' was Source A, with the various cuts and insertions described above. Like many of the Purcell autographs in Lbl Add. 30931–3, that of *My Beloved Spake* may instead have been a 'transmission copy' prepared by Purcell in order to provide Daniel Henstridge with a copy, following the practice by which most provincial cathedrals and other establishments seem to have acquired new repertoire.[95]

Both Isaack's score in Cfm 117 and Badham's in Ob T 1031, meanwhile, are examples of 'file copies': large, bound volumes containing collections of works copied in score for the purposes of storage and preservation, perhaps as exemplars for future performing materials or simply as part of a personal collection.[96] Finally, Tucker's bass part to *My Beloved Spake* in Lbl Add. 50860 provides an example of performance materials. Thus the only one of Herissone's five categorizations of Purcell autographs not represented among the sources for *My Beloved Spake* is that of teaching materials.[97] As Herissone acknowledges, there are other relevant manuscript functions; a good example would be Thomas Tudway's copy of the anthem in Lbl Harleian 7338, fol. 224, a particular kind of file copy often referred to as a 'presentation copy' (this manuscript is one of a six-volume set entitled *Services and Anthems*, compiled by Tudway between 1715 and 1720 for his patron Edward, Lord Harley).[98] Finally, even entrepreneurial 'manuscript publications' may preserve variants that cast light on the creative history of a piece.[99]

---

93 A slightly different interpretation of sources based on musical function is outlined in Robert Thompson's chapter in this volume, pp. 31–53 above.

94 Herissone, '"Fowle Originalls"': 586.

95 Ibid.: 587; on the practice of dissemination among cathedrals see Ian Spink, *Restoration Cathedral Music, 1660–1714*, Oxford Studies in British Church Music (Oxford: Clarendon, 1995), p. 77; see also the discussion in Robert Thompson's chapter, this volume, pp. 31–53.

96 Herissone, '"Fowle Originalls"': 587.

97 Ibid.: 587–8.

98 See Spink, *Restoration Cathedral Music*, pp. 87–8.

99 See Robert Thompson, 'Manuscript Music in Purcell's London', *Early Music* 23 (1995): 605–18; and Alan Howard, 'Manuscript Publishing in the Commonwealth Period: A Neglected Source of Consort Music by Golding and Locke', *Music & Letters* 90 (2009): 35–67.

Herissone applies these terminological distinctions to two genres of music by Purcell: liturgical sacred music with organ accompaniment, and odes and welcome songs. The different relationship between 'fowle originalls' and autograph file copies in these genres is marked, serving to demonstrate her thesis concerning the importance of source function. In the liturgical music, 'fowle originalls' are complete texts showing evidence of some revision, particularly to imitative passages; the file copy Cfm 88 preserves these changes but also demonstrates Purcell's habitual revision of details when copying from his originals into his score-book.[100] Variants in Cfm 88 fall into one of three categories: pre-copying revisions, made before or in the process of copying and thus not visible as corrections; post-copying revisions, involving crossings-out and other self-evident alterations that Herissone suggests may have been prompted by Purcell's intention to allow Isaack access to his score-book;[101] and planned revisions, which are similar to pre-copying revisions except that Purcell had evidently not decided exactly what was needed; he therefore left gaps in works like *Save me, O God, O God, Thou hast Cast me Out* and perhaps *Blessed is He whose Unrighteousness is Forgiven*, some of which he never returned to complete. Apart from Herissone's observation that many of the pre- and post-copying revisions in Cfm 88 seem to have been made without any prospect of performance, then, the pattern in this repertoire is intuitively familiar from many later repertoires; the difference is the absence of a logically determinable 'definitive' version of each work.

The odes and welcome songs, by contrast, seem to suggest a situation in which Purcell made his file copies in Lbl R.M. 20.h.8 simultaneously with the copying of the 'fowle originalls'.[102] While there are few surviving loose-leaf copies of these works, those that are extant show a common pattern: they tend to contain relatively neatly copied vocal parts, with very few corrections, and singers' names inserted for the solos, yet have instrumental parts that are poorly laid out, heavily corrected and often incomplete, as if composed directly into the manuscript. The Lbl R.M. 20.h.8 file copies, on the other hand, have much more complete instrumental parts, and vocal parts that are sometimes insufficiently notated to provide a complete record of the work.[103] The implication, Herissone argues, is that the loose-leaf 'fowle originalls' were used as copy texts for the vocal parts, and the file copies for the instrumental, with time pressures prompting Purcell to work on both copies together in order to facilitate a division of labour in the preparation of performance materials. Here, then, is a compositional process that is fundamentally different from that of the liturgical sacred music, and one that can only be understood through the examination of the sources in the context of their likely intended uses.

Herissone's focus on the specific intended functions of manuscript sources has the potential to move the study of Purcell's creative strategies beyond the kinds of subjective accounts of his supposed motivations for making particular

---

100　For the discussion of liturgical sacred music with organ accompaniment, see Herissone, '"Fowle Originalls"': 588–604.

101　Ibid.: 603.

102　Ibid.: 612.

103　Ibid.: 616.

revisions discussed above, and towards a much more profound understanding of the relationship between his music and the sources in which it is preserved. Her conceptualization of the Restoration musical work as inhabiting a state of constant flux, furthermore, with sources recording only its state at a given point in time and even then only with sufficient completeness to fulfil the source's intended functions, points to a more fundamental reconsideration of the nature of musical creativity in late seventeenth-century England. An important ingredient in this new approach is our increased understanding of the implications of what was predominantly a manuscript rather than a printed-music culture, and the effects of scribal habits upon the texts they transmitted: not only might the specific notated details of a given source be expected to reflect the circumstances behind its creation and intended use, but variation could also result from the act of manuscript reproduction itself. The classic treatment of this topic by Harold Love contains much that is directly relevant to this kind of musical creativity; indeed, in the following passage he could almost be describing the same set of practices that Herissone found in Purcell's liturgical sacred music:

> The ideal of creativity revealed in such cases is a gradualistic one … the scribal author is able both to polish texts indefinitely and to personalize them to suit the tastes of particular recipients. This practice denies the sharp distinctions which can be drawn for print-published texts between drafts, the 'authorized' first-edition text, and revisions which are fully reflected on and well-spaced in time. It also militates against our identifying any particular text as the embodiment of a 'final intention', for while the process of revision may in some instances be one of honing and perfecting, it may equally be one of change for change's sake or of an ongoing adaptation to the expectations of readers. Versions produced in this way do not so much replace as augment each other. In some instances they seem to grow from a lifestyle in which the activity of altering a text was more important than its outcome.[104]

It might be objected that the situation with Restoration music is really not all that different from that in the nineteenth century, if one allows for the fact that the kinds of compositional manuscripts found among the sketches and drafts of Mozart, Beethoven and Schumann (for example) are simply not available for Blow and Purcell. Is this idea of 'gradualistic creativity' really all that different from the kinds of changes and revisions that were also made to nineteenth-century works in response to specific performance demands, and recorded in manuscript emendations and insertions to printed editions? Clearly one possible answer is that it is not. In many ways it would be helpful to view Restoration music practices as a specific instance of a much wider principle, one that begins to look increasingly important as we seek new ways to understand the core eighteenth- and nineteenth-

---

104 Harold Love, *The Culture and Commerce of Texts: Scribal Publication in Seventeenth-Century England* (Amherst: University of Massachusetts Press, 1998; originally published as *Scribal Publication in Seventeenth-Century England* (Oxford: Clarendon, 1993)), p. 53.

century repertoires without uncritically accepting the ideologies of monumental objectification that we have inherited along with them.

Nevertheless, there are issues of both scale and kind that set seventeenth-century music apart somewhat from this later repertoire, which concern the status of the written text in relation to its realization in performance in the respective traditions. Any nineteenth-century adaptation of music to fit particular performance circumstances is likely to have drawn on a notionally definitive printed version whose contents were carefully controlled by the composer. However imperfectly this printed version encoded the music, and however inaccurate its contents turned out to be, it was nevertheless understood as a fixed exemplar. For Restoration works, the likelihood of variation in performance and the comparative imprecision of musical notation at the time meant that this concept of fixity simply did not exist.[105]

This is borne out not only in the amount of information that is typically missing from a seventeenth-century music manuscript (instrumentation, thoroughbass realization, ornamentation, tempo, dynamics, and so on) but also in the degree to which these and other details typically vary between sources, even between autographs of the same work. An excellent example is Blow's *Venus and Adonis*, recently edited by Bruce Wood for the Purcell Society's new 'Companion Series' in a parallel edition that shows the differences between the two extant versions, including both 'background variation' of this type and genuine revisions.[106] Such works present an intriguing problem for modern editors, since to select one version or the other risks imposing an unwarranted sense of textual stability, whereas to print both tends to suggest self-critical reworking on the part of the composer when many of the variants are in truth simply alternative realizations of an underlying concept of the piece that is less circumscribed than that for later musical works.[107]

What Boorman calls the 'allusive' nature of musical texts can help us to an even more radical reinterpretation of the comparative authority of different Restoration musical sources. In his words, the particular details notated in any score '[are] there because the composer (or some intermediary) regarded them as essential indicators of some aspect of the execution, as stimuli, rather than as binding instructions. ... The text represents an amalgam of decisions about only the essential components

---

105 For a recent discussion of this issue see Stanley Boorman, 'The Musical Text', in Nicholas Cook and Mark Everist (eds), *Rethinking Music* (Oxford and New York: Oxford University Press, 1999), p. 407.

106 John Blow, *Venus and Adonis*, ed. Bruce Wood, The Purcell Society Edition Companion Series, vol. 2 (London: Stainer and Bell, 2008). For an overview of the kinds of notational features that seem to have been regarded by composers as interchangeable, see Herissone, 'The Theory and Practice of Composition in the English Restoration Period', pp. 159–62.

107 See also my comments in 'John Blow in Parallel Texts', Review of John Blow, *Venus and Adonis*, ed. Bruce Wood, Purcell Society Companion Series, vol. 2 (London: Stainer & Bell, 2008), in *Early Music* 37 (2009): 319. My own edition of Blow's anthem *Jesus Seeing the Multitudes*, which attempts to differentiate between genuine revisions and 'background variation' of details of this type, is available in the Society for Seventeenth-Century Music's *Web Library of Seventeenth-Century Music*, http://aaswebsv.aas.duke.edu/wlscm.

of a work'.[108] While this is true of all notated music – the main difference being the amount of information considered essential at a given time or place – the absence of a sense of the definitive or authorized version of a work in much music of the seventeenth and early eighteenth centuries means that the qualitative distinction between variants introduced by the composer and by other individuals can be eroded almost to the point of elimination. This is why, for example, many of the variants in the Isaack score of *My Beloved Spake* deserve serious consideration rather than simply being dismissed as corruptions: given Purcell's own propensity to make similar changes when copying his own music (as shown by works like the Funeral Sentences, for which multiple autographs survive), there is no clear reason to deny Isaack's text of *My Beloved Spake* the authority afforded to Purcell's autograph as a record of the piece as it would have been understood by his contemporaries. Non-autograph versions of a Restoration work therefore potentially carry an authority equal to that of autographs, not only in cases where corroboration suggests a common autograph source (as with *My Beloved Spake*), but even where they can be confidently attributed to someone other than the composer.

In effect this extends Love's notion of 'gradualistic creativity' to a kind of decentralized concept of the Restoration musical work as the sum of all possible realizations. In order to understand works by Purcell and his contemporaries better, therefore, we need to study their treatment by others who were literate in his musical style and its notated essentials, rather than relying on literal readings of autograph texts. What this must not become, however, is a blandly relativistic attitude to the sources in which it is no longer possible to discern differing levels of authority among them. As well as examining the working methods of composers in general and the specific decisions they made about individual works, then, the study of Restoration musical creativity will be fundamentally about assessing the reliability and competence of individual scribes. It will also be concerned with establishing the validity of a source as evidence of musical activity in a given context, since even a text that seems comparatively distant from the origins of a musical work may preserve much of interest in the context of the culture in which it originated.

Two specific areas for further research present themselves in the light of this wider definition of the Restoration musical work. First, if the notated sources preserve notionally essential aspects of a given work, exactly what were the defining characteristics that were considered specific to a given composition? Second, and furthermore, how did composers and other musicians realize these characteristics in performance? Recent work on Restoration keyboard music has suggested a way into this topic by examining those aspects that remain comparatively constant in disparate sources of the same pieces and transcriptions of pieces. Good examples are Jeremiah Clarke's *Shore's Trumpet Tune* and Robert King's settings of songs from Thomas Clayton's *Arsinoe*, as noted by Andrew Woolley: it seems that the 'gists' of such compositions are confined to as little as their general melodic contour and harmonic structure, and even quite considerable variation of rhythmic, melodic

---

108   Boorman, 'The Musical Text', p. 419.

and harmonic details within this framework could be accommodated without altering the identity or ascription of a work.[109] Keyboard music is particularly open to such observations, given the large number of concordances, the common practice of arranging music from other genres for keyboard, and the likelihood that this was a genre in which repertoire was transmitted at least partly orally among professional musicians, being written down only for the benefit of their pupils. This, of course, has a profound effect upon the problems of producing modern editions, and the inclusive approach to Restoration sources I have described is thus increasingly obvious in this field.[110]

The usefulness of the 'gist' idea in other areas of the repertoire is as yet difficult to assess. There is some evidence of a similar notion in Purcell's transcriptions of his solo songs in the 'Gresham' score-book, Lg Safe 3, another case involving the transcription and arrangement of works for use in new generic and functional contexts.[111] The fact remains, however, that cases that do not involve changes of genre and, in particular, some degree of transmission by memory, rarely seem to produce such extreme textual variation. In works like the odes and welcome songs discussed by Herissone, in which the creation of the earliest sources seems to have been closely tied to the preparation of performance materials, there is little evidence of textual variation in later sources. It may be that the lack of opportunity for repeated performance of these works simply meant that the kind of variation found in the keyboard music simply never came about. Nevertheless, the idea of the 'gist' might profitably be used in this context as a way of probing the likely earlier stages in the compositional process that are not recorded in the sources; after all, we know from passages of incomplete copying that the first things to be written down were very often the outer parts – in other words, the very parts that defined the 'gist' of the music.[112]

---

109 Andrew Woolley, 'English Keyboard Sources and their Contexts, c.1660–1720' (PhD dissertation, University of Leeds, 2008), pp. 89–93. The concept of the 'gist' and the related idea of 'family resemblances' among related melodies and pieces is a common one among scholars of earlier lute music and popular songs; see, for example, John M. Ward, *Music for Elizabethan Lutes: Osborn Commonplace-book Tablatures and Related Sources* (2 vols, Oxford: Oxford University Press, 1992), and his earlier articles also making use of related ideas: 'The British Broadside Ballad and its Music', *Journal of the American Musicological Society* 20 (1967): 28–86; 'The Hunt's Up', *Proceedings of the Royal Musical Association* 106 (1979–80): 1–25; 'The Morris Tune', *Journal of the American Musicological Society* 39 (1986): 294–331; and 'And who but Ladie Greensleeues', in Edward D. Olleson, Susan Wollenberg and John Caldwell (eds), *The Well Enchanting Skill: Music, Poetry and Drama in the Culture of the Renaissance – Essays in Honour of F.W. Sternfeld* (Oxford: Clarendon, 1990), pp. 181–212.

110 See Christopher Hogwood, 'Creating the Corpus: the "Complete Keyboard Music" of Henry Purcell', in Hogwood (ed.), *The Keyboard in Baroque Europe* (Cambridge and New York: Cambridge University Press, 2003), pp. 67–89.

111 See Henry Purcell, *The Gresham Autograph*, Introduction by Margaret Laurie and Robert Thompson (facsimile edition, London: Novello, 1995), pp. viii–ix.

112 An example from the odes is the final chorus of *Swifter Isis, Swifter Flow* in Purcell's

Conversely, it may be that better understanding of the practices surrounding the 'gist' concept in keyboard music can lead to a richer sense of the possibilities for performing some of the music that is preserved in less elaborate states; in other words (illuminating my second question), it could help us investigate the actual realization of the 'notated essentials' in performance. The propriety of added divisions and other extempore elements in the performance of Restoration music has been hotly debated, and it may seem difficult to reconcile the apparent freedom of some examples from the keyboard music with reported injunctions from some contemporary composers that performers avoid excessive divisions.[113] In part, this apparent contradiction may be attributed to the differing agendas of composers and virtuoso performers in late seventeenth-century England, but it might also be useful to consider whether the issue here was primarily one of imposing fidelity to the written text, or rather of asserting the principles of tasteful performance.

Central to the resolution of such questions, and arguably at the heart of all of the issues discussed above, is the problem of whether and to what extent seventeenth-century English musical culture can be said to have had what we would recognize as a 'work concept' at all, and if so, how it was balanced with the textual variation observable throughout the repertoire to different degrees. The idea of a polarization in seventeenth-century music between composer- and performer-related types, suggested by Anthony Newcomb and expanded by John Butt in *The Cambridge History of Seventeenth-Century Music* to encompass a contrast between 'reified abstractions' and 'events', might be a useful starting point.[114] Yet there are problems here: we have seen that in one sense each notated instance of a Restoration piece constitutes an 'event' in its own right; yet even in cases of quite wide textual variation, certain aspects (certain musical elements, an attribution, perhaps some variant of a title) remain that seem to suggest a firm sense of identity. It may be that all Restoration music stands somewhere between these poles or, perhaps more usefully, is capable of being appropriated by either one at a given moment, and thus carries the potential to embody both functions.[115]

Apart from such general issues surrounding the status of Restoration music and its notated guises, it seems likely that much research in the near future will be devoted to the reinterpretation of source-based evidence in the light of increasingly refined understandings of the contexts in which they were produced, and of the various social roles played by Purcell and his contemporaries: the composer as student, and the continued role of the Renaissance principle of *imitatio* in the creation of new

---

autograph, Lbl R.M. 20.h.8; see Herissone, '"Fowle Originalls"': 611–12. More examples abound in Purcell's instrumental and sacred music (see Herissone, 'Purcell's Revisions of his Own Works', pp. 56–8), although the actual relationship of these to Purcell's creative process has yet to be reconsidered in the light of the functions of their sources.

113 See, for example, Locke's preface to *The Little Consort* (London, 1656).

114 See John Butt, 'The Seventeenth-Century Musical "Work"', in Tim Carter and John Butt (eds), *The Cambridge History of Seventeenth-Century Music* (Cambridge: Cambridge University Press, 2005), pp. 28–33.

115 I am grateful to Stephen Rose for this suggestion.

musical works and styles; the impact upon composition of relationships among patrons, publishers, printers and the composers themselves; changing attitudes to authorship, and the roles of various scribal networks in the gestation, transmission and evolution of works, texts of works, and even whole repertoires.[116]

Analytical Approaches to Creativity

Although, as we have seen, Kerman's criteria for materials relevant to 'sketch studies' ignore the importance of earlier versions that are preserved in non-autograph sources, it is hard to ignore the fact that in one sense his model holds true for Purcell's music. 'Palaeographical' approaches have little to offer in the way of insight into the earliest stages of the creative process, since, for some of the reasons described above, 'sketches' for this repertoire on the whole simply do not seem to have survived. In order to probe these aspects of Restoration creativity, then, an alternative approach is needed.

The language of 'creative intention', to return to Nicholas Cook's term as discussed at the beginning of this chapter, has always played a significant role in the analysis of Purcell's music, whether as its principal aim – as in Peter Holman's study of *Three Parts upon a Ground* – or more generally through the vocabulary used to make analytical observations about the music – as in Martin Adams's *Henry Purcell: The Origins and Development of his Musical Style*.[117] Neither of these studies, however, is primarily concerned with the detail of how Purcell actually composed his music. Holman's focus is principally upon the kinds of decisions Purcell had to make even before he began writing, such as scoring and choice of idiom; Adams, meanwhile, is mainly concerned with the critical appraisal of Purcell's achievements from a modern perspective, and the development of the composer's style in the course of his career. Both nevertheless harbour some interesting implications if one

---

116 Three projects on the horizon at the time of writing all promise to deal with these issues and more: *Concepts of Creativity in Seventeenth-Century England*, a collection of essays edited by Rebecca Herissone, arising out of the September 2008 conference of the same name at the University of Manchester; Herissone's monograph *Musical Creativity in Restoration England* (Cambridge: Cambridge University Press, forthcoming); and Stephanie Carter's 'Music Publishing and Compositional Activity in Restoration England, 1650–1700' (PhD dissertation, University of Manchester, 2011).

117 Peter Holman, 'Compositional Choices in Henry Purcell's *Three Parts upon a Ground*', *Early Music* 29 (2001): 250–61; Adams, *Henry Purcell*. See, for example, p. 100 (on Fantazia no. 6): 'Purcell now uses this association to drive a series of entries'; and p. 195 (on the song 'I take no pleasure'): 'Purcell "bends" the harmonic progress for expressive purposes'. In addition, Purcell's agency is also implicit in many passages of Adams's book that do not specifically invoke his name, such as on p. 161 (on the relationship between the canzona of Sonata 7 from the 1697 set and that in the 'Trumpet Overture' from *The Indian Queen*): 'The changes in the subject are significant: they avoid the earlier work's clipped, two-bar phrasing.'

reads between the lines: Holman's discussion of Purcell's use of the four canonic passages in *Three Parts upon a Ground* 'as structural reference points', for example, strongly implies that these canonic sections must have been worked out separately and then incorporated into the overall plan.[118]

More recently, analytical study of Purcell's music has formed part of a wider interest in the idea of developing analytical tools based on techniques that demonstrably informed the activities of contemporary musicians, thereby opening up a new avenue of inquiry into Purcell's creative strategies.[119] Because the success of this kind of analysis depends upon the identification of specific compositional problems in the context of which decisions made by the composer can be examined and evaluated, there are potentially many different approaches that might be taken. In vocal music, for example, one might start with the nature of the text to be set, examining its metrical patterns, imagery and structural organization, and the relationship between these and the musical idioms selected by the composer. Katherine Rohrer's study of the connections between textual metre and dance styles in Purcell's songs offers a glimpse of the potential rewards of this topic, and indeed Purcell's treatment of different dance genres in both his vocal and instrumental music would be a good starting point in its own right for this kind of approach.[120] The remainder of this chapter, however, will focus on one aspect of Purcell's compositional technique that provides a clear window onto his creative strategies: his use of imitative counterpoint and canon. My own research on this topic forms part of an expanding body of literature – centred mainly on earlier composers but also including Laurence Dreyfus's work on J.S. Bach – which is largely devoted to the analysis of contrapuntal music through the discovery of its inventive origins and the mechanisms that determined the treatment of the resulting materials.[121]

---

118 Holman, 'Compositional Choices': 258.

119 The background to this development is rehearsed in Bent, 'The Grammar of Early Music', pp. 15–59.

120 Katherine T. Rohrer, 'Poetic Metre, Musical Metre, and the Dance in Purcell's Songs', in Curtis Price (ed.), *Purcell Studies* (Cambridge: Cambridge University Press, 1995), pp. 207–42. Much might be learned about Purcell's engagement with dance idioms by adopting an approach similar to that taken by Meredith Little and Natalie Jenne in *Dance and the Music of J.S. Bach*, Music Scholarship and Performance (Bloomington, IN: Indiana University Press, 1991); I analyse the third movement of Purcell's Sonata 5 from the 1683 set in the context of its juxtaposition of contrapuntal demands with dance-derived rhythmic considerations in my PhD thesis, 'Purcell and the Poetics of Artifice: Compositional Strategies in the Fantasias and Sonatas' (PhD dissertation, King's College, London, 2006), pp. 219–23.

121 In addition to the examples cited above in n. 17, examples include Laurence Dreyfus, 'Bachian Invention and its Mechanisms', in John Butt (ed.), *The Cambridge Companion to Bach* (Cambridge: Cambridge University Press, 1997), pp. 171–92; Julian Grimshaw, 'Morley's Rule for First-Species Canon', *Early Music* 34 (2006): 661–6; Grimshaw, 'Sixteenth-Century English *Fuga*: Sequential and Peak-Note Subjects', *Musical Times* 148 (2007): 61–78; Grimshaw, '*Fuga* in Early Byrd', *Early Music* 37 (2009): 251–65; John Milsom, 'Analysing Josquin', in Richard Sherr (ed.), *The Josquin Companion* (Oxford:

Traditional accounts of Purcell's most concentrated contrapuntal passges have tended to use them as examples of the composer's ingenuity, often citing them as evidence of a conservatism of style manifested in his fascination for and familiarity with the techniques of 'Ancient' music.[122] This notion is a prickly one, since although he was admittedly unusual among his musical colleagues, Purcell's interest in the extreme forms of artifice he found in the older music he studied aligned him closely with ideas current in Restoration literature, theatre and architecture.[123] Putting this issue aside, however, it remains the case that the frequent admiring references to such passages in Purcell's music are rarely followed through in analytical study. Yet even very simple questions asked of familiar examples can result in interesting revelations. Consider the opening section of Fantazia 8, and the first movement of Sonata 1 from the 1683 set, both examples of Purcell's so-called 'conservative' style, and both founded on astonishingly varied combinations of their respective imitative materials. If we look at those materials themselves, outside the confines of the passages Purcell created from them, it emerges that he systematically exhausted the contrapuntally viable two-voice canonic combinations of his subjects in each case.[124] As a simple observation this is interesting; when viewed from the point of view of creative process it is critical, since it demands consideration of exactly how Purcell was able to achieve such a methodical working. Either, it seems, he was able to perceive and retain large amounts of contrapuntal information in his head, keeping track of its use as he wrote down his music, or he undertook some sort of written pre-compositional 'research' into the contrapuntal possibilities of his material.

Setting aside for a moment the question of exactly what form Purcell's investigation of his materials might have taken, consideration of how Purcell arranged them into an actual piece raises another set of questions. Here we can turn to Christopher Simpson's *Compendium of Practical Musick* (1667) as a possible model, since it gives by far the most detailed practical advice on the composition of imitative and canonic passages of all Restoration treatises. Specifically, Simpson presents an 'Example of the first Platform of a Fuge', in which the imitative parts

Oxford University Press, 2000), pp. 431–84; Milsom, 'Absorbing Lassus', *Early Music* 33 (2005): 305–20; Joshua Rifkin, 'Miracles, Motivicity, and Mannerism: Adrian Willaert's *Videns Dominus flentes sorores Lazari* and Some Aspects of Motet Composition in the 1520s', in Dolores Pesce (ed.), *Hearing the Motet: Essays on the Motet of the Middle Ages and Renaissance* (New York and Oxford: Oxford University Press, 1997), pp. 243–64; and Peter N. Schubert, 'Hidden Forms in Palestrina's *First Book of Four-Voice Motets'*, *Journal of the American Musicological Society* 60 (2007): 483–556.

122 See, for example, Peter Holman, *Henry Purcell*, Oxford Studies of Composers (Oxford: Oxford University Press, 1994), pp. 74–85; see also Adams, *Henry Purcell*, p. ix.

123 For an amplification of this point, see Howard, 'Purcell and the Poetics of Artifice', pp. 224–33.

124 See ibid., pp. 113–14 and 121–6; I make a similar observation about the second section of the sacred partsong 'Since God so Tender a Regard' in my article 'Composition as an Act of Performance: Artifice and Expression in Purcell's Sacred Partsong *Since God so tender a regard'*, *Journal of the Royal Musical Association* 132 (2007): 47–9.

alone are notated.[125] This, he advises, should be the first stage of composing a passage of imitative counterpoint; once the subject entries are fixed, the composer may return in order to 'fill up the empty places with such Concords and Bindings [i.e. suspensions] as you think fittest for carrying on your Composition'.[126] However, while this method works well for simple passages in which the subject entries are confined to one or two parts, it soon loses its explanatory power for music that contains complexes of three, four or even five subject entries. To give an extreme example, the many three-part canons in the first movement of Sonata 6 from the 1683 set – including the famous opening passage in which augmentation and double augmentation are used simultaneously – can hardly have been composed in this way: rather, the first and most artificial of the canons in this movement was surely fundamental to the very conception of the piece, a guiding principal of Purcell's melodic invention.[127]

Similarly, the passage in bb. 16–18 of Fantazia 8, in which all four parts present the subject in one large complex of entries overlapping on successive minims, seems highly likely to represent the key creative impulse behind the whole opening section of this piece.[128] Once this is recognized, moreover, it becomes possible to account – in a surprisingly simple yet highly persuasive manner – for the range of contrapuntal invention in this section of the fantazia, and thus the form of 'research' undertaken by Purcell. In fact, not only is this passage constructed according to the principals of what John Milsom calls 'stretto *fuga*' – according to which such four-part canons can always be constructed from melodic material composed of the correct 'interval stock' – but also nearly all of the imitative combinations in this whole section are related either to this passage, or to the opening combination of the point in prime and inverted forms, by simple melodic or intervallic inversions and rotations of part order.[129] The great feats of memory or laborious notation of large numbers of combinations suggested above can therefore largely be replaced with simple 'tricks of the trade' that Purcell could easily have learnt from his studies of older music, or even from older contemporaries. Indeed, alongside the improvisatory techniques already discussed, Locke's Gloria in Ob Mus.Sch.c.138 actually contains a short

---

125 Christopher Simpson, *A Compendium of Practical Musick in Five Parts … The Third Editio[n]* (London, 1678; originally published 1667), p. 111.

126 Ibid.

127 In 'Purcell and the Poetics of Artifice', pp. 245–9, I demonstrate that a different technique recommended by Simpson, this time for the composition of canons in all parts simultaneously (*A Compendium of Practical Musick*, pp. 120–21 and 124–5), could easily have been adapted to compose this passage; in fact, this most cited of instances of Purcell's contrapuntal mastery was probably comparatively simple to compose.

128 Howard, 'Purcell and the Poetics of Artifice', p. 124.

129 Milsom gives a concise summary of the principles of 'stretto *fuga*' in 'Absorbing Lassus': 313. For a more detailed analysis of this section of Fantazia 8, see Howard, 'Purcell and the Poetics of Artifice', pp. 121–32 (a full discussion of the observation made in the present chapter, which is updated from the original treatment in my thesis, will be included in my forthcoming book on Purcell's 'artificial' techniques.

passage of imitation for four voices on a subject constructed on the same principles of 'stretto *fuga*' found in Purcell's Fantazia 8.

Observations like these are difficult to internalize in the absence of greater detail, but something of the explanatory potential of the ideas advanced here can be gained from a closer assessment of the end of the 'alleluia' in bb. 134–55 of *My Beloved Spake*. Any appeal to strict contrapuntal procedures in the analysis of this work may appear surprising, given that it dates from well before Purcell's documented interest in contrapuntal techniques at the end of the 1670s, and indeed there is no question of this passage even approaching the virtuosity of the fantazias and sonatas. Nevertheless, Purcell's methodology in this, one of the few sustained passages of imitation in the work, provides an opportunity to see some of these ideas in action and demonstrates that they formed part of Purcell's musical education even at a very early age.

In a procedure that was typical of the verse anthem in the 1670s, this section begins with a series of phrases based on the same material, sung by verse parts alone (see Example 3.3).[130] Here, Purcell's compositional approach is simple: he composes four verse entries, each based on the same dotted motif; he is careful to vary the harmonic content by contriving his phrases to end in different keys,[131] and he maintains momentum by overlapping each new entry with the preceding cadence (a device that is facilitated by the design of the motif, whose falling third fits easily when begun on the fifth degree).

The first imitative writing appears in bb. 146–8, and is accomplished by the simplest means: the alto part echoes the second bass an octave higher and a crotchet later, and there is no reason to suppose that Purcell did not fit these entries in around an already-composed bass part in a manner similar to the technique he would later call 'imitation, or reports' in 'The Art of Descant'.[132] Note, however, that this form of the dotted 'alleluia' motif, as used by Purcell in the first-bass and tenor entries in the preceding bars, was already predisposed to such treatment, given that it comprises two successive intervals of a falling third and thereby meets the requirements for 'stretto *fuga*'; thus Purcell may have designed the motif for its ease of contrapuntal combination from the outset. A final lone entry of the subject in these bars, in the first bass at b. 149³, is again designed to sustain momentum by overlapping with the cadence.

---

130 On this technique see, for example, Shay, 'Purcell's Revisions to the Funeral Sentences Revisited': 461.

131 See Simpson's advice for the composition of music 'in strains' (i.e. dance forms with repeated sections), *A Compendium of Practical Musick*, p. 116. Although this passage of *My Beloved Spake* is not strictly 'in strains', its idiom is clearly dance-derived and the need to avoid 'Reiterat[ing] the Aire too much', as Simpson puts it, is equally valid in this context.

132 Henry Purcell, 'The Art of Descant', in John Playford, *An Introduction to the Skill of Musick. In Three Books ... The Twelfth Edition. Corrected and Amended by Mr. Henry Purcell* (London, 1694), p. 108. In the treatise Purcell defines this technique as the addition of imitative lower parts to an already-composed treble, but the method is equally applicable to the present case in which the bass, as the leading solo part, clearly has compositional priority.

Example 3.3   *My Beloved Spake*, bb. 135–55.

Much more interesting is what happens in bb. 150³–53, a span of just over three bars in which the 'alleluia' subject is heard no fewer than nine times, five of which are complete entries and four are either truncated or have intervallic alterations. If we isolate the imitative content of bb. 146–55 (as in Example 3.4), it soon becomes apparent that even this density of entries is achieved very simply using the results of the initial imitative work in bb. 146–8. Example 3.4(a) shows both of the two-voice interlocks that resulted from the imitation of the bass in bb. 146–8: interlocks A, at the octave one unit later (between second bass and alto), and B, at the lower seventh two units later (between alto and the next second-bass entry). As shown in Example 3.4(b), every interlock in bb. 150–53 is formed either from one of these two complexes or from their inversions at the octave, tenth or twelfth (also shown in Example 3.4(a) for ease of reference), including one passage that uses the principles of four-part 'stretto *fuga*' to dictate the pitches of four successive entries (shown boxed in Example 3.4(b)). This whole passage, then, could easily have been composed with great fluency directly into the original manuscript in which Purcell first notated the piece: just like the Locke Gloria and the more ambitious examples in Fantazia 8 and Sonata 6 of the 1683 set, it uses simple imitative commonplaces and transformations of material to create complex-sounding textures with the minimum of effort.

As well as explaining the density of complete subject entries, this analysis of the relationship between the various interlocks also provides a framework within which to examine Purcell's decisions about when to depart from the exact melodic content of the 'alleluia' motif (instances of which are shown in Example 3.4(b) by the replacement of altered pitches with crossed noteheads to show the notional exact form of a given entry). An initial example is the second-bass entry beginning at b. 147³, which we might speculate was altered in order to accommodate the entry on g' in the tenor a crotchet later: as Example 3.4(a) shows, the resulting interlock A10 is not viable due to consecutive octaves. In this instance it should be noted that the tenor entry in fact only doubles the alto a third lower, and in any case the intervallic content of the motif in the previous three solo entries is not sufficiently consistent to rule out the possibility that Purcell always intended to alter it in b. 147 in order to strengthen the bass's harmonic motion; thus the tenor entry may well be opportunist rather than playing an active role in the imitation.

Harmonic considerations may also have led Purcell to alter the second-bass entry in b. 152, although in this case the imitative role of the part seems more significant, given that complex A between the two bass parts here is a sequential repetition down a step (and metrically displaced) from the statement in the basses beginning in bar 150³, and also forms part of the 'stretto *fuga*'-derived complex identified earlier.[133] In other words, Purcell here subordinates strict imitative treatment to

---

133 In case the reader wonders why such 'altered' subject entries are not accompanied by amendments in the autograph score of *My Beloved Spake*, it may be helpful to recall that the Lbl Add. 30932 score, while made by Purcell, is clearly itself a copy, as demonstrated above. Whether the original autograph, Source A, contained such amendments would depend on the extent to which Purcell was able to hold such textures in his head before notating them (thus removing the need for written changes), and whether he used

Example 3.4   Imitative materials in *My Beloved Spake*, bb. 146–55: (a) two-part interlocks; (b) 'skeleton' score showing disposition of these materials.

considerations of harmonic direction. Another example with similar implications is the alteration of the first-bass entry beginning in b. 152, which would not be necessary were it not for the alto part doubling the tenor entry a crotchet later at the upper third (thereby creating another instance of the unusable interlock A10). Although this alto entry seems less important in imitative terms, however, it forms a crucial part of a rising sequence beginning in the second bass with entries on a, b♭ and c from b. 146³ onwards. After a short gap, this sequence is resumed with

---

any sketch-like materials as he did for *Let mine Eyes Run Down with Tears*; as already discussed, this is a matter for speculation.

an altered entry on e' in the tenor at bar 150³, leading to entries on f' and g' in the alto from bar 151³. By juxtaposing the two sequences identified here, the rising one in the alto and tenor and the falling one in the basses (which continues as far as the truncated entry on A in the first bass in b. 153), Purcell is able to build a strong sense of momentum towards the cadence in b. 155; no wonder, then, that he allowed this process to override the potential for a more exact imitative entry in the first-bass part.

Such a detailed account of a very short and in some ways unrepresentative passage may seem an insignificant advance in our understanding of the creative processes that informed the composition of *My Beloved Spake*. There are, nevertheless, other sections of the work that are open to similar considerations: the canon between tenor and violin at the start of 'The fig tree putteth forth', for example, is an interesting early instance of Purcell's interest in this technique; the construction of the subjects used in some of the other imitative passages, meanwhile, can be used to explain why he did not introduce more thorough imitative writing of the kind found in bb. 146–55 elsewhere; this may indicate inexperience, or simply different compositional priorities.[134] Furthermore, even short excerpts from a work as early as *My Beloved Spake* can help illuminate some of the changes to Purcell's technique that occurred over a very short period. By the time he wrote the fantazias around 1680, he had already developed the techniques of melodic invention that made possible the imitation in bb. 146–55 to such an extent that he was rarely forced to sacrifice strict imitation, and hence the degree of artifice on display, for the sake of harmonic concerns.

There remains much work to be done in order to understand Purcell's contrapuntal techniques, not to mention the other possible ways of studying his creative decisions suggested at the start of this section. One aspect of Purcell's approach to contrapuntal invention that has not been discussed here, for example, is the extent to which he relied on a relatively circumscribed range of melodic subjects in his imitative writing, testing these to the limits of their potential for contrapuntal elaboration.[135] This is a logical extension of the observations made above about the suitability of particular kinds of material for this kind of treatment, and it might ultimately provide new ways of understanding some of Purcell's most accomplished music of the 1690s in the context not only of techniques but also of specific materials he first developed in the instrumental music of the late 1670s and early 1680s. The problems of incorporating such materials into the very different stylistic context of music like *Hail, bright Cecilia* or the Te Deum and Jubilate in D themselves present further opportunities for the future interrogation of Purcell's creative practices.[136]

---

134 See, in particular, the later 'alleluia' at bb. 254–76, where the intervallic content of the subject prevents the formulation of large numbers of alternative interlocks.

135 I explore this topic in 'Purcell and the Poetics of Artifice', pp. 132–48.

136 My book on Purcell's 'artificial' creative strategies, incorporating material from my thesis, will also extend the topic to consider this later vocal music.

Purcell's ability to make use of these 'artificial' techniques is also in urgent need of contextualization within the wider corpus of Restoration music. We know that few other composers seem to have cultivated these approaches to such a degree, but there are nevertheless indications that Locke in particular was familiar with many of them. Blow is also a key figure in this regard: certain passages in his music (the canonic passages of the Service in G, for example, and perhaps even the instrumental parts of some symphony songs) suggest considerable contrapuntal skill, yet he clearly chose to exercise it much less than did Purcell. Apart from simply contrasting Purcell's style with those of his contemporaries, such questions are important since they provide possible contexts in which to explore the possibility of finding source evidence for the kinds of creative strategies found in Purcell's fantazias and similar works: some of Daniel Henstridge's attempts at canonic writing preserved in Lbl Add. 30933, for example, clearly show him working in the way suggested by Christopher Simpson.[137] Such an approach might also shed light on the mechanisms by which these kinds of skills were passed between different generations of musicians: did Purcell learn everything he knew about counterpoint from his copying of Byrd's and Orlando Gibbons's music, or might it be that Locke, and perhaps Christopher Gibbons, provided a direct link with the pre-Commonwealth generation by which these skills were maintained?

Conclusions

The example of *My Beloved Spake* demonstrates the possible rewards of approaches to studying Restoration creativity that no longer rely on the principles of a discipline – 'sketch studies' as conventionally defined – that is principally concerned with much later repertoires. Given a greater contextual understanding of the sources and their intended functions, we can learn more about why the music is notated as it is; when we recognize the different reasons why composers and copyists made changes to the music they notated, we can better evaluate the relationships among the resulting texts and possibilities for their realization in performance; and by deepening our knowledge of the musical techniques that they used, we can begin to comprehend the kinds of issues composers were faced with as they created new works, and hence offer critical readings of their resulting decisions in many cases, even if these are not directly recorded in the surviving sources.

It remains the case, however, that some of the very factors that set Restoration music apart from later repertoires also present fundamental obstacles to the development of the kind of detailed knowledge of creative practices that have been possible in studies of late eighteenth- and nineteenth-century music. The scarcity of 'sketches' is itself a corollary of the likely importance of memory and other non-notated musical practices and skills; for all that we can capture something of these through written accounts, and even recover some of them by attempting to master

---

137 Simpson, *A Compendium of Practical Musick*, pp. 120–21 and 124–5.

them ourselves, the actual processes that gave rise to particular passages and pieces of music are likely to be irretrievable.

Despite such problems, it may be possible to illuminate further the creative activities of composers like Purcell in a philosophical sense, a topic not hitherto explored in this essay, but nevertheless likely to provide another important starting point for future study. We know, for example, that Dryden maintained a fairly consistent tripartite model of creativity throughout his career, described most vividly in the preface to *Annus Mirabilis* as consisting of 'invention', 'fancy' or 'variation', and 'elocution'.[138] That these derive ultimately from the five-part 'divisions' of classical rhetoric (the remaining two usually expressing memory and delivery in some form) comes as no surprise; indeed, as a possible model for musical creation this is promising given the importance that German theorists like Joachim Burmeister and Christoph Bernhard attached to similar conceptualizations of the act of musical composition.[139] There are problems with the application of these ideas to Purcell and his contemporaries, not least concerning their educational background: no Restoration musicians received the university education from which Dryden profited, and neither would they have been systematically exposed to humanist literature through public schooling of the kind enjoyed by aspiring musicians in Lutheran parts of Germany.[140] Furthermore, no Restoration musicians seem to have devoted space in published treatises to discussions of this nature, concerned as they tended to be with the more practical aspects of musical performance and composition.

On the other hand, it is clear that such ideas can help us to understand both manuscript evidence and analytical observations better. The consideration of how Purcell's demonstrable activities and approaches relate to this kind of model of creativity is essential to their logical interpretation: it matters a great deal, for example, whether the addition of the inner parts to a four-part homophonic texture or the creation of an intricate contrapuntal texture are considered to belong to the realm of 'invention' or of 'elocution', since this fundamentally alters our understanding of how Purcell approached these tasks and how they related to the other creative strategies he pursued.

There are other approaches to understanding creativity that have been adopted in modern scholarship on Restoration literature that also have potential to inform future studies of Purcell and his musical colleagues. This is a large topic, which will require detailed investigation by scholars with a much broader knowledge of the

---

138 See Robert D. Hume, 'Dryden on Creation: "Imagination" in the Later Criticism', *The Review of English Studies* 21 (1970): 309–11.

139 See Dreyfus, *Bach and the Patterns of Invention*, pp. 3–4, and, for a more detailed discussion of the importance of rhetoric in eighteenth-century descriptions of compositional process, Ian Bent, 'The "Compositional Process" in Music Theory 1713–1850', *Music Analysis* 3 (1984): 29–55.

140 See Bettina Varwig, '"Mutato Semper Habitu": Heinrich Schütz and the Culture of Rhetoric', *Music & Letters* 90 (2009): 215–39; and Varwig, 'One More Time: J.S. Bach and Seventeenth-Century Traditions of Rhetoric', *Eighteenth-Century Music* 5 (2008): 183–5.

literature than my own, but I can at least report that preliminary forays reveal the potential riches of this approach. In terms of the general issues of textual instability and the importance of social contextualization of individual sources and texts, many of the concepts raised by the more recent approaches to the 'palaeographical' study of Purcell's creativity seem to have been central to the debate surrounding the similar reform of textual criticism in the early 1990s.[141] More specifically, the interest of musicology in the crossings-out, emendations and marginalia found in autograph sources has a clear parallel in work on late seventeenth- and early eighteenth-century literature. In his essay on Pope's *Essay on Man*, prefaced to a series of source facsimiles and parallel transcriptions published among similar materials for Pope's wider output, Maynard Mack uses Dryden's distinction between 'wit writing' and 'wit written' to characterize what Mack calls the full 'terrain of the imagination', from the search for ideas stored in the memory through to the eventual creation of a refined and polished work.[142] Mack is able to observe the full gamut of creative modes between these opposite poles in Pope's manuscripts for the *Essay on Man*. Even if this is rarely possible with musical works, the polarization of creative activity in this way is strongly reminiscent of the similar division of musical creativity explored earlier, between performer-centred, 'event-like' domains and more highly 'composed' works, and also – recalling Mace's description of how he composed his lesson 'My Mistress' – between improvisatory and notational stages of the creative process.

The principal difference, perhaps, is Dryden's emphasis upon 'the finding of the thought' as against the apparent free fancy of musical improvisation. Yet the more one probes this difference, the less problematic it in fact becomes, for, as Roger North well understood, the 'excellent art of voluntary' was as much a skill of recall and successful combination of existing fragments as it was one of invention and fantasy. His description of the skills of the master 'voluntiere' might be equally applicable to the early stages of all creative processes in Restoration music:

> It is not to be expected that a master invents all he plays in that manner. No, he doth but play over those passages that are in his memory and habituall to him. But the choice, application, and connexion are his, and so is the measure, either grave, buisy, or precipitate; as also the severall keys to use as he pleaseth. And among the rest, in the spirit of zeal when he is warme and

---

141 See, for example, G. Thomas Tanselle, 'Textual Instability and Editorial Idealism', *Studies in Bibliography* 49 (1996): 1–61.

142 Maynard Mack (ed. and trans.), *The Last and Greatest Art: Some Unpublished Poetical Manuscripts of Alexander Pope* (Newark: University of Delaware Press; London and Toronto: Associated University Presses, 1984), pp. 190–202. Dryden's descriptions of 'wit writing' ('which, like a nimble Spaniel … ranges through the field of Memory till it springs the Quarry it hunted after') and 'wit written' ('that which is well defin'd, the happy result of thought, or product of that imagination') are also from the preface to *Annus Mirabilis*; see Hume, 'Dryden on Creation': 296–7.

engaged, he will fulfil of his owne present invention a musick which, joined with the rest, shall be new and wonderfull.[143]

How we understand the results of this process, and their subsequent refinement in the many stages of revision and reinvention at the hands of composers like Purcell, will always be a topic of great interest to scholars of Restoration music. With the methods suggested by recent approaches both to the interpretation of sources and the analysis of the music, there is every reason to suppose that our knowledge of Purcell's musical creativity will continue to deepen.

---

143 Roger North, 'Notes Concerning the Excellent Art of Voluntary', Lbl Add. 32536, fols 83v–88; in John Wilson (ed.), *Roger North on Music: Being a Selection from his Essays Written during the Years c.1695–1728* (London: Novello, 1959), p. 141.

Performance Practices

Stephen Rose

When systematic research into performance practice began in the 1950s and 1960s, many scholars neglected the styles suitable for seventeenth-century composers such as Henry Purcell. Frederick Neumann's *Ornamentation in Baroque and Post-Baroque Music* (1978) aimed to elucidate the ornaments appropriate for J.S. Bach's music, viewing the previous century's embellishment practices largely as a prelude to those of Bach.[1] Robert Donington's *Performer's Guide to Baroque Music* (1973) implied that there was a single style valid throughout the period 1600–1750, using such terms as 'the Baroque Attitude' and 'Baroque Style'.[2] Yet it is anachronistic to impose an all-purpose 'Baroque Style' on Purcell's music, not least because his output was created before the major changes in instruments and performing techniques that occurred around 1700. All the same, until the 1990s many performers tackled Purcell's music in ways more appropriate for Handel, for instance by adding oboes and a double bass to the orchestra in *Dido and Aeneas*.[3]

Only in the 1990s did a strong awareness emerge of the performance practices characteristic of Restoration music. In part this change was fostered by research published around 1995, the tercentenary of Purcell's death. Peter Holman's study of the violin band at the English court illuminated the performing environment and repertory of the royal orchestra during the seventeenth century;[4] the anthology *Performing the Music of Henry Purcell* was the first set of essays to focus on aspects of vocal and instrumental performance specific to the composer;[5] and Andrew

---

For advice and assistance during the writing of this chapter, I am grateful to Rebecca Herissone, Christopher Hogwood, Peter Holman, Alan Howard, Margaret Laurie, Graham Sadler and Andrew Woolley.

1   Frederick Neumann, *Ornamentation in Baroque and Post-Baroque Music: with Special Emphasis on J.S. Bach* (Princeton: Princeton University Press, 1978).

2   Robert Donington, *A Performer's Guide to Baroque Music* (London: Faber, 1973), pp. 15 and 18.

3   As, for instance, on Henry Purcell, *Dido and Aeneas*, English Concert, dir. Trevor Pinnock (Archiv 289 427 6242 8, *rec.* 1988).

4   Peter Holman, *Four and Twenty Fiddlers: The Violin at the English Court 1540–1690*, Oxford Monographs on Music (Oxford: Clarendon, 1993).

5   Michael Burden (ed.), *Performing the Music of Henry Purcell* (Oxford: Clarendon, 1996).

Parrott assembled an invaluable summary of the main choices facing historically informed performers of Purcell.[6] Also significant were Parrott's recordings with the Taverner Consort and Players, in which he offered thoughtful solutions to the problems of pitch and voice types posed by Purcell's odes and stage works. Other recordings of the 1990s, such as Robert King's surveys of the complete odes and church music, paved the way for a more nuanced understanding of Purcell's vocal output, although (as will be discussed below) some of King's decisions relied on dubious scholarship.

Taking its starting point from these seminal studies and recordings, this chapter draws on more recent research – as well as investigating areas hitherto little studied, such as vocal ornamentation – to emphasize the variety of performance styles in Purcell's London. Singers and instrumentalists of the period followed their individual tastes: in the case of string playing, for instance, the court violinist John Lenton wrote: 'It would be a difficult undertaking to prescribe a general rule for Bowing, the humours of Masters being very Various, and what is approved by one would be condemned by another.'[7] Furthermore, different performance styles were used for different genres. As will be discussed below, vocal music and instrumental music had their own types of ornamentation. Church music used a different pitch standard from secular music. Polyphonic writing as found in viol fantazias and many anthems required a style of keyboard accompaniment whereby the player doubled the parts of the texture, as opposed to the chordal continuo realization used for more modern genres such as theatre songs.

Diversity was also caused by the changes underway in musical life in the second half of the seventeenth century, leading to a mix of old and new practices in Purcell's milieu. The old system of proportional notation (in which tempo was implied by time signatures) was disappearing, replaced by the use of English or Italian tempo words such as *Slow* or *Adagio*. New instruments were increasingly being used, such as the oboe and the Baroque recorder recently imported from France. Another reason for the heterogeneity of performance styles was the influx of continental performers into London, creating a melting pot of different national traditions. The vocal styles used by French and Italian émigrés co-existed with indigenous approaches to singing. In violin playing, Italians such as Nicola Matteis used techniques such as the *messa di voce*, whereas a French style of playing (following Lully's rule of the downbow) was described by Lenton in his *Gentleman's Diversion* (1693).[8] Visiting French performers brought their country's traditions of

---

6   Andrew Parrott, 'Performing Purcell', in Michael Burden (ed.), *The Purcell Companion* (London: Faber, 1995; Portland, OR: Amadeus Press, 1995), pp. 387–444.

7   John Lenton, *The Gentleman's Diversion, or the Violin Explained* (London, 1693), p. 7.

8   On Matteis, see John Wilson (ed.), *Roger North on Music: Being a Selection from his Essays Written during the Years c.1695–1728* (London: Novello, 1959), pp. 164 and 355; on Lenton, see Peter Walls, 'The Baroque Era: Strings', in Howard Mayer Brown and Stanley Sadie (eds), *Performance Practice: Music after 1600*, The New Grove Handbooks in Music (Basingstoke: Macmillan, 1989), p. 51.

rhythmic alteration to England, but it is unclear to what extent English musicians adopted the techniques of *notes inégales* and overdotting.

Further diversity resulted from performers adapting pieces for different performing contexts, ensembles and tastes. Restoration symphony anthems were originally performed in the Chapel Royal with string accompaniment, but many were later arranged with organ-only accompaniment for use in cathedrals outside London or at the Chapel Royal when the string players were not available.[9] Purcell's opera *Dido and Aeneas* was performed in *c*.1687–88 at Josias Priest's girls' school in Chelsea with a cast of 'young gentlewomen',[10] but it was modified for public performance at Lincoln's Inn Fields in 1700, with a changed order of movements and a mixed cast that probably included a bass in the role of the Sorceress.[11] If *Dido* had been performed at court earlier in the 1680s, as some scholars have suggested, the performing conditions there would have been different again.[12] To take a third example, in 1692 the ode *Hail, bright Cecilia* received a lavish premiere at Stationers' Hall, London, with a large choir and orchestra, and 12 of the finest soloists who could be mustered from the Chapel Royal and the theatre. Subsequently it was sometimes performed in pared-down versions, possibly with one performer per part, as for instance at the music club in Canterbury from 1698 onwards.[13]

Thus Purcell wrote his music within a culture of adaptation, in which he would not necessarily have had a fixed conception of how a piece should sound. Consequently this chapter does not attempt to give hard-and-fast rules as to how specific compositions should be performed. Rather, it outlines the range of options available to performers during Purcell's lifetime and in the first few decades after his death. The details of performance practices in Purcell's immediate environments – the court and the London theatres – are of particular interest. But the performance styles used for his music in the early eighteenth century are also informative, in particular showing the continuities and changes from late seventeenth-century conventions.

---

9   For examples see Henry Purcell, *Sacred Music, Part II: Nine Anthems with Strings*, ed. Lionel Pike, The Works of Henry Purcell, vol. 14 (new edn, London: Novello, 2003).

10   On the date of the Chelsea performance, see Bryan White, 'Letter from Aleppo: Dating the Chelsea School Performance of *Dido and Aeneas*', *Early Music* 37 (2009): 417–28.

11   Curtis Price and Irene Cholij, 'Dido's Bass Sorceress', *Musical Times* 127 (1986): 615–18. For an exploration of the implications of this recasting of gender, see Amanda Eubanks Winkler's chapter in this volume, pp. 279–80.

12   On a possible court performance, see Bruce Wood and Andrew Pinnock, '"Unscarr'd by Turning Times"? The Dating of Purcell's *Dido and Aeneas*', *Early Music* 20 (1992): 372–90.

13   Purcell's autograph score of *Hail, bright Cecilia* (Ob Mus.c.26) gives the names of the vocal soloists for two separate performances, and the large size of the chorus and orchestra is implied by the instructions during the first chorus to reduce to two or four performers per part. The performing materials preserved as Ob Tenbury 1309 consist of a single copy of each part, suggesting a one-per-part performance. Copied by the Canterbury organist Daniel Henstridge, these parts were probably used at the town's music club. See the critical notes to Henry Purcell, *Ode for St Cecilia's Day 1692*, ed. Christopher Hogwood (London: Eulenburg, 2009).

A major challenge of researching performance practices from eras before the advent of sound recording is that many aspects of playing and singing styles were never written down, so cannot be easily reconstructed. Indeed, several repertories in Restoration England were extemporized, and can nowadays be documented only with great difficulty. Organ music was typically improvised – Roger North vividly described the extempore 'art of voluntary'[14] – and this explains why only a handful of Purcell's notated organ pieces survive. Singers often accompanied themselves – John Evelyn described how the Italian castrato Siface 'touch'd the Harpsichord to his Voice rarely well'[15] – and such self-accompaniment lent itself to improvised or memorized performances. Pepys reported how Giovanni Battista Draghi, when performing a preview of part of 'a play in Italian for the Opera', 'did sing the whole from the words without any Musique pricked, and played all along upon a Harpsicon most admirably'.[16] One wonders if Draghi ever wrote this piece down. Extemporized elements were also present in works for larger ensembles, such as *Dido and Aeneas*: the libretto of the Chelsea performance specifies two guitar dances for which no music survives, and these are likely to have been improvised, probably over well-known bass patterns such as the chaconne and the passacaglia. Present-day performers sometimes omit the dances and sometimes include their own improvisations.[17]

Extant notated music remains the major source for the study of Purcellian performance practice, but it has its limitations. Seventeenth-century notation usually does not specify elements of performance such as articulation, dynamics and ornaments, and can be imprecise regarding other features, such as rhythm. Players and singers in Purcell's time read the notation in the light of conventions whereby much performance information was implied. Modern researchers can recover some of these conventions from treatises, as for instance in Ellen T. Boal's

---

14   Wilson (ed.), *Roger North on Music*, p. 143.

15   *The Diary of John Evelyn: Now First Printed in Full from the Manuscripts Belonging to Mr John Evelyn*, ed. E.S. De Beer (6 vols, Oxford: Clarendon, 1955), vol. 4, p. 547 (19 April 1687).

16   *The Diary of Samuel Pepys: a New and Compleat Transcription*, eds Robert Latham and William Matthews (11 vols, London: Bell, 1970–83), vol. 8, p. 55 (12 February 1667).

17   *An Opera Perform'd at Mr. Josias Priest's Boarding-School at Chelsey. By Young Gentlewomen* (n.p., n.d.), undated libretto (Royal College of Music, shelfmark D.144) reproduced in facsimile in Henry Purcell, *Dido and Aeneas*, ed. Margaret Laurie, The Works of Henry Purcell, vol. 3 (new edn, Sevenoaks: Novello, 1974), pp. xiii–xx. Laurie's performing edition of the opera (London: Novello, 1961) includes suggested bass-patterns for the two guitar improvisations (see p. 103). For two contrasting examples of guitar improvisations, compare the vigorous strumming on Henry Purcell, *Dido and Aeneas*, Le Concert d'Astrée and European Voices, dir. Emmanuelle Haïm (Virgin Classics 5-45605-2, *rec.* 2003), with the improvisations on themes taken from the seventeenth-century guitarists Francesco Corbetta and Robert de Visée on Henry Purcell, *Dido and Aeneas*, Orchestra of the Age of Enlightenment, dir. Elizabeth Kenny and Steven Devine (Chandos CHAN 0757, *rec.* 2008).

investigation of how tempo could be indicated by time signatures.[18] Other scholars have inferred performing styles from textual discrepancies between different copies of the same piece. The section below on rhythmic alteration shows how Robert Donington deduced Purcell's use of *notes inégales* by collating passages that are notated in equal rhythms in some sources and as dotted figures in other sources. Variants between manuscripts are also a valuable and hitherto untapped source of information about vocal embellishment, as I show in the section below on ornamentation. In all cases, such notational variants prompt reflections on the relationship between copyist, notation and performer.

But if an investigation into performance practice is to be based on a study of notation, a particular problem with Purcell is that few sources directly connected with performance survive for his odes, symphony anthems or theatre music. Extant performing materials can be highly informative about playing and singing styles. Peter Holman has reached important conclusions about continuo practices and ensemble sizes from the original sets of parts for odes and Act Songs performed at Oxford University in the late seventeenth century.[19] Or, to take an example from Germany, scholars have deduced much information about continuo scoring, melodic articulation and chorus size from the performing parts of Bach's cantatas.[20] Had the original performing materials of Purcell's court odes and symphony anthems survived, they might have supplied answers to some of the questions raised in this chapter about pitch, transposition and continuo instrumentation. Yet almost all these manuscripts are lost, presumably destroyed in the Whitehall fire of 1698.[21]

The source situation is even worse for Purcell's theatre music. For many productions neither the performance material nor an authoritative manuscript score survives. Nor is there any archival information, such as financial records, which would inform us about the size of the orchestra or the continuo instrumentation originally used in Purcell's stage works. Yet many manuscripts and printed editions survive in which Purcell's theatre dances and songs were adapted for performance in domestic or other non-theatrical environments. Sometimes these arrangements include ornaments or rhythmic alterations that suggest how Purcell's texts were

---

18   Ellen T. Boal, 'Purcell's Clock Tempos and Fantasias', *Journal of the Viola da Gamba Society of America* 20 (1983): 24–39.

19   Peter Holman, 'Original Sets of Parts for Restoration Concerted Music at Oxford', in Michael Burden (ed.), *Performing the Music of Henry Purcell* (Oxford: Clarendon, 1996), pp. 9–19.

20   See, for instance, Laurence Dreyfus, *Bach's Continuo Group: Players and Practices in His Vocal Works*, Studies in the History of Music, vol. 3 (Cambridge, MA and London: Harvard University Press, 1987); John Butt, *Bach Interpretation: Articulation Marks in Primary Sources of J.S. Bach*, Cambridge Musical Texts and Monographs (Cambridge: Cambridge University Press, 1990); Andrew Parrott, *The Essential Bach Choir* (Woodbridge: Boydell and Brewer, 2000).

21   This suggestion was made by Peter Holman in *Henry Purcell*, Oxford Studies of Composers (Oxford: Oxford University Press, 1994), p. 150. The exception is the group of partial-autograph instrumental parts for the symphony-anthem version of *My Song shall be Alway* in Och Mus. 1188–9, discussed below.

treated in performance. Equally, such arrangements can show how theatre music was modified for different venues or for the idioms of different instruments: a recorder player and a singer, for example, would use different ornamentation when performing the same melody.[22]

This chapter focuses on six areas of performance practice that have been the focus of recent research or that warrant further investigation: tempo and rhythm; pitch standards; vocal techniques and voice types; ornamentation; rhythmic alteration; and the scoring and realization of continuo parts. Other aspects of Purcellian performance, such as bowing techniques or keyboard temperaments, have not attracted fresh research since the 1990s, and here Andrew Parrott's chapter still serves as the best introduction.[23] Compared to the studies that were published in the 1990s, this chapter stresses the diversity of practices in Purcell's London. I also offer new insights into singers' techniques and ornamentation in the period, drawing on sources hitherto unstudied such as the treatise *The Art of Singing* (1677) by the Italian émigré Pietro Reggio (1632–85),[24] who was active in Oxford and London from the mid-1660s until his death. Not all of the options used by instrumentalists and singers in Purcell's time will be to the taste of modern-day performers or listeners, but the multiplicity of seventeenth-century practices is a measure of how Purcell's music was being adapted and creatively reworked in his own time.

Metre and Tempo

A performer's choice of tempo can be crucial to the character of a piece: the selection of an appropriate tempo goes hand-in-hand with identifying the harmonic rhythm, and by extension the relationship between melodic ornament and harmonic structure. Purcell's output straddles a period of change in the notation of metre. The mensural system of fifteenth- and sixteenth-century music (in which mensuration signs indicated how a uniform tactus should be divided) was gradually being replaced by time signatures (where the upper figure indicates the number of beats in a bar, and the lower figure shows the note value of the beat); the signatures preserved in Purcell's sources correspondingly demonstrate an eclectic mix of new and old types of sign, as well as signatures associated with England, France and Italy. Since the 1980s scholars such as Bruce Wood and Margaret Laurie have recognized that some of the signatures used by Purcell were derived from old mensuration signs

---

22   See, for instance, the five theatre tunes arranged and ornamented for solo recorder in *The Compleat Flute-Master, or the Whole Art of Playing on ye Rechorder* (London, 1695); two examples are transcribed in David Lasocki, 'The *Compleat Flute-Master* Reincarnated', *American Recorder Magazine* 11 (1970): 83–5.

23   Parrott, 'Performing Purcell', pp. 393–7 and 406–7.

24   Pietro Reggio, *The Art of Singing or a Treatise, Wherein is Shown How to Sing Well any Song Whatsoever* (Oxford, 1677).

and hence often imply both tempo and proportional relationships, particularly in vocal works. It is therefore regrettable that the Purcell Society edition of the Works of Henry Purcell continues to modernize time signatures as a matter of policy, although recent volumes do indicate the original signs between the staves. Less research has been done on tempos appropriate to Purcell's instrumental works, least of all his dance movements. Nor has there been any systematic published study of Purcell's use of time signatures in all his autograph manuscripts.

The starting point for all studies of the tempos suitable for Purcell's music is the chapter entitled 'On the *Moods* or *Proportions* of the *Time*' that he contributed to the twelfth edition of Playford's *Introduction to the Skill of Musick* in 1694.[25] For duple metre, Purcell listed time signatures derived from proportional notation: c, ¢ and ⊘. In sixteenth-century theory, each successive sign indicated a diminution (doubling) of the pace. By the time of the 1694 *Introduction*, these exact proportions had been replaced by a looser sense of gradually increasing tempos. Purcell described c as 'the first and slowest of all' types of common time, ¢ as 'a little faster', and ⊘ as 'quickest of all'; the sign ⊘ could also be expressed as 2 ('the *French Mark* for this retorted *Time*').[26] A similarly non-arithmetic definition of duple time-signatures is found in the preface to Purcell's *Choice Collection of Lessons* (1696): c is 'a very slow movement', ¢ 'a little faster' and ⊘ 'a brisk & airy time'. Purcell's definitions suggest there was only a slight difference of tempo between c and ¢, but a greater acceleration from ¢ to ⊘.[27] This would correlate with the attempts of some musicians such as John Lenton to propose a new proportional relationship between the slowest and fastest duple metres, where c is half the speed of ⊘ instead of one quarter the speed, as in the strict mensural system.[28]

As for triple-time metres, theorists of the late seventeenth century again grouped these in a sequence of increasing tempos. In the preface of Purcell's *Choice Collection of Lessons*, 3/2 consists of 'three Minums in a barr, and is commonly play'd very slow', 3i 'has three Crotchets in a barr, and they are to be play'd slow', 3 'has ye same as ye former but is play'd faster', and 6/4 'has six Crotchets in a barr & is Commonly to brisk tunes as Jiggs and Paspys [Passepieds]'.[29] A simpler classification is found in Purcell's chapter in Playford's *Introduction* (1694), where 3/2 is the 'slowest' type of triple time, and 3 and 3i (with three crotchets in a bar) collectively form a 'faster'

---

25 John Playford, *An Introduction to the Skill of Musick. In Three Books … The Twelfth Edition. Corrected and Amended by Mr. Henry Purcell* (London, 1694), pp. 25–6. For evidence of Purcell's authorship of the chapter on tempo, see Rebecca Herissone, *Music Theory in Seventeenth-Century England*, Oxford Monographs on Music (Oxford: Oxford University Press, 2000), p. 265.

26 In some of Purcell's earlier works (particularly introductory symphonies), 2 probably indicates a moderate tempo. See A. Margaret Laurie, 'Continuity and Tempo in Purcell's Vocal Works', in Curtis Price (ed.), *Purcell Studies* (Cambridge: Cambridge University Press, 1995), p. 200.

27 Henry Purcell, *A Choice Collection of Lessons for the Harpsichord or Spinnet* (London, 1696).

28 Herissone, *Music Theory in Seventeenth-Century England*, pp. 66–7.

29 Purcell, *A Choice Collection of Lessons*, sig. [a4].

metre.[30] As with Purcell's descriptions of duple metres, there is no mention of arithmetic relationships between these triple-time tempos.

Several scholars have tried to calculate the metronome marks appropriate for the various tempos as listed by Purcell. Indeed, Purcell himself defined the speeds for two of the duple-time signs with reference to the motion of clocks and watches. He likened the tempo of c to 'the slow motions of the Pendulum' of 'a large Chamber-Clock', without specifying whether he meant the minim or crotchet beat. Less ambiguously, he described a crotchet in ϕ as 'almost as fast as the regular Motions of a Watch';[31] Ellen T. Boal states that this is 'the first written indication by a renowned composer of an exact, dependable small unit of time',[32] and argues that these descriptions of clock tempos suggest a speed of $\downarrow$ = 120 in c and $\downarrow$ = 240 in ϕ.[33] Rebecca Herissone, however, clarifies Purcell's description of common time via reference to Daniel Robinson's *Essay upon Vocal Musick* (1715), suggesting a speed of $\downarrow$ = 60 in c.[34] Klaus Miehling relates Purcell's definition of c to a 'fundamental-beat-tempo' of between 60 and 80 beats per minute.[35] But whatever values are assigned to Purcell's clock tempos, it is unrealistic to expect these speeds to be valid throughout his output, given the variety of note lengths and rhythmic patterns found in different movements with the same time signatures in this period. As Daniel Robinson stated: 'I never heard of any certain Standard of Time, by which the length of Notes were to be strictly squared or adjusted, nor do I conceive how such a Thing can be devised, by Reason of the copious Variety of Air which is comprehended in this Art, and the great diversity of Mens Fancies in their allowance of Time to the Measure of this or that Mood.'[36]

If Purcell's time signatures cannot indicate exact tempos, they nonetheless may suggest tempo relationships within his multi-sectional vocal works. As Margaret Laurie and Bruce Wood have shown, establishing such relationships can give a sense of a constant tactus between different sections, thus ensuring continuity in performance.[37] In many multi-sectional vocal works, the implications of Purcell's time signatures are clear. For instance, in the first chorus of *Welcome to All the Pleasures*, there is a change from c to ϕ during the line 'Hail great assembly of

---

30   Playford, *An Introduction to the Skill of Musick … The Twelfth Edition*, p. 27.

31   Ibid., pp. 25–6.

32   Boal, 'Purcell's Clock Tempos': 25–6. An earlier reference to measuring tempo according to a second-hand of a watch was made by the composer Christopher Simpson in his *Compendium of Practical Musick in Five Parts* (London, 1667).

33   Boal, 'Purcell's Clock Tempos': 25–6 and 30–32.

34   Herissone, *Music Theory in Seventeenth-Century England*, p. 52. Lionel Sawkins arrives at the same metronome mark for c in his 'Trembleurs and Cold People: How Should They Shiver?', in Michael Burden (ed.), *Performing the Music of Henry Purcell* (Oxford: Clarendon, 1996), p. 252.

35   Klaus Miehling, 'Das Tempo bei Henry Purcell', *Basler Jahrbuch für historische Musikpraxis* 15 (1991): 118 and 123.

36   Daniel Robinson, *An Essay upon Vocal Musick* (Nottingham, 1715), pp. 14–15.

37   Laurie, 'Continuity and Tempo in Purcell's Vocal Works'; Bruce Wood's comments can be found in his introductions to editions for the Purcell Society as listed in n. 44 below.

Apollo's race' in the printed score of 1684 (bb. 64–7). Occurring in the middle of the phrase, the tempo change is best interpreted as strictly proportional, with the speed doubling at 'of Apollo's race'.[38]

Yet one problem with inferring tempos from time signatures is that the extant non-autograph sources often seem to contain errors or discrepancies, implying that not all copyists, typesetters or performers adhered to the proportional system. Lionel Sawkins notes that in the Frost Scene from *King Arthur* some of the earliest sources notate the Cold Genius's 'What Power art Thou' in c, whereas the Chorus of Cold People (which uses a similar shivering figure) is written in ¢. Sawkins considers the initial c to be illogical, and suggests that ¢, as found in some slightly later sources, is more appropriate for the Cold Genius's air; this would imply a faster tempo than that adopted by many performers. Sawkins also uses proportional relationships to advocate a brisk tempo for the Cold Genius's subsequent air 'Great Love' (notated in 2 in all the principal manuscript sources).[39]

Another example of possible errors in time signatures is found in the early sources of Purcell's mad song Bess of Bedlam ('From Silent Shades'). The piece represents Bess's mood swings and sudden hallucinations via a highly sectional structure, with many changes between different types of duple and triple time. The version printed in the fourth book of Playford's *Choice Ayres and Songs* (1683)[40] uses two duple-time signatures, ¢ (for the recitative sections, and also the more tuneful 'I'll lay me down and rest') and 𝄵 (for the hallucinatory 'Bright Cynthia kept her revels'). Margaret Laurie suggests that the recitative sections 'originally bore the time signature c', which would create a different time signature for each of the three styles of duple-time writing, and imply a tempo relationship of 1:2:4 between these passages.[41] Such extremes of tempo are entirely appropriate for the song's subject-matter, as Amanda Eubanks Winkler's chapter in this book demonstrates.[42] Manuscript copies of the song further emphasize the need for contrasts in tempo by adding instructions 'Slow' or 'Quick' to the triple-time sections.[43]

Like Bess of Bedlam, most of Purcell's multi-sectional works contain a mix of passages in duple time and in triple time. In his editions of Purcell's odes and symphony songs, Bruce Wood argues that these contrasting metres can often be linked via proportional relationships.[44] Although no Restoration treatises explain

---

38   As suggested by Bruce Wood in Henry Purcell, *Three Odes for St Cecilia's Day*, The Works of Henry Purcell, vol. 10 (new edn, London: Novello, 1990), p. x. See Henry Purcell, *A Musical Entertainment Perform'd on November XXII, 1683* (London, 1684), p. 7.

39   Sawkins, '*Trembleurs* and Cold People', pp. 253–7.

40   John Playford, *Choice Ayres and Songs to Sing to the Theorbo-lute, or Bass-viol ... The Fourth Book* (London, 1683).

41   Laurie, 'Continuity and Tempo in Purcell's Vocal Works', p. 199.

42   See the section 'Lovesick Madness' in Chapter 7 below.

43   These scribal additions are listed in Henry Purcell, *Secular Songs for Solo Voice*, ed. Margaret Laurie, The Works of Henry Purcell, vol. 25 (new edn, Borough Green: Novello, 1985), pp. 280–82.

44   See Henry Purcell, *Birthday Odes for Queen Mary, Part I*, ed. Bruce Wood, The Works of Henry Purcell, vol. 11 (new edn, London: Novello, 1993), p. xiii; Purcell, *Birthday Odes*

precisely how to link duple with triple time, the older mensural tradition allowed for two types of relationship: sesquialtera (where three triple-time crotchets occupy the same duration as two duple crotchets) and tripla (where three triple-time crotchets occupy the same duration as one duple crotchet). Vestiges of these conventions appear in Christopher Simpson's *Compendium of Practical Musick* (1667), where the sesquialtera proportion is described as signifying 'a *Tripla* Measure of three Notes to two such like Notes of the Common Time'.[45] But, as Wood notes, arithmetic ratios are not always applicable to Purcell's music. For instance, in the symphony song *If ever I more Riches did Desire*, the triple-time section 'Me, O ye Gods' (b. 148) shows no proportional relationship with the surrounding sections: in his autograph manuscript, Lbl R.M. 20.h.8, Purcell notates the section in 3 but uses the verbal modifier 'Very slow' to cancel the time signature's usual connotations of a fast tempo.[46]

In her edition of *Dido and Aeneas*, Ellen Harris explores the feasibility of proportional tempo relationships across the opera, suggesting how a constant tactus might underpin sequences of movements in duple and triple metres.[47] Harris's imposition of these arithmetic relationships is particularly appropriate given that the earliest source of the opera's music (Ob Tenbury 1266) uses time signatures typical of the late seventeenth century, despite itself dating from the second half of the eighteenth century. Many of Harris's suggestions work well and lend continuity to the piece: in the first Witches scene, for example, she suggests that the Sorceress's duple-time passages relate to the triple-time chorus 'Harm's our Delight' via a sesquialtera relationship, and to the triple-time 'Ho ho ho' choruses via a tripla relationship. Elsewhere, however, the old system of proportions is too rigid for the opera. As Peter Holman writes, 'Sesquialtera surely produces much too jaunty an effect for "In our deep vaulted cell", which seems to demand the modern constant-crotchet relationship with the preceding Witches' duet. Nor does it work for the first section of the overture to be half the speed of the fugue; either the former ends up too slow or the latter too quick.'[48] Because the mensural system was gradually breaking down, it is not an infallible guide to tempo relationships in Purcell's works.

In contrast with these many studies of proportional relationships in vocal works, less research has been done on the tempos suitable for Purcell's instrumental music. In his chamber works, the disintegration of the mensural system is particularly evident: since tempos are indicated by note values or verbal markings, the time

---

    for Queen Mary, Part II, ed. Bruce Wood, The Works of Henry Purcell, vol. 24 (new edn, London: Novello, 1998), pp. xii–xiii; Purcell, *Royal Welcome Songs, Part II*, ed. Bruce Wood, The Works of Henry Purcell, vol. 18 (new edn, London: Novello, 2005), pp. xiv–xv.

45   Simpson, *Compendium of Practical Musick*, p. 34.

46   Henry Purcell, *Symphony Songs*, ed. Bruce Wood, The Works of Henry Purcell, vol. 27 (new edn, London: Stainer and Bell, 2007), pp. xiii–xiv.

47   Henry Purcell, *Dido and Aeneas*, ed. Ellen Harris, Oxford Operas (Oxford: Oxford University Press, 1987), p. vii.

48   Peter Holman, Review of Purcell, *Dido and Aeneas*, ed. Harris, in *Music & Letters* 71 (1990): 618.

signatures may give little clue as to suitable speeds. The only time signatures used in the viol fantazias of *c*.1680 are c and ¢ and Ellen Boal suggests that there is little distinction between these signs, although ¢ may indicate a slighter faster tempo.[49] In addition, Purcell denotes the speed of individual sections with English terms such as 'brisk', 'slow' and 'drag'. Usually these terms correspond with changes to faster or slower note values, and – as Peter Holman comments – they should be thought of as descriptive (denoting a change of motion already implicit in the notation) rather than prescriptive (instructing the performer to do something otherwise not indicated).[50]

Purcell's *Sonnata's of III Parts*, published in 1683, require performers to make more decisions about tempo: each sonata contains a mix of duple-time and triple-time sections and uses Italian tempo markings. As in the fantazias, the time signatures do not seem to imply tempos: Mary Cyr shows that c and ¢ are used for duple-time passages whether fast or slow, with little apparent distinction between the signs.[51] More important are the tempo markings, which (as explained in the edition's Preface) fall into three categories: *Adagio* and *Grave* for 'a very slow movement' (usually in duple time); *Presto Largo*, *Poco Largo* and *Largo* for 'a middle movement' (a moderate tempo, usually in triple time); and *Allegro* or *Vivace* for 'a very brisk, swift or fast movement'.[52] Tempo changes may be indicated by these words rather than by new time signatures. Thus in Sonata 1 the adjoining Adagio and Presto sections (bb. 67–119) are both in ¢; the same time signature is also used for the adjacent Adagio and Vivace sections in Sonata 2 (bb. 78–118). With the gradual abandonment of the system of proportions, the choice of exact tempo was increasingly at the musician's discretion; this multiplied the diversity of practices in the period, and may also have vexed inexperienced and amateur performers. As Roger North wrote, of all the difficulties encountered in music-making, 'none are found greater than to attain a true knowledge and setled habit of keeping musicall time.'[53] For modern-day performers and scholars, the tempos suitable for Purcell's music – in particular his instrumental works – continue to be an area for experiment and inquiry.

---

49   Boal, 'Purcell's Clock Tempos': 36.

50   Holman, *Henry Purcell*, p. 77.

51   Mary Cyr, 'Tempo Gradations in Purcell's Sonatas', *Performance Practice Review* 7 (1994): 187 and 193.

52   Henry Purcell, *Sonnata's of III Parts: Two Viollins and Basse* (London, 1683), Preface 'To the Reader'. The Preface refers to Purcell in the third person, so may not have been written by him.

53   Mary Chan and Jamie C. Kassler (eds), *Roger North's The Musicall Grammarian 1728*, Cambridge Studies in Music (Cambridge: Cambridge University Press, 1990), p. 126. See also Herissone, *Music Theory in Seventeenth-Century England*, pp. 53–4.

Pitch Standards

The diversity of performance practices in Purcell's lifetime is particularly evident with regard to pitch. Multiple pitch standards were used in seventeenth-century Europe, in contrast to the modern expectation of a universal norm. It is certainly inappropriate for today's performers to tackle all of Purcell's music at what has colloquially become known as 'Baroque pitch' (a' = 415 Hz). Bruce Haynes and Dominic Gwynn have shown that at least two pitch standards existed in Purcell's London: a high pitch in church music, and a low pitch in secular music that was particularly associated with the new woodwind instruments arriving from France. However, any discussion of pitch standards is hampered by the patchy and contradictory nature of the surviving evidence. Although some extant recorders and organ pipes indicate possible pitch levels of the period, it is hard to establish which (if any) of these instruments represent common practice, particularly as small variations of pitch can occur within an accepted standard. Furthermore, the late seventeenth century was a time of change in pitch levels used in England, evident in the rebuilding of many church organs from the 1670s onwards. Despite these uncertainties, research into pitch standards remains vitally important for performers of Purcell's music, not least because it can help clarify which voice types are suitable for his countertenor lines (see the section 'Voices', below).

Until the end of the seventeenth century, most church music was probably performed at what Bruce Haynes calls Quire Pitch, between one and two semitones above modern pitch.[54] Evidence for the existence of this pitch has been assembled by Dominic Gwynn and Martin Goetze from extant organ pipes and also archival documents concerning church organs.[55] But the pitches of organs in the years before and after the Commonwealth constitute a complex subject, so a few words of introduction are necessary here. Church organs built before the Commonwealth and a few from the 1660s were so-called 'five-foot' or 'transposing' instruments which incorporated two pitch standards, Quire Pitch and Organ Pitch (a fourth higher). The pipes sounded at pitches a fourth higher than those indicated by the keys, so an organist played a C in order to accompany a choir singing an F.[56] Purcell's organ at Westminster Abbey was of this kind, and – as Gwynn remarks – it is hard to envisage 'the problems of pitch, compass and tuning which Purcell must have encountered' on it.[57] After 1660, however, most new organs were non-

---

54 Bruce Haynes, *A History of Performing Pitch: The Story of 'A'* (Lanham: Scarecrow, 2002), pp. 86–92 and 129–32.

55 Dominic Gwynn, 'Organ Pitch in Seventeenth-Century England', *BIOS Journal* 9 (1985): 65–78; Martin Goetze, 'Transposing Organs and Pitch in England', *FoMRHI Quarterly* 78 (1995): 61–7.

56 Dominic Gwynn, 'Lost Worlds: The English Organ before 1700', in Thomas Donahue (ed.), *Music and its Questions: Essays in Honor of Peter Williams* (Richmond, VA: Organ Historical Society Press, 2007), pp. 23–47; Andrew Johnstone, '"As It Was in the Beginning": Organ and Choir Pitch in Early Anglican Church Music', *Early Music* 31 (2003): 506–26.

57 Dominic Gwynn, 'Purcell's Organ at Westminster Abbey: A Note on the Cover

transposing instruments, tuned to Quire Pitch.[58] Indeed, Purcell signed a contract in 1694 with Bernard Smith for the alteration of the Westminster Abbey organ to a non-transposing system.[59] Yet even after the abandonment of the transposing system, extant organ pipes show that Quire Pitch did not have an exact value, but varied by up to a tone between churches.[60]

Purcell wrote most of his sacred music for performance in the Chapel Royal at Whitehall. The organ here was built in 1662, presumably as a non-transposing instrument, and in 1676 Bernard Smith was paid 'for taking half a note lower the Organ'.[61] There is no evidence of the original or altered pitch of the instrument (which was destroyed in the Whitehall fire of 1698), but Gwynn suggests it was built at approximately two semitones above modern pitch.[62] That sacred music was performed at a different pitch from secular music at court is implied by a 1664 payment for two violins and a bass viol for use specifically in the Chapel Royal, shortly after the introduction of string accompaniment in anthems.[63] Peter Holman suggests that the violins were at the same pitch as the organ, whereas Bruce Haynes speculates that they were tuned a tone lower to facilitate transposition.[64] A further unresolved question is how the organ's pitch related to that of the cornetts and sackbuts still used at the Chapel Royal in the 1660s.[65]

Haynes hypothesizes that the new pitch of the Whitehall organ after its 1670s rebuilding was a' = 473 Hz, 'in order to put it within transposing reach' of the lower-pitched instruments used by French wind players.[66] Three French woodwind players were officially appointed to the Chapel Royal in 1678, and two anthems by John Blow exist with recorder parts; but these wind players left England in 1682, and none of Purcell's music for the Chapel Royal has notated wind parts.[67] Haynes

Illustration', *Early Music* 23 (1995): 550.

58 Stephen Bicknell, *The History of the English Organ* (Cambridge: Cambridge University Press, 1996), pp. 117–19.

59 Franklin B. Zimmerman, *Henry Purcell, 1659–1695. His Life and Times* (2nd edn, Philadelphia: University of Pennsylvania Press, 1983), p. 235.

60 See the lists of pitches in Gwynn, 'Organ Pitch in Seventeenth-Century England': 68–9, and Gwynn, 'The English Organ in Purcell's Lifetime', in Michael Burden (ed.), *Performing the Music of Henry Purcell* (Oxford: Clarendon, 1996), p. 32.

61 Andrew Freeman, *Father Smith, otherwise Bernard Schmidt, being an Account of a Seventeenth Century Organ Maker*, edited, annotated and with new material by John Rowntree (Oxford: Positif Press, 1977; first published London: Musical Opinion, 1926), p. 13.

62 Gwynn, 'Organ Pitch in Seventeenth-Century England': 69.

63 Andrew Ashbee, *Records of English Court Music, vol. 1: 1660–1685* (Snodland, Kent: Ashbee, 1986), p. 60.

64 Peter Holman, 'Purcell and Pitch', *Early Music* 24 (1996): 366; Haynes, *A History of Performing Pitch*, p. 154 n. 84.

65 On the continuing use of cornetts and sackbuts, see Holman, *Four and Twenty Fiddlers*, pp. 394–7.

66 Haynes, *A History of Performing Pitch*, pp. 130–31.

67 Ibid., pp. 407–11.

conjectures further that 'all of Purcell's music prior to 1690 that involves organ was probably performed by singers at *Quire Pitch* (A = 473) and (except for the organist) transposed upwards by any instrumentalists who accompanied'.[68] But because no performing parts from the Whitehall chapel survive for Purcell's symphony anthems, it is impossible to know if such transpositions occurred in practice. The only material directly associated with Purcell that does survive for this repertory, his partial-autograph parts for *My Song shall be Alway* (Och Mus. 1188–9), which were possibly made for use at Windsor, show no evidence of transposition.[69] (By contrast, the extant performing material for Bach's Leipzig cantatas shows that the organ part was always transposed.)

Some modern-day ensembles have successfully performed Purcell's church music at high pitch. In his complete recording of the sacred music, Robert King performs those pieces associated with the Chapel Royal at a' = 466 Hz. This pitch, an exact semitone above a' = 440 Hz, facilitates transposition relationships that are more convenient for modern performers than Haynes's suggestion of a' = 473 Hz: King's string players used instruments tuned at a' = 415 Hz with parts transposed up a tone.[70] The high pitch gives King's interpretations a brilliance absent at lower pitches, and also has important implications for the vocal lines. King asserts that the high pitch 'makes sense of Purcell's improbably (and uncharacteristically) low vocal writing in his Chapel Royal works'.[71] Furthermore, it puts the countertenor lines more comfortably in the range of a falsettist such as James Bowman, who features throughout King's recordings.

Many questions remain about the pitch at which Purcell's church music was performed outside London. At Worcester Cathedral, the organ of 1666 was 'the most obviously conservative of the post-war organs', with a stop list similar to its 1613 predecessor, and a Quire Pitch that was probably one or two semitones higher than a' = 440 Hz.[72] This may be why the Worcester organ-book WO A.3.10 contains Purcell's *Thy way, O God* and *My Song shall be Alway* a tone lower than in most other sources. On the other hand, the same book contains Purcell's anthem *Blessed is the Man* in D minor, a tone higher than 11 other sources.[73] Such transpositions

---

68 Ibid., pp. 131–2.

69 Holman, *Four and Twenty Fiddlers*, p. 406.

70 See Bruce Wood, Review of *The Complete Sacred Music of Henry Purcell*, The King's Consort, dir. Robert King, vols 1 and 2 (Hyperion CDA66585 and CDA66609, *rec.* 1991–92), in *Early Music* 20 (1992): 693–4.

71 Robert King, CD booklet, *The Complete Sacred Music of Henry Purcell*, The King's Consort, dir. Robert King (Hyperion CDS44141–51, *rec.* 1991–94), p. 13.

72 Gwynn, 'The English Organ in Purcell's Lifetime', p. 35.

73 See the modern editions of these three anthems in Henry Purcell, *Sacred Music, Part IV: Anthems*, eds Anthony Lewis and Nigel Fortune, The Works of Henry Purcell, vol. 28 (London: Novello, 1959), p. 189; Purcell, *Sacred Music, Part V: Anthems*, eds Anthony Lewis and Nigel Fortune, The Works of Henry Purcell, vol. 29 (rev. edn, London: Novello, 1967; new edn first published 1959), p. 193; Purcell, *Sacred Music, Part VII: Anthems and Miscellaneous Sacred Music*, eds Anthony Lewis and Nigel Fortune, The Works of Henry Purcell, vol. 32 (London: Novello, 1962), p. 183.

have implications for keyboard temperament and vocal tessitura, and need to be thoroughly researched.

By contrast with the high pitch of church music, a lower pitch was used for secular repertories. Haynes uses the term Consort Pitch, as found in the writings of Roger North, Alexander Malcolm and Peter Prelleur. According to Haynes, this pitch level was approximately a' = 400 Hz, a minor third below Quire Pitch (or one-and-a-half semitones below a' = 440 Hz). His main evidence comprises the pitches of extant recorders from the period c.1690–1730: 'thirty-three range from 395 to 405 at an average of 402, and fifteen are pitched from 408 to 418, averaging 411.'[74] He conjectures that this low Consort Pitch was current throughout the seventeenth century and possibly even earlier, being preserved by such traditions as viol playing.[75] A low pitch would thus be suitable for Purcell's viol fantazias.

Haynes shows that the low pitch was strongly associated with secular works of the late seventeenth century that include woodwind parts. Recorders and oboes arrived in England in the early 1670s, played by French instrumentalists such as James Paisible. Haynes argues that the pitch standard for these French players was the *Ton de la chambre du Roy*, which he defines as a' = 404–409 Hz, or in other words, sufficiently close as to be considered equivalent to the English Consort Pitch.[76] From 1690 onwards, Purcell regularly used oboes and/or recorders in his odes and stage works, so these were presumably performed at low pitch.

Andrew Parrott has used the low pitch of a' = 392 Hz for his recordings of Purcell's odes *Hail, bright Cecilia* (1692), *Come ye Sons of Art* (1694) and *Welcome to All the Pleasures* (1683).[77] The 1692 and 1694 odes include oboes and are obvious candidates for performance at low pitch. Parrott made his decision partly on the basis of the earliest extant English-made oboe, the so-called 'Galpin oboe' (attributed to the 1680s or 1690s), which has a possible pitch of a' = 392 Hz.[78] (Haynes, however, argues that old oboes are unreliable indicators of historical pitches, given that the original reeds are missing, and embouchure can influence pitch.[79]) Parrott's choice of a' = 392 Hz (a whole tone below today's concert pitch) is also more pragmatic for modern performers than Haynes's suggestion of a' = 400 Hz, because it allows players to use their usual instruments with the music transposed down a tone or semitone. Moreover, at a' = 392 Hz most of the countertenor lines in these odes are accessible to high tenors (see the section 'Voices', below).

William Christie has also experimented with low pitches in his performances of Purcell's stage works. His recordings of *The Fairy Queen* and *King Arthur*, made

---

74 Haynes, *A History of Performing Pitch*, p. 127.
75 Ibid., pp. 95–6.
76 Ibid., pp. 119 and 128.
77 Henry Purcell, *Ode on St Cecilia's Day 1692*, Taverner Choir, Taverner Players, dir. Andrew Parrott (EMI CDC 7474902, *rec.* 1985); Purcell, *Come Ye Sons of Art, Welcome to All the Pleasures, Funeral Music for Queen Mary, Funeral Sentences*, Taverner Consort, Taverner Choir, Taverner Players, dir. Andrew Parrott (EMI Reflexe CDC 7496352, *rec.* 1988).
78 Parrott, 'Performing Purcell', p. 414.
79 Haynes, *A History of Performing Pitch*, p. 27.

respectively in 1989 and 1995, use a' = 392 Hz.[80] At this pitch airs in *The Fairy Queen* such as 'A Thousand Ways we'll Find' (notated range g–b♭') and 'Let the Fifes and the Clarions' (notated range a–b') are brought within the reach of a high tenor. Other voice parts also benefit: in *King Arthur*, 'Fairest Isle' (notated range f'–a♭'' or a'') is more comfortable for a soprano at the lower pitch.[81] But in Christie's recording of *The Fairy Queen*, the low pitch puts some of the bass notes below the reach of the soloist: in the duo 'Come let us leave the town', for example, the bass Thomas Lander was forced to transpose his low Gs up an octave. In his 2009 performances of *The Fairy Queen* at Glyndebourne and at the BBC Promenade Concerts, Christie opted for the slightly higher pitch of a' = 405 Hz. This is closer to the figure identified by Haynes's research, and perhaps also recognizes that a' = 392 Hz is a little too low for Purcell's dramatick operas.

Whereas a high pitch is suitable for Purcell's church music and a low pitch for his secular works written from 1690 onwards, there is little scholarly agreement on the pitch levels appropriate for his secular vocal works of the 1680s, such as the odes and symphony songs. These pieces would have been accompanied by the Twenty-Four Violins, who almost certainly played at low pitch. Indeed, all the odes have been recorded by Robert King at the so-called 'Baroque pitch' of a' = 415 Hz.[82] But Andrew Parrott's brief study of vocal range suggests that a higher pitch may have been used in the 1680s: Parrott notes that the choral ranges in Purcell's secular works before 1690 are often a tone lower than in secular works written after that date.[83] Timothy Morris's more detailed study of vocal range produces more ambiguous results: for him, a possible shift of pitch standards is evident, mainly in the decreasing use of low notes in choral bass parts as the 1680s proceeds.[84] Unfortunately, the range of bass parts may have largely depended on the abilities of individual singers such as John Gostling, who, as is well known, had an unusually low range; hence they cannot provide watertight evidence of pitch standards. Further research is thus needed on the pitch levels of Purcell's secular works of the 1680s, particularly given the importance of pitch to the colour of his music in performance.

---

80 Henry Purcell, *The Fairy Queen*, Les Arts Florissants, dir. William Christie (Harmonia Mundi, HMC 901308.09, *rec.* 1989); Purcell, *King Arthur*, Les Arts Florissants, dir. William Christie (Erato, 4509-98535-2, *rec.* 1995).

81 Interestingly, 'Fairest Isle' also appears transposed down by a minor third in an early eighteenth-century manuscript, Lbl Add. 40139, fols 41v–42r.

82 *The Complete Odes and Welcome Songs of Henry Purcell (1659–1695)*, The King's Consort, dir. Robert King (Hyperion CDS 44031–8, *rec.* 1988–92).

83 Parrott, 'Performing Purcell', pp. 416–17.

84 Timothy Morris, 'Voice Ranges, Voice Types, and Pitch in Purcell's Concerted Works', in Michael Burden (ed.), *Performing the Music of Henry Purcell* (Oxford: Clarendon, 1996), p. 133.

Voices

Research into the performing styles and voice types of Purcell's singers poses a particular set of challenges. Although the names of Purcell's solo singers are recorded in some of the sources of his odes from the late 1680s onwards, virtually nothing is known about how they sounded. Whereas players can experiment with original instruments, there are no surviving singers from the seventeenth century to investigate. And although we might assume that modern-day vocalists have the same type of larynx as those of past centuries, it is possible that the physiology of the voice has altered, given the changes in diet, health and lifestyle in the intervening centuries. Perhaps partly because of these imponderables, there has been relatively little published research into the singing styles and techniques used in Restoration England. The most detailed study is Edward Huws Jones's 1978 doctoral dissertation on English vocal techniques up to 1670, but this covers only the first decade of the Restoration era.[85] The following paragraphs offer my own summary of how Purcell's contemporaries may have drawn on Italian and French singing styles, using sources such as Pietro Reggio's treatise *The Art of Singing* that have only recently come to light, and demonstrating the lines of enquiry that might be developed by future researchers. I then summarize the vigorous debate about which voice type is most suitable for the parts that Purcell assigned to 'countertenors'.

It is well known that seventeenth-century Europe was dominated by two schools of singing: the Italian and French.[86] In his aforementioned dissertation, Jones shows how these continental styles influenced English vocal techniques between 1610 and 1670, but no detailed research has yet been carried out to determine how far these foreign models shaped English approaches to singing during Purcell's lifetime. In the early seventeenth century the Italianate vocal style popular in England involved a highly nuanced declamation, in which singers used many small crescendos and diminuendos to give shape to notes and phrases. This style was first codified in the 1664 edition of Playford's *Brief Introduction to the Skill of Musick*, in the form of a translation of part of the preface to Giulio Caccini's *Le nuove musiche* (1602), with the information that these Italian vocal methods 'have been used here in England by most of the Gentlemen of His Majesties Chappel above this 40 years'.[87] Although the translation of Caccini appeared in subsequent editions of Playford's *Introduction* up to and including that of 1694, it is unclear if this old method of singing remained in widespread use throughout Purcell's lifetime. As a boy Purcell

85 Published as Edward Huws Jones, *The Performance of English Song, 1610–1670*, Outstanding Dissertations in Music from British Universities (New York: Garland, 1989).

86 Sally A. Sanford, 'A Comparison of French and Italian Singing in the Seventeenth Century', *Journal of Seventeenth-Century Music* 1/i (1995), http://sscm-jscm.press.illinois.edu/v1/no1/sanford.html (last accessed 9 October 2009).

87 John Playford, *A Brief Introduction to the Skill of Musick ... The Fourth Edition, much Enlarged* (London, 1664), p. 77.

may have learned the nuanced Italianate singing style from his teacher Henry Cooke, Master of the Children at the Chapel Royal from 1660. Cooke was named by Playford as a particular exponent of it, and was also described by Evelyn as 'the best singer after the *Italian* manner of any in *England*'.[88] However, some of the other English singers whom Playford associated with the early Italian vocal style – for instance Henry Lawes (d. 1662) and Charles Coleman (d. 1664)[89] – died shortly after the Restoration, and their compositions were not widely published after the 1660s. This may suggest that the Caccini-esque manner of singing was falling into disuse by the 1670s, along with the mid-century repertory of continuo song.

From the 1660s a new Italian vocal style was brought to England by émigré performers. An Italian opera troupe arrived in London around 1664, recruited by Thomas Killigrew with the support of Charles II: it included at least one castrato, plus the brothers Bartolomeo and Vincenzo Albrici, the bass Pietro Reggio, and the harpsichordist Giovanni Battista Draghi.[90] Draghi, Reggio and Bartolomeo Albrici settled in England for the rest of their lives and promoted Italianate vocal styles through their teaching; both Reggio and Bartolomeo Albrici taught John Evelyn's daughter Mary.[91] Other Italian-born or Italian-trained singers were associated with the Catholic Chapels of Catherine of Braganza, Mary of Modena or James II, among them the organist and tenor Giovanni Sebenico (in London 1666–73) and Innocenzo Fede (director of the choir in James II's Catholic Chapel). Much of the repertory of these Italians is lost, but a profitable topic for future research would be to investigate Draghi's extant compositions for evidence of a move towards writing for trained singers. Whereas the English continuo songs of the first half of the century contain simple but subtle declamation suitable for amateur voices, Draghi's vocal lines have a wider tessitura and a greater variety of note values. In his 1682 song 'Where art thou, God of Dreams?', for example, the soprano soloist is pitted against an active continuo line and two obbligato violins; the vocal part contains melismatic figuration, repeated phrases and also long sustained notes over the moving bass.[92]

Possible evidence of the singing styles of the Italian émigrés clustered around Draghi can be found in Reggio's *The Art of Singing* (1677), the earliest treatise published in England on the subject of vocal technique. Reggio's book emphasizes dynamic shading, in particular the *messa di voce*:

> a general Rule, [is] to sing all long Notes in the beginning of them soft, and then increase your Voice till you come up to the full strength of it … but when

88   *The Diary of John Evelyn*, ed. De Beer, vol. 3, p. 144 (28 October 1654).
89   These are two of the singers named in the version of the Caccini translation in John Playford, *A Brief Introduction to the Skill of Musick* (London, 1666), p. 58.
90   Margaret Mabbett, 'Italian Musicians in Restoration England (1660–1690)', *Music & Letters* 67 (1986): 238.
91   *The Diary of John Evelyn*, ed. De Beer, vol. 4, pp. 421–2 (14 March 1685).
92   For a score of 'Where art thou, God of Dreams?', see Peter Holman, 'The Italian Connection: Giovanni Battista Draghi and Henry Purcell', *Early Music Performer* 22 (2008): 9–10.

you are come unto the full strength of your Voice, you must decrease again till you bring it back again to the same softness as you began first.[93]

He suggests other ways to vary dynamics, such as crescendos through phrases, and includes many musical examples where individual notes are marked with 'L' ('lowd') or 'S' ('soft'). Perhaps because English was not his first language, Reggio does not say how these 'pointillistic' dynamics should relate to the text. Nor does he discuss techniques of vocal production, although his description of dynamic shading presupposes a flexible breathing technique where the volume and pressure of air varies with the declamation.[94]

In his emphasis on dynamic shading, Reggio describes a vocal style that appears to have changed little from the techniques demonstrated by Caccini in the early seventeenth century. Playford's 1664 translation likewise explained the *messa di voce* ('Encreasing and Abating the voyce') and its opposite, the *Exclamation* ('the slacking of the Voice, to reinforce it somewhat more').[95] Moreover, the musical examples that Reggio includes in his treatise, mostly taken from his own continuo songs such as 'Underneath this Myrtle Shade', are reminiscent of the ayres of the generation of Henry Lawes, with syllabic lines and a restricted compass. The only work quoted by Reggio that approaches the rhythmic variety or wide tessitura of Draghi's or Purcell's music is his song for *The Tempest* (1674), 'Arise, ye Subterranean Winds'.[96] Yet the circumstances of Reggio's career might explain why he seems to have adhered to an older style of Italian singing. In England he earned his livelihood partly through teaching amateurs and partly through his domestic performances as described by Pepys and Evelyn.[97] Both contexts required an intimate style of performance, in which simple melodies could be sung with great subtlety; but these techniques were not necessarily typical of all Italian singers in Restoration England.

Compared to Reggio's music, Purcell's Italianate songs are more ambitious in their compositional style and their demands on the vocalist. Take, for example, his song 'Ah me! To many Deaths Decreed', sung by Mrs Ayliff in the 1692 production of *Regulus*. The song was described by Peter Motteux as being set 'the *Italian* way',[98]

---

93   Reggio, *The Art of Singing*, p. 16. The sole surviving copy of *The Art of Singing* has been in private ownership since its rediscovery and sale at Sotheby's in 1997, but photocopies are held at the British Library, London, shelfmark D.621.s, and the Bodleian Library, Oxford, shelfmark Rec.d.129.

94   On this Italian approach to breathing, see Sanford, 'A Comparison of French and Italian Singing', para. 2.2.

95   Playford, *Brief Introduction to the Skill of Musick … The Fourth Edition*, pp. 61 and 64.

96   Reggio, *The Art of Singing*, p. 8; for a modern edition of the song, see Matthew Locke, *Dramatic Music*, ed. Michael Tilmouth, Musica Britannica, vol. 51 (London: Stainer and Bell, 1986), p. 44.

97   *The Diary of Samuel Pepys*, eds Latham and Matthews, vol. 5, p. 217 (22 July 1664); *The Diary of John Evelyn*, ed. De Beer, vol. 4, p. 220 (23 September 1680).

98   *The Gentleman's Journal*, August 1692, p. 26. On the ambiguities of Motteux's remarks, see Curtis A. Price, *Henry Purcell and the London Stage* (Cambridge: Cambridge

probably because of its combination of florid semiquavers, long-held notes and repeated phrases for the soprano (see Example 4.1). In singing the piece, Ayliff may have used some of the techniques described by Reggio: the *messa di voce*, for instance, would give shape to the long notes in bb. 1 and 4. But the semiquaver figuration and the changes of pace in each phrase demand a vocal agility that Reggio's treatise does not discuss, although it was certainly a technique prized by Italian vocalists in this period: the castrato Pier Francesco Tosi (who himself was working in London by 1693) recommended that singers practise divisions to gain an 'easy velocity and true intonation'.[99] Furthermore, Ayliff performed 'Ah me!' at London's Drury Lane Theatre, a much bigger venue than those typically used by Reggio. This did not necessarily mean that she had a big voice: small voices were preferred because they had the flexibility necessary for divisions and ornaments.[100] But the 'pointillistic' dynamic shading recommended by Reggio would be lost outside a domestic setting; instead, Purcell's writing invites dynamics on the level of phrases, perhaps with the repeat of the initial phrase being sung as an echo.[101] In short, Purcell's 'Ah me!' probably requires an Italianate style of singing closer to that described by Tosi in his 1723 treatise than that outlined by Reggio in 1677.

Alongside the Italian singers discussed above, French vocalists were also present at the English court in the seventeenth century. It is well known that French musicians were employed by Queen Henrietta Maria in the 1620s and 1630s, including the lutenist Jacques Gaultier, and also the singer Madame Coniack who appeared in the 1632 masque *Tempe Restored*.[102] After the Restoration, the continuing political and personal contacts between the English and French courts encouraged an appreciation of French song, although the implications of this have been little studied. In the 1660s the court had an ensemble of six French musicians, mostly singers;[103] and in 1676 Louis XIV sent three French singers to entertain Charles II with extracts from Lully's operas.[104] The 1676 performances would almost certainly have come to the attention of the 17-year-old Purcell and may explain some of his knowledge of Gallic music. French singers also appeared in the 1671 'Concert

---

University Press, 1984), pp. 19 and 69.

99   Pier Francesco Tosi, *Opinioni de' cantori antichi e moderni, o sieno osservazioni sopra il canto figurato* (Bologna, 1723). English translation as *Observations on the Florid Song: or, Sentiments on the Ancient and Modern Singers*, ed. John Ernest Galliard (2nd edn, London, 1743), p. 51.

100   Jones, *The Performance of English Song*, p. 21; Parrott, 'Performing Purcell', p. 424.

101   For examples of notated echo phrases, see 'When first I saw' and 'Strike the viol' in Purcell's autograph song-book (Lg Safe 3, fols 50r and 56v; facsimile available in Henry Purcell, *The Gresham Autograph*, Introduction by Margaret Laurie and Robert Thompson (facsimile edition, London: Novello, 1995)).

102   Karen Britland, *Drama at the Courts of Queen Henrietta Maria* (Cambridge and New York: Cambridge University Press, 2006), pp. 91–2.

103   Holman, *Four and Twenty Fiddlers*, p. 290.

104   John Buttrey, 'New Light on Robert Cambert in London, and his *Ballet en Musique*', *Early Music* 23 (1995): 220.

Example 4.1   Henry Purcell, 'Ah me! To many Deaths decreed' (from John Crowne, *Regulus*, as printed in *Orpheus Britannicus* (1698), p. 179), bb. 1–5.

of Nations' held at Whitehall for Charles II,[105] the opera *Ariane* staged by Robert Cambert in 1674 and the court performance of *Calisto* in 1675.[106] There may also have been a London performance of Lully's *Cadmus et Hermione* by a French company in 1686, according to circumstantial evidence gathered by W.J. Lawrence.[107] Furthermore, French singers were employed by several members of the aristocratic coterie that surrounded Charles II's court. The Duchesse de Mazarin (who was briefly Charles's mistress in the 1670s) had a French page-boy named Dery, whose singing was admired by the French exile Saint-Évremond.[108] John Wilmot, Earl of Rochester, retained a French singing boy, Jean-Baptiste de Belle-Fasse, whose musical skills he described with homosexual innuendo.[109] French singers were renowned for their close adherence to the prosody of the sung text, avoiding the

105 Chan and Kassler (eds), *Roger North's The Musicall Grammarian*, p. 262; Holman, *Four and Twenty Fiddlers*, pp. 361–6.

106 For a list of French musicians in *Calisto*, see Andrew Walkling, 'Masque and Politics at the Restoration Court: John Crowne's *Calisto*', *Early Music* 24 (1996): 34–6 and 51.

107 W.J. Lawrence, 'The French Opera in London – A Riddle of 1686', *Times Literary Supplement* 1782 (28 March 1936): 263.

108 C.M. de Saint-Denis Saint-Évremond, *Letters of Saint-Évremond*, ed. John Hayward (London: Routledge, 1930), p. 266. Dery may be 'the French boy' described by Evelyn as 'fam'd for his singing'; see *The Diary of John Evelyn*, ed. De Beer, vol. 4, pp. 404 and 413 (28 January 1685 and 6 February 1685).

109 James Johnson, *A Profane Wit: The Life of John Wilmot, Earl of Rochester* (Rochester: University of Rochester Press, 2004), pp. 43, 116 and 214–15.

elisions of syllables and repetition of words characteristic of Italian performers.[110] Above all, they were admired for their melodic elegance: as Saint-Évremond said, they 'find in the beauty of their performance, as it were a charm for our souls'.[111] A profitable topic for future research would be to gauge the influence of these French singers on Purcell and his contemporaries.

One of the most contentious questions in Purcellian performance practice is whether voice parts designated as 'countertenor' in contemporary sources should be sung by high tenors or male falsettists. For Purcell, the term 'countertenor' did not have the connotations of a falsetto voice that it carries today; it merely denoted the voice part above the tenor line. The debate about which voice type should sing these lines is clouded by the fact that since 1950 many performers and listeners have regarded the falsetto voice as ideal for Purcell. As Michael Tippett claimed, on first hearing the falsettist Alfred Deller sing 'Music for a While': 'I recognized absolutely that this was the voice for which Purcell had written.'[112] With the current boom in male falsettists, many of these singers have a personal investment in proving the validity of their vocal technique for Purcell. Yet the evidence assembled by Andrew Parrott suggests that falsetto voices are appropriate for only a small proportion of Purcell's countertenor lines. Indeed, many falsettists have to transpose Purcell solos upwards to fit their register. Even Deller performed 'Music for a While' between a tone and a major third higher than notated by Purcell, which, given the fact that theatre music of this period used the low Consort Pitch described previously, means that his recordings would have been pitched considerably above the level at which the music would have been heard in Purcell's day.[113]

When investigating Purcell's countertenors, it is important to distinguish between choral and solo parts. Falsettists were used in choirs in the early years of the Restoration: Matthew Locke reported that on the reopening of the Chapel Royal, 'the superiour Parts of their Musick' were supplied by cornetts and 'Mens feigned Voices', in the absence of trained choristers.[114] As for Purcell's choral countertenor lines in his odes and anthems, these often lie in a range comfortable for a falsettist such as c'–a', particularly in the case of sacred music that would be performed at Quire Pitch.[115] However, Purcell usually avoids the top and bottom extremes of the register, allowing the parts to be sung by either falsettists or high tenors.

---

110 Bénigne de Bacilly, *Remarques curieuses sur l'art de bien chanter* (Paris, 1668), English translation as *A Commentary upon the Art of Proper Singing*, ed. Austin B. Caswell, Music Theorists in Translation, vol. 7 (New York: Institute of Medieval Music, 1968), p. 42.

111 *Letters of Saint-Évremond*, ed. Hayward, p. 214.

112 Michael Tippett, Obituary of Alfred Deller, in *Early Music* 8 (1980): 43.

113 See, for instance, Henry Purcell, *Musique de scène – Airs d'opéras – Odes et Chants sacrés*, Deller Consort dir. Alfred Deller (Harmonia Mundi HMD 218, *rec. c.*1969).

114 Matthew Locke, *The Present Practice of Musick Vindicated against the Exceptions and New Way of Attaining Musick Lately Publish'd by Thomas Salmon, M.A.* (London, 1673), p. 19.

115 Morris, 'Voice Ranges, Voice Types, and Pitch', p. 132; Elisa Fraser Wilson, 'The Countertenor Voice in the Symphony Anthems of Henry Purcell: A Study of Range and Tessitura' (DMA dissertation, University of Illinois at Urbana-Champaign, 2003), p. 79.

Solo countertenor lines are another matter. Examining the range of Purcell's countertenor solos, Andrew Parrott argues that these lines were generally sung by high tenors.[116] Many of Purcell's countertenor solos descend as low as f or g (notes that require chest voice), yet they go no higher than a' or b' (notes available to a high tenor, particularly at the low Consort Pitch). Parrott's recordings and those by William Christie (mentioned above) successfully employ high tenors for almost all of these lines. The use of high tenors has a historical precedent in the form of the French *haute-contre* voice, which Neal Zaslaw and Mary Cyr have argued to be a high tenor, with the possible use of falsetto for the highest notes.[117] However, as yet there is no research on how the *haute-contre* might have influenced Restoration writing for countertenors. One of the French musicians employed at the English court in the 1660s, Nicholas Fleuri, was described as an *haute-contre*;[118] and there was also an *haute-contre*, Bertrand Gillet, in the group of French singers sent in 1676 by Louis XIV to entertain Charles II. In addition, two of the Chapel Royal countertenors – Alexander Damascene and Josiah Bouchier – were probably of French origin,[119] but nothing is known about where they trained as singers, so it is impossible to say whether or not they were exponents of the *haute-contre*. More research in this area would be welcome.

Alongside this tradition of high tenor voices, Parrott suggests that solo falsetto singing became established in England by the 1680s, probably inspired by the example of Italian falsettists and castratos. Two English singers who visited Italy seem subsequently to have cultivated the falsetto voice, if John Evelyn's reports can be trusted. In 1682 Evelyn described John Abell, 'newly return'd from Italy', as 'the famous Trebble. ... I never heard a more excellent voice, one would have sworne it had ben a Womans it was so high, & so well & skilfully manag'd'.[120] Three years later, Evelyn wrote that a Mr Pordage, again recently returned from Italy, sang 'with an excellent voice both Treble and Bass'.[121] Abell appeared as a soloist in Purcell's ode *Ye Tuneful Muses* (1686) with the range g–b', and also in *Sound the Trumpet, Beat the Drum* (1687) with the range b–b'. Little can be concluded from these notated ranges, however, because it is uncertain whether the odes of the 1680s were performed at high or low pitch.

Clearer evidence of the use of falsetto soloists is found in three of Purcell's odes of the 1690s. Here the range of solo parts has led Andrew Parrott to suggest that Purcell wrote for two types of countertenor – a 'high countertenor' who must have been a falsettist, plus the normal countertenor who probably sang with a chest

---

116 Parrott, 'Performing Purcell', p. 418; also see Olive Baldwin and Thelma Wilson, 'Alfred Deller, John Freeman and Mr Pate', *Music & Letters* 50 (1969): 103–10.

117 Neal Zaslaw, 'The Enigma of the Haute-Contre', *Musical Times* 115 (1974): 939–41; Mary Cyr, 'On Performing Eighteenth-Century Haute-Contre Roles', *Musical Times* 118 (1977): 291–5.

118 Holman, *Four and Twenty Fiddlers*, p. 290.

119 Peter Giles, *The History and Technique of the Counter-tenor: A Study of the Male High Voice Family* (Aldershot: Scolar, 1994), pp. 60 and 72.

120 *The Diary of John Evelyn*, ed. De Beer, vol. 4, p. 270 (27 January 1682).

121 Ibid., p. 403 (27 January 1685).

voice. The emergence of the solo falsettist is exemplified by the Chapel Royal singer John Howell (d. 1708), who was described as a 'High Countratenor' in Purcell's autograph of *Hail, bright Cecilia*.[122] Howell's solos in Purcell's works include the upper part in 'Hark each Tree' (*Hail, bright Cecilia*), with the range c'–d", and 'Crown the Altar' (*Celebrate this Festival*) with the range d'–d". In both cases Howell's parts are notated in the C2 clef, rather than the C3 clef that Purcell normally used for countertenor parts. Indeed, in French operas of the period, the *haute-contre* was always notated in the C3 clef, so here Purcell made a clear departure from French practice. Timothy Morris suggests other high countertenors available to Purcell were William Turner (whose solo in *Hail, bright Cecilia* has the range g–c") and possibly also Josiah Bouchier (whose solo in *Hail, bright Cecilia* has the range a–d").[123] But their parts use lower notes that would require chest voice, and none is notated in the C2 clef that is characteristic of Howell. (Interestingly, the C2 clef had already been used in Louis Grabu's *Albion and Albanius* for the part of Hermes, whose range g–c" goes almost as high as Howell's solos, but also a fourth lower. Unfortunately nothing is known about Grabu's cast, apart from the fact that it consisted of English performers.[124])

On the basis of the range of solo parts, Parrott suggests that Purcell juxtaposes the two types of countertenor in the duet 'Sound the Trumpet' in *Come ye Sons of Art* (1694).[125] The Countertenor 1 part (c♯'–e") suits a falsetto 'high countertenor', while the Countertenor 2 part (a–c♯") suits a high tenor if sung at low pitch. Unfortunately, because the duet does not survive in any seventeenth-century sources, there is no record of the original singers, or indeed whether Purcell distinguished the two parts via different clefs. On Parrott's 1988 recording, the upper part is sung by Timothy Wilson (falsettist) and the lower part by John Mark Ainsley (tenor).[126] As Bruce Wood remarks, dividing the duet between two different voice types:

> causes the lower type of countertenor line, when performed at an appropriate pitch, to spring into focus: its bottom notes, involving falsettists as they do in awkward changes of gear, lie perfectly for tenors, while in those duet passages in which both types of voice interweave lines often a third apart, the problems of balance, intractable if both singers are falsettists, simply melt away.[127]

---

122 Ob Mus.c.26, fol. 32r. The same designation of 'High Countratenor' was used for the upper vocal part in 'Hark each Tree' when it was published in *Orpheus Britannicus: A Collection of the Choicest Songs, for One, Two, and Three Voices ... The Second Book* (London, 1702), p. 157.

123 Morris, 'Voice Ranges, Voice Types and Pitch', pp. 140–41.

124 For details of the performance of *Albion and Albanius*, see Bryan White's Preface to Louis Grabu, *Albion and Albanius*, ed. Bryan White, The Purcell Society Edition Companion Series, vol. 1 (London: Stainer and Bell, 2007).

125 Parrott, 'Performing Purcell', p. 420.

126 Purcell, *Come Ye Sons of Art*, dir. Parrott.

127 Bruce Wood, Review of Purcell, *Come Ye Sons of Art*, dir. Parrott, in *Early Music* 18 (1990): 499.

Parrott's argument that there was a division between falsettists and high tenors is supported by the ranges of Purcell's countertenor parts and the clefs he used; nevertheless, another possibility remains to be researched – namely that tenors went into falsetto for their highest notes. Although such blending of registers does not seem to have occurred in France,[128] it was encouraged in the newer styles of Italian singing. Tosi recommended that singers should 'leave no Means untried, so to unite the feigned [falsetto] and the natural [chest] Voice'.[129] By the mid-eighteenth century it was usual for English tenors to sing falsetto at the top of their register, with a technique that was used by Robert Nugent Owenson (1744–1812) and Charles Dibdin (1745–1814). Indeed, Michael Kelly (1762–1826) was described as being unusual for using full voice rather than falsetto at the top of his range.[130] The history of the English tenor in the eighteenth century still needs to be written, but it is possible that some singers were beginning to blend their falsetto and tenor registers in the 1690s. Such blending may have been necessary for the two soloists in John Blow's 'Ode on the Death of Mr Henry Purcell', for instance, since it has some of the widest ranging countertenor parts of the period, spanning two octaves from d to d". A profitable topic for further research would be the ranges of tenor and countertenor parts in the music of Blow and his successors, which would place Parrott's hypotheses about Purcell's countertenors in a broader context.

Ornamentation

Purcell's contemporaries regarded ornamentation as a vital element of performance. As Roger North wrote, the 'sprinkling of discord or error' created by trills and other ornaments 'is like damask, grotesque, or any unaccountable variegation of colours, that renders a thing agreeable'.[131] Yet despite the importance of such adornments, they are notoriously difficult to describe verbally or represent in musical notation, a problem that North again described vividly:

> It is the hardest task that can be, to pen the manner of artificiall Gracing an upper part. It hath bin attempted, and in print, but with woefull effect. One that hears, with a direct intent to learne, may be shew'd the way by a notation, but

128 Andrew Parrott, 'Falsetto and the French: "Une toute autre marche"', *Basler Jahrbuch für historische Musikpraxis* 26 (2002): 135–6.

129 Tosi, *Observations on the Florid Song*, ed. Galliard, p. 23.

130 'In vigorous passages he never cheated the ear with the feeble wailings of falsetto'; James Boaden, *Memoirs of the Life of John Philip Kemble Esq. Including a History of the Stage from the Time of Garrick to the Present Period* (2 vols, London, 1825), vol. 1, p. 350. See also John Potter, 'The Tenor–Castrato Connection, 1760–1860', *Early Music* 35 (2007): 97–110.

131 Roger North, *Notes of Me: the Autobiography of Roger North*, ed. Peter Millard (Toronto: University of Toronto Press, 2000), p. 158; see also Wilson (ed.), *Roger North on Music*, p. 28.

> no man ever taught himself that way. The spirit of that art is incommunicable by wrighting, therefore it is almost inexcusable to attempt it.[132]

Over three centuries after Purcell's time, however, scholars have no option but to try to garner clues about ornamentation from written sources such as explicatory tables and annotated manuscripts. This section summarizes the existing state of research on Purcell's keyboard ornaments, then explores some avenues for future research on the hitherto little-studied area of vocal embellishments.

As with the other aspects of performance practice studied in this chapter, ornamentation conventions in Purcell's time were subject to considerable diversity. Individual performers were likely to have their own tastes in adornment, and different instruments or voices required different types of ornaments. Some performers used florid divisions in the Italian manner; others favoured small graces such as appoggiaturas and passing notes inspired by the French *agréments*; and there were also indigenous English traditions of embellishment. One risk in the study of historical ornamentation is that, as researchers seek to discern norms behind the multiplicity of individual musicians' habits, they may falsely assimilate local traditions with the perceived conventions of a period. This is the case with Howard Ferguson's 1964 study of Purcell's keyboard ornamentation.[133] In the late seventeenth century there existed a distinctive set of English keyboard ornaments with idiosyncratic symbols and names.[134] Yet Ferguson failed to recognize several of these English embellishments, notably the prepared mordent known as the 'beat'. By the 1990s Ferguson's re-reading of Purcell's ornaments had attained the status of orthodoxy, being followed by scholars such as Geoffrey Cox, Robert Klakowich and Barry Cooper, as well as by many performers.[135] Ferguson's theories were even repeated in Davitt Moroney's 1999 edition of Purcell's keyboard autograph, despite having been discredited several years earlier.[136] It is therefore important

132 Wilson (ed.), *Roger North on Music*, p. 149.
133 Printed in Henry Purcell, *Eight Suites* ed. Howard Ferguson, Purcell Complete Keyboard Works, vol. 1 (London: Stainer and Bell, 1964); and Henry Purcell, *Miscellaneous Keyboard Pieces*, ed. Howard Ferguson, Purcell Complete Keyboard Works, vol. 2 (London: Stainer and Bell, 1964).
134 Outlined in Kah-Ming Ng, 'Ornaments, §6: English Baroque', *Grove Music Online*, http://www.oxfordmusiconline.com, accessed 9 October 2009.
135 Geoffrey Cox (ed.), *Faber Early Organ Series: European Organ Music of the 16th and 17th Centuries, vol. 3: England 1660–1710* (London: Faber, 1986), pp. v–vi; Giovanni Battista Draghi, *Harpsichord Music*, ed. Robert Klakowich, Recent Researches in the Music of the Baroque Era, vol. 56 (Madison: A-R Editions, 1986), pp. xiii–xiv; Barry Cooper, 'Keyboard Music', in Ian Spink (ed.), *The Blackwell History of Music in Britain, vol. 3: The Seventeenth Century* (Oxford: Blackwell, 1992), p. 361. For a performance that follows Ferguson's prescriptions, see Henry Purcell, *Suites and Transcriptions for Harpsichord*, Terence Charlston (Naxos 8.553982, *rec.* 1997).
136 Henry Purcell, *Twenty Keyboard Pieces; and One by Orlando Gibbons: From Purcell's Autograph Manuscript in the British Library, MS Mus.1.*, ed. Davitt Moroney (London: Associated Board, 1999), pp. 12–14.

to devote a few paragraphs to the changing scholarly interpretations of Purcell's ornamentation practices in this genre.

Purcell's vocabulary of keyboard ornaments is defined in the 'Rules for Graces' first published in *The Harpsichord Master* (1697), which claimed they had been 'written by ye late famous Mr H Purcell at the request of a perticuler friend, & taken from his owne *Manuscript*'.[137] Subsequently the 'Rules' appeared in the posthumous third edition of Purcell's *Choice Collection of Lessons for the Harpsichord or Spinnet* (1699). The 'Rules' use the English terminology ('Shake', 'Beat', 'Forefall', and so on) as well as indigenous symbols, although some of the actual ornaments are very close to French keyboard practice. However, Ferguson declared that the 'Rules for Graces' were 'not altogether reliable'.[138] Besides correcting a misprint in the explanation of the broken chord ('Battery'), Ferguson emended Purcell's 'plain Note and Shake', renaming it the 'Backfall and Shake' and tying the initial appoggiatura to the following note (see Example 4.2). This emendation made Purcell's ornament into the equivalent of a French *tremblement appuyé*, a trill that lingers on the first upper note. H. Diack Johnstone, however, argues that Purcell's notation should be taken at face value, with a reiterated upper auxiliary, on the basis of the analogy to the 'Forefall and Shake' described by Matthew Locke in the prefatory material to *Melothesia* (1673).[139] The repeated upper auxiliary can help establish a pulse on long-held notes, and is particularly idiomatic on the harpsichord.

Ferguson was even more interventionist in his interpretation of Purcell's 'Beat'. Purcell's 'Rules' define the beat as a mordent approached by a lower auxiliary. Ferguson, however, argued that the beat should be a plain mordent akin to the French *pincé* (see Example 4.3). He speculated that Purcell's explanation of the beat should correspond to an ornament that he calls the 'Forefall and Beat' (which is not mentioned in the 'Rules'), suggesting that the 'correct explanation of the *Beat* and the name and sign for a *Forefall-&-Beat* were left out of the original engraving by mistake'.[140] One reason for Ferguson's emendation was that Purcell does indeed use a sign for a 'Forefall and Beat' (⁗) elsewhere in his keyboard music. Furthermore, Ferguson was convinced that the plain mordent was commonly used in seventeenth-century England.[141]

Johnstone, however, once again argues that Purcell's instructions for the beat should be taken at face value. Surveying a variety of definitions found in English manuscripts and printed treatises, he concludes that 'prior to 1749, the simple

---

137 *The Harpsichord Master* exists in a unique copy in the Auckland Public Library, New Zealand; a modern edition including facsimile reproductions of Purcell's instructions was published as *The Harpsichord Master 1697: Containing Instructions for Learners by Henry Purcell*, ed. Robert Petre (Wellington: Price Milburn Music; London: Faber, 1980).

138 Purcell, *Eight Suites*, ed. Ferguson.

139 H. Diack Johnstone, 'Ornamentation in the Keyboard Music of Henry Purcell and his Contemporaries', in Michael Burden (ed.), *Performing the Music of Henry Purcell* (Oxford: Clarendon, 1996), pp. 94–100.

140 Purcell, *Eight Suites*, ed. Ferguson, p. 26.

141 Howard Ferguson, *Keyboard Interpretation from the 14th to the 19th Century: an Introduction* (London: Oxford University Press, 1975), p. 150.

Example 4.2   'Plain Note and Shake': (a) as defined by Purcell; (b) as emended by Howard Ferguson.

Example 4.3   'Beat': (a) as defined by Purcell; (b) as emended by Howard Ferguson.

mordent was virtually unknown in England.'[142] Indeed, French authors such as Guillaume Nivers (1665) and Gilles Jullien (1690) defined the mordent as being prepared by an initial lower auxiliary in the same manner as Purcell.[143] According to Johnstone, the symbol described by Ferguson as the 'Forefall and Beat' should in fact be a compound ornament, where the lower auxiliary is restruck.[144] Example 4.4 shows his realization for the ornaments at the opening of Purcell's Voluntary for Double Organ, with lower auxiliaries for the beats and a repeated lower auxiliary for the symbol that indicates a forefall and beat. Very few organists nowadays start these ornaments with any lower auxiliaries at all, although this may reflect the difficulty of playing so many decorative notes on a nineteenth- or twentieth-century instrument with a sluggish action.

Johnstone's claim that the simple mordent was unknown in England is nevertheless contradicted by some sources from the early eighteenth century. A few harpsichordists of continental origin did equate the beat with a plain mordent. Charles Dieupart, who taught the Countess of Sandwich around 1700 and then worked in London from 1703 onwards, published his *Six Suittes* (1701)[145] with a bilingual *Explication des Marques* / *Rules for Graces*, in which a plain mordent is described as a *pincé* and also as a beat. A similar mingling of continental and English traditions is seen in the Babell manuscript, Lbl Add. 39569, copied by Charles Babell in the early 1700s. Babell came to England after working in

---

142 H. Diack Johnstone, 'The English Beat', in Robert Judd (ed.), *Aspects of Keyboard Music: Essays in Honour of Susi Jeans on the Occasion of her Seventy-Fifth Birthday* (Oxford: Positif Press, 1992), p. 42.

143 Neumann, *Ornamentation in Baroque and Post-Baroque Music*, pp. 419–20.

144 Johnstone, 'Ornamentation in the Keyboard Music of Henry Purcell', pp. 101–2.

145 Charles Dieupart, *Six suittes de clavessin* (Amsterdam, 1701).

Example 4.4   Purcell, Voluntary for Double Organ, bb. 1–2, with H. Diack Johnstone's realization of the ornaments.

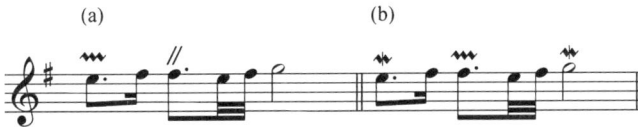

(a)   (b)

Example 4.5   Purcell, *A New Ground*, b. 6: (a) ornaments notated in *The Second Part of Musick's Hand-maid* (1689); (b) ornaments given by Charles Babell (Lbl Add. 39569, p. 35).

Hanover and The Hague, and he used a French notational style (including French ornament signs) in the manuscript.[146] The volume contains several Purcell keyboard movements, probably copied from the printed editions but with altered ornamentation.[147] The ornaments that are notated as beats in English printed sources are written by Babell in continental notation either as a plain mordent (*pincé*) or as a mordent with an initial lower auxiliary (*cheute et pincé*). Thus in *A New Ground* (the keyboard transcription of 'Here the Deities' from the 1683 St Cecilia's Day ode), the version in *The Second Part of Musick's Hand-maid* (London, 1689) uses a beat, whereas Babell prefers a simple mordent (see Example 4.5). In contrast, in the jig from *Abdelazer*, Purcell uses the English symbol and Babell uses the continental sign to indicate the same ornament – a mordent with initial lower auxiliary (see Example 4.6). Significantly, in Example 4.6 the ornamented note is approached by a rising step, and so the initial lower auxiliary is part of the overall melodic motion. With his own interpretation of English ornaments, Babell's manuscript shows an individuality that is typical of keyboard sources of the period. Such individuality

---

146 On Babell's biography and background, see Bruce Gustafson's preface to the facsimile edition of Lbl Add. 39569 in *London, British Library MS Add. 39569: Babell MS*, Introduction by Bruce Gustafson, 17th-Century Keyboard Music, vol. 19 (New York: Garland, 1987); see also Bruce Gustafson, 'Charles Babel', *Die Musik in Geschichte und Gegenwart. Personenteil* (17 vols, Kassel: Bärenreiter, 1999–2007), vol. 1, col. 1250; and Andrew Woolley, 'English Keyboard Sources and Their Contexts, c.1660–1720' (PhD dissertation, University of Leeds, 2008), pp. 198–221.

147 Purcell, *Eight Suites*, ed. Ferguson, p. 24.

Example 4.6   Purcell, Keyboard jig transcribed from *Abdelazer*, bb. 1–2: (a) ornaments notated in *A Choice Collection of Lessons* (1696), p. 60; (b) ornaments given by Charles Babell (Lbl Add. 39569, p. 61).

should warn scholars against making sweeping generalizations about keyboard ornamentation.

Compared to Johnstone's exhaustive study of keyboard ornamentation, the graces suitable for Purcell's vocal works have been little researched.[148] Some commentators maintain that extra ornamentation is unnecessary in Purcell's songs. In 1776 John Hawkins observed: 'We see in many of Purcell's songs the graces written at length and made a part of the composition'; for Hawkins, this was 'a manifest proof that in the performance of them little was meant to be trusted to the singer'.[149] In modern times Robert Donington and Bruce Wood have reiterated the belief that Purcell's vocal lines need little additional ornamentation.[150] Yet treatises of the late seventeenth century contain much advice on vocal ornamentation, and several manuscript song-books of the period embellish Purcell's vocal works with an array of graces.

The older style of Italianate singing, as practised until at least the mid seventeenth century, used such ornaments as the *trillo* (a rapid repetition of a single note) and the *gruppo* (an upper-note trill). Both were included alongside the *messa di voce* in the translation of Caccini's preface to *Le nuove musiche* printed in successive editions of Playford's *Introduction*, as discussed above. Similar ornaments seem to be described in Reggio's *Art of Singing* (1677), although his account is obscured by ambiguous terminology: he notates an upper-note trill and a single-note tremolo as vocal exercises, but does not define which of these ornaments he means by the term 'trill'.[151] However, some of these ornaments were clearly becoming obsolete during Purcell's lifetime. In the Italian singing styles of the later seventeenth century as

---

148 As Robert Shay comments in his review of Michael Burden (ed.), *Performing the Music of Henry Purcell*, (Oxford: Clarendon, 1996), in *Journal of Seventeenth-Century Music* 4/i (1998), para. 4.1, http://sscm-jscm.press.illinois.edu/v4/no1/shay.html (accessed 9 October 2009).

149 John Hawkins, *A General History of the Science and Practice of Music*, reprinted with a new introduction by Charles Cudworth (2 vols, New York: Dover, 1963; first published London: Novello, 1853), vol. 2, pp. 754 and 816.

150 Robert Donington, 'Performing Purcell's Music Today', in Imogen Holst (ed.), *Henry Purcell 1659–1695: Essays on his Music* (London: Oxford University Press, 1959), p. 81; Bruce Wood's advice can be found in his prefaces to volumes of the Purcell Society Edition, such as Purcell, *Symphony Songs*, p. xii.

151 Reggio, *The Art of Singing*, pp. 8, 13 and 20–21.

documented by Tosi, 'Divisions' and 'Shakes' were used sparingly.[152] Significantly, the 1697 edition of Playford's *Introduction* omitted the translation of Caccini and made no mention of the single-note *gruppo*, instead singling out the upper-note trill as 'the most principal Grace in Musick'.[153] Furthermore, copious Italianate ornamentation was not suitable for all types of songs. The *Synopsis of Vocal Musick* (1680) included a summary of the Caccini/Playford instructions, but the author explained that the *trillo* and *gruppo* 'are not to be used in Airy Songs, which require only a lively and cheerful kind of Singing, carried by the Air it self: but [only] in Passionate Musick, wherein must be kept a command of the breath'.[154] In other words, Purcell's tuneful theatre songs – such as 'When I have often Heard', from *The Fairy Queen* – could be sung with minimal use of trills.

Another aspect of Italianate ornamentation comprised the various techniques that were used for decorating cadences. Pepys was probably referring to this skill when he described Henry Cooke's 'strange mastery ... in making of extraordinary surprizing closes, that are mighty pretty'.[155] Reggio's treatise includes six examples of how to grace cadences, four of which are quoted in Example 4.7. Once again, the gap between the musical language of Reggio and Purcell is apparent: Reggio's unadorned cadences are simpler than those found in Purcell, with a slower harmonic rhythm, and only one of his examples has the melodic 4–3 motion favoured by Purcell. Yet the techniques used by Reggio – rhythmic intensification created by adding semiquavers, and the filling of melodic gaps with passing notes – remain relevant to Purcell, and occur in such song manuscripts as the Gresham autograph (see below).

Alongside the vocabulary of Italianate ornamentation, English singers also seem to have used adornments similar to those found in France, notably one-note appoggiatura-like figures. Many of these graces had been part of English ornamentation since the early seventeenth century (probably reflecting the influence of the French singers and lutenists who worked for Henrietta Maria) and had gained English names: thus the rising appoggiatura (*port de voix*) was termed a forefall, while the falling appoggiatura (*coulé*) was termed a backfall. The addition of appoggiaturas required less skill from a singer than trills, and could also enhance the points of emphasis in a melody. A well-known example of the application of one-note graces occurs in Purcell's 'If Music be the Food of Love', which exists in a G minor version without backfalls (published in *The Gentleman's Journal* in 1692) and in an A minor version with backfalls (*Comes Amoris ... The Fourth Book*,

---

152 Tosi, *Observations on the Florid Song*, ed. Galliard, pp. 51 and 58.

153 John Playford, *An Introduction to the Skill of Musick: In Three Books ... The Thirteenth Edition* (London, 1697), p. 31.

154 A.B., *Synopsis of Vocal Musick* (London, 1680), p. 44, reprinted in *Synopsis of Vocal Musick by A. B. Philo-Mus*, ed. Rebecca Herissone, Music Theory in Britain, 1500–1700: Critical Editions (Aldershot: Ashgate, 2006), p. 97; see also pp. 22 and 165–6.

155 *The Diary of Samuel Pepys*, eds Latham and Matthews, vol. 8, p. 59 (13 February 1667).

Example 4.7   Plain and ornamented cadences from Pietro Reggio, *The Art of Singing or a Treatise, Wherein is Shown How to Sing Well any Song Whatsoever* (Oxford, 1677), p. 31. 'L' and 'S' denote 'Loud' and 'Soft'.

1693).[156] Liberal use of forefalls and backfalls was also recommended in treatises on instrumental playing, notably John Lenton's violin tutor.[157]

Many clues about vocal ornamentation can be gleaned from manuscript versions of Purcell's songs. These sources vary greatly in their quantity of notated embellishments, but as yet have not been the subject of any systematic research. An example of a song-book with a small but significant amount of added embellishment is Purcell's Gresham autograph (Lg Safe 3). The book contains 45 songs by Purcell, mostly from his theatre works and odes, and mainly arranged for soprano and continuo. Robert Thompson and Margaret Laurie suggest that the book was perhaps intended for use in the informal concerts given at court by Purcell and various singers.[158] Whatever its exact function, the fact that this manuscript is an autograph source gives particular authority to its melodic lines, which often differ in ornamental detail from other sources of the same songs. Example 4.8 compares two passages of the song 'Lucinda is Bewitching Fair'

---

156 Both versions are quoted in Parrott, 'Performing Purcell', p. 428 and Robert Spencer, 'Singing Purcell's Songs', *Early Music Performer* 2 (1999): 13.

157 Lenton, *The Gentleman's Diversion*, p. 13; a facsimile of the relevant page is reproduced in Holman, *Four and Twenty Fiddlers*, p. 377.

158 See Laurie and Thompson's Preface to Purcell, *The Gresham Autograph*, pp. viii–ix. Thompson puts forward an alternative hypothesis linking the book with Lady Annabella Howard in Chapter 2, p. 49 of this volume.

Example 4.8   Purcell, 'Lucinda is Bewitching Fair' (from *Abdelazer*), bb. 1–2 and 16–17. Plain version as published in *Thesaurus Musicus: Being, a Collection of the Newest Songs Performed at His Majesties Theatres … The Fourth Book* (1695), pp. 6–7; ossia ornaments from the Gresham autograph, Lg Safe 3, fols 66v–67r.

(from *Abdelazer*) as found in *Thesaurus Musicus … The Fourth Book* (1695)[159] and the Gresham manuscript. In several places the Gresham manuscript introduces a four-note semiquaver flourish on the second beat of the bar (for the last syllable of a word), sometimes a third higher than the melodic line in *Thesaurus Musicus*. Example 4.9 compares extracts of 'Thus the Gloomy World' (from *The Fairy Queen*) as it appears in Purcell's partial autograph score (Lam 3) and the Gresham autograph. Variants in the Gresham autograph include rhythmic alterations (bb. 63–4), elaborated roulades (b. 88) and the filling in of thirds with passing notes (bb. 75 and 91). For both songs, the small adornments in the Gresham autograph should not be regarded as textual variants; such minor alterations were regularly introduced by scribes when copying music, and reflect the liberties taken by performers when interpreting a written text. Alan Howard describes these small notational discrepancies as the 'background variation' between different sources of the same piece.[160]

By contrast with the Gresham autograph, other manuscripts of the 1680s and 1690s show profuse ornamentation of the vocal line, usually with small graces such as appoggiaturas. Lbl Add. 29397 (*c.*1682–90) has embellished versions of Purcell's 'O Solitude' and 'From Silent Shades', as well as decorated songs by other composers such as Reggio's 'Arise, ye Subterranean Winds'.[161] Also rich in

---

159 John Hudgebutt, *Thesaurus Musicus: Being, a Collection of the Newest Songs Performed at His Majesties Theatres … The Fourth Book* (London, 1695).

160 See this volume, Chapter 3, p. 97. Rebecca Herissone suggests in her forthcoming monograph *Musical Creativity in Restoration England* that aspects of the notation of the Gresham autograph imply that Purcell was notating some pieces from memory, so it is possible that some of the ornamentation reflects memorized performances.

161 For Lbl Add. 29397's ornaments in 'O Solitude', see Henry Purcell, *Thirty Songs in Two Volumes*, ed. Timothy Roberts (2 vols, Oxford: Oxford University Press, 1995), vol. 1, pp. 30–35.

Example 4.9   Purcell, 'Thus the Gloomy World' (from *The Fairy Queen*), bb. 63–4 and 88–91. Plain version as in Lam 3, fol. 87r; ossia ornaments from the Gresham autograph, Lg Safe 3, fols 4r–5v (transposed to facilitate comparison).

appoggiaturas and other small graces is the version of 'Fairest Isle' found in Lbl Add. 40139, fols 41v–42r.[162] The Purcell songs in the Elizabeth Segar song-book (US-NH Osborn 9, dated 1692) – including 'From Silent Shades', 'If Love's a sweet Passion' (from *The Fairy Queen*), and 'Come if you Dare' and 'Fairest Isle' (from *King Arthur*) – are even more lavishly adorned.[163] Example 4.10 shows sections of 'From Silent Shades' (Bess of Bedlam) as embellished in Add. 29397 and the Segar song-book. The printed version of this mad song (*Choice Ayres ... The Fourth Book*, 1683) has virtually no ornaments, either because of the difficulty of representing trills and other graces in movable type, or because the printed edition needed to appeal to the broadest possible market of amateur singers. The manuscript versions add trills on the dotted notes at cadences (as in b. 2), and use forefalls and backfalls to fill leaps of a third or to emphasize significant notes (such as the g' on 'shades', b. 1). The Segar song-book also notates portamento (with a slide from g' to d' at the start of b. 2), as well as the melodic decoration known as a 'springer' (b. 25).

---

162 For a specimen of these ornaments, see the critical notes in ibid., vol. 1, p. 55.
163 For general comments on the Segar song-book, see Gloria Rose, 'A New Purcell Source', *Journal of the American Musicological Society* 25 (1972): 230–36.

Example 4.10   Purcell, 'From Silent Shades' (Bess of Bedlam), bb. 1–3 and 23–6:
(a) ornaments from Lbl Add. 29397, fol. 71r; (b) ornaments from
Elizabeth Segar Songbook, US-NH Osborn 9, fol. 7r.

It is hard to gauge to what extent these heavily adorned songs are typical.
They may represent one extreme of performance practice, namely those singers
who favoured the most florid ornamentation; or the embellished versions might
be explained as rare instances when all the ornaments usually improvised were
written down. This second explanation is plausible for the Elizabeth Segar song-
book, which was presumably made for an amateur who would need ornaments
notated as part of her lessons.[164] Professional singers, by contrast, would look
askance at written-down graces. Tosi asserted that a 'well instructed' singer should
be 'so familiar' with appoggiaturas 'by continual Practice, that ... he will laugh at
those Composers that mark them'.[165] Similarly, Roger North wrote in the 1720s:
'There are elegances in passing from one note or syllable to another, well knowne
to all good singers, which by imitation may be communicated to beginners, but

---

164 Writing of the first half of the seventeenth century, Edward Huws Jones likewise notes
that 'manuscripts compiled for amateur singers ... usually give the fullest indications
of ornamentation'; see *The Performance of English Song*, p. 52.
165 Tosi, *Observations on the Florid Song*, ed. Galliard, pp. 38–9.

otherwise scarce expressible. The most skillfull of the elder Itallians leav all those matters to the performers, and write their musick plain.'[166]

Further evidence supporting the use of plentiful embellishment is found in treatises that instruct where to place ornaments. Reggio suggested in his *Art of Singing* that trills be put on every dotted note, particularly those in descending passages.[167] The 1697 edition of Playford's *Introduction to the Skill of Musick* recommended trills 'on all Descending *Prick'd Crotchets*, also when the *Note* before is in the same Line or Space with it, and generally before a Close, either in the middle, or at the end of a Song'.[168] Similar incitements to copious ornamentation are found in treatises directed at instrumentalists. A manuscript set of 'Rules' for recorder ornaments (partly derived from the *Compleat Flute-Master*, 1695) recommended that 'all Ascending Prick't Notes are Beaten. [A]ll Descending are shaked; all sharpes are shaked ascending or falling. Never shake a quaver nor Semiquaver.'[169] The cumulative weight of such evidence challenges Hawkins's view that Purcell's melodic lines need no further ornamentation. Indeed, recent recordings show how historically informed performers are increasingly willing to incorporate graces into their performances. Carolyn Sampson, for example, makes judicious use of forefalls and backfalls in her 2006 recording of 'From Silent Shades' and 'O Solitude';[170] the 2008 recording of *Dido and Aeneas* by Sarah Connolly (Dido) and the Orchestra of the Age of Enlightenment also makes good use of appoggiaturas, as well as some more ambitious ornaments such as the quaver divisions introduced by Belinda (Lucy Crowe) in 'Thanks to these Lonesome Vales'.[171] Such adornments are not the only way to sing Purcell, but they are certainly in the spirit of several of the manuscript song-books of the 1680s and 1690s. For singers experimenting with historically appropriate ornamentation, a thorough study of embellishment in manuscript sources would be a valuable addition to the existing research on Restoration performance styles.

Rhythmic Alteration

French musicians of the seventeenth century were renowned for their subtle modification of notated rhythms in performance. The principal forms of rhythmic alteration are *notes inégales* (in which pairs of notes notated in equal values are

---

166 Chan and Kassler, *Roger North's The Musicall Grammarian*, p. 203.

167 Reggio, *The Art of Singing*, pp. 18–21. Reggio's printed collection of *Songs* (1680) indicates frequent trills with the symbol 'tr.', sometimes found in every bar, as in 'The Thief' (p. 5).

168 Playford, *An Introduction to the Skill of Musick … Thirteenth Edition*, p. 31.

169 Lbl Add. 35043, fol. 125r; transcribed in Thurston Dart, 'Recorder "Gracings" in 1700', *Galpin Society Journal* 12 (1959): 93–4.

170 Henry Purcell, *Victorious Love*, Carolyn Sampson (BIS-SACD-1536, *rec.* 2006).

171 Purcell, *Dido and Aeneas*, dir. Kenny and Devine.

performed unevenly) and overdotting (in which dotted notes are held for longer than their notated value). From the mid 1960s until the early 1990s there was heated scholarly debate both about the precise nature of rhythmic alteration in France, and about whether such practices were used elsewhere in Europe.[172] The debate was strongest with regard to Germans such as Bach, but it also uncovered evidence from England. As we have seen, Restoration musicians were strongly influenced by French performance styles (notably with the court's enthusiasm for singers and instrumental techniques from France), but they were not completely Frenchified. The scholarly debate about rhythmic alteration petered out in the mid 1990s without any firm conclusions being reached about English practices; however, modern-day performers have offered a variety of rhythmic interpretations of Purcell's music, ranging from William Christie's generous use of *notes inégales* to Robert King's literal adherence to the notated rhythms.

In the mid 1960s Howard Ferguson and Robert Donington assembled evidence for the use of *notes inégales* in England.[173] By contrast with the wealth of documentation available in France, there are only three English treatises that mention rhythmic alteration. Mary Burwell's manuscript lute tutor (c.1668–71) recommends playing a passage of ascending quavers in 3/4 as dotted rhythms, because 'by stealing halfe a note from one note and bestoweing of it upon the next note that will make the playing of the Lute more aerie and skipping'.[174] Roger North makes some rather vague comments on rhythmic alteration, suggesting that a passage of stepwise rising crotchets 'differs not much from' dotted rhythms or lilting triplet rhythms.[175] Finally, Anselm Bayly's *Practical Treatise on Singing and Playing* (1771) recommends that unequal notes be avoided in semiquaver melismas in Purcell's anthem *O Give Thanks*, implying that some singers were still using inequality at this late date.[176]

More convincing than these scattered treatises is the evidence of rhythmic inequality that can be found in the notation of compositions by Purcell and other Restoration musicians. Several pieces survive in two versions – one notated with even notes, the other with dotted rhythms – suggesting that copyists struggled to notate the subtle lilting rhythms of *notes inégales*. (As Bacilly advised French singers, dotted rhythms should be performed 'as delicately and subtly as possible', avoiding the 'jerky or jumping style typical of the old "Gigue"'.[177]) Examples of Purcell's rhythmic discrepancies were listed by Ferguson and Donington in the 1960s, and more have been unearthed by editors in subsequent decades. For pieces

---

172 The debate is summarized in Stephen Hefling, *Rhythmic Alteration in Seventeenth- and Eighteenth-Century Music: Notes Inégales and Overdotting* (New York: Schirmer, 1993), p. xi.

173 Howard Ferguson, 'Purcell's Harpsichord Music', *Proceedings of the Royal Musical Association* 91 (1964–65): pp. 7–9; Robert Donington, 'A Problem of Inequality', *Musical Quarterly* 53 (1967): pp. 514–17.

174 Quoted in Ferguson, 'Purcell's Harpsichord Music': 7; Hefling, *Rhythmic Alteration in Seventeenth- and Eighteenth-Century Music*, pp. 51–2.

175 Wilson (ed.), *Roger North on Music*, pp. 223–4.

176 Hefling, *Rhythmic Alteration in Seventeenth- and Eighteenth-Century Music*, pp. 53–4.

177 Bacilly, *A Commentary upon the Art of Proper Singing*, ed. Caswell, p. 118.

Example 4.11   Purcell, 'Fairest Isle', bb. 1–4: (a) rhythms as notated in *Orpheus Britannicus* (1698), p. 83; (b) rhythms given in *Apollo's Banquet ... The Second Book* (1691), sig. F1v.

in 3/4, it is usually the quavers in stepwise passages that are subject to inequality, particularly if marked by slurs. This is in keeping with the French tradition that inequality should be applied to notes half the length of the beat in triple time. One of the best-known examples is the song 'Fairest Isle': in *Orpheus Britannicus* (1698)[178] the melisma on 'isles' is notated with even quavers, whereas the instrumental version in *Apollo's Banquet ... The Second Book* (1691)[179] uses dotted rhythms here (see Example 4.11).[180] Similarly, the ritornello in 'With Trumpets and Shouts' from the 1684 ode *From those Serene and Rapturous Joys* is found in a keyboard version with dotted rhythms, rather than the equal quavers of Purcell's autograph score in Lbl R.M. 20.h.8.[181] Although these occurrences of notated inequality are mostly found in stepwise passages, they sometimes appear on disjunct figures, as in the Second Act Tune of *Distress'd Innocence*. Here the slurred falling quaver figure in Ob Tenbury 785 is given as a dotted rhythm in the printed *Collection of Ayres, Compos'd for the Theatre* of 1697 (see Example 4.12, bb. 4–5).[182]

There are fewer examples of rhythmic inequality in Purcell's duple-metre works. One instance observed by Ferguson is in the keyboard Almand in G major (Z662/ii): this is notated with equal semiquavers in Och Mus. 1177, and with dotted semiquavers and demisemiquavers in Purcell's *Choice Collection of Lessons* (1696).[183] As Ferguson suggested, 'something halfway between the two rhythms may well

---

178   Henry Purcell, *Orpheus Britannicus: A Collection of all the Choicest Songs for One, Two, and Three Voices* (London, 1698).

179   Henry Playford, *Apollo's Banquet: Containing Variety of the Newest Tunes, Ayres, Jiggs and Minuets, for the Treble-Violin ... The Second Book* (London, 1691).

180   This variant was first noted by Margaret Laurie in a letter in *Musical Times* 105 (1964): 198. As can be seen from Example 4.11, the 1691 instrumental version also lowers the a" in b. 3.

181   Christopher Hogwood, 'Creating the Corpus: The "Complete Keyboard Music" of Henry Purcell', in Christopher Hogwood (ed.), *The Keyboard in Baroque Europe* (Cambridge and New York: Cambridge University Press, 2003), p. 89.

182   Henry Purcell, *A Collection of Ayres, Compos'd for the Theatre* (London, 1697).

183   Both versions are printed in Purcell, *Eight Suites*, ed. Ferguson, pp. 7–8.

Example 4.12   Purcell, Second Act Tune from *Distress'd Innocence*, bb. 3–5: (a) rhythms as notated in Ob Tenbury 785; (b) rhythms given in *A Collection of Ayres* (1697).

have been played, that is to say, triplets (more or less)'.[184] The Almand shows that Purcell was following the French convention whereby inequality in duple metres was applied at the level of the quarter beat (in other words, the semiquavers here; the beat is evidently a crotchet, despite the ¢ time signature).[185]

All the above instances are of long–short inequality, but Purcell also used the short–long rhythm (the so-called Scotch Snap or Lombardic rhythm). Often he notated this pattern, but elsewhere it can be implied by a slurred pair of quavers. In his autograph score of the symphony anthem *My Heart is Inditing*, for example, the first treble has Scotch Snaps in bb. 128–9, whereas Violin 1 has pairs of slurred quavers that should be synchronized with the voices (see Example 4.13). A similar example can be found in the air 'One charming Night' in Act II of *The Fairy Queen*, as copied by the anonymous scribe FQ1 in the partial autograph manuscript Lam 3 (fol. 31r): here the Scotch Snaps in the vocal part are written as slurred pairs of quavers in the recorders (bb. 1 and 12). Thus rhythmic notation in Purcell's music is ambiguous: a slurred pair of quavers may indicate a Scotch Snap as in these examples here, or long–short rhythms as in the Second Act Tune from *Distress'd Innocence*. The exact type of inequality may have been left to the discretion of the performer, which might explain why no hard and fast rules about *notes inégales* are found in English treatises of the period.

Certainly modern-day performers have shown considerable diversity in their attitude towards *notes inégales*. Robert King's recordings mostly follow the rhythms as notated; by contrast, William Christie makes extensive use of *notes inégales* in his 1989 account of *The Fairy Queen*. In the air 'If Love's a sweet Passion' he interprets the slurred pairs of quavers as *notes inégales* – mostly long–short, but with Scotch Snaps on the pairs immediately before the cadences in bb. 29 and 41. In 'Now the Night is chas'd away', the soprano soloist uses the same lilting

---

184   Ferguson, 'Purcell's Harpsichord Music': 8. John Byrt suggests in 'Writing the Unwritable', *Musical Times* 138 (1997): 18–24 that this almand requires a gentle inequality, as opposed to the sharper *saccadé* effect he recommends for the dotted rhythms in the D minor 'Bell-barr' almand (marked 'Very slow').

185   Hefling, *Rhythmic Alteration in Seventeenth- and Eighteenth-Century Music*, p. 7.

Example 4.13 Purcell, *My Heart is Inditing*, bb. 128–9. Violin 1 and Treble 1 parts from Purcell's autograph manuscript, Lbl R.M. 20.h.8, fols 56v–57r.

rhythms regardless of whether passages are notated as slurred semiquavers (bb. 22–3) or as dotted semiquavers and demisemiquavers (bb. 16–17).[186] This *inégale* interpretation of the slurred pairs is in keeping with Purcell's use of the slur elsewhere, although Curtis Price criticized Christie for obliterating the complexity of the composer's rhythms: 'Poor Purcell needn't have bothered with all those dots and beams, because in this performance the intricate lines are forced into regular patterns.'[187] In Christie's defence, it must be said that he takes the piece at such a rapid tempo that the singer could not have projected the subtle differences in rhythm that Price favours.

Particular challenges of rhythmic interpretation are posed by the first sections of Purcell's overtures. Since the 1950s much scholarly ink has been spilt over how to interpret the eighteenth-century French overture: Thurston Dart and his followers suggested that the dotted rhythms should be exaggerated by lengthening the dotted note and compressing any upbeat tirades, whereas Frederick Neumann lambasted such overdotting as a 'delusion'.[188] Most of these discussions focused on a repertory slightly later than Purcell, although Dart declared that Purcell's overtures 'bear the clear impress of the French style' and he consequently recommended the use of 'double-dotting' and 'the rhythmical French style of bowing'.[189] But no researcher has as yet uncovered any clear-cut evidence from Restoration England to support the use of overdotting in overtures. A manuscript instruction to recorder players to 'stay long on yᵉ Prickt Crotchet'[190] can be read either as a direction to apply overdotting or as a description of the difference between normal and dotted crotchets. The first English writer who can

186 Purcell, *The Fairy Queen*, dir. Christie.
187 Curtis Price, Review of Henry Purcell, *The Fairy Queen*, Les Arts Florissants, dir. William Christie (Harmonia Mundi, HMC 901308.09, *rec.* 1989), in *Early Music* 18 (1990): 494.
188 For a summary of the debate, see Hefling, *Rhythmic Alteration in Seventeenth- and Eighteenth-Century Music*, pp. x–xi and 145.
189 Thurston Dart, *The Interpretation of Music*, Hutchinson's University Library, Music Series (4th edn, London: Hutchinson, 1967), p. 125.
190 Dart, 'Recorder "Gracings" in 1700': 93.

plausibly be interpreted as referring to overdotting is Roger North in his *Musicall Grammarian* of 1728, which describes the sharp rhythms (♩. ♪) of 'branles' in the style of Lully.[191]

Moreover, many of Purcell's overtures eschew the fiery French style so suited to overdotting. In an early overture such as that of *Welcome to All the Pleasures* (1683), the ♪♫ rhythms are part of the contrapuntal texture, rather than upbeat tirades that can be easily compressed. In later overtures such as those to *Bonduca* (1695) or *Abdelazer* (1695), the ♪♫ rhythms have a melodious character in which anything more than a slight sharpening seems inappropriate. Yet the rhythms of Purcell's overtures can be interpreted in a variety of ways, as is evident on recordings of *Dido and Aeneas*. Trevor Pinnock (1988) adheres strictly to the notation of the first section of the overture; Emmanuelle Haïm (2003) performs the first section at a vigorous tempo, with overdotting; Elizabeth Kenny and Steven Devine (2008) favour a slower tempo, slightly sharpening the dotted rhythms and interpreting the slurred quavers in b. 7 as Scotch Snaps.[192] Given the lack of consensus about rhythmic alteration, there remains plenty of scope for further experimentation in this area by modern-day performers.

Continuo Practices

Diversity can also be observed in continuo playing, which was not a single unified technique in Purcell's day. Rather, it drew on a variety of traditions, including the practice of doubling the parts of a polyphonic texture. The heterogeneity of continuo techniques is evident even in terminology: the Italianate 'basso continuo' was found alongside the Frenchified 'Bass Continued' and the native 'thorough-bass' and 'throughbass' in 1680s London. Furthermore, in the years immediately after Purcell's death there were major changes in continuo playing in England: from the late 1690s figures were used far more frequently in bass lines, as is evident from posthumously published sources of Purcell's music such as *Orpheus Britannicus*;[193] and in the 1700s the arrival of Italian string players in London led to the first regular use of violoncellos and double basses. It is hence important to disentangle the continuo practices of Purcell's lifetime from those used in early eighteenth-century performances of his music. The following section outlines the current state of research on the bass instruments likely to have been used in Purcell's time and at which points in a piece they played. It also offers evidence for how styles of realization varied according to genre, with

---

191 Chan and Kassler (eds), *Roger North's The Musicall Grammarian*, p. 184; Hefling, *Rhythmic Alteration in Seventeenth- and Eighteenth-Century Music*, pp. 80–81.

192 Purcell, *Dido and Aeneas*, dir. Pinnock; Purcell, *Dido and Aeneas*, dir. Haïm; Purcell, *Dido and Aeneas*, dir. Kenny and Devine.

193 Price, *Henry Purcell and the London Stage*, p. 243.

the tradition of polyphonic keyboard accompaniment still strong in church music and consort pieces.

A wide variety of instruments was available to play the bass line in Restoration London. Andrew Parrott lists the continuo instruments recommended in song publications during Purcell's lifetime, noting that the theorbo, lute and/or bass viol are almost always named; keyboard instruments such as the harpsichord and organ start to be advertised on the title pages of printed song-books only from 1687 onwards.[194] As is well known, organs were found in many taverns as well as private homes – Purcell owned a chamber organ, to judge from his widow's will[195] – and thus could be used for secular songs and consort music as well as sacred genres.

The most likely bowed instruments used for bass lines in Purcell's day were the bass viol and bass violin. By the 1680s the bass viol was associated mainly with amateur players; for instance, North records how his brother Francis (Lord Keeper of the Great Seal) played the bass viol in private performances of Purcell's trio sonatas, with the composer on the harpsichord.[196] In contrast, the bass violin was usually played by professional musicians; it was distinguished by the fact that its lowest string was tuned to B♭, and it was a slightly larger and more powerful instrument than the violoncello. Purcell specified the bass violin in the printed score of *Dioclesian* and his autograph of *Hail, bright Cecilia*, and its use is also implied by the low B♭s found in the Symphony and the bass solo 'The Father's brave' of the 1695 ode *Who can from Joy Refrain?* in Purcell's manuscript score. It seems that the violoncello arrived in London as late as the 1700s, brought by Italians such as Nicola Haym.

There is no evidence of the double bass being used in London during Purcell's lifetime. The first player to be named as a specialist double bassist in London was the Italian Joseph Saggione (also known as Giuseppe Fedeli), who in 1707 was listed as the 'Double Base' in the Haymarket theatre orchestra.[197] An earlier apparent reference to a 'Double Base', in John Blow's anthem *Lord, Who shall dwell in Thy Tabernacle?* (probably written in the early 1680s), probably denotes a viol tuned a fourth or fifth lower than the normal bass viol and used to play bass parts at written pitch.[198] Given the lack of evidence for a 16 ft bass, ensembles such as Andrew Parrott's Taverner Players have performed Purcell's music without double bass;[199] this enhances the lightness of the music, particularly where bass lines are swift moving, as in the second half of the overture to *Dido and Aeneas*.

---

194   Parrott, 'Performing Purcell', pp. 395–7.

195   Zimmerman, *Henry Purcell, 1659–1695. His Life and Times*, p. 283.

196   Wilson (ed.), *Roger North on Music*, p. 47.

197   Peter Holman, 'Purcell's Orchestra', *Musical Times* 137 (1996): 18; Philip H. Highfill, Kalman A. Burnim and Edward A. Langhans, *A Biographical Dictionary of Actors, Actresses, Musicians, Dancers, Managers and Other Stage Personnel in London 1660–1800* (16 vols, Carbondale: Southern Illinois University Press, 1973–93), vol. 13, pp. 169–70; Judith Milhous and Robert Hume, *Vice Chamberlain Coke's Theatrical Papers 1706–1715: Edited from the Manuscripts in the Harvard Theatre Collection and Elsewhere* (Carbondale: Southern Illinois University Press, 1982), pp. 30–31.

198   Holman, *Four and Twenty Fiddlers*, p. 410; Parrott, 'Performing Purcell', p. 404.

199   As on Parrott's recordings from his earliest reading of Purcell, *Dido and Aeneas*, Taverner

Nevertheless, a surprising number of ensembles continue to use a double bass for Purcell's music. A 16 ft bass is present throughout Robert King's recordings of the odes, and on recent accounts of *Dido and Aeneas* directed by Emmanuelle Haïm and Valentin Radu.[200] A possible justification for using the double bass in some of Purcell's works of the 1690s is that several of these pieces were performed in subsequent decades with the addition of a 16 ft bass. For *Hail, bright Cecilia* (1692), for instance, an incomplete set of performing parts (Ob Mus.c.27, fols 3–25, possibly copied by Bernard Gates (1686–1773)) includes a part for the 'Contr: Bass'. The double bass plays throughout the ode (except in ''Tis Nature's Voice'), although in some movements, such as the opening Symphony, it doubles the timpani part.[201] The same ode also exists in a mid eighteenth-century orchestration in Lbl R.M. 24.e.9, again with use of the double bass.[202] Nowadays, however, such eighteenth-century re-orchestrations are often regarded as inauthentic bastardizations of Purcell's originals.

A further question regarding continuo instrumentation is whether the bowed bass should play throughout pieces for voices and instruments. The few wisps of surviving evidence suggest that the bowed bass is a member of the string band and should play primarily in those instrumental sections and choruses where the rest of the band is playing. In concerted music for the court such as odes and symphony anthems, Peter Holman suggests that solo vocal sections were accompanied by chordal instruments alone. He bases this interpretation partly on his examination of the Oxford collection of performing parts for university odes, with the caveat that Oxford practices may not have applied at the court.[203] Evidence of Purcell's own practice can be found in the part-autograph parts for the symphony anthem *My Song shall be Alway*; here the bowed bass plays only with the upper strings.[204] It is hard to gauge the representativeness of one set of parts, but Holman's evidence raises the possibility that many vocal solos, even those with active bass lines or ground basses, should not use a bowed bass.

Similar considerations about the allocation of continuo instruments apply to Purcell's stage music. In the theatre there may have been a division between movements for string band (played without chordal continuo instruments) and the vocal numbers (played with chordal accompaniment). Such a separation is implied by the text for Thomas Shadwell's adaptation of *The Tempest* (1674), where the opening stage direction states that 'the Band of 24 Violins, with the Harpiscals and Theorbo's which accompany the Voices, are plac'd between the Pit and the

---

Choir and Players, dir. Andrew Parrott (Chandos ABRD 1034, *rec.* 1981) onwards.

200 Purcell, *Complete Odes and Welcome Songs*, dir. King; Purcell, *Dido and Aeneas*, dir. Haïm; Purcell, *Dido and Aeneas*, Ama Deus Baroque Ensemble, dir. Valentin Radu (Lyrichord LEMS 8057, *rec.* 2007).

201 For details, see Purcell, *Ode for St Cecilia's Day 1692*, ed. Hogwood.

202 See Sandra Mangsen, 'New Sources for Odes by Purcell and Handel from a Collection in London, Ontario', *Music & Letters* 81 (2000): 38–9, where the manuscript shelfmark is incorrectly given as Lk.24.e.9.

203 Holman, 'Original Sets of Parts for Restoration Concerted Music at Oxford'.

204 Och Mus. 1188–9; Holman, *Four and Twenty Fiddlers*, p. 406.

Stage', thus implying that only the chordal instruments played with the singers.[205] This division partly reflects the origin of the violin band as a self-sufficient string consort, playing dance music without any need for a chordal instrument.[206] By contrast, instruments such as the lute and harpsichord were strongly associated with singers, being used with them for rehearsals before a production opened. The division of continuo instruments was prevalent in the operas of Lully, in which Graham Sadler argues that the dances and overtures were played by strings alone, whereas chordal continuo instruments were used for the solo vocal numbers, the choruses and some *ritournelles* scored for less than the full five-part string band.[207] Such practices were brought to England by Grabu's *Albion and Albanius* (1685). The printed score of Grabu's opera is modelled on the Ballard scores of Lully's stage works, and makes a similar division between continuo instruments. While the vocal sections, choruses and ritornelli have a figured bass part labelled 'The BASS continued' (a literal translation of the French *basse continue*), the Overture and most of the dances have a bass line that lacks figures and is not labelled as 'The BASS continued'.[208] As Holman notes, this distinction may suggest that 'the songs were accompanied by the continuo with an associated group of two violins and oboes/recorders to play the symphonies and ritornelli, while the dances were played by the string band alone'.[209] Interestingly, the choruses (which are doubled by the strings) are printed with two bass lines, suggesting that here the bowed bass and the chordal continuo instruments played together.

It is debatable how far this division in continuo instrumentation can be mapped onto Purcell's major stage works. His printed score of *Dioclesian* is not as clear in its patterns of figuring and labelling bass lines as *Albion and Albanius*. Although the First Music and Second Music have no figuring (as in Lully's and Grabu's operas), there are two bars of figuring in the Overture.[210] Nonetheless, the notion of a split orchestra is a thought-provoking one, and would accord with Michael Burden's recent suggestion that 'the more elaborate the drama, the more likely the band was to be found employed in a variety of locations and ensembles' around the playhouse.[211] Furthermore, if bowed bass instruments are excluded from the airs for voice and continuo, the lutenist or harpsichordist must devise realizations that give sufficient emphasis and momentum to active bass lines. So a ground bass air,

205 Thomas Shadwell, *The Tempest, or, The Enchanted Island. A Comedy* (London, 1674), p. 1.
206 Peter Holman, 'Reluctant Continuo', *Early Music* 9 (1981): 75–8.
207 Graham Sadler, 'The Role of the Keyboard Continuo in French Opera, 1673–1776', *Early Music* 8 (1980): 148–57; see also Sadler, 'The *Basse Continue* in Lully's Operas: Evidence Old and New', in Jérôme de La Gorce and Herbert Schneider (eds), *Quellenstudien zu Jean-Baptiste Lully/L'oeuvre de Lully: Etudes des Sources – Hommage à Lionel Sawkins*, Musikwissenschaftliche Publikationen, vol. 13 (Hildesheim: Olms, 1999), pp. 382–97.
208 Lewis Grabu, *Albion and Albanius: an Opera. Or, Representation in Musick* (London, 1687).
209 Holman, 'Reluctant Continuo': 77.
210 Henry Purcell, *The Vocal and Instrumental Musick of The Prophetess, or the History of Dioclesian* (London, 1691), p. 9.
211 Michael Burden, 'Where Did Purcell Keep his Theatre Band?', *Early Music* 37 (2009): 436.

such as 'Music for a While' (from *Oedipus*), could be realized with a broken-chord accompaniment similar to that in Purcell's keyboard transcription of 'Here the Deities' (from the 1683 St Cecilia's Day Ode).

The strongest evidence that the string band in the theatre might play without chordal continuo is found in the posthumous *Collection of Ayres, Compos'd for the Theatre* (1697). This collection of theatre overtures and dance movements consists of four printed part-books for the four string parts; there is no mention of the continuo, nor any figures in the Bassus part. It thus could be performed by just the string band. Yet within a decade of Purcell's death, figured basses were being added to the *Ayres*, probably for concert or domestic use rather than theatre performance. Margaret Laurie explains that one copy of the bass part of the *Ayres* has figures added in an early eighteenth-century hand, and a manuscript scored up from the printed part-books contains figures (US-LAuc fP985/M4/C697).[212] Peter Holman's recording performs the *Ayres* in their concert order (starting each suite with the Overture, rather than the First and Second Act Tunes that would herald a theatre performance) and he also adds keyboard continuo (as was evidently used in some concert performances of the 1700s).[213]

As for the continuo instruments used to accompany singers in Purcell's stage works, Curtis Price and Judith Milhous suggest that in ordinary dramas there probably was little need for a harpsichord. There are only four documented occasions in Purcell's lifetime of harpsichords being used in theatre music.[214] For simple songs without instrumental ritornelli, the theorbo and guitar would have been convenient options, particularly as they could easily be used on stage or by the singers for self-accompaniment.[215] The guitar may have been the continuo instrument of choice in *Dido and Aeneas*: as already mentioned, the Chelsea libretto specifies two guitar dances, and a strummed accompaniment suits the harmonic and rhythmic patterns of several movements. There is no direct evidence of the continuo instruments used in Purcell's dramatick operas of the 1690s; but given the scale of the productions at the Dorset Garden Theatre, performers should not feel bound to follow Price and Milhous's scepticism about the use of harpsichords. What is clear is that Purcell's stage works require more variety of continuo scoring than is suggested by the Purcell Society's editions, which supply a keyboard realization for every movement.

The question of how continuo players realized their parts has been complicated by recent research that has demonstrated that techniques differed depending on the

---

212 Henry Purcell, *Dramatic Music, Part I*, ed. Margaret Laurie, The Works of Henry Purcell, vol. 16 (new edn, London: Novello, 2007), p. xii.

213 Henry Purcell, *Ayres for the Theatre*, The Parley of Instruments, dir. Peter Holman (Hyperion CDA66212, *rec.* 1986).

214 Curtis Price and Judith Milhous, 'Harpsichords in the London Theatres, 1697–1715', *Early Music* 18 (1990): 39.

215 Curtis A. Price, *Music in the Restoration Theatre: with a Catalogue of Instrumental Music in the Plays, 1665–1713*, Studies in Musicology, vol. 4 (Ann Arbor: UMI Research Press, 1979), pp. 78–80.

genre and style of a piece. This diversity reflects the varied origins of continuo playing in the late sixteenth and early seventeenth centuries. Contrapuntal pieces such as motets required polyphonic accompaniment, where the keyboard player doubled all the contrapuntal lines in the texture, often reading from a score or tablature of the piece. (The continuo part in such a piece is sometimes called *basso seguente*, because it doubles whichever is the lowest voice.) Opera and monodic songs were accompanied by basso continuo, where the player added chords above the (usually figured) bass line. The division between these two styles of playing was made by German and Italian theorists of the seventeenth century,[216] but can also be observed in England during Purcell's time. A chordal realization is appropriate for Purcell's secular vocal works, including his theatre songs and odes; advice on making such a realization can be found in John Blow's manuscript 'Rules for Playing of a Through Bass upon Organ & Harpsicon'.[217] For Purcell's consort music and church compositions, however, the older style of polyphonic doubling is appropriate, as is explained below.

Peter Holman has traced a tradition of polyphonic keyboard accompaniment in English consort music of the seventeenth century. The organ was used to double all or some of the parts in viol fantazias, partly as a way to keep the players in tune. Much consort music from between 1620 and 1660 has written-out organ parts; where such parts do not exist – as with the consort music of Orlando Gibbons, Christopher Gibbons and Matthew Locke – Holman suggests that the composers accompanied viol performances of their consort works by playing from a score. Purcell's fantazias belong to the same tradition and are similarly preserved in his score. Holman comments that although these 'are normally played just with viols today … it is easy to imagine the composer accompanying them on the organ from his score'.[218] Sadly, no recordings of the fantazias have as yet experimented with the possibility of organ accompaniment.

A residue of this practice of polyphonic keyboard accompaniment can be detected in Purcell's *Sonnata's of III Parts* (1683). Even though these trio sonatas draw on Italian models, they show many continuities with the English consort tradition, which explain several idiosyncrasies of the continuo part. The sonatas were published as four part-books (Violin I, Violin II, plus a part for a melodic Basso and a figured Basso Continuo part). The preface, however, indicates that the provision of the figured part was 'quite besides [Purcell's] first Resolutions'. As Holman comments, 'Perhaps Purcell originally intended to publish just the string parts, expecting the organist to read from a manuscript score or a keyboard reduction'.[219] The tradition of polyphonic

---

216 Gregory S. Johnston, 'Polyphonic Keyboard Accompaniment in the Early Baroque: an Alternative to Basso Continuo', *Early Music* 26 (1998): 51–3.

217 Lbl Add. 34072, fols 1–5; transcribed in F.T. Arnold, *The Art of Accompaniment from a Thorough-Bass as Practised in the XVIIth and XVIIIth Centuries* (2 vols, New York: Dover, 1965; first published London: Oxford University Press, 1931), vol. 1, pp. 163–72.

218 Peter Holman, '"Evenly, Softly and Sweetly Acchording to All": The Organ Accompaniment of English Consort Music', in Andrew Ashbee and Peter Holman (eds), *John Jenkins and his Time: Studies in English Consort Music* (Oxford: Clarendon Press, 1996), pp. 368 and 372.

219 Ibid., p. 372. The same point was made by Arnold, *The Art of Accompaniment from a*

Example 4.14   Purcell, Sonata 12 in D major, bb. 15–19, from *Sonnata's of III Parts* (1683).

doubling explains why the continuo part shadows the violin parts at the start of fugal movements or in passages when the bowed bass is silent. Whereas Roger Fiske described the continuo notes at the start of fugal movements as 'almost certainly cues showing the keyboard player where to come in',[220] these passages should be played; indeed, sometimes they also contain notes that are essential harmonic support, as with the initial d' in Example 4.14. The practice of polyphonic accompaniment further suggests that the continuo should simply double the violins at the end of movements, where they typically come together in a unison, rather than filling in the final chord with a major or minor third.[221]

Thorough-Bass, vol. 1, pp. 93–4.

220 Henry Purcell, *Sonatas of Three Parts*, ed. Roger Fiske (2 vols, London: Eulenburg, 1975), p. vi.

221 David Wulstan, 'Purcell in Performance, I', *Leading Notes: Journal of the National Early Music Association* 5 (1995): 10.

Yet the figuring of the *Sonnata's* suggests that exact doubling of the detail of upper parts is often inappropriate. Example 4.15 shows how the upper parts frequently clash with the continuo harmonies: the violins may play dissonances while the continuo simultaneously sounds the note of resolution. In Purcell's idiom, the sustained chords put harmonic detail into sharper relief. As Michael Tilmouth commented: 'For their full and proper effect, [the] notes of anticipation [and the] changing and passing notes, must be heard in conflict with the supporting harmony ... Purcell's sparse figuring is there by design, not accident.'[222] In this respect Purcell's sonatas go beyond the principle of polyphonic accompaniment, espousing an Italianate sense of contrast between soloist and accompaniment.

Rebecca Herissone has demonstrated that polyphonic keyboard accompaniment was also used in Restoration church music, including Purcell's anthems. The accompaniments for this repertory are notated in organ-books that typically contain skeletal scores of pieces, showing the top and bottom parts, and sometimes also the beginning of imitative entries. Between the 1960s and 1990s most scholars and performers believed that organists should regard these scores as indications of the vocal texture, and that the player should supply an independent accompaniment that avoided doubling the lines of vocal soloists. Such a realization can be seen in the Purcell Society volumes edited by Lionel Pike.[223] Herissone, however, argues that an organist playing from an original organ-book could not tell which notes indicated the choir's parts and which notes indicated the independent accompaniment. Instead the accompaniment would be based closely upon what was notated in the organ-book, doubling the outer voices and filling in the texture where appropriate.[224] Herissone's research confirms the importance of choosing a style of accompaniment appropriate to the genre being performed.

Conclusions

Since the tercentenary of Purcell's death in 1995, research into performance practice has emphasized the diversity of performing styles and techniques in Restoration England. Scholars and performers are increasingly aware that performance practices varied according to genre. Further investigation of the practices specific to individual genres or particular places is required – for instance, the pitch standards used for Purcell's secular music of the 1680s, or for performances of his church music outside London. More research into performance practice in the decade after Purcell's death might also shed light on some of the debates relating to his music, for instance concerning the nature of the countertenor voice.

---

222 Henry Purcell, *Twelve Sonatas of Three Parts*, ed. Michael Tilmouth, The Works of Henry Purcell, vol. 5 (new edn, Borough Green: Novello, 1976), p. xi.

223 For instance, Purcell, *Sacred Music, Part II*, ed. Pike.

224 Rebecca Herissone, *'To Fill, Forbear, or Adorne': The Organ Accompaniment of Restoration Sacred Music*, RMA Monographs, vol. 14 (Aldershot: Ashgate, 2006).

Example 4.15   Purcell, Sonata 7 in E minor, bb. 107–10, from *Sonnata's of III Parts* (1683). Shading denotes melodic dissonance not indicated by the continuo figuring.

Much can also be discerned from manuscripts of the late seventeenth and early eighteenth centuries – even those sources that Purcell Society editors regard as corrupt – about how Purcell's music was adapted in performance. Nevertheless, in many areas of performance practice scholars are unlikely to be able to reach firm conclusions about period styles due to the lack of surviving evidence, and here experimentation by modern-day performers remains valuable. In addition, the evidence of the diversity of seventeenth-century performances can also inspire today's practitioners, offering a range of options for those who seek historical precedents for their interpretations, and stimulating other performers to devise their own creative adaptations of Purcell's music.

Theatre Culture

Andrew Pinnock

Purcell turned 30 in 1689. By then his professional reputation had been established. He was a leading court and church composer, an occasional supplier of commercial theatre music and an energetic networker, assiduously cultivating amateur contacts in an effort to build his teaching practice (this business-orientated sociability was misconstrued by his early biographers: meetings sometimes took place in taverns). Yet he was very far from famous. Apart from the court insiders present when royal odes and welcome songs were performed, only people with specific musical interests were likely to have heard of him.

This was about to change. In 1689–90 reductions in staffing at court – which cost a number of his colleagues their jobs, and Purcell himself £40 per year[1] – forced him to reassess his career. John Blow and Nicholas Staggins were both in robust health: Purcell had little immediate hope of succeeding to their comfortably paid positions.[2] An entrepreneurial way forward was apparently the only one open to him. Career necessity, coupled with 'tremendous self-confidence and … aware[ness] of his talent',[3] led him to the theatre, on which his work remained focused for the rest of his life. Purcell produced a string of theatrical successes between 1690 and 1695 and became a celebrity – the first such famous composer in British musical history.[4]

Purcell researchers cannot escape the theatre, therefore. Much of his best music is theatrical in origin. The highest-profile modern Purcell performances take place in opera houses, where they are visible and accessible to audiences and to critics in ways his ecclesiastical and chamber music simply are not. Modern media interest in evidence 'relevant' to the production, marketing and appreciation of Purcell's

---

1   See Bruce Wood, *Purcell: An Extraordinary Life* (London: ABRSM Publishing, 2009), p. 132.
2   For details of these positions see Bruce Wood, 'Blow, John', and Watkins Shaw, 'Staggins, Nicholas', in *Grove Music Online*, http://www.oxfordmusiconline.com (last accessed 1 April 2011).
3   Curtis Price, 'In Search of Purcell's Character', in Curtis Price (ed.), *Purcell Studies* (Cambridge: Cambridge University Press, 1995), p. 3.
4   For more on Purcell's fame as a composer, see Andrew Pinnock, 'The Purcell Phenomenon', in Michael Burden (ed.), *The Purcell Companion* (London: Faber, 1995; Portland, OR: Amadeus Press, 1995), pp. 3–17; and the section 'Purcell and the Restoration Context' in Chapter 8 of this volume.

operas, stimulates research effort likely to produce such evidence, subtly (perhaps not so subtly) distracting from possible alternative uses of the researchers' time. But the 'superstar' aura surrounding Purcell leads to serious critical and historical distortion, denying the inherently interdisciplinary and collaborative nature of the theatre business and downplaying the importance (to Restoration audiences) of non-musical production inputs. The aim of this chapter is thus to consider the theatrical environment in which Purcell operated. I assess the evidence base on which academically respectable accounts of Restoration theatre-history rest, warning of gaps in the evidence where I think people might fall into them; try to show why theatre research findings matter; and seek to identify themes for possible future research.

Theatrical Reference Tools

The Restoration theatre invites study as a performance space, as a workplace, a social hub, a place of entertainment (obviously), and as a cultural institution helping to define – perhaps tending to corrupt – the nation's moral tone (so the nature of the entertainment mattered even to non-attenders). Equally it invites investigation as an economic engine (consuming resources, human and financial; stimulating activity in other sectors of the economy such as play- and music-publishing), as a powerful advertising medium (with potential to be harnessed for personal, political or commercial advantage), and as a propaganda machine that rival political and religious groupings tried either to control or to subvert. Some of these avenues have been extensively explored; others seem to me to offer greater scope for new, original contributions.

Two of the most approachable starting points for work on the Restoration theatre are *The London Theatre World*, edited by Robert D. Hume and published in 1980,[5] and *A Companion to Restoration Drama*, edited by Susan J. Owen and published in 2001;[6] both supply excellent and non-duplicating overviews. They are recognizably modern in comparison with Montague Summers's *The Restoration Theatre* (1934),[7] for instance, a book that is still useful (like much of the rest of Summers's work),[8] but is more a miscellany of insights into the Restoration theatre world than a systematic exploration of it.

---

5   Robert D. Hume (ed.), *The London Theatre World 1660–1800* (Carbondale: Southern Illinois University Press, 1980).

6   Susan J. Owen (ed.), *A Companion to Restoration Drama*, Blackwell Companions to Literature and Culture, vol. 12 (Oxford: Blackwell, 2001).

7   Montague Summers, *The Restoration Theatre* (London: Kegan Paul, Trench and Trübner, 1934).

8   See Robert D. Hume, 'The Uses of Montague Summers: A Pioneer Reconsidered', *Restoration: Studies in English Literary Culture, 1660–1700* 3 (1979): 59–65.

Introducing *The London Theatre World*, Hume noted major advances in scholarly understanding of the Restoration theatre, all 'fairly recent' from the perspective of 1979/80:

> The current high estimation of … the best-known [Restoration] plays largely follows from the exciting critical readings which started to appear in the 1950s in books by Thomas H. Fujimara, Dale Underwood and Norman Holland. Renewed interest in these plays led next to questions about the stage history of the plays and about the nature of the theatre that spawned them. Publication of the five parts of *The London Stage, 1660–1800*, in the course of the 1960s opened up whole new worlds of possibilities … [leading] naturally to the monumental Highfill-Burnim-Langhans *Biographical Dictionary of Actors, Actresses, Musicians, Dancers, Managers and Other Stage Personnel in London, 1660–1800*.[9]

Thanks to *The London Stage* and the *Biographical Dictionary*,[10] from the 1970s onwards critics searching for meaning in Restoration play-texts, and musicologists deriving information about the use of music in the Restoration theatre from play-texts, have had much more and much better organized contextual information available to them. Part 1 of *The London Stage* covers the period 1600–1700; Part 2, in two volumes, runs from 1700 to 1729, a period equally interesting to Purcellians because his theatre music remained popular throughout it, and because many of the music sources on which modern editors of his theatre music have to rely were printed or copied posthumously.[11] Occasional later eighteenth-century revivals figure in Parts 3, 4 and 5.[12]

---

9 Hume (ed.), *The London Theatre World*, p. xi.

10 Philip H. Highfill, Kalman A. Burnim and Edward A. Langhans, *A Biographical Dictionary of Actors, Actresses, Musicians, Dancers, Managers and Other Stage Personnel in London 1660–1800* (16 vols, Carbondale: Southern Illinois University Press, 1973–93).

11 William Van Lennep (ed.), with a Critical Introduction by Emmett L. Avery and Arthur H. Scouten, *The London Stage, 1660–1800: A Calendar of Plays, Entertainments and Afterpieces, together with Casts, Box-receipts and Contemporary Comment. Part 1: 1660–1700* (Carbondale: Southern Illinois University Press, 1965); Emmett L. Avery (ed.), *The London Stage, 1660–1800: A Calendar of Plays, Entertainments and Afterpieces, together with Casts, Box-receipts and Contemporary Comment. Part 2: 1700–1729* (2 vols, Carbondale: Southern Illinois University Press, 1960).

12 Arthur H. Scouten (ed.), *The London Stage, 1660–1800: A Calendar of Plays, Entertainments and Afterpieces, together with Casts, Box-receipts and Contemporary Comment. Part 3: 1729–1747* (2 vols, Carbondale: Southern Illinois University Press, 1961); George Winchester Stone Jr. (ed.), *The London Stage, 1660–1800: A Calendar of Plays, Entertainments and Afterpieces, together with Casts, Box-receipts and Contemporary Comment. Part 4: 1747–1776* (3 vols, Carbondale: Southern Illinois University Press, 1962); Charles Beecher Hogan (ed.), *The London Stage, 1660–1800: A Calendar of Plays, Entertainments and Afterpieces, together with Casts, Box-receipts and Contemporary Comment. Part 5: 1776–1800* (3 vols, Carbondale: Southern Illinois University Press,

The London Theatre World successfully distilled the documentary world-view of *The London Stage* into a single reader-friendly volume, and established lines of authority along which reputations for academic expertise could be passed from *The London Stage*'s founder-editors to approved successors. Meant to 'serve the dual function of summing up where scholarship now stands [*c*.1980] and inspiring new research',[13] it defined the Restoration theatre-research field with unprecedented clarity and helped to consolidate personal positions within that field. Since *The London Theatre World* appeared, many of the research questions raised or implied in Hume's preface to the book have been answered by contributors to it (often by Hume himself, often by Hume in highly productive collaboration with Judith Milhous), leaving other would-be annalists with relatively little to do.

Drama criticism happens in a world beyond annals, of course. This distinction is an old-established and important one. Unlike *The London Theatre World*, Owen's *Companion to Restoration Drama* aims to 'introduce the reader to the full range and diversity of criticism in this field as well as to the variety of drama'.[14] Leaving *The London Theatre World*'s version of theatre history more or less untouched (significantly, Edward A. Langhans covers 'The Theatres' and 'The Post-1660 Theatres as Performance Spaces' in both handbooks), Owen's *Companion* presents a series of exemplary essays designed to stimulate independent critical thinking and potentially endless further reading.

Their very different treatments of the actress question are symptomatic, and probably to be expected bearing in mind the many developments in scholarship that occurred in the two decades after Hume's collection was published. Hume's introduction notes the 'introduction of actresses … mak[ing] a sharp differentiation from the Caroline theatre closed by the Puritans in 1642';[15] while Philip Highfill, in *The London Theatre World*'s chapter 'Performers and Performing', discusses actresses' career patterns alongside those of actors, but does not engage with wider critical and gender-theoretical questions (nor, strangely, does John Loftis, in the chapter 'Political and Social Thought'). *The Companion to Restoration Drama* picks up where *The London Theatre World* leaves off, including whole chapters on 'Libertinism and Sexuality' (Maximilian E. Novak), 'The Restoration Actress' (Deborah Payne Fisk) and 'Masculinity in Restoration Drama' (Laura J. Rosenthal). Male playwrights wrote most of the words that Restoration actresses were given to speak, but actresses could gloss the words in performance, using gesture, facial expression, tone and timing to encourage audience reactions other than those intended. Female playwrights offered different takes on sex, love and (often forced) marriage. Playwrights and actresses collaborated to create strong female characters, with input from composers if the characters were required to sing. Women in the audience reacted to plays just as much as men, and, like men's their

---

1968).

13   Hume (ed.), *The London Theatre World*, p. xii.

14   Owen (ed.), *A Companion to Restoration Drama*, p. xv.

15   Hume (ed.), *The London Theatre World*, p. xi.

reactions mattered.[16] As socio-historical documents giving   for their date – a public voice of unprecedented prominence to 'Female Wits', Restoration play-texts cry out for feminist or feminized criticism.[17] In *The Companion to Restoration Drama* that cry is heeded. *The London Theatre World* holds back.

Readers to whom *The Companion to Restoration Drama*'s critical adventurousness appeals are likely to find Derek Hughes's *English Drama 1660–1700*[18] a more sympathetic survey of 'virtually all extant, performed plays from 1660–1700'[19] than Robert D. Hume's genre-orientated alternative, *The Development of English Drama in the Late Seventeenth Century*.[20] Both are formidable intellectual achievements: extant performed plays from 1660 to 1700 number over five hundred. They render Allardyce Nicoll's *A History of Restoration Drama* (first published in 1923) more or less redundant. While some of Nicoll's appendices are still useful – in particular 'Documents Illustrative of the History of the Stage' and 'Hand-list of Restoration Plays'[21] – his pre-Humean notions of development now come across as 'simplistic nonsense'.[22]

For more than a century before *The London Stage* appeared, John Genest's *Some Account of the English Stage from the Restoration in 1660 to 1830* served British theatre historians' post-Restoration reference needs.[23] This was astonishingly detailed for a one-man compilation, efficiently summarizing thousands of play plots, dating premieres, listing casts, sifting cast lists to identify roles with which particular actors were associated, reviewing playwrights' careers, revealing disagreements between earlier authorities and correcting the factual record whenever he thought he could. Genest (a Church of England minister turned gentleman scholar, retired to Bath for the sake of his health) relied on published sources almost entirely – on printed play-

16   See David Roberts, *The Ladies: Female Patronage in Restoration Drama 1660–1700*, Oxford English Mongraphs (Oxford: Clarendon; New York: Oxford University Press, 1989).

17   Such issues of gender and gender roles, and recent developments in the literature in this field, are discussed below in Chapter 7 of this volume.

18   Derek Hughes, *English Drama 1660–1700* (Oxford: Clarendon, 1996).

19   As described in Robert D. Hume, 'Theatres and Repertory', in Joseph Donohue (ed.), *The Cambridge History of British Theatre: Vol. 2 – 1660 to 1895* (Cambridge: Cambridge University Press, 2004), p. 60 n. 9. Hume has written a number of theatres-and-repertory pieces over the years, changing his story very little from one to the next. Donohue's volume includes an excellent bibliography, at present one of the most up to date available.

20   Robert D. Hume, *The Development of English Drama in the Late Seventeenth Century* (Oxford: Clarendon, 1976).

21   These are Appendix B and Appendix C respectively. The fourth revised edition of Nicoll's *A History of Restoration Drama, 1660–1700* was published by Cambridge University Press in 1952, as Volume 1 in Nicoll's five-volume set *A History of English Drama 1660–1900* (5 vols, Cambridge: Cambridge University Press, 1952–59). As such it has been reprinted many times.

22   Hume, *The Development of English Drama*, p. 15.

23   John Genest, *Some Account of the English Stage from the Restoration in 1660 to 1830* (10 vols, Bath: H.E. Carrington, 1832).

books, and on sources including Samuel Pepys's *Diary* (first published in 1825),[24] John Downes's *Roscius Anglicanus*,[25] Gerard Langbaine's *English Dramatick Poets*,[26] Charles Gildon's *Life of Betterton*,[27] Colley Cibber's *Apology*,[28] and Edmond Malone's 1800 edition of Dryden's prose works and letters.[29] Until scholars gained access to government archives, later in the nineteenth century, Genest's work, in the words of Ward, stood 'unrivalled as the consistent execution of a comprehensive scheme'.[30]

Slowly, however, as indexed volumes covering the Restoration period began to appear in the *Calendar of State Papers: Domestic Series*,[31] researchers realized that a wealth of manuscript material unavailable to Genest needed reading and assimilating into theatre history. This was a daunting task, primarily taken up by a new generation of American scholars, in particular Leslie Hotson and Eleanore Boswell. Hotson's *The Commonwealth and Restoration Stage* (1928) published the results of doctoral work begun in 1922, work financially supported at different

---

24 Richard, Lord Braybrooke (ed.), *Memoirs of Samuel Pepys ... Comprising his Diary from 1659 to 1669, Deciphered by the Rev. John Smith, A.B., from the Original Short-hand MS. in the Pepysian Library, and a Selection from his Private Correspondence* (2 vols, London: Henry Colburn, 1825).

25 John Downes, *Roscius Anglicanus, or an Historical Review of the Stage* (London, 1708); republished in Francis Waldron (ed.), *Roscius Anglicanus, or an Historical Review of the Stage after it had been Suppress'd by means of the late Unhappy Civil War .. 'till the ... Restoration ... Giving an Account of its Rise Again* (London, 1789). Milhous and Hume have since produced a modern, fully annotated scholarly edition of Downes's account: see John Downes, *Roscius Anglicanus*, eds Judith Milhous and Robert D. Hume (London: Society for Theatre Research, 1987).

26 Gerard Langbaine, *An Account of the English Dramatick Poets: Or, some Observations and Remarks on the Lives and Writings, of all those that have been Publish'd ... in the English Tongue* (Oxford, 1691); [Charles Gildon] (ed.), *The Lives and Characters of the English Dramatick Poets ... First Begun by Mr. Langbain, Improv'd and Continued Down to the Present Time, by a Careful Hand* (London, 1699).

27 [Charles Gildon], *The Life of Mr. Thomas Betterton, the Late Eminent Tragedian. Wherein the Action and Utterance of the Stage, Bar, and Pulpit, are distinctly consider'd* (London, 1710).

28 Colley Cibber, *An Apology for the Life of Mr. Colley Cibber, Comedian ...With an Historical View of the Stage During his Own Time* (London, 1740).

29 Edmond Malone (ed.), *The Critical and Miscellaneous Prose Works of John Dryden ... With Notes and Illustrations; an Account of the Life and Writings of the Author ... and a Collection of his Letters* (4 vols, London, 1800).

30 Adolphus William Ward, *A History of English Dramatic Literature to the Death of Queen Anne* (3 vols, 2nd edn, London: Macmillan, 1899), vol. 1, p. 2 n. 1.

31 Mary Anne Everett Green, et al. (eds), *Calendar of State Papers, Domestic Series, of the Reign of Charles II ... Preserved in the State Paper Department of Her Majesty's Public Record Office* (28 vols: vols 1–7, London: Longman, Green, Longman and Roberts, 1860–66; vols 8–28, London: Her/His Majesty's Stationery Office, 1893–1939); Francis Bickley, et al. (eds), *Calendar of State Papers Preserved in the Public Record Office, Domestic Series, James II* (3 vols, London: Her Majesty's Stationery Office, 1960–72); William John Hardy (ed.), *Calendar of State Papers, Domestic Series, of the Reign of William and Mary ... Preserved in the Public Record Office* (6 vols, London: Her/His Majesty's Stationery Office, 1895–1908).

times by Harvard and by Yale Universities.[32] Boswell's research – funded by the John Simon Guggenheim Memorial Foundation and the American Association of University Women – produced *The Restoration Court Stage (1660–1702)* in 1932.[33] Both books remain standard reference works to this day. Together they set a new professional standard for Restoration theatre research, to which others (regardless of nationality or financial means) would have to rise if they wanted to be taken seriously. The English maverick Montague Summers suffered badly by comparison. Allardyce Nicoll took a job at Yale.

Starting just post Hotson, the *London Stage* project had 1930s origins recalled in the preface to Part 1 and (with some interesting extra information) in the July 2001 preface to the revised Part 2 by Milhous and Hume.[34] It required determined teamwork, substantial amounts of American university and foundation funding, over thirty years and a hugely supportive publisher for its successful completion. Rightly, Milhous and Hume praise Southern Illinois University Press for taking it on and seeing it through. In paperback reprint form, the editorial introductions opening each part of *The London Stage* have been widely influential: 'wonderfully full, vivid, and detailed ... they present a view of the London theatre by scholars who know its nuts-and-bolts underside'.[35] *The London Stage* presented its 'Calendar of Plays, Entertainments & Afterpieces' in unbranching chronological order. As Milhous and Hume note, this allowed the user to 'see at a glance what plays were performed at each theatre on any given day. Consequently one can study competition and competitive devices as they evolved, day by day, week by week, month by month. This was Genest's greatest failing: he presented a separate list for each theatre, making comparisons vastly more difficult'.[36] Competition between theatres emerged as far and away the most important spur to theatrical innovation in the Restoration period, as in most others.

With some simplification and reordering, *The London Theatre World* adopted the fact-categorizing framework constructed by Emmett L. Avery and Arthur H. Scouten in their Critical Introduction to Part 1 of *The London Stage*. Categories included theatre management, the playhouses, scenery and technical design, performers and production of plays, the repertory, and the audience. The Critical Introduction to *The London Stage* covered a huge range of topics, but two significant gaps had been identified and largely filled by the time *The London Theatre World* appeared. First, the editors of *The London Stage* had assumed, 'when an exact date for the premiere of a play is not known ... [that] the first performance preceded

---

32   Leslie Hotson, *The Commonwealth and Restoration Stage* (Cambridge, MA: Harvard University Press, 1928).

33   Eleanore Boswell, *The Restoration Court Stage (1660–1702), with a Particular Account of the Production of 'Calisto'* (Cambridge, MA: Harvard University Press; London: Allen and Unwin, 1932).

34   Judith Milhous and Robert D. Hume (eds), *The London Stage 1660–1800: A New Version of Part 2, 1700–1729 ... Draft of the Calendar for Volume I, 1700–1711*, http://www.personal.psu.edu/hb1/London%20Stage%202001/, Preface, p. iii (last accessed 1 April 2011).

35   Ibid., p. iv.

36   Ibid., p. iv.

publication usually by at least a month'.[37] Testing this assumption in 'Dating Play Premières from Publication Data, 1660–1700',[38] Milhous and Hume found it far from universally valid, concluding that '[t]he dates given in *The London Stage* appear very solid and exact … [b]ut in fact they are nothing of the sort'.[39] The rule followed in *The London Stage* hardly ever holds for Restoration 'opera': here, word-book publication coincided with the work's stage premiere as closely as possible, and in some cases may even have preceded it.

Second, as the time lag between stage premiere and play-text publication varied appreciably, so too did the closeness of fit between performed and published versions of (supposedly) the 'same' play. Surviving Restoration prompt-books – mostly manuscripts of playhouse origin, sometimes published play-texts bought and marked up for prompt-book use when repertoire pieces were revived – show researchers what sorts of performing material actors and stage crews had to work with. Plays published in full literary form, for leisurely consumption at home, were often performed in cut versions, their action tightened up to pull dramatic or comedic high spots closer together. The practical and stage-aesthetic principles guiding Restoration script editors when they went to work can be inferred from prompt-book evidence; and the extent to which play-texts surviving only in published literary form might have been altered prior to performance can be very roughly estimated.[40] *The London Theatre World* included a chapter on 'The Evidence from Promptbooks', by Leo Hughes. Edward Langhans's handsome collection of prompt-book facsimiles appeared the following year – *Restoration Promptbooks* (1981).[41]

Another indispensable Milhous and Hume contribution to Restoration theatre scholarship – *A Register of English Theatrical Documents 1660–1737* – catalogues nearly 1,700 documents of proven or potential evidential value to theatre historians covering the period 1660–1700.[42] Volume 1 runs from 1660 to 1714, volume 2 from 1714 to 1737. The *Register* is, as Milhous and Hume explain, 'a preliminary attempt to provide a chronological list of all known documents [manuscript and printed] concerning the management and regulation of the theatre in England between 1660 and 1737'.[43] Most of these documents concern management and regulation of theatrical activity in London. As is so often the case with Milhous and Hume, their preliminary effort is unlikely to be improved on by anyone else for the foreseeable future. They avoid unnecessary overlap with James Arnott and John Robinson's bibliography *English Theatrical Literature 1559–1900*, which remains the

37   Lennep (ed.), *The London Stage, Part 1*, p. 3.
38   Judith Milhous and Robert D. Hume, 'Dating Play Premières from Publication Data, 1660–1700', *Harvard Library Bulletin* 22 (1974): 374–405.
39   Ibid.: 405.
40   For a specifically Purcellian application of prompt-book evidence see Andrew Pinnock, 'Play into Opera: Purcell's *The Indian Queen*', *Early Music* 18 (1990): 3–21.
41   Edward A. Langhans, *Restoration Promptbooks* (Carbondale: Southern Illinois University Press, 1981).
42   Judith Milhous and Robert D. Hume (eds), *A Register of English Theatrical Documents, 1660–1737* (2 vols, Carbondale: Southern Illinois University Press, 1991).
43   Ibid., vol. 1, p. xiii.

primary reference tool for researchers solely interested in books and pamphlets about the Restoration theatre.[44] Equally, they omit letters and diary entries – since these are cited in *The London Stage* – and prologues and epilogues, since these were conscientiously collected, edited and annotated by Pierre Danchin in *The Prologues and Epilogues of the Restoration, 1660–1700*.[45] The *Register*, thoroughly indexed, is easy to mine for documentary evidence furthering specific research purposes. 'Betterton … allowed to import opera materials' for instance;[46] 'French musicians to be arrested; French musicians to be discharged from custody';[47] 'Purcell … *Fairy Queen* score lost'.[48] But it is also worth reading patiently through, to gain a feel both for theatre-administrative routine in Restoration London and for the sorts of semi-predictable disruption to which routine was subject.

With such a wide range of reference tools available, today's Restoration theatre historians are well supplied with documentary evidence, much of it 'trivial, formulaic, and internally redundant',[49] some of it (particularly the lawsuits) gratifyingly colourful; most is straightforwardly accessible to researchers equipped with standard bibliographical tools. Yet as Milhous and Hume remark in another context, even with all this evidence available 'we know no more than about 7 per cent of all the [public theatrical] performances that were given in the period 1660–1700', 7 per cent rising to 'nearly 100 per cent after 1706' thanks to printed playbill production and daily newspaper advertisements from then on.[50] Knowing the length of the Restoration theatre season, and knowing how many London theatre companies were in operation, we can tell how many performance slots needed filling. Which play or opera filled which particular slot is known only occasionally.

Matters get worse when court productions are taken into account. Although documents cited in the Milhous and Hume *Register* very frequently refer to works undertaken in the Hall Theatre, Whitehall (sometimes called the Theatre Royal Whitehall – the king's private theatre), the documents hardly ever tell us with which play, opera or masque the works were associated. *Calisto* is a rare, highly conspicuous exception. London had 'two separate operatic hubs', as Rebecca Herissone points out, 'the court and the public theater'. This was a recipe for conflict 'over precisely what "opera" in England should be',[51] but lack of information about court activity makes the true causes of conflict hard to unravel, and the trend-setting significance of court theatrical initiatives hard to assess.

44   James F. Arnott and John W. Robinson, *English Theatrical Literature, 1559–1900: A Bibliography* (London: Society for Theatre Research, 1970).

45   Pierre Danchin (ed.), *The Prologues and Epilogues of the Restoration, 1660–1700: A Complete Edition* (7 vols, Nancy: Presses Universitaires de Nancy, 1981–88).

46   Milhous and Hume, *A Register of English Theatrical Documents*, vol. 2, p. 963.

47   Ibid., vol. 2, p. 1000.

48   Ibid., vol. 2, p. 1049.

49   Ibid., vol. 1, p. xiv.

50   Milhous and Hume (eds), *The London Stage 1660–1800: A New Version of Part 2*, Preface, p. iv.

51   Rebecca Herissone, 'Playford, Purcell, and the Functions of Music Publishing in Restoration England', *Journal of the American Musicological Society* 63 (2010): 273.

Writers of Restoration theatre history face an unenviable task. They have to invent plausible narrative threads joining widely scattered evidential dots, imposing explicit or implicit cause-and-effect relationships on events that seventeenth-century witnesses to those events might not have thought to connect. The opposite is also true, of course: they may possibly (frequently?) miss connections obvious to seventeenth-century observers. When small new pieces of evidence come to light whole swathes of historical inference with which the new evidence is inconsistent may have to be cut away and replaced. Recent scholarly controversy surrounding *Dido and Aeneas* taught Purcell scholars a salutary lesson in this respect. Since the publication of Sir John Hawkins's *A General History of the Science and Practice of Music* in 1776, it had been common music-historical knowledge that 'One Mr. Josias Priest ... [who] kept a boarding-school for young gentlewomen ... got [Nahum] Tate to write, and Purcell to set to music, a little drama called Dido and Æneas'.[52] But a single fresh discovery triggered question after question: evidence that John Blow's court masque *Venus and Adonis* (?1683)[53] had been restaged at Priest's school in April 1684.[54] Might *Dido* also have been written for court before transferring to the school? Might *Venus* and *Dido* have been composed around the same time, as deliberate companion pieces? This suggestion seemed to fit the facts fairly well until Bryan White's 2009 paper 'Letter from Aleppo: dating the Chelsea School performance of *Dido and Aeneas*' stirred more new information into the mix.[55] White's overseas correspondent, writing in February 1689, seemed to think that Dido was a fairly recent composition, not five or six years old.

Disinterested readers looking at articles on *Dido and Aeneas* written over the past twenty years and possibly wondering about their combative tone should remember the scale of the trauma with which their authors (this one included) were trying to deal. Everything we thought we knew about Purcell's greatest hit needed thinking through again. A safe post-revisionist consensus has yet to emerge. Similarly, although with less fuss, Michael Burden's 2003 article 'Casting Issues in the Original Production of Purcell's Opera "The Fairy-Queen"' – presenting eye-witness evidence that, in 1692, child actors played Oberon and Titania – significantly changed scholarly perceptions of the whole piece.[56] There may be more such shocks to come: Purcell scholars still have a good deal to learn from the

---

52   Sir John Hawkins, *A General History of the Science and Practice of Music*, reprinted with a new introduction by Charles Cudworth (2 vols, New York: Dover, 1963; first published London: Novello, 1853), vol. 2, p. 745.

53   This is the likely date of the first performance given in Bruce Wood's Preface to John Blow, *Venus and Adonis*, ed. Bruce Wood, The Purcell Society Edition Companion Series, vol. 2 (London: Stainer & Bell, 2008), pp. xii–xiv.

54   This evidence was first presented in Richard Luckett, 'A New Source for "Venus and Adonis"', *Musical Times* 130 (1989): 76–9.

55   Bryan White, 'Letter from Aleppo: Dating the Chelsea School Performance of *Dido and Aeneas*', *Early Music* 37 (2009): 417–28. See also the discussion of the implications of *Dido*'s dating in Chapter 6, pp. 222–4, and Chapter 7, pp. 279–80 below.

56   Michael Burden, 'Casting Issues in the Original Production of Purcell's Opera "The Fairy-Queen"', *Music & Letters* 84 (2003): 596–607.

vast amounts of contextual data on performances, casts and other extra-musical factors that influenced, and in many cases governed, the composition of music for the Restoration theatre.

The Restoration Theatre as Commercial Venture

To scholars investigating Purcell's theatre music, especially his opera scores, the significance of earlier seventeenth-century court masque antecedents seems obvious: as Moore observed, '[t]he masque is without any doubt the strongest formative influence on Restoration opera'.[57] Edward J. Dent's old but not yet superseded *Foundations of English Opera* gives a useful introduction to the masques 'out of [which] ... English opera developed',[58] astutely noting the economic and administrative adjustments needed to get from one to the other:

> the ingenuity of Inigo Jones [masque designer under James I and Charles I] may be said to have made for economy as well as extravagance, and it was due to him and his pupil John Webb that [Sir William Davenant] was in later years enabled to present the public with plays and masques, elaborated into what were given the name of operas, on a scale ... compatible with financial success.[59]

By 'economy as well as extravagance' Dent presumably refers to the painted scenes and scene-changing machinery ingeniously developed (or imported) by Jones, which enabled small teams of theatre professionals to achieve hugely impressive effects.

The masque was the precursor of English opera on every level – generic, organizational and socio-political – demanding forcefully coordinated multimedia collaboration for its successful realization. The Civil War did not 'put an end to these royal *divertissements*' (*pace* Westrup).[60] Budgets tightened for a period, and overtly royalist appearances were avoided, but masques survived intact. The conventional division of scholarly labour preventing experts in Shakespearean and post-Shakespearean drama from looking forward to the Restoration, and preventing Restoration drama experts looking back, puts an inconvenient mid-century blockage in the way of Purcell researchers that it is worth trying to dislodge. For masque background Paul Reyher's impressively detailed 1909 French-language study *Les Masques anglais* is still worth consulting (it covers the whole seventeenth

57   Robert Etheridge Moore, *Henry Purcell and the Restoration Theatre* (Cambridge, MA: Harvard University Press; London: Heinemann, 1961), p. 24.
58   Edward J. Dent, *Foundations of English Opera: A Study of Music Drama in England during the Seventeenth Century* (Cambridge: Cambridge University Press, 1928), p. 42.
59   Ibid.
60   Jack A. Westrup, *Purcell*, The Master Musicians (rev. edn, Oxford: Oxford University Press, 1995; originally published London: Dent, 1937), p. 105.

century),[61] along with Peter Walls's *Music in the English Courtly Masque, 1604–1640*,[62] David Lindley's edited essay collection *The Court Masque*,[63] Barbara Ravelhofer's *The Early Stuart Masque*,[64] and salient chapters in Peter Holman's *Four and Twenty Fiddlers*.[65] *Inigo Jones: The Theatre of the Stuart Court*, an imposing two-volume set edited by Stephen Orgel and Roy Strong, is indispensable.[66] Including 'the complete designs for productions at court for the most part in the collection of the Duke of Devonshire together with their texts and historical documentation', it nevertheless excludes music – leaving a large gap for Andrew Sabol to fill with *Four Hundred Songs and Dances from the Stuart Masque*.[67]

The barrier that has for a long time existed between masque-related research before and after the Civil War has resulted in a number of gaps in our perception of the relationships between court and commercial music theatre. The key transitional figure was William Davenant, and he remains central to our understanding of the way in which the Restoration theatre developed as a business, which in turn influenced the way in which public opera developed in England. He created the theatre company to which Purcell later attached himself, he built an audience hungry for innovation and, as Dent explained, he blended plays and masques to produce an economically viable hybrid marketable as opera. Well connected at court, he succeeded Ben Jonson as Poet Laureate under Charles I, and for self-promotional reasons pretended to be Shakespeare's illegitimate son. He had 'good friends in high positions [even] under Cromwell'.[68] In spring 1639 he obtained a royal licence to 'exercise action, musical presentments, scenes, dancing, and the like' in a purpose-built theatre off Fleet Street,[69] allowing him to run a commercial masque heavily reliant on changeable scenery and musical attractions for its drawing power. Davenant planned to open up the world of the court masque to a paying public. Although the Civil War set him back by two decades, he lived to fulfil that ambition.

---

61   Paul Reyher, *Les Masques anglais: étude sur les ballets et la vie de cour en Angleterre (1512–1640)* (Paris: Hachette, 1909).

62   Peter Walls, *Music in the English Courtly Masque, 1604–1640*, Oxford Monographs on Music (Oxford: Clarendon, 1996).

63   David Lindley (ed.), *The Court Masque*, Revels Plays Companions Library (Manchester: Manchester University Press, 1984).

64   Barbara Ravelhofer, *The Early Stuart Masque: Dance, Costume, and Music* (Oxford: Oxford University Press, 2006).

65   Peter Holman, *Four and Twenty Fiddlers: The Violin at the English Court 1540–1690*, Oxford Monographs on Music (Oxford: Clarendon, 1993).

66   Stephen Orgel and Roy Strong (eds), *Inigo Jones: The Theatre of the Stuart Court including the Complete Designs for Productions at Court, for the most part in the Collection of the Duke of Devonshire, together with their Texts and Historical Documentation* (2 vols, London: Sotheby Parke Bernet; Berkeley and Los Angeles: University of California Press, 1973).

67   Andrew J. Sabol (ed.), *Four Hundred Songs and Dances from the Stuart Masque* (Providence, RI: Brown University Press, 1978).

68   Hotson, *The Commonwealth and Restoration Stage*, p. 148.

69   W.J. Lawrence, *The Elizabethan Playhouse and Other Studies*, 2nd Series (Stratford-upon-Avon: Shakespeare Head Press, 1913), p. 125.

In 1656, near the end of the Cromwell interregnum period, Davenant produced England's first ever through-composed opera in the dining hall of his London mansion, Rutland House: *The Siege of Rhodes*.[70] He could afford to take entrepreneurial risks, having married twice more since 1639 (to a wealthy widow on each occasion). Singing in lieu of speaking enabled him to evade the parliamentary ban on public play performances then in force. Although the opera's music has been lost, surviving scene designs by John Webb place it unmistakeably in the masque tradition. Two of the five composers hired to work on it – Henry Lawes and Charles Coleman – had prior masque experience, which they passed on to Matthew Locke, a younger member of the compositional team; Locke himself would later pass on his own experience to Henry Purcell.

Reactions to *The Siege of Rhodes* must have been fairly positive, for shortly afterwards Davenant applied for permission to transfer his operation from home to a long-vacant commercial theatre, the Cockpit in Drury Lane.[71] In January 1657 he wrote a memorandum to Cromwell's Secretary of State, John Thurloe, in which he justified the enterprise, using public-interest and economic arguments with a strikingly modern ring:

> Mechanicks and retaylers ... are chiefly maintain'd by the superfluous expence of the gentry in garments and ornaments.
>
> That superfluous expense, States ... never restraine, ... [except] when costly manufactures are wrought by forraine hands. ...
>
> The countrey doth not provoke that expence which flowes from the gentry in cities: because those who are expencive in habits and ornaments, weare them to be seene by a numerous concourse of others not by a thinne society of themselves. ...
>
> The People of England are observ'd ... to require continuall divertisements, being otherwise naturally inclin'd to that melancholy that breeds sedition. ... Which example and the former reasons may (especially at this time) put the publique authority in minde that the city hath occasion for divertissements. ...
>
> And offers of this kinde may evade that imputation of levity, since the People were this way guided to assist their owne interests by the Athenians and the Romans; the one laying aside a third part of the publique revenue for representations to divert them, and the other a treasure not to be computed.[72]

---

70 Before staging *The Siege of Rhodes* at Rutland House, Davenant trialled a similar form of entertainment – entitled *The First Day's Entertainment at Rutland House* – combining 'music and declamations after the manner of the ancients'; see ibid., p. 129.

71 Once established in the Cockpit, to reduce the strain on his musical collaborators he followed *The Siege of Rhodes* with two more speaking-and-singing productions: *The Cruelty of The Spaniards in Peru*, and *The History of Sir Francis Drake*; see Hotson, *The Commonwealth and Restoration Stage*, pp. 133–63.

72 C.H. Firth, 'Sir William Davenant and the Revival of the Drama during the Protectorate', *English Historical Review* 18 (1903): 320–21.

Here, Davenant articulated the economic impact of theatrical divertissements. He acknowledged protectionist objections to the import of luxury goods produced abroad (making home-produced opera preferable, therefore). He argued that arts activity could promote greater social cohesion. He made a clever (if strategically understated) case for public subsidy. And he sought an exclusive licence – permission to present shows of a sort nowhere else on offer. This was straightforward 'mercantilist' logic;[73] and Davenant, growing to manhood at the height of the mercantilist economic era in England, knew the theory perfectly well.

In the hope of securing monopoly privileges, projectors like Davenant brought lobbying and other forms of persuasive pressure to bear on government officials in a position to do them favours. They sought out 'rents', as modern political economists say.[74] From time to time through to the end of the seventeenth century, and of course beyond, English opera promoters returned to the subsidy question, hoping to persuade either the court or court-emulative members of the gentry to underwrite their operations. Robert Cambert and other London-based French musicians trying to found a 'Royal Academy of Music' in 1673–74 made their rent-seeking intentions plain. Published French and English versions of the libretto to *Ariane, ou le mariage du Bacchus* (an all-sung opera performed in March 1674, in the Theatre Royal Drury Lane) included a dedication to Charles II 'incorporat[ing] a plea for state-supported opera … appealing directly to his absolutist aspirations':[75] '*You would compleat the Splendor and Magnificence of Your Imperial Seat, by establishing within her stately Walls Your* [French!] *Academy of* Opera's, *the fairest and most charming of all Publick Showes.*'[76] The preface to the *Fairy Queen* word-book (published 1692), a shameless rent-seeking prospectus, is a favourite citation of cultural economists as well as musicologists. Motives for opera investment in an era of pervasive patronage were not wholly 'commercial': loss-leading investment in opera would have paid off, had potential sponsors responded. Rebecca Herissone's recent work on composer self-publication also suggests that theatre music may have been produced with longer-term promotional goals in view.[77]

In 1660 Davenant obtained one of two theatrical patents awarded by Charles II's reconstituted monarchical government, allowing him to present plays and operas

---

73   'Mercantilism is economic nationalism that seeks to limit the competition faced by domestic producers. The tools of mercantilist policies include the granting of monopoly privileges, regulation of prices and business practices and especially prohibitions, tariffs, subsidies and other regulations regarding the conduct of international trade'; Laura LaHaye, 'Mercantilism', in Steven N. Durlauf and Lawrence Blume (eds), *The New Palgrave Dictionary of Economics* (2nd edn, Basingstoke: Palgrave Macmillan, 2008), pp. 568–9.

74   See William D. Grampp, *Pricing the Priceless: Art, Artists, and Economics* (New York: Basic Books, 1989), pp. 206–20.

75   Herissone, 'Playford, Purcell, and the Functions of Music Publishing': 273.

76   Pierre Perrin, *Ariadne, or, the Marriage of Bacchus. An Opera, or a Vocal Representation* (London, 1674), sig. A2v–A3; quoted in Herissone, 'Playford, Purcell, and the Functions of Music Publishing': 274.

77   Herissone, 'Playford, Purcell, and the Functions of Music Publishing'.

in public. Unfortunately for Davenant, another theatrical projector with pre-Civil War experience and strong court connections, Thomas Killigrew, had also applied for a licence, and also succeeded in securing one. Theatrical duopoly resulted: not much competition by modern standards, but enough to depress profits on both sides. Killigrew had smarter premises, the newly built Theatre Royal in Bridges Street off Drury Lane. Davenant, poorly housed by comparison (in a converted indoor tennis court), had to innovate to survive. Masque-inspired opera was his solution. Two particularly successful productions, *Macbeth* (1663–64) and *The Tempest, or the Enchanted Island* (1667), were repeatedly revived until well into the eighteenth century.[78]

Both houses employed musicians and, although Davenant used his more imaginatively, Killigrew put on enough of a show to stay in competition. Both impresarios subcontracted music-directing responsibility to specialists, of course. Peter Holman has assembled evidence showing that, in the early Restoration period, 'the orchestras of both theatres were made up of the [king's] Twenty-four Violins', distributed equally between the theatres by order of the Lord Chamberlain.[79] This was done in the interests of fairness, presumably, and to guarantee the king a pleasant musical experience whichever theatre he chose to attend. The arrangement seems to have survived until Killigrew's company started its slide toward bankruptcy in the late 1670s (see below), and the two principal composers for the Twenty-four Violins, Matthew Locke and John Banister, also supplied most of the incidental music for both theatres until their deaths in the mid 1670s.[80] Theatrical earning opportunities were parcelled out between court musicians in predictable hierarchical order, as the young Purcell must have been well placed to observe. He exploited court connections in the same business-like way a decade and a half later, when his own career in the theatre took off.

Complex contractual agreements governed employer–employee relations and profit-sharing systems in both theatres. They cannot be reconstructed fully at this distance. Disputes were frequent and often required arbitration before the Lord Chamberlain, the crown-appointed theatre licenser. Surviving legal depositions are detailed, and very revealing. Both Davenant and Killigrew sold shares to raise start-up funds. In Davenant's theatre expenditure on instrumental music was initially capped at 30s per day to keep costs under control and ensure the shareholders an adequate return.[81] Davenant and Killigrew were both shareholders in their respective enterprises. Davenant's leading actors were shareholders also; helpfully, from the management point of view, their personal financial interests aligned with those of non-performing shareholder colleagues, focusing creative minds on money as much as art. Shares were bought and sold as personal fortunes fluctuated.

---

78   For their stage and publication histories see Christopher Spencer (ed.), *Five Restoration Adaptations of Shakespeare* (Urbana: University of Illinois Press, 1965).
79   Holman, *Four and Twenty Fiddlers*, pp. 333–7.
80   Ibid., p. 336.
81   Hotson, *The Commonwealth and Restoration Stage*, p. 207.

When Davenant died in 1668 title to his patent (his theatre operating-licence) passed to Charles, Davenant's oldest son by his third wife; but until Charles came of age his mother was effectively in control. Sensibly, Lady Davenant delegated day-to-day management of the company to Thomas Betterton and Henry Harris, two of Davenant's leading actors, paying them 20s a week each; this arrangement continued even when Charles Davenant came properly into his inheritance. Sir William's heirs and the two actor-managers remained on productively good terms for many years and were able to press ahead with the founder's expansion plans, raising funds to build the new Dorset Garden theatre, which opened in 1671, and presenting a series of productions of unprecedented ambition at Dorset Garden from 1674 onwards. Dorset Garden's state-of-the-art stage machinery made hitherto unrealizable scenic transformations, flying and lighting effects possible. These were key ingredients of opera, as well-travelled audience members recognized. Indeed, it is important to be aware that productions at Dorset Garden passed as operas whenever they had sufficient musical content and lavish staging, even though long sections of the show were still spoken.[82] Conspicuous production expenditure defined the genre, very largely.[83]

We can be practically certain that Purcell witnessed all of Dorset Garden's main musical productions. Although he would have been just too old to sing with the Chapel Royal choir in Dorset Garden's 1674 extravaganza *The Tempest* (his voice had broken the year before), he surely knew it was happening and would have had no trouble gaining entry to see it, had he so wished. Likewise he would surely have been well aware of *Psyche*, the 1675 English riposte to the French self-styled Royal Academicians, Cambert and Perrin. Thomas Shadwell produced an English text based on the Lully–Molière tragédie-ballet *Psyché* (premiered in Paris in 1671), but Matthew Locke took an aggressively nationalistic musical line, writing Anglo-Italianate music and scoring it up for an eccentric array of old English instruments.[84]

Thomas Killigrew (thoroughly corrupt in his business dealings, it emerged) was forced to rebuild his theatre after it burned down in 1672. To conceal the extent of his indebtedness, he fed shareholders a stream of misinformation; he also quarrelled catastrophically with Charles, his oldest son and heir. In 1676/7 Charles seized control of the Killigrew business (he fought his father in court, and won), but was unable to manage it either to fellow shareholders' or to the actors' satisfaction.

---

82   For an idea of how lavish they could be, see Judith Milhous, 'The Multimedia Spectacular on the Restoration Stage', in Shirley Strum Kenny (ed.), *British Theatre and the Other Arts, 1660–1800* (Washington DC: Folger Shakespeare Library; London: Associated University Presses, 1984), pp. 41–66.

83   As Hume states, 'What the [modern] interpreter needs to understand above all is a simple but disconcerting truth: in seventeenth-century England "opera" was less a genre than a mode of production'; Robert D. Hume, 'The Politics of Opera in Late Seventeenth-Century London', *Cambridge Opera Journal* 10 (1998): 43.

84   See Holman, *Four and Twenty Fiddlers*, pp. 345–55; and Herissone, 'Playford, Purcell, and the Functions of Music Publishing': 274–5. For a modern edition of Locke's vocal music for *Psyche*, see Matthew Locke, *Dramatic Music*, ed. Michael Tilmouth, Musica Britannica, vol. 51 (London: Stainer & Bell, 1986).

Company morale plummeted; funds dried up. The Davenant company proposed a merger (more or less a takeover); the extreme weakness of his negotiating position led Charles Killigrew to agree to it, and necessary royal approval was obtained. So in May 1682 London's two rival theatres came under joint management and stopped competing. An absolute monopoly was established, and it survived until late 1694 – almost to the end of Purcell's career. The United Company owned two theatres but only performed in one at a time. Drury Lane – not so well equipped for opera, cheaper to run – was its main play-house. Occasional spectacular shows, making extensive use of music and scenery and requiring careful technical preparation, could be rehearsed in Dorset Garden without disrupting Drury Lane operations. By restricting the supply of dramatick opera, public interest in it could be inflamed; and opera tickets could now be sold at elevated prices.

At this point in the story Thomas Betterton came fully into his own as the 'natural leader' of the United Company.[85] His Dorset Garden co-manager, Henry Harris, had just retired from acting; no one in the former Killigrew company could match his experience. Betterton's authority was unassailable. He and his actress wife lived in an apartment forming part of Dorset Garden Theatre from 1671 to 1694, literally above the shop. As well as acting in many of his own productions, Betterton selected scripts for the company, some from stock (old plays revived), some newly commissioned. He reviewed scripts before submitting them to the Lord Chamberlain for licensing, removing material likely to offend the censor in advance. He trimmed scripts too long or tedious for performance in uncut form.[86] He sketched out plans for scenery, perhaps taking inspiration from prints in his library, as Julie and Frans Muller have suggested.[87] At Charles II's expense he travelled to Paris to learn as much as he could about French opera-production techniques. Roger North called him 'the cheif ingineer of the stage'.[88] He owned shares in the company, and amassed a personal fortune. For one so powerful he

---

85   Hotson, *The Commonwealth and Restoration Stage*, p. 281.

86   Dryden's *Don Sebastian* (1689, publ. 1690) is a famous example. According to Dryden, newly appointed Lord Chamberlain the Earl of Dorset *'was pleas'd to read the Tragedy twice over before it was Acted; and did me the favour to send me word, that I had written beyond any of my former Plays; and that he was displeas'd any thing shou'd be cut away. ... Above twelve hunder'd lines ha[d] been cut off ... since it was first deliver'd to the Actors'* [before Dorset got to see it?] *'judiciously lopt by Mr.* Betterton'. See Dryden's Preface to *Don Sebastian*, in John Dryden, *Plays: Albion and Albanius, Don Sebastian, Amphitryon*, eds Earl Miner, George R. Guffey and Franklin B. Zimmerman, The Works of John Dryden, vol. 15 (Berkeley, Los Angeles and London: University of California Press, 1976), pp. 70–71 and 66.

87   Julia and Frans Muller, 'Purcell's *Dioclesian* on the Dorset Garden Stage', in Michael Burden (ed.), *Performing the Music of Henry Purcell* (Oxford: Oxford University Press, 1996), p. 238.

88   John Wilson (ed.), *Roger North on Music: Being a Selection from his Essays Written during the Years c.1695–1728* (London: Novello, 1959), p. 353.

was surprisingly popular. Judith Milhous notes that '[t]he only subject that could focus criticism of Betterton was money, a risk endemic to his position'.[89]

Betterton's importance to the Restoration theatre is well known to theatre historians. An impression of his working methods can be gained from James Winn's thoroughly indexed Dryden biography,[90] while the latter part of Betterton's career has been extensively researched by Judith Milhous.[91] Until very recently no book-length modern study covering his long pre-1695 career existed (Robert Lowe's 1891 biography was the best available),[92] but David Roberts's *Thomas Betterton: The Greatest Actor of the Restoration Stage* has filled the gap, published in 2010 to coincide with the three hundredth anniversary of Betterton's death.[93] What needs stressing here is Betterton's significance as an advocate for music within the United Company. He opened the door to a new breed of musical rent-seeker, and watched (perhaps approvingly, perhaps unwittingly) as more and more of the audience's money drained away into musicians' pockets.

By 1680 a successful format for the public concert had been established in Restoration London, and audiences were growing. For the theatres, this competition demanded retaliatory action: productions began to incorporate more and more impressive theatre music to ensure that the theatre remained the entertainment destination of choice, even for audience members primarily interested in music.[94] Political demands had to be accommodated also. As the twenty-fifth anniversary of the Restoration approached, Charles II planned a series of self-aggrandizing celebratory statements (some artistic, some architectural) and looked to Betterton for operatic support.[95] The result was the first all-sung English-language opera to be performed on the Dorset-Garden stage, *Albion and Albanius*, with a libretto by Poet Laureate John Dryden, and music by the French-trained Catalan Louis Grabu. As is well known, Charles's unexpected death before the public premiere of

---

89   Judith Milhous, 'Betterton, Thomas', in *Oxford Dictionary of National Biography*, http://www.oxforddnb.com (last accessed 1 April 2011).

90   James Anderson Winn, *John Dryden and his World* (New Haven and London: Yale University Press, 1987).

91   See Judith Milhous, *Thomas Betterton and the Management of Lincoln's Inn Fields, 1695–1708* (Carbondale: Southern Illinois University Press, 1979).

92   Robert W. Lowe, *Thomas Betterton*, Eminent Actors, vol. 2 (London: Kegan Paul, Trench and Trübner, 1891).

93   David Roberts, *Thomas Betterton: The Greatest Actor of the Restoration Stage* (Cambridge and New York: Cambridge University Press, 2010).

94   See Anthony A. Olmsted, 'The Capitalization of Musical Production: The Conceptual and Spatial Development of London's Public Concerts, 1660–1750', in Regula Burckhardt Qureshi (ed.), *Music and Marx: Ideas, Practice, Politics*, Critical and Cultural Musicology (New York: Routledge, 2002), pp. 106–38.

95   See Andrew R. Walkling, 'The Apotheosis of Absolutism and the Interrupted Masque: Theater, Music, and Monarchy in Restoration England', in Julia Marciari Alexander and Catharine MacLeod (eds), *Politics, Transgression, and Representation at the Court of Charles II* (New Haven and London: Yale Center for British Art/Yale University Press, 2007), pp. 193–231.

Albion and Albanius forced a lengthy delay, during which time Dryden and Grabu had to rework the ending. Monmouth's landing delivered the *coup de grâce*: real-world political turmoil upstaged dramatic allegory, and when *Albion* eventually opened, its hoped-for audience failed to materialize. The opera was a commercial flop. But for Betterton and for other company members involved in the production, *Albion and Albanius* was a hugely valuable learning experience – the logical end of a chain of development pushing straight plays more and more in the direction of all-sung opera. Although Betterton backtracked to dramatick opera subsequently, reinserting spoken roles for actors like himself, both his musical ambitions and audience expectations had been permanently changed.

As a shareholder in the United Company, Betterton's ambitious creative instincts and personal financial interests were opposed. However, in the late 1680s his grip on the company reins in any case loosened. Charles Davenant sold out, and his brother Alexander bought Charles's shares, ostensibly with his own money, but in practice with funds supplied by two speculators, Sir Thomas Skipwith and Christopher Rich. Alexander Davenant, Skipwith and Rich tried to drive up profits by cutting costs. Betterton was relieved of managerial duties and the stage roles in which he was used to starring were reallocated to younger actors. In Autumn 1691 he surrendered his shares and went on salary – while nevertheless continuing to direct shows.[96] From that point, Betterton's incentives were realigned: heavy spending on music and spectacle would burnish Betterton's visionary reputation without affecting his personal earnings. Financial pain was visited on the remaining shareholders, and Betterton probably thought they deserved to suffer. The Purcell–Betterton dramatick operas can therefore be interpreted as, among other things, acts of economic revenge perpetrated by a highly aggrieved and highly experienced company insider, sacrificing shareholder profits on the altar of art. Knowledge of theatre practicalities and theatre personalities suggests new perspectives from which to view Purcell's operatic output.

Purcell's success with *Dioclesian* in 1690 – the production that marked Dorset Garden's proud return to dramatick opera after the disaster of *Albion and Albanius* – made him Betterton's composer of choice for all subsequent high-budget productions through to 1695. As we saw at the beginning of this chapter, musical cutbacks at court encouraged Purcell to look for opportunities elsewhere, so Betterton signed him up at the perfect moment. Purcell's staggering productivity in the last five years of his life – three full-scale dramatick-opera scores plus *The Indian Queen*, together with incidental music for more than fifty plays – required equally extraordinary economic and administrative foundations to sustain it.

The economic and administrative circumstances underpinning Purcell's musical achievement in the theatre were inherently unstable. Tension between actors and management in the United Company escalated as production costs soared and actors' salaries were eroded. In December 1694 Betterton, along with most of

---

96   See Nicoll, *A History of English Drama 1660–1900: Vol. 1*, pp. 334–5. Nicoll notes some rather puzzling vacillation: apparently 'Betterton came into share again' in September 1692, and went back on salary in January 1693.

the United Company's best-known actors, petitioned the Lord Chamberlain for a licence to run their own theatre, breaking the United Company's monopoly. With permission granted, Betterton and his fellow rebels decamped to Lincoln's Inn Fields – reoccupying Davenant's first post-Restoration theatre building, the converted tennis court – and started acting there at the end of April 1695. Purcell stayed with the former United Company, working with its 'raw young Actors' and singers as best he could. Before the full implications of resurgent musical competition between Purcell at Dorset Garden/Drury Lane and Betterton's house composers at Lincoln's Inn Fields had time to sink in, Purcell fell ill and died. How he might have fared against younger English challengers for the 'Orpheus Britannicus' title, or indeed against Handel, seem to me to be valid questions: they were avoided by Purcell's contemporaries out of respect for his memory – not because they are musically uninteresting and not because they are unanswerable.[97]

The Restoration Theatre as Physical Space

The best available introduction to Restoration theatre architecture is Richard Leacroft's *The Development of the English Playhouse*.[98] Some of Leacroft's ideas have been challenged since the book appeared in 1973, but his beautifully drawn pictures – practically informed attempts at theatre reconstruction, interpreting incomplete and sometimes contradictory evidence in the light of professional stage-design experience – are hugely helpful aids to the visual imagination. The evidence with which theatre reconstructors have to work is of various sorts. It includes small-scale evidence from entrance/exit and scene-change directions in prompt-books and published play-texts, which often have architectural implications since they signal the existence of features such as doors opening onto the stage or trapdoors.[99] Careful measurements recorded in sale or lease documents for plots of land bought or leased for theatrical development also sometimes survive. London maps not

---

97 See Andrew Pinnock and Bruce Wood, 'A Mangled Chime: The Accidental Death of the Opera Libretto in Civil War England', *Early Music* 36 (2008): 265–84, and compare against Westrup, *Purcell*, p. 149: 'If Purcell had lived twenty years longer he might himself have led the invasion of Italian opera [!] and by adapting the style to the peculiar exigencies of the English tongue have given us a national opera able to withstand all the assaults of the alien.' This is a tragic misunderstanding grounded in Westrup's belief that the score of *The Tempest* (since de-attributed) was 'Purcell's most mature work for the theatre ... exhibit[ing] ... the complete absorption of the Italian style' (Westrup, *Purcell*, p. 145).

98 Richard Leacroft, *The Development of the English Playhouse: an Illustrated Survey of Theatre Building in England from Medieval to Modern Times* (London: Eyre Methuen, 1973).

99 In Chapter 4 ('The Curtain; The Prologue; Changes of Scene') of *The Restoration Theatre* (London: Kegan Paul, Trench and Trübner, 1934), Summers brings together a large collection of stage directions from which architectural and technical-mechanical information can be gleaned.

only show where the theatres were located but also illustrate their size and shape relative to other buildings in the area. A theatre drawing by Sir Christopher Wren survives in the library of All Souls College, Oxford,[100] beautifully executed but torn along the bottom. Although Wren very likely would have been called in to design a new Theatre Royal, Drury Lane when fire destroyed the old one (January 1672), this particular drawing is not explicitly labelled. It may have been superseded by a later plan, no longer extant; it may relate to a different project altogether. Still, as Leacroft establishes, all its key architectural features were, on other evidence, demonstrably present in the new Theatre Royal as built and operated. Leacroft's reconstruction, largely based the Wren drawing, looks both elegant and practicable. Clearly it was influenced by Richard Southern's earlier model reconstruction, pictured in *Changeable Scenery*, a book that, although it was published 60 years ago, remains extremely useful, not least for its detailed explanations of how Restoration and other early stage machinery worked.[101]

Leacroft assumes that Restoration theatre architects would have been influenced by earlier seventeenth-century practice – that of Inigo Jones and John Webb above all[102] – which in turn was influenced by classical amphitheatre models and a desire to recreate them in more comfortable modern form. Curved rather than straight-row seating had classical precedent, allowing clearer sightlines and minimizing the distance between performers and spectators. Yet the Restoration theatre's changeable scenery looked more convincing seen head on. Leacroft's new Drury Lane reconstruction achieves a shapely compromise – the 'fan-shaped auditorium', as he calls it – optimizing both the view and the acoustic experience for almost everyone in the audience. The only conspicuous losers out were those in gallery seats close to the proscenium arch; and since their conspicuousness was intentional (they were there not to see but to be seen), complaints from that quarter were very unlikely.

Leacroft briefly describes the Dorset Garden theatre without attempting to reconstruct its interior appearance, presumably because Edward Langhans's cut-away model of Dorset Garden was well known by the time Leacroft published his book. Researchers interested in Langhans's reconstructive reasoning have to turn to journal articles for explanations, starting with Robert D. Hume's overviews, 'The Dorset Garden Theatre: A Review of Facts and Problems' and 'The Nature of the Dorset Garden Theatre'.[103] Photographs of the Langhans model are reproduced in Langhans's essay in *The London Theatre World*, but have subsequently also been

---

100 A retouched version of the drawing is given in ibid., facing p. 94; The image is reproduced without enhancement in Michael Burden, 'Where Did Purcell Keep his Theatre Band?', *Early Music* 37 (2009): 432.

101 Richard Southern, *Changeable Scenery: Its Origin and Development in the British Theatre* (London: Faber, 1952), picture facing p. 176.

102 See John Orrell, *The Theatres of Inigo Jones and John Webb* (Cambridge and New York: Cambridge University Press, 1985).

103 Robert D. Hume, 'The Dorset Garden Theatre: A Review of Facts and Problems', *Theatre Notebook* 33 (1979): 4–17; Hume, 'The Nature of the Dorset Garden Theatre', *Theatre Notebook* 36 (1982): 99–109.

published in *Henry Purcell's Operas: The Complete Texts*,[104] and in Bruce Wood's *Purcell: An Extraordinary Life*.[105] Recently, Frans and Julie Muller have suggested a number of refinements adapting the Langhans model for greater functionality in Purcell's dramatick operas.[106] Frans Muller is, as was Leacroft before him, a professional theatre architect with technical as well as scholarly expertise.

Alistair Potts's 1998 Cambridge University PhD dissertation, 'The Development of the Playhouse in Seventeenth-Century London', explores differences of opinion between rival Restoration theatre reconstructors over the past few decades.[107] Potts's suggestion – that, for play performance purposes, Drury Lane was far superior to Dorset Garden, in terms of its design, appointment and location – may surprise Purcell scholars, but it is well supported by evidence. Dorset Garden fell into disrepair soon after Purcell's death, following the break-up of the United Company, and was demolished in 1709; Drury Lane survived until 1791. Nevertheless, as far as theatre musicians were concerned, Dorset Garden was advantageous for containing a 'music room' prominently positioned above the proscenium arch.[108] In Drury Lane the musicians occupied side boxes level with the proscenium (one or more, possibly, depending on the number of performers involved). An orchestra pit was created for Dorset Garden's 1674 production of *The Tempest*: 'the Band of 24 Violins, with the Harpsichals and Theorbo's which accompany the Voices' sat between the front row of stall seats and the stage itself, since '[t]he Front of the Stage [had been] open'd', allowing some to tuck themselves right underneath'. Unusually, however, a choir 'above 30 Warbling voyces' took part in the same production (seconded from the Chapel Royal, as noted above): instrumentalists may have been removed from the music room merely so that singers could use it instead. Curtis Price argued in 1979 that 'the orchestra pit was a common feature of the Restoration playhouse' when large musical forces were required: 'the modest hideaway of the musicians of an earlier age … became the lover's balcony, only occasionally occupied by a serenading band'.[109] But more recent investigations

---

104 Michael Burden (ed.), *Henry Purcell's Operas: The Complete Texts* (Oxford and New York: Oxford University Press, 2000), plate 4 (between pp. 270 and 271).

105 Wood, *Purcell: An Extraordinary Life*, p. 45.

106 Frans and Julie Muller, 'Completing the Picture: The Importance of Reconstructing Early Opera', *Early Music* 33 (2005): 667–81.

107 Alistair James Potts, 'The Development of the Playhouse in Seventeenth-Century London', (PhD dissertation, University of Cambridge, 1998), http://playhousehistory. co.uk (last accessed 1 April 2011).

108 This and the following paragraph are adapted from Henry Purcell, *The Fairy Queen*, eds Bruce Wood and Andrew Pinnock, The Works of Henry Purcell, vol. 12 (new edn, London: Stainer & Bell, 2009), pp. xxx–xxxi, to which readers are referred for further information about Purcell's dramatick-opera orchestration and the physical placement of instrumentalists in Dorset Garden.

109 Curtis A. Price, *Music in the Restoration Theatre: with a Catalogue of Instrumental Music in the Plays, 1665–1713*, Studies in Musicology, vol. 4 (Ann Arbor: UMI Research Press, 1979), pp. 86–7.

have rehabilitated the Dorset Garden music room as a viable workspace for 'two dozen players and the continuo group', with a floor area 'over 200 square feet'.[110]

Seventeenth-century composers, performers, playwrights, librettists and theatre audiences shared a thorough understanding of the symbolic associations surrounding certain classes of instrument. '[F]lutes figure in sacred or pastoral scenes ... trumpets, sometimes accompanied by the *timbales*, announce the presence of warriors or [heroes]. Oboes ... play military marches or announce the descent of the Zephyrs ... But generally they are more suitable for rural tableaux' – in this respect Jérôme de La Gorce's notes on Lully's orchestra apply equally to Purcell's.[111] Yet, although Lully's use of costumed instrumentalists on stage is well documented, the Purcell opera word-books mention them infrequently and ambiguously.[112] Other English opera word-books earlier and later in date – including *Psyche*, *The Tempest* and *The Island Princess* – are more explicit, and in regular plays on-stage instrumentalists were fairly common.[113] '[T]here were alternatives on offer for the Restoration composer', as Michael Burden points out: '[t]he [theatre] band could be moved around; it could be split; it could be put on stage, the use of on-stage music being greater than at any time since.'[114]

Frustratingly little is known about set and costume design in the Restoration theatre, for reasons explained by Sybil Rosenfeld:

> Scene designers were not employees of wealthy principalities, but of struggling public theatres and their work was made for the rough and tumble of a continuous repertoire of performances and not for occasional magnificent productions ... [the latter far more likely to be] recorded in commemorative volumes for the honour and glory of [theatre patrons].[115]

Of the set designs that have been preserved, William Dolle's engraved views of scenes in the Dorset Garden tragedy *The Empress of Morocco* (1673) have been

---

110 See Mark A. Radice, 'Theater Architecture at the Time of Purcell and its Influence on his "Dramatick Operas"', *Musical Quarterly* 74 (1990): 129; see also Julia and Frans Muller, 'Purcell's *Dioclesian* on the Dorset Garden Stage'.

111 Jérôme de La Gorce, 'Some Notes on Lully's Orchestra', in John Hajdu Heyer (ed.), *Jean-Baptiste Lully and the Music of the French Baroque: Essays in Honor of James R. Anthony* (Cambridge: Cambridge University Press, 1989), pp. 103–106.

112 See, for example, *Dioclesian*, Act II, Scene [ii], lines 804–806: 'While they invest him with the Imperial Robes, this Martial Song is sung: Trumpets and Ho-Boys joyning with them'; *Dioclesian*, Act II, Scene [ii], lines 937–938: 'Exeunt Trumpets and Drums, sounding and beating a dead March'; and *King Arthur*, Act II, Scene [ii], line 502: 'Here the Men offer their Flutes to the Women, which they refuse'. Line numbers are those assigned in Burden (ed.), *Henry Purcell's Operas: The Complete Texts*.

113 See Price, *Music in the Restoration Theatre*, pp. 73–81.

114 Burden, 'Where Did Purcell Keep his Theatre Band?': 440.

115 Sybil Rosenfeld, *Georgian Scene Painters and Scene Painting* (Cambridge: Cambridge University Press, 1981), pp. 3–4.

extensively reproduced,[116] as has the engraved frontispiece to *Ariane, ou le mariage de Bacchus*, showing a small group of performers on the Drury Lane stage in 1674.[117] Beyond these, however, scholars have to look to English source evidence earlier and later in date than the Restoration, and at roughly contemporary mainland European evidence, in order to attempt more or less plausible reconstructions of Restoration scenery and costumes.

Inigo Jones's early seventeenth-century masque scenery and costume designs, referred to above, are probably the most significant resources in this respect. As John Peacock shows,[118] most of Jones's designs were copied from Italian and other continental originals – unsurprisingly, since his patron Charles I was busy amassing and proudly displaying a huge collection of paintings bought from all over Europe.[119] Similar scenic internationalism in the Restoration period seems highly likely. Researchers keen to visualize the scenic splendours of *Psyche*, *Dioclesian* and *The Fairy Queen* can also take inspiration from surviving designs by Jean Berain, Giacomo Torelli and Carlo Vigarani, much discussed by art historians and extensively reproduced.[120] Sir James Thornhill's four early eighteenth-century sketch-designs for *Arsinoë* (Drury Lane, 1705) are also suggestive: they include 'a garden scene by Moonlight', 'a room of state with statuary', 'a hall with ... coupled columns leading through an arch to a garden', and 'another garden scene with ... a perspective back scene of a parterre with a haven and ships beyond'.[121] Roger Savage's pioneering article 'The Shakespeare-Purcell *Fairy Queen*: A Defence and Recommendation' – very imaginatively and variously illustrated – shows how far a historically minded stage designer could hope to go in the direction of visual 'authenticity'.[122] Frans and Julie Muller add movement in their animations

---

116 They occur, for instance, in Allardyce Nicoll, *The Development of the Theatre: A Study of Theatrical Art from the Beginnings to the Present Day* (5th rev. edn, London: Harrap, 1966), pp. 155–6; and in Locke, *Dramatic Music*, ed. Tilmouth, pp. xxvii–xxix.

117 This is reproduced, for instance, in Westrup, *Purcell*, facing p. 108; and in Price, *Music in the Restoration Theatre*, p. 91.

118 John Peacock, *The Stage Designs of Inigo Jones: The European Context* (Cambridge: Cambridge University Press, 1995).

119 See Chapter 1 of Jonathan Brown, *Kings and Connoisseurs: Collecting Art in Seventeenth-Century Europe*, The A.W. Mellon Lectures in the Fine Arts, vol. 43 (New Haven and London: Yale University Press, 1995).

120 For a selection of these images, see the illustrations accompanying Jérôme de La Gorce, 'Quelques rapports entre les dessins d'opéras français du règne de Louis XIV et l'architecture, la sculpture et la peinture', in Jérôme de La Gorce (ed.), *Iconographie et arts du spectacle: actes du séminaire CNRS (G.D.R. 712), Paris, 1992*, Histoire de l'art et iconographie, vol. 2 (Paris: Klincksieck, 1996), pp. 135–54. See also Per Bjurström, *Giacomo Torelli and Baroque Stage Design*, Figura, New Series, vol. 2 (Stockholm: Nationalmuseum, 1961); Chapter 4 of Nicoll, *The Development of the Theatre*; and Jérôme de La Gorce, *Berain, dessinateur du Roi Soleil* (Paris: Herscher, 1986).

121 See Sybil Rosenfeld, *A Short History of Scene Design in Great Britain*, Drama and Theatre Studies (Oxford: Blackwell, 1973), pp. 63–5.

122 Roger Savage, 'The Shakespeare-Purcell *Fairy Queen*: A Defence and Recommendation', *Early Music* 1 (1973): 201–21.

for *Dioclesian* and *The Fairy Queen*,[123] and in their 2005 article 'Completing the Picture' put forward further fascinating evidence suggesting deliberate use of visual imagery domestically familiar to William and Mary.[124] The Mullers are indefatigable campaigners for historically informed opera production, rightly if not always conveniently reminding Purcellians that Restoration 'whole shows' involved a great deal more than words and music.

Research Tools for Music in the Restoration Theatre

Curtis Price's *Henry Purcell and the London Stage* was the first published book-length survey exploring Purcell's entire theatre-music output.[125] Nothing like it has appeared since its publication in 1984. It is essential reading for researchers, even though more recent investigations inspired by Price have redrawn large parts of the landscape that he set out bravely to map. *Henry Purcell and the London Stage* is partly a critical appreciation of Purcell's theatre music, taking methodological inspiration from a number of US literary scholars working in the Restoration field (Hume and Milhous of course, James Winn and Steven Zwicker), partly an exploration of the varied uses to which music was put in the Restoration theatre, and partly a survey of source evidence, clearing the ground for critical appreciation and correcting ancient editorial misapprehensions. Via Price, Margaret Laurie's thinking on chronology and source relationships became much better known.[126] Price also developed some of John Buttrey's PhD dissertation suggestions for political-allegorical interpretation in Purcell operas.[127] British Purcell theatre-music research conducted in the 1950s and 1960s had to wait a quarter of a century for recognition outside specialist circles, and Price's intellectual advocacy was hugely important in this respect.

His earlier study, *Music in the Restoration Theatre* (1979),[128] did an even more ambitious pioneering job. The reference tool at its heart – 'a Catalogue of Instrumental Music in the Plays 1665–1713' – lists all the theatrically associated

---

123 These are accessible via http://www.julieandfransmuller.nl/Dioclesianmasque_eng. html and http://www.julieandfransmuller.nl/FQ_act5_masque_eng.html (last accessed 1 April 2011).

124 Muller and Muller, 'Completing the Picture'.

125 Curtis A. Price, *Henry Purcell and the London Stage* (Cambridge: Cambridge University Press, 1984).

126 A. Margaret Laurie, 'Purcell's Stage Works', (PhD dissertation, University of Cambridge, 1962). In his Preface, Price noted 'I owe special thanks to A. Margaret Laurie, whose doctoral thesis on Purcell's theatre music provides the foundation for this book'; Price, *Henry Purcell and the London Stage*, p. xii.

127 John Buttrey, 'The Evolution of English Opera between 1656 and 1695: A Re-investigation' (PhD dissertation, University of Cambridge, 1967). Price's interpretations are explored in Chapter 6 below.

128 See n. 109.

Restoration instrumental music that Price had managed to locate (thousands of individual items), shows where the music can be found in both manuscript and printed sources, and demonstrates through silent omission how much music has gone missing. If a play listed in Allardyce Nicoll's 'Hand-list of Restoration Plays'[129] or in Montague Summers's *A Bibliography of Restoration Drama*[130] is not listed in Price's Catalogue, its instrumental music is unlikely to have survived. Price's Catalogue was designed to complement two other reference books: Day and Murrie's *English Song Books 1651–1702: A Bibliography*,[131] and Zimmerman's *Henry Purcell, 1659–1695: An Analytical Catalogue of his Music*.[132] Price reported the existence of Purcell theatre-music concordances only when Zimmerman had overlooked them. Detailed indices in Day and Murrie make it fairly easy to connect published theatre songs (including Purcell's) with the plays in which they originally featured, but Price also included a song-list for each catalogued play, adding Day and Murrie numbers when early printed versions of the songs exist (but omitting songs by Henry Purcell).

For Restoration theatre-music researchers, the catalogues of Day and Murrie, Zimmerman and Price are essential navigational aids.[133] All three – like *The London Stage* and Milhous and Hume's *Register of English Theatrical Documents* – were produced on US scholarly initiative and with US foundation backing. In Britain a different system of reward – centred on the combined activities of the Purcell Society edition, BBC broadcasting opportunities and commercial recording contracts – resulted in forms of output focusing on practically orientated performance research. Purcell Society committee members and editors from Arnold Goldsbrough, Thurston Dart and Anthony Lewis through to Christopher Hogwood and Peter Holman have invested as much energy in performing, broadcasting and recording activities as in book- and article-writing. Landmark theatre-music recordings thus produced include Lewis's *Fairy Queen*, *King Arthur* and *Indian Queen*, Hogwood's complete theatre music, and Holman's *Ayres for the Theatre*.

My own work on the texts of Henry Purcell's dramatick operas, pursued in collaboration with Michael Burden, Margaret Laurie and (especially) Bruce

129 See n. 21.

130 Montague Summers, *A Bibliography of Restoration Drama* (London: Fortune Press, [1935]).

131 Cyrus Lawrence Day and Eleanore Boswell Murrie, *English Song-Books, 1651–1702: A Bibliography, With a First-Line Index of Songs* (London: for the Bibliographical Society at Oxford University Press, 1940 (for 1937)).

132 Franklin B. Zimmerman, *Henry Purcell, 1659–1695: An Analytical Catalogue of his Music* (London: Macmillan; New York: St Martin's Press, 1963).

133 Nevertheless, Zimmerman's work-by-work commentaries are now 50 years out of date, and the introductory chapters prefacing Price's catalogue (although not the catalogue itself) have been largely superseded. Only one song ('Dear pretty youth') in Z631, *The Tempest*, is now thought to be by Purcell. The rest of this dramatick-opera score was disowned by most Purcell experts soon after the publication of Margaret Laurie's 1964 article 'Did Purcell set *The Tempest*?', *Proceedings of the Royal Musical Association* 90 (1963–64): 41–57.

Wood, has tried to bring editorial and prior analytical order to source evidence inconveniently heterogeneous in origin – bringing together printed word-book evidence, textual evidence from music manuscripts and publications, and all available contextual evidence, finding explanations for conflicting evidence wherever possible, and aiming to produce a scholarly amalgam useful for critical and for practical performing purposes. My extended essay in *Henry Purcell's Operas: The Complete Texts*, 'From Rosy Bowers: Coming to Purcell The Bibliographical Way',[134] used 'new bibliographical' reasoning of the sort championed by Walter Greg and Fredson Bowers, to re-frame the editorial problems specific to dramatick opera and to suggest that different approaches to problem-solving suited different editorial purposes. Stage-to-page issues have attracted much scholarly attention in literary studies, of course;[135] in applying Stephen Orgel's motto '[t]he text ... was not the play' to Purcell's operas,[136] I sought to draw Purcell scholars into this wider debate.

Eight of the thirty-two volumes comprising the Purcell Society edition of Purcell's complete works contain theatre music, reflecting the fact that roughly a quarter of his output was theatrically commissioned. Three volumes of 'Dramatic Music' collect together songs and instrumental pieces written for plays not musical or scenically elaborate enough to count as dramatick operas when first produced, almost all performed in Drury Lane rather than Dorset Garden.[137] The original Purcell Society editions of Dramatic Music Parts I, II and III have now been thoroughly superseded by the revised editions of 1998–2010, edited by Margaret Laurie and Ian Spink, who have considerably updated information on the dates of composition, early performances, and the location and state of source materials. Apart from the sheer quantity of music these volumes show Purcell to have written in the last five years of his life, they also illustrate something of the practical conditions in which he must have worked. Purcell could well have composed suites of instrumental music for plays such as *Distress'd Innocence* and *The Virtuous Wife* without reading their scripts or meeting their authors: here integration into

---

134 Andrew Pinnock, 'From Rosy Bowers: Coming to Purcell the Bibliographical Way', in Michael Burden (ed.), *Henry Purcell's Operas: The Complete Texts*, (Oxford and New York: Oxford University Press, 2000), pp. 31–93.

135 See, for example, George Winchester Stone, Jr. (ed.), *The Stage and the Page: London's 'Whole Show' in the Eighteenth-Century Theatre*, Publications from the Clark Library Professorship, UCLA, vol. 6 (Berkeley and London: University of California Press, 1981); and Julie Stone Peters, *Theatre of the Book 1480–1880: Print, Text, and Performance in Europe* (Oxford: Oxford University Press, 2000). Nevertheless, the former covers a slightly later period than the Restoration, and the latter a much wider one.

136 Stephen Orgel, 'Acting Scripts, Performing Texts', in Randall McLeod (ed.), *Crisis in Editing: Texts of the English Renaissance – Papers given at the Twenty-Fourth Annual Conference on Editorial Problems* (New York: AMS Press, 1994), p. 251.

137 Henry Purcell, *Dramatic Music, Part I*, ed. Margaret Laurie, The Works of Henry Purcell, vol. 16 (new edn, London: Novello, 2007); Purcell, *Dramatic Music, Part II*, ed. Ian Spink, The Works of Henry Purcell, vol. 20 (new edn, London: Novello, 1998); Purcell, *Dramatic Music, Part III*, ed. Margaret Laurie, The Works of Henry Purcell, vol. 21 (new edn, London: Stainer and Bell, 2010).

the drama was barely an issue. Single songs setting self-explanatory words also required little or no collaborative effort. But in some cases, usually when writing a mad song or song of conjuration, Purcell does seem to have worked knowingly with a playwright to create boundary-transcending artistic effects, little moments of 'real opera' by Edward J. Dent's sternly naturalistic definition – 'speech intensified into song under stress of emotion'; music (for a short while) 'the ideal language in which the persons in the drama express themselves'.[138]

Dido and Aeneas, Dioclesian, King Arthur, The Fairy Queen and The Indian Queen have volumes to themselves. The current Purcell Society Dido and Aeneas volume, edited by Margaret Laurie – continuously in print since 1979 – appeared long before the redating Dido controversy arose.[139] It presents a version of the work that I and many others now think is one of several that might tentatively be reconstructed.[140] There is scope for a new edition along the lines of Bruce Wood's parallel text Venus and Adonis, and to prove the point Bruce Wood has already prepared one in draft form. The original Purcell Society editions of Dioclesian (eds Frederick Bridge and John Pointer, 1900) and of King Arthur (ed. Dennis Arundell, 1928) were revised by Margaret Laurie, in 1961 and 1971 respectively.[141] Laurie provided new introductions, compiled new and very extensive textual commentaries, and edited brand new vocal scores for both works, but in both cases pages from the old editions, amended as necessary, were photographically reproduced: this saved money but it also constrained re-editorial freedom to some extent. Both operas are consequently now due to be re-edited from scratch (Dioclesian, eds Rebecca Herissone and Sandra Tuppen, is in preparation), making use of the new approach adopted for The Indian Queen and The Fairy Queen in the editions of 1994 (eds Margaret Laurie and Andrew Pinnock) and 2009 (eds Bruce Wood and Andrew Pinnock) respectively.[142] Here full critical editions of the complete play-texts as well as all surviving music for the dramatick opera in question are printed together for the first time.

As editor, co-editor or moderator of all five new Purcell Society theatre-music volumes published since Curtis Price's Henry Purcell and the London Stage appeared, Margaret Laurie – many of whose ideas were also incorporated into Price's book,

---

138 Dent, Foundations of English Opera, pp. 2–3.
139 Henry Purcell, Dido and Aeneas, ed. Margaret Laurie, The Works of Henry Purcell, vol. 3 (new edn, Sevenoaks: Novello, 1979).
140 For a 'Suggested Movement List for a Reconstructed "Complete" Production of Dido and Aeneas', including some 'speculative interpolations deriving no authority from any original source', see the Appendix in Andrew Walkling, 'The Masque of Actaeon and the Antimasque of Mercury: Dance, Dramatic Structure, and Tragic Exposition in Dido and Aeneas', Journal of the American Musicological Society 63 (2010): 235–7.
141 Henry Purcell, Dioclesian, ed. Margaret Laurie, The Works of Henry Purcell, vol. 9 (rev. edn, London: Novello, 1961); Purcell, King Arthur, ed. Margaret Laurie, The Works of Henry Purcell, vol. 26 (rev. edn, London: Novello, 1971).
142 Henry Purcell, The Indian Queen, eds Margaret Laurie and Andrew Pinnock, The Works of Henry Purcell, vol. 19 (new edn, London: Novello, 1994); Purcell, The Fairy Queen, eds Wood and Pinnock.

as noted above – has continued her research right to the present, embedding the results in prefaces and critical commentaries rather than books and articles more ostentatiously angling for citation and review. Against expectations perhaps (especially if expectations were shaped by unfortunate experience with old Purcell Society material), theatre-music researchers familiar with relevant volumes in the new Purcell Society edition may turn out to be better informed than those looking mainly to journals for cutting-edge contributions to debate.

Non-Purcell Society editions of all his operas exist, of course, some printed and published, others made solely for recording purposes.[143] Along with her book *Henry Purcell's 'Dido and Aeneas'*, researchers will find Ellen Harris's two editions interesting, even though both predate the *Dido* redating controversy.[144] Michael Burden's recent edition of *The Fairy Queen* is a work of real scholarship, presenting a version of the piece differing from the Purcell Society's in some thought-provoking ways.[145]

Future Research

This chapter has so far considered four different aspects of research on the Restoration theatre: the production of reference tools; consideration of the theatre as a commercial venture; studies of the physical and technical features of the playhouse; and research into the music composed for plays and operas. Much self-contained research continues in each of these discrete fields, and there are many aspects of what might be termed 'purely' musicological research into Restoration theatre music in which our understanding could be further enhanced. Music-editorial research continues to identify and assess specific problems through the close attention to detail that such source-work requires. Editors look for signs of disturbance in the sources, hinting at early production difficulties that would otherwise remain hidden: the Dance of Monkeys in *The Fairy Queen* is a good example of this sort of problem, since it is located differently in different sources.[146] Editors try to fill gaps in the surviving sources: Michael Burden's interest in missing dance tunes, for example, produced a useful article on untexted repeats of choral/orchestral numbers in dramatick opera, along with most of the dance tunes he set out to recover.[147]

---

143 See Andrew Pinnock, 'Fairest Isle™ – Land of the Scholar-Kings', *Early Music* 23 (1995): 651–65.

144 Ellen T. Harris, *Henry Purcell's 'Dido and Aeneas'* (Oxford: Clarendon, 1987); Henry Purcell, *Dido and Aeneas*, ed. Ellen Harris, Oxford Operas (Oxford: Oxford University Press, 1987); Purcell, *Dido and Aeneas*, ed. Ellen T. Harris, Eulenburg Miniature Scores (London: Eulenburg, 1987).

145 Henry Purcell, *The Fairy-Queen: An Opera*, ed. Michael Burden, Eulenburg Miniature Scores (New York and London: Eulenburg, 2009).

146 For possible reasons behind its shift, see Purcell, *The Fairy Queen*, ed. Wood and Pinnock, p. xxi.

147 Michael Burden, 'To Repeat (or Not to Repeat)? Dance Cues in Restoration English

Recent Purcell Society dramatick-opera editions have sought to distinguish as far as possible between different versions of the 'same' work, so that the early stage-histories of these works have been opened up for source-based study. As is discussed in Chapter 8 below, interest in later revivals is also increasing,[148] but the reception history of Purcell's theatre music remains largely untold: this line of enquiry could be stretched to the present, and widened out to include revivals in countries other than England, not least because Purcell's dramatick operas have exerted insufficiently appreciated influence over nineteenth- and twentieth-century composers busy reviving Purcell pieces while writing their own.

New documentary discoveries continue to be made, and very occasionally documents formerly in private hands pass into academic-institutional ownership – improved access prompting questions which scholars are more likely to ask when in a position to answer them. The English version of Cavalli's *Erismena* is a case in point, preserved in a handsome manuscript score that the Bodleian Library acquired in 2009 (from the estate of J. Stevens Cox). Who obtained a copy of the original Italian version of the opera? Who made the English translation? Was it prepared for production in Killigrew's Theatre Royal, Drury Lane around the time of the much better documented *Ariane* – Killigrew positioning his venue as a receiving house for bought-in opera while Betterton at Dorset Garden produced his own? These are just three of many intriguing questions raised by Michael Burden, which overseas archival evidence might help researchers answer.[149] Material unearthed in archives outside the UK might also shed light on foreign operatic trade routes leading to London.

Similarly, editorial work has begun to move firmly away from the notion of Purcell-centred research, chiefly designed to create contexts reaffirming the incomparable greatness of his music, in favour of wider cultural-environmental research revealing his partial dependence on others and acknowledging the continuing professional success of many who outlived him. Volumes 1 and 2 in the Purcell Society Companion Series present much-needed modern editions of

---

Opera', *Early Music* 35 (2007): 397–417.

148 See, for example, Ellen T. Harris, '*King Arthur's* Journey into the Eighteenth Century', in Curtis Price (ed.), *Purcell Studies* (Cambridge: Cambridge University Press, 1995), pp. 257–89; Michael Burden, '"Gallimaufry at Covent Garden": Purcell's *The Fairy Queen* in 1946', *Early Music* 23 (1995): 268–84; Burden, 'Purcell Debauch'd: the Dramatick Operas in Performance', in Michael Burden (ed.) *Performing the Music of Henry Purcell* (Oxford: Clarendon, 1996), pp. 145–62; Burden, 'Purcell's *King Arthur* in the 1730s', *Restoration: Studies in English Literary Culture, 1660–1700* 34 (2010): 117–38; Todd Gilman, 'David Garrick's *Masque of King Arthur* with Thomas Arne's Score (1770)', *Restoration: Studies in English Literary Culture, 1660–1700* 34 (2010): 139–62. These are discussed in the sections 'Purcell in Early Eighteenth-Century Performance Culture', 'Purcell in Later Eighteenth-Century Performance Culture' and 'Purcell and the English Musical Renaissance', in Chapter 8 of this volume.

149 For more on New College Oxford's June 2010 *Erismena* study day, organized by Michael Burden and Suzanne Aspden, see David Stuart and Greg Skidmore, 'Cavalli's *Erismena*', *Early Music* 38 (2010): 482–3.

Albion and Albanius (ed. Bryan White),[150] and *Venus and Adonis* (ed. Bruce Wood).[151] A complete edition of John Eccles's work is underway – a high proportion of it theatrical[152] – while Mark Humphreys's 2005 Oxford DPhil research work on Daniel Purcell produced a new biography and a complete thematic catalogue of a composer most of whose music was again written for the theatre.[153] The music described by Kathryn Lowerre, in *Music and Musicians on the London Stage, 1695–1705*, is increasingly accessible, awaiting further study and inviting practical revival.[154] In a post-Purcell-anniversary environment free from hagiographic distractions there is a chance that some of it will interest audiences. 'Purcell's big operas were not written in a vacuum', as Burden points out. They 'come at the beginning of a series ... which began with ... *Dioclesian* in 1690, and ended with Gottfried Finger's music to [Elkanah] Settle's *The Virgin Prophetess* in 1701'.[155]

As specialists from different backgrounds seek each other out and team up, interdisciplinary research into the theatre culture of the Restoration gains in effectiveness. One example of this trend was the 1993 Oxford conference 'Performing the Music of Henry Purcell', which Michael Burden and I co-organized two years ahead of the 1995 Purcell tercentenary, and in which performance-practice issues relating to the operas were a major focus. Emphasis was placed firmly on the multimedia nature of these works: notable contributions on stage singers, dancing, costumes and staging appeared in the book published soon afterwards, which remains the most significant single resource on multimedia performance in the Restoration theatre.[156] My own research work on *King Arthur*, undertaken in the hope of provoking debate from which future Purcell Society *King Arthur* editors could learn, has uncovered more of Dryden's literary and historical sources, has identified seventeenth-century book illustrations which Dryden may have had in mind, or open in front of him,

---

150 Louis Grabu, *Albion and Albanius*, ed. Bryan White, The Purcell Society Edition Companion Series, vol. 1 (London: Stainer & Bell, 2007).

151 See n. 53.

152 A-R Editions, Middleton. Michael Burden, Amanda Eubanks Winkler and Kathryn Lowerre are among those driving this edition forward.

153 Mark Humphreys, 'Daniel Purcell: A Biography and Thematic Catalogue' (DPhil dissertation, University of Oxford, 2005).

154 Kathryn Lowerre, *Music and Musicians on the London Stage, 1695–1705*, Performance in the Long Eighteenth Century: Studies in Theatre, Music, Dance (Farnham and Burlington: Ashgate, 2009).

155 Michael Burden, 'Aspects of Purcell's Operas', in Burden (ed.), *Henry Purcell's Operas: The Complete Texts*, (Oxford and New York: Oxford University Press, 2000), p. 4. Arguably the series began with Dorset Garden's 1674 production of *The Tempest*.

156 Michael Burden (ed.), *Performing the Music of Henry Purcell* (Oxford: Clarendon, 1996). The chapters in question are: Olive Baldwin and Thelma Wilson, 'Purcell's Stage Singers' (pp. 105–29); Richard Semmens, 'Dancing and Dance Music in Purcell's Operas' (pp. 180–96); Ruth-Eva Ronen, 'Of Costume and Etiquette: Staging in the Time of Purcell' (pp. 197–211); Roger Savage, 'Calling Up Genius: Purcell, Roger North, and Charlotte Butler' (pp. 212–31); and Julia and Frans Muller, 'Purcell's *Dioclesian* on the Dorset Garden Stage' (pp. 232–42).

when writing some of the scene descriptions in *King Arthur*, and – more recently – has focused attention on licensing issues with which Dryden, Betterton and possibly Purcell would have had to deal.[157] Words for which no authentically Purcellian music seems to have survived may have been censored out.

Wider historical research is also deepening contextual understanding of the theatre works. As thinking on seventeenth-century English history develops, so does scope for mapping new historical understanding onto play and dramatick-opera plots, something that is already being demonstrated by the increasingly sophisticated allegorical interpretations being applied to Restoration drama, which are investigated in detail in Andrew Walkling's chapter in this book. Walkling's own work in this field seems set to continue.[158] Steven Zwicker's recent piece on *King Arthur* is a notably broad-minded contribution to Purcellian political-allegorical literature,[159] cleverly avoiding the pitfalls against which Hume warns in 'Politics of Opera in Late Seventeenth-Century London'.[160] Research bringing music into investigations of larger cultural discourses – including representations of women, of madness and of witchcraft – which largely focuses on the Restoration theatre, is explored by Amanda Eubanks Winkler in Chapter 7 below.

'[I]n the contemporary world ... economic considerations are playing an ever stronger role in assigning value [including critical value?] to the things people make, consume, enjoy, buy, and sell' – this observation, for which two well-known academic economists are responsible,[161] holds true even in the Restoration theatre-research field. Hume's article 'The Economics of Culture in London, 1660–1740'[162] sets an ambitious agenda both for his and for other people's research, but its opening assumption – mirroring the 'libertarian economist' position of US cultural economist Tyler Cowen – seems to me to be slightly anachronistic when projected back to the patronage and rent-suffused seventeenth century: 'Culture is a commodity produced for gain (whether pecuniary or otherwise) and offered for sale to the public, with or without success.'[163] While a transition to commercial

---

157 Andrew Pinnock, '*King Arthur* Expos'd: A Lesson in Anatomy', in Curtis Price (ed.), *Purcell Studies* (Cambridge: Cambridge University Press, 1995), pp. 243–56; Pinnock, 'A Double Vision of Albion: Allegorical Re-Alignments in the Dryden-Purcell Semi-Opera *King Arthur'*, *Restoration: Studies in English Literary Culture, 1660–1700* 34 (2010): 55–81.

158 See the sections 'Purcell's "Court" Music: Theatre Music' and 'Purcell's "Public" Music: Theatre Music' in Chapter 6 below.

159 Steven N. Zwicker, 'How Many Political Arguments Can Dance on the Head of a Pin?', *Restoration: Studies in English Literary Culture, 1660–1700* 34 (2010): 103–16.

160 Hume, 'The Politics of Opera': 15–43.

161 Michael Hutter and David Throsby (eds), *Beyond Price: Value in Culture, Economics, and the Arts*, Murphy Institute Studies in Political Economy (Cambridge and New York: Cambridge University Press, 2008), p. xv.

162 Robert D. Hume, 'The Economics of Culture in London, 1660–1740', *Huntington Library Quarterly* 69 (2006): 487–533.

163 Ibid.: 487. According to Cowen, 'Artists work to achieve self-fulfillment, fame, and riches. The complex motivations behind artistic creation include love of the beautiful, love of money, love of fame, personal arrogance, and inner compulsions. ... More

cultural activity had clearly begun in the Restoration period, a large amount of art not meant for sale to the public was still being produced, as it is today. But Hume's 'blunt, financially-orientated counterview to common scholarly [critical] approaches'[164] will be essential reading when it appears in his forthcoming book *The Economics of Culture in London, 1660–1820*, and in the volume he is preparing with Milhous, *Theatre Finances in London, 1660–1800*.[165]

Complex economic interrelationships linked theatre producers in Restoration London, specialist suppliers to producers (including musicians like Purcell), theatre audiences, producers of theatrical spin-off goods such as play- and song-books, theatre-trained or theatre-imitating service providers such as singing and dancing teachers, and their many overlapping client groups. Although there is much still to be learned about precisely how such relationships were managed, most functions fulfilled by specialist intermediaries in the modern music industry seem to have been identified and efficiently covered by their seventeenth-century forebears. Artists' agents had yet to emerge – with relatively little work on offer, and all of it in or around London, artists could represent themselves – but the equivalent of fixers (booking agents) probably did exist. The royal birthday odes which Purcell continued to write from 1690 on, after losing his job as harpsichordist in the King's Private Music,[166] may have been intended as payment in kind to Nicholas Staggins, Master of the King and Queen's Music and royal orchestra manager *ex officio*. Staggins was an indifferent composer (despite his concurrent Cambridge music professorship) who, but for Purcell, might have been expected to produce the odes himself. Purcell spared Staggins's blushes; Staggins shared information, enabling Purcell to plan theatre rehearsals and performances involving musicians from the royal court in full awareness of possible clashes.[167]

Marketing was also relatively well developed. Rumours about the extravagant cost of dramatick operas were deliberately spread, providing invaluable publicity through word of mouth. Previews and reviews were planted in the press. Betterton's 'public-relations' machine (making allowance for the relatively primitive stage of

---

generally, I treat artists as pursuing a complex mix of pecuniary and non-pecuniary returns'; see Tyler Cowen, *In Praise of Commercial Culture* (Cambridge, MA and London: Harvard University Press, 1998), p. 15. Cowen defines his 'libertarian economist' position in *Good and Plenty: The Creative Successes of American Arts Funding* (Princeton: Princeton University Press, 2006), p. 2.

164 Taken from Hume's description of his forthcoming book, at http://www.personal.psu. edu/hb1/.

165 This will include 'one chapter devoted to an overview of opera in London', extending and updating Milhous's well-known paper 'Opera Finances in London, 1674–1738', *Journal of the American Musicological Society* 37 (1984): 567–92. Information about Hume's and Milhous's forward plans is taken from Hume's self-published bibliography, available at http://www.personal.psu.edu/hb1/ (last accessed 1 April 2011).

166 See n. 1.

167 These suggestions are elaborated in Andrew Pinnock and Bruce Wood, 'Come ye Sons of Art – Again: Court Cross-Subsidy for Purcell's Opera Orchestra, 1690–1695', *Early Music* 37 (2009): 445–66.

available communications technology) worked much like a modern one, and was every bit as effective.[168] From a more specifically musical perspective, Dorset Garden (and to a lesser extent Drury Lane) served as multimedia advertising sites for musical wares. Content was constantly refreshed. Instrumentalists appeared on stage and in boxes framing the stage, to give compelling, highly visible demonstrations of virtuoso skill. This encouraged the sale of instruments to amateurs, the sale of tutor books and sheet music, and it fuelled demand for one-to-one lessons.

The music-publishing business was also central to the marketing of the theatre. Theatre songs were published in a variety of formats, but the most frequently produced were single-sheet songs, bought by amateur performers to sing at home, making dramatick opera an interactive medium, accessible both to those who had attended and wanted a 'souvenir' of the event, and also to people who lived too far from London to attend in person. From the commercial perspective, however, modern thinking on copyright and the beginnings of modern copyright legislation had yet to crystallize. Music publishers sold music, either printed or in manuscript copies made by professional scribes, but they did not deal in performing rights (the modern publishers' *raison d'être*). Pirate publishers were therefore able to bring out unauthorized editions. Theatre music prints and manuscripts passed from friend to friend for free recopying.

Although not protected by any equivalent of intellectual property rights, Purcell understood the advantages of publishing his music. His full score of *Dioclesian*, self-published in 1691, was an expensive loss leader, not selling as well as he might have hoped, but boosting his reputation hugely. In France the sumptuous Ballard editions of Lully operas were produced under royal privilege and Lully's stage shows enjoyed royal subsidy. Publishing his own score of *Dioclesian*, Purcell bid for a place in the front rank of European composers, not just of his English colleagues. Fame, once attained, would transmute naturally into money.[169]

With *Some Select Songs as they are Sung in the Fairy Queen*, self-published the following year, Purcell began to recoup. In contrast to the expensive full score of his first opera, this was an anthology of popular numbers from *The Fairy Queen*, available for sale in the theatre while the show was running. Its first edition rapidly sold out, so Purcell produced 'The Second Edition, with Additions' also in 1692. Reprinting gave him an opportunity to switch songs originally published in the alto clef into the treble clef (making them more accessible to inexperienced singers, and arguably also playable on domestic instruments like the recorder); but he advertised new music without including any.[170] Popular numbers picked for inclusion in *Some Select Songs* were meant to be popular, undoubtedly: they were composed with that aim in mind. *The Fairy Queen* – Purcell's last full-scale dramatick opera – was the most overtly crowd-pleasing, featuring juvenile actors in cute fairy parts, animals (the dancing monkeys),[171] and slapstick humour in

---

168 For contemporary press coverage see Michael Burden, *Purcell Remembered* (London and Boston: Faber, 1995), pp. 77–109.

169 See Herissone, 'Playford, Purcell, and the Functions of Music Publishing'.

170 See Purcell, *The Fairy Queen*, eds Wood and Pinnock, p. xxxvii (sources L1, L1a and L2).

171 See Michael Burden, 'Dancing Monkeys at Dorset Garden', *Theatre Notebook* 57 (2003):

Coridon and Mopsa. Like many of the single-sheet songs produced from theatre productions, *Some Select Songs* attached a singer's name to each song, implicitly providing celebrity endorsement. Dorset Garden employed the top performers in London, flaunted its royal warrant, had royals in the audience from time to time, and had court musicians on its payroll. Late seventeenth-century English celebrity culture centred on the theatre, and Purcellian dramatick opera was theatre at its most glamorous. As Sir William Davenant had before, Betterton and Purcell understood a basic trick of arts marketing, 'selling the audience to itself'.[172]

Hume – 'financially-orientated' as he admits – is expertly equipped to track the flow of money from hand to hand, as recorded or otherwise demonstrated in contracts, receipts, published price-lists, household account books itemizing cultural expenditure, and so on. He assumes commercial motives for cultural production, and corresponding payment expectations on the part of would-be consumers. Other forms of analysis – non-financial but still recognizably economic – will appeal to researchers with different intellectual sympathies and different skill sets. Economic sociologists might want to study the personal acquisition and group consolidation of social capital through cultural consumption behaviour;[173] economic psychologists might study seventeenth-century 'economies of esteem'. D.F. McKenzie's warning to fellow bibliographical theorists is worth bearing in mind: 'we have perhaps failed in our historical sense, too readily imputing our own ... ideas and interests and the assumptions of our own society – especially our economic assumptions – to men whose attitudes to work were quite different from ours.'[174] Cultural economic research has the potential greatly to enrich our understanding of Purcell's achievement in the theatre.[175] I think it would be a pity to limit that potential by defining 'economics' too narrowly.

119–35.

172 John Pick and Malcolm Anderton, *Arts Administration* (2nd edn, London and New York: Spon, 1996), p. 95.

173 See, for instance, Chapter 5 of Harold Love, *The Culture and Commerce of Texts: Scribal Publication in Seventeenth-Century England* (Amherst: University of Massachusetts Press, 1998; originally published as *Scribal Publication in Seventeenth-Century England* (Oxford: Clarendon, 1993)).

174 Donald F. McKenzie, 'Printers of the Mind: Some Notes on Bibliographical Theories and Printing-House Practices', *Studies in Bibliography: Papers of the Bibliographical Society of the University of Virginia* 22 (1969): 10.

175 It also has the potential to keep researchers busy for 'twenty or thirty years ... collect[ing] and publish[ing] additional evidence', as Hume realizes: see 'The Economics of Culture': 488.

Politics, Occasions and Texts

Andrew R. Walkling

Henry Purcell lived in an intensely political age. Although his birth in the chaotic year 1659 precluded his having direct experience either of the mid-century turmoil of Civil War and republican rule, or of the commotion surrounding Charles II's restoration in 1660, he came of age during the acute political and religious crises of the 1670s and 1680s. In his adulthood he did not simply witness, but become a peripheral participant in, a revolution in his country's constitution and government, and the early stages of a profound transformation in the nature of English politics, economics and society. Passing most of his life in such interesting times, and at such proximity to the centre of power, Purcell can hardly have failed to be influenced in some way or other by the grand events swirling about him.

Yet in speaking of the 'political context' of Purcell's musical output, it is dangerously easy to oversimplify. Rumours of his Roman Catholic sympathies abound,[1] but we know little about the political beliefs of the man himself. As a servant of the Crown (and a resident of Westminster, as opposed to the more politically volatile city of London), he most likely maintained a solid, or at least pragmatic, loyalism. But that loyalism would itself have been tested by the kaleidoscopic shifts from the dissolute, profligate Anglican Charles II to the rigid, stubborn Roman Catholic James II to the dour Calvinist military man William III – whose edge, admittedly, was taken off by his more relaxed and culturally sophisticated consort Mary II. As a child of the court from his earliest chorister days, Purcell was probably fully versed in the complex acrobatics of serving and pleasing his royal masters, and he would have known all too well the need for discretion. Unlike some of the more tangential artistic servants of the Crown – the patent theatrical players or the Poet Laureate, for example – musicians were an integral part of the household staff, alongside officers of the Royal Works, officers of the Robes, the Sergeant Painter and the Master Cook; they were not expected to function in any kind of overt political capacity. Purcell seems to fit this profile: if he had independent political opinions, he successfully kept them to himself. And while

---

1   W. Douglas Newton, *Catholic London* (London: Hale, 1950), p. 74; see also Franklin B. Zimmerman, *Henry Purcell, 1659–1695: His Life and Times* (2nd edn, Philadelphia: University of Pennsylvania Press, 1983), pp. 160–61 and 95–6.

he might have bridled at the staff reductions imposed on the court establishment in 1689, he remained a faithful court servant despite his diminished responsibilities, continuing to cater for his new monarchs' wishes even as he supplemented his income with more public, commercial work.

The search for a political approach to Purcell's music must, therefore, depend upon our consideration of certain external forces, in particular patrons (such as the court and the theatrical companies) and librettists. Purcell's primary responsibility to his patrons was to compose music for specific occasions – occasions that could carry a variety of political implications. His primary responsibility to his librettists was to create musical settings of their pre-existing texts – texts that might evince political meaning in a multiplicity of ways, ranging from the overt to the surreptitious. If Purcell's music is to be viewed through a political lens, then, it is necessary to consider how he responded to such occasions and texts.

The first step is to ask what constitutes a political text, both from our modern, analytical perspective and from the point of view of those who actually experienced the politics of the late seventeenth century. It is perhaps difficult for us, living in an age characterized by individual rights and freedom of expression, to comprehend how political discourse was articulated in the early modern period. In England in particular, the theory of divine-right monarchy and hierarchical social structures that emphasized deference and passive obedience came increasingly into conflict with a growing popular awareness of and engagement with political concerns, fostered by the development of a 'public sphere' that was itself a product of enhanced economic prosperity and a marketplace of ideas driven in part by a lively culture of print and manuscript circulation.[2] Both of these competing forces found an outlet in cultural expression, with the arts serving as an essential conduit for the dissemination of information. Thus literary (and, by extension, musical) texts were an important source of factual knowledge, opinion and debate, particularly given the virtual absence of any equivalent to the highly developed news media and communications networks prevalent in our own time.

Seventeenth-century texts – including those associated with Purcell, which are our focus here – incorporated political content in a variety of ways. Some used overt statements in order to convey a clear propagandistic point, such as the passage 'And now every tongue shall make open confession / That York, royal York is the next in succession' from the court ode *What shall be Done in Behalf of the Man?*

---

2 The classic articulation of the 'public sphere' is Jürgen Habermas's *The Structural Transformation of the Public Sphere: An Inquiry into a Category of Bourgeois Society*, trans. Thomas Burger with Frederick Lawrence, Studies in Contemporary German Social Thought (Cambridge, MA: MIT Press; Cambridge: Polity, 1989), first published as *Strukturwandel der Öffentlichkeit: Untersuchungen zu einer Kategorie der bürgerlichen Gesellschaft*, Politica, vol. 4 (Neuwied: Luchterland, 1962). Habermas takes a broad view of early modern culture, but has spawned a substantial scholarly subfield in which specific cases have been examined in detail, often necessitating refinements to Habermas's original formulation.

(1682). Another example of this kind of explicit reference occurs in the 'Catch upon Charleroy', written in 1692 during the time of King William's Continental wars:

> Is Charleroy's siege come to? Who wou'd a thought it?
> Then the rumours was false that Lewis had bought it.
> Then charge all your guns, boys, as high as they can be,
> With the briskest champagne rammed down with Nantz brandy.
> Let engineer Vauban shoot the Devil and all,
> Yet his Marshal shan't dance at old Maintenon's ball.

Others sought to express the majesty of royal power by enveloping their message in elaborate rhetorical tropes. Nahum Tate, for example, likened the king and queen to the classical deities Phoebus and Venus in the prologue to *Dido and Aeneas* (discussed below), while the anonymous song text 'If Pray'rs and Tears', subtitled 'Sighs for our late Sovereign *King Charles* the Second', describes the public's vain entreaties to God during the final hours of that monarch's life, and compares the sinful English nation to the wayward people of Israel:

> Albion is now become a holy land,
> And wages holy war to stay the threat'ning hand;
> > Oh! that we might prevail:
> Such well appointed numbers never us'd to fail.
> ...
> Alas, we'd conquer'd too, but, for our former crimes,
> > Treasons, rebellions, perjuries,
> With all the iniquities of the times,
> > Whole legions do against us rise:
> These are the pow'rs that strike the kingdom dead,
> And now the crown is fall'n from our Josiah's head.

Still other texts were considerably more obscure, their meaning constructed in such a way that readers and auditors had to apply a broader contextual perspective in order to begin to make sense of them.

The distinctions among these types of political expression, which map out a continuum ranging from explicit to concealed meaning, present a way of considering the mutually supporting techniques of propaganda and allegory, both of which were a staple of early modern political discourse. The deployment of these devices depended to a great degree upon the nature of a given work's audience: as I have argued elsewhere in discussing Restoration theatrical culture, works intended for public consumption generally presented their political content in a straightforward manner – ranging from open satire, in which little or no attempt was made to conceal the work's purpose, to 'impressionistic' allegory, in which familiar themes, tropes, allusions and parallels provoked sometimes fleeting moments of recognition in the reader or audience, thus creating an opportunity for the application of political meaning. At the other end of the scale, however, lies the *roman à clef* – a literary form in which the articulation of a political message is achieved through the establishment of an intricate system of one-to-one correspondences between fictional characters and real-life figures – which is only infrequently found outside of a courtly context in the latter half of the seventeenth century.[3]

The idea that early modern cultural products functioned in political ways has been well established for some time now, and has been extensively studied in relation to mid and late seventeenth-century England by Annabel Patterson, Steven Zwicker, Lois Potter and Susan Owen, among others.[4] What these scholars have shown is that seventeenth-century authors and readers instinctively viewed cultural production at least in part through a political lens: issues of genre, structure, narrative and linguistic choice (defined broadly in terms of verbal, musical and visual language) were seen as markers of meaning and guides to interpretation for an audience finely attuned to such cues and fundamentally grounded in a hermeneutic model that demanded a search for the underlying meaning of a text. In this context, the absence of documentary evidence that readers or audiences understood particular texts as political should not be taken to indicate that such interpretation did not occur; rather, our focus should be on *how* texts functioned as conveyors of political meaning, bearing in mind the inherent tensions between authorial intent and reader response, as well as the particularities of individual texts. Besides taking into account modes of reading and interpretation, such explorations must necessarily consider the ideology and practice of early modern absolutism and the functioning of structures of censorship, both of which varied over time and according to circumstance.[5]

Musicologists have come somewhat belatedly to this table, and those who have sought to explore the political implications of works set to music by Purcell and others have tended to treat these pieces in isolation, without being fully cognisant of the theoretical and interpretative models deployed by scholars in other fields,

---

3   Andrew R. Walkling, 'Politics and Theatrical Culture in Restoration England', *History Compass* 5 (2007): 1500–1520, esp. 1504–10.

4   Annabel Patterson, *Censorship and Interpretation: The Conditions of Writing and Reading in Early Modern England* (rev. edn, Madison and London: University of Wisconsin Press, 1990); Steven N. Zwicker, *Politics and Language in Dryden's Poetry: The Arts of Disguise* (Princeton: Princeton University Press, 1984); Zwicker, *Lines of Authority: Politics and English Literary Culture, 1649–1689* (Ithaca and London: Cornell University Press, 1993); Lois Potter, *Secret Rites and Secret Writing: Royalist Literature, 1641–1660* (Cambridge: Cambridge University Press, 1989); and Susan J. Owen, *Restoration Theatre and Crisis* (Oxford: Clarendon, 1996).

5   For example, the regime of print censorship in Restoration England, which was established under the Licensing Act of 1662 and relied upon the cooperation of London's Worshipful Company of Stationers, was considerably more lax than the censorship of plays in performance, which fell under the purview of the Lord Chamberlain and the Master of the Revels, both officials of the royal household. Consequently, plays frequently appeared in print with passages clearly marked as having been excised in performance. This distinction became even more marked during the lapse of the Licensing Act between 1679 and 1685.

in particular literary studies. This is unfortunate, given that in musical settings of literary texts it was the texts rather than the music that were normally given primacy by contemporaries and which thus require our attention if we are to understand the political reception of seventeenth-century vocal music (which is where much – although, as we shall see, not all – of the political content can be found). The assessment of musical texts as political has hitherto focused principally on theatrical works, especially the larger operas and masques of the late 1680s and 1690s. Particularly noteworthy are John Buttrey's 1967 doctoral dissertation,[6] a frequently cited article of 1987 by Curtis Price,[7] and a wide-ranging exploration of the topic by Robert Hume that casts a more sceptical eye over the field and the claims of some of its exponents.[8] In each of these studies, Purcell himself emerges almost synecdochically as the leading representative of the Restoration musical world, the importance of which in the eyes of modern scholarship would seem to be substantially diminished without the invigorating presence of the British Orpheus.[9] Thus the most comprehensive exploration of Restoration theatrical music with respect to textual and political considerations is a work dealing exclusively with Purcell, Curtis Price's indispensible *Henry Purcell and the London Stage*,[10] whose detailed survey of the composer's vocal music for the theatre offers a wealth of insights into the political issues pertinent to that particular genre.[11] Notably, although Price's book is now a quarter of a century old, no equivalent studies have yet appeared for composers such as John Banister, Matthew Locke, John Blow, John Eccles, Daniel Purcell or Jeremiah Clarke, all of whom made significant contributions to Restoration theatrical music, and whose output was no less affected by political considerations than Purcell's.

6   John Buttrey, 'The Evolution of English Opera between 1656 and 1695: A Re-investigation' (PhD dissertation, University of Cambridge, 1967).

7   Curtis A. Price, 'Political Allegory in Late-Seventeenth-Century English Opera', in Nigel Fortune (ed.), *Music and Theatre: Essays in Honour of Winton Dean* (Cambridge: Cambridge University Press, 1987), pp. 1–29.

8   Robert D. Hume, 'The Politics of Opera in Late Seventeenth-Century London', *Cambridge Opera Journal* 10 (1998): 15–43.

9   See, for example, my own article laying out general arguments in favour of allegorical interpretation, which appears in a volume specifically dedicated to Purcell scholarship: 'Performance and Political Allegory in Restoration England: What to Interpret and When', in Michael Burden (ed.), *Performing the Music of Henry Purcell* (Oxford: Clarendon, 1996), pp. 163–79.

10   Curtis A. Price, *Henry Purcell and the London Stage* (Cambridge: Cambridge University Press, 1984).

11   Earlier studies of Purcell's theatre music, including Robert Etheridge Moore, *Henry Purcell and the Restoration Theatre* (Cambridge MA: Harvard University Press; London: Heinemann, 1961) and A. Margaret Laurie, 'Purcell's Stage Works' (PhD dissertation, University of Cambridge, 1962), as well as Curtis Price's *Music in the Restoration Theatre: with a Catalogue of Instrumental Music in the Plays, 1665–1713*, Studies in Musicology, vol. 4 (Ann Arbor: UMI Research Press, 1979), are concerned less with politics and interpretation than with attribution, musical analysis and performance circumstances. They are described in Chapter 5 above.

Purcell's theatre music is thus well covered in the scholarly literature, but the frequently complex political qualities of the texts, particularly those that were in some way oppositional, ensure that debates over individual interpretations, as well as interpretative contexts more broadly, continue. Ironically, it is those works of Purcell with more overt political applicability that have tended to be either denigrated or ignored in modern scholarship. This may be because they seem largely unremarkable from our interpretative standpoint: a loyal catch or a court ode looks functionally similar to the kind of open, uncensored political statements we might expect to hear every day in our own lives, in conversations with friends or in the media, and thus appears to warrant less analytical attention than a convoluted political allegory. Judged by modern standards, such texts come across either as commonplace statements of political belief or affiliation, unworthy of textual or contextual evaluation, or as ridiculously sycophantic utterances whose stilted rhetoric, devoid of literary nuance, would fool no intelligent hearer and hence merit little more than scorn. The problem is that, while the function of these pieces is similar to what we experience in the modern world, the rhetoric and context are not, and it is a mistake to assume that these works had the same resonances for contemporaries as they do for us. For all its seeming transparency to our eyes, early modern propaganda had evolved by the late seventeenth century into a highly developed form, as successful at transmitting its desired messages as any commercial advertising campaign or political spin machine of our own day. There is no evidence that Purcell considered the composition of welcome songs or loyal catches beneath him, or that contemporary audiences snickered behind their painted fans at the extravagant invocation of the monarch as 'Caesar' in song. Significant work thus remains to be done to enhance our understanding of both the mechanics of these works and their effects on early modern British politics and society.

It is also worth noting that the predominant emphasis on Purcell's theatre music rather than other genres reflects broader trends in seventeenth-century British cultural studies. The theatre has long been of great interest to scholars of literature and history, and the allied contributions of musicologists fit neatly into this context. Court studies, on the other hand, has only recently emerged as a reputable field, divested of the anecdotalism and lack of analytical rigour that had long characterized the subject. Similarly, the discipline of social history, which incorporates the study of public discourse, has now begun to concern itself with the interpretation of cultural materials through the investigation of print culture, but has as yet paid scant attention to performative contexts, such as music-making in domestic, public and sacred spaces. Potential developments in these fields provide welcome opportunities for advancements to be made in the study of music as a feature of political expression and political activity more generally.[12] But, given the

---

12   Of particular interest in this regard is the work of Stacey Houck on royalist undercurrents in the publications of John Playford; see for example her essay 'John Playford and the English Musical Market', in Jessie Ann Owens (ed.), 'Noyses, Sounds and Sweet Aires': Music in Early Modern England (Seattle and London: Folger Shakespeare Library, 2006), pp. 48–61.

special status of Purcell in musicological scholarship, a more wide-ranging and nuanced understanding of Purcell's music and its role in contemporary politics may in fact help musicologists themselves to push the boundaries of our understanding of Restoration culture. In the remainder of this chapter I will seek to indicate a way forward by offering an exploration of Purcell's musical output as it relates to late seventeenth-century political considerations, placed within the context of the existing literature in the field.

Purcell's political output is best considered first and foremost as a function of the purpose and audience for which he was composing, with the primary distinction being between those works he wrote in his capacity as a servant of the crown and those he produced for public consumption. Genre is also of relevance to this taxonomy: the 'court' category includes the majority of the composer's odes and nearly all of the anthems (including those that we might deem political), while the theatre music, apart from the special case of court masque, falls under the 'public' rubric. Similarly, most of Purcell's political songs appear to have a court provenance, while the catches – a type of song with a specialized structure and set of performance requirements – can be considered germane to the public sphere. Thus, we will survey Purcell's political output according to provenance, considering first 'court' and then 'public' works, subdividing each by genre.

Purcell's political works are an important avenue by which to understand the composer more fully: they allow us to see him immersed in his contemporary context, responding musically in the moment to newsworthy events and deeply enmeshed in the networks of patronage that were so fundamental to his career development. Moreover, an investigation of these most event-driven of Purcell's compositions helps us to challenge unwarranted modern value judgements that relegate them to lower status on account of their supposedly compromised universality. While it is true that the immediate currency of any political work is liable to decrease with the passage of time, it is to be regretted that scholars and performers of our own day have tended to consider such pieces less compelling as objects of aesthetic investigation and performable works of art than those 'ageless' compositions that transcend the mundanities of seventeenth-century specificity – witness the fate of Purcell's royal odes, or his political catches, both discussed below. Yet this is to a large degree less about whether or not a work might have been political in its original conception than about how readily its political features can be submerged under other considerations – or, better yet, simply overlooked. Thus, of Purcell's 18 court odes, the one by far the most widely performed and recorded over the past 60 years is *Come ye Sons of Art*, whose quasi-Cecilian rhetoric largely obscures its purpose as the sixth in an annual sequence of birthday songs for Queen Mary. Similarly, the sometimes contentious debate over the dating and allegorical interpretation of *Dido and Aeneas* is fed in part by a reluctance to 'debase' one of the great operatic works of the seventeenth century by associating it with a transitory political controversy whose details, however pressing they may have been at the time, seem far less important to us now.

The case of *Dido and Aeneas* raises fundamental questions about the ways in which a play can or cannot be considered political. Only a very few dramatic works of the Restoration (musical or otherwise) present themselves unambiguously as commentaries on recent events,[13] and thus the political features of a play, when they can be shown to exist, are usually bound up in a matrix of literary, dramaturgical and performance considerations that may have nothing to do with politics or current affairs. Whether or not *Dido* has a political bent, it is also much more than a political work, as the abstruse nature of its supposed political message – and, we might argue, its continued popularity with modern audiences – clearly attests. Given such variety of function, is it appropriate to describe a play as political if some, but by no means all, aspects of the work can be shown to have been inspired by contemporary events? Even a play banned from performance by the authorities for alleged political content or applicability, such as Tate's Shakespearean adaptation *The History of King Richard the Second* (to which Purcell contributed music in 1680), cannot be characterized simply as a political play and nothing more – an argument on which authors such as Tate themselves relied heavily when seeking to disavow any political applicability in their works so as to blunt the effects of censorship.[14]

Our focus on Purcell, of course, raises an even more difficult question. Even if we might accurately describe a play as political on the basis of a reading of its text or an understanding of its production history, to what extent can we consider its *music* as political? Indeed, the same question applies equally to Purcell's musical settings of unabashedly political, *non*-theatrical texts, such as those of catches or odes. As an abstract language, music does not readily lend itself to analysis along such lines, and thus we are left to regard the majority of Purcell's compositions as political by association: by virtue of his collaboration with a poet or playwright who produced a political text, Purcell might be said, in some sense, to have composed political music. This is not meant, however, to absolve Purcell of any taint of politics in these cases: the composer's choice to participate in such projects – and in many cases to put his name to them publicly – must be seen as an indication of some level of complicity in the political message being transmitted. Of course, complicity is a matter of degree. In the case of court works (including nearly all of the political odes, anthems and songs) Purcell might be said to have been merely 'doing his job'. With the catches, however, his motivations are not as clear: were these works – intended for public consumption – also commissioned by the court, or do they represent a personal act of patriotism on the composer's part? Either way, we can be in no doubt that he understood the implications of what he was creating. With regard to the theatre music, on the other hand, the extent of Purcell's contribution to political plays (which were, more often than not, oppositional) is sufficiently limited as to leave us uncertain whether he was even aware of the political nature of works to which his name was being attached. Hence, our search for traces of the

---

13   See Walkling, 'Politics and Theatrical Culture': 1504–6, where three such works are briefly discussed: John Tatham, *The Rump: Or The Mirrour of the Late Times* (1660); John Dryden, *Albion and Albanius* (1685); and the anonymous play *The Abdicated Prince: Or, the Adventures of Four Years* (1690).

14   As Patterson, Zwicker and others have argued, however, such disavowals were frequently disingenuous; see n. 4 above.

political in Purcell's *oeuvre* might take cognisance of this additional distinction: instances in which the composer clearly knew of the political content with which he was being associated and those (primarily theatrical works) in which he probably or possibly did not.

The difficulty of reading a piece of music, independently of words, as political – a problem that is only exacerbated in Purcell's case by the ambiguity of the composer's own political inclinations – has thus forced scholars to focus not so much on Purcell's music *per se*, but upon the texts he set, which were not, generally speaking, under his purview. As we have already noted, the differing characteristics of the texts (and, by extension, their perceived quality) have determined the varying levels of scholarly engagement with the different generic categories to be explored below under the broader rubrics of 'court' and 'public', and have thus strongly affected our understanding of what constitutes the political in Purcell's music. However, there are some ways in which Purcell's own musical choices might actually be read as political in and of themselves, and the final section of this chapter will seek to illustrate two possible ways of approaching such an issue.

Purcell's 'Court' Music

Odes

The most obviously political of the genres to which Purcell contributed is the court ode, which came to maturity in the early years of the Restoration, reaching what might be considered its pinnacle in the hands of Purcell and his colleague John Blow. From the late 1670s Blow took up the composition of odes to celebrate New Year's Day and the king's birthday, while Purcell, beginning in 1680, assumed responsibility for a new sub-genre of ode, the welcome song, designed to greet the monarch on his return to Whitehall Palace after a sojourn away from the capital. With the disappearance of the welcome song after the Glorious Revolution of 1688–89, Purcell undertook the composition of birthday odes for Queen Mary, while Blow retained primary responsibility for King William's birthday odes and those for New Year's Day.[15]

Purcell's odes have attracted a fair amount of scholarship, most of it dedicated to historical and contextual considerations and/or to the analysis of the music.

---

15 Besides his fifteen strictly 'royal' welcome songs and birthday odes for Charles, James and Mary, Purcell also composed a welcome song addressed to the Duke of York on his return from Scotland in 1682 (*What shall be Done in Behalf of the Man?*), an ode to celebrate the wedding of Princess Anne and Prince George of Denmark in 1683 (*From Hardy Climes*) and a birthday ode for the Duke of Gloucester in 1695 (*Who can from Joy Refrain?*).

In the former case, the composer's work has been placed within the context of the developing genre and individual odes assigned, sometimes speculatively, to particular occasions.[16] In some instances, the leading manuscript source (Purcell's autograph Lbl R.M. 20.h.8, in which nine of the pre-1689 odes appear) offers helpful descriptive rubrics, such as 'A Welcome Song for his Majesty at his return from New Market October yᵉ 21 – 1682' (for *The Summer's Absence Unconcerned we Bear*); in other instances, crucial details are missing – for instance the rubric for *From those Serene and Rapturous Joys* simply describes it as 'The Welcome Song perform'd to his Majesty in yᵉ year 1684' – leaving scholars guessing as to which of several arrivals of the king was being celebrated. Most of the welcome songs seem to have been performed in the autumn (usually September or October, when Charles II and James II returned from their summer holidays in Windsor, Winchester or Newmarket), although debates continue over a few, in particular *Swifter, Isis, Swifter Flow*, whose text was long believed to refer to Charles II's return from Oxford after the dissolution of the parliament held there in March 1681, but which Bruce Wood has more recently connected to events the following August.[17] Needless to say, Purcell's birthday odes for Queen Mary do not present the same problems of dating.

Although William Turner, Giovanni Battista Draghi and Nicholas Staggins composed a few court odes during this time, the otherwise strict division of labour between Purcell and Blow is noteworthy, and would seem to deserve further consideration. Ian Spink wonders 'whether there was some personal reason why Purcell never wrote an ode for King William', speculating that 'he may … have preferred to set birthday odes for the queen, thus leaving uncompromised (or less compromised) any Stuart sympathies he may have felt.'[18] Yet the composition of music for annual odes, whether on New Year's Day or a royal birthday (or even the more variable welcome home) more strongly implies an officially assigned duty than a personal choice and, given the scale of these works, it may simply have been deemed convenient to divide up the responsibilities according to a sort of rota system. No one but Blow, we should note, is known to have written a New Year ode between 1678 and 1700,[19] and Purcell maintained his own near-monopoly, composing all but one or two of the welcome songs and every 'secondary' birthday ode (for Queen Mary and William, Duke of Gloucester) known to have been presented between 1680 and his death in 1695.[20]

---

16   See, for example, Rosamond McGuinness, *English Court Odes, 1660–1820*, Oxford Monographs on Music (Oxford: Clarendon, 1971); and Ian Spink, 'Purcell's Odes: Propaganda and Panegyric', in Curtis Price (ed.), *Purcell Studies* (Cambridge: Cambridge University Press, 1995), pp. 145–71.

17   Henry Purcell, *Royal Welcome Songs, Part I*, ed. Bruce Wood, The Works of Henry Purcell, vol. 15 (new edn, London: Novello, 2000), p. x.

18   Spink, 'Purcell's Odes', p. 157.

19   New Year odes are not known to exist for the years 1689, 1691, 1695, 1697, 1699 and 1701.

20   Curiously, the main royal birthday odes seem to have been more promiscuously assigned and more haphazardly performed, although Blow is known to have written

Existing alongside the questions of circumstance and dating is the analysis of Purcell's music. Here Purcell's odes – the only large-scale genre in which he remained consistently active throughout his career – have been considered a fertile field for the composer's experimentation with varying vocal and instrumental textures and in particular the development of his facility with the ground-bass form.[21] Political considerations are less at play here, but it is worth observing the extent to which praise for Purcell's musical abilities as displayed in these works is invariably coupled with denigration of the supposedly stilted and fawning texts he was obliged to set. In this critical environment, Rosamond McGuinness's description of the texts as 'examples of mediocre poetry' seems positively indulgent: Bruce Wood deplores the 'naked literary poverty' of these 'flatulent encomia', while Spink simply dismisses them as 'doggerel'.[22] The euphuistic style and obsequious tone of the ode texts set by Purcell and his contemporaries are certainly not to modern tastes, but they epitomize the rhetorical and formal extravagance of the high Baroque. This was no doubt exactly what Charles II and his successors were looking for after the Restoration when they promoted the adaptation of the so-called Pindaric ode, a form pioneered in English by the poet Abraham Cowley in the 1650s, for use with multisectional musical settings and semi-public performance in a court context. In responding to the royal mandate the poets, most of whom remain anonymous,[23] succeeded in heightening certain defining features of the genre. These included an acrobatic prosodic style, tactical dexterity, semantic obscurity punctuated by the use of complex, extended metaphor, an elevated rhetorical tone (described by one commentator as 'the poetics of transport')[24] and an almost visual sensibility governed by the constant reiteration of fundamental themes pertaining to the articulation of monarchical power. The syntactic and prosodic complexity of the odes is well illustrated by the following example from Thomas Shadwell's text for *Now does the Glorious Day Appear* of 1689, the earliest of the six odes for Mary's birthday:

---

three or possibly four of them (for 1678, 1681, 1692 and possibly 1699).

21   See Bruce Wood, 'Purcell's Odes: A Reappraisal', in Michael Burden (ed.), *The Purcell Companion* (London: Faber, 1994; Portland, OR: Amadeus Press, 1995), pp. 200–253; Martin Adams, 'Purcell, Blow and the English Court Ode', in Curtis Price (ed.), *Purcell Studies* (Cambridge: Cambridge University Press, 1995), pp. 172–91; Adams, *Henry Purcell: The Origins and Development of his Musical Style* (Cambridge: Cambridge University Press, 1995), pp. 222–71; and also Rosamond McGuinness, 'The Ground Bass in the English Court Ode', *Music & Letters* 51 (1970): 118–40 and 265–78.

22   McGuinness, *English Court Odes, 1660–1820*, p. 62; Wood, 'Purcell's Odes', p. 200; Spink, 'Purcell's Odes', p. 145.

23   Of the 18 royal odes Purcell composed, 11 were set to texts whose authors remain unidentified; of the remaining seven, one each was provided by Thomas Flatman, Thomas Shadwell, Thomas D'Urfey and Sir Charles Sedley, while three (or perhaps only two) were written by Nahum Tate.

24   Patterson, *Censorship and Interpretation*, p. 165.

> On this bless'd day was our restorer born:
> Far above all let this the calendar adorn.
> It was a work of full as great a weight –
> And did require the self-same pow'r
> Which did frail humankind create –
> When they were lost them to restore;
> For a like act, Fate gave our princess birth,
> Which adding to the saints, made joy in Heav'n
> As well as triumph upon Earth
> To which so great, so good a queen was giv'n.

This passage epitomizes the grand machinery of the ode text. The essential point being made is simple and is expounded in the first couplet of the quoted passage, which can be paraphrased, 'This is the birthday of our restorer; let it be celebrated above all other days.' Everything that follows is merely an elaboration upon this main point which, despite its superficially bombastic rhetoric, is actually quite adroit, flattering the Queen by likening her advent to that of Christ, while at the same time deftly avoiding the stigma of blasphemy. But the hearer's efforts to grasp the passage's meaning are persistently impeded by pronouns with ambiguous antecedents, and deferred by nested subordinate clauses that introduce elaborate similes whose presence in the text's linear progression is signalled and effectuated by seemingly insignificant comparative prepositions and adjectives ('as', 'self-same', 'like') upon which the whole colossal mechanism suddenly and gracefully pivots. Thus, the listener is carried along on the eddies of the language, awash in the sublimity of an elevated poetic discourse set to a lilting prosody ($A_5A_6B_5C_4B_4C_4D_5E_5D_4E_5$, but with a subtle internal echo that interposes the 'B' rhyme ('weight'/'create') into the 'D–E' quatrain ('Fate'/'great'), thus binding the entire structure more tightly together), while simultaneously struggling to parse the dense syntax. Ultimately, the sense of the text becomes clear, and can be articulated in more comprehensible, prosaic terms: 'It was an equally momentous task to redeem frail humankind when they had gone astray – that work required the same power [i.e. God's] that had created them in the first place. Our princess was given birth by Fate for the same redemptive purpose; this event increased the number of the saints, thereby causing celebration in heaven and among those on earth, to whom she was sent.' Yet the outcome has been achieved only through an intellectual juggling act in which the hearer is compelled to rearrange poetic phrases on the fly and hold half-articulated ideas in reserve to await their consummation – all within an evanescent performative setting, and to the accompaniment of Purcell's ravishing and harmonically sophisticated music. It is this potent combination of rigorous cerebral challenge and rapturous abandon that gives the ode such transcendent power, particularly in performance, thereby establishing it as a fundamental expression of royal ideology in the Baroque age. Textually speaking, the ode serves as a locus of the kind of rhetoric associated in the earlier part of the seventeenth century with the court masque, a genre also long denigrated by modern scholars on similar grounds, but whose skilful exploitation of political nuance in the context of divine-right kingship has in recent years come to be better understood and appreciated.[25] In the Restoration court ode, the marriage of text with musical settings by Purcell and others only served to enhance the efficacious, almost mystical qualities of these works.

Despite the obvious political content of the odes, there has as yet been no scholarly study that fully addresses the question of their engagement with contemporary issues or their impact as vehicles for royalist propaganda. Such a task would require sustained consideration of the texts, something they have yet to receive. But even on a superficial level the content and tone of the odes can give us a sense of the court's political concerns, as is made clear in examples such as this passage from the 1683 welcome song *Fly, bold Rebellion*:

> Come then, change your notes, disloyal crowd,
> You that already have been too loud
> With importunate follies and clamours!
>   'Tis no business of yours
>   To dispute the high pow'rs
> As if you were the government framers;
>   But with heart and with voice
>   Join all to rejoice,
> With welcomes redoubled to see him appear
>   Who brings mercy and peace
>   And all things to please
> A people that know not how happy they are.

Purcell's later birthday odes for Mary focus more on praising the queen's beauty, virtue and steadfastness and less on denouncing the opposition, but the political content of their texts is similarly transparent, particularly since Mary's exalted detachment (the putative source of her wisdom and beauty) is contrasted in every ode with the martial strivings of her husband. The following passage from *Arise, my Muse* of 1690 illustrates the point:

> To quell his country's foes,
> Behold! the god-like hero goes,
> Fated and born to conquer all,
> Both the great, the vulgar, and the small;
>   To hunt the savages from dens,
>   To teach them loyalty and sense,
> And sordid souls of the true faith convince.

---

25   The Restoration court ode is more than just a distant relation of the masque: see for example the opening of the 1685 welcome song for James II, *Why are all the Muses Mute?*, where the king's physical presence is necessary to 'inspire / And animate … the vocal choir' before the ode proper (including the overture) can begin.

No one in 1690 would have missed the reference to the new king's ongoing campaign against the Irish 'savages', whose rejection of 'the true faith' justified English efforts to 'hunt [them] from [their] dens' and impose both spiritual and physical conquest on their 'sordid souls'. Such brutal rhetoric may seem to be partially mitigated by the concurrent celebration of 'gracious Gloriana' and her 'Bright … virtue and charming … eyes', but D'Urfey's text clearly reflects the uncertainty of a nation newly at war against both internal and external enemies. Every one of Mary's six birthday odes brings William on the scene, usually granting him a perfunctory few lines near the end (in which his consort is normally also mentioned) before the text returns to its main honoree for a final encomium.[26] *Arise, my Muse*, however, is exceptional in that it seems to abandon Mary entirely a little more than halfway through, focusing instead on an imagined dialogue between 'Eusebia' (the Church of England) and the personified figure of Glory. Eusebia laments that William 'must … fatal dangers undertake' on her behalf, while Glory urges the king forward ('go on, illustrious man: / Leave not the work undone / Thou hast so well begun'). With Glory's final admonition to William, 'Go on, great prince, go on!', the ode abruptly comes to an end, as if to underscore the unfinished state of England's endeavours at this critical historical juncture.[27]

Two other apparently court-focused works deserve consideration in the context of the ode, although they are smaller-scale single songs. 'High on a Throne of Glitt'ring Ore', for soprano with continuo accompaniment and a soprano/bass 'chorus' at the end, sets a short encomiastic text that Thomas D'Urfey published as 'An Ode to the Queen' in 1690, the same year *Arise, my Muse* was performed.[28]

---

26   As in *Now does the Glorious Day Appear* (1689), *Love's Goddess sure was Blind* (1692), *Celebrate this Festival* (1693; referring to William alone at the end) and *Come ye Sons of Art* (1694). *Welcome, welcome, Glorious Morn* (1691), a sizeable portion of which is taken up with a prophecy uttered by the unnamed 'mighty Goddess of this wealthy isle', gives William more substantial exposure, alternating its focus back and forth between the two monarchs throughout the last third of the piece. Note that Sir Charles Sedley's text for *Love's Goddess sure was Blind* is, uniquely for this period, not Pindaric, consisting instead of eight regular four-line stanzas (ABAB, in iambic tetrameter). Here, William's stanza (the sixth, 'May her hero bring us peace') is balanced textually against the previous stanza, which is devoted to Mary ('May her blest example chase'), a structural element that must have been apparent to Purcell, since he chose to set this pair of stanzas for a rapid-fire delivery to a single tune (the famous 'Cold and Raw' contrafactum; see n. 162 below), whereas every other stanza in the ode receives its own independent setting.

27   In fact, Purcell left unset the final two stanzas of D'Urfey's poem, in the second of which Mary is reinstated: see *Poems on Affairs of State from Oliver Cromwell to this Present Time … Part III* (London, 1698), p. 66. As Bruce Wood has observed (in his Preface to Henry Purcell, *Birthday Odes for Queen Mary, Part I*, ed. Bruce Wood, The Works of Henry Purcell, vol. 11 (new edn, London: Novello, 1993), p. x), it is surprising that Purcell would have resisted the opportunity to compose music for this text, which practically bursts with musical references, including 'tuneful Harmony' and 'skilful Melody', as well as voices, lutes and flutes.

28   Thomas D'Urfey, *New Poems, Consisting of Satyrs, Elegies, and Odes: Together with a Choice*

Like the full-scale ode, this work eulogizes Mary as the virtuous 'Gloriana', whose edifying pronouncements move even unseen deities to sing her praises. The song seems to have been created as a vehicle for praising the queen in general, rather than for any specific event, and nothing is known about the occasion or setting of its performance.

The other political 'mini-ode' is more complicated: the solo song 'Lovely Albina's come ashore' seems to refer to a political event or circumstance, but in allegorical terms that are difficult to unravel:

> Lovely Albina's come ashore
>   To enter her just claim;
> Ten times more charming than before,
>   To her immortal fame.
>
> The Belgic Lion, as he's brave,
>   This beauty will relieve,
> For nothing but a mean blind slave
>   Can live, and let her grieve.

Jack Westrup reports that this poem 'is supposed to refer to the ... reconciliation between Princess Anne and [William]' in 1695, without offering further details.[29] The allegory is certainly opaque, but James Winn has recently proposed that the song should indeed be seen in the light of the ongoing warming of relations between Anne and her brother-in-law, which began in early 1695, when Anne moved into St James's Palace with her husband and five-year-old son. However, it was only later in the year, after William had achieved military success in the capture of Namur in the Low Countries and Anne returned to London from Windsor, where she had spent the summer, that the reconciliation strengthened.[30] The Princess's disembarkation on 27 September might have provided a pretext for this mini-welcome song, although the coupling of an unambiguous reference to the king ('the Belgic Lion') with a veiled threat that only 'a mean blind slave' would treat Anne poorly seems impolitic at best. Purcell's association with the piece might thus have been interpreted as taking sides, but contemporaries seem to have focused more on the fact that it was, as one manuscript source describes it, 'The last Song

---

    Collection of the Newest Court Songs (London, 1690), pp. 19–21. The table of contents (sig. A8r) describes the piece as '*An Ode to the Queen, excellently set to Musick; by M. H. Purcel.*'

29   Jack A. Westrup, *Purcell*, The Master Musicians (rev. edn, Oxford: Oxford University Press, 1995; originally published London: Dent, 1937), p. 84. Zimmerman asserts that the text, without the music, appears in the manuscript Lbl Add. 30303, which may predate this event, but James Winn has kindly informed me that there is in fact no trace of 'Lovely Albina' in this source; see Franklin B. Zimmerman, *Henry Purcell, 1659–1695: An Analytical Catalogue of his Music* (London: Macmillan; New York: St. Martin's Press, 1963), p. 193.

30   James Winn, personal communication, 9 May 2010; this issue will be explored in greater detail in Winn's forthcoming study *Queen Anne Style*.

M^r. Henry Purcell Sett before his Sickness',[31] and the composer's premature death soon afterwards certainly precluded any tangible consequences for what might be described as his final essay in the genre of court ode.[32]

Despite the seemingly thorough scholarly treatment of Purcell's odes as compared to some of his other genres, significant work remains to be done, particularly with regard to textual considerations, and to the ideological implications of both text and performance.[33] Such investigation needs to move beyond a subjective assessment of the 'quality' of the texts, either as poetry or as encomiastic articulations of political allegiance or royalist propaganda, in order to consider *how* the odes worked – textually, musically and performatively – and why, if they really were so transparently sycophantic, the genre seems to have had such extraordinary staying power.[34] Purcell's odes, while providing some of the best examples of the form, are only one piece of this larger puzzle, and it is unfortunate that, with a few exceptions, his odes are the only ones widely available in modern printed scores and recordings.

Anthems

Considerably less attention has been paid to the potential political application and meaning of Purcell's anthems. Nearly all of his anthems and divine service settings were composed for use in the Chapel Royal, but in this case royal provenance is not sufficient to mark a work as 'political' *per se*.[35] To narrow the field, we can take note of a group of anthems whose association with the court is combined

---

31 US-Ws V.b.197, p. 127; see also Henry Purcell, *Orpheus Britannicus. A Collection of all the Choicest Songs for One, Two, and Three Voices* (London, 1698), p. 133. This seems to be more accurate than the description 'The last Song that Mr. *Henry Purcell* Sett before he Dy'd' found in John Hudgebutt, *Thesaurus Musicus: Being, a Collection of the Newest Songs Performed at His Majesties Theatres … The Fifth Book* (London, 1696), p. 28; compare 'From Rosy Bow'rs', which is described in *Orpheus Britannicus*, p. 90, as 'the last Song that Mr. *Purcell* Sett, it being in his Sickness'.

32 James Winn has noted that within a few months the work had been printed, not only in *Thesaurus Musicus* (pp. 28–9) but also as a single-sheet song by the engraver Thomas Cross (personal communication). I am grateful to Professor Winn for taking the time to discuss this topic with me.

33 For an instructive example of this type of approach, see Anthony Miller, 'The Roman Triumph in Purcell's Odes', *Music & Letters* 83 (2002): 371–82.

34 I hope to address some of these considerations in a forthcoming article, 'Reading the Restoration Court Ode', which will seek both to contextualize the pre-1689 odes more fully and provide a detailed analysis of their texts.

35 The same might be said of Purcell's symphony songs – multi-part songs with full instrumental accompaniment – which Peter Holman has suggested may have been 'written to be performed by members of the Private Music in the royal apartments at Whitehall'; see Peter Holman, *Henry Purcell*, Oxford Studies of Composers (Oxford: Oxford University Press, 1994), p. 47.

with an occasional purpose. Such a purpose is not always easy to ascertain, since anthems generally set pre-existing scriptural texts and fall within the context of religious worship, so they do not announce their applicability to contemporary political events in the same way that odes do. In certain special instances, of course, anthems are clearly associated with important events: Purcell's career saw two royal coronations in rapid succession (James in 1685 and William and Mary in 1689) as well as the deaths of two monarchs slightly less than a decade apart (Charles in 1685 and Mary in 1694). To one degree or another, each of these demanded his compositional attentions. For James's lavish coronation, Purcell is now believed to have composed two anthems, the full anthem *I was Glad*[36] and the unusual concerted anthem *My Heart is Inditing*.[37] The latter, based primarily on a text from Psalm 45, climaxes with the exhortation 'Praise the Lord, O Jerusalem; praise thy God, O Zion, for kings shall be thy nursing fathers, and queens thy nursing mothers', a pastiche of Psalm 147:12 and Isaiah 49:23. This same textual pairing, conventionally associated with royal coronations, was reused to open Purcell's concerted anthem *Praise the Lord, O Jerusalem*, written for William and Mary's coronation four years later. On this occasion, *I was Glad* was once again sung as an introit at the beginning of the ceremony, but the more spectacular *My Heart is Inditing* seems to have carried too much Jacobite baggage to be deployed a second time; moreover, its text, which had been assembled for the coronation of James II's consort, Maria Beatrice d'Este, was less appropriate for Mary, who was being crowned as queen regnant alongside her husband.[38]

Purcell's music for royal funerals is more fragmentary. As Bruce Wood has compellingly demonstrated, the composer's setting of one section of the Anglican burial service, *Thou knowest, Lord*, was created to fill in a gap in the old setting by Thomas Morley, dating from the reign of Elizabeth I.[39] Purcell also wrote the

---

36 Bruce Wood, 'A Coronation Anthem – Lost and Found', *Musical Times* 118 (1977): 466–8. Purcell's other *I was Glad*, the symphony anthem, is not known to be associated with any particular royal event, *pace* Andrew Gant's thought-provoking argument in his sleeve notes to the CD recording *Music for the Coronation of James II, 1685*, The Choir of the Chapel Royal, The Musicians Extra-Ordinary, dir. Andrew Gant (Signum Classics SIGCD094, *rec*. 2007), pp. 5–6. See also Zimmerman's unconvincing attempt to explain away its presence in Cfm 117 in *Henry Purcell, 1659–1695: An Analytical Catalogue*, pp. 18–19; Zimmerman describes *I was Glad* as a 'full anthem' in *Henry Purcell, 1659–1695. His Life and Times*, p. 124, despite providing a reference to the symphony anthem from his catalogue.

37 In categorizing Purcell's anthems by type, I rely upon the taxonomy outlined in Eric Van Tassel, 'Music for the Church', in Michael Burden (ed.), *The Purcell Companion* (London: Faber, 1994; Portland, OR: Amadeus Press, 1995), pp. 103–4.

38 For a discussion of Purcell's concerted coronation anthems and how Purcell seems to have responded differently to the different circumstances of the two coronations, see ibid., pp. 187–9.

39 Bruce Wood, 'The First Performance of Purcell's Funeral Music for Queen Mary', in Michael Burden (ed.), *Performing the Music of Henry Purcell* (Oxford: Clarendon, 1996), pp. 61–81. Because it is not technically an anthem, but rather constitutes service music,

instrumental March and Canzona to accompany the funeral procession.[40] When Charles II died in 1685, on the other hand, there was no state funeral, allegedly on account of the late king's deathbed conversion to Roman Catholicism. As Shay and Thompson suggest, this fact may explain the existence of Purcell's incomplete full anthem *Hear my Prayer, O Lord*, which is now thought to date from early 1685, and hence may preserve the opening for a larger funeral anthem that is no longer extant.[41]

The foregoing political associations are obvious enough, but other Restoration anthems with less explicit links to grand occasions were also apparently created to mark political events. The strongest evidence for this practice is provided by the 'Gostling Manuscript' (US-AUS HRC 85), which includes a number of anthems by Purcell's contemporaries to which Gostling added revealing annotations. John Blow's *O Lord, thou art my God* (p. 134 inv.), for example, is dated 19 June 1688, nine days after the birth of the Prince of Wales (James Francis Edward, later known as the 'Old Pretender'); Blow's *We will Rejoice in thy Salvation* (p. 102 inv.) is described as an 'Anthem made upon yᵉ discovery of yᵉ plot against King William Sung April 16: 1696 the Thanksgiving Day'; and Gostling notes that Jeremiah Clarke's A minor setting of *I will Love thee, O Lord my Strength* (p. 213 inv.) was composed as a 'Thanksgiving Anthem Sept 23 . 1705 at St Pauls yᵉ Queen present for yᵉ victory & success in fflanders, in passing yᵉ ffrench lines'. One of Purcell's anthems, *Blessed are They that Fear the Lord*, is marked similarly: Gostling tells us it was written 'for yᵉ Thanksgiving appointed Jan: 15ᵗʰ 1687/8 for yᵉ Queens being wᵗʰ child',[42] a reference to Queen Maria Beatrice's pregnancy that resulted in the birth of the Prince of Wales on 10 June.

Three other anthems Purcell composed prior to the Glorious Revolution may have political overtones. *The Lord is my Light and my Salvation; Whom then shall I Fear?*, believed to date from around 1683, might in some way be associated with the

---

this piece should be recatalogued in any future revision of Zimmerman's *Analytical Catalogue*, perhaps as Z234; this is one example demonstrating how Zimmerman's 1963 catalogue, while remaining an indispensable source, is now much in need of updating, as Andrew Pinnock also notes in Chapter 5, n. 133 above.

40   The appearance of the March (Z860/1) in Purcell's music for a revival of Thomas Shadwell's play *The Libertine* (Z600/2a) is now believed to post-date Mary's funeral: see Wood, 'The First Performance of Purcell's Funeral Music for Queen Mary', pp. 61–72.

41   Robert Shay and Robert Thompson, *Purcell Manuscripts: The Principal Musical Sources* (Cambridge: Cambridge University Press, 2000), p. 46. Shay and Thompson note that Purcell's customary practice was to notate his anthems first in 'a rough separate score', so it is possible that the anthem was completed but that Purcell did not finish entering it into Cfm 88, fols 83v–83r inv.

42   US-AUS HRC 85, p. 105; see John Gostling, *The Gostling Manuscript*, introduction by Franklin B. Zimmerman (Austin: University of Texas Press, 1977). On p. 109 (second instance), Gostling wrote: 'Composed by Mʳ Henry Purcell. Jan: 12. 1687[/8]. for yᵉ Thanksgiving – Appointed in London & 12 miles round, upon her Majesties being wᵗʰ Child. & on yᵉ 29 following over England.' See also William Gostling's similar annotation in Purcell's autograph manuscript Lbl Add. 30931, fol. 66v, as described in Shay and Thompson, *Purcell Manuscripts*, p. 143.

discovery of the Rye House Plot against Charles II in the early summer of that year; *O Lord, Grant the King a Long Life* is one of two anthems that appear in the index to Purcell's autograph manuscript Lbl R.M. 20.h.8 immediately before the 1685 coronation anthem *My Heart is Inditing*, but were never copied into the volume, so it is possible that it was composed during Charles II's final illness;[43] and the joyful *O Sing unto the Lord* of 1688 may also be associated with the Prince of Wales, perhaps having been written to celebrate his nativity. In these cases we have no hard evidence to support such a proposition, either in a contemporary annotation or in the text itself, but in discussing *O Sing unto the Lord* Zimmerman observed that '[t]he alteration and re-arrangement of the verses of the text to this anthem suggests that it may have been an occasional composition. Ordinarily, Purcell followed the biblical text rather closely as far as the original order was concerned.'[44] This unusual practice of setting 'discontinuous' excerpts from a scriptural source also applies to *The Lord is my Light* and *O Lord, Grant the King a Long Life*, and it may provide a clue to the identification of other anthems Purcell composed to mark specific occasions. As Eric Van Tassel has suggested, 'politics probably underlay, far more often than we can now prove, the selection or editing of anthem texts for ordinary or special Chapel Royal services, to support the official line on the issues of the day.'[45] Van Tassel's survey of Purcell's liturgical music reveals a total of 11 anthems composed prior to 1689 that set discontinuous texts and thus merit further investigation.[46]

In the wake of the Revolution, Purcell's duties as a composer of sacred works were substantially curtailed: aside from the coronation and funeral music discussed above, he seems to have composed no more than five or six anthems. However, three of these present discontinuous texts, and thus may also have been written to serve a political purpose. Indeed, one of them also contains an annotation by Gostling demonstrating its political associations: he records that the verse anthem *The Way of God is an Undefiled Way* was performed 'November yᵉ 11ᵗʰ 1694 / King William then returnd from Flanders'.[47] In addition, Peter Holman has recently suggested that the symphony anthem *My Song shall be Alway* was probably written for William's triumphal entry into Windsor on 9 September 1690, after the Siege of Limerick,[48] a battle about which Purcell composed several political catches for public consumption.[49] This leaves the verse (or possibly symphony) anthem *O Give*

---

43 See Shay and Thompson, *Purcell Manuscripts*, pp. 140 and 157.

44 Zimmerman, *Henry Purcell, 1659–1695: An Analytical Catalogue*, p. 42.

45 Van Tassel, 'Music for the Church', p. 102.

46 See ibid., pp. 106–13 (Lists 1–4). Besides the coronation anthem *My Heart is Inditing* and the three symphony anthems already mentioned, this list includes three other symphony anthems (*In Thee O Lord do I put my Trust*; *Praise the Lord, O my Soul, and All that is within me*; and *Praise the Lord, O my Soul, O Lord my God*); three verse anthems (*Bow Down thine Ear*; *O Lord, thou art my God*; and *Hear my Prayer, O Lord*); and the full-with-verse anthem *Lord, how Long wilt thou be Angry?*.

47 US-AUS HRC 85, p. 102 inv.

48 Peter Holman, *Four and Twenty Fiddlers: The Violin at the English Court, 1540–1690*, Oxford Monographs on Music (Oxford: Clarendon, 1993), p. 406.

49 See the discussion below, p. 234. Another Purcell composition, the First Act Tune from

Thanks of 1693, which – while it also seems to have a celebratory purpose – cannot yet be linked with a specific event.

Of course, a discontinuous text is not a *sine qua non* for an anthem to have potential political implications, something that is demonstrated by anthems such as *Blessed are They that Fear the Lord* that were associated with specific events by Gostling, but that do not have rearranged texts. Given the exceptional nature of all of Purcell's post-1689 anthems, we might also want to scrutinize the other three he is believed to have produced during that period,[50] and similar questions might be asked of some of the earlier anthems, even those whose dates are less certain and whose texts seem perfectly conventional on first inspection.[51]

Apart from the factual observations noted above, there have to date been no significant scholarly efforts to situate these, and possibly other, Purcell anthems in a political context, let alone to explore more generally how an occasional anthem performed as part of a divine service might have been received or understood by its hearers. This is a significant lacuna, and although contextualizing such works is certainly no easy task, a well-informed and comprehensive approach to the problem – preferably one that takes in not only Purcell's work but the entire corpus of Restoration and late-Stuart anthems – might yield important results regarding not merely the details of individual works but, more broadly, the place of anthems and other church music in contemporary political discourse and royalist ideology.

Dioclesian (also fitted with words by William Mountfort around 1691 as the 'mock' song 'O! how happy's he, who from bus'ness free') appeared under the title 'Siege of *Limerick*' in Henry Playford, *The Dancing-Master: or, Directions for Dancing Country Dances, with the Tunes to each Dance for the Treble-Violin. The Ninth Edition Corrected* (London, 1695), p. 173, and also in the tenth edition of 1698.

50 These are *The Lord is King, and hath put on Glorious Apparel; The Lord is King, be the People never so Impatient;* and *O Lord, Rebuke me Not.*

51 However, two early Purcell anthems that have been tentatively associated with the Anglican Feast of Charles I, King and Martyr (30 January), and thus might be considered quasi-political, are probably not: *Turn thou us, O good Lord* and *Blow up the Trumpet in Sion* both set texts from the Ash Wednesday service in the 1662 *Book of Common Prayer*, the former a collect and the latter an excerpt from the appointed epistle reading. The similarities in Purcell's setting of the words 'spare thy people', which appear in both texts and are noted in Van Tassel, 'Music for the Church', p. 199 n. 67, are more likely attributable to this connection, since the text of *Blow up the Trumpet* (from Joel 2:15–17) is not in fact included in the liturgy for the Charles I feast, while only the opening phrase of the 'Turn thou us' collect is used there, as part of the litany. Shay and Thompson demonstrate that *Blow up the Trumpet* cannot have been written after 1677, thereby effectively demolishing Zimmerman's theory that the anthem was written to celebrate the court's capture of the Lord Mayoralty of London in 1682; see Shay and Thompson, *Purcell Manuscripts*, p. 199 and Zimmerman, *Henry Purcell, 1659–1695. His Life and Times*, pp. 89–90.

Songs

One of the curious qualities of Purcell's compositional output with respect to political meaning and applicability is the near absence of explicit political content from the large body of single songs in his *oeuvre*. Aside from the two 'mini-odes' ('High on a Throne of Glitt'ring Ore' and 'Lovely Albina's come ashore') noted above, and two loyal drinking songs associated with plays discussed below, there are only three single songs by Purcell that can clearly be shown to have a political context. All three were written as occasional pieces to memorialize deceased monarchs: the declamatory solo song 'If Pray'rs and Tears' mourns the death of Charles II, while two Latin works, the single-voice 'Incassum, Lesbia, incassum rogas' (also entitled 'The Queen's Epicedium') and the duet 'O dive custos Auriacae domus', appeared alongside a work by John Blow (setting an English version of 'Incassum, Lesbia') in *Three Elegies upon the Much Lamented Loss of Our Late Most Gracious Queen Mary*, published in May 1695.[52] 'If Pray'rs and Tears' falls into a more general (largely non-political) category of declamatory memorial songs, most of which Purcell wrote for less exalted colleagues, such as Matthew Locke, John Playford and Thomas Farmer.[53] The elegies for Queen Mary are also exceptional as highly classicized, almost academic works – the 1695 folio print carefully presents each text in poetic form alongside its musical score, and 'O dive custos' is described on the title page as being excerpted 'out of the *Oxford Verse*', that is, the university publication *Pietas Universitatis Oxoniensis in Obitum Augustissimae*, which prints the full ten-stanza text, by Henry Parker (a student at New College) – of which Purcell set only the first four stanzas.[54]

These exceptional court-associated works aside, the absence of politics from Purcell's body of single songs may itself be a noteworthy phenomenon. We know little about the composer's motivation for composing non-theatrical songs in the first place: some may have been a source of trifling financial benefit, such as those that appeared in *The Gentleman's Journal* in the early 1690s; others may have been written for friends and colleagues, only incidentally finding their way into print later on. Either way, their apoliticality raises broader questions about the composer's own political inclinations: Purcell's pointed avoidance of politics in these 'discretionary' creations might be taken as an indication of his desire to remain out of the fray

---

52 Henry Playford, *Three Elegies upon the Much Lamented Loss of Our Late Most Gracious Queen Mary* (London, 1695).

53 At the same time, it also forms part of a general outpouring of poetic grief, in English and Latin, brought about by Charles's death. John Alden has counted nearly seventy such works, many of which (like 'If Pray'rs and Tears') are anonymous; see John Alden, *The Muses Mourn: A Checklist of Verse Occasioned by the Death of Charles II* (Charlottesville: Bibliographical Society of the University of Virginia, 1958). 'If Pray'rs and Tears', the only work Alden found that was set to music, is no. 59 (pp. 52–3).

54 *Pietas Universitatis Oxoniensis in Obitum Augustissimae et Desideratissimae Reginae Mariae* (Oxford, 1695) sig. X2v. Purcell's small output of Latin works, which span several generic categories, but seem to be mostly non-political, deserve further study as a group.

whenever possible, and as evidence that his settings of political texts may have been created largely as a consequence of his official responsibilities.[55]

Theatre Music

In any consideration of the potentially political qualities of Purcell's compositional output, *Dido and Aeneas* must perforce loom large, if only on account of the intense interest and controversy that it has generated over the last half-century. It is well known that *Dido and Aeneas* is a conundrum: its origins are obscure, its performance history is hazy and it survives only in an incomplete state. Although it is now widely believed to have originated as a court masque, that theory is no more than speculative, and the date of its composition (and hence the identity of the monarch for whom it may have been composed) remains a contested issue. With so much uncertainty, it is not surprising that the political meaning(s) of *Dido* have been the subject of a wide range of interpretations. It will probably never be possible to establish a definitive political reading of *Dido* (or, conversely, to prove that no such reading can be advanced); yet the work and its critical history provide an opportunity to investigate the contingency of such readings and to ask how they come to be articulated.

The first step in such a process is to clarify what is certainly known about the work's earliest textual sources, since the issue of *Dido*'s political meaning and the question of its date of composition – which themselves exist in a symbiotic relationship – are both dependent upon what the text itself can tell us. The surviving text of *Dido and Aeneas* can be considered in three parts: an allegorical prologue featuring classical deities and pastoral figures, seemingly intended as a compliment to a monarch and his consort; a three-act tragedy based on Book IV of Virgil's epic poem *The Aeneid*; and a satirical spoken epilogue written for a performance of the work at a boarding school for young ladies in Chelsea, on the outskirts of London. The epilogue, written by Thomas D'Urfey, was published in D'Urfey's *New Poems* of 1690 and identifies the speaker as Lady Dorothy Burke, a student at the school who may also have taken a role in the main production.[56] The first two components, apparently written by Nahum Tate, survive in a printed, undated libretto issued

---

55   Ian Spink doubts the authenticity of the unaccompanied two-part patriotic drinking song 'To this Place We're now Come'; see Henry Purcell, *Duets, Dialogues and Trios*, ed. Ian Spink, The Works of Henry Purcell, vol. 22b (London: Novello, 2007), p. 228. Nonetheless, it is perhaps worth noting the generic similarities between this song and the two theatre-associated songs 'How Great are the Blessings' and 'Here's a Health to the King', discussed below.

56   '*Epilogue to the Opera of* DIDO *and* ÆNEAS, *performed at Mr.* Preist's *Boarding-School at* Chelsey; *Spoken by the Lady* Dorothy Burk', in D'Urfey, *New Poems*, pp. 82–3. The volume's table of contents (sig. A8r) identifies the school's proprietor as '*Mrs.* Preist'. Although it is dated 1690, *New Poems* was advertised in the Term Catalogue for Michaelmas 1689, and thus was most likely published very early in the year announced on the title page.

for a performance of the work at the same school.[57] Apart from these basic facts, our understanding of *Dido* is dependent entirely on speculation and inference.[58] Much of this speculation has centred around the work's supposed date, which has been revised a number of times in the modern era as new documents have come to light. Following some confusion on the part of scholars in the nineteenth century, in 1904 William Barclay Squire proposed a date of 1689 for the boarding-school performance, which was then assumed, by default, to be the premiere.[59] That theory held sway until 1989, when Richard Luckett and Paul Hopkins made the tangential discovery that John Blow's *Venus and Adonis* had been performed first at court and then at Priest's boarding school, leading many to conclude that *Dido*'s origins also lay not at the boarding school, but at the royal court.[60] Thus began a new round of debates over the likely date of the supposed court premiere, while Barclay Squire's date of 1689 for the boarding-school performance continued to stand as an unchallenged point of faith.[61] In 2009, however, Bryan White announced the discovery of a letter of February 1689, written far from London, in which the Chelsea production of *Dido* seems unambiguously to be mentioned.[62] Although his argument still depends on a

---

57 *An Opera Perform'd at Mr. Josias Priest's Boarding-School at Chelsey. By Young Gentlewomen* (n.p., n.d.). Both sections reappeared in slightly altered form in [Charles Gildon], *Measure for Measure. Or Beauty the Best Advocate. As it is Acted at the Theatre in Lincolns-Inn-Fields* (London, 1700), where Tate and Purcell's work was interpolated into the play as a sequence of four paradramatic entertainments.

58 Michael Burden put the problem succinctly in 1989 when he observed that 'the most that can be said is that the work was "Perform'd at Mr. Josias Priest's Boarding-School at Chelsey", that Dorothy Burke probably took part in the performance, and that it is possible that Priest did too'; see Michael Burden, Review of Ellen T. Harris, *Henry Purcell's 'Dido and Aeneas'* (Oxford: Clarendon, 1987), in *Musical Times* 130 (1989): 85–6.

59 W. Barclay Squire, 'Purcell's Dramatic Music', *Sammelbände der Internationalen Musikgesellschaft* 5 (1903–04): 506–14. Squire wryly catalogues the earlier theories about the date of *Dido*, as propounded by Hawkins (1677), Macfarren (1675), Rimbault (1675, revised to 1680), Cummings (1680) and Husk (1675, with a supposed second performance in 1680). Squire's theory is restated, with some additional facts, in W. Barclay Squire, 'Purcell's "Dido and Aeneas"', *Musical Times* 59 (1918): 252–4.

60 See Richard Luckett, 'A New Source for "Venus and Adonis"', *Musical Times* 130 (1989): 76–9. See also Chapter 5, p. 174 above.

61 Bruce Wood and Andrew Pinnock, '"Unscarr'd by Turning Times"?: The Dating of Purcell's *Dido and Aeneas*', *Early Music* 20 (1992): 372–90, proposing a date of 1684; Curtis Price, '*Dido and Aeneas*: Questions of Style and Evidence', *Early Music* 22 (1994): 115–25; and Andrew R. Walkling, '"The Dating of Purcell's *Dido and Aeneas*"?: A Reply to Bruce Wood and Andrew Pinnock', *Early Music* 22 (1994): 469–81, arguing for a date of 1687. See also the other responses to Wood and Pinnock: John Buttrey, 'The Dating of *Dido*' (Correspondence), *Early Music* 20 (1992): 703; and Martin Adams, 'More on Dating *Dido*' (Correspondence), *Early Music* 21 (1993): 510; and Wood and Pinnock's replies to Price and Walkling: '"Singin' in the Rain": Yet More on Dating *Dido*' (Correspondence), *Early Music* 22 (1994): 365–7; and 'Not Known at this Address: More on the Dating of *Dido*' (Correspondence), *Early Music* 23 (1995): 188–9.

62 Bryan White, 'Letter from Aleppo: Dating the Chelsea School Performance of *Dido*

---

chain of inference, White has credibly demonstrated that the Chelsea performance had almost certainly taken place by July 1688, and not in 1689 as was long believed. This, of course, has done nothing to lift the cloud of uncertainty over the dating, or even existence, of the putative earlier court premiere.[63]

All this has a direct impact on the question of *Dido*'s politics, particularly since the range of plausible dates for the various performances – 1684, 1687, 1688, 1689 – spans a period of significant political change, encompassing the last years of Charles II, the brief reign of James II and the Glorious Revolution: depending on when *Dido and Aeneas* was actually performed, contemporary viewers would have understood the text in quite different ways. In the years prior to Luckett and Hopkins's 1989 discovery, the standard interpretation, articulated by John Buttrey in 1967, held that the 'opera', as composed expressly for performance at the boarding school, was intended to compliment the newly installed William and Mary by allegorizing them in the prologue as the deities Phoebus and Venus; the prologue's emphasis on the coming of Spring was taken to suggest a performance around the beginning of May, perhaps in conjunction with Queen Mary's twenty-seventh birthday on 30 April,[64] or, as Margaret Laurie subsequently proposed, with the coronation of the joint monarchs nine days earlier.[65] D'Urfey's epilogue, with its references to Rome promoting 'strange Tricks' and to the unshakeable Protestantism of the young ladies, who remain 'Unscar'd by turning Times' served as a linchpin of this argument.[66] Aware that, as Curtis Price later observed, 'the story of a prince who seduces and abandons a neurotic queen would seem a tactless way to honour the new monarchs',[67] Buttrey read the main portion of the work as an allegorized

---

and Aeneas', Early Music 37 (2009): 417–28. The information considered by White casts doubt on whether another document initially thought by Mark Goldie to refer to *Dido*'s performance at the school actually refers to that event at all; see Mark Goldie, 'The Earliest Notice of Purcell's *Dido and Aeneas*', *Early Music* 20 (1992): 392–400.

63   For a discussion of this matter, see my exchange of communications with Curtis Price in *Journal of the American Musicological Society* 64 (2011): 266–74.

64   John Buttrey, 'Dating Purcell's Dido and Aeneas', *Proceedings of the Royal Musical Association* 94 (1967–68): 51–62.

65   Henry Purcell, *Dido and Aeneas*, ed. Margaret Laurie, The Works of Henry Purcell, vol. 3 (new edn, Sevenoaks: Novello, 1979), p. ix.

66   Wood and Pinnock's rendering, without comment, of 'Unscar'd' as 'Unscarr'd' in the title of their article serves to obscure the potentially important question of whether D'Urfey intended to refer to the (presumably emotional) scars inflicted by 'turning Times' ('unscarred') or to the fear the turning of those times might engender ('unscared'). Although Wood and Pinnock do signal the emendation in their transcription of D'Urfey's epilogue on p. 374, the article's title has caused subsequent ambiguities, for example in White's 'Letter to Aleppo', where the title is cited accurately in n. 1, but is given with D'Urfey's original spelling in the references in nn. 38, 40 and 46.

67   Price, *Henry Purcell and the London Stage*, p. 229; in Price, 'Political Allegory in Late-Seventeenth-Century English Opera', p. 17, Price opines that although the main story of *Dido* was 'probably not a deliberate allegory (even though it alludes to the new monarchs) … there were simply too many uncomfortable coincidences' for the work to have been appropriate for public performance during (and immediately after) Purcell's lifetime.

warning to William and Mary of 'the possible fate of the British nation should Dutch William fail in his responsibilities to his English queen'.[68]

Such an approach reveals both the opportunities and the dangers associated with allegorical reading. On the one hand, certain noteworthy phrases in the text, such as Phoebus's assertion that Venus's 'Lustre … half Eclipses' his own radiance, or the aphoristic choral statement, 'When Monarchs unite how happy their State, / They Triumph at once [o'er] their Foes and their Fate' in Act I, would seem to offer straightforward encomiastic references to the new king and queen, similar to the kind of commendatory language normally found in Baroque operatic prologues. At the same time, Buttrey's 'cautionary tale' (as Price later described it) relies on a different allegorical mechanism, one based on the *roman à clef*, in which Aeneas becomes a metonymic stand-in for William, and Dido, presumably, for Mary. The two models are not mutually exclusive: in England and elsewhere other examples can be found of theatrical works with satirical or otherwise subversive meanings that were preceded by prologues whose ingenuous and heartfelt praise of their subject betrays no hint of the irony that is to come. The English court masque form of the early seventeenth century had moved with ease between these modes, as a number of scholars have amply demonstrated,[69] but the conflicting languages of adoration and admonition were more promiscuously intermixed in this earlier form, while the structural separation of allegorical techniques used in the later period offered considerably greater opportunities for meticulously assembled, sustained critiques whose more dangerous implications were meant to be blunted, or perhaps camouflaged, by the rhetoric of unstinting praise offered in the prologue. Given the strong cultural propensity for the writing and reading of underlying, often semi-concealed, meaning in the early modern period, it is not outside the realms of probability, the objections of some modern commentators notwithstanding, that oblique criticism of this nature existed, and indeed was recognized by its target audience, including monarchs and their ministers.

The problem with Buttrey's argument is really that it does not incorporate sufficient nuance or coherence: by the late seventeenth century the courtly *roman à clef* had become a finely tuned instrument of political commentary, and the unspecific formula 'fail in his responsibilities' divined by Buttrey in the alleged message to William is not sufficient to stand on its own as a *raison d'être* for the supposed political thrust of the work. Any such reading, at least in the case of a courtly *roman à clef*, must consider the whole set of themes that the text presents, which need to come together as part of a consistent referential structure. Thus, if

---

68   Buttrey, 'Dating Purcell's Dido and Aeneas': 60.

69   See, for example, Kevin Sharpe, *Criticism and Compliment: The Politics of Literature in the England of Charles I*, Cambridge Studies in Early Modern British History (Cambridge: Cambridge University Press, 1987), esp. Chapter 6; Martin Butler, 'Politics and the Masque: *The Triumph of Peace*', *The Seventeenth Century* 2 (1987): 117–41; and Butler, 'Politics and the Masque: *Salmacida Spolia*', in Thomas Healy and Jonathan Sawday (eds), *Literature and the English Civil War* (Cambridge: Cambridge University Press, 1990), pp. 59–74.

William were indeed being counselled not to 'fail in his responsibilities', the text should be expected to delineate those responsibilities. Other related questions should similarly admit of answers that can illuminate the work's intentions on a detailed level: what, specifically, does this retelling of the well-known episode from the *Aeneid* advise the king to do? How will the consequences play out if he does not follow this advice? How do we account for the role of 'fate' in the story, the mournful composure of the already doomed Queen Dido at the beginning of the work, to say nothing of her rage at Aeneas and her tragic demise at the end? How can we explain the presence of the Sorceress and her enchantresses, and their evil trick that drives the work's catastrophic dramatic machinery? What about the well-intentioned but ultimately deleterious importunities of Belinda and the 'Second Woman', and the 'hero' Aeneas's infuriating weakness of character?[70] Without consideration of these specific aspects of the story and its supposed allegorical parallels, it is no wonder that Buttrey's interpretation leaves much to be desired – particularly when we recall that it was being applied to an opera he assumed had been written for a girls' boarding school, which therefore had nothing at all to do with the king to whom its purported counsel was addressed.

This last concern, along with a more general nagging discomfort among scholars about why Tate and Purcell would have expended so much creative energy on a school production, seemed to be alleviated by the 1989 discovery mentioned above, which showed that *Dido* had more in common with its companion work, Blow's court masque *Venus and Adonis*, than had hitherto been thought, and thus might itself have originated under royal auspices. This new perspective on *Dido*'s origins, however, seemed to create its own set of problems, particularly with regard to the interpretation of the prologue, whose application to William and Mary had only recently been characterized by Ellen Harris as something that 'cannot be seriously doubted'.[71] Curtis Price responded to the changed scholarly landscape by suggesting that the prologue might still have been written in 1689 to compliment the new monarchs, even if the main body of *Dido* itself had an earlier provenance.[72] At the same time, he commented favourably on my own theory that the prologue could be much more effectively and coherently read in the context of the reign of James II, whose consort Maria Beatrice d'Este, while not

---

70 Such questions, of course, must always be asked with a view to how seventeenth-century writers and readers would have understood and interpreted the issues, something we are still only beginning to understand adequately, and Michael Burden's warning that 'simply producing a "better" or more consistent construct in the twentieth century does not mean that that was the one intended' is well taken; see Michael Burden, '"Great Minds Against Themselves Conspire": Purcell's Dido as Conspiracy Theorist', in Michael Burden (ed.), *A Woman Scorn'd: Responses to the Dido Myth* (London: Faber, 1998), p. 229.

71 Ellen T. Harris, *Henry Purcell's 'Dido and Aeneas'* (Oxford: Clarendon, 1987), p. 18. In the section immediately following, Harris firmly established her anti-allegorical credentials by rejecting Buttrey's Aeneas-as-William analysis as well as Price's attempt to render Buttrey's ideas more plausible.

72 Price, '*Dido and Aeneas*: Questions of Style and Evidence': 122.

a reigning monarch, was frequently acclaimed for her near-coequal status with her husband and her Venus-like beauty.[73] Both of these ideas came in response to the most radically revisionist theory, that of Bruce Wood and Andrew Pinnock, whose proposal of a 1684 date for the newly conjectured court premiere was predicated in part on an outright rejection of the possibility of allegorical content in any part of *Dido*, including the prologue, the second half of which is read as a non-political commentary on the extreme weather conditions in 1684.[74] The allegoresis of the prologue to *Dido and Aeneas* remains a problematic issue, not least because, unlike most of its progenitors – including the prologues to numerous contemporary French *tragédies en musique*, as well as several associated with operatic productions at the Restoration court, including *Ballet et musique* (1674), *Ariane* (1674), *Calisto* (1675) and *Rare en tout* (1677), to say nothing of the entire opera *Albion and Albanius* (1685) – the *Dido* prologue is exceptionally opaque in its meaning.[75]

Aside from the proliferation of opinions on what the prologue might or might not be taken to mean, the seemingly welcome opportunity after 1989 to rethink the allegorical implications of *Dido* as a whole was not immediately seized upon. Wood and Pinnock's theory represented the final nail in the coffin (already partially assembled by Price and Harris) of Buttrey's problematic Williamite reading of the work's main plot, but Price responded to this challenge by recanting his earlier speculation about political reading, arguing that *Dido* 'should be read as neither partisan nor even politicized because its language is chastely untopical, its plot and characters too faithful to the fourth book of the *Aeneid*'.[76] Price might be forgiven for attempting so valiantly to make sense of a rapidly fracturing scholarly consensus, particularly given Wood and Pinnock's vigorous efforts to defend their preferred analysis,[77] but the implied claim that Nahum Tate made no substantive changes to Virgil's story is unjustified. In fact, Tate reworked the plot in significant ways, changing the chronology and causality of the original, modifying the personality traits of the lead characters, altering the circumstances of Dido's death, and, most notably, introducing the '*Sorceress and her Inchanteress[es]*' as the driving force

---

73   Walkling, '"The Dating of Purcell's *Dido and Aeneas*"?': 473–80.

74   Wood and Pinnock, '"Unscarr'd by Turning Times"?': 374–6; and '"Singin' in the Rain"': 365. This denial of allegorical meaning extended even to D'Urfey's epilogue, whose apparent political references were dismissed as conventional tropes that 'can be taken entirely at face value' ('"Unscarr'd by Turning Times"?': 375).

75   The prologue to Blow's *Venus and Adonis* (?1683) is also unique, albeit in a different way: the text is entirely pastoral (the only god present is Cupid); there are no spectacular scenic effects or allegorical characters; and the rhetoric is satirical rather than encomiastic. This may be a function of the work's librettist, whom James Winn has argued was Anne Finch, a Maid of Honour to Maria Beatrice, then Duchess of York: see James Winn, '"A Versifying Maid of Honour": Anne Finch and the Libretto for *Venus and Adonis*', *Review of English Studies*, New Series 59 (2008): 67–85.

76   Price, '*Dido and Aeneas*: Questions of Style and Evidence': 122.

77   See Wood and Pinnock, '"Singin' in the Rain"' and 'Not Known at this Address'; neither of these responses, however, addresses the very significant concerns raised by Martin Adams in 'More on Dating *Dido*'.

behind the work's tragic momentum.[78] It can be argued that these textual signals were intended to direct the audience's attention to the presence of an underlying political message in this redaction of the well-known story, while at the same time retaining enough faithfulness to the original to protect the author from unwelcome consequences should the encoded meaning provoke a negative response in its audience (particularly the king).

Working in the context of this dynamic – a process closely associated with the 'hermeneutics of censorship' identified by Annabel Patterson – and using Tate's revisions as a point of entry, I have read *Dido and Aeneas* as a courtly *roman-à-clef* allegory designed to comment on the political events of the 1680s, in particular James II's rapidly disintegrating authority in 1687–88, a product of his susceptibility to the malign influence of his Roman Catholic advisors.[79] Such an interpretation is naturally controversial, although most of the criticism to date has originated from those who feel that *Dido* cannot mean anything at all (an unlikely assumption, given how much we now know about seventeenth-century habits of writing and reading) and/or from those whose view is that the work cannot be reduced to a single authorially determined position (almost certainly true, but not germane to the question of what Tate may potentially have been aiming to say).[80] Thus far, no scholar has advanced an alternative reading that meets the tests of nuance and coherence outlined above, features that would have been deemed essential to the functioning of a *roman-à-clef* allegory at the time (and which were not evident in the interpretation advanced by Buttrey, as has long been recognized).

Despite, or perhaps on account of, the steady trickle of new discoveries and insights over the last two decades, *Dido and Aeneas* remains a perplexing puzzle whose elements are only partially implicated in the issue of political meaning or interpretation. *If* we accept that Tate's libretto contains political elements, and *if* it is true (as most scholars believe) that Purcell originally or subsequently composed music for the prologue, we still have little insight into the question of whether Purcell himself regarded his participation in the project as politically charged – much less how he felt about it if he did. Although I have argued that the main *Dido* libretto can be read as mildly oppositional in its response to a moment of emerging political crisis, this kind of rhetoric – skilfully crafted and carefully deployed – is no less inconsistent with the expectations and practices of a Baroque court than are

---

78   A well-informed exploration of these changes can be found in Hugh M. Lee, 'Purcell's *Dido and Aneas* [sic]: Aeneas as Romantic Hero', *Vergilius* 23 (1977): 21–9.

79   Andrew R. Walkling, 'Political Allegory in Purcell's "Dido and Aeneas"', *Music and Letters* 76 (1995): 540–71; an earlier, less detailed presentation of this argument can be found in Walkling, 'Politics and the Restoration Masque: The Case of *Dido and Aeneas*', in Gerald MacLean (ed.), *Culture and Society in the Stuart Restoration: Literature, Drama, History* (Cambridge: Cambridge University Press, 1995), pp. 52–69.

80   See for example Hume, 'The Politics of Opera': 39–40, and Burden, '"Great Minds Against Themselves Conspire"', p. 229. Burden, however, agrees that 'a Restoration audience would have expected to look for such an allegory'; he also sagely speculates on the self-interested motives of all those who seek to couple allegorical readings (or non-readings) with the distinction of becoming 'the one to redate the opera'.

the unvarnished encomia of operatic prologues (including *Dido's*) or of court odes. Thus, Purcell's involvement in the production, whenever it took place, should actually surprise us less than his participation in the creation of politically sensitive works for the public theatres, whose function as conduits for potentially seditious ideas was of far greater concern to the authorities than were the court's own self-reflexive private dramatic endeavours. Whatever else it may have been, the masque represented the supreme articulation of courtly ideals in which a wide array of artistic techniques – literary text, music, dance, oral declamation, gesture, stage machinery, painting, costume design, lighting technology – were brought together to create a dramatic performance that presented a spectacular and profoundly intellectual exploration of the attributes of early modern kingship.[81] As modern audiences implicitly understand, while they may not always be aware of it, the celebrated grandeur, beauty and pathos of Purcell's music for *Dido and Aeneas* are themselves functions of the work's inherently political milieu.

Besides his significant, if still poorly understood, work on *Dido and Aeneas*, Purcell appears to have contributed at least a small amount of music to one other theatrical production to have originated at the Restoration court. Thomas D'Urfey's 'New Opera' *Cinthia and Endimion* is only known from its commercial representation at the Drury Lane theatre in 1696–97,[82] but it has long been noted that settings of two songs from the play, including Purcell's 'Musing on Cares of Human Fate', appear in the second book of Henry Playford's song collection *The Theater of Music*, published in 1685, and that the earliest version of D'Urfey's drama may thus have been written around that time.[83] If so, it was probably originally created to be a court masque, as the overtly allegorical qualities of the characters, as well as the remains of an embedded Restoration-era operatic prologue (somewhat

---

81   See, for example, my examination of the phenomenon of the 'interrupted masque' in *Dido* and elsewhere: Andrew R. Walkling, 'The Apotheosis of Absolutism and the Interrupted Masque: Theater, Music, and Monarchy in Restoration England', in Julia Marciari Alexander and Catharine MacLeod (eds), *Politics, Transgression, and Representation at the Court of Charles II* (New Haven and London: Yale Center for British Art/Yale University Press, 2007), pp. 193–231, and the more detailed exploration of *Dido's* structural and ideological intricacies in Walkling, 'The Masque of Actaeon and the Antimasque of Mercury: Dance, Dramatic Structure, and Tragic Exposition in *Dido and Aeneas*', *Journal of the American Musicological Society* 63 (2010): 191–242.

82   Thomas D'Urfey, *A New Opera, Call'd Cinthia and Endimion: Or, the Loves of the Deities* (London, 1697).

83   The other song is 'The Poor Endymion Lov'd too Well', by the very obscure composer David Underwood. Cyrus L. Day was the first to propose a considerably earlier date for *Cinthia and Endimion* on this basis; see Thomas D'Urfey, *The Songs of Thomas D'Urfey*, ed. Cyrus Lawrence Day, Harvard Studies in English, vol. 9 (Cambridge MA: Harvard University Press, 1933), pp. 21–2. For a more comprehensive discussion, see Carolyn Kephart, 'Thomas Durfey's *Cinthia and Endimion*: A Reconsideration', *Theatre Notebook* 39 (1985): 134–9, and Olive Baldwin and Thelma Wilson, 'The Music for Durfey's *Cinthia and Endimion*', *Theatre Notebook* 41 (1987): 70–74.

uncomfortably resituated in the second act in the 1696–97 version), suggest.[84] As with a number of the examples of 'political' plays from the public theatres to be discussed below, Purcell's contribution here is only tangentially related to politics, despite the apparent courtly circumstances of its creation and the likelihood that the text was politically meaningful on one or more levels, akin to the situation with *Dido and Aeneas* discussed above. Nevertheless, it is interesting to consider the possibility that Purcell was involved in a (probably abortive) project to create a comic, part-sung, part-spoken masque featuring Olympian and pastoral characters for Charles II, along the lines of the 1675 court extravaganza *Calisto*, and to wonder what other portions of D'Urfey's text the composer may have set before the production was abandoned.

Purcell's 'Public' Music

Catches

The majority of Purcell's political works produced for public consumption fall into two categories: catches and theatre music. The former group, in particular, bears comparison with the political odes and anthems written for the court. Despite the obvious contrast between those musically and programmatically sophisticated compositions and the catches – which are short, succinct and intended for impromptu unaccompanied performance – these works share a common purpose: the propagandistic reinforcement of royal authority. Like the odes, Purcell's 60 or so catches span his entire compositional career, from the late 1670s to the mid 1690s.[85] The greater part of them offer a mad romp through the subjects of drinking, sex and scatology, with a few touching upon more refined topics; however, Purcell also composed about a dozen political catches, some of which are explicitly occasional while others speak more generally to contemporary political concerns. They constitute a sadly overlooked genre: while many of the more bawdy catches have appeared multiple times on records and CDs, only one of the political catches has ever been recorded commercially.[86] Moreover, scholars have shown no more

---

84   I will be exploring *Cinthia and Endimion* in detail in my forthcoming book *Masque and Opera in Restoration England*.

85   Zimmerman catalogues 53 catches and lists 8 more as 'doubtful' in his Appendix I. In addition, 4 catches are associated with plays (*Bonduca*, *The English Lawyer*, *The Knight of Malta* and *The Richmond Heiress*, whose catch Zimmerman lists at Z608/2 but inexplicably also catalogues as an independent catch, Z243), and one appears in an early manuscript as a contrafactum of an Alleluia canon (Z101).

86   This is the exceptional 'True Englishmen, Drink a good Health to the Mitre' (see below), recorded by the Deller Consort and now available on the multi-disc CD set *Folk Songs and Ballads*, Alfred Deller, The Complete Vanguard Recordings, Vol. 1 (Musical Concepts MC193, 2008). The catch 'Down with Bacchus' appears on *A Baroque Celebration: Music*

than passing interest in these works, although they offer a unique window into Purcell's day-to-day existence, particularly during volatile times.[87]

With one exception (discussed below), Purcell's political catches fall neatly into two groups determined by chronology and subject matter and divided by the political watershed of the Glorious Revolution. Those written prior to 1688 focus on patriotism and allegiance to the Stuart crown, while those of the 1690s are more jingoistic and mostly address the early stages of William's war against the French/Catholic menace (see Table 6.1).[88] All of the pre-1689 catches found their way into print, most in the 1685 collection *Catch that Catch Can*,[89] whereas the later works survive in a somewhat more haphazard fashion, in some cases only in manuscript sources.

The catches labelled 'occasional' in Table 6.1 are especially interesting sources of information on Purcell's engagement with contemporaneous political events: the meeting of Parliament during the Exclusion Crisis, the return of the Duke of York from exile in Scotland in 1682 and William's battles with Jacobite forces in Ireland all elicited catches whose texts, invariably anonymous, feature the kind of swaggering,

---

by *Bach, Handel, Lully, Purcell and Others*, New York Kammermusiker, Double Reed Ensemble, dir. Ilonna Pederson (Dorian Sono Luminus DOR-90189, *rec.* 1993), but is arranged as a binary, instrumental piece.

87　The most thorough treatment is in Henry Purcell, *Catches*, ed. Ian Spink, The Works of Henry Purcell, vol. 22a (London: Novello, 2000). Spink predictably focuses on matters of dating, but also offers a few relevant textual emendations and interpretative points. Not all of these are incontrovertible: for example, his argument that the phrase 'I pray for him too, but wish him out o'th'land', from 'God Save our Sov'reign Charles', refers to the Duke of York ('wished "out o'th'land" for his own good', p. 49) rather than to the putatively disloyal Whig or Trimmer 'Who to his pious votes denies his hand' is unconvincing. The problem in this instance is compounded by Spink's mistaken rendering of 'pray' as 'play' (p. 7; in Paul Hillier (ed.), *The Catch Book: 153 Catches, Including the Complete Catches of Henry Purcell* (Oxford: Oxford University Press, 1987), no. 70, 'pray' is printed correctly, but 'wish' is mistaken for 'with').

88　One other, semi-political catch is 'Who comes there? Stand!' ('The London Constable', probably dating from the early 1680s), in which one interlocutor assures a suspicious officer of the watch that 'I am an honest Tory', a declaration that, accompanied by a bribe, quickly defuses the song's tense dramatic situation.

89　John Playford, *Catch that Catch Can: or, the Second Part of the Musical Companion* (London, 1685). The texts of three of the catches – 'Now England's Great Council's assembled', 'Since the Duke is Return'd' and 'Come, my Hearts, Play your Parts' – appeared earlier in Henry Playford, *Wit and Mirth. An Antidote against Melancholy … The Third Edition, Enlarged with several New Songs and Catches* (London, 1684); 'Come, my Hearts, Play your Parts' was subsequently reprinted in John Playford, *The Second Book of the Pleasant Musical Companion: Being a New Collection of Select Catches, Songs, and Glees for Two and Three Voices* (London, 1686/1687), the retitled second edition of *Catch that Catch Can*. The slightly later catch 'Now we are Met and Humours Agree' (?1687) appeared in Henry Playford, *The Banquet of Musick: or, a Collection of the Newest and Best Songs Sung at Court, and at Publick Theatres … The First Book* (London, 1688) and in an appendix (printed in 1687) to John Carr, *Comes Amoris: Or the Companion of Love … The Second Book* (London, 1688).

Table 6.1   Political catches by or attributed to Purcell.[a]

Incipit	Date	Occasional	Title	Z no.
Now England's Great Council's assembled	?1679	Y	'A Catch Made in the Time of Parliament, 1676'	261
God Save our Sov'reign Charles	?1681	?	'A Loyal Catch'	250
Since the Duke is Return'd we'll Damn all the Whigs	1682	Y	'Upon the Duke's Return'	271
Come, my Hearts, Play your Parts	1684	N	'A Loyal Catch'	246
Let's Live good honest Lives	*Early 1680s*	N	'A True Catch'	D102
Now we are Met and Humours Agree	?1687	N		262
True Englishmen, Drink a good Health to the Mitre	?1688–89	Y	'Song with Music on the 7 Bishops'	284
Let us Drink to the Blades Intrench'd on the Shannon	1690–91	Y		259
Room for th'Express, at Length here it Comes	?1691	Y	'Written on the Fall of Limerick, July 1694'	270
The Surrender of Lim'rick and the Flight of the Bassa	1691	Y		278
Is Charleroi's Siege come to?	1692	Y	'A Catch upon Charleroy'	257
Down with Bacchus	?1692	N		247
The Glass was just Tim'd to the Critical Hour	*?1690s*	Y		D105

[a] Items shown in italics are those whose attribution to Purcell is uncertain.

opinionated rhetoric that would surely have gone down well among an all-male gathering of inebriated (but musically inclined) citizens, tradesmen or apprentices. Examples include:

> Let's drink to the Senate's best thoughts,
> For the good of the king and the nation:
> > May they dig on the spot
> > As deep for the Plot
> As the Jesuits have laid the foundation

from 'Now England's Great Council's assembled' (?1679);[90]

> Since the Duke is return'd we'll damn all the Whigs,
> And let them be hang'd for politic prigs:
> Both Presbyter Jack and all the whole crew
> That lately design'd 'Forty-One to renew

from 'Since the Duke is Return'd' (1682); and

> To our conquering army loud praises let's sing,
> And now, Monsieur Frenchman, have at you next spring!

from 'Room for th'Express, at Length here it Comes' (?1691).[91] In most instances these works quickly appeared in print, nearly always with Purcell's name prominently

---

90   The text for this catch first appeared in J. H., *A Choice Compendium, Or, An Exact Collection of the Newest, and Most Delightful Songs* (London, 1681), sig. A1v–A2r. In the version subsequently printed in the 1684 edition of *Wit and Mirth*, pp. 140–41, the final words have been changed from 'Dye like a Traytor' to 'dye like a Rogue, or a Traitor', which would only fit Purcell's tune if an additional three-beat bar were added, in turn necessitating the addition of a bar in each of the other two verses. The date given in *Catch that Catch Can*, no. 36 ('A Catch Made in the Time of Parliament, 1676') is undoubtedly an error: the 'Cavalier Parliament' of 1661–78 never met during 1676, having been prorogued from November 1675 to February 1677, and the reference to Parliament unearthing information on 'the Plot' definitively places this catch after the revelations of the 'Popish Plot' in the summer of 1678. The most likely date of composition is March 1679, when the 'First Exclusion Parliament' began its session. Purcell's catch would have been less apt for either of the other two possibilities: the 'Second Exclusion Parliament' finally opened in October 1680 after a year of successive prorogations and increased partisan tension, and by the time of the 'Oxford Parliament' of March 1681 the notion of 'dig[ging] ... for the Plot' had become highly controversial. Spink's reference in Purcell, *Catches*, ed. Spink, p. 53 to the reconstitution of the Privy Council in April 1679 is probably irrelevant: 'England's great council' is almost certainly meant as a reference to Parliament, as the title of the work indicates.
91   The date given in the title of this catch in one source, 'Written on the Fall of Limerick, July 1694', is certainly in error, since Limerick had definitively surrendered to the Williamite forces in October 1691; the source is cited in Zimmerman, *Henry Purcell,*

affixed to them. The overt partisanship of the texts would have associated him unambiguously with the royal faction, perhaps more so than any other body of work to which he put his hand. However, this faction changed its orientation dramatically in 1688–89, which meant that having written Tory catches in support of Charles II and James II throughout the 1680s, Purcell was suddenly writing Williamite, anti-Jacobite catches (including three associated with the pivotal siege of Limerick in Ireland).[92] Thus the catches still leave us with no clear sense of his actual political sympathies.

The most problematic case is the one that sits at the cusp of this momentous political shift. 'True Englishmen, Drink a good Health to the Mitre', first printed in 1701,[93] celebrates the acquittal at the Court of King's Bench of the 'Seven Bishops' who petitioned against James II's Declaration of Indulgence in May 1688. This crucial tactical defeat for James, who had imprisoned the bishops in the Tower of London and charged them with seditious libel, played an important role in the king's loss of popular support and ultimately helped bring about the Glorious Revolution later that year. Purcell's catch denounces the enemies of the Anglican Church ('May their cunning and forces no longer prevail, / But their malice, as well as their arguments, fail'), urging all 'true Englishmen' to 'remember the Seven, who supported our cause'. While popular opinion was heavily in favour of the bishops during the waning days of James's ill-fated reign, Purcell's composition of music for such an enthusiastically oppositional piece seems oddly out of character, leading some to speculate that the catch may not have been written until some months later, after the Glorious Revolution had been accomplished. Yet despite their continued celebrity as intrepid supporters of the established church against King James's arbitrary actions, five of the seven bishops subsequently became non-jurors, refusing to swear allegiance to the new monarch William, and were consequently deposed from their sees in February 1690. Thus, the catch would appear even more inappropriate in a post-Revolutionary context, given its call for 'a health to the mitre' at a time when the shine was rapidly beginning to wear off the seven bishops, the majority of whom viewed William as a usurper. A more likely explanation is that 'True Englishmen' was composed during that uncertain

---

1659–1695: An Analytical Catalogue, p. 122.

92   It is not clear why Zimmerman and Spink unquestioningly follow the lead of W. Barclay Squire in definitively attributing 'The Surrender of Lim'rick and the Flight of the Bassa' to Purcell but relegating 'The Glass was just Tim'd to the critical hour' to the 'doubtful' category; see Henry Purcell, *Catches, Rounds, Two-Part and Three-Part Songs*, ed. W. Barclay Squire and J.A. Fuller-Maitland, The Works of Henry Purcell, vol. 22 (London: Novello, 1922), pp. xv and xx. Both works appear, together, only in sources dating from the latter half of the eighteenth century: John Walsh's *The Catch Club or Merry Companions. A Collection of Favourite Catches for Three and Four Voices Compos'd by Mr Henry Purcell, Dr Blow, and the most Eminent Authors. Book II* (London, 1762), and the manuscripts Lbl Add. 29386 and Lbl Add. 31462.

93   Henry Playford, *The Second Book of the Pleasant Musical Companion: Being a Choice Collection of Catches, for Three and Four Voices ... The Fourth Edition* (London, 1701), no. 20.

period in the autumn of 1688 when William's imminent invasion was being welcomed not as an opportunity to overthrow James, but simply as a means to free him from the influence of his 'wicked advisors', who were deemed responsible for the king's unpopular policies, including the persecution of the bishops earlier that year.[94] Interestingly, the text of the first and third verses of Purcell's catch is closely mirrored in a stanza from a broadside ballad of December 1688, entitled *The Prince of Orange VVelcome to London*:[95]

Catch: 'True Englishmen, drink a good health to the mitre'	Ballad: 'The Prince of Orange VVelcome to London'
True Englishmen, drink a good health to the mitre, Let our church ever flourish, though her enemies spite her.	And now let us drink a good Health to the Mitre, And may that Church flourish, tho' enemies spight her
...	...
Then remember the Seven who supported our cause, As stout as our martyrs and as just as our laws.	Next Health to that Seven that stood by our Cause, As stout as our Martyrs, as just as our Laws.

While it is impossible to determine which of these versions was written first, we might reasonably assume some proximity in the dating of the two. In any case, Purcell's catch would seem to illustrate the composer's sensitivity to the rapidly changing political landscape as the events of the Glorious Revolution unfolded.

As Table 6.1 demonstrates, the majority of Purcell's political catches are occasional, but a few articulate more generalized expressions of loyalty, usually appropriately lubricated with strong beverages. Two examples are:

A health to the king,
Round let it pass;
Fill it up, and then
Drink it off like men;
Never balk your glass

from 'Now we are Met' (?1687); and

---

94 See for example the broadside ballad *A New Song Made in the Praise of the West of England. To the Tune of, The Protestant Prince; or, Up the green Forrest* (London, [1688]), whose final line offers the otherwise seemingly contradictory invocation 'God bless the King & the Prince of Orange'. The ballad is no. 899 in Angela J. McShane, *Political Broadside Ballads of Seventeenth-Century England: A Critical Bibliography* (London: Pickering and Chatto, 2011). I am grateful to Angela McShane for her valuable assistance in discussing the broadside ballad repertoire with me.

95 *The Prince of Orange VVelcome to London. To the Tune of, The two English Travellers* (London, 1688), stanza 12 (McShane, *Political Broadside Ballads*, no. 895). William entered the capital on 18 December.

... since all flesh is grass,
Let's merrily drink our glass.
God bless our noble king;
What need we fear the Pope,
The Jesuits, Jews, or Turks,
For we defy the Devil and all his works

from 'Let's Live good honest Lives', which is probably from the early 1680s, although not definitively attributable to Purcell.[96] The generic nature of these particular texts allowed them to weather changes of regime and political circumstance: the late seventeenth-century manuscript source Y M12(S) contains four Williamite catches but also reproduces the two pre-1689 catches excerpted above, both of which are sufficiently non-specific to have been equally applicable to either period.[97]

It is normally difficult to ascertain precisely how these catches were used and what political effect they might have had on those singing or hearing them; however, we can sometimes glimpse political catches in a performance setting. One such case is Purcell's highly occasional 'Since the Duke is Return'd we'll Damn all the Whigs',[98] which was probably written in spring 1682 to commemorate the return of James, Duke of York, from a three-year exile on the Continent and in Scotland, an event for which Purcell also produced the court ode *What shall be Done in Behalf of the Man?*. 'Since the Duke is Return'd' is an exceptionally forthright partisan statement for Purcell to have made. The opening line, which would have been sung prominently by a solo voice when the catch was begun in performance, offers an unambiguous attack on the opposition Whigs; moreover, as Zimmerman has observed, the first four bars of Purcell's triple-time tune contain precisely the same sequence of 11 notes as the duple-metre ballad tune 'Hey Boys, up go We', which had emerged in early 1682 as one of England's most popular melodies, used over and over again in political broadsides, particularly by Tory polemicists (see

---

96   This catch is actually based on a tune by William Cranford ('Mark how these knavish rests'), printed in John Playford's catch collections of the 1650s and 1660s. The version with political text here attributed to Purcell was reprinted in subsequent editions of *The Second Book of the Pleasant Musical Companion* (the third edition of 1695, the fourth of 1701 and the fifth of 1707) but, as Spink points out, 'it was probably omitted from the 1686 edition ... because its anti-papist sentiments would have been offensive to James II, who came to the throne the previous year'; see Purcell, *Catches*, ed. Spink, p. 66.

97   'Now we are Met' was reprinted in 1695, 1701, 1707 and 1709; in the latter two instances, during Anne's reign, the word 'King' in the first line quoted above was appropriately changed to 'Queen'.

98   The word 'damn' in the opening line first appears in the 1685 edition of *Catch that Catch Can* (no. 38), published after the Duke of York's accession to the throne as James II; the two earlier versions give the less provocative verbs 'slight' and 'defie': they occur respectively in [?Thomas Jordan], *The Lord Mayor's Show: Being a Description of the Solemnity at the Inauguration of the truly Loyal and Right Honourable Sir William Prichard, K^t* (London, 1682), p. 5; and H. Playford, *Wit and Mirth* (1684), p. 142, which makes no mention of Purcell as the composer.

Example 6.1).[99] This tune also appeared under the title 'an Old Tune of 41', referring to the beginning of the English Civil War in 1641 – a point also emphasized in Purcell's catch, which accuses the Whigs of having 'lately design'd 'Forty-One to renew'. Elsewhere it was referred to as 'York and Albany's Welcome to England', a reference to one of several songs using this tune to have been written, like Purcell's catch, expressly to welcome the Duke of York (who was also Duke of Albany in the Scottish peerage) home from exile.[100] In addition, the second musical strain of the catch, which would normally not have been heard sung by itself in performance, rises to a high point as the tune modulates to the dominant on the words 'God save the King ... and Duke', thus giving further prominence to the catch's loyalist, Tory message.[101] The continued relevance of 'Since the Duke is Return'd' as a declaration of loyalty to the royal family was acknowledged later in the year when the text was printed among several songs of a similar tenor supposedly sung at the inauguration dinner of the Tory Lord Mayor of London, Sir William Pritchard.[102] The description of the day's events explicitly mentions Purcell as the author of the catch (although none of the other four songs receives any attribution).[103] As Zimmerman points out,

---

99 Zimmerman, *Henry Purcell, 1659–1695: An Analytical Catalogue*, p. 122.

100 *York and Albany's Welcome to England: Or, The Loyal Subjects Joy for his Most Miraculous Deliverance. To a New Play-house Tune, Much in Request* (London, [1682]) (McShane, *Political Broadside Ballads*, no. 631); see also *Great York and Albany: Or, The Loyal Welcom to His Royal Highness on His Return from Scotland. To the Tune of, Hey Boys Up Go We* (London, 1682) (McShane, *Political Broadside Ballads*, no. 632). For an overview of the history of 'Hey Boys, up go We', see Claude M. Simpson, *The British Broadside Ballad and its Music* (New Brunswick: Rutgers University Press, 1966), pp. 304–8.

101 Insufficient punctuation in the printed versions of the text has created a minor interpretative problem in this passage. Whereas in *The Lord Mayor's Show* the phrase is given as '*To God save the* King, *and* Duke *they reply'd*', in *Wit and Mirth* it is rendered as '*To God save the King and the Duke, they reply'd*', and in the 1685 *Catch that Catch Can* as 'to *God save the King and Duke, they reply'd*'. Hillier gives the most logical modern transcription of the phrase (in Purcell, *The Catch Book*, ed. Hillier, no. 92): 'To "God save the King" – "and Duke!" they reply'd'. Spink acknowledges that this version makes good sense but himself gives 'To "God Save the King and Duke" they replied' (Purcell, *Catches*, ed. Spink, pp. 23 and 56), a reading clearly dependent on that in *Catch that Catch Can*, the only one of the three original sources to print the text with music.

102 [?Jordan], *The Lord Mayor's Show*, p. 5; see Michael Burden, '"For the Lustre of the Subject": Music for the Lord Mayor's Day in the Restoration', *Early Music* 23 (1995): 600. Due most likely to a compositor's eye skip, two half-lines of text from the catch are missing near the end. Spink (in Purcell, *Catches*, ed. Spink, p. 56) points out that the wording of the pamphlet does not explicitly state that these particular songs were performed; rather it gives them as examples of loyal songs 'such as' those sung for the Lord Mayor and by the spectators after the feast had ended.

103 Inexplicably, the printed pamphlet gives the date of the celebration as 'Monday, *September* XXX. 1682', thus seemingly placing it on the day immediately following Pritchard's hotly contested election, rather than on the usual 'Lord Mayor's Day' of 29 October (according to the Julian calendar then in use). 30 September 1682 was, however, a Saturday, not a Monday, and since 30 October did fall on a Monday, that

Example 6.1   Comparison of opening note-sequences of Purcell's catch 'Since the Duke is Return'd' and the ballad tune 'Hey Boys, up go We'.

this catch was not the only piece of music by Purcell associated with this pivotal event in the ferocious political battle for control of the City of London, since his tune 'Now the fight's done' from the play *Theodosius* was appropriated for a pro-Pritchard ballad.[104]

Few of Purcell's political catches offer the kind of contextual richness found in 'Since the Duke is Return'd', but even those that are non-occasional can reward further study, particularly if publication history is taken into account. One example is the loyal catch 'Come, my Hearts, Play your Parts', Purcell's only Exclusion-era political catch to have retained its currency sufficiently to merit reprinting in the second edition of *The Second Book of the Pleasant Musical Companion* of 1686/1687.[105] At first sight, the text of this catch seems oddly constructed, with the first and

---

was probably the date of the rather paltry Lord Mayor's Show of that year (displaced, as we might expect, from Sunday). How a seventeenth-century London printer could have mixed up the months remains a mystery. I am grateful to Gary De Krey for taking the time to explore this problem with me; for more details on the 1682 mayoral election, see Gary S. De Krey, *London and the Restoration, 1659–1683*, Cambridge Studies in Early Modern British History (Cambridge: Cambridge University Press, 2005), pp. 343–5.

104   [Joseph Martin], *The Contented Subjects; Or, the Citizens Joy* (London, [1682]), beginning 'Now, now the time's come, Noble *Prichard* is chose'. See Zimmerman, *Henry Purcell, 1659–1695. His Life and Times*, pp. 92–4; however, we have already noted (n. 51 above) that Zimmerman's theory connecting the anthem *Blow up the Trumpet in Sion* with this event is untenable.

105   See n. 89 above; the catch did not, however, appear in subsequent editions of this publication, most likely because, as Spink suggests (in Purcell, *Catches*, ed. Spink, p. 49), 'after 1688 it was liable to be construed in a Jacobite sense, and, for those who had switched allegiance to King William, an embarras[s]ing reminder of their "treasons"'. As we have noted above (n. 96), the Purcell-attributed catch 'Let's Live good honest Lives', first published in 1685, was excluded from the 1686/1687 edition of *The Second Book of the Pleasant Musical Companion*, but did reappear in later editions, beginning with the third of 1695, when its anti-Catholic rhetoric would again have been in vogue. None of the other early political catches of Purcell was ever reprinted after 1685.

third stanzas giving the unusual rhyme scheme AAAAB ... EEEEB, interrupted in the middle stanza by the completely unrelated rhyme scheme CCDDD.[106] As transcribed using modern spelling and punctuation, the text reads as follows:

> Come, my hearts,
> Play your parts
> With your quarts;
> See none starts:
>   For the king's health is a-drinking   5
>
> Then to his Highness
> See there wine is
> That has passed the test
> Above the rest,
> For those healths deserve the best   10
>
> They that shrink
> For their chink
> From their drink
> We will think
>   That of treasons they are thinking.   15

Despite its lack of specific references, this catch serves well as a statement of political loyalty: the singer's drinking companions ('my hearts') are urged to remain respectfully in their places ('see none starts') while those present drink to the king's health, followed by that of the Duke of York ('his Highness'); only the best wine should be expended on this activity,[107] and anyone who pleads poverty as an excuse not to participate ('They that shrink / For their chink / From their drink') is to be suspected of disloyalty.[108] Yet if we look at the earliest printed source of the

---

106 The same is true of the very complex metrical structure of the text, which I have not illustrated here.

107 Spink suggests (in Purcell, *Catches*, ed. Spink, p. 48) that the 'reference to wine "that has pass'd the test" may be an ironic allusion to the Test Act of 1673', which prohibited Roman Catholics such as the Duke of York from holding public office. However, the Duke himself had effectively circumvented the provisions of the Test Act in May 1684 when he rejoined the Privy Council and was reappointed Lord High Admiral – although, as Maurice Ashley points out, Charles II himself had to sign all admiralty documents so as to keep his Catholic brother technically in compliance with the law; see Maurice Ashley, *James II* (Minneapolis: University of Minnesota Press, 1977), p. 150. The obscurity of the text, in which the relative pronoun 'that' refers most obviously to the wine – 'the best' wine, appropriate for drinking the Duke's health – but could also take 'his Highness' as its antecedent, aptly reflects the legal grey area in which James found himself at the time this catch was presumably written.

108 This sense of 'chink' is defined in the *Oxford English Dictionary* (http://www.oed.com) as 'A humorous colloquial term for money in the form of coin; ready cash. Exceedingly

text, entitled '*A New SONG of the* KINGS *Health*',[109] we discover that the words of Purcell's catch are in fact drawn from a longer poem whose political message is more pointed:

> Come, my hearts,
> Play your parts
> With your quarts;
> See none starts:
>   For the king's health is a-drinking.   5
> Then to's Highness
> See there wine is
> That has passed the test
> For those healths require the best
> They that shrink   10
> For their chink
> From their drink
> We will think
>   Of treasons they are thinking:
> Pox upon 'em: 15
> Let us sham 'em[110]
> As we would cutthroats
> Or the pious Doctor Oates.
>
> Could they but bend the laws
> To the Good Old Cause,   20
>   What plundering
> Should we have of the princes
>   And our nobles
>   And our bishops?
> But Heaven will confound 'em   25
> And their damn'd designs. *Amen.*

The poetic structure of '*A New SONG*' helps to clarify some of the questions raised by the text of the Purcell setting: in this, presumably earlier, version, the first nine lines – lacking 'Above the rest', which thus may have been Purcell's own interpolation into the catch[111] – constitute a single AAAABCCDD stanza that is

---

common in the dramatists and in songs of the 17th c.'. Spink (in Purcell, *Catches*, ed. Spink, pp. 5 and 49) unnecessarily follows the 1686/1687 edition in emending 'For their chink' to 'From their chink'.

109 H. Playford, *Wit and Mirth* (1684), pp. 131–2; despite the title, no music is provided.

110 The verb 'to sham' is defined in the *Oxford English Dictionary* (http://www.oed.com) as 'To cheat, trick, deceive, delude with false pretences; to impose upon, take in, hoax', citing numerous examples from the 1680s.

111 The only other substantive differences between the two versions in the 14 lines they

then repeated in lines 10–18 (EEEEBFFGG), the second stanza being linked to the first by the 'B' rhyme 'drinking/thinking'. Although no musical setting for 'A New SONG' is known to survive, any setting that was composed must have been completely independent of Purcell's catch: the catch tune could potentially accommodate lines 15–18 to the music of the second strain, but it would not work at all with the highly anomalous final eight-line stanza, which seems to break down after the first couplet (HH) into a jumble of unrhymed and rhythmically irregular lines that read almost like prose. An examination of this text can provide some insights into Purcell's compositional process: evidently Purcell chose to extract a portion of the larger text, creating an A–B–A stanzaic form where none had existed before, thereby freeing himself to add a line to the B stanza so as to equalize the lengths of the three stanzas at five lines each, a congruent structure well suited to the catch form. In the process, he eliminated the original text's most controversial political references – to the plotmonger Titus Oates (here likened to a common criminal), and to the alleged socially revolutionary tendencies of the Whigs, which are deemed to have placed their very souls in peril – while retaining the text's more generic loyalist (and drink-related) rhetoric.

While the poetic quality of their texts is undoubtedly variable, Purcell's political catches are no less worthy of study than the more well-known bawdy catches for which the composer is justly famous.[112] Moreover, the political catches constitute an integral part of the thriving public discourse of the day, particularly with reference to the Exclusion struggle of the early 1680s and the Williamite wars of the early 1690s. In this regard, we might learn a good deal about Purcell himself by exploring the political catches more comprehensively, while at the same time coming to a better understanding of the composer's place in the marketplace of ideas and opinion that constitutes the early modern 'public sphere'.

Odes

Purcell's successful run of court odes, beginning in 1680 and continuing to the end of his life, spawned a parallel body of public odes, mostly dating from 1689 or later, which were composed at the behest of institutions including the school run by Lewis Maidwell in King Street, Westminster and the 'Musical Society' that sponsored the annual celebrations of the Feast of St Cecilia. While these non-court

---

share are relatively minor: 'to's' for 'to his' (line 6, where the absence of the extra syllable in the original makes for better scansion); 'require' for 'deserve' (line 9/10); and 'Of treasons' for 'That of treasons' (line 14/15, where the addition of the word 'That' to create a two-syllable anacrusis in the later version actually enhances the metrical affinity between this line and line 5, thus making the catch version preferable, poetically speaking).

112 As Spink points out (in Purcell, *Catches*, ed. Spink, p. ix), Purcell was a prolific catch composer, whose five dozen or so catches amount to nearly double the entire combined (estimated) output of John Blow (14), Henry Aldrich (12) and Michael Wise (8).

odes share some of the musical and poetic features enumerated in the discussion of Purcell's court odes presented above, the works themselves are generally non-political. There are, however, two exceptions: the Yorkshire Feast Song (*Of Old, when Heroes thought it Base*), composed for the annual London feast of Yorkshiremen held on 27 March 1690, and *Great Parent, hail!*, written to celebrate the centenary of Trinity College, Dublin on 9 January 1694. The former, whose text is by D'Urfey, traces the history of York and its denizens through the Roman invasion, the dynastic struggles of the Wars of the Roses and, finally, the conjunction of these two thematic threads in 'the knell of falling Rome' brought about by William's overthrow of the Catholic James. The assembled Yorkshiremen are lauded for the fact that 'when the renown'd Nassau / Came to restore our liberty and law' they had boldly welcomed him as 'our deliv'rer'.

The manifestly political tone and content of the text closely mirrors that of the royal odes, despite this work's different provenance; King William is mentioned, but 'our mighty defender' shares the acclaim with 'all the heroes [who] invited him in'. The latter formulation acknowledges the 'Immortal Seven' who sent the famous letter of invitation to William in June 1688, and implicitly pays tribute to one of their number in particular: the Yorkshireman Thomas Osborne, formerly Earl of Danby. Osborne had recently been elevated to Marquess of Carmarthen for his significant role in supporting William's invasion, and at the time the ode was written he was beginning a new rise to pre-eminence in Parliament and the royal administration.[113] While we do not know for certain that the Marquess was actually present at the feast where the ode was performed, the compliment implied in the text would certainly not have been lost on those in attendance, and Purcell might justifiably have been pleased to associate himself with such a major public event, for which he created what D'Urfey subsequently described as '*One of the finest Compositions he ever made, and cost* 100l. *the performing*'.[114]

The Trinity College ode, whose text is by Nahum Tate, is similarly configured. At first it works its way through the history of the institution, culminating in an offering of praises to William and Mary ('For surely no Hibernian muse / – Whose isle to him her freedom owes – / Can her restorer's praise refuse'). The ode then briefly focuses on a pair of royal subordinates: the late James Butler, First Duke of Ormond, Ireland's long-time Lord Lieutenant, who had died in July 1688, and his grandson, also James, the Second Duke, who had assumed his forebear's position as Chancellor of the University of Dublin.[115] Although the younger Duke would later be exiled as a Jacobite plotter, in 1694 he was a leading political and military

---

113 Andrew Browning, *Thomas Osborne, Earl of Danby and Duke of Leeds 1632–1712* (3 vols, Glasgow: Jackson, 1944–51), vol. 1, pp. 474–5.

114 Thomas D'Urfey, *Songs Compleat, Pleasant and Divertive* (5 vols, London, 1719), vol. 1, p. 114; D'Urfey, *Wit and Mirth: or Pills to Purge Melancholy … The Fourth Edition* (5 vols, London, 1719), vol. 1, p. 114.

115 See *The London Gazette*, 22–5 January 169[4], p. 2, where the ode is described as being 'in Praise of their Foundress [i.e. Elizabeth I] and Benefactors, of Their Majesties King *William* and Queen *Mary* … and of their Chancellors'.

figure in the Williamite regime, a position reinforced by his family connections with the joint monarchs.[116] Like Carmarthen in 1690, he might have been expected to grace the performance of Purcell's ode with his presence, although there is no clear evidence that he did: the account in *The London Gazette* names many of those in attendance, but says nothing of Ormond himself.[117]

Theatre Music

As we have already noted, the 'genre' of theatre music is determined primarily by contextual function rather than internal features, and this circumstance requires us to consider the political qualities of Purcell's contributions to the theatre under a variety of headings: first, plays with political implications for which Purcell wrote only small amounts of seemingly non-political music; second, plays to which he contributed songs with explicit political texts; and third, theatrical works with political overtones that contain substantial amounts of music by Purcell and thus were more closely associated with his name and reputation.[118]

As is well known, Purcell wrote comparatively little dramatic music before the last six years of his life. It is therefore notable that, with the exception of one ephemeral piece – a misogynistic catch written for or after Edward Ravenscroft's 1677 play *The English Lawyer* – all of his pre-1690 theatrical compositions can be associated in one way or another with contemporary politics. On the other hand, only a select few items from his more substantial later output meet these criteria, although this is perhaps not surprising, given the exceptionally politicized nature of the London theatres in the early 1680s. In a few instances Purcell's participation in the creation of political plays may be entirely innocent. He wrote three songs for plays that were banned by the authorities on account of their political content – Nahum Tate's *The History of King Richard the Second* (banned in December 1680 and January 1681 after two days' acting in each instance, but approved for performance in 1682),[119] Nathaniel Lee's *The Massacre*

---

116 Ormond's mother was William's second cousin, and his first wife Anne Hyde (d. 1685) had been cousin to Mary; see Stuart Handley, 'Butler, James, Second Duke of Ormond (1665–1745)', in *Oxford Dictionary of National Biography*, http://www.oxforddnb.com (last accessed 12 July 2010).

117 In his retrospective account of the festivities, John Dunton provides the text of 'Part of the Ode', but notably stops short after the stanza celebrating William and Mary, thus making no mention of the Ormonds, despite Dunton's having offered multiple favourable comments on the Second Duke elsewhere in his book; see John Dunton, *The Dublin Scuffle: Being a Challenge sent by John Dunton, Citizen of London, to Patrick Campbel, Bookseller in Dublin … To which is added … Some Account of his Conversation in Ireland* (London, 1699), pp. 415–16 and *passim*.

118 A fourth category will be discussed below, under 'intertextuality'. In considering the two court masques of the 1680s, discussed above, we might place *Cinthia and Endimion* in the first category, *Dido and Aeneas* in the third.

119 Based on Shakespeare's *Richard II*, the play was presented at its premiere under the

of Paris (supposedly banned prior to its performance in *c.*1679–81 and finally acted in 1689)[120] and John Dryden's *Cleomenes, The Spartan Hero* (banned prior to performance at the behest of Mary in April 1692, but allowed to go forward after about a week, following the intervention of two powerful politicians).[121] None of these songs appears to advance the supposed political agenda of its respective play, and thus Purcell's exposure to the official disapproval associated with their prohibitions on political grounds must have been minimal.[122] Only in the case of *Cleomenes* is his name attached directly to the play in any near-contemporary published copy of the song.[123]

---

title *The Sicilian Usurper*, with the characters' names and the location changed. After the first banning, it reopened the following month as *The Tyrant of Sicily*, 'but the Cheate being found out it was forbid acting againe', and the King's Company was subjected to a mandatory ten-day closure: see William van Lennep, Emmet L. Avery, Arthur H. Scouten, et al. (eds), *The London Stage, 1660–1800* (11 vols, Carbondale: Southern Illinois University Press, 1960–68), Part I, pp. 293–4, quoting US-Ws L.c.1032 (Newdigate Newsletters, 20 January 168[1]). Purcell's strophic song 'Retir'd from any Mortal's Sight' is sung during the prison scene in Act V, as King Richard (the Sicilian 'Oswald') contemplates his impending death. For a recent consideration of the play's politics, see Leticia Álvarez-Recio, 'Nahum Tate's *The History of King Richard the Second* (1681): Politics and Censorship during the Exclusion Crisis', *Restoration and Eighteenth-Century Theatre Research* 24/1 (Summer 2009): 17–30.

120 Purcell composed his multisectional song 'Thy Genius, lo!' for the appearance of the prognosticating spirit to King Charles IX at the beginning of Act V. For a 1695 revival of the play, he wrote a new, entirely declamatory setting of the same text, and may also have written the song 'To Arms, heroic Prince' (formerly thought to be for Shadwell's *The Libertine*) to follow it on this occasion. See Ian Spink, 'Purcell's Music for "The Libertine"', *Music & Letters* 81 (2000): 520–31.

121 For a discussion of the controversy and a reading of the play as political statement see David Bywaters, *Dryden in Revolutionary England* (Berkeley: University of California Press, 1991), pp. 93–103. Purcell's strophic song 'No, no, poor suff'ring Heart' was written to add colour to a voluptuous scene in Act II introducing the Egyptian court; the scene also calls for a dance that does not appear to survive, although Price suggests that the four-part instrumental arrangement of the song tune found in Lbl Add. 24889, fol. 21v, might have been used for it; see Price, *Music in the Restoration Theatre*, pp. 77–8.

122 A fourth play, Dryden's *The Spanish Fryar* (originally performed in 1680 and revived in 1681, 1684, 1689 and 1698), had also been banned – for its anti-Catholicism – in 1686, during the reign of James II. However, Purcell's song 'Whilst I with Grief did on you Look', which is associated with the play only by an undated single-sheet engraved print entitled '*A new Song in the Play call'd the* Spanish *Fryer*', must date from a revival after 1694 since the text, by D'Urfey, celebrates Anne Bracegirdle's famous interpretation of the mad song 'I Burn, I Burn', composed in that year; see Price, *Henry Purcell and the London Stage*, p. 86.

123 'No, no, poor suff'ring Heart' appears in the single-sheet collection *Joyful Cuckoldom, or the Love of Gentlemen, and Gentlewomen* (supposedly London, 1695), no. 19, as 'A New Song, in the Play called, The Tragedy of CLEOMENES, The Spartan Heroe. Sung by M[rs] Butler.', composed by 'M[r] H. Purcell.' The song was also printed in John Carr, *Comes*

Of a similar character is his contribution to Thomas D'Urfey's *Sir Barnaby Whigg*, the song 'Blow, Boreas, blow'. Probably presented early in the summer of 1681,[124] *Sir Barnaby Whigg* was offered as a loyalist reply to the work of the Whig playwright Thomas Shadwell, whose spectacular anti-Catholic polemic *The Lancashire Witches* had premiered earlier in the season, probably sometime between March and June.[125] Shadwell, the 'true-blue Protestant poet', who would become Poet Laureate under William and Mary in 1689, is brutally satirized in the title character by D'Urfey, who emphasizes not only his pomposity but also his notorious obesity and his pretensions to musical skill.[126] In Act III, scene 2, Sir Barnaby sings a self-parodying song about his lack of poetic or musical ability, the tune for which is the song 'The Delights of the Bottle' from the closing grand masque of Shadwell's and Matthew Locke's 1675 opera *Psyche*.[127] Despite its attempt to incorporate several conventional comic plotlines, *Sir Barnaby Whigg* is a fundamentally political work from the opening salvo of its prologue to Sir Barnaby's rapid-fire conversions to Roman Catholicism and then Islam in Act V, which culminate in his arrest for treason.[128] Unlike the plays mentioned above,

---

Amoris: Or the Companion of Love … The Fourth Book (London, 1693), p. 1 ('The Words by Mr. *Dryden*. Set by Mr. *Purcell*'). Purcell's music was reused as a (non-political) ballad tune on at least two occasions: see Simpson, *The British Broadside Ballad*, pp. 513–14. For the status of *Joyful Cuckoldom*, see Donald W. Krummel, *English Music Printing, 1553–1700* (London: Bibliographical Society, 1975), p. 166 n. 50, where it is suggested that the manuscript copy of the work's title page (dated '1671' and identifying Henry Playford as the publisher) may be a hoax created by the nineteenth-century scholar–forger Edward F. Rimbault.

124 For this and other premiere dates, see Judith Milhous and Robert D. Hume, 'Dating Play Premières from Publication Data, 1660–1700', *Harvard Library Bulletin* 22 (1974): 374–405.

125 In his dedicatory epistle to the Earl of Berkeley, D'Urfey bemoans the fact that *'in this Age 'tis not a Poets Merit, but his Party that must do his business; so that if his Play consists of a Witch, a Devil, or a Broomstick, so he have but a Priest at one end of the Play, and a Faction at 'tother end of the Pit, it shall be fam'd for an excellent piece'*; Thomas D'Urfey, *Sir Barnaby Whigg: or, No Wit like a Womans* (London, 1681), sig. A3r.

126 The classic attack on Shadwell, John Dryden's poem *Mac Flecknoe*, highlights many of these same qualities.

127 Price claims in *Henry Purcell and the London Stage*, p. 154, that 'no setting of this devastating lyric survives', but see D'Urfey's *A New Collection of Songs and Poems. By Thomas D'Urfey* (London, 1683), p. 11, where the connection to 'The Delights of the Bottle' is made clear.

128 Just after Sir Barnaby is hustled away, one of the characters remaining on stage refers dismissively to his ilk as 'Rogues that speak Treason by allusion and *simile*' (p. [51]). For an assessment of *Sir Barnaby Whigg* as one of D'Urfey's 'most political and, dramatically speaking, … most damaged' plays, in which 'political controversy cuts across Durfey's comedy of relationships, causing mismatches of tone, inadequate motivation and characterization and gratuitous scenes', see John McVeagh, *Thomas Durfey and Restoration Drama: The Work of a Forgotten Writer*, Studies in Early Modern English Literature (Aldershot and Burlington: Ashgate, 2000), p. 83.

D'Urfey's Tory concoction was favoured by the government and hence was not banned. Nevertheless, Purcell's participation in this politically charged work resembles in its basic features the previous examples: his single contribution to the play is not in itself political, being sung as part of a convivial scene involving a voluble sea-captain in Act I, before the title character has even made his first appearance; and in the two contemporary publications in which the song was printed his association with the play was not made explicit,[129] thus (whether intentionally or not) shielding the composer from the taint of partisanship in which D'Urfey himself seems to have so revelled.

Two other Purcell songs associated with the theatre are somewhat different from the examples already noted in that they offer public expressions of loyalty to the crown in a straightforward rhetoric similar to that found in the composer's political catches, discussed above. Both fall chronologically into the politically charged 1680s – specifically, during the reign of James II – and seem to have little to do with the dramatic works with which they are associated. The duet 'How Great are the Blessings of Government Made', subtitled 'A Health to King James II', appeared in Tate's farce *Cuckolds-Haven* (July 1685),[130] and the solo 'Here's a Health to the King' may be connected with D'Urfey's *A Fool's Preferment* (?April 1688).[131] Both are essentially loyalist drinking songs, similar in function (but not in musical structure) to the catches, and it is not clear how they might have been incorporated into the stage performances, assuming they actually were: 'How Great are the Blessings' seems to have been sung between the second and third acts of its play,[132] and may have been written and inserted at the last minute in response to the recent defeat of Monmouth's Rebellion in the West Country. The song resurfaced in 1687 as part of that year's Lord Mayor's Show, where it was sung 'At Dinner before the Banquet' to entertain the assembled luminaries, including James himself.[133] Whether Purcell had any hand in this

---

129 D'Urfey, *A New Collection of Songs and Poems*, p. 49: 'The Storm, a Song in Sir Barnaby Whigg' (text only); D'Urfey, *A Third Collection of New Songs, Never Printed Before. The Words by Mr D'Urfey* (London, 1685), p. 1: 'The STORM: Set to Music by Mr. Henry Purcell'. Even in *Orpheus Britannicus*, p. 185 it is simply labelled 'The STORM, a single SONG'. There is no record of *Sir Barnaby Whigg* having been revived after its initial run in 1681.

130 This play, an adaptation of the 1605 collaboration between Ben Jonson, John Marston and George Chapman, *Eastward Ho*, was performed at Dorset Garden (the theatre usually reserved, after 1682, for large-scale musical works such as operas), and may have been the first play put on there after the premature closing of the elaborate opera *Albion and Albanius* on 13 June.

131 The evidence for this song as a Purcell composition is circumstantial, hence Zimmerman's classification of it as a 'doubtful' work: see *Henry Purcell, 1659–1695: An Analytical Catalogue*, pp. 428 and 242. There is a good deal of confusion surrounding Purcell's contributions to *A Fool's Preferment*, a subject I hope to address in a future article.

132 N[ahum] Tate, *Cuckolds-Haven: or, an Alderman No Conjurer* (London, 1685), p. 29.

133 M[atthew] Taubman, *London's Triumph, or the Goldsmiths Jubilee* (London, 1687), p. 12

later performance is uncertain: the song had already appeared in print, and the composer's name is nowhere mentioned in the published pamphlet recounting the day's events. The Lord Mayor's Show version gives a second stanza not found in either the *Cuckolds-Haven* playbook or the printed music,[134] and it is possible that this new text, which includes a line describing 'Caesar' (i.e. King James) as 'He who crowns with His Presence the state of this Day', was fitted to Purcell's music after the fact. Perhaps the most interesting aspect of 'How Great are the Blessings' is the striking similarity of its concluding strain to the final solo and chorus of the 1687 welcome song *Sound the Trumpet, Beat the Drum*, 'To Urania and Caesar Delights without Measure':

'How Great are the Blessings' (1685/1687)	'To Urania and Caesar' (1687)
Since all we enjoy to his bounty we owe,	Since the joys we possess to his goodness we owe,
'Tis fit all our bumpers like that should o'erflow.	'Tis but just our best wishes like that should o'erflow.

The textual echo is reinforced by similar musical treatments (see Example 6.2), with the C major passage from the song written in 1685 and performed at the Guildhall on Lord Mayor's Day, 29 October 1687, recast into its relative minor and substantially elaborated for the welcome song offered to James at Whitehall only two and a half weeks earlier, on 11 October. Whether or not Purcell knew that his work was going to be featured at the Lord Mayor's festivities, it is possible that both he and his anonymous librettist had this unusual theatrical song from 1685 in mind when he fashioned the concluding section of their ode for the king two years later.[135]

('SONG. / To the *KING*.'). Curiously, the song was revived in the Lord Mayor's Show held two years later, in the wake of the Revolution: see M[atthew] T[aubman], *Londons Great Jubilee Restor'd and Perform'd on Tuesday, October the 29th 1689* (London, 1689), pp. 13–[14]. In only one instance was the text altered on this occasion to reflect the dual monarchy of William and Mary – from 'his Majesty's health' to 'Their MAJESTIES Health'; otherwise, all pronoun references in the song to 'Our PRINCE' remain singular and male. Burden seems to have missed the Purcell connection with this song in both instances in Table 1 of '"For the Lustre of the Subject"': 597.

134 J. Playford, *The Second Book of the Pleasant Musical Companion* (1686/1687), 'The Third Part', no. 10 (sig. H3v–H4r).

135 The recycling of 'How Great are the Blessings' for the post-Revolutionary Lord Mayor's Show of 1689, noted above (n. 133), and the song's connection with *Sound the Trumpet, Beat the Drum* would be made even more interesting if further evidence were to emerge for the claim, found in Lbl RM 24.e.7, that 'After Mr. Purcell's death other words were adapted to the music [of *Sound the Trumpet*] and it was performed as a Welcome Song on King William's return from Flanders'; this inscription is reported in Zimmerman, *Henry Purcell, 1659–1695: An Analytical Catalogue*, p. 160.

Example 6.2   Comparison of passages from 'To Urania and Caesar Delights without Measure' and 'How Great are the Blessings of Government Made'.

In all of the instances enumerated above, Purcell's contributions are on a small scale and are largely tangential to the drama; their contemporary sources frequently do not explicitly associate the name of the composer with the play at all. On the other hand, Purcell was a high-profile contributor to several works that, it has been argued, contemporary playgoers would have understood as political. Indeed, Purcell's earliest substantial theatrical commission seems to fall into this category. In 1680 the 21-year-old composer supplied several pieces for Nathaniel Lee's tragedy *Theodosius* (acted in the summer or early autumn), including a song and a multisectional religious ceremony in Act I and four Act Songs that were apparently performed in place of the usual instrumental Act Tunes after each of the first four acts of the play.[136] Although Purcell's name received no mention in the printed playbook, his music quickly achieved fame. Much of it appeared in a twelve-page supplement to the playbook, one of the earliest examples in Restoration England of notated music accompanying a play in print.[137] In addition, the three strophic Act Songs (those for Acts I, III and IV)[138] were all printed in the third book of Playford's *Choice Ayres and Songs* (1681) and rapidly gained currency as ballad tunes, appearing in multiple sources with a wide variety of texts, both political and non-political.[139] But as Jack Armistead has argued, *Theodosius* may itself be read as a political play, in which Charles II is subtly criticized under the guise of the early fifth-century Byzantine emperor Theodosius II for his supposed indolence and his withdrawal into an insulated bucolic life at Windsor Castle during the politically volatile summer of 1680.[140]

The crisis of the early 1680s may have engendered more political instability, and hence more political drama, than that of a decade later, but the aftermath of the Glorious Revolution of 1688–89 was also a time of political contestation that manifested itself on the stage and, this time, fell just at the moment when Purcell was finally coming into his own as a theatrical composer. Purcell contributed music to nearly four dozen plays between 1689 and 1695, and any number of them – even those that were revivals of older plays – could potentially have been susceptible to some sort of political application. However, three in particular with which Purcell was closely and publicly associated in the early years of the post-revolutionary period have received attention from scholars seeking to understand the politics of

---

136 In fact, there may have been more. No settings survive for two other songs called for as part of the action in Acts III and IV respectively. For the debate over whether Purcell's five-part G minor overture and the five-movement dance suite associated with it in US-NH Filmer 8, pp. 95–7, are also associated with *Theodosius*, see Layton Ring, Correspondence, 'Malice Afterthought', *Musical Times* 134 (1993): 614–15; Peter Holman, Response to Layton Ring, Correspondence, 'Malice Afterthought', *Musical Times*, 134 (1993): 615; and Silas Wollston, 'New Light on Purcell's Early Overtures', *Early Music* 37 (2009): 652.

137 Nat[haniel] Lee, *Theodosius: Or, The Force of Love* (London, 1680): 'WITH THE MUSICK betwixt the ACTS.'

138 Because of a typographical anomaly in the print, scholars have generally identified two songs to be performed after Act II; however, 'Sad as death at dead of night/Curse the night, then, curse the hour' and 'Dream no more of pleasures past' are in fact all part of one song, as a careful reading of the song's text makes clear.

139 See Simpson, *The British Broadside Ballad*, pp. 4–6 ('Ah Cruel Bloody Fate', no. 3); pp. 285–7 ('Hail to the Myrtle Shades', no. 178); and pp. 523–5 ('Now, now the Fight's Done', no. 333). The appropriation of Purcell's tunes by ballad-writers throughout the late seventeenth century and well into the eighteenth – perhaps most clearly demonstrated by the frequent reuse (often for political purposes) of Purcell's martial song 'Let the Soldiers Rejoice' from *Dioclesian*, discussed in ibid., pp. 440–42 – is a topic that has only recently begun to be explored; see Chapter 8, p. 322 below.

140 J.M. Armistead, *Nathaniel Lee*, Twayne's English Authors Series, vol. 270 (Boston: Twayne, 1979), pp. 127–9.

English drama at the beginning of the 1690s. These are the opera *The Prophetess, or the History of Dioclesian* (June 1690; adapted from John Fletcher and Philip Massinger probably by Thomas Betterton) and two works by John Dryden, the adapted comedy *Amphitryon* (October 1690) and his original dramatick opera *King Arthur* (?June 1691).

The Prophetess (usually known to Purcell scholars as *Dioclesian*) was the first of a long run of these dramatick operas that continued into the early years of the eighteenth century, and offers an example of the kind of multilevel allegorical structure that many English operas seem to have developed in this period, an amalgam of the courtly *roman à clef* style of allegoresis inherited from the masque and what I have called the 'impressionistic' allegory frequently found in plays written for the public theatres.[141] In this hybrid form, well suited to the special qualities of the emerging genre of spectacular public opera, certain aspects of the *roman à clef* style might be deployed in the service of a more diffuse, satirical allegory appropriate to an entertainment presented to the general public. The intended outcome would, of course, be different from that of a court masque: no specific counsel was being offered regarding the potential future consequences of royal policy, whether well- or ill-advised; rather, events in the past (both distant and recent) could be depicted in a propagandistic way in order to help form public views about the state of affairs in the present. This had certainly been the case with John Dryden and Louis Grabu's sycophantic royal opera *Albion and Albanius* of 1685, which ended with the apotheosis of the recently deceased Charles II ('Albion'), and devoted nearly all of its substance to establishing a justification for the accession of James II ('Albanius') in his place.

With respect to *Dioclesian*, a quarter of a century ago Curtis Price proposed a reading of the main characters in the opera that accords well with the ways in which *roman à clef* allegories traditionally operated: Charinus is Charles II, Diocles is the Duke of York, Maximinian is the Duke of Monmouth (note the system of alliteration).[142] In suggesting these identifications, Price offered a credible analysis

---

141   See Walkling, 'Performance and Political Allegory in Restoration England', pp. 163–79 and Walkling, 'Politics and Theatrical Culture in Restoration England': 1506–9.

142   Price, *Henry Purcell and the London Stage*, pp. 265–72. Julia Muller reports private correspondence in which Price retracts his political reading of the opera: see Julia Muller, *Words and Music in Henry Purcell's First Semi-Opera*, Dioclesian: *An Approach to Early Music through Early Theatre*, Studies in the History and Interpretation of Music, vol. 28 (Lewiston, Queenston and Lampeter: Edwin Mellen Press, 1990), p. 37. In fact, Price's analysis is entirely plausible and, indeed, helps to shed much light on the work. I would propose only a minor correction to Price's 'key' as laid out in his diagram of the drama's characters and their relationships to one another (Fig. 2, p. 271): where Price read the crucial minor character of Aper ('the boar') as Oliver Cromwell, I take this figure to refer not to a single individual, but rather to an idea, such as faction, political discord or civil war – and thus by association the entire gamut of political rebels and religious radicals who were responsible for Charles I's downfall and the destruction of the monarchy. This would be in keeping with personified characterizations such as Democracy and Zelota in *Albion and Albanius*, and would also be consistent with other Restoration political allegories in which a boar was used to represent the threat of

of the later, post-revolutionary work as a kind of reply to *Albion and Albanius*, which helps to explain both *Dioclesian*'s oddly telescoped account of both the Restoration of 1660 and the Exclusion Crisis of 20 years later and the ambiguous and somewhat perplexing way in which the *roman à clef* style of allegory appears to be used. The sense of duplicity and chaos that pervades the allegory in *Dioclesian* serves to highlight the satirical treatment being meted out to the unabashedly loyalist (and uncharacteristically blatant) allegory of *Albion*. Of course, *Dioclesian*'s allegory is also somewhat diffuse because Thomas Betterton, the work's adaptor, was merely updating an early seventeenth-century play, and did little to modify the structure of the original in any substantive way. Yet as Price pointed out, the changes Betterton did make demonstrate his interest in creating a political allegory out of his source.[143] Moreover, the confusion expressed by Price over the masque's real purpose[144] may be the very response intended by the work's adaptors: it might be argued that one important objective of the allegory in *Dioclesian* may have been to highlight the ambiguity of James's role in the return of political stability at the Restoration, particularly given the fact that James was very nearly responsible, through his intransigence in the events leading up to both the crisis over Exclusion and the Glorious Revolution, for that stability's undoing. In light of these possibilities, *Dioclesian* can be read as a kind of perverse parody, both of *Albion and Albanius* and of Restoration allegorical drama in general. With William and Mary safely in power in 1690, we can imagine that participation in such a project would have had few negative consequences for Purcell, and it is perhaps a mark of his comfort with the now relatively anodyne politics of *Dioclesian* that he was willing to trumpet his musical contribution to the opera with the publication of a sumptuous folio score the following year.[145]

---

chaos or civil strife. By this formula, Diocles as a Duke-of-York figure would be credited with overcoming the civil war and mob rule that had led to the death of the Emperor Numerianus (Charles I). The obvious lack of historical accuracy in this supposed parallel underscores the satirical intentions of the opera, as does the lengthy and seemingly ill-placed masque that interrupts Diocles's progress from hapless saviour of the state to incompetent co-emperor – a characterization of James II that would surely have delighted audiences in 1690.

143 Price, *Henry Purcell and the London Stage*, pp. 271–2. In 'The Politics of Opera', p. 37, Robert Hume derides Price's reading, asking: 'How often do seventeenth-century dramatic satires depict *past* events *covertly*? What would be the point? How many viewers would see the parallels of events ten years old, or care if they did?' Hume's fiercely logical objections, however, both here and throughout his article, are grounded in a late twentieth-century rational empiricist hermeneutic, and do not adequately consider the subtleties of seventeenth-century modes of discourse.

144 Price, *Henry Purcell and the London Stage*, p. 273: 'Should the music celebrate the death of Aper or underscore his vilification? Should it solemnize Diocles's coronation or rejoice in it? Or should it lament the death of Numerianus instead?'

145 See ibid., p. 263 and Rebecca Herissone, 'Playford, Purcell, and the Functions of Music Publishing in Restoration England', *Journal of the American Musicological Society* 63 (2010): 243–89.

In contrast to *Dioclesian*, Purcell's contribution to *Amphitryon* – John Dryden's 1690 version of a Molière play that was itself an adaptation of a work by the Roman comic playwright Plautus – was limited to the provision of three songs, an eight-movement instrumental 'theatre suite' and possibly one or two miscellaneous dances or other tunes.[146] Nevertheless, it is often considered to mark a watershed moment in the public recognition of Purcell's pre-eminence as a theatre composer. This is largely because of John Dryden's well-known statement in the dedication acclaiming 'the Excellent Composition of Mr. *Purcell*; in whose Person we have at length found an *English-man*, equal with the best abroad', an opinion Dryden may have developed after seeing *Dioclesian* the previous spring.[147] All three of the songs (as well as the dance that is probably associated with them) seem rather arbitrarily inserted into the third and fourth acts of a play that is otherwise devoid of musical elaboration of the dramatic action.[148] Yet Dryden must have considered Purcell's contribution important, since the title page of the printed playbook prominently announced the inclusion in an appendix of 'The MUSICK of the SONGS. Compos'd by Mr. *Henry Purcel*'.[149] As we have seen, Purcell's music for the political play

---

146 Uncertainty remains about the authorship of the dance described as 'MR. *Purcell*'s Tune in *Amphitrion*' in Henry Playford, *Apollo's Banquet: Containing Variety of the Newest Tunes, Ayres, Jiggs and Minuets, for the Treble-Violin … The Second Book* (London, 1691), no. 25, since it is attributed in another source to James Paisible; there are also doubts about whether Purcell wrote the 'Dance for Tinkers', which is included in the most authoritative manuscript source for the play's music. For a discussion of the latter piece, see Price, *Henry Purcell and the London Stage*, pp. 150–51.

147 John Dryden, *Plays: Albion and Albanius, Don Sebastian, Amphitryon*, eds Earl Miner, George R. Guffey and Franklin B. Zimmerman, The Works of John Dryden, vol. 15 (Berkeley, Los Angeles and London: University of California Press, 1976), p. 225. In his commentary, Miner offers the interesting suggestion that Dryden's remark 'may also imply some difficulty before Purcell was engaged, in getting satisfactory music for the play' (p. 460 n. 5). However, it is more clearly related to Dryden's earlier challenge to his own 'Country-men' to equal Grabu's achievement in *Albion and Albanius*, a challenge to which Dryden also responded when he ghostwrote Purcell's dedication to *Dioclesian*; see Price, *Henry Purcell and the London Stage*, p. 147 and Bryan White, '"Studying a little of the *French* Air": Louis Grabu's *Albion and Albanius* and the Dramatic Operas of Henry Purcell', in Rachel Cowgill, David Cooper and Clive Brown (eds), *Art and Ideology in European Opera: Essays in Honour of Julian Rushton* (Woodbridge: Boydell and Brewer, 2010), pp. 17–18 and 38.

148 The Purcell Society edition that includes *Amphitryon* does not consider the single-sheet version of the song 'For Iris I sigh' (*The Indifferent Lover, Or, The Roving Batchelor. To a Pleasant New Tune, Sung in the Last New Comedy, Called Amphytrion, Or, Fond Boy* (London, [c.1690]), which includes an additional six verses of text, although the music printed with the song is a meaningless typographical pastiche; see Henry Purcell, *Dramatic Music, Part I*, ed. Margaret Laurie, The Works of Henry Purcell, vol. 16 (new edn, London: Novello, 2007), p. 272.

149 John Dryden, *Amphitryon; Or, The Two Socia's* (London, 1690); a nearly identical second issue of 1691 includes the same announcement. The songs, printed by John Heptinstall, who had recently produced Purcell's lavish score for *Dioclesian*, were issued with a

Theodosius had been published in the same format in 1680, but without attribution. Several of his songs in *A Fool's Preferment* had similarly been included in the playbook printed in 1688, this time with a title-page credit comparable to that for *Amphitryon*,[150] but the play itself does not seem to have had a political bent, and the loyal song 'Here's a Health to the King' (which may or may not be by Purcell) was not included in the publication. *Amphitryon*, therefore, represented a new level of prominence for Purcell's public identification with politically sensitive drama, particularly given the association with Dryden, the deposed Poet Laureate whose agonized protestation that despite 'adhering to a lost Cause ... I am a patient Sufferer, and no disturber of the Government' stands side by side in the dedication with his fulsome praise for Purcell.

As recent research on Dryden has demonstrated, the poet's declarations of innocence often mask an ulterior purpose, and David Bywaters has read *Amphitryon* as an extended topical commentary on the Williamite seizure of power and its aftermath as perceived by Jacobites like the ex-Laureate.[151] Of particular interest is his identification of the chorus to Purcell's duet 'Fair Iris and her Swain' as the play's only overt expression of Dryden's hope for an eventual return of the exiled James II:

> Thus at the height we love and live,
> And fear not to be poor:
> We give, and give, and give, and give,
> Till we can give no more:
> > But what today
> > Will take away,
> Tomorrow will restore.

Given the obvious need for circumspection, it is small wonder that Dryden chose to embed the articulation of such a potentially sensitive statement 'at several removes from the action' in this dramatically autonomous 'Pastoral Dialogue betwixt *Thyrsis* and *Iris*'.[152] Whether Purcell knowingly consented to provide the vehicle for this elaboration upon Dryden's concerted assault on 'the specious bases for William's authority and the irresistible power that actually enforce[d] that authority',[153] on the other hand, is something about which we can only speculate.

Dryden's thorny oppositional stance is no less in evidence in his major collaboration with Purcell of the following year. The gestation history of *King*

---

separate register and title page: *The Songs in Amphitryon, With the Musick. Composed by Mr. Henry Purcell* (London, 1690).

150 Thomas D'Urfey, *A Fool's Preferment, Or, the Three Dukes of Dunstable* (London, 1688): 'Together, with all the SONGS and NOTES to 'em, Excellently Compos'd by Mr. HENRY PURCELL. 1688'.

151 Bywaters, *Dryden in Revolutionary England*, pp. 56–74.

152 Ibid., p. 72.

153 Ibid., p. 65.

Arthur – which seems originally to have been designed for Charles II in the early 1680s but was abandoned when its allegorical prologue was expanded into the full-scale opera *Albion and Albanius* – is difficult to unravel, given Dryden's evasive comments on the subject, and we have no evidence like that which exists for *Cinthia and Endimion* to show Purcell's involvement in the project prior to the 1690s. Dryden did, however, state clearly that the post-Revolutionary version embodied substantial revisions,[154] and a number of scholars have found evidence of a sustained – albeit veiled and sometimes contradictory – political message in the work as produced.[155] As Bywaters argues, the opera's strident patriotism itself becomes a tool for the playwright, as he lavishes effusive praise on his country 'for precisely those qualities it most obviously lacks' under the new regime.[156] The intricacies of the possible allegorical parallels remain open to further exploration,[157] but the underlying themes of 'war and peace, engagement and detachment, action and resignation'[158] that inform the opera are undoubtedly political in their implications, and would thus infuse Purcell's musical contributions to at least some degree. Whatever Dryden's ultimate intention with respect to veiled allegories, the sequence of musical numbers that make up the extravagant final masque – a series of tableaux designed to celebrate Britain as a uniquely favoured home of military, economic and social vitality and seat of exemplary beauty, love and valour – is even more apposite. This nationalistic paean – the closest Purcell ever came to penning a grand patriotic composition with the possible exception of *Bonduca*'s 'Britons Strike Home' – must surely stand as a crowning example of the composer's public music with a political bent. Although we may never know whether or not

---

154 John Dryden, *Plays: King Arthur, Cleomenes, Love Triumphant, contributions to The Pilgrim*, ed. Vinton A. Dearing, The Works of John Dryden, vol. 16 (Berkeley, Los Angeles and London: University of California Press, 1996), p. 6: 'I have been oblig'd so much to alter the first Design … that it is now no more what it was formerly, than the present Ship of the *Royal Sovereign*, after so often taking down, and altering, is the Vessel it was at the first Building'. Immediately following this passage, Dryden praised Purcell's music in terms similar to those expressed in *Amphitryon*, quoted above.

155 Price, *Henry Purcell and the London Stage*, pp. 290–95, with additional thoughts in Price, 'Political Allegory in Late-Seventeenth-Century English Opera', pp. 10–17; James Anderson Winn, *John Dryden and his World* (New Haven and London: Yale University Press, 1987), pp. 448–51; Bywaters, *Dryden in Revolutionary England*, pp. 75–93; Walkling, 'The Apotheosis of Absolutism', p. 226.

156 Bywaters, *Dryden in Revolutionary England*, p. 79 (regarding Dryden's dedication to the Marquess of Halifax) and pp. 89–90 (with respect to the opera's final resolution and grand concluding masque).

157 In *Henry Purcell and the London Stage*, pp. 293–5, Price identifies two conflicting allegorical systems in the opera (Arthur = William / Oswald = James, and *vice versa*), an analysis endorsed by Winn in *John Dryden and his World*, p. 619 n. 58. Bywaters deftly reads this apparently contradictory situation as an indication of 'the complexity, indeed the inconsistency, of Dryden's purposes', which included his desire to re-establish his court connections while at the same time maintaining his Jacobite loyalties; see *Dryden in Revolutionary England*, pp. 81–2.

158 Bywaters, *Dryden in Revolutionary England*, p. 75.

his own breast swelled with pride upon hearing the work he had created, it would certainly have had an impact on many members of its audience, regardless of their political inclinations.[159]

A crucial point to make about Purcell's involvement in all of the public theatrical works in which political meaning might be descried is that, in stark contrast to *Dido and Aeneas*, the main characters who might constitute the primary focus of the play's allegorical or satirical intentions rarely appear in the musical episodes Purcell was responsible for setting.[160] Thus in most instances his compositions must be seen to play little more than a supporting role in the political agendas of their parent literary works. Although, as Curtis Price has ably shown in *Henry Purcell and the London Stage*, Purcell's music often does contribute to the psychological elaboration of dramatic situations and to deepening our understanding of or identification with the plights of individual characters, this function of subtly enhancing or undermining the more comprehensively articulated message of dramatic poetry and prose is at best ancillary to the connotative power and the artistic primacy of the spoken or sung word, John Dryden's (possibly disingenuous) protestations in the dedicatory epistle to *King Arthur* notwithstanding.[161] We are only beginning to understand, if such a thing is even possible, how the language of music as wielded by Purcell and his contemporaries could be said to function in a political way in the absence of more comfortingly legible verbal texts. However, as we shall see in the final section of this chapter, certain new approaches to Purcell's work might ultimately yield some interesting answers.

Music as Political Statement

Intertextuality

The evident adaptation of the closing strain of the theatrical catch 'How Great are the Blessings' for use in the court ode *Sound the Trumpet, Beat the Drum*, illustrated

---

159 For a brief discussion of other possible political implications of the final two movements of the *King Arthur* masque, see Andrew Pinnock and Bruce Wood, 'Come, Ye Sons of Art – Again: Court Cross-Subsidy for Purcell's Opera Orchestra, 1690–1695', *Early Music* 37 (2009): 455.

160 An exception might be the speaking–singing character Philidel in *King Arthur*, whom Winn reads as a stand-in for Dryden himself; see *John Dryden and his World*, pp. 449–50.

161 '[T]he Numbers of Poetry and Vocal Musick, are sometimes so contrary, that in many places I have been oblig'd to cramp my Verses, and make them rugged to the Reader, that they may be harmonious to the Hearer' (Dryden, *Plays*, ed. Dearing, p. 6). This, of course, is as much a statement concerning matters of prosodic decorum in an 'Entertainment ... principally design'd for the Ear and Eye' as it is a relative valuation of the expressive powers of music and poetry, but we should note the potentially broader applicability of Dryden's concession to Purcell's contributions to their joint operatic endeavour: 'my Art on this occasion, ought to be subservient to his.'

above in Example 6.2, offers a glimpse into another aspect of Purcell's musical engagement with political issues: intertextuality. Purcell was no Handel with respect to borrowing, but his selective reuse of musical material, particularly in what appear to be political contexts, deserves further consideration. The multiple appearances of the theme shown in Example 6.2, and the better-known example of Purcell's incorporation of the ballad tune 'Cold and Raw' into Queen Mary's birthday ode *Love's Goddess sure was Blind* following the queen's request to hear the tune, offer only a glimpse of the vast sonic landscape of memorable popular tunes, both ascribed and anonymous, that suffused the consciousness of seventeenth-century Englishmen and women.[162] When those present at the welcoming of James from Windsor on 11 October 1687 heard the final bars of *Sound the Trumpet, Beat the Drum*, they may have been reminded, consciously or unconsciously, of the earlier song and, by extension, its theme of loyalty to the king. This example is not altogether atypical: the vast majority of Purcell's self-borrowings involve court odes and public theatrical works, although they are primarily focused on instrumental movements such as overtures, symphonies and dance tunes.[163] There may be multiple reasons covering a range of circumstances for Purcell to have reused his own thematic material in this way: Andrew Pinnock and Bruce Wood, for example, have recently advanced a provocative utilitarian explanation for Purcell's frequent recycling of thematic and conceptual materials over short time-spans between his odes and theatre pieces during the 1690s, which may shed

---

162 On 'Cold and Raw' see Sir John Hawkins, *A General History of the Science and Practice of Music*, reprinted with a new introduction by Charles Cudworth (2 vols, New York: Dover, 1963; first published London: Novello, 1853), vol. 2, p. 564 n. *. For a general discussion of the sonic and psychological features of ballads in a social context, see Bruce R. Smith, *The Acoustic World of Early Modern England: Attending to the O-Factor* (Chicago: University of Chicago Press, 1999), pp. 168–205.

163 Examples of instrumental music from odes reused in theatrical productions are given in Pinnock and Wood, 'Come Ye Sons of Art – Again': 447, which includes pieces with direct melodic echoes together with some in which 'gestural or ideational connectedness registers, rather than note-for-note musical correspondence' (ibid.: 449). To these can be added the overture to *Love's Goddess sure was Blind* (1692), which is related to the overture to *The Rival Sisters* (1695). There are also two more exceptional borrowings of a similar type: between the overture to *My Heart is Inditing*, and that of *Celestial Music* (both 1689); and between the March Purcell wrote for the funeral of Queen Mary in 1694 and the Act V symphony in *The Libertine* (1695). There remains some question as to whether the overture to *Arise, my Muse* (1690) was intended to serve in the same capacity for *King Arthur* (1691), or whether this is a result of a modern misreading of the sources: see Pinnock and Wood, 'Come Ye Sons of Art – Again': 464 n. 22. Alon Schab argues that two other purely theatrical borrowings – the Magicians' Dance from *Circe* (?1690), which is also the 'Slow Aire' in *The Married Beau* (1694); and 'Ah! How Sweet it is to Love' from *Tyrannick Love* (1694), which occurs as what may have been the Fourth Act Tune in *The Virtuous Wife* (1694) – did not originate with Purcell himself, but rather with the anonymous compiler/arranger of the posthumous publication *A Collection of Ayres, Compos'd for the Theatre* (London, 1697); see Schab, 'Distress'd Sources?: A Critical Consideration of the Authority of Purcell's *Ayres for the Theatre*', *Early Music* 37 (2009): 636.

light on developments in the configuration and duties of the court orchestra in the wake of the Glorious Revolution.[164] Similarly, the emergence of more accurate chronologies for Purcell's compositions may help us better to assess the composer's workload at particular moments in his career, how that issue may have affected his decisions to reuse material, and what those decisions may say about how he prioritized different projects.[165]

Just as our understanding of the political contours of Purcell's music is heavily weighted towards vocal works, so too the composer's thematic borrowing assumes greater interest when texted material is involved. For example, his reuse of passages from the early mad song 'From Silent Shades' ('Bess of Bedlam') in D'Urfey's play *A Fool's Preferment*[166] may be relevant to a reading of portions of the text as a satirical volley against Charles II as a potential cuckolder/cuckoldee 'made under the protection of feigned madness' on the part of the (genuinely insane) character Lyonel, as Curtis Price points out.[167] As already mentioned, the echo of 'Hey Boys, up go We' in the catch 'Since the Duke is Return'd' and the musical edifice he constructed for Queen Mary on the tune 'Cold and Raw' also suggest a possible political context for Purcell's creative employment of ballads and other popular tunes in his compositions, but there may be other thematic echoes that remain to be traced – or, conversely, unambiguously demonstrated to be no more than coincidental, and hence not relevant to a consideration of Purcell's politics.[168]

We might also take note of some instances in which instrumental and song tunes by Purcell were fitted with new texts as 'mock songs', albeit not necessarily with the composer's knowledge or consent. Many of these texts focus on drinking and other scurrility, but one example of particular interest involves the alto solo 'I Envy not the Pride of May' from the 1693 Marian birthday ode *Celebrate this Festival*, a self-justifying declaration by the embodied month of April (in which the queen had been born) that the following month's flowers are nothing in comparison to the 'saint and beauty' over which April can lay claim. A mere five months after the ode was performed, the *Gentleman's Journal* printed the song as 'I Envy not a Monarch's Fate', whose text explicitly rejects 'the vain honours of the great' in

---

164 Pinnock and Wood, 'Come Ye Sons of Art – Again'.
165 The chronology presented by Zimmerman in *Henry Purcell, 1659–1695: An Analytical Catalogue*, pp. 529–35 (Appendix V), while helpful, is now in need of substantial revision – a process that will be greatly aided by Robert Shay and Robert Thompson's important work on the sources, which has established more accurate chronologies for some groups of pieces; see Shay and Thompson, *Purcell Manuscripts*.
166 See Olive Baldwin and Thelma Wilson, 'A Purcell Problem Solved', *Musical Times* 122 (1981): 445.
167 Price, *Henry Purcell and the London Stage*, pp. 156 and 159.
168 For example, I have serious doubts about the association claimed by Zimmerman between the chorus 'Long live great Charles' from the welcome song *What shall be Done in Behalf of the Man?* and the opening bars of the anonymous canon 'Long live King Charles', published 19 years earlier; see Zimmerman, *Henry Purcell, 1659–1695: An Analytical Catalogue*, p. 171, and John Hilton, *Catch that Catch Can, or a New Collection of Catches, Rounds, and Canons* (London, 1663), section 2, p. [18].

favour of a life of pastoral simplicity, a view in diametric opposition to the usual rhetoric of court odes. This issue of 'mock-song' adaptations of Purcell runs along similar lines to the adaptation of the composer's tunes as broadside ballads and has equal potential as a field for further investigation.

As we have seen throughout this chapter, the main loci of politics in Purcell's compositional output are the (somewhat paradoxically) related genres of court music – in particular the odes – and 'popular' music – a category that includes catches but is also closely associated with ballad tunes and other convivial forms of musical entertainment. In fact, an examination of the composer's reuse of thematic material drawn from both instrumental and vocal sources within these two genres reveals clusters of intertextual links that may, upon further study, shed light on the first decade of Purcell's career, when his close affiliation with the court coincided with a period of significant political turmoil. We have already observed this with regard to 'How Great are the Blessings' and *Sound the Trumpet, Beat the Drum*, which ode is also the source for the 'first music' chaconne of *King Arthur*.[169] An even more intricate nexus of intertextual relations seems to centre around 1682, the year in which the celebrated ballad tune 'Hey Boys, up go We' first appeared. As we saw in Example 6.1, Purcell subtly quoted the opening of this tune in his catch 'Since the Duke is Return'd'. But he also penned an instrumental dance movement that employs the 'Hey Boys' melody as its bass line, transforming the common-time tune into a swinging 6/4 jig. The jig forms the final section of a fragmentary five-movement orchestral suite in G major now also believed to date from 1682.[170] In the work's sole surviving source, the autograph manuscript Lbl Add. 30930, Purcell wrote out only the treble and bass lines of the last three movements, leaving the two inner staves blank, but a complete version of the suite (if it ever existed) would almost certainly have been intended for the court violin band.[171] In 1686 the jig re-emerged, this time in 6/8 and fully scored, as part of the solo–chorus– ritornello complex 'Be Lively, then, and Gay' from the welcome song *Ye Tuneful Muses*, written for James II.[172] Peter Holman is certainly right to read the presence of the 'Hey Boys, up go We' tune here as a compliment or message of some sort to James,[173] the broader political implications of which would seem to be inescapable, but the appearance of the tune in the earlier courtly orchestral suite, and the expansion of the jig into a full-scale movement in the later welcome song, is also potentially noteworthy for what it could have contributed to this potential web of political associations.

---

169 See Pinnock and Wood, 'Come Ye Sons of Art – Again': 447.

170 Shay and Thompson, *Purcell Manuscripts*, pp. 297–8. In *Henry Purcell*, pp. 66–7, Holman suggests a date for the suite of between 1686 and 1690, based on the concordance with *Ye Tuneful Muses*, discussed below.

171 Holman, *Henry Purcell*, p. 13.

172 The Suite in G also contains movements that reappear in the suites for the plays *Distress'd Innocence* (October 1690) and *The Gordian Knot Unty'd* (November 1690). For a discussion of the latter, see below.

173 Holman, *Henry Purcell*, p. 168.

All of the elements seen in the foregoing discussion – the importance of court odes as a source of politically charged references; the retrospective nod to the early court instrumental repertoire; the use of partially concealed ballad tunes to convey political messages – come together in a case that may be of particular relevance to the question of political intertextuality. Purcell's suite of instrumental music for the lost play *The Gordian Knot Unty'd* offers a striking example of the reuse of material from earlier court works. As Table 6.2 shows, four of the suite's seven dance movements represent wholesale quotations from works Purcell composed for the royal court during the first half of the 1680s,[174] a striking coincidence for a play believed to have been presented in November 1690, almost two years after the Glorious Revolution. It is unfortunate that we know nothing about the content of this play, which is believed to be by William Walsh,[175] a gentleman-poet who wrote no other complete dramatic works and the bulk of whose literary output remained unpublished during his lifetime.[176] Walsh, who would later serve as an important conduit of literary influence between John Dryden and Alexander Pope, was a skilled satirist and, politically speaking, 'a low-church whig, devoted to the revolution settlement, and war against France'.[177] Thus, the play may be presumed

---

174 In *Henry Purcell … An Analytical Catalogue*, pp. 80 and 175, Zimmerman additionally notes a similarity between the beginning of the Second Act Tune and the opening of Purcell's Latin motet *Beati omnes qui timent Dominum*, and Robert Shay observes a further correspondence between the 'opening melodic shape and key' of this movement and that of the rondeau–minuet in the fragmentary five-part suite, probably of court provenance, preserved in US-NH Filmer 8, p. 96; see Robert Shay, 'Bass Parts to an Unknown Purcell Suite at Yale', *Notes*, Series 2/57 (2000–01): 828. In examining the Third Act Tune, Peter Holman shows (*Henry Purcell*, p. 67) that Purcell altered the three lower parts in the last four bars in order better to coordinate the harmony with a change he had previously made to the first-violin part in the earlier manuscript copy of the four-part Suite in G.

175 Dennis Arundell, 'The Gordian Knot Untied', *Times Literary Supplement* 1220 (4 June 1925): 384, with responses by W.J. Lawrence and Felix White in *Times Literary Supplement* 1221 (11 June 1925): 400 and Arundell in *Times Literary Supplement* 1222 (18 June 1925): 416. Arundell argues, on the grounds that Walsh had elsewhere used the phrase 'Gordian Knot' to refer to the bonds of marriage, that the lost play was an adaptation by Walsh of Molière's *Monsieur de Pourceaugnac*, but he does not attempt to explain why, in 1704, Walsh participated in a collaborative version of the very same play, entitled *Squire Trelooby*, alongside William Congreve and Sir John Vanbrugh, rather than simply re-using the adaptation he had allegedly produced fourteen years earlier.

176 For details on Walsh, see James Sambrook, 'Walsh, William (*bap.* 1662, d. 1708)', in *Oxford Dictionary of National Biography*, http://www.oxforddnb.com (last accessed 8 August 2010). Sambrook observes: 'it seems that Walsh had a gentlemanly negligence about publication: most of his verse appeared in miscellanies and journals after his death, or remains unpublished.' Oddly, *The Gordian Knot Unty'd* is not mentioned in this article.

177 Ibid.

Table 6.2   Purcell's reuse of musical material in *The Gordian Knot Unty'd* (1690).

Movement	Type (Key)	Concordance
1st Music	Chaconne (d)	
2nd Music (i)	Air (D)	
2nd Music (ii)	Minuet (D)	*From Hardy Climes* (1683)
Overture	[Grave–Canzona] (g)	
1st Act Tune	Air (g)	*What shall be Done in Behalf of the Man?* (1682)
2nd Act Tune	Rondeau–Minuet (g)	*Why are all the Muses Mute?* (1685)
3rd Act Tune	Air (G)	Suite a4 (?1682)
4th Act Tune	Jig (G)	'Liliburlero'

to have been an unabashedly pro-Williamite work, if indeed it had a political bent – as is implied by the title, which alludes to the hard-won resolution of a seemingly intractable dilemma such as, perhaps, the actions of the former King James.

Such an interpretation is strengthened by the fact that Purcell turned once again to the ballad repertoire, this time deploying the anti-James smash hit 'Liliburlero' as the bass line for the Fourth Act Tune. This rollicking jig, in which the highly political ballad tune is prominently audible, may have punctuated some catastatic dramatic moment near the end of the play, and might thus have been expected to garner cheers from the 1690 audience. What is less clear is why Purcell chose to exploit other tunes so closely associated with the pre-Revolutionary court, and in particular with the now-disgraced and exiled James. Peter Holman regards the music for *The Gordian Knot Unty'd* as 'a compilation suite',[178] presumably cobbled together while the composer was busy with more important commissions. Certainly *The Gordian Knot Unty'd* is not one of Purcell's major works, and the play most likely appeared immediately in the wake of several other theatrical productions with which he was involved, including the high-profile *Amphitryon*, as well as *Distress'd Innocence* and *Sir Anthony Love*.[179] The selections Purcell made for *The Gordian Knot Unty'd*, none of which have been transposed from their original sources, are also appropriate to

---

178 Holman, *Henry Purcell*, p. 170; he also suggests that the Liliburlero jig might have been taken 'from a lost ode of 1689–90 – perhaps even from one that celebrated the Glorious Revolution'.

179 Purcell may also have been writing music for the revival of *Circe* at this time (although the dating is uncertain), and could even have begun work on *King Arthur*, whose premiere occurred the following May or June.

the key structure he was concerned to establish of D minor–major in the First and Second Music, and G minor–major in the Overture and Act Tunes (a configuration potentially well suited to a play that may have moved dramatically from a situation of extreme danger to a happy ending).[180] But the sheer density of references to the court repertoire must raise some questions about the possible political implications of this music for what may well have been a political play. Could Purcell have been intentionally offering a surreptitious oppositional comment to undermine the play's overt political message? And while the anti-Jacobite 'Liliburlero' reference would have been the one clearly recognizable to most in the audience, might there have been some – courtiers in attendance at the theatre, or perhaps even musicians in the orchestra – who would have recognized the tunes associated with the old regime and felt a smug satisfaction at the subversive musical message they were hearing, or a twinge of nostalgia for the world that had been so recently swept away? This is not to argue that there is any definitively articulated political message lurking in the individual movements, especially the Act Tunes, as they were placed in the play.[181] Rather, I want to suggest the possibility of a particularly diffuse 'impressionistic' political meaning based solely in the evanescent thematic echoes that we have already seen at work in other theatrical circumstances and which, I believe, formed such an important part of seventeenth-century musical and sonic consciousness.[182]

Abstract Music and Contrapuntal Language: The Politics of the Fantazias?

The issue of intertextuality brings us closer to the prospect of assessing specifically Purcell's music as a focus of political expression and analysis, rather than its verbal texts and performance contexts. This is, admittedly, highly speculative territory, but having come this far we would be remiss not to hazard one further, if tentative, step into the uneasy realm of abstract music by considering what may be the epitome of that form in Purcell's output, the fantazias for viol consort, and how they might point the way towards potential future lines of scholarly investigation into the question of Purcell's musical politics (and musical politics generally). As is well known, Purcell's fantazias constitute a remarkable phenomenon in a number of ways. They were the last of their kind, representing the final gasp of a long and

---

180 For a discussion of Purcell's associational use of keys see Price, *Henry Purcell and the London Stage*, pp. 22–3.

181 Such interpretation is in any case very difficult to substantiate, as is demonstrated, for example, in Curtis Price's only partially successful efforts to contextualize the instrumental music in the near-contemporary suite for *Distress'd Innocence*; see ibid., pp. 65–6.

182 A good example of this 'sonic consciousness' might be the familiar cries of London street vendors, something Purcell seems to have avoided, but which was of great interest to a number of other composers, particularly early in the century; see Smith, *The Acoustic World of Early Modern England*, pp. 64–70.

distinguished tradition of English viol consort music stretching back at least as far as the middle of the sixteenth century. Yet, rather than being the culmination of the genre as it had developed by the middle of the seventeenth century, they marked a return to what was in Purcell's time a stylistically archaic tonal language. As Peter Holman has observed, the sheer harmonic density displayed in Purcell's fantazias 'had not been a regular part of English consort music for generations, and one has to go back to the reign of James I ... before encountering a body of English music so taken up with formal contrapuntal techniques'.[183] Perhaps on account of this quality, Purcell's fantazias seem to have been largely unknown to his viol-playing contemporaries, including Roger North, who famously remarked that the last of such works to have been composed was Matthew Locke's *Consort of Four Parts*.[184] It is also striking that in Purcell's autograph, Lbl Add. 30930, each of the ten four-part fantazias is given a precise date, presumably the date of composition, in Purcell's hand.[185] Most of the dates, which fall in chronological order, are in June 1680 (10, 11, 14, 19, 22, 23, 30), with two in August of the same year (18 or 19,[186] 31), while the final, incomplete four-part fantazia is dated 24 February 1683.

Scholarship on the fantazias has focused on their possible function as contrapuntal exercises,[187] written without hope of wide circulation or financial gain by a young composer coming to terms with the legacy of his illustrious predecessors, in

---

183 Holman, *Henry Purcell*, pp. 81–2.

184 Mary Chan and Jamie C. Kassler (eds), *Roger North's The Musicall Grammarian 1728*, Cambridge Studies in Music (Cambridge: Cambridge University Press, 1990), p. 260: 'he composed a magnifick consort of 4 parts after the old style which was the last of the kind that hath bin made[,] so wee may rank him with Cleomenes, King of Sparta who was styled ultimus heroo[r]um.' It should be pointed out that the transmission paths of manuscript sources for this repertoire were fairly restricted, which could also explain North's ignorance of Purcell's work in this area; for a brief treatment of this subject, see Harold Love, *The Culture and Commerce of Texts: Scribal Publication in Seventeenth-Century England* (Amherst: University of Massachusetts Press, 1998; originally published as *Scribal Publication in Seventeenth-Century England* (Oxford: Clarendon, 1993)), pp. 23–31.

185 Nigel Fortune and Franklin B. Zimmerman, 'Purcell's Autographs', in Imogen Holst (ed.), *Henry Purcell 1659–1695: Essays on his Music* (London: Oxford University Press, 1959), p. 111; see also Shay and Thompson, *Purcell Manuscripts*, pp. 84–100.

186 Purcell seems to have altered this date at least once: Zimmerman reads the final version of the number as '18' in *Henry Purcell, 1659–1695: An Analytical Catalogue*, pp. 377–8, but it is given as '19' in Henry Purcell, *Fantazias and Miscellaneous Instrumental Music*, ed. Michael Tilmouth with Alan Browning and Peter Holman, The Works of Henry Purcell, vol. 31 (rev. edn, London and Sevenoaks: Novello, 1990), p. 119 and in Shay and Thompson, *Purcell Manuscripts*, p. 96. Holman, without providing further comment, offers all three possible readings of the number in *Henry Purcell*, p. 82, citing '16, 18, 19'.

187 See for example Holman, *Henry Purcell*, p. 75: 'The most likely explanation is that Purcell wrote his fantazias more as composition exercises than as material for performance. Only [the second three-part fantazia, in F Major] survives in parts as well as score.' Robert Thompson, however, offers evidence of a minor revision to fantazia 5 in US-NYp Drexel 5061 that 'may reflect an experiment carried out when the music was played through'; see 'The Sources of Purcell's Fantasias', *Chelys* 25 (1996–97): 92.

particular Locke and Jenkins. Yet this approach does not satisfactorily address a number of questions that arise from this exceptional repertoire and its sources. Why, for example, do Purcell's fantazias not deploy a more Lockean idiom, particularly given that the composer is known to have owned a manuscript containing the *Consort of Four Parts* (probably Locke's autograph, now Lbl Add. 17801)?[188] Alternatively, why did Purcell not follow Jenkins in composing fantazia–dance pairs, rather than this unusual assemblage of independent fantazias, devoid of the harmonically and rhythmically regular or predictable dance movements that usually served to take the edge off the fantazias' complex abstractedness?[189] What was Purcell's original plan for his fantazias, given that the manuscript as ultimately organized and bound contains blank pages and sectional headings that seem to anticipate multiple fantazias in five, six, seven and eight parts, even though the composer ultimately wrote no eight-part fantazias and composed only one in each of the other three scorings?[190] And, perhaps most perplexingly, why did Purcell assiduously date each of the four-part fantazias, including the incomplete one he wrote three years after the others, and yet offer no dates of any kind for any of the three-, five-, six- and seven-part fantazias that were ultimately included in the same volume?

Although no definitive answer to these questions can be posited here, it is surely worth considering the larger context, including the political circumstances, in which Purcell's composition of the four-part fantazias occurred. The summer of 1680 was a time of deep political division and uncertainty in England, marked not so much by overt social and civil unrest as by a foreboding that such things might potentially occur in the immediate future. Despite elections for a parliament (what would come to be known as the 'Second Exclusion Parliament') the previous September, Charles II had successively delayed the body's meeting for many months while seeking to shore up his political position *vis-à-vis* the opposition Whig faction through the appointment of the so-called 'Chits' ministry and attempts to

---

188 Thompson, 'The Sources of Purcell's Fantasias': 94, quoting annotations in Lbl Add. 31435 referring to Lbl Add. 17801 as 'Mr: Purcells Score book'. Purcell did follow Locke in eliminating the organ continuo (an early seventeenth-century innovation) and in emphasizing the four-part form (in which 10 of the 16 surviving fantazias are scored); on the other hand, his planned expansion into larger scorings up to eight parts, as well as his apparent interest in the long neglected 'In Nomine' form, are further evidence of a curiously retrospective approach.

189 This question cannot simply be answered with reference to Purcell's supposedly leapfrogging back to the earlier repertoire. As Thompson points out, 'what is conspicuous … in the evidence of [the] manuscripts … is not how much but how little of the huge existing repertory he definitely knew'; see 'The Sources of Purcell's Fantasias': 95.

190 Robert Thompson has recently drawn attention to the fact that Lbl Add. 30930, despite its seemingly painstaking organization – including blank space left for the insertion of other, unwritten fantazias in various scorings – may actually have been assembled *in medias res* from loose sheets on which some of the volume's contents had already been copied; see Thompson, 'The Sources of Purcell's Fantasias'; Shay and Thompson, *Purcell Manuscripts*, pp. 88–100.

refashion his network of foreign alliances.[191] The apparent weakening of the Whigs, particularly their leader, Anthony Ashley Cooper, First Earl of Shaftesbury, had led earlier in the year to a general perception that the festering political crisis (commonly known as the Exclusion Crisis) might be coming to an end.[192] By June, however, the opposition's frustration had led them to take new, more drastic measures, including mass petitions to the king demanding that Parliament finally be allowed to sit, as well as a series of public dinners, particularly in London, with leading nobility and gentry hosted by James Scott, Duke of Monmouth, Charles's eldest illegitimate son, who had been put forward as the Whigs' chief candidate for the throne in opposition to the king's Roman Catholic brother James, Duke of York.[193] By the end of the month, having secured the election of two Whigs as sheriffs of London,[194] Shaftesbury and his compatriots took the extraordinary step of presenting the Duke of York to a Middlesex grand jury as a Catholic recusant, and the king's mistress, Louise de Kéroualle, Duchess of Portsmouth, as a prostitute.[195] Although the king and his ministers managed to get the jury dismissed before actual charges could be brought, this brazen manoeuvre underscored the extraordinarily rancorous political atmosphere that continued to develop as the tense weeks progressed.

In the summer of 1680 Henry Purcell would certainly not have been alone in feeling, if not outright despair at the increasingly portentous events taking place around him, at least some generalized sense of anxiety or apprehension that may have found an outlet in his withdrawal into a reflective, even contemplative compositional exercise.[196] We can only speculate how the restless, intricate

---

191 Mark Knights, *Politics and Opinion in Crisis, 1678–81*, Cambridge Studies in Early Modern British History (Cambridge: Cambridge University Press, 1994), p. 69.

192 Ibid., pp. 69–70 and 264.

193 Ibid., pp. 268–75; for Monmouth, see Tim Harris, 'Scott [Crofts], James, Duke of Monmouth and First Duke of Buccleuch (1649–1685)', in *Oxford Dictionary of National Biography*, http://www.oxforddnb.com (last accessed 12 August 2010).

194 The initial shreival election was on 24 June (see De Krey, *London and the Restoration*, p. 192), but the new sheriffs, Slingsby Bethel and Henry Cornish, were retrospectively disqualified from standing for having failed to take the oaths and sacramental 'test' required by the 1661 Corporation Act. A new election was held on 14 July, at which Bethel and Cornish, having fulfilled the 'test' requirements, were handily returned again; see Knights, *Politics and Opinion in Crisis*, p. 271.

195 Ronald Hutton, *Charles the Second: King of England, Scotland and Ireland* (Oxford: Clarendon, 1989), p. 392.

196 Compare, for example, Ralph Josselin's diary entry for 18 July 1680: 'dull heavy weather. worse times. but worst hearts. god is not minded and no wonder he minds not us'; Alan Macfarlane (ed.), *The Diary of Ralph Josselin, 1616–1683*, Records of Social and Economic History New Series, vol. 3 (Oxford: Oxford University Press for The British Academy, 1976), p. 629. Bruce Wood and Andrew Pinnock speculate that Purcell might have been attending the king at Windsor (and hence had extra time on his hands) during the summer of 1680, but he is not included in the warrant for 'riding charges and other expenses' covering that period; see Bruce Wood and Andrew Pinnock, sleeve notes to Henry Purcell, *Fantazias and In Nomines*, Fretwork (Virgin Veritas, 7243 5 45062 2 2, *rec.* 1995), p. 7, and National Archives, London, LC5/144, p. 45, calendered in Andrew

melodic and harmonic weavings of this seemingly abstract instrumental genre may have been intended to convey the composer's – or the nation's – disquiet,[197] or even sought to articulate particular musical associations between Purcell and his predecessors who had also turned to the intimate viol repertoire in earlier periods of political turmoil. There is considerable room for exploration of the possible political contexts and implications of the tortuous contrapuntal language of early modern viol consort music, particularly in the cases of composers such as William Lawes, Jenkins and Locke, all of whom lived through politically and socially turbulent times. David Pinto has offered some provocative questions along these lines in his study of Lawes's consort music,[198] and we should note Thomas Mace's description, a mere four years before Purcell wrote his fantazias, of viol music as 'so many *Pathettical Stories, Rhetorical, and Sublime Discourses; Subtil, and Accute Argumentations; … Suitable, and Agreeing to the Inward, Secret, and Intellectual Faculties of the Soul and Mind'*,[199] a revealing characterization to which Purcell would almost certainly have had access.[200]

In considering how Purcell's fantazias might be understood as something more than simply private compositional exercises – miniature 'masterpieces' in which Purcell exhibited the depth of his newly matured skill while simultaneously paying tribute to his musical forebears – we might also take notice of the parallel and precisely contemporaneous repertoire of sacred partsongs, whose more than coincidental associations with the fantazias have long been recognised.[201] Alan Howard's recent appraisal of the most virtuosic of these works provides an image of Purcell responding in deeply personal ways to the opportunities afforded by both the texts and the performance circumstances of this intimate chamber music, even to the extent of replacing the subjective voice of the performer with that of

Ashbee, *Records of English Court Music, vol. 1: 1660–1685* (Snodland, Kent: Ashbee, 1986), pp. 191–2.

197 We might consider, in a different but related vein, Thomas Tomkins's famous 'A Sad Pavan: For these Distracted Times', written in the aftermath of another moment of acute national crisis, the execution of Charles I in 1649.

198 David Pinto, *For the Violls: The Consort and Dance Music of William Lawes* (Richmond: Fretwork, 1995), pp. 70–73; see also John Cunningham, *The Consort Music of William Lawes, 1602–1645* (Woodbridge: Boydell and Brewer, 2010).

199 Thomas Mace, *Musick's Monument, or a Remembrancer of the Best Practical Musick* (London, 1676), p. 234.

200 Aside from the fact that the book was on sale at John Carr's shop at the Middle Temple gate, at least two of Purcell's colleagues, the singer/composer James Hart and the shadowy sometime court violinist Henry Dove (who surrendered his place in the Twenty-Four Violins in 1676), were original subscribers to the volume: see ibid., sig. d1r.

201 See Nigel Fortune, 'Purcell: The Domestic Sacred Music', in F.W. Sternfeld, Nigel Fortune and Edward Olleson (eds), *Essays on Opera and English Music in Honour of Sir Jack Westrup* (Oxford: Blackwell, 1994), pp. 65–6. Most of these works were – like the fantazias – copied by Purcell into Lbl Add. 30930.

the composer himself.[202] Howard's nuanced assessment of Purcell's exceptionally elaborate displays of compositional virtuosity in these private, introspective pieces, and his identification of related techniques in the fantazias themselves,[203] represent a significant contribution to our understanding of the distinctive repertoires of the early 1680s, while the added dimension of political contextualization might help further to illuminate the composer's motivations and approaches in this realm.

Beyond this, the possibility that Purcell may have turned to the writing of intricate and in some respects self-consciously antiquated contrapuntal music at a moment of political crisis – a crisis that also held personal ramifications for a loyal court servant, living and working in the London area – offers yet another way to think about the 'politics' of his work. So much of what he wrote music for the court and the church; music for the theatres and for corporate institutions; music for publishers, colleagues and students – was produced at the behest of others. Yet here and there we find, in the darker recesses of his *oeuvre*, traces of a more personal motivation: private compositions that might, in some instances, have been created at least in part as intimate meditations on public occasions. Such individual musical expressions should provoke us to consider how Purcell might have conceived of his own place in the conjoined worlds of music and politics when he chose to turn inward in the summer of 1680 to explore the most intimate and personal manifestations of his craft, even while he laboured to fill his first major theatrical commission (*Theodosius*) and to create his earliest royal welcome song (*Welcome, Vicegerent of the Mighty King*), both of which must have been well underway as Purcell rounded out the set of four-part fantazias that, it would seem, he never intended to offer up for public consumption.

Conclusions

The consideration of Purcell's 'private' music in succession to the earlier explorations of the composer's 'court' and 'public' music in this chapter brings us full circle by reopening the question of how Purcell's music itself might be deemed political, and what this can tell us about the composer's responses to the political events and opportunities with which the often turbulent world of Restoration England presented him. As the foregoing survey demonstrates, Purcell's works exist within a complex matrix of political modalities of which we are only beginning to achieve

---

202 Alan Howard, 'Composition as an Act of Performance: Artifice and Expression in Purcell's Sacred Partsong *Since God so tender a regard*', *Journal of the Royal Musical Association* 132 (2007): 53: 'the text's protagonist must be understood to be Purcell himself; we are required to accept the composer's setting of the text as a vehicle of his personal expression.'

203 See Alan Howard, 'Purcell and the Poetics of Artifice: Compositional Strategies in the Fantasias and Sonatas' (PhD dissertation, King's College, London, 2006), esp. pp. 132–59. See also the section 'Analytical Approaches to Creativity' in Chapter 3 above.

an adequate understanding. At the moment, the primacy of the literary over the musical text remains an obstacle to be surmounted, as does the relatively meagre supply of genuinely personal biographical details that might help to illuminate the composer's motives or intentions. While Purcell studies have by no means remained static over the last 20 years, few of the most recent discoveries or insights have brought us appreciably closer to breaking this *impasse* and subjecting the composer and his works to a genuinely new way of thinking. Such an approach, I would suggest, demands that we move beyond the music as received object and seek to gain a greater understanding of Purcell's creative process. We still know far too little about Purcell's actual relationships with his librettists, both living and dead, although some interesting work has begun to be carried out on his own textual tinkering and prosodic choices,[204] and the recent initiative, spearheaded by Rebecca Herissone, to understand the mechanics of musical creativity in seventeenth-century England promises to advance our knowledge in significant ways.

However, in order to reap the benefits of these potentially important scholarly developments, we must have a sense of where we are going. Hitherto, the question of Purcell's role in the translation of poetic text to musical text has too often been obscured by larger, ideologically freighted critical concerns or outright misconstrual, as a study of the sizeable body of work on *Dido and Aeneas* amply demonstrates. We need, instead, to seek out answers to some basic questions regarding motivation and process: why Purcell composed what he did, how he went about it and what impressions and reactions he might have expected from his audiences. From here it is a small step to deciphering the political implications of his work, where they exist, and thereby to understanding more fully how Purcell may have conceived of himself as, if not a political composer as such, then certainly a composer existing in, and inextricably bound to, a political world.

---

204 See for example Katherine T. Rohrer, 'Poetic Metre, Musical Metre, and the Dance in Purcell's Songs', in Price (ed.), *Purcell Studies* (Cambridge: Cambridge University Press, 1995), pp. 207–42.

Society and Disorder

Amanda Eubanks Winkler

Purcell was born into a period marked by violence and upheaval, and his short life was punctuated by intermittent religious and political crises. Yet the seventeenth century was also an age of more positive transitions, an age in which old epistemes began to be replaced by knowledge systems that, from our perspective, seem more recognizably modern. The Royal Society explored acoustics using the new empirically grounded science;[1] and anatomical discoveries challenged, but did not completely overthrow, the notion that women and men existed on an ontological continuum, with men occupying the top of the hierarchy (the widely discussed 'one-sex' model described by medical historian Thomas Laqueur).[2] Changing mores, as well as practical considerations, led to the introduction of structural changes on the English stage, as members of both sexes began to act in public. And music became increasingly important, as actors and actresses became thoroughly trained in the art of song and a new crop of performers known solely for their singing graced the London theatres.[3]

As a musician working for the court and the Chapel Royal in the 1680s, Purcell's fortunes had been directly linked to those of the monarchs he served. However, as noted in Chapter 5, upon the accession of William and Mary, his role at court diminished and the focus of his compositional activity switched to the theatre. Purcell's compositions for the theatre, the primary focus of this chapter, are a rich site for investigation, since in his work for the stage he collaborated with those of all religious and political stripes: Whigs and Tories, Anglicans and Catholics, including the famous Catholic convert and former poet laureate John Dryden. It

---

1   For a discussion of the Royal Society and its connection to music, see Penelope Gouk, *Music, Science and Natural Magic in Seventeenth-Century England* (New Haven: Yale University Press, 1999).

2   Thomas Laqueur, *Making Sex: Body and Gender from the Greeks to Freud* (Cambridge, MA: Harvard University Press, 1990). See the section 'Gender and Gender Roles' below.

3   For invaluable discussions of Purcell's singers see Olive Baldwin and Thelma Wilson, 'Richard Leveridge, 1670–1758. 1: Purcell and the Dramatic Operas', *Musical Times* 111 (1970): 592–4; Baldwin and Wilson, 'Purcell's Sopranos', *Musical Times* 123 (1982): 602–9; and Baldwin and Wilson, 'Purcell's Stage Singers', in Michael Burden (ed.), *Performing the Music of Henry Purcell* (Oxford: Clarendon, 1996), pp. 105–29.

seems a foregone conclusion to assert that both aesthetic concerns and larger social, political and religious forces shaped musical conventions and modes of listening in Purcell's time. Yet, with the exception of the political allegory question considered by Andrew Walkling in Chapter 6, until recently research on Purcell has shied away from interpretative approaches incorporating methodologies from literary and cultural studies that would allow these contexts to be considered. This infrequent engagement with the rich scholarship being conducted in other fields has in turn caused Purcell to be largely ignored outside the discipline of musicology, or, at best, to be relegated to the margins. A telling example is *The Cambridge Companion to English Restoration Theatre* of 2000, which does not include an essay on music, and barely mentions Purcell.[4]

In some respects our reluctance to engage with interdisciplinary approaches as musicologists is understandable: music is a highly specialized discipline and methodologies that work well for literature and history do not necessarily help us to comprehend music when applied indiscriminately. However, early modern opera scholars have benefited tremendously from their engagement with a broad range of approaches,[5] and since the 1990s some Purcell scholars have also taken the proverbial bull by the horns. Interdisciplinary collections such as Michael Burden's *A Woman Scorn'd* and the forthcoming book *Concepts of Creativity in Seventeenth-Century England* suggest that the time may be ripe for Purcell to take a more central role in late seventeenth-century cultural studies.[6] This chapter demonstrates how interdisciplinary scholarship can enrich our understanding of Purcell's music and the contexts in which it was performed, concentrating first on the central issue

---

4   Deborah Payne Fisk (ed.), *The Cambridge Companion to English Restoration Theatre* (Cambridge: Cambridge University Press, 2000). There are notable exceptions to this lamentable rule: both James A. Winn and Dianne Dugaw, scholars of English literature, have written about Purcell's music. See, for example, James Anderson Winn, *'When Beauty Fires the Blood': Love and the Arts in the Age of Dryden* (Ann Arbor: University of Michigan Press, 1992); and Winn, 'Dryden's Songs', in Jayne Lewis and Maxmillian E. Novak (eds), *Enchanted Ground: Reimagining John Dryden* (Toronto: University of Toronto Press, 2004), pp. 290–317. See also Dianne Dugaw, '"Critical Instants": Theatre Songs in the Age of Dryden and Purcell', *Eighteenth-Century Studies* 23 (1989–90): 157–81; and Dugaw, '"The Rationall Spirituall Part": Dryden and Purcell's Baroque *King Arthur'*, in Lewis and Novak (eds), *Enchanted Ground: Reimagining John Dryden* (Toronto: University of Toronto Press, 2004), pp. 273–89. Theatre historians Robert Hume and Judith Milhous have also long been interested in issues concerning late seventeenth-century English music and their contributions to Restoration theatre music scholarship are invaluable, as is made clear in Chapter 5 above.
5   See, for example, Wendy Heller, *Emblems of Eloquence: Opera and Women's Voices in Seventeenth-Century Venice* (Berkeley: University of California Press, 2003).
6   Michael Burden (ed.), *A Woman Scorn'd: Responses to the Dido Myth* (London: Faber, 1998). This collection, which includes essays from classicists, literary scholars and musicologists, considers the *Dido* narrative from multiple perspectives. *Concepts of Creativity* has contributions from historians of art, architecture, drama and music and considers the nature of invention in the period.

of gender, and then assessing in turn the topics of melancholia, madness and witchcraft.

Gender and Gender Roles

Gender has been a particular node of interest in early modern cultural studies and the number of books and articles produced in the past ten years on this subject is staggering. There are literary studies that consider gender roles in plays, historical works that examine changes in gender construction during the period, and analyses of same-sex desire: even a casual perusal of the book reviews section of *Renaissance Quarterly* or *Eighteenth-Century Studies* demonstrates the vibrancy of this area of enquiry. Alongside a substantial body of publications, professional organizations have emerged that are specifically interested in gender issues, such as the Society for the Study of Early Modern Women.[7] Yet in Purcell scholarship this area has only recently begun to be explored. A consideration of seventeenth-century gender, sex and modes of desire can only enhance our understanding of Purcell's music, particularly in the context of the stage, where actors and actresses sang words shaped by the anxieties and debates of their time. In fact, early modern notions of gender profoundly affected each category of Purcell's output discussed below – laments, mad songs and witches' music and incantations.

Ideas about gender in Purcell's England were in flux. The upheavals of the Civil War and Interregnum had led many to question not only the absolute authority of the king, but also hierarchical structures in general. The ultimate challenge to the status quo came when Charles I was put on trial for treason and beheaded in 1649. With husbands in exile or at war, women gained visibility and access to power during this tumultuous period. They took care of estates, preached in 'radical' religious sects such as the Ranters and Quakers, and became famous as prophetesses who predicted future political, religious and societal events.[8] This erosion of long-held beliefs about the social power structure had far-reaching effects, leading eventually to the development of a constitutional monarchy – which required a reformulation of the relationship between monarch and subject – and also a questioning and in some cases loosening of gender paradigms.

Political theorists and other writers concerned with reformulating the relationship of monarch to subject also considered the relationship of man to woman. In *Leviathan* (1651) Thomas Hobbes argued that women and children

---

7   See http://www.ssemw.org.

8   The changing role of women at this time is explored in Anthony Fletcher, *Gender, Sex and Subordination in England, 1500–1800* (New Haven: Yale University Press, 1995), pp. 384–5; Keith Thomas, 'Women and the Civil War Sects', *Past and Present* 13 (1958): 42–62; Patricia Crawford, *Women and Religion in England, 1500–1720* (London: Routledge, 1993); and Sara Mendelson and Patricia Crawford, *Women in Early Modern England, 1550–1720* (Oxford: Clarendon, 1998).

subordinated themselves to the will of their husband or father because the force of 'Civill Lawes', created by men with power, induced them to submit.[9] John Locke's *Two Treatises on Government* (1690) took a slightly different (and more conservative) view. Women, he believed, were 'naturally' subordinate to men, so the relationship was not simply a function of 'Civill Laws' – for example, when marital conflict arose, Locke advises that 'the last Determination, *i.e.* the Rule, should be placed somewhere, it naturally falls to the Man's share, as the abler and the stronger'.[10] Notably, neither Locke nor Hobbes claimed female equality: the question they explored was *why* women were subordinate (by nature or by law), not whether they should be subordinate in the first place.[11]

The normativity of female submission did meet with resistance in some quarters. In 1700, slightly after the time of Purcell, proto-feminist Mary Astell decried the hypocrisy of the men who resisted unfettered absolutism and developed the underpinnings of constitutional monarchy yet did nothing to alleviate the suffering and oppression of women. Looking to the past, she singled out John Milton, an adamant critic of Charles I's supposed political tyranny:

---

9   For a comparison of the 'Artificiall Chains' that bind subject to king and wife to husband see Chapter 20 of Thomas Hobbes, *Leviathan (1651)*, ed. Richard Tuck, Cambridge Texts in the History of Political Thought (Cambridge: Cambridge University Press, 1991). Hobbes posited that 'Dominion is acquired by two wayes; By Generation, and by Conquest. The right of Dominion by Generation, is that, which the Parent hath over his Children; and is called PATERNALL. ... And whereas some have attributed the Dominion to the Man onely, as being of the more excellent Sex; they misreckon in it. For there is not alwayes that difference of strength, or prudence between the man and the woman, as that the right can be determined without War. In Commonwealths, this controversie is decided by the Civill Law: and for the most part, (but not alwayes) the sentence is in favour of the Father; because for the most part Common-wealths have been erected by the Fathers, not by the Mothers of families'; ibid., pp. 139–40.

10 John Locke, *Two Treatises on Government (1690)*, ed. Peter Laslett, Cambridge Texts in the History of Political Thought (Cambridge: Cambridge University Press, 1988), p. 321. Thomas Laqueur discusses the impact of social contract theory (the idea that contracts or agreements bind people together in a civil society) upon gender construction in *Making Sex*, pp. 156–7. His account of Hobbes closely follows Carole Pateman's reading in *The Sexual Contract: Aspects of Patriarchal Liberalism* (Stanford: Stanford University Press, 1988), particularly p. 49.

11 For these reasons, among others, Pateman has argued that contract theory is antithetical to feminism, a claim she makes throughout *The Sexual Contract*. Recently, Rachel Weil has examined the relationship between political thought and gender in late seventeenth- and early eighteenth-century England; as she demonstrates, liberal political ideas were not always tied to liberal notions of gender: 'In some cases Whig ideology promoted the freedom of women as individuals; in others, it played into male anxieties about women's power. Often it did both'; *Political Passions: Gender, the Family and Political Argument in England, 1680–1714* (Manchester: Manchester University Press, 1999), p. 51; see also her excellent discussion of Whig writers Algernon Sidney, William Lawrence, James Tyrrell and John Locke, pp. 50–84.

For whatever may be said against Passive–Obedience in another Case, I suppose there's no Man but likes it very well in this; how much soever Arbitrary Power may be dislik'd on a Throne, Not Milton himself wou'd cry up Liberty to poor Female Slaves, or plead for the Lawfulness of Resisting a Private Tyranny.[12]

Despite their differences, Astell, Locke and Hobbes all discussed the relationship between man and woman in political terms that resonated with the formulation of a constitutional monarchy, a system that could be overthrown if 'arbitrary power' were exercised too freely.[13] Naturally, the emergence of such ideas had a profound effect on patriarchy and marriage, and in turn these social changes had far-reaching political, personal, theatrical and musical ramifications. As Susan Staves has noted, the late seventeenth century saw a secularization of both monarchy and marriage. No longer did the monarch rule by divine right: he (or she) ruled by consent of the people's representatives in Parliament. Likewise, marriage was no longer a sacred contract between man and woman for the sole purpose of 'being fruitful and multiplying' (or, more cravenly, for economic benefit). Rather, marriage could be an emotionally fulfilling partnership – a companionate marriage – whose bonds could be dissolved or modified by the state. If the union was unhappy, men could petition Parliament for a divorce or the woman could be granted maintenance to keep separate lodgings.[14]

Although bonds could now be broken, some elements of the marriage institution were untouched by the new progressivism. While some scholars believe that companionate marriage undermined patriarchy, as men and women took 'separate but equal' roles in the relationship, others, such as Anthony Fletcher, have observed that single women still had more autonomy than their married counterparts, who were legally their husband's property.[15] Married women of the upper classes were

---

12 Mary Astell, *Some Reflections upon Marriage, Occasion'd by the Duke and Dutchess of Mazarine's Case; Which is also Consider'd* (London, 1700), 29.

13 As she was an ardent Tory, it is somewhat surprising to find Astell recycling criticisms of absolutism to support a reform of marriage. Several authors have explored this seeming contradiction, including Patricia Springborg, 'Astell, Masham, and Locke: Religion and Politics', in Hilda L. Smith (ed.), *Women Writers and the Early Modern British Political Tradition* (Cambridge: Cambridge University Press, 1998), pp. 105–25. See also the recent collection William Kolbrener and Michal Michelson (eds), *Mary Astell: Reason, Gender, Faith* (Aldershot and Burlington: Ashgate, 2007), and Sarah Apetrei, '"Call No Man Master Upon Earth": Mary Astell's Tory Feminism and an Unknown Correspondence', *Eighteenth-Century Studies* 41 (2008): 507–23.

14 Susan Staves, *Players' Scepters: Fictions of Authority in the Restoration* (Lincoln: University of Nebraska Press, 1979), pp. 155–6.

15 Fletcher, *Gender, Sex, and Subordination in England*, p. 395. For opposing viewpoints see Edward Shorter, *The Making of the Modern Family* (New York: Basic Books, 1977); Lawrence Stone, *The Family, Sex, and Marriage in England 1500–1800* (New York: Harper and Row, 1977); and Randolph Trumbach, *The Rise of the Egalitarian Family* (New York: Academic Press, 1978). For a summary of recent research on marriage, gender

supposed to eschew the public sphere and were expected to be pious and chaste, revelling in their domestic duties and (God willing) motherhood, while single women and widows could participate more fully in the public discourse, even becoming playwrights – the widow Aphra Behn being one of the most famous examples.[16] And of course the double standard was still very much in play: men committed adultery with few repercussions; women who cuckolded men were cited, both on stage and off, as examples of moral turpitude. For patriarchy to survive, men had to be sure of female chastity to confirm that their male heirs were legitimate, something that female adultery seriously undermined.[17]

The complicated and imperfect shift towards a companionate model of marriage mirrored the gradual move away from the Galenic or one-sex theory in the late seventeenth century to a perception of biological sex that is more recognizably modern. According to the one-sex model, sexual difference was of degree, not kind: there was but one body that revealed the perfection of nature and it was male. In this episteme, a woman's ovaries and uterus were merely an inverted penis and testicles, an inversion that occurred because woman was cold and moist, and thus lacked the vital heat to 'perfect' her organs, causing her to retain them inside her body.[18] New discoveries made by anatomists in the mid-seventeenth century began to undermine such notions of the woman as a less perfect man; by the late seventeenth-century writers had begun to posit a clear biological division between the sexes, which explained radically different modes of behaviour.[19] In this new model, sexual difference was not just determined by the external or internal placement of a set of organs, it was systemic: men and women were ontologically distinct creatures.

Both the new notion of companionate marriage and the gradual shift to a two-sex model encouraged writers to describe the separate and supposedly equal spheres occupied by men and women. Although neither older theories nor established notions of marriage disappeared, conduct-book writers from the period began clearly to describe separate male and female behavioural traits, often claiming that these differences were rooted in 'nature'.[20] In 1673 Richard Allestree articulated

---

and sexuality, see Katherine Crawford, *European Sexualities, 1400–1800*, eds William Beik, T.C.W. Blanning and Brendan Simms, New Approaches to European History (Cambridge: Cambridge University Press, 2007).

16   Fletcher explains how this idealized gendered division of labour frequently broke down or was subverted because of socio-economic exigencies; see *Gender, Sex, and Subordination in England*, pp. 223–79.

17   Jacqueline Pearson, *The Prostituted Muse: Images of Women and Women Dramatists, 1642–1737* (New York and London: Harvester-Wheatsheaf, 1988), pp. 70–74.

18   On the one-sex model, see Laqueur, *Making Sex*, Chapters 1–5. For a summary of late seventeenth- and early eighteenth-century scientific thought on gender, see Londa Schiebinger, 'The Philosopher's Beard: Women and Gender in Science', in Roy Porter (ed.), *The Cambridge History of Science, vol. 4: Eighteenth-Century Science* (Cambridge: Cambridge University Press, 2003), pp. 184–211.

19   Laqueur, *Making Sex*, pp. 154–63.

20   See, for example, Edward Waterhouse, *The Gentlemans Monitor; or, a Sober Inspection into*

these ideas in his conduct book, *The Ladies Calling*. Although Allestree based his conclusions on older theories of gender, his explanation of the differences between the sexes was notable for its detail and essentialism, and represents a transitional stage between past scholasticism and empirical rationalism.[21] For Allestree sexual difference was systemic and rooted in nature. Women were naturally feeble, 'smooth and soft', but the softness of their natures made them predisposed to great piety, mercy and compassion. Nevertheless, following the authority of the ancients, he ultimately believed women were flawed beings, and the best correctives for their imperfect natures were modesty and chastity.[22] He also asserted that women were both intellectually and physically weaker than their male counterparts.

Allestree's descriptions illustrate that the new theory, in which men and women occupied separate spheres behaviourally and ontologically, did not alter the prevailing view that the body and temperament of a woman were inferior to those of a man. Even an avid proponent of the education of women, the bluestocking Margaret Cavendish, Duchess of Newcastle, espoused such modes of gendered thinking. In the preface to *The Worlds Olio* (1655), she described the 'great difference between the Masculine Brain and the Feminine'. Like Allestree, she used the rhetoric of 'nature' to make her point, stating that nature had created 'Mans Brain more clear to understand and contrive than Womans. ... Women can never have so strong Judgment nor clear Understanding nor so perfect Rhetorick.'[23] Both Allestree's and Cavendish's descriptions of gender traits clearly indicate that they believed and readily accepted the premise that men were superior: strong, rational, intelligent beings fit to rule over women by the virtue of their God-given 'natures'.

---

the Vertues, Vices, and Ordinary Means, of the Rise and Decay of Men and Families (London, 1665); William Ramesey, *The Gentlemans Companion: Or, a Character of True Nobility and Gentility* (London, 1672); S[arah] F[yge], *The Female Advocate: or, an Answer to a late Satyr against the Pride, Lust and Inconstancy, &c. of Woman* (London, 1686); George Savile, Marquis of Halifax, *The Lady's New-Years Gift, or, Advice to a Daughter* (London, 1688); Abel Boyer, *Characters of the Virtues and Vices of the Age; or Moral Reflections, Maxims, and Thoughts Upon Men and Manners* (London, 1695); and Lady Anne Halket, *Instructions for Youth* (Edinburgh, 1701).

21 Fletcher, *Gender, Sex, and Subordination in England*, pp. 383–4.

22 On Allestree's views of women see ibid., pp. 384–7.

23 Margaret Cavendish, *The Worlds Olio* (London, 1655), sig. A4r–v. For a discussion of Cavendish's fraught position within feminist scholarship, see John Rogers, *The Matter of Revolution: Science, Poetry, and Politics in the Age of Milton* (Ithaca and London: Cornell University Press, 1996), pp. 182–3. On her complicated views on gender (and her relationship to the work of Astell) see Catherine Gallagher, 'Embracing the Absolute: The Politics of the Female Subject in Seventeenth-Century England', *Genders* 1 (1988): 24–39. For an outline of her relationship to Hobbes, see Anna Battigelli, 'Political Thought/Political Action: Margaret Cavendish's Hobbesian Dilemma', in Hilda L. Smith (ed.), *Women Writers and the Early Modern British Political Tradition* (Cambridge: Cambridge University Press, 1998), pp. 40–55; and Battigelli, *Margaret Cavendish and the Exiles of the Mind* (Lexington: University of Kentucky Press, 1998).

The ongoing explication of distinct gender roles, the refashioning of patriarchal ideology and the reformulation of marriage all inform the theatrical milieu in which Purcell worked. The most obvious indication of these changes was the introduction of actresses onto the Restoration stage.[24] During the Elizabethan and Jacobean eras, the bodies of young boys were concealed under female garb, and therefore songs for female characters were performed by potentially volatile, cracking male soprano voices. Although women were barred from performing on the public stage for moral reasons, their replacement by boys masquerading as women caused another set of problems.[25] Anti-theatricalist William Prynne proclaimed in *Histriomastix* (1633):

> Yea witnes … *that Players and Play-haunters in their secret conclaves play the Sodomites:* together with *some moderne examples of such, who have been desperately enamored with Players' Boyes thus clad in womans apparell, so farre as to solicite them by words, by Letters, even actually to abuse them.*[26]

The fear of such 'abuses' was evident in the patent granted to Thomas Killigrew for his theatrical company on 25 April 1662, which made it possible for women to play female characters:

> And for as much as many plays formerly acted do contain several profane, obscene and scurrilous passages, and the women's parts therein have been acted by men in the habit of women, at which some have taken offence, for the preventing of these abuses in the future, we do hereby strictly command and enjoin that from henceforth … we do … permit and give leave that all the

---

24   Both the lack of trained boys as female impersonators following the Civil War and Commonwealth and changing views of gender contributed to the introduction of actresses after the Restoration. For the material reasons why women were introduced, see Michael Shapiro, 'The Introduction of Actresses in England: Delay or Defensiveness?', in Viviana Comensoli and Anne Russell (eds), *Enacting Gender on the English Renaissance Stage* (Urbana: University of Illinois Press, 1999), pp. 177–200.

25   Women did perform in courtly and public venues before the Restoration; for a useful discussion, see Pamela Allen Brown and Peter Parolin (eds), *Women Players in England, 1500–1660: Beyond the All-Male Stage* (Aldershot: Ashgate, 2005) and Sophie Tomlinson, *Women on Stage in Stuart Drama* (Cambridge: Cambridge University Press, 2005). On Anna of Denmark and female performance in masques, see Leeds Barroll, *Anna of Denmark Queen of England: A Cultural Biography* (Philadelphia: University of Pennsylvania Press, 2001), and Clare McManus, *Women on the Renaissance Stage: Anna of Denmark and Female Masquing in the Stuart Court 1590–1619* (Manchester: Manchester University Press, 2002). For recent discussions of Henrietta Maria as a patron and performer in masques and pastorals see Erica Veevers, *Images of Love and Religion: Queen Henrietta Maria and Court Entertainments* (Cambridge: Cambridge University Press, 1989), and Karen Britland, *Drama at the Courts of Queen Henrietta Maria* (Cambridge and New York: Cambridge University Press, 2006).

26   William Prynne, *Histriomastix: The Player's Scourge, or Actor's Tragedy* (London, 1633), pp. 211–12.

women's parts to be acted in either of the said two companies for the time to come may be performed by women, so long as their recreations, which by reason of the abuses aforesaid were scandalous and offensive, may by such reformation be esteemed not only harmless delight, but useful and instructive representations of human life.[27]

Despite the assurances of 'harmless delight' and 'useful and instructive representations of human life' found in the patent, the Restoration theatre was not known for its morality. In response to the new theatrical reality, playwrights and composers created stock roles, such as the libidinous rake, the suffering, loving wife and the bantering couple, to exploit opportunities for displaying heterosexual desire – sometimes quite graphically – in all its permutations.[28] During this period the protagonists of tragedies were often already married when the action began; comedies revolved around the attempt to secure marriage based on loving companionship rather than monetary gain.[29] Yet the use of actresses in women's

---

27 For Killigrew's patent see Public Record Office, London, PRO C66/3013, no. 20, quoted in Elizabeth Howe, *The First English Actresses: Women and Drama 1660–1700* (Cambridge: Cambridge University Press, 1992), pp. 25–6. As Shapiro notes, the patent, which was issued in 1662, codified a practice that had already been in place for several years; see 'The Introduction of Actresses in England', p. 187.

28 The scholarship on the influence of the actresses and the introduction of these character types is voluminous; what follows is a selection of some of the most frequently cited sources. On the rake and his meaning in Restoration culture see Harold Weber, *The Restoration Rake-Hero: Transformations in Sexual Understanding in Seventeenth-Century England* (Madison: University of Wisconsin Press, 1986); Richard Braverman, 'Libertines and Parasites', *Restoration: Studies in English Literary Culture, 1660–1700* 11 (1987): 73–86; and Braverman, *Plots and Counterplots: Sexual Politics and the Body Politic in English Literature, 1660–1730* (Cambridge: Cambridge University Press, 1993). The libertine rake was an ambivalent figure off-stage, sometimes being associated with unbridled sexual activity that spilled over into sodomy (as demonstrated in Ian MacCormick (ed.), *Secret Sexualities: A Sourcebook of Seventeenth- and Eighteenth-Century Writing* (London: Routledge, 1997), p. 105) or was used to criticize the arbitrary power possessed by Charles I; see Paul Hammond, 'The King's Two Bodies: Representations of Charles II', in Jeremy Black and Jeremy Gregory (eds), *Culture, Politics, and Society in Britain, 1660–1800* (Manchester: Manchester University Press, 1991). On the bantering, so-called 'gay couple' see John Harrington Smith, *The Gay Couple in Restoration Comedy* (New York: Octagon Books, 1971; first published Cambridge, MA: Harvard University Press, 1948); and Howe, *The First English Actresses*, pp. 66–74.

29 The predominant kind of newly written tragedy during Purcell's time was the 'she-tragedy'. While some feminist scholars have identified the 'she-tragedy' as a form designed to give women and their problems a voice, others have viewed it as another medium of oppression. For the former arguments see Staves, *Players' Scepters*, p. 172, and Howe, *The First English Actresses*, Chapter 5. For feminist critiques of she-tragedy see Pearson, *The Prostituted Muse*, p. 49; Laura Mandell, *Misogynous Economies: The Business of Literature in Eighteenth-Century Britain* (Lexington: University of Kentucky Press, 1999), Chapter 2; and Jean I. Marsden, *Fatal Desire: Women, Sexuality, and the*

roles often reinforced, rather than undermined, popular conceptions of the female nature as irrational, overly sexual and immoral: actress-singers literally embodied and gave voice to the vices society believed were inherent to their sex.[30]

Nevertheless, Restoration-era playwrights did not always reaffirm patriarchy and heterosexual courtship, and the women and men playing these roles were not mere puppets or victims. Various studies of the actress (and to a lesser extent the actor) demonstrate how their reputations and particular talents shaped both the drama and contemporary notions of gender and desire, including Kristina Straub's *Sexual Suspects*,[31] Elizabeth Howe's *The First English Actresses*, and, more recently, Cynthia Lowenthal's *Performing Identities on the Restoration Stage*,[32] Jean Marsden's *Fatal Desire*, and Gilli Bush-Bailey's *Treading the Bawds*.[33] Unfortunately, music – a crucial element on the Restoration stage – has largely been absent from these discussions. In fact, authors, composers and performers all played with normative notions of gender for the titillation and entertainment of their audiences, although this was a double-edged sword. From early in the Restoration era actresses made their names playing bawdy roles in comedies, cross-dressing (and sometimes singing and dancing) in breeches to show off their legs, which, under normal circumstances, were modestly hidden.[34] This performance practice increased their popularity, but it also caused them to be labelled as whores (an epithet that had some truth, as some actresses granted sexual favours to audience members in exchange for money, status and gifts). Other actress-singers such as Letitia Cross made their names by accentuating their sexual and musical charms: Purcell's famous feigned mad song 'From Rosy Bow'rs', performed by Cross when she was perhaps as young as 12 in Thomas D'Urfey's *The Comical History of Don Quixote*,

---

English Stage, 1660–1720 (Ithaca: Cornell University Press, 2006).

30   Actresses were an extremely popular innovation on the Restoration stage, and placing them in titillating situations brought in revenue for the playhouses. Their performances could also bring lucrative personal arrangements. Actresses Nell Gwyn and Moll Davies, both known for their singing and dancing, became mistresses of Charles II, and many other actresses had liaisons or left the stage altogether to become mistresses of noblemen. See Howe, *The First English Actresses*, p. 73, and Pearson, *The Prostituted Muse*, pp. 27–8. Katharine Eisaman Maus believes that the primary reason for the actresses' success was their sexual exploitation on and off stage; see '"Playhouse Flesh and Blood": Sexual Ideology and the Restoration Actress', *ELH: A Journal of English Literary History* 46 (1979): 595–617.

31   Kristina Straub, *Sexual Suspects: Eighteenth-Century Players and Sexual Ideology* (Princeton: Princeton University Press, 1992).

32   Cynthia Lowenthal, *Performing Identities on the Restoration Stage* (Carbondale: Southern Illinois Press, 2003).

33   Gilli Bush-Bailey, *Treading the Bawds: Actresses and Playwrights on the Late-Stuart Stage* (Manchester: Manchester University Press, 2006). These are but a few sources; the literature on the subject is vast.

34   On cross-dressing actresses, see John Harold Wilson, *All the King's Ladies: Actresses of the Restoration* (Chicago: University of Chicago Press, 1958) and Pat Rogers, 'The Breeches Part', in Paul-Gabriel Bouce (ed.), *Sexuality in Eighteenth-Century Britain* (Manchester: Manchester University Press, 1982), pp. 244–58.

The Third Part,[35] showcased the young singer's vocal talents even as she became a sexual object for the enjoyment of those in the audience.[36]

When Purcell was composing for the stage in the 1680s and 1690s, a number of new star actors and actresses had emerged who were extremely competent singers. Purcell composed music both for them and for the professional singers who had also begun to grace the stage during the same period. He wrote music for new tragedies – some in the 'she-tragedy' mould that featured female suffering – tragedies in revival (such as Dryden and Nathaniel Lee's bloodthirsty *Oedipus*), comedies by the prolific and profane Thomas D'Urfey and others, dramatick operas, and even the *sui generis* opera possibly first performed at court, *Dido and Aeneas*. The music Purcell wrote for these works was all inflected and affected by predominant notions of gender during his time.

As one might expect, the richest gendered readings of Purcell's music in the literature focus on his only all-sung opera, *Dido and Aeneas*. Several studies have considered how the gender of the performers affected the meaning or creation of the work, although many are problematic in that they assume that Dido's first performance was given at Josias Priest's boarding school for girls, a claim that is now acknowledged to be unsafe.[37] In her 1989 book-length study of the opera, Ellen Harris considers the all-girl performance context of *Dido* and suggests that the opera may have served a didactic or moralistic function for the schoolgirls who performed it at Josias Priest's school, teaching them about the dangers of extramarital affairs. While Harris's reading presupposes a boarding-school premiere, one could still read Priest's production as being didactic in nature, even if *Dido* was not originally conceived for this purpose.[38] In theory, the girls at Priest's school would have been expected to learn the proper mode of female comportment, although as Thomas D'Urfey's scandalous *Love for Money* (1691) illustrates, that did not always occur in practice.[39] Robert Mullally has also investigated the school performance of *Dido*, using the preface and epilogue of the Chelsea libretto to claim that the work must have had an all-female cast, although he does not attempt an interpretation of the work through this lens.[40] More recently, Judith Peraino has interpreted the work

---

35 Thomas D'Urfey, *The Comical History of Don Quixote. The Third Part. With the Marriage of Mary the Buxome* (London, 1696), p. 48.

36 For more on Cross's performance, see Amanda Eubanks Winkler, 'Gender and Genre: Musical Conventions on the English Stage, 1660–1705' (PhD dissertation, University of Michigan, 2000), pp. 224–31; and Baldwin and Wilson, 'Purcell's Stage Singers', pp. 124–5. For Cross's other roles, see Baldwin and Wilson, 'Purcell's Sopranos': 606–7.

37 Many scholars now believe *Dido* was first performed at court. Recent epistolary evidence discovered by Bryan White may imply that Purcell composed *Dido* for Priest's school after all, but, as White makes clear, the wording of the letter is not conclusive; see 'Letter from Aleppo: Dating the Chelsea School Performance of *Dido and Aeneas*', *Early Music* 37 (2009): 417–28. For more on this debate, see Chapter 5, pp. 174–5 and Chapter 6, pp. 223–4 above.

38 Ellen T. Harris, *Henry Purcell's 'Dido and Aeneas'* (Oxford: Clarendon, 1987).

39 Thomas D'Urfey, *Love for Money: Or, the Boarding School* (London, 1691).

40 Robert Mullally, 'A Female Aeneas?', *Musical Times* 130 (1989): 80–92.

from a lesbian perspective and suggests that *Dido* 'allows for the "working out" of the underlying homosexual dynamics at play in the homosocial environment of the boarding school'.[41] Expanding upon an idea first suggested by Roger Savage,[42] Peraino carries out a close reading of the relationship between Dido and the Sorceress. Whereas Savage read the Sorceress as the dark anti-self to Dido (and noted the connection between the scenes at court and coven, suggesting that Dido and the Sorceress might even effectively be played by the same singer), Peraino interprets their relationship as a homosexual sadomasochistic dyad. Although Peraino's reading is adventurous, it is deeply flawed: it is highly unlikely that Josias Priest and the girls at his boarding school would have thought about the work in these modern terms (for this reason, Michael Burden among others calls Peraino's approach 'wrong-headed').[43] Finally, one must mention Irena Cholij and Curtis Price's discovery that the role of the Sorceress was probably played by a man in the 1700 revival of the work at Lincoln's Inn Fields.[44] Although Cholij and Price do not contextualize this information within seventeenth-century theories on gender, their discovery, as we shall see below, stimulated subsequent research.

Another strand of criticism focuses particularly on the character of Dido, sometimes viewing her through early modern notions of femininity and sexuality. Through a close analytic reading of Dido's lament, Janet Schmalfeldt claimed that the heroine became the most compelling character in the opera. She was not the 'crazed' woman of Virgil's *Aeneid* (perhaps, as Schmalfeldt suggests, for political reasons); rather she became a self-sacrificing heroine through Purcell's ennobling music.[45] Wendy Heller argues on similar lines, reading Dido as a stoic heroine, connecting her portrayal to writings on female virtue by Tate and Montaigne.[46] Andrew Pinnock's interpretation, however, takes a different approach, using seventeenth-century parodies of the *Aeneid* to demonstrate that the retelling of the story (and the portrayal of Dido) was neither as decorous nor as moralistic as scholars such as Harris have claimed. Instead, according to Pinnock, Tate uses

41   Judith A. Peraino, 'I am an Opera: Identifying with Henry Purcell's *Dido and Aeneas*', in Corinne E. Blackmer and Patricia Juliana Smith (eds), *En Travesti: Women, Gender Subversion, Opera*, Between Men – Between Women: Lesbian and Gay Studies (New York: Columbia University Press, 1995), p. 127.

42   Roger Savage, 'Producing *Dido and Aeneas*', *Early Music* 4 (1976): 393–404; later republished as 'Producing *Dido and Aeneas*: An Investigation into Sixteen Problems', in *The Purcell Companion*, ed. Michael Burden (London: Faber, 1995; Portland, OR: Amadeus Press, 1995), pp. 445–68.

43   Michael Burden, '"Great Minds against Themselves Conspire": Purcell's Dido as a Conspiracy Theorist', in Burden (ed.), *A Woman Scorn'd: Responses to the Dido Myth* (London: Faber, 1998), pp. 243–4.

44   Curtis Price and Irena Cholij, 'Dido's Bass Sorceress', *Musical Times* 127 (1986): 615–18.

45   Janet Schmalfeldt, 'In Search of Dido', *Journal of Musicology* 18 (2001): 584–618.

46   Wendy Heller, '"A Present for the Ladies": Ovid, Montaigne, and the Redemption of Purcell's Dido', *Music & Letters* 84 (2003): 189–208.

vocabulary that readers of the travesty tradition would have recognized as being sexual or humorous.[47]

Beyond the juggernaut of *Dido and Aeneas*, other parts of Purcell's output have yet to be considered from the perspective of contemporary gender perceptions and are ripe for investigation. For example, a study of Purcell's comical dialogues – linked both to the action of the play and to the contemporary notions of patriarchy, courtship and marriage outlined above – would be particularly fruitful, since gendered behaviour was at its most subversive in the comedic tradition (one need only conjure the image of John Pate in drag singing the role of Mopsa in an early revival of *The Fairy Queen*). Here scholarship on gender, love relationships and Restoration comedy would be particularly useful. John Harrington Smith's classic study of the bantering 'gay couple' in Restoration comedy is a good starting point, but more recent studies such as Harold Weber's *The Restoration Rake-Hero*, which considers the relationship between male and female sexual libertinism in comedy and the larger Restoration culture, or J. Douglas Canfield's *Tricksters and Estates*, which examines seventeenth-century ideology in comedy, are invaluable resources for contextualizing the smutty banter frequently found in these duets.[48] Many feminist scholars such as Jacqueline Pearson, Elizabeth Howe and Pat Gill, have analysed the relationship between men and women in Restoration comedy, noting the ambiguous place women occupy in these works, as they simultaneously push sexual and moral boundaries yet serve as the butt of the playwrights' jibes about their supposedly unruly behaviour.[49]

An analysis of Purcell's on- and off-stage drinking songs and catches through a gendered lens would also be enlightening.[50] Men in Restoration comedy sometimes sang drinking songs or catches together, a behaviour that mirrored what was happening offstage in the homosocial environs of the catch club. The subject matter of Purcell's drinking songs is obvious, frequently extolling the pleasures of 'wine, women, and song'; the subjects of his catches, however, are broader, as Peter Holman has observed, ranging from the political ('Since the Duke is Return'd'), to the ages of man ('An Ape, a Lion, a Fox and an Ass'), to the blatantly sexual ('My

---

47   Andrew Pinnock, 'Book IV in Plain Brown Wrappers: Translations and Travesties of Dido', in Michael Burden (ed.), *A Woman Scorn'd: Responses to the Dido Myth* (London: Faber, 1998), pp. 249–71.

48   Harold Weber, *The Restoration Rake-Hero* and J. Douglas Canfield, *Tricksters and Estates: On the Ideology of Restoration Comedy* (Lexington: University of Kentucky Press, 1997).

49   Pearson, *The Prostituted Muse*, pp. 49–57, 83–118; Howe, *The First English Actresses*, pp. 37–90. This point comprises the central argument of Pat Gill's, *Interpreting Ladies: Women, Wit and Morality in the Restoration Comedy of Manners* (Athens: University of Georgia Press, 1994). See also many of the essays in Katherine M. Quinsey (ed.), *Broken Boundaries: Women and Feminism in Restoration Drama* (Lexington: University of Kentucky Press, 1996).

50   Linda Phyllis Austern considers the catch and homosociality in 'Music and Manly Wit in Seventeenth-Century England', in Rebecca Herissone (ed.), *Concepts of Creativity in Seventeenth-Century England* (Woodbridge: Boydell and Brewer, forthcoming).

Lady's Coachman, John').[51] Recent scholarship has sought to understand the catch within a rich social context. Catch clubs emerged in the mid-seventeenth century and, as Brian Robins described in his *Catch and Glee Culture in Eighteenth-Century England*, the meetings took place in:

> a hostelry of some description, ensuring the necessary juxtaposition of music making and a convivial atmosphere where drinking played an essential part in the entertainment, and the willing support of the landlord. Those who attended comprised both performer and auditor, but entry was restricted to males only.[52]

After the Restoration tradesmen and gentleman amateurs alike participated in catch culture,[53] although as Holman points out, Purcell's catches are quite difficult, and therefore may have been intended for 'professional musicians off-duty'.[54] In order to understand catch culture more fully within the context of early modern notions of masculinity, musicologists would do well to consult the pioneering work of Eve Kosofsky Sedgwick on homosociality and more recent studies by Thomas King and others on constructions of English masculinity during the Restoration period.[55]

Lamenting Melancholics

As with gender studies, a vibrant interdisciplinary literature investigating madness and melancholy in early modern England has flourished in the wake of new historicist methodologies and the growing field of cultural studies. This literature can be tremendously useful for a Purcell scholar interested in understanding the composer's laments and mad songs within the context of early modern ideas about

51   Peter Holman, *Henry Purcell*, Oxford Studies of Composers (Oxford: Oxford University Press, 1994), p. 30. See also the section 'Purcell's "Public" Music: Catches' in Chapter 6 above.

52   Brian Robins, *Catch and Glee Culture in Eighteenth-Century England* (Woodbridge: Boydell and Brewer, 2006), p. 13. See also Ian Spink's introduction to Henry Purcell, *Catches*, ed. Ian Spink, The Works of Henry Purcell, vol. 22a (London: Novello, 2000).

53   Robins notes that during the Civil War 'the exile of skilled musicians into inns and taverns following the closure of theatres and the mix of displaced professional musicians and gentleman enthusiasts … not only raised performance levels, but also introduced convivial music making to a new social class'; Robins, *Catch and Glee Culture*, pp. 10–11. For more on musical clubs, see Emanuel Rubin, *The English Glee in the Reign of George III: Participatory Art Music for an Urban Society* (Warren, MI: Harmonie Park Press, 2003), pp. 87–90.

54   Holman, *Henry Purcell*, p. 30.

55   See Eve Sedgwick, *Between Men: English Literature and Male Homosocial Desire* (New York: Columbia University Press, 1985); and Thomas A. King, *The Gendering of Men, 1600–1750, vol. 1: The English Phallus* (Madison: University of Wisconsin Press, 2004).

these afflictions. Although there is no evidence to suggest that Purcell was an avid reader of medical texts, many of the ideas described below were commonly known in early modern England. Mental illness has been considered from art-historical, medical-historical, theatre-historical and literary points of view, while Linda Austern and Penelope Gouk have analysed music's relationship to melancholy and madness in early modern culture.[56] According to Austern, Gouk and others, music was simultaneously a cause of, a symptom of and a cure for mental illness and thus it was a central part of seventeenth-century people's understanding of the disorder. As we shall see, gender also played a crucial role in the categorization and depiction of the various mental disorders seen on Purcell's stage.

Understanding and historicizing melancholy has been a preoccupation for literary scholars since at least the 1950s,[57] and the secondary literature on the subject is voluminous. The central text outlining an early modern perspective on the disease nevertheless remains Robert Burton's compendious *Anatomy of Melancholy*, first issued in 1621, but reissued numerous times throughout the seventeenth century.[58] Burton's encyclopedic work draws together learned and popular conceptions of melancholy, since the author quotes both hearsay and ancient authority in his tome. To describe the thinking of Burton and other contemporary writers such as André du Laurens (Laurentius), Timothy Bright and Gideon Harvey[59] is obviously beyond the scope of this chapter. At the risk of simplifying a tremendously complex topic, early modern beliefs on melancholy, which followed the premises of humoural theory, can be summarized as follows: four humours were believed to circulate throughout the body, and each was associated with a specific temperament:

---

56   Penelope Gouk, 'Music, Melancholy, and Medical Spirits in Early Modern Thought', in Peregrine Horden (ed.), *Music as Medicine: The History of Music Therapy since Antiquity* (Aldershot and Brookfield: Ashgate, 2000), pp. 173–94; Linda Phyllis Austern, '"For, Love's a Good Musician": Performance, Audition, and Erotic Disorders in Early Modern Europe', *Musical Quarterly* 82 (1998): 614–53; Austern, 'Musical Treatments for Lovesickness: The Early Modern Heritage', in Peregrine Horden (ed.), *Music as Medicine: The History of Music Therapy since Antiquity* (Aldershot and Brookfield: Ashgate, 2000), pp. 213–45; and Austern, '"No Pill's Gonna Cure My Ill": Gender, Erotic Melancholy, and Traditions of Musical Healing in the Modern West', in Penelope M. Gouk (ed.), *Musical Healing in Cultural Context* (Aldershot: Ashgate, 2000), pp. 113–36.

57   See, for example, Lawrence Babb, *The Elizabethan Malady: A Study of Melancholia in English Literature from 1580 to 1642* (East Lansing: Michigan State College Press, 1951).

58   The most recent scholarly edition is Robert Burton, *Anatomy of Melancholy*, eds Thomas C. Faulkner, Nicholas K. Kiessling and Rhonda L. Blair (6 vols, Oxford, 1989–2000).

59   T[imothy] Bright, *A Treatise of Melancholie* (London, 1586); Andreas Laurentius, *A Discourse of the Preservation of the Sight; of Melancholike Diseases; of Rheumes, and of Old Age* (London, 1599); James [Jacques] Ferrand, *Erotomania: Or a Treatise Discoursing of the Essence, Causes, Symptomes, Prognosticks, and Cure of Love or Erotique Melancholy*, trans. Edmund Chilmead (Oxford, 1640); Gideon Harvey, *Morbus Anglicus: Or, the Anatomy of Consumptions* (London, 1666). For a useful compendium of writings on melancholy by Pseudo-Aristotle, Galen, Avicenna, Ficino, Bright, Burton and others see Jennifer Radden (ed.), *The Nature of Melancholy: From Aristotle to Kristeva* (New York: Oxford University Press, 2000).

blood (sanguine), phlegm (phlegmatic), yellow bile (choleric) and black bile (melancholic). A person existed in a healthy state when the four humours were properly balanced; melancholy was caused by an overabundance of black bile in the body. Black bile could either naturally occur in excess in the body (as was the case in 'natural melancholy') or an excess of black bile could be produced through outside influences which overheated the body, causing it to burn one of the other humours, which created an 'adust' noxious, blackened version. This effect, caused by diet, lack of exercise and even the fires of love, could produce 'accidental' or 'unnatural' melancholy. Regardless of cause, the symptoms were the same: sighing, paleness, obsessive thoughts and lack of appetite, among others. In severe cases, melancholy could lead to madness – a complete break with reality.[60]

In general, melancholy tended to be the preserve of men, in particular learned men. The link between melancholia and masculine genius can be traced back to *Problemata XXX* by an author whom early moderns believed to be Aristotle (an attribution that has since been questioned). Pseudo-Aristotle asks 'Why is it that all men who have become outstanding in philosophy, statesmanship, poetry or the arts are melancholic, and some to such an extent that they are infected by the diseases arising from black bile, as the story of Heracles among the heroes tells?'[61] This question was taken up by Neoplatonists such as Ficino, who further linked melancholia with 'great men'. Of course, in the Elizabethan era this connection was widespread: composers such as John Dowland actively cultivated the idea of themselves as melancholic, yet remarkable, artists.[62] As Juliana Schiesari has shown, women, because of their 'defective' natures, were excluded from this kind of melancholy.[63]

While melancholics possessing special talents or insight were a frequent presence in Elizabethan and Jacobean drama (for example, Jaques in Shakespeare's *As You Like It* or the eponymous character in John Marston's *The Malcontent*), during the more cynical Restoration era this exalted sort of melancholy was largely neglected. Instead, playwrights focused on what Burton describes as love melancholy, also known as 'heroic melancholy' or, as French physician Jacques Ferrand termed it in the title of his well-known treatise on the subject translated into English in 1640, 'erotomania'. This malady could afflict both men and women,

---

60 For a lucid summary of the causes and effects of melancholy see Stanley Jackson, *Melancholia and Depression: From Hippocratic Times to Modern Times* (New Haven: Yale University Press, 1986).

61 From 'Problems Connected with Thought, Intelligence, and Wisdom', reproduced in Radden (ed.), *The Nature of Melancholy*, pp. 57–60.

62 See for example, Robin Headlam Wells, 'John Dowland and Elizabethan Melancholy', *Early Music* 13 (1985): 514–28; and Peter Holman, *Dowland: Lachrimae (1604)*, Cambridge Music Handbooks (Cambridge: Cambridge University Press, 1999).

63 See Juliana Schiesari, *The Gendering of Melancholia: Feminism, Psychoanalysis, and the Symbolics of Loss in Renaissance Literature* (Ithaca: Cornell University Press, 1992). Other feminist scholars have also analysed melancholy; see for example, Julia Kristeva, *Black Sun: Depression and Melancholy*, trans. Leon S. Roudiez (New York: Columbia University Press, 1989).

although the symptoms were believed to have different causes. Men who suffered from the affliction became deranged because of an overheating of their body by the passion of love, which burned the humours, producing a sludge and noxious fumes that clouded the brain. 'Erotomania' could become very serious, leading to delusion and even madness. Women's symptoms, on the other hand, were sexual in nature, and were sometimes thought be caused by an unruly womb, which wandered the body freely (an affliction known as *furor uterinus* or hysteria), filling their heads with vapours that rendered them distracted.[64] These sexually voracious women, out of control with desire, captured the early modern imagination and their suffering was transformed into art and musical entertainment, both on the continent and in England.

Erotomania undermined the masculinity of male sufferers, as men were supposed to be rational and in control of their passions.[65] Ferrand derisively calls male erotomaniacs 'effeminate weake spirited fellowes',[66] a description that I have argued applies to Aeneas' highly problematic behaviour in Purcell's *Dido and Aeneas*.[67] Scholars have long been puzzled by the character's perceived weakness and have often criticized Tate's portrayal.[68] However, while Aeneas behaves heroically elsewhere in the *Aeneid*, he does not cover himself in glory in Virgil's Book IV, and early modern English translators of the work essentially exploited and even amplified Aeneas' already present lovesick effeminacy. In the opera the character shows irrationality and a lack of discernment, as he first eschews his duty for pleasure and then, later, believes the false Mercury sent by the Sorceress. Purcell's tonally unstable music for the character accurately represents his irrational (ignoble) drive to consummate his desire for the queen: for example, the 'Trojan prince' slitheringly modulates to E minor as he declares, 'Aeneas has no fate but

---

64 Edward Jorden's *A Briefe Discourse of a Disease Called the Suffocation of the Mother* (London, 1603) focuses exclusively on this ailment. For a modern summary of the causes and effects of the disease, as well as its portrayal in art, see Laurinda S. Dixon, *Perilous Chastity: Women and Illness in Pre-Enlightenment Art and Medicine* (Ithaca: Cornell University Press, 1995). See also Ilza Veith, *Hysteria: The History of a Disease* (Chicago: University of Chicago Press, 1965).

65 On masculinity and the problem of effeminacy, see Fletcher, *Gender, Sex and Subordination in England*, pp. 83–98 and 322–46.

66 Ferrand, *Erotomania*, p. 215. Effeminacy was a term frequently used to refer to the behaviour of men who desired women too much, and thus became like them.

67 For my analysis of Aeneas' character, see Winkler, *O Let Us Howle Some Heavy Note: Music for Witches, the Melancholic, and the Mad on the Seventeenth-Century English Stage* (Bloomington: Indiana University Press, 2006), pp. 139–42.

68 Joseph Kerman famously refers to him as 'a complete booby' in 'A Glimmer from the Dark Ages', in Curtis Price (ed.), *Purcell: 'Dido and Aeneas' – An Opera*, Norton Critical Score (New York: Norton, 1986), p. 224 (originally published in Joseph Kerman, *Opera as Drama* (New York: Kopf, 1956)). See also Price's comment that he is 'a glorified pawn' in Curtis Price, *'Dido and Aeneas* in Context', in Price (ed.), *Purcell: 'Dido and Aeneas'– An Opera*, Norton Critical Score (London: Norton, 1986), p. 4.

you! / Let Dido smile, and I'll defy / The feeble stroke of Destiny'.[69] Later in the opera he sings a similar melismatic lamenting outburst as Dido does in her final lament ('Ah'), a musical gesture that marks his emotionality as being no different from that of his female counterpart.

Apart from in *Dido and Aeneas*, men suffering from erotomania lament their fate on the Restoration stage verbally: unless they run mad they do not usually burst into song. They are therefore saved from perpetuating their supposed emasculation, as music was thought to promote effeminacy.[70] Instead, their emotions are often given voice by boys, thought to be 'less perfect' according to early modern theories of gender, as they had not yet achieved sexual maturity and were therefore more like a woman in their temperament, being colder and wetter than adult men.[71] Purcell's 'Celia has a Thousand Charms', written for Robert Gould's *The Rival Sisters* (1695), exemplifies this tradition of the ventriloquized lament. The song is sung by a boy at the request of Alonzo and indicts the behaviour of Alonzo's supposedly fickle lover, Alphanta, in thinly veiled pastoral terms. The first half of the piece, a florid recitative, describes the ecstasy found in Celia's (that is, Alphanta's) welcoming arms. The second half of the song shifts into the language of lament as it portrays the effects of suspicion of the beloved's falseness, revealing Alonzo's bodily imbalance through sighing figures, as well as dissonant cross-relations and chromaticism. In essence, the boy replicates and explains through his music and text the symptoms and the reason for his master's affliction, literally internalizing Alonzo's pain. While Alonzo was spared the humiliation of public musical lamenting, he did not fully escape the emasculating effects of music. Seventeenth-century audiences would have understood that listening to music, particularly music sung by a boy in an alluringly high register, could actually stir up lust, befuddle the mind, and further unman the listener.[72] Indeed, Alonzo's affliction becomes worse upon hearing the boy's song, revealing his overly emotional, effeminized state as he rants:

---

69   Price reads this moment in similar terms, saying it 'herald[s] the intrusion of desire', in *'Dido and Aeneas* in Context', p. 26. I would claim desire had already intruded; see Dido's description of Aeneas in 'Whence could so much Virtue Spring?'. Harris rightly observes that Aeneas' music in his first two appearances is 'interruptive of the tonality of the scene' and she connects his unstable tonal presence to the disruptive role he plays within the dramatic fabric of the opera; *Henry Purcell's Dido and Aeneas*, p. 74.

70   Linda Phyllis Austern, '"Alluring the Auditorie to Effeminacie": Music and the Idea of the Feminine in Early Modern England', *Music & Letters* 74 (1993): 343–54.

71   Linda Phyllis Austern, '"No Women are Indeed": The Boy Actor as Vocal Seductress in Late Sixteenth- and Early Seventeenth-Century English Drama', in Leslie C. Dunn and Nancy A. Jones (eds), *Embodied Voices: Representing Female Vocality in Western Culture*, New Perspectives in Music History and Criticism (Cambridge: Cambridge University Press, 1994), pp. 86–7. See also Stephen Greenblatt's discussion of effeminacy and boys in *Shakespearean Negotiations: The Circulation of Social Energy in Renaissance England* (Oxford: Clarendon, 1988), p. 78 and Stephen Orgel, *Impersonations: The Performance of Gender in Shakespeare's England* (Cambridge: Cambridge University Press, 1996).

72   Austern, '"No Women are Indeed"', pp. 90–91.

I'm cold! I starve with cold!
My heart is turn'd to Ice with her Disdain!
Oh! It oppresses – but I'll tear it out.[73]

Women were the more frequent victims of erotomania on stage and, unlike their male counterparts, they often sang their own laments and almost always died from their unseen wounds. Following his Italian counterparts, Purcell frequently used a ground bass for these movements (for example, in the Plaint in *The Fairy Queen* and Dido's two laments in *Dido and Aeneas*). According to Ellen Rosand, who has analysed the lament tradition in Italian opera, the ground-bass aria, with its inherent repetition and opportunities for chromaticism and suspensions, was a perfect musical analogue of the obsessively painful thoughts of the grieving lover.[74] While scholars have long acknowledged Purcell's participation in the pan-European musical language of lament, until recently the place of these pieces within the larger discourse surrounding lovesickness has not been investigated. In the 1990s feminist musicologists such as Suzanne Cusick first began thinking about the lament as part of larger early modern discourses on women.[75] Others quickly followed; in fact, the whole August 1999 issue of *Early Music* was devoted to the subject of lament, but strangely, English musical traditions were not considered in this primarily Italianate group of essays.[76] Recent scholarship has investigated the English lament tradition in the seventeenth century more broadly, focusing on its musical and theatrical parameters and its connection to medicine and gender.[77]

Within this context, *Dido and Aeneas* has again received the most attention. Previously mentioned studies by Heller and Schmalfeldt focus heavily on Dido's famous final lament in their analyses, although they do not connect her utterance directly with the contemporary medical tradition; instead they praise Dido's stoic nobility as she succumbs to her 'fate'. Irving Godt believes quite the opposite: Purcell's Dido is a 'headstrong woman' who puts love before duty and therefore, according to 'the standards of the age' must be punished.[78] For Michael Burden, Dido is a problematic and unattractive figure, a 'conspiracy theorist' whose

---

73   [Robert] Gould, *The Rival Sisters: Or, the Violence of Love* (London, 1696), p. 14. For more on the ventriloquized lament tradition for men, see Winkler, *O Let Us Howle*, pp. 134–9. A similar tradition also existed for women on the earlier seventeenth-century English stage, but this tradition fell somewhat out of favour later in the century when proficient singing-actresses used laments as a showcase for their talents; ibid., p. 85.

74   Ellen Rosand, 'The Descending Tetrachord: An Emblem of Lament', *Musical Quarterly* 65 (1979): 346–59.

75   Suzanne G. Cusick, '"There Was Not One Lady Who Failed to Shed a Tear": Arianna's Lament and the Construction of Modern Womanhood', *Early Music* 22 (1994): 21–41.

76   *Early Music* 27/1 (1999).

77   Rebecca Crow Lister, '"Wild Thro' the Woods I'le Fly": Female Mad Songs in Seventeenth-Century English Drama' (DMA dissertation, Florida State University, 1997); Winkler, *O Let Us Howle*, Chapters 3 and 4.

78   Irving Godt, 'Purcell and Dido (and Aeneas)', *Studies in the History of Music* 2 (1988): 60–82, particularly p. 75.

suspicions and distrust cause her own 'spiritual' demise.[79] Other scholars, such as Curtis Price, puzzle over Dido's death, wondering why and how she dies: in Virgil's original tale, the queen of Carthage plunges a dagger into her chest, but in Tate's libretto she simply seems to wither away.[80]

Recently, I sought to understand Dido's death by placing the opera within a larger seventeenth-century cultural context. Both Burton and Ferrand considered Virgil's Dido to be an archetypal lovesick woman and her behaviour within Tate's opera is easily understandable if we view her as suffering from the affliction of erotomania. Ferrand describes the typical symptoms:

> And if the Lovers eyes be thus discomposed and out of order; how much more thinke you is his heart? For you shall see him now very jocund and laughing; and presently within a moment he falls a weeping, and is extreame sad: then by and by againe he entertaines himselfe with some pleasant merry conceipts, or other; and within a short space againe is altogether as sad, pensive, and dejected as before. This Passion you may observe drawn out to the life by *Virgill*, in his *Dido Aeneid*.4.[81]

Indeed, Tate and Purcell's Dido exhibits the wide mood-swings characteristic of the disorder as she veers from extreme, seemingly irrational sadness ('Ah! Belinda, I am pressed with torment') to lust ('Anchises's valour mix'd with Venus' charms') before her sexual consummation with Aeneas. After a brief period of contentment (sex was considered a sure cure for lovesickness),[82] she is thrust once again into irrationality when she learns of her lover's imminent departure. Although Aeneas vacillates about leaving, the imperious Dido sends him packing and the chorus that follows his departure diagnoses her problem in medical terms: she has shunned the cure she most desires. Her final lament, 'When I am Laid in Earth', serves as yet another signifier of her erotomania as it was an operatic genre associated almost exclusively with women deserted by their lovers. Singing this sort of music in fact perpetuates her problem, as its slow tempo and obsessive ground bass pattern sympathetically mimic the sluggish humour of black bile and the symptoms it produced. As Burton explains of those suffering from acute erotomania, 'Death is the common *Catastrophe* to such persons.'[83]

---

79 Burden, '"Great Minds against Themselves Conspire"', p. 237.
80 Price wonders if Dido dies at all; see *'Dido and Aeneas* in Context', pp. 39–41; Burden also notices this fascination with Dido's manner of death, claiming that the Virgilian original colours Purcell scholars' view of her demise; see '"Great Minds against Themselves Conspire"', pp. 235–6.
81 Ferrand, *Erotomania*, pp. 107–8.
82 For this reason, parents were encouraged to let their daughters marry; see Fletcher, *Gender, Sex and Subordination in England*, p. 52.
83 Burton, *Anatomy of Melancholy*, vol. 3, p. 199; for a fuller discussion of erotomania and Dido see Winkler, *O Let Us Howle*, pp. 105–13.

Madness

Madness has also been a focus of attention within early modern studies, as scholars both inside and outside the field of musicology have sought to historicize the trope of unreason. Michel Foucault's seminal study *Madness and Civilization* looms large in the study of madness,[84] and his theory – that notions of madness changed around 1656 when the Hôpital Général was founded in Paris – has affected many scholars who followed in his wake. According to Foucault, madmen wandered freely during the Middle Ages and were sometimes even thought to possess wisdom that others did not have. Gradually, unreason became more of a threat until establishments such as the Hôpital Général and Bedlam in London were founded to contain madness, separating the abnormal from the normal. Although some scholars quibble with the Francocentrism, ahistoricism and strict periodicity of Foucault's formulation, the attempt to understand early modern madness in historical, not modern post-Freudian terms has led scholars to carry out significant archival research, reading long-forgotten treatises on the subject.[85] Two of the primary studies on historical madness in England, Michael MacDonald's *Mystical Bedlam* of 1981 and Roy Porter's *Mind-Forg'd Manacles* of 1987, are still widely consulted by medical historians, literary scholars and musicologists.[86] As Porter notes, madness was an enormously broad category in seventeenth- and eighteenth-century England;[87] in Purcell's music, however, we generally encounter two sorts of madness: that caused by acute lovesickness (which produces musical raving rather than lamenting) and, to a far lesser extent, the madness of religious enthusiasm.

Ellen Rosand and Paolo Fabbri have identified the conventions for musical madness within seventeenth-century Italian opera and the English musical tradition is similar in many respects.[88] Madness is conveyed both through text (irrational

---

84   Michel Foucault, *Madness and Civilization: A History of Insanity in the Age of Reason*, trans. Richard Howard (New York: Vintage Books, 1988).

85   After praising Foucault's insight into the relationship between 'the normal' and the mad, Michael MacDonald declares, '[*Madness and Civilization*'s] major weaknesses are that abstractions confront abstractions in his book and his description of how real men and women thought and acted is often vague or fanciful. It is easier to grasp the shape of Foucault's personal vision of history than it is to see how actual people interpreted madness and how they treated the insane persons whom they encountered'; *Mystical Bedlam: Madness, Anxiety, and Healing in Seventeenth-Century England* (Cambridge: Cambridge University Press, 1981), p. xi. Roy Porter has also criticized Foucault's assertion that after the mid-century people did not experience the mad because they were locked away, demonstrating instead that people had frequent exposure to the mad and the sad, and even viewed their plight as instructive; see Roy Porter, *Mind-Forg'd Manacles* (London: Athlone, 1987).

86   In his classic study, MacDonald analyses the records of physician Richard Napier, who treated over 2,000 mentally disturbed patients between 1597 and 1634, revealing seventeenth-century attitudes towards those suffering from mental illness.

87   Porter, *Mind-Forg'd Manacles*, p. x.

88   Ellen Rosand, 'Operatic Madness: A Challenge to Convention', in Steven Paul Scher

delusions, mythological allusions, references to bodily distress) and music (strange harmonic progressions, unprepared and angular leaps, dissonances, rapid shifts of metre and affect). However, only recently have scholars considered why these musical conventions developed, how they represent the symptoms of madness, and what the music can tell us about conceptions of insanity within the larger culture. In the section that follows I discuss scholarship in three areas: lovesick madness (a species of the erotomania described above); music as a cure for madness; and the madness of religious fanaticism, often called 'enthusiasm' in contemporary discourses.

Lovesick Madness

Just as lovesickness was gendered as a feminine or effeminizing disorder in medical treatises, so musical lovesickness was gendered during the Restoration, with different modes of mad behaviour for men and women. Rebecca Lister was the first to identify and explore this gender divide in madness in her DMA dissertation, although she primarily focused on the plight of on-stage musical madwomen.[89] Others soon followed her lead, identifying specific dramatic and musical conventions associated with male and female mad songs.

Some of Purcell's finest mad songs were composed for male characters and, as I have explained elsewhere, these musical madmen behave quite differently from their female counterparts.[90] While madmen do not die from their affliction, they do not escape unscathed. They are gently mocked by onlookers and are generally portrayed as effeminate: for example, in Thomas D'Urfey's *A Fool's Preferment* (1688), the stage direction describes the unhappy lover Lyonel 'crown'd with Flowers, and Antickly drest, sitting on a Green Bank'. Here we see the effeminizing effect of madness – Lyonel has, Ophelia-like, bedecked himself with a garland of flowers. It was far more problematic for a man to behave in this way than for a woman. As William Mountfort, the actor who portrayed Lyonel, demurs in the epilogue to the play:

> Fond of his Art; the Poet has to day
> Mistook, and made me mad the silliest way;
> Pride, Wealth, or Wine, may Frenzy often move:
> But that's a strange Brute that runs mad for Love,

(ed.), *Music and Text: Critical Inquiries* (Cambridge: Cambridge University Press, 1992), pp. 241–87; Paolo Fabbri, 'On the Origins of an Operatic Topos: The Mad-Scene', in Iain Fenlon and Tim Carter (eds), *Con Che Soavità: Studies in Italian Opera, Song, and Dance, 1580–1740* (Oxford: Clarendon, 1995), pp. 157–95.

89   Lister, '"Wild Thro' the Woods I'le Fly"', pp. 52–4.

90   For a fuller discussion of male musical madness in the seventeenth century see Winkler, *O Let Us Howle*, Chapter 4.

Few now, Thank Heaven, such lewd examples find,
'Tis forfeiting the Charter of our Kind.[91]

In Purcell's series of mad songs for this play, one of his first forays into theatrical writing, one can see the musical tropes of male madness emerging, as Lyonel veers wildly between delusions of grandeur ('I'll Sail upon the Dog Star'), lamentation ('I Sigh'd and I Pin'd') and misogyny ('There's Nothing so Fatal as Woman'). Notably, Lyonel's beloved, Celia, must listen to these songs; thus, Lyonel's madness, while emasculating, actually functions as a punishment for the woman who left him.[92] To return to D'Urfey's epilogue:

> Shall Men have all, and Women no remorse?
> Then let the Cart hereafter drag the Horse.
> Let each Eve wrest the Scripture false, and swear;
> She was not made for Man, but Man for Her;
> No, this had been a most unpardon'd Crime;
> Did not the Lady here repent in time.[93]

Purcell's other famous madman, Cardenio in D'Urfey's *The Comical History of Don Quixote, Part I* also follows the pattern established in *A Fool's Preferment*. Cardenio, raving because of the desertion of Luscinda, sings 'Let the Dreadful Engines', in which the series of affects presented in Lyonel's airs are contracted into one long multisectional *tour de force*, in this case for the talented actor-singer John Bowman. Indeed, the musical virtuosity and extreme contrasts found in this air are characteristic of the genre.

Women suffer lovesick madness, both feigned and real, far more frequently on the Restoration stage. Given the prominent presence of female mad songs in this period, it is surprising that Purcell wrote relatively few examples compared to his contemporary John Eccles, but this is probably because Eccles composed music for the most celebrated portrayer of erotomania, the actress-singer Anne Bracegirdle. Still, Purcell's first mad song, 'From Silent Shades' (Bess of Bedlam), is for a woman, and although it was not intended for the theatre it still incorporates the common musical tropes associated with mad songs: rapidly shifting affects and delusions of grandeur coupled with *double entendres*.[94] The music and text of this piece resonated

91 Thomas D'Urfey, *A Fool's Preferment, or the Three Dukes of Dunstable* (London, 1688), p. [86].
92 Celia was also a victim: she was forced to leave her beloved by the king, who made her a 'gift' to his favourite; see Winkler, *O Let Us Howle*, p. 152. Curtis Price erroneously states that Celia leaves Lyonel for the king; see *Henry Purcell and the London Stage* (Cambridge: Cambridge University Press, 1984), p. 156.
93 D'Urfey, *A Fool's Preferment*, p. [86].
94 Although not written for a play, 'Bess of Bedlam' was performed in the theatres. According to the play-text of *A Fool's Preferment*, Lyonel sings two snippets from the piece, and singers in the eighteenth century often performed it on stage. On 'Bess' and *A Fool's Preferment*, see Olive Baldwin and Thelma Wilson, 'A Purcell Problem Solved',

with larger cultural notions of disorder: as Peter Holman claims, 'Bess of Bedlam' is textually and musically related to 'Mad Tom of Bedlam', which incorporates a Jacobean masque tune.[95] Although 'Bess' undoubtedly bears a musical resemblance to 'Mad Tom', Dolly MacKinnon, who reads 'Bess' through the lens of seventeenth-century notions of madness, has found the direct textual source for 'From Silent Shades': the poem/ballad 'Mad Maulkin' which dates from 1682, the year before 'Bess' was published.[96] Yet another source for Purcell's female mad songs can be found in the *double-entendre*-filled ballads of differing affects sung by Ophelia in Shakespeare's *Hamlet*. The lovesick Ophelia, singing madly before her death, had a tremendous influence on theatrical portrayals of madness, and it seems likely that well-known theatrical precedents informed Purcell's practice as well.[97]

Still, theatrical female madness signified differently from a song performed in a concert or domestic setting: costumes, stage action and the theatrical context all coloured audience perceptions of the piece. Such is the case with Purcell's final mad song 'From Rosy Bow'rs', from *The Comical History of Don Quixote, The Third Part*. As I explained above, the young Letitia Cross performed the piece, and while her madness was feigned, her behaviour incorporated all the typical tropes of female madness, including sexual profligacy. As she declares:

> Younger I'm sure by far [than Dulcinea] – Perhaps too young; but I'll so swell my Breasts, and heave and fall, and mould 'em with my Hands to make 'em grow – pull down my Stays, that they may shew themselves, and Jett it up and down.[98]

In this context, as I have argued elsewhere, 'From Rosy Bow'rs' is simply the musical icing on the erotically charged cake, as D'Urfey and Purcell exploited notions of female sexual and musical excess so common in portrayals of lovesick madness.[99] This song proved to be tremendously popular, and, detached from its theatrical context, enjoyed a long afterlife, as Patricia Köster has shown, in eighteenth-century women's fiction, where it was used to suggest 'female weakness'.[100]

Musical Times 122 (1981): 445; and on the song's popularity on the stage in the eighteenth century, see Baldwin and Wilson, 'Purcell's Mad Songs in the time of Handel, Haydn and Mendelssohn' (Unpublished paper presented at conference Purcell, Handel, Haydn, Mendelssohn: Anniversary Reflections, Oxford, 27–29 March 2009), and also Chapter 8, pp. 321–2 below.

95 Holman, *Henry Purcell*, pp. 40–41. Holman identifies the melody as a Jacobean masque tune, 'Gray's Inn Masque'.

96 Dolly MacKinnon, '"Poor Senseless Bess, Clothed in Her Rags and Folly": Early Modern Women, Madness, and Song in Seventeenth-Century England', *Parergon* 18 (2001): 119–51.

97 See Winkler, *O Let Us Howle*, Chapter 3.

98 D'Urfey, *The Comical History of Don Quixote. The Third Part*, p. 48.

99 Winkler, 'Gender and Genre', pp. 224–5.

100 Patricia Köster, 'Purcell's Swan Song: A Long Reverberation in Women's Fiction', in Thomas R. Cleary (ed.), *Time, Literature and the Arts: Essays in Honor of Samuel L. Macey*

Music as a Cure

One area of Purcell's *oeuvre* that has been neglected thus far is his music designed to cure lovesickness or to flee from it. Just as music could perpetuate melancholic diseases, it was also thought to mitigate their effects, as Linda Austern and Penelope Gouk have shown. Gouk explains:

> Music was recognized as having a particular affinity with the passions of the mind. These were thought to lie midway between the reason and the sense, and were responsible for bringing about alterations in the body's humours.[101]

Thus appropriate mirthful music might stir the passions, sympathetically promoting bodily harmony through its harmonious sounds by altering the mood of the listener and restoring his humoural balance. That Purcell was aware of music as a curative agent seems clear; it was frequently used as such in Restoration drama and he set several texts to music that use medicalized language. For instance, in the jaunty 'I Attempt from Lovesickness to Fly' from *The Indian Queen* (1695), Purcell provides the appropriate music for curing melancholic disorders (swift-moving music to counteract sluggish black bile), although the text claims the impossibility of cure (the singer flies in 'vain'). Another example of a Purcellian song to purge melancholy is the catch ''Tis Women make us Love', whose simple style, C major tonality and 6/4 metre Austern reads as an antidote for the disorder. Although the text laments the sadness women bring and the madness caused by alcohol, 'here the singers have it all: … mirth, strong drink, a merry company (of fellow sufferers) to join in a witty celebration of the purgation of the madness and sadness arising from heterosexual love.'[102] Obviously, more research can be done in this area: long ago Robert Noyes and then Curtis Price noted the prevalence of scenes of curative music on the Restoration stage and thus a more thorough study of this element seems overdue.[103]

Religious Enthusiasm

A third type of musical madness was sometimes represented on the English stage, although with far less frequency than lovesickness: religious enthusiasm. Like melancholy, such enthusiasm was thought to have positive and negative properties.

(Victoria: University of Victoria, 1994), pp. 140–56.

101 Gouk, 'Music, Melancholy, and Medical Spirits', p. 185. See also Austern, '"No Pill's Gonna Cure my Ill"'; Austern, 'Musical Treatments for Lovesickness'.

102 Austern, 'Musical Treatments for Lovesickness', p. 239.

103 Robert Gale Noyes, 'Conventions of Song in Restoration Tragedy', *Proceedings of the Modern Language Association* 53 (1938): 162–88; and Curtis A. Price, *Music in the Restoration Theatre: with a Catalogue of Instrumental Music in the Plays 1665–1713*, Studies in Musicology, vol. 4 (Ann Arbor: UMI Research Press, 1979), p. 22.

The ancients believed that one could have access to spiritual insight through ecstatic communion with the divine – Plato's notion of divine furor. These ideas were spread during the Renaissance by Neoplatonists such as Marsilio Ficino, Heinrich Cornelius Agrippa and others. For them, divine furor facilitated enlightenment and artistic achievement.[104] However, such practices fell out of favour among mainstream religious figures in mid-to-late seventeenth-century England. Radical Protestants used communion with the divine to support their own disruptive political agendas during the Civil War, Commonwealth and Protectorate.[105] Their sectarianism drew fire from members of the Church of England, who sought to discredit the prophecies that they believed had contributed to dissent, regicide, revolution and the suppression of their Church.[106] Even earlier in the century, writers such as Burton had begun to conflate enthusiasm with melancholy as a way of discrediting this mode of religious experience.[107] Meric Causabon, Henry More and others treated enthusiasm with similar disdain and recently I have argued that we should think about musical enthusiasm on the Restoration stage not through a classical humanistic lens, but rather in the context of these anti-enthusiastic discourses.[108]

Purcell's song of musical enthusiasm, Cumana's 'Beneath a Poplar's Shadow' from an early 1690s revival of Nathaniel Lee's *Sophonisba*, supports this assertion. Rather than Cumana being genuinely infused with the divine, speaking genuine prophecy, both Purcell and Lee portray her as a lunatic. The musical rhetoric of her song, with its rapid shifts of affect, subverts musical logic. These elements, while characteristic of enthusiastic speech (which featured hyperbole and extreme disjunctiveness), are also associated with the musical and rhetorical conventions of the mad song.[109] Indeed, 'Beneath a Poplar's Shadow' is labelled a 'mad song' in Purcell's *Orpheus Britannicus*, Book 2.[110] Still, much work remains to be done on

---

104 Gary Tomlinson, *Music in Renaissance Magic: Toward a Historiography of Others* (Chicago: University of Chicago Press, 1993), pp. 65 and 172–3; and Gretchen Ludke Finney, *Musical Backgrounds for English Literature: 1580–1650* (New Brunswick: Rutgers University Press, 1962), pp. 47–75.

105 The religious situation in mid-to-late seventeenth-century England is too complicated to explain fully here, but for a lucid summary, see Horton Davies, *Worship and Theology in England from Andrews to Baxter and Fox, 1603–1690*, Worship and Theology in England, vol. 2 (Princeton: Princeton University Press; London: Oxford University Press, 1975).

106 Keith Thomas, *Religion and the Decline of Magic* (London: Weidenfeld and Nicolson, 1971), p. 144.

107 In volume 3 of *The Anatomy of Melancholy*, Burton devotes a whole section to 'religious melancholy'.

108 Amanda Eubanks Winkler, 'Enthusiasm and Its Discontents: Religion, Prophecy, and Madness in the Music for *Sophonisba* and *The Island Princess*', *Journal of Musicology* 23 (2006): 307–30.

109 On enthusiastic speech, see Clement Hawes, *Mania and Literary Style: The Rhetoric of Enthusiasm from the Ranters to Christopher Smart* (Cambridge: Cambridge University Press, 1996), p. 11.

110 For a fuller discussion of on-stage representations of musical enthusiasm, see Winkler, 'Enthusiasm and Its Discontents': 307–30.

the actual musical practices of dissenters and how mainstream perceptions of their rituals affected on-stage performance.

Magic and Witchcraft

Cumana's enthusiastic scene with its blood-magic and bizarre ritual can also be viewed within the tradition of seventeenth-century scenes of witchcraft and incantations.[111] As Phyllis Mack has noted, 'female sectarians were frequently depicted as witch figures, animalistic creatures who were never seen to think but whose bodies secreted polluted substances as false notions.'[112] During a period filled with religious conflict and tumult such notions proved particularly potent, especially for those invested in shoring up religious orthodoxy. However, we must be careful not to use the term 'witch' indiscriminately, for within Purcell's *oeuvre* there are at least two distinct kinds of magic user: sorcerers and sorceresses who use their learned magic to call up spirits, demons and ghosts; and hag-type witches who cackle excessively, and almost comically, at their evil-doing. Often, as Linda Austern has observed of early seventeenth-century theatre music, these categories break down along gender lines, with male sorcerers more often participating in an ancient noble tradition and female magic-users resorting to the dark arts to work their charms.[113] While Purcell and his contemporaries often treat these categories of magic user quite differently in musical and dramatic terms, there is considerable overlap between the two.

The first category of magician is treated with more seriousness than his hag-like counterpart, possibly in part because elites had a long-standing engagement with learned magical traditions. Penelope Gouk has demonstrated that there was in fact a significant overlap in seventeenth-century England between older magical practices and the new experimental science.[114] Descended from a noble Neoplatonic line stretching from Ficino through Agrippa, this sort of magus could uncover and manipulate the occult (hidden) secrets of creation. He made his way onto the stage in works such as Shakespeare's *The Tempest*. Neoplatonists such as Ficino believed that the adept could unlock the secrets of the natural and supernatural realms with the correct sort of sympathetic music. As D.P. Walker and Gary Tomlinson have shown, music was thought to have the power to call

---

111 On the connection between *Macbeth* and *Sophonisba*, see Thomas B. Stroup and Arthur L. Cooke, 'Introduction to *Sophonisba*', in *The Works of Nathaniel Lee*, eds Thomas B. Stroup and Arthur L. Cooke, vol. 1 (New Brunswick: Scarecrow Press, 1954), p. 76.

112 Phyllis Mack, *Visionary Women: Ecstatic Prophecy in Seventeenth-Century England* (Berkeley: University of California Press, 1992), p. 48.

113 Linda Phyllis Austern, '"Art to Enchant": Musical Magic and Its Practitioners in English Renaissance Drama', *Journal of the Royal Musical Association* 115 (1990): 191–206.

114 Gouk, *Music, Science, and Natural Magic in Seventeenth-Century England*. For more on learned magic in early modern England and its relationship to scientific enquiry, see Thomas, *Religion and the Decline of Magic*.

forth spirits or demons, summoning them with harmonious musical strains.[115] On the seventeenth-century English stage this Neoplatonic ethos was frequently combined with pagan ritualistic behaviour, including in *Oedipus*, *The Indian Queen* and *The Indian Emperour*.[116]

Although the philosophical tradition dictated that the learned magus might use music as an incantatory device, within the stage tradition these enchanters and enchantresses are not consistently singing characters, although the spirits, demons and ghosts they summon often are.[117] However, when they do sing, their music is complex – a demonstration of their rhetorical skill. Ismeron's remarkable incantation, 'Ye twice Ten Hundred Deities' in *The Indian Queen* (1695) is a good example of this trope, since Purcell here uses mimetic declamatory air and quasi-liturgical language to summon the reluctant God of Dreams.[118] Purcell and the playwrights writing these scenes drew on the religious music and liturgical formulas they knew. Although these practices were distorted by paganism (and were thus clearly inferior to Christianity according to the ethos of Purcell's time), they are presented seriously, even nobly, on stage. Indeed, Purcell accords some of his finest and most complicated music to these scenes of conjuration: a prime example can be found in the music he wrote for a 1692 revival of John Dryden and Nathaniel Lee's *Oedipus*, which features contrapuntal choruses (sometimes using responsorial effects) as well as the famous air for alto priest, 'Music for a While', set to one of the most bizarre ground basses in Purcell's *oeuvre*.[119] While the conjuration scene has elements aligned with witchcraft (they are, after all, summoning the 'sullen powers below' and the ghost of the deceased Laius), its solemn style separates it from the witches' music discussed below. Steven Plank and I have studied these conjuration scenes within a larger cultural and theatrical context, but much remains to be done in this area in order to uncover the multiple ways seventeenth-century audiences may have understood these scenes. Did their quasi-liturgical language give them

---

115 D.P. Walker, *Spiritual and Demonic Magic: From Ficino to Campanella* (Notre Dame: University of Notre Dame Press, 1975); Tomlinson, *Music in Renaissance Magic*.

116 These types of magic-user carried over from the English Renaissance stage; on the earlier tradition, see Austern, '"Art to Enchant"', and Sarah Williams, '"Now Rise Infernal Tones": Representations of Early Modern English Witchcraft in Sound and Music' (PhD dissertation, Northwestern University, 2006).

117 On this sort of incantation scene in Restoration drama, see Amanda Eubanks Winkler, 'Sexless Spirits?: Gender Ideology and Dryden's Musical Magic', *Musical Quarterly* 93 (2010): 297–328, and Steven E. Plank, '"And Now About the Cauldron Sing": Music and the Supernatural on the Restoration Stage', *Early Music* 18 (1990): 392–407.

118 Plank, '"And Now About the Cauldron Sing"': 402. In a recent essay, James A. Winn points out the poetic indebtedness of Ismeron's charm to the witches' charms in *Macbeth*: the 'weird sisters' of Shakespeare's play chant in trochaic tetrameter 'a heavy, hypnotic verse form'. Ismeron's 'Ye twice Ten Hundred Deities' is primarily in tetrameter, and contains a trochaic section in the middle, but the charm shifts to trochees for 'By the Croaking of the Toad'; see Winn, 'Dryden's Songs', p. 294.

119 For more on this scene see Winkler, 'Gender and Genre', pp. 100–114.

an anti-Catholic flavour, as Plank has suggested,[120] or were they interpreted as a less-perfect precursor to the fully realized Christian faith, as some Dryden scholars have claimed?[121] Perhaps audiences at the time would have recognized both strands in Purcell's musical settings of these ritualized texts.

Far more attention has been paid both within and outside of the field of musicology to the so-called 'hag' type witch: the base creature who supposedly relied on a nefarious pact with the Devil to accomplish her evil deeds. Understanding this sort of witch from an anthropological, sociological, historical and particularly a theatrical/literary perspective is helpful for Purcell scholars seeking to interpret the wayward sisters in *Dido* and the female sorcerers featured in *Circe* and *Dioclesian*. Historians have tackled the question of witches and witchcraft from several viewpoints. Some have attempted localized studies (of Lancashire and Scotland),[122] while others have cast the net more broadly, considering witchcraft and witch-hunting in England over the course of a century or more.[123] Recent witch scholarship has focused on the reasons why witch-hunts were undertaken, exploring who was persecuted and why, and what ideological purposes the figure of the witch served within early modern culture.

Scholars have arrived at several answers, as Robin Briggs suggests in his article, '"Many Reasons Why": Witchcraft and the Problem of Multiple Explanation'.[124] In this insightful essay Briggs assesses the work of those who preceded him, claiming that monothematic explanations (that the state sought to curtail popular beliefs through witch-hunting, enforcing their own Christian notion of the sacred in its attempt to eradicate paganism) simply do not work for our understanding of

---

120 Plank, '"And Now About the Cauldron Sing"': 400.

121 See the writings of J.M. Armistead, particularly 'The Occultism of Dryden's "American" Plays in Context', *Seventeenth Century* 1 (1986): 127–52.

122 See for example Edgar Peel and Pat Southern, *The Trials of the Lancashire Witches: A Study of Seventeenth-Century Witchcraft* (New York: Taplinger, 1969); Alan Macfarlane, *Witchcraft in Tudor and Stuart England: A Regional and Comparative Study* (London: Routledge and Kegan Paul, 1970); Brian P. Levack, 'The Great Scottish Witch Hunt of 1661–1662' *Journal of British Studies* 20 (1980): 90–108; and Julian Goodare (ed.), *The Scottish Witch-Hunt in Context* (Manchester: Manchester University Press, 2002).

123 Wallace Notestein, *A History of Witchcraft in England from 1558 to 1718* (New York; Russell and Russell, 1965; first published Washington: American Historical Association, 1911); H.R. Trevor Roper, *Religion, the Reformation and Social Change: The European Witch-Craze of the Sixteenth and Seventeenth Centuries and Other Essays* (New York: Harper, 1969); Christina Larner, *Witchcraft and Religion: The Politics of Popular Belief* (New York: Blackwell, 1984); James Sharpe, *Instruments of Darkness: Witchcraft in England, 1550–1750* (London: Hamish Hamilton, 1996); and Stuart Clark, *Thinking with Demons: The Idea of Witchcraft in Early Modern Europe* (Oxford: Oxford University Press, 1997). One classic study that encompasses witchcraft, Thomas's *Religion and the Decline of Magic*, still has a significant influence on witchcraft studies.

124 Robin Briggs, '"Many Reasons Why": Witchcraft and the Problem of Multiple Explanation', in Jonathan Barry, Marianne Hester and Gareth Roberts (eds), *Witchcraft in Early Modern Europe: Studies in Culture and Belief* (Cambridge: Cambridge University Press, 1996), pp. 49–63.

witchcraft.[125] Instead he suggests a multicausal approach that takes into account localized situations and disconnects the mode of and impetus for prosecution from the practices (or supposed practices) of the purported witch. In the 1990s feminist scholars did much to enhance our understanding of this complicated issue. According to Francis Dolan's *Dangerous Familiars*, which considers historical and literary discourses about domestic crime, the witch was but another sort of criminal: a familiar person within a village or domestic setting who somehow broke communal codes of behaviour. As Dolan explains:

> the conflict often began when a poor, elderly, unmarried woman demanded charitable assistance and was denied; those who denied her, fearing her bitterness and vengefulness, ameliorated their panic and guilt by turning the tables: They accused her of bewitching them.[126]

Deborah Willis takes a slightly different approach in *Malevolent Nurture*, positing a psychological reason for the accusation that goes beyond mere guilt: taking her cue from the theories of Melanie Klein, she believes that witchcraft accusations stemmed from pre-Oedipal anger against the mother. Children, according to this theory, always resent their mothers because they can never fully meet their narcissistic needs.[127] While some critics have taken Willis to task for assuming static notions of childhood (that is, applying twentieth-century post-Freudian theory to early modern culture), she is surely correct to view the witch as a deformed maternal figure, one who, as Gail Kern Paster has observed, allows demonic familiars to suckle corrupted matter from an extra teat rather than nourishing children.[128]

Many accused witches of personal or domestic malfeasance – deaths of livestock, agricultural failures, infanticide, causing bodily harm or impotence – and they were also thought to cause large-scale societal problems, threatening those in power as they undermined or usurped legitimate government.[129] Diane Purkiss has particularly focused on this strand of belief, demonstrating how accusations of witchcraft were deployed to vilify the opponent during the Civil

---

125 This idea was first put forward by Thomas in *Religion and the Decline of Magic*. As Briggs notes, subsequent scholars have flattened the nuances of his argument.

126 Francis E. Dolan, *Dangerous Familiars: Representations of Domestic Crime in England, 1550–1700* (Ithaca: Cornell University Press, 1994), p. 172.

127 Deborah Willis, *Malevolent Nurture: Witch-Hunting and Maternal Power in Early Modern England* (Ithaca: Cornell University Press, 1995).

128 Gail Kern Paster, *The Body Embarrassed: Drama and the Disciplines of Shame in Early Modern England* (Ithaca: Cornell University Press, 1993), p. 249.

129 As Stuart Clark notes, witches could reinforce the status quo, shoring up authority; however, during periods when 'when circumstances rendered the structures of authority unstable and vulnerable to challenge', they might perform a subversive role; see Clark, *Thinking with Demons*, p. 25. However, as Clark cautions, focusing only on the social function of such behaviours limits us: we must also consider how witchcraft was made intelligible. Clark argues that rigid social structures and hierarchies must be in place in order for people to recognize the 'inversion' of witchcraft; see ibid., pp. 25–6.

War (even Cromwell was labelled a witch).[130] Of course the impulse to regard witches as usurpers did not begin with this mid-century conflagration. As Purkiss has shown, discourses of the witch as a subverter of 'natural' hierarchies and masculine privilege had a long history both on and off stage (one need only think of Shakespeare's *Macbeth* for an example of the prototypical witch as malevolent sponsor of bad government – a role William Davenant makes explicit in his Restoration-era revision of the work when the witches sing a celebratory chorus of 'We shall Rejoice when Good Kings Bleed').[131]

The reasons for indicting witches in the early modern period were complicated and multicausal and the supposed crimes perpetrated by these women were also varied; it is unproductive to believe that our ancestors were simply duped into believing in things that we, from our position of enlightenment, know do not exist. While many did believe in the existence of witches, from James I at the beginning of the century to Joseph Glanvill at the end of it, opinion on witches was by no means univocal.[132] Even in the late sixteenth century Johannes Weyer and Reginald Scot questioned whether the sorry old women prosecuted for witchcraft were actually capable of magic. Instead, they suggest, these decrepit creatures may have been suffering from melancholic delusions. As Scot states:

> For as some of these melancholike persons imagine, they are witches, and by witchcraft can worke wonders, and doo what they list: so doo others, troubled with this disease, imagine manie strange, incredible, and impossible things.[133]

This scepticism about the existence of witches increased over the course of the seventeenth century, and by Purcell's time many in elite society no longer believed in witchcraft, a situation lamented by Glanvill, who declares in *Saducismus Triumphatus* (1681): 'And those that know any thing of the World, know, that most of the looser *Gentry*, and the small pretenders to *Philosophy* and *Wit*, are generally deriders of the *belief of Witches* and *Apparitions*.'[134] Indeed, Glanvill had reason to

---

130 Diane Purkiss, 'Desire and Its Deformities: Fantasies of Witchcraft in the English Civil War', *Journal of Medieval and Early Modern Studies* 27 (1997): 103–32; and Purkiss, *The Witch in History: Early Modern and Twentieth-Century Representations* (London: Routledge, 1996), pp. 199–230. Anthony Harris also covers this terrain in *Night's Black Agents: Witchcraft and Magic in Seventeenth-Century English Drama* (Manchester: Manchester University Press, 1980), a book well known to Purcell scholars. While this is still a useful study, feminist scholars have done much to complicate and nuance the arguments Harris made.

131 On Davenant's witches see Winkler, *O Let Us Howle*, Chapter 2 and Amanda Eubanks Winkler (ed.), *Music for Macbeth*, Recent Researches in the Music of the Baroque Era, vol. 133 (Middleton: A-R Editions, 2004).

132 King James the First, *Daemonologie* (Edinburgh, 1597); Joseph Glanvill, *Saducismus Triumphatus: Or Full and Plain Evidence Concerning Witches and Apparitions* (London, 1681).

133 Reginald Scot, *Discouerie of Witchcraft* (London, 1584), pp. 52–3.

134 Glanvill, *Saducismus Triumphatus*, sig. F3r.

worry about the disbelief of his contemporaries, but, as Ian Bostridge (a brilliant interpreter of Britten and Purcell and a noted historian of witchcraft) has shown in *Witchcraft and its Transformations*, after the Glorious Revolution 'Catholicism with all its horrors (dominion by grace, absolutism, equivocation) replaces the witch as the defining outsider.'[135] This conflation of witches and Catholics did not, however, begin with the Glorious Revolution. It has even been suggested that Shakespeare's 'weird sisters' were nasty political lampoons of the Jesuits who had just attempted to blow up Parliament as part of the thwarted Gunpowder Plot.[136]

So what effect did this conglomeration of beliefs – the witch as deformed and grotesque mother figure, the witch as manipulator and thwarter of desire, the witch as usurper of monarchical privilege, the witch as deluded melancholic, the witch as Catholic – have upon Purcell's witches, the witches in *Dido and Aeneas*? As Steven Plank and I have both observed, the Sorceress seems to occupy a slightly different plane from her jolly troop of followers.[137] With her expert musical rhetoric and the use of the special texture of accompanied recitative, she seems to transcend the base category of witch, at least upon her first appearance in Act II ('Wayward Sisters'). Yet her text still uses common tropes found in other conjuration scenes, including its references to 'ravens' (recalling Davenant's revision of *Macbeth*) and calls to 'appear' (occurring in numerous conjuration scenes including the one from *Oedipus*). When she appears in Act III, her essential feminine irrationality has overtaken her as she gleefully cackles in the rhythmically off-kilter 'Our next Motion'. Despite this lapse,[138] in general the Sorceress possesses a certain gravitas, making her a worthy adversary to the Queen of Carthage.

The members of her coven, however, are humorous creatures and many scholars have puzzled over their seemingly light-hearted musical rhetoric (Jack Westrup famously commented 'the choruses are jolly rather than frightening').[139] Indeed, modern audiences frequently laugh at the witches' antics. Seventeenth-century audiences, however, would not have been confused: the witches' behaviour was perfectly in keeping with long-standing musical/theatrical conventions for witchcraft. Witches generally sang light-hearted, major-key music that often incorporated dance rhythms, particularly those of the rustic jig. They often showed their lack of mastery of rhetoric as they spouted nonsense sounds ('Ho, ho, ho') and took special glee in subverting authority figures, showing an unmotivated hatred for their betters.

Complicating our interpretation of these witches is the long-standing performance convention whereby hags were played by male actors. From

---

135 Ian Bostridge, *Witchcraft and Its Transformations, c.1650–c.1750* (Oxford: Clarendon, 1997), pp. 102–3.
136 Garry Wills, *Witches and Jesuits: Shakespeare's Macbeth* (New York: Oxford University Press, 1995), particularly pp. 35–49.
137 Plank, '"And Now About the Cauldron Sing"': 398; Winkler, *O Let Us Howle*, p. 59.
138 Price and Cholij suggest this tune may not have been sung by the Sorceress; see 'Dido's Bass Sorceress': 617.
139 For a summary of these queries, see Winkler, *O Let Us Howle*, p. 55.

Shakespeare's *Macbeth* into the eighteenth century, men often took witches' roles not just in *Dido* (the bass Wiltshire performed the role of the Sorceress in the 1700 interpolation of the opera into Gildon's *Measure for Measure*),[140] but also in John Eccles's and Richard Leveridge's music for Hecate in *Macbeth* (John Bowman sang Eccles's music; Leveridge and/or Marcellus Laroon the Leveridge version).[141] Given the travesty performance tradition and their 'jolly' music, were these witches meant to be taken seriously? As I have argued elsewhere, while musical and dramatic conventions emerged to marginalize the witches or demonstrate their subversion, their popularity suggests that audiences were entertained by their antics. After all, Nahum Tate *added* the Sorceress and her coven to Virgil's *Dido* story. Dolan suggests (somewhat simplistically in my opinion) that the comical treatment of witches shows a reluctance to take them or their powers seriously – they are presented as rustic bumpkins, hicks, definitively separated from the urban elite.[142] But as Freud noted long ago, people sometimes laugh at what scares them.[143] And if we believe the numerous scholars who have discussed the conflation of witches with Catholics, perhaps by laughing at the witches in *Dido*, English audiences would have exorcised some of their fears of Catholicism, even though, disturbingly, the Sorceress and her coven triumph in the end.

While *Dido*, as always, has received a vast amount of attention, other works would benefit from a more nuanced reading of their musical content within the broader musical/theatrical context of other magic users. For example, Purcell wrote some puzzlingly cheerful C major music for the Act I conjuration scene in a revival of Charles Davenant's *Circe*, where the eponymous sorceress asks her priestly minions to conjure demons and Pluto, the god of the underworld. And Maximinian mocks the 'holy druid' Delphia in *Dioclesian*, questioning her powers and describing her in grotesque terms often applied to witches ('she sits grunting at us, / And blowing out her Prophecies at both Ends').[144] Her devils and furies cavort to infernal, but – in the case of the 'Butterfly Dance' – harmonically complex music, and at the end of the play her power is subordinated to masculine will: she must conjure a masque to apologize for her trouble-making.[145] How are such characters positioned within the witch/learned sorceress matrix? These cases are certainly ambiguous and would benefit from additional exegesis.

---

140   As noted on p. 301 above, this observation was first made by Cholij and Price in 'Dido's Bass Sorceress'.

141   Winkler (ed.), *Music for Macbeth*, pp. 98–9.

142   Dolan, *Dangerous Familiars*, p. 217. She also suggests, perhaps correctly, that humorous on-stage portrayals of witchcraft defused the perceived real-life threat of maleficium, thereby saving women's lives.

143   Sigmund Freud, *Jokes and Their Relation to the Unconscious*, trans. James Strachey (New York: Norton, 1960), pp. 289–90.

144   Quotation taken from Act I, Scene ii, lines 276–7; see Julia Muller's edition, 'Thomas Betterton, *The Prophetess: Or, the History of Dioclesian*', in Michael Burden (ed.) *Henry Purcell's Operas: The Complete Texts* (Oxford: Oxford University Press, 2000).

145   For a discussion of *Circe* and *Dioclesian* through a gendered lens, see Winkler, 'Gender and Genre', pp. 131–43.

Purcell's Music in Context

This chapter has laid out some of relationships between scholarship on Purcell's music and larger cultural discourses about gender, mental illness and witchcraft. A sceptic might wonder if Purcell was aware of these larger cultural discourses and, even if he was, to what extent they informed his musical practices. Of course we cannot know what Purcell read, but we do know that, at the very least, he knew the texts he was expected to set. These texts, as many of the interdisciplinary scholars discussed above have shown, clearly participated in larger cultural discourses about gender, melancholy and madness, and witchcraft in early modern England. Purcell, as a gifted composer whose livelihood was in part dependent upon the success of his works, would have wanted to set these texts appropriately, and so he crafted music that conveyed their meaning or affect. In doing so, he shaped his audience's perceptions. His catches helped men perform masculinity appropriately, challenging them to sing difficult music even when in their cups; his comedic, bantering duets cast a sometimes-cynical eye toward romance, the rollicking tunes only partially ameliorating the sometimes subversively sour messages of the texts; his laments promoted audience sympathy for the lamenter, even as he turned cries of pain into aesthetically pleasing musical entertainment (the pornography of grief); his mad songs for men and women reinforced notions of male irrationality and effeminacy and female sexual voraciousness through their rapidly shifting affects, even as the actors and actresses who performed them got to show off their considerable musical talents; his conjurors were rendered in familiar and recognizable quasi-liturgical terms as they conjured their pagan gods, elevating their musical discourse; and his witches, while jolly and comedic on the surface, perhaps masked deeper cultural anxieties over unruly women and usurpation of power. By continuing these efforts to understand Purcell not just in musical and stylistic terms but also in broader cultural terms, we will enrich our comprehension of our Orpheus Britannicus and the musical decisions he made.

Performance History and Reception

Rebecca Herissone

For many composers other than Purcell, the study of reception has long since been what Jim Samson has described as a standard 'part of the tool-kit of historical research', so that even rudimentary textbooks usually include some consideration of reception within the broader narrative of composer- or work-based studies.[1] Yet even the most thoughtful and forward-looking volumes of this type within the Purcellian literature stop more or less dead in 1695,[2] and it is probably fair to say that – despite some important exceptions that will be considered in this chapter – consideration of the broader context in which Restoration music was heard, disseminated and appropriated by later generations and came to shape our own perceptions of it today has been largely overlooked within the narratives attached to Purcell's music. This situation has potentially serious consequences because it has become clear for composers whose reception has been more thoroughly investigated just how profound an effect posthumously developed opinions about their music can have on subsequent reception to the present day. As this chapter will demonstrate, the 'afterlife' of Purcell's music is no exception in this respect.[3]

---

1   Jim Samson, 'Reception', in *Grove Music Online*, http://www.oxfordmusiconline.com (last accessed 27 August 2009). Samson mentions in particular the Cambridge Music Handbooks series, which has yet to include a volume on a work by Purcell.

2   See, for example, Peter Holman, *Henry Purcell*, Oxford Studies of Composers (Oxford: Oxford University Press, 1994), as well as Peter Holman and Robert Thompson, 'Purcell: (3) Henry Purcell (ii)' in *Grove Music Online*, http://www.oxfordmusiconline.com (last accessed 27 August 2009).

3   The term 'afterlife', which Dahlhaus attributes to Walter Benjamin, is intended here to connote both performance of Purcell's works (with related activities such as the publishing of editions), and their critical reception; I would not go so far as to agree with Dahlhaus's definition, which is that that the term refers to 'the evolution of [art works'] inner truths, which, especially in major works, remain largely latent at first and only gradually come to light'. See Carl Dahlhaus, *Foundations of Music History*, trans. J.B. Robinson (Cambridge, London and New York: Cambridge University Press, 1983), p. 155.

As is well known, the most significant and substantial body of work on reception within musicology has focused on nineteenth-century composers (Beethoven, Wagner, Schumann, Chopin), although Bach reception has also been studied in detail. While the predominant emphasis on figures from the Germanic tradition is perhaps a straightforward reflection of the origins of reception study in German literary scholarship,[4] the emphasis on figures active within the last 200 years has a more practical explanation: there are distinct advantages to considering reception of this relatively recent music, since the body of evidence – particularly surviving critical opinion – is so much greater than for earlier periods when published reviews and appreciations were rare and preservation of material haphazard. Attempting a comprehensive study of the reception of a seventeenth-century composer like Purcell is an inherently difficult task, since sources from the first century of his 'afterlife' are limited and are often more factual than critical. Nevertheless, a relatively extensive range of primary sources and databases has been readily available for some time – notably Michael Tilmouth's 'Calendar of References to Music in Newspapers published in London and the Provinces (1660–1719)',[5] *The London Stage*, which catalogues theatrical productions in London theatres to the end of the eighteenth century,[6] and all the most significant British eighteenth-century historical writings on music, including those in manuscript by Thomas Tudway[7] and Roger North,[8] and of course Burney's and Hawkins's published

---

4   See the references to Hans Robert Jauss's theories in Chapter 2 of Robert C. Holub, *Reception Theory: a Critical Introduction*, New Accents Series (London: Routledge, 2003; first published London: Methuen, 1984).

5   Michael Tilmouth, 'A Calendar of References to Music in Newspapers published in London and the Provinces (1660–1719)', *Royal Musical Association Research Chronicle* 1 (1961): ii–vii, 1–107; 2 (1962): 1–15.

6   *The London Stage, 1660–1800*, eds William van Lennep, Emmet L. Avery, Arthur H. Scouten, et al. (11 vols, Carbondale: Southern Illinois University Press, 1960–68). More limited catalogues were published previously in Alfred Jackson, 'Play Notices from the Burney Newspapers, 1700–1703', *Proceedings of the Modern Language Association* 48 (1933): 815–49, and, specifically relating to performances of Purcell, Eric Walter White, 'Early Theatrical Performances of Purcell's Operas, with a Calendar of Recorded Performances, 1690–1710', *Theatre Notebook* 23 (1958–59): 43–65. Higney also provides an extensive appendix to his thesis listing references to Purcell and his music in London newspapers from 1683 to 1771; see John Higney, 'Henry Purcell: A Reception/Dissemination Study, 1695–1771' (PhD dissertation, University of Western Ontario, 2008), pp. 278–382.

7   Tudway's historical introductions to the volumes of sacred music he compiled for Lord Harley are partially transcribed in Christopher Hogwood, 'Thomas Tudway's History of Music', in Christopher Hogwood and Richard Luckett (eds), *Music in Eighteenth-Century England: Essays in Memory of Charles Cudworth* (Cambridge: Cambridge University Press, 1983), pp. 19–48.

8   Most of North's historical memoirs were published in John Wilson (ed.), *Roger North on Music: Being a Selection from his Essays Written during the Years c.1695–1728* (London: Novello, 1959), but his edition has since been superseded by Mary Chan and Jamie C. Kassler (eds), *Roger North's The Musicall Grammarian 1728*, Cambridge Studies in Music

General History volumes.[9] In addition, a selection of more recent comments on Purcell was made readily available by Michael Burden in his *Purcell Remembered* of 1995.[10] It is surprising, indeed, that so little has been made in studies of Purcell's music of the considerable scholarly effort that has been expended on compiling these primary materials. In the last decade the work of gathering information on performances, editions and opinion has become considerably easier through the creation of a fully searchable form of the Retrospective Index to Music Periodicals, and the digitization of a wide range of complete primary texts of journals and newspapers. These electronic resources make comprehensive research possible for the first time, and recent trends correspondingly show studies of Purcell reception and the performance history of his music to be growing in both number and volume, although the published literature remains small.

The first substantial investigation of Purcell's posthumous fortunes, an essay that remains central to any assessment of his reception today, was Richard Luckett's '"Or Rather Our Musical Shakespeare": Charles Burney's Purcell' of 1983, which, despite the title, in fact sketches much of the earlier reception history of the composer in the eighteenth century as well as Burney's account.[11] Prior to this publication there were probably only three studies that touched on aspects of Purcell's reception, and two of those did so only by implication: Eric Walter White's account of the 1700 adaptation of *Dido and Aeneas* as a series of insertions between acts of Charles Gildon's production of *Measure for Measure* focused primarily on how this version can inform us about differences between surviving sources of the opera and its original form, but did not consider what the incorporation of *Dido* into a public-stage production five year's after Purcell's death tells us about Purcell's reputation at the time;[12] and Margaret Laurie's important exposé of the misattribution of the music from *The Tempest* to Purcell convincingly established the cause of the mistake – the 1786 score published by Harrison and co., which probably followed the designation to Purcell given in a manuscript source of *c.*1750 – but again did not fully explore why Purcell's name might have become attached to the music in the eighteenth century in preference to those of other composers

---

(Cambridge: Cambridge University Press, 1990).

9   Charles Burney, *A General History of Music from the Earliest Ages to the Present Period*, ed. Frank Mercer (2 vols, New York: Dover, 1957; first published London: Foulis, 1935); John Hawkins, *A General History of the Science and Practice of Music*, reprinted with a new introduction by Charles Cudworth (2 vols, New York: Dover, 1963; first published London: Novello, 1853).

10 Michael Burden, *Purcell Remembered* (London and Boston: Faber, 1995), pp. 80–83, 99, 105–9, and 118–71.

11 Richard Luckett, '"Or Rather Our Musical Shakspeare": Charles Burney's Purcell', in Christopher Hogwood and Richard Luckett (eds), *Music in Eighteenth-Century England: Essays in Memory of Charles Cudworth* (Cambridge: Cambridge University Press, 1983), pp. 59–77.

12 Eric Walter White, 'New Light on *Dido and Aeneas*', in Imogen Holst (ed.), *Henry Purcell (1659–95): Essays on his Music* (London: Oxford University Press, 1959), pp. 14–34.

associated with the piece.[13] This leaves only the article by Alec Hyatt King on Benjamin Goodison's abortive attempt to publish a complete edition of Purcell's works around 1789.[14] Although King's essay is very brief, it provides a valuable first glimpse of the way in which Purcell's works were included in early attempts to imbue music with a historical context through the publication of modern editions of 'ancient' repertory – albeit by an amateur of no great editorial talent who was probably capitalizing on Arnold's burgeoning Handel edition and who was unable to muster sufficient support for his edition to be completed.

Luckett's essay, however, gives a much fuller contextualization of Purcell's reputation in the eighteenth century, focusing particularly on the evidence that suggests Purcell's fortunes gradually declined as the century progressed. While this perception is now being challenged in some quarters,[15] Luckett's identification of the central documents, events and individuals that help us to understand Purcell's reception in the century after his death form the foundation for most later research in the field. To this should be added important contributions by four other scholars: Ellen Harris was the first to consider the posthumous performance history of a work by Purcell in her 1989 book *Henry Purcell's 'Dido and Aeneas'*, which was also the only publication at the time to include research into performances from the nineteenth century and beyond; this was complemented by her study of the eighteenth-century staged performances of *King Arthur* in *Purcell Studies*,[16] and both pieces of research are notable for their detailed accounts of the alterations and adaptations that were made to Purcell's music for later productions and concerts. Michael Burden's research has also been primarily in the field of performance history, but until recently his focus has been on the staged productions of the dramatick operas in the late nineteenth and twentieth centuries – particularly Edward Gordon Craig's *Dido and Aeneas* of 1900 and the Covent-Garden production of *The Fairy Queen* of 1946.[17] Like Harris he considers interpretation and

---

13 Margaret Laurie, 'Did Purcell set *The Tempest?*', *Proceedings of the Royal Musical Association* 90 (1963–64): 43–4 and 46. Laurie does point out, however, that the copyist of the mid-eighteenth-century manuscript, Ob Tenbury 1266, may have been confused by the inclusion in the *Tempest* music of 'Dear pretty Youth', a single song that is by Purcell and is attributed to him in *Orpheus Britannicus*.

14 Alec Hyatt King, 'Benjamin Goodison and the First "Complete Edition" of Purcell', in Richard Baum and Wolfgang Rehm (eds), *Musik und Verlag: Karl Vötterle zum 65. Geburtstag* (Kassel: Bärenreiter, 1968), pp. 391–6.

15 In his thesis, discussed below, John Higney perceives a shift in Purcell's fortunes rather than a straightforward decline; see 'Henry Purcell: A Reception/Dissemination Study', pp. 207–8.

16 Ellen T. Harris, '*King Arthur*'s Journey into the Eighteenth Century', in Curtis Price (ed.), *Purcell Studies* (Cambridge: Cambridge University Press, 1995), pp. 257–89.

17 Michael Burden, '"Gallimaufry at Covent Garden": Purcell's *The Fairy Queen* in 1946', *Early Music* 23 (1995): 268–84; Burden, 'Purcell's Operas on Craig's Stage: the Productions of the Purcell Operatic Society', *Early Music* 32 (2004): 443–58. More recently Burden has been researching performance of Purcell's operas in the eighteenth century: see, for example, Michael Burden, 'Purcell's *King Arthur* in the 1730s', *Restoration: Studies in*

adaptation, in particular assessing the way in which the dramatick operas have been misinterpreted and misunderstood by producers more used to grand opera than seventeenth-century part-sung, part-spoken works.[18] In contrast, William Weber's important book of 1992, *The Rise of Musical Classics in Eighteenth-Century England*,[19] placed Purcell among other composers within the broader context of the developing historicization of music in the eighteenth century and the political situations that influenced the people who became involved in that process. Finally, Andrew Pinnock's 'The Purcell Phenomenon' from 1995, although brief, is so far the only published account of Purcell's posthumous history to include general consideration of the nineteenth and twentieth centuries.[20]

The marked emphasis on theatrical productions and concert performances in the existing literature has been balanced to some extent in recent years by new contributions, such as Christopher Hogwood's assessment of editions of Purcell's keyboard music from Goodison to the twentieth century,[21] and Alan Howard's perceptive analysis of the reception of Purcell's instrumental music.[22] Indeed, the emphasis on reception by both Howard and John Higney in his 2008 PhD thesis, 'Henry Purcell: A Reception/Dissemination History, 1695–1771' – to date the only dissertation focusing exclusively on the posthumous history of Purcell's music – indicates a burgeoning interest in this field among scholars educated during the post-Kerman era. The number and strength of papers on Purcell's performance history and reception at the March 2009 conference Purcell, Handel, Haydn, Mendelssohn: Anniversary Reflections[23] suggests that such research is also being cultivated more broadly, and that a more complete account of the afterlife of Purcell's music is a real possibility. Nevertheless, research on this topic currently

---

English Literary Culture, 1660–1700 34 (2010): 117–38.

18   Michael, Burden, 'Purcell Debauch'd: The Dramatick Operas in Performance', in Michael Burden (ed.), *Performing the Music of Henry Purcell* (Oxford: Clarendon, 1996), pp. 145–62.

19   William Weber, *The Rise of Musical Classics in Eighteenth-Century England: a Study in Canon, Ritual and Ideology* (Oxford: Clarendon, 1992).

20   Andrew Pinnock, 'The Purcell Phenomenon', in Michael Burden (ed.), *The Purcell Companion* (London: Faber, 1995; Portland, OR: Amadeus Press, 1995), pp. 3–17. Burden's *Purcell Remembered* does also include brief commentaries on the selected extracts, which include nineteenth- and twentieth-century writings, but Burden does not seek to provide a narrative or fully to contextualize the cited excerpts.

21   Christopher Hogwood, 'Creating the Corpus: The "Complete Keyboard Music" of Henry Purcell', in Christopher Hogwood (ed.), *The Keyboard in Baroque Europe* (Cambridge and New York: Cambridge University Press, 2003), pp. 67–89.

22   This forms Chapter 1 of Howard's thesis, 'Purcell and the Poetics of Artifice: Compositional Strategies in the Fantasias and Sonatas' (PhD dissertation, King's College, London, 2006), pp. 14–71.

23   The conference was held at New College, Oxford, from 27–29 March 2009 and included papers on Purcell reception and performance history by Olive Baldwin and Thelma Wilson, Michael Burden, John Higney, Andrew Pinnock and Will Lingard, Vanessa Rogers, and Sandra Tuppen. I am grateful to them all for agreeing to provide copies of their unpublished papers for use in this book.

remains relatively fragmented. The purpose of this chapter is to draw together the strands of scholarship focusing on the performance history and reception of Purcell's music in the existing literature – in particular to collect and reflect on ideas and interpretations that have been expressed in diverse sources – in order to create a more rounded picture of the factors that have contributed to current perceptions of the composer, and to identify and consider aspects of research on this topic that have so far been neglected.

Purcell and the Restoration Context

A cursory glance at the popular literature on Baroque music, the available commercial recordings and modern editions makes abundantly clear the extent to which Purcell's reputation has outlasted those of his Restoration colleagues, even though many of them – particularly John Blow – were also highly esteemed in their lifetimes and held prestigious posts. Famously, indeed, the eulogy to Purcell by his fellow former chorister at the Chapel Royal, Henry Hall, published in *Orpheus Britannicus* in 1698, claimed 'Yet only *Purcell* e're shall <u>equal</u> *Blow*'.[24] The fundamental question we need to ask when considering Purcell's reception, therefore, is why his music entered the historical canon when theirs did not. Although detailed comparison between the posthumous fortunes of the music of Restoration composers has not yet been carried out, the key to the answer has been highlighted by a number of scholars: the major shift in Purcell's compositional activities and employment circumstances in the last five years of his life, following the Glorious Revolution and the decline of court music-making under William and Mary.[25] The transformation of Purcell's career from traditional, patronage-based

---

24 Henry Hall, *'To the Memory of my Dear Friend Mr.* Henry Purcell', in Henry Purcell, *Orpheus Britannicus: A Collection of all the Choicest Songs for One, Two, and Three Voices* (London, 1698), p. vi (my emphasis underlined). This line was used by Bruce Wood as the inspiration behind an analysis of ways in which Purcell's music may have been influenced by Blow's recent compositions in 'Only Purcell e're shall equal Blow', in Curtis Price (ed.), *Purcell Studies* (Cambridge; Cambridge University Press, 1995), pp. 106–44. There may, however, be an element of disingenuousness to Hall's sentiment here, since Oliver Pickering revealed in an article of 1994 that Hall's elegy was adapted from two earlier poems in tribute to Purcell that survive in manuscript, and that all the references to Blow in the 1698 printed version were later additions, apparently made by Hall in an attempt to curry favour with Blow who had, of course, become the pre-eminent composer in England following Purcell's death. See Oliver Pickering, 'Henry Hall of Hereford's Poetical Tributes to Henry Purcell', *The Library: The Transactions of the Bibliographical Society* 16 (1994): 27–8. Higney analyses in detail Hall's poem in 'Henry Purcell: A Reception/Dissemination Study', pp. 66–72, but does not draw significance from Pickering's observations.

25 See Pinnock, 'The Purcell Phenomenon', pp. 4–5 and cf. also the remarks to this effect in Pinnock's and Amanda Eubanks Winkler's chapters in this volume, pp. 165–6 and

employment at court to the commercial life of the musical entrepreneur – a new world in which 'those with an eye to the future were busy reinventing themselves as self-employed, self-directing professionals'[26] – not only brought his music outside the confines of court and chapel to a wider audience, but also gave it frequent exposure in the press, and made it prime material for cheap prints bought for use in the home by an even broader public. It showed him to be a flexible composer, as happy producing verse anthems as lengthy operas and simple catches, and able to produce music for all available outlets within his environment,[27] including the genres of entertainment that were to grow in importance as the public consumption of culture grew after his death. All these factors – his adaptability, his public face and his published output – combined to ensure his longevity into the eighteenth century and beyond.

Of course, Purcell did not set out to create a lasting reputation for himself, coming as he did from a tradition in which music was 'composed, used, and discarded':[28] in his lifetime it was virtually unheard of for the music of a composer who had been dead for a century still to be performed. But the effects of his personal career shift gave him a distinct advantage over his contemporaries who had not moved into the new commercial sphere: in becoming a musical entrepreneur he anticipated the new direction in which England's cultural production was moving, and therefore produced music that was in genres that became increasingly popular after his death and that was disseminated through the most widespread channels. As the momentum created by the decline of court patronage in the 1690s continued to grow throughout the eighteenth century, so the burgeoning forms of public theatre and concert for which Purcell had composed music became the mainstay of musical activities, creating a long-term outlet for his works, which were readily available to interested parties because they already existed in print. There were, as Higney has pointed out, many parts of Purcell's output that did not fit within the new environment and that were not preserved into the eighteenth century,[29] but

---

pp. 269–70. The broader picture of the rise of the entrepreneur as the cultural significance of the English court declined in the last years of the seventeenth century is well known, and is alluded to in, among others, Weber, *The Rise of Musical Classics*, pp. 7–9; R.O. Bucholz, *The Augustan Court: Queen Anne and the Decline of Court Culture* (Stanford: Stanford University Press, 1993); and Michael Foss, *Man of Wit to Man of Business: The Arts and Changing Patronage 1660–1750* (Bristol: Bristol Classic Press, 1988; first published as *The Age of Patronage*, London: Hamish Hamilton, 1971).

26 Andrew Pinnock and Will Lingard, 'Seeking the Bubble: The Economic Basis of Musical Reputation, and the role of the Anniversary as Value Inflator' (Unpublished paper presented at conference Purcell, Handel, Haydn, Mendelssohn: Anniversary Reflections, Oxford, 27–29 March 2009).

27 The importance of the wide range of Purcell's compositional activities to his later reputation is noted by Pinnock in 'The Purcell Phenomenon', p. 5; by Higney in 'Henry Purcell: A Reception/Dissemination Study', p. 11; and by Pinnock and Lingard in 'Seeking the Bubble'.

28 Weber, *The Rise of Musical Classics*, p. 2.

29 Higney, 'Henry Purcell: A Reception/Dissemination Study', pp. 12–17.

there can be no doubt that it was Purcell's forward-looking approach to his change of circumstances after the accession of William and Mary that led ultimately to his entry into the developing canon of historical 'great' composers in England.

The importance of his printed output in this respect cannot be overestimated. During the Restoration period the appearance of music in print was rarely in itself an indication of the esteem in which the music was held, but rather a reflection of what the publishers thought would sell, which essentially meant pieces that could be used in the domestic environment.[30] Consequently composers who wrote music in suitable genres – particularly secular song and theatre music from which tunes could be extracted – found much more of their material printed than did composers who specialized in, say, choral church music, which had no market beyond the limited group of cathedrals and collegiate institutions where choirs were maintained. The output of these more traditional court- and church-based composers remained primarily functional and often event-led – it was written for specific purposes and/or performers, sometimes for one-off performances, and did not require broad dissemination beyond its immediate environment, therefore remaining in a small number of hand-written copies. In his early career Purcell was primarily a composer of this type, and most of his sacred music and court odes survive only in manuscript; but his late career shift led him to produce large quantities of 'publishable' music, the result of which was that far more of his output was printed than was the case for his contemporaries. This gave him three advantages: first, this published music stood a much greater chance of surviving in the long term than did works that were preserved in only a few manuscript sources. Second, it was more accessible both to historians of music like Burney and Hawkins and to musicians interested in performing old music, most of whom seem to have relied heavily on printed music. Third, because the role of music printing changed during the course of the eighteenth century, the fact that he had larger amounts of music in print than his contemporaries gave the impression that he was a better composer. As printing became more profitable and modern copyright law developed to give composers control over their published output during the course of the eighteenth century,[31] it gradually became the norm for most, if not all, of a composer's mature output to be printed and given opus numbers; print therefore came to represent authority and esteem. Musicians and music historians working from the late eighteenth century onwards seem to have been largely unaware that printing in earlier periods sometimes had quite a different function, and they were therefore inclined to attribute more value and significance to prints of earlier music than perhaps they had had at the time of publication.

---

30 I have addressed this issue elsewhere in 'Playford, Purcell, and the Functions of Music Publishing in Restoration England', *Journal of the American Musicological Society* 63 (2010): 243–89.

31 The most significant event in this respect was the test case for the application of literary copyright laws to music brought by J.C. Bach and C.F. Abel in 1774. See David Hunter, 'Music Copyright in Britain to 1800', *Music & Letters* 67 (1986): 278–80.

More than any of his contemporaries, Purcell seems to have embraced the change from private to commercial music-making at the end of the seventeenth century, and, as Higney postulates, 'one wonders if his life and works would have been so venerated if he had died even a few years earlier',[32] before his career took its new turn. None of his composer colleagues profited to such an extent from the shift away from traditional patronage: the most notable comparison is with John Blow, who reacted to the decline in court music in the 1690s by consolidating his church appointments, and entered a kind of semi-retirement from about 1700, so was never a prominent figure on the commercial music scene. While his music did remain in circulation within sources of sacred music, it never became part of the repertory of the concert rooms, and his lack of theatre output also meant that his music was little known amongst the broader public, even though he did publish a number of collections of his music late in his life.[33]

There was a third factor that aided the development of Purcell's posthumous reputation and that seems to have been influenced by his strong public profile in the later part of his career: his early and sudden death at the age of 36. While this event could hardly be described as lucky, the sense that the composer had been cut down in his prime does seem to have had a significant impact on Purcell's continuing popularity in the early eighteenth century. Again music printing is important here, for two reasons: first, Frances Purcell seems to have decided that printing as many of her late husband's works as possible was her best chance of earning an income from his music after his death; consequently five volumes of his works were published by her between 1696 and 1698, almost doubling the number of collections dedicated to his music and considerably augmenting the amount of his output that was easily available to later generations. Second, although there were at least two commemorative performances for Purcell,[34] and several

---

32   Higney, 'Henry Purcell: A Reception/Dissemination Study', p. 38.

33   Eighteenth- and nineteenth-century reception of Blow's music, however, is much more complicated than this sketch would suggest, partly because he seems to have been judged by many writers in comparison with Purcell: see the section 'Critical Comment on Purcell in the late Eighteenth Century', below.

34   The clearest documentation is for an event that took place at York Buildings on 13 January 1695/6, which seems to have consisted merely of a performance of Gottfried Finger's ode for Purcell; however, it was a public commemoration to which attention was drawn in the press, since there was an advertisement in *The Post Boy*, 7–9 January 1695/6; the commemoration is cited in Higney, 'Henry Purcell: A Reception/Dissemination Study', p. 42. In addition, an inscription written by William Croft at the beginning of Jeremiah Clarke's ode *Come, come Along for a Dance and a Song* in Lbl Add. 30934 notes that 'The following piece of musick was compos'd by Mr Jeremiah Clarke (when organist of Winchester Colledge) upon the Death of the famous Mr. Henry Purcell, and perform'd upon the stage in Druery Lane play house', suggesting an additional event. See Peter Holman, sleeve notes to *Odes on the Death of Henry Purcell*, The Parley of Instruments and Parley of Instruments Choir, dir. Roy Goodman and Peter Holman (Hyperion CDA 66578, *rec.* 1992). I am grateful to Alan Howard for this information.

odes were set to music to mourn his death,[35] it was the publication of the last of Frances's prints – the two-volume collection of vocal music *Orpheus Britannicus*, which appeared in 1698 and 1706, and in which Henry Playford printed a series of elegies to the composer – that seems to have established this passing as exceptional. Richard Luckett was the first to draw attention to the importance of these books, which, he suggested, was due less to the contents of the volumes than to the way in which they were presented.[36] Elegiac poems in themselves were regularly produced to commemorate the lives of significant individuals in this period, and even the endowment of the title 'Orpheus' was not unique to Purcell.[37] What seems to have made *Orpheus Britannicus* stand apart was the way in which the entire two-volume set was designed to act as a monument to Purcell's memory – a function for music printing that was very rare in England in this period[38] – allowing many of the poems to be published together alongside a substantial collection of Purcell's vocal music, often also bound with a portrait of the composer, as a permanent commemoration and symbol of the way in which his death had been mourned. Luckett goes so far as to suggest that the two *Orpheus* volumes were intended as a musical equivalent of a literary first folio.[39]

Such a link with literary icons has been drawn upon particularly by John Higney, who sees attempts in both the *Orpheus Britannicus* poetry itself, and in later tributes from the early eighteenth century, to associate Purcell with the emerging literary canon.[40] While he locates the earliest such comparison in Henry Hall's tribute, in which Purcell was viewed as combining the talents of Abraham Cowley and Francis Quarles, by the beginning of the eighteenth century the composer was more often being grouped with the central playwrights of the past century, something that

---

35   As well as Clarke's *Come, come Along for a Dance and a Song*, these were by Blow (*Mark how the Lark and Linnet Sing*) and Henry Hall (*Yes my Aminta, 'tis too True*). A poem by Tate, 'A Gloomy Mist o'erspreads the Plains' is described in *Orpheus Britannicus*, p. iv as '*A Lamentation for the Death of Mr.* Henry Purcell. *Sett to Musick by his Brother, Mr.* Daniel Purcell', but this setting no longer survives.

36   Luckett, '"Or Rather Our Musical Shakspeare"', p. 62.

37   Ibid.; a similar point is made in Weber, *The Rise of Musical Classics*, p. 76, and Howard notes the significance of the Orpheus trope in 'Purcell and the Poetics of Artifice', pp. 18–19. Such poems were not uncommon forms of tribute for musicians: William Lawes's death at the Siege of Chester was commemorated in poems printed at the front of Henry and William Lawes, *Choice Psalmes put into Musick, for Three Voices* (London, 1648), for example, and Purcell himself wrote music for Tate's ode 'Gentle Shepherds' on the death of John Playford in 1686. Higney considers the rhetorical traditions within which the major literary figures who contributed odes to *Orpheus Britannicus* worked in 'Henry Purcell: A Reception/Dissemination Study', pp. 44–56.

38   See my 'Playford, Purcell and the Functions of Music Publishing'.

39   Richard Luckett, 'The Playfords and the Purcells', in Robin Myers, Michael Harris and Giles Mandelbrote (eds), *Music and the Book Trade from the Sixteenth to the Twentieth Century* (New Castle, DE: Oak Knoll; London: British Library, 2008), pp. 59 and 61. Luckett considers at length whether Playford intended the volumes to be put to practical use.

40   Higney, 'Henry Purcell: A Reception/Dissemination Study', pp. 69–74.

is depicted vividly in the following description of a ceiling frieze at the Theatre Royal, printed in *The British Journal* in 1722:

> London. On Saturday last, several of the most eminent Painters met at the Theatre-Royal in Lincolns-Inn-Fields, to take a View of the Cieling [*sic*], the House being thoroughly lighted for that Purpose; and gave their Opinion, That the Performance excels any Thing of that Kind, both as to Design and Beauty. Over the Stage, Apollo and the Muses are represented, and over the Pit, a magnificent Piece of Architecture, with a Groop of Figures leaning over a long Gallery, viz. Shakespear, Johnson, Beaumont, Fletcher, Dryden, Purcell, &c. in conference with Betterton.[41]

Such evidence, Higney writes, suggests that 'the English theatrical canon, which emerged well before that of music, appears to have acted as both an exemplar and a conduit for Purcell's entry into the musical canon':[42] while the development of a set of modern English literary classics was well underway by the early eighteenth century, the same could not yet be said for composers, and the appropriation of Purcell into the literary fold prepared the path for a musical canon to begin to develop in England.[43]

It is significant also that many of the early discourses about Purcell's 'classic' status were written by literary rather than musical figures. This was due in principle to the simple fact that there was no tradition of writing about music in these terms until the latter half of the eighteenth century,[44] but there were implications for the development of Purcell's reputation, since those literary writers who drew on his legacy did so from a particular perspective that proved to have lasting influence. In fact the characteristic of his music on which they predominantly drew seems to have been established initially in *Orpheus Britannicus*, although not, interestingly enough, in the elegies: in his own preface, Henry Playford had described Purcell, *'that great Master'*, as having *'a peculiar Genius to express the Energy of English Words, whereby he mov'd the Passions of all his Auditors'*.[45] As we shall see, this identification of Purcell with the effective setting of English texts was to become both an important

---

41 *The British Journal*, 22 September 1722, p. 3, quoted in part in Higney, 'Henry Purcell: A Reception/Dissemination Study', p. 73.

42 Higney, 'Henry Purcell: A Reception/Dissemination Study', p. 73.

43 Weber assesses in detail the relationship between the literary and musical canons in England in the eighteenth century in 'The Intellectual Origins of Musical Canon in Eighteenth-Century England', *Journal of the American Musicological Society* 48 (1994): 491–504. He locates the development of the modern literary canon in the crisis epitomized by the Quarrel of the Ancients and Moderns at the turn of the eighteenth century, as a result of which recent as well as classical authors became able to enter the canon. This, he says, allowed the musical canon to develop, since 'a canon could now arise without ancient origins' (ibid.: 503–4), but he sees comparisons between musical and literary figures as largely superficial (see ibid.: 502).

44 Both points are made (although not specifically in relation to Purcell) in ibid.: 492–3.

45 Henry Playford, 'The Bookseller to the Reader', in *Orpheus Britannicus*, p. iii.

factor in the solidification of his classic status, and a useful political tool in the eighteenth century. Perhaps it was also partly responsible for the fact that – as Luckett has clearly demonstrated and despite claims to the contrary by English figures who valued Purcell – the composer did not develop a significant reputation in continental Europe, where his music seems to have remained virtually unknown.[46]

It is clear, then, that the seeds of Purcell's posthumous reception in England were sewn in the last five years of his career. The fact that they grew predominantly from his new commercial activities and the higher public profile and printed legacy they produced meant that certain parts of his output were strongly privileged in this process, while other genres for which he had also written copious amounts of music – most of his sacred repertory, court odes and instrumental music, for example – became largely forgotten. Ultimately, it led to an imbalanced view of Purcell as a composer, which we can see reflected in the performances of his music that were mounted during the three centuries after his death, the nature of the published editions and the critical discourse preserved in his historiography.

Purcell in Early Eighteenth-Century Public Performance Culture

By far the largest proportion of the existing research on Purcell's reception in the eighteenth century concentrates on the fortunes of his theatre music in performance. This is largely due to Harris's studies of specific performances of *Dido and Aeneas* and *King Arthur*, now added to by Michael Burden and Todd Gilman,[47] and to Weber's extensive exploration of the politics of the stage in the period and the establishment of the historical concerts of the Academy of Ancient Music and the Concert of Antient Music – work that has since been augmented by Sandra Tuppen[48] – as well as research on specific works within Purcell's theatrical *oeuvre* that became popular during the century after his death for a variety of reasons.[49]

---

46   Luckett, '"Or Rather Our Musical Shakspeare"', pp. 64–5. Luckett notes that both Roger North and John Hawkins stated Purcell was famous abroad, but that their claims are not supported by the surviving evidence. Howard attributes Purcell's obscurity in Europe partly to the types of music that he wrote, since genres such as Anglican sacred music, court odes and dramatick opera 'were not only unique to English culture but [also] strongly tied to specific social functions'; Howard, 'Purcell and the Poetics of Artifice', p. 30.

47   Burden, 'Purcell's *King Arthur* in the 1730s'; Todd Gilman, 'David Garrick's *Masque of King Arthur* with Thomas Arne's Score (1770)', *Restoration: Studies in English Literary Culture, 1660–1700* 34 (2010): 139–62.

48   Sandra Tuppen, 'Purcell in the Eighteenth Century: Music for the "Quality, Gentry, and Others"' (Unpublished paper presented at conference Purcell, Handel, Haydn, Mendelssohn: Anniversary Reflections, Oxford, 27–29 March 2009).

49   Olive Baldwin and Thelma Wilson, 'Purcell's Mad Songs in the time of Handel, Haydn

As with other aspects of Purcell's reception, no overarching narrative has been written to assimilate these studies, but in drawing them together here it is possible to construct a remarkably coherent story. It is best understood divided into the period when Purcell's theatre music was still regarded as part of a current and continuing tradition (covered in this section), and a later period when certain pieces began to be revived as antiquarian works (assessed in the section 'Purcell in Later Eighteenth-Century Performance Culture').

Given the extent to which Purcell's tremendous success as a theatre composer in the last five years of his life influenced his later reception, it is somewhat ironic that, by the time of his death in 1695, the dramatick opera tradition in which he had been such a major figure was in trouble. As is well known, financial difficulties were the prime cause of this decline: the cost of mounting multimedia productions was immense and, even though new works had only ever been occasional highlights of theatre seasons consisting mostly of spoken drama, the size of the potential audience was not sufficient for dramatick operas to be viable in the long term.[50] In 1695 the United Company, for which Purcell had worked in his heyday, split into two weakened groups because of quarrels over performers' pay. Although both companies had some notable successes around the turn of the eighteenth century – most particularly *The Island Princess*, mounted by the Patent Company under Christopher Rich in 1699, with music by Jeremiah Clarke, Richard Leveridge and Daniel Purcell – by 1700 lack of finance restricted the number of new works that could be produced, which made revivals of Restoration dramatick opera an important part of the repertory of both companies. Purcell's *Dioclesian*, for example, was given four performances at Drury Lane in 1700, appeared again in 1702 and 1705, with additional excerpts included in entertainments in 1703 and 1704, and had a lengthy run of ten performances at the newly reopened Lincolns Inn Fields theatre under John Rich in 1715, with further performances in 1716 and 1717.[51] *King*

---

and Mendelssohn' and Vanessa Rogers, '"Britons Strike Home": Ballad Opera and the Eighteenth-Century Purcell Revival, 1728–1760' (Unpublished papers presented at conference Purcell, Handel, Haydn, Mendelssohn: Anniversary Reflections, Oxford, 27–29 March 2009).

50   Although such a study has yet to be carried out for Restoration opera, detailed consideration of likely audience numbers for opera in Handel's day is published in David Hunter, 'Patronizing Handel, Inventing Audiences: The Intersections of Class, Money, Music, and History', *Early Music* 28 (2000): 32–49; and Robert D. Hume investigates the wider economic problems facing opera companies in the late seventeenth and early eighteenth centuries in 'The Economics of Culture in London, 1660–1740', *Huntington Library Quarterly* 69 (2006): 515–17.

51   White, 'Early Theatrical Performances of Purcell's Operas': 47, 53, 55 and 59; Tilmouth, 'A Calendar of References to Music in Newspapers': 33, 35, 44, 53, 61 and 92–3; see also Jackson, 'Play Notices from the Burney Newspapers': 820 and Julia Muller, *Words and Music in Henry Purcell's First Semi-Opera, Dioclesian: An Approach to Early Music through Early Theatre*, Studies in the History and Interpretation of Music, vol. 28 (Lewiston, Queenston and Lampeter: Edwin Mellen, 1990), p. 479. It is difficult to reconcile these figures with Weber's statement that Purcell's works had 'fallen from stage repertories'

Arthur was also regularly featured on the public London stage, as were extracts (usually masques) from Purcell's music for *The Indian Queen, Bonduca, Timon of Athens* and *Oedipus*.[52] There were frequent references in advertisements for these revivals to the esteem in which Purcell was held – he was regularly described as 'the late famous Mr. Henry Purcell', for instance[53] – and the composer's name was clearly considered to have commercial value, as Luckett points out.[54] However, Purcell's was not the only 'old' operatic music being revived on the stage in this period: Locke's *Psyche* was produced at Drury Lane in June 1704,[55] for example, and *The Island Princess* received almost annual performances from its premiere in 1699 until 1728.[56] Until the 1720s, when Italian opera began to gain in both popularity and success, Restoration dramatic music was essentially part of a continuous tradition, and there is little evidence to suggest that Purcell's music was given particular emphasis during this period.

The strength of Purcell's reputation in the first decades of the eighteenth century led his music to remain popular in several other public spheres outside the theatre, and it is here that we can see the first clear indication of his legacy outlasting that of his contemporaries. His Te Deum and Jubilate, which had been composed for the St Cecilia's Day festival of 1694, and which (importantly) had been published posthumously by Frances Purcell in 1697, became an annual feature of the grand Festival of the Sons of the Clergy, a major event that took place each year from 1697 at St Paul's Cathedral. As Weber notes, not only was Purcell the sole dead composer whose music continued to be used at the ceremony, its regular exposure in this context also led to the piece becoming widely performed elsewhere – particularly within the growing tradition of provincial musical events, of which he singles out the Three Choirs Festival.[57] The high profile of the Festival of the Sons of the Clergy, which Higney identifies as 'the single most advertised Purcell event of the first half of the eighteenth century',[58] led the piece to become

---

between his death and 1704; Weber, *The Rise of Musical Classics*, p. 91.

52   See White, 'Early Theatrical Performances of Purcell's Operas': 53–65 *passim*; and Jackson, 'Play Notices from the Burney Newspapers': 839 and 842.

53   See the references in White, 'Early Theatrical Performances of Purcell's Operas': 54 and 55, for instance, and similar examples given in Luckett, '"Or Rather Our Musical Shakspeare"', p. 64.

54   He notes that Rich's company was prepared to pay an exceptionally large reward of 20 guineas for the return of the score of *The Fairy Queen* in 1701; '"Or Rather Our Musical Shakspeare"', pp. 63–4.

55   Tilmouth, 'A Calendar of References to Music in Newspapers': 56.

56   See the references to the opera in *Index to the London Stage, 1660–1800*, compiled by Ben Ross Schneider, Jr (Carbondale: Southern Illinois University Press, 1979), p. 310, although it should be noted that not all the references given here are to staged performances, a minority denoting only the appearance of excerpts from the music in concerts.

57   Weber, *The Rise of Musical Classics*, pp. 110–20.

58   Higney, 'Henry Purcell: A Reception/Dissemination Study', p. 115.

one of Purcell's best-known works in the period, so it is no surprise that Thomas Tudway singled it out for praise.[59]

Purcell also began to gain an exceptionally high profile in the public concerts mounted regularly as benefits or subscription series by professional musicians. While these programmes predominantly contained contemporary music,[60] excerpts from Purcell's theatre music, often performed by the famous theatre singers of the moment, seem to have been extremely popular, to judge from the evidence of the advertisements and stage records in which they were mentioned. Weber's remark that there is much research still to be done on the nature of these concert programmes remains valid today,[61] but Higney's research has highlighted some of the key evidence and issues on which such a study might focus: the patterns of references to Purcell in newspaper announcements of these concerts; possible links between concert programmes and the use of Purcell's music as entr'actes in theatrical performances in the period;[62] and the way in which Purcell's songs were programmed alongside performances of Italian music in the first decade of the eighteenth century, apparently as a way of enticing audiences to hear the new imported music.[63]

Ultimately, however, Italian opera's rise to popularity on the English stage was what led Purcell's music to decline in significance, as 'the glamour vanished' by the mid eighteenth century.[64] Although his reputation had lasted longer than those of most of his contemporaries, he began to be superseded, particularly by Handel. There is clear evidence for this trend in performances of Purcell's works: for example, Luckett notes that Purcell's Te Deum ceased to be included each year at the Sons of the Clergy by 1713 when Handel's Utrecht setting began to be used in alternation with Purcell's, and that in 1743 the Dettingen Te Deum became the standard choice.[65] Higney charts the decline in publications of Purcell's music from the 1720s,[66] and contemporary comment from this period also points clearly to the

---

59 See Hogwood, 'Thomas Tudway's History of Music', p. 45.

60 Weber comments that 'the only other dead composer often represented on these programmes was Corelli'; see *The Rise of Musical Classics*, p. 92.

61 Ibid.

62 Higney, 'Henry Purcell: A Reception/Dissemination Study', pp. 107–11.

63 Ibid., pp. 125–6.

64 Luckett, '"Or Rather Our Musical Shakspeare"', p. 67.

65 Ibid., pp. 67–8.

66 Higney, 'Henry Purcell: A Reception/Dissemination Study', p. 35. Note, however that Higney's Appendix V, 'A Preliminary List of Late Seventeenth[-] and Eighteenth-Century Purcell Publications', on which his Table is based, is provisional and appears not to be fully inclusive, being compiled from data in the British Union Catalogue of Early Music, Cyrus Lawrence Day and Eleanore Boswell Murrie's *English Song-Books, 1651–1702: A Bibliography, With A First-Line Index of Songs* (London: For the Bibliographical Society at Oxford University Press, 1940 (for 1937)) and bibliographical work by David Hunter (presumably his *Opera and Song Books Published in England, 1703–1726: A Descriptive Bibliography* (London: Bibliographical Society, 1997)), but apparently without reference to the Répertoire International des Sources Musicales

rejection of music from Purcell's era in favour of the new fashion for Italian music: Roger North, who became a keen advocate of the new operas, bemoaned the fact that Purcell had not lived long enough to adopt Italian styles wholeheartedly, writing of 'Mr H. Purcell, who unhappily began to shew his Great skill before the reform of musick al Italiana, and while he was warm in the pursuit of it, Dyed';[67] and the travel writer and spy John Macky wrote similarly in 1722 that, although Purcell's works were held in great esteem, 'the Taste of the Town being at this day all *Italian*, it is a great Discouragement to them'.[68]

Opinion is divided, however, on the extent and progress of the decline. While Luckett sees a gradual but inexorable path towards obscurity demonstrated in the substitution of Purcell with Handel as 'our British Orpheus', the replacement of performances of his works with Handelian concertos, and the lack of references to Purcell in many mid and late eighteenth-century commentaries on music,[69] Weber considers this view to be unduly influenced by 'printed commentary', which means that it 'does not take into account the extraordinary extent to which his music was performed throughout the century'.[70] In fact, both writers cite largely the same evidence of the most significant Purcell performances in the latter half of the eighteenth century, and it seems likely that the shift to which they are alluding should be understood more in terms of the place Purcell's music was felt to occupy: whereas in the first part of the century he was still being regarded as part of an essentially contemporary repertory – albeit that his music had remained there longer than that of most other musicians at the time – slowly, as it began to sound more and more old-fashioned, it became 'antiquarian' music that was quite unlike current musical styles. For Higney, indeed, Purcell's 'otherness' grew out of a gradual aesthetic move away from mimesis as the principal mode of creation towards free expression.[71] It was the fact that at least some of Purcell's music survived this transition and continued to be performed repeatedly that allowed him to enter the English canon. In addition, once it was identified as *unlike* contemporary music, it could also be used by commentators as a political tool, both in the fight against Italian opera and for nationalist purposes.

Series A catalogue of printed books.

67   Quoted in Wilson (ed.), *Roger North on Music*, p. 307, from the first *Musicall Grammarian* of *c*.1726.

68   *A Journey Through England. In Familiar Letters from a Gentleman Here, to his Friend Abroad ... The Second Edition, Considerably Improv'd* (London, 1722), p. 171, quoted in Luckett, '"Or Rather Our Musical Shakspeare"', p. 67. Macky's eventful political life is documented in J.D. Alsop, 'Macky, John (d. 1726)', in *Oxford Dictionary of National Biography*, http://www.oxforddnb.com (last accessed 10 September 2009).

69   Luckett, '"Or Rather Our Musical Shakspeare"', pp. 67–70.

70   Weber, *The Rise of Musical Classics*, p. 90. Weber, however, agrees with Luckett that Handel replaced Purcell as a British national icon by mid-century; see ibid., p. 101.

71   Higney, 'Henry Purcell: A Reception/Dissemination Study', pp. 142–68.

Purcell's Role in Mid Eighteenth-Century Comment

Italian opera in eighteenth-century England is well known for its popular success and commercial instability, but, until the 1740s, it was heavily criticized by many commentators, particularly English literary figures, who saw it as a threat to everything from playwrights' wages to national security. Weber assesses in detail the role Purcell's music played in this debate, and identifies the most significant protagonists,[72] including the Whig writer John Dennis,[73] and the poet and writer Joseph Addison who, in 1711, wrote a series of polemical essays on opera in *The Spectator*, the magazine he co-founded with Richard Steele. His objections to Italian opera centred on the problems of translation into English, and of comprehension when works were performed in Italian or in bilingual productions, so that 'We no longer understand the Language of our own Stage'.[74] This concern later led him to criticize the inability of the Italian musicians to appreciate Purcell's superior text-setting capabilities – thus drawing directly on the reputation that had been established for Purcell by Henry Playford and setting him up as a representative of the expressive setting of English texts:

> the *Italian* Artists cannot agree with our *English* Musicians, in admiring *Purcell's* Compositions, and thinking his Tunes so wonderfully adapted to his Words, because both Nations do not always express the same Passions by the same Sounds.[75]

Other literary commentators soon joined Addison in expressing their regret at the declining popularity of English music, choosing Purcell to represent the ideal of the past. The playwright and commentator Charles Gildon, in his *Complete Art of Poetry* of 1718, not only referred to Purcell's text-setting powers in describing him as having 'the Genius of *Greek* Musick' with which 'he touch'd the Soul',[76] but also used Purcell to defend the tradition of part-sung, part-spoken opera in contradistinction to the Italian all-sung form. He sets up one character against another, allowing one to comment:

---

72 Weber, *The Rise of Musical Classics*, pp. 94–9. See also Luckett, '"Or Rather Our Musical Shakspeare"', p. 67 and Higney, 'Henry Purcell: A Reception/Dissemination Study', pp. 98–102 and 125–30.

73 *An Essay upon Publick Spirit; Being a Satyr in Prose upon the Manners of Luxury of the Times* (London, 1711), cited in Weber, *The Rise of Musical Classics*, p. 97.

74 *The Spectator*, 21 March 1711, pp. 1–2, quoted in Weber, *The Rise of Musical Classics*, p. 95. On bilingual productions, Addison notes that when Italian performers were first brought to London 'the King or Hero of the Play generally spoke in Italian, and his Slaves answer'd him in English'; *The Spectator*, 21 March 1711, p. 1.

75 *The Spectator*, 3 April 1711, p. 1; partly quoted in Luckett, '"Or Rather Our Musical Shakspeare"', p. 66.

76 Quoted in Luckett, '"Or Rather Our Musical Shakspeare"', p. 67.

But then I think nothing can be more absurd, than his preferring the ridiculous Qualities of an *Opera* after the *Italian*, to that after the Way of *Harry Purcel* [in which] ... what was proper for Musick, was sung, and the *Drama* performed as all other *Drama's* were.[77]

In the case of Henry Carey in his well-known poem 'The Poet's Resentment', first published anonymously in *The Universal Journal* in July 1724, the concern was the decline in the setting of native texts:

> Untuneful is our Native Language now,
> Nor must the Bays adorn a *British* Brow:
> The wanton Vulgar scorn their Mother-Tongue,
> And all our *British* Bards have bootless sung.
> Ev'n Heav'n-born *Purcel* now is held in scorn;
> *Purcel!* Who did a brighter Age adorn.
> That Nobleness of Soul, that manly Fire,
> That did our *British Orpheus* once inspire
> To rouse us all to Arms, is quite forgot:
> We're, now, for something soft – We know not what.[78]

Carey's poem inspired an unprecedented response a fortnight later, when a letter from an anonymous author was published in the *Journal* defending Purcell's memory against 'the modern Fops, who seem resolv'd to tear the Laurel from his Brow, and lay his Memory low in Oblivion'.[79] This lengthy letter is significant in several respects: like the painting at the Theatre Royal, it drew explicit comparison between Purcell and Shakespeare, referring to him, indeed, as a '*Shakespear* in Music', whose works had yet to be surpassed. Crucially, the author does not see why the fact that the music was now old-fashioned should lead it to fall into obscurity:

> The first and chief Reflection they cast on his Musick, is, that 'tis Old Stile:
> I grant it; (all the World knows it was not made Yesterday;) but I cannot
> comprehend these Gentlemens nice Distinction of Old Stile and New Stile,
> unless they would infer that the three Sister-Arts never flourished 'till now,

---

77 Charles Gildon, *The Complete Art of Poetry. In Six Parts* (2 vols, London, 1718), vol. 1, pp. 104–5, quoted in Weber, *The Rise of Musical Classics*, p. 95; Weber gives the date of Gildon's work as 1722.

78 *The Universal Journal*, 11 July 1724, p. 3, partly quoted in Weber, *The Rise of Musical Classics*, pp. 97–8 and in Burden, *Purcell Remembered*, p. 156, in the slightly revised form in which it appeared in the third edition of Carey's *Poems on Several Occasions ... The Third Edition, Much Enlarged* (London, 1729); the original publication is reproduced in facsimile in Higney, 'Henry Purcell: A Reception/Dissemination Study', p. 224, although without attribution. Burden notes Carey's apparent later role in promoting English opera in the 1730s; see 'Purcell's *King Arthur* in the 1730s': 132–3.

79 *The Universal Journal*, 25 July 1724, p. 3.

or that the Music, Painting and Poetry of the last Age is Old Stile, (*i.e.*) out of Date, and therefore ought to be kick'd out of Doors.

We have doubtless many good Painters now living; must therefore *Rubens*, *Vandyke*, *Lilly*, and *Kneller* be forgot? Must *Spencer*, *Milton*, *Shakespear*, and *Addison* be never read, because there are Writers of a later Date? And must *Corelli*, *Bird*, and *Purcel* never be sung, because they are Old Stile?[80]

For the first time in critical writings, then, Purcell's name was being evoked in canonical terms sitting alongside great literary figures and artists, and the two composers the author identified as having equal status, Byrd and Corelli.[81] Whereas for the other commentators Purcell was simply associated with a nostalgic view of an English music written by native composers, whose music was, in short, the antithesis to Italian opera, this author was arguing for the preservation of his music as an 'ancient', but still valid, repertory.

Purcell in Later Eighteenth-Century Public Performance Culture

Once Purcell began to be viewed as an antiquarian composer, his music took on two distinctive characteristics in performance: it was subjected to the common practice that developed in England of 'updating' old music to make it more palatable to mid and late eighteenth-century ears, and it became increasingly restricted to a relatively small number of works that were performed repeatedly. The latter tradition of course began in the very earliest years after Purcell's death because of the emphasis at that time on his works designed for the public domain, but it became gradually more exaggerated as the eighteenth century progressed. This can be explained partly through Purcell's association with specific nationalistic sentiments (not unrelated to the anti-Italian-opera faction), and partly by the continuing attraction of some works because of their musical or textual content. Two groups of songs, for example, were performed repeatedly at concerts and in the theatre: the first comprised those with patriotic texts, chiefly 'Fairest Isle' from *King Arthur*, 'Genius

---

80 Ibid., reproduced in facsimile in Higney, 'Henry Purcell: A Reception/Dissemination Study', p. 225, and in transcription in Burden, *Purcell Remembered*, pp. 136–8. Higney analyses the rhetoric of the letter in 'Henry Purcell: A Reception/Dissemination Study', pp. 27–9. Weber also comments on the response in *The Rise of Musical Classics*, p. 99, but surprisingly does not emphasize the significance of the author's views on musical canon. Burden points out that the letters need to be seen in the context of the personal links between the editors of *The Universal Journal* and Purcell: Leonard Welstead, who worked alongside Ambrose Philips, had been married to Purcell's daughter Frances before her death in 1724. See Burden, 'Purcell's *King Arthur* in the 1730s': 132.

81 On the development of the canonical status of Corelli in England in this period, see Weber, *The Rise of Musical Classics*, pp. 77–89.

of England', from *The Comical History of Don Quixote*, 'Britons Strike Home' from *Bonduca* and 'Let the Soldiers Rejoice' from *Dioclesian*, which Weber demonstrates were sometimes even 'used to celebrate national events';[82] the second was a set of 'mad songs' – Bess of Bedlam ('From Silent Shades'), and 'From Rosy Bow'rs' and 'Let the Dreadful Engines' from *The Comical History of Don Quixote*.[83] According to Baldwin and Wilson, it was the length of these songs and their virtuosic character, with extreme contrasts, that led to their prolonged popularity, particularly among professional theatre singers:[84] certain famous performers – including John Beard, Elizabeth Linley, Sarah Harrop and Elizabeth Billington – adopted the songs as highlights of their concert repertory, a strategy which, from the evidence of the newspaper advertisements, clearly drew audiences.[85]

Purcell's mad songs inspired imitations in the operas of Handel and in *The Beggar's Opera*,[86] but his music was also incorporated more directly into the ballad-opera genre that grew out of the success of the latter work, and this is an aspect of Purcell's reception that has remained entirely unexplored until recently. Vanessa Rogers's preliminary research has uncovered at least 17 of Purcell's songs and instrumental tunes in ballad operas produced between 1728 and 1760, making Purcell the best-represented composer in the genre after Handel.[87] While some of the chosen pieces were otherwise little performed in the period – such as 'Fair Iris and her Swain' from *Amphitryon* – and others were used because they had already been adapted as ballads,[88] many belonged to the popular subset of Purcell 'favourites'. The emphasis on those songs with nationalistic potential – 'Fairest Isle', 'Let the Soldiers Rejoice' and 'Britons Strike Home' (which even provided the title for a ballad opera of 1739) – is notable, and might be linked to the use of ballad opera as a counter-attack on Italian opera, although *Britons Strike Home* itself was in fact inspired by the declaration of war against Spain.[89]

---

82   Ibid., p. 94. For example, he notes: 'When George II visited Covent Garden on 27 October 1739, immediately after declaring war on Spain, he was greeted by "Britons, strike home" and an enthusiastic response from the audience.'

83   Weber names the first two among Purcell's popular songs in ibid., pp. 94–5; 'Let the Dreadful Engines' was performed relatively less frequently.

84   Baldwin and Wilson, 'Purcell's Mad Songs in the time of Handel, Haydn and Mendelssohn'.

85   Ibid. Baldwin and Wilson also list several singers in addition to Billington who were well known for performing the songs in the 1790s. See also Luckett, '"Or Rather Our Musical Shakspeare"', p. 70.

86   Baldwin and Wilson, 'Purcell's Mad Songs in the time of Handel, Haydn and Mendelssohn'.

87   Rogers, '"Britons Strike Home"'. Rogers's list is tentative because there are some 3,500 tunes printed in ballad operas, usually given as a single line of music and set to new text with no indication of their origin, thus making identification difficult.

88   Rogers cites several instrumental tunes from Purcell's dramatic works that appeared with new texts in ballad collections like *Pills to Purge Melancholy*; ibid.

89   Ibid. See also n. 82 above.

The selections of Purcell's music included in the programmes of the Academy of Ancient Music and later the Concert of Antient Music also attest to the idea that his antiquarian identity was being built around a limited group of works. The Academy's 1761 catalogue *The Words of Such Pieces as are Now Most Usually Performed by the Academy of Ancient Music* includes two anthems by Purcell, but the remaining pieces are masques from *King Arthur*, *The Indian Queen* and *Oedipus*, plus the misattributed music from *Macbeth* and *The Tempest*, all of which suggest that the Academy was reliant on the excerpts from Purcell's theatre works that had remained in the repertory in the early part of the eighteenth century,[90] and whose popularity often derived simply from their subject matter, works with supernatural themes being particular favourites.[91] Sandra Tuppen's recent work on the programmes of the Concerts of Antient Music reveals that an even narrower group from among these pieces was included regularly within their repertory, comprising scenes from *King Arthur*, *The Indian Queen* and *Bonduca*, plus the misattributed *Tempest* music.[92] Some additional music was incorporated into the concert programmes – of which 'Fear no Danger' from *Dido and Aeneas* and the 1693 birthday ode *Celebrate this Festival* were the most frequently performed – but Tuppen demonstrates clearly that these pieces were introduced by individual enthusiasts, so their inclusion should not be interpreted as indicative of a more general broadening of the Purcellian repertory at the end of the eighteenth century. In particular, she tracks a path from the Noblemen and Gentlemen's Catch Club, founded in 1761, to the Concerts, which were run by many of the same individuals. The surviving archive of minute books, membership lists and manuscripts (now held at the British Library) makes it possible to identify which Purcell works were introduced by whom, and she thereby concludes that it was chiefly one Sir Watkin Williams Wynn who brought these new pieces to the Catch Club, and who later (alongside the Earl of Sandwich himself) promoted Purcell's music in the programmes of the Concert.[93] Since music

---

90   The Academy's Purcellian repertory is described by Weber, *The Rise of Musical Classics*, p. 64, where it is noted that very few other seventeenth-century composers were included regularly in the Academy's concerts, the emphasis being mainly on sixteenth-century vocal music. Much of our knowledge of the programmes is reliant on the 1761 catalogue and its second edition of 1768.

91   For example, the regular revivals of at least parts of *King Arthur* seem to have occurred partly by virtue of its magic elements, something that is emphasized in the major production by Henry Giffard at Goodman's Theatre in 1736, when it was retitled *King Arthur, or Merlin, the British Enchanter*. See Harris, '*King Arthur*'s Journey', p. 282 and also Burden, 'Purcell's *King Arthur* in the 1730s'. A later interpretation of *King Arthur* for topical purposes was explored by Michael Burden in 'Fox and Pitt as Grimbald and Philidel: an 18th-century Political Use for *King Arthur*' (Unpublished paper presented at conference Purcell, Handel, Haydn, Mendelssohn: Anniversary Reflections, Oxford, 27–29 March 2009).

92   Tuppen, 'Purcell in the Eighteenth Century'.

93   Ibid. Tuppen demonstrates that programming for each concert was determined by the director for each concert, and that the amount of music by Purcell included in the programmes correspondingly fluctuated according to the individuals involved.

performed at the Concerts sometimes appeared in public events shortly after it had been included in the more select subscription series, and was also taken to provincial concerts by members who had country houses outside London,[94] it is possible that these individuals encouraged a wider appreciation of Purcell's music than might have occurred otherwise. Nevertheless, it remains the case – despite the fact that he was the most frequently performed English composer at the Concerts – that Purcell was very much a minority figure within the programmes, which were heavily dominated by Handel, Italian instrumental works and German and Italian opera extracts.[95]

Although relatively little of Purcell's music was performed in the historical repertory of either the Academy or the Concert, there is evidence that at least one piece included by the Academy had a lasting influence into the nineteenth century. An eighteenth-century manuscript of *Dido and Aeneas*, Lbl Add. 31450, is inscribed 'Concerts of Antient Music', and appears to be the copy referred to in the 1827 *Catalogue of the Musical Library belonging to His Majesty's Concert of Antient Music*. That it in fact originally belonged to the Academy rather than the Concert is demonstrated by the close relationship between this score and two printed librettos from Academy performances of 1774 and 1787, the first of which is entitled *The Loves of Dido and Aeneas: an Opera ... with several other pieces by the Academy of Ancient Music on Thursday, April 21, 1774*.[96] Ellen Harris has carried out a detailed comparison between these sources and the Tenbury score now acknowledged to derive from the earliest surviving version of the opera. Her analysis demonstrates that the two concert performances of *Dido* mounted by the Academy of Ancient Music incorporated a wide variety of changes into both the text and the music of the opera.[97] When G. Alexander Macfarren produced the first published edition of *Dido* for the Musical Antiquarian Society in 1841, however, he was clearly unaware of the complex textual history of the work, and based his edition on the Academy score, or one of its close relations.[98] Since no further scores of *Dido* were produced

---

94   Ibid.
95   Working on the basis of the figures given in Weber's analysis of the repertory of the Concerts in *The Rise of Musical Classics*, pp. 248–57, Tuppen determines that just 4 per cent of the items on the programmes from 1776 to 1790 comprised Purcell's music, and her analysis of the programmes from 1791–1800 shows this figure falling to 2 per cent; Tuppen, 'Purcell in the Eighteenth Century'. My own analysis of Weber's figures as related to Restoration composers suggests that minor adjustment may be needed now that the surviving programmes are all available via Eighteenth-Century Collections Online. Tuppen notes a letter in the *General Advertiser* of 17 March 1786 complaining at the neglect of Purcell in the programme of the Academy of Ancient Music's subscription series that year, which indicates that at least one individual was keen to hear more Purcell at the time, but there is no evidence that his/her view represented the tastes of a wider audience; Tuppen, 'Purcell in the Eighteenth Century'.
96   Ellen Harris, *Henry Purcell's 'Dido and Aeneas'* (Oxford: Clarendon, 1987), pp. 124–6.
97   Ibid., pp. 127–9 and 130–47 (although Harris deals with other eighteenth-century scores not related to the Academy here also).
98   Ibid., p. 148. The related scores are Lbl Add. 15979, US-Ws F 770, and the parts Lam 25

until 1889, and Macfarren's edition remained in use even then,[99] wider knowledge of the opera throughout most of the nineteenth century was therefore based on the Academy's heavily adapted version.

Harris's research has demonstrated that the patterns of revision and reworking detectable in the Academy's score of *Dido* in fact form part of a common approach to performance of Purcell's works in the latter half of the eighteenth century, since many of the same types of alteration can also be found in Thomas Arne's version of *King Arthur*, published around the time of the production mounted by Garrick with Arne in 1770–71.[100] There are some differences between the methods used in the two adaptations: the fragmentary survival of the music for *King Arthur* required replacement of missing music that was not undertaken for *Dido and Aeneas*,[101] and there is also no direct parallel in the alternative settings Arne provided for some other movements, nor his extra recitatives and arias;[102] on the other hand the smaller-

---

A and 25 D; ibid., p. 129. The date Harris gives for the publication of Macfarren's *Dido* edition is contradicted by Palmer, who cites it as 1843, but cross-reference with Turbet's article on the Musical Antiquarian Society confirms that Harris is correct. The edition itself bears no date, and Turbet notes that the dates given for the Society's volumes in the first edition of *Grove's Dictionary* by William Chappell are incorrect; his own list is 'based on numbered lists in the annual reports' of the Society, and 'corrects all others'. See Fiona M. Palmer, *Vincent Novello (1781–1861): Music for the Masses*, Music in Nineteenth-Century Britain (Aldershot: Ashgate, 2006), p. 167 and n. 180; and Richard Turbet, 'The Musical Antiquarian Society, 1840–1848', *Brio* 29 (1992): 16–18.

99   For instance, it was used for the 1895 performance of *Dido* mounted by Stanford at the Royal College of Music, described below. See Harris, *Henry Purcell's 'Dido and Aeneas'*, p. 151.

100   The engraved score is entitled *The Songs, Airs, Duets & Chorusses in the Masque of King Arthur: as Perform'd at the Theatre Royal in Drury Lane. Compos'd by Purcel & Dr. Arne* ([London], [c.1771]). According to the surviving libretto, an earlier revival of *King Arthur* in Dublin in 1763 also included omissions and additions, principally songs incorporated into Acts I, II and V for the star soprano Signora Passerini. See Harris, *'King Arthur's Journey'*, p. 283. The Garrick–Arne production has recently been revisited in Gilman, *'David Garrick's Masque of King Arthur'*: 139–44; later productions including both Purcell's and Arne's music, most of which were based on Kemble and Lindley's further adaptation of 1784, *Arthur and Emmeline*, are briefly discussed in ibid.: 144–5 and 147–53.

101   Since the early eighteenth-century version of *Dido* represented by the Tenbury score seems to have been the source for the Academy's version, the arrangers do not seem to have been aware of the missing music at the end of Act II, although they cut Aeneas' monologue 'Jove's command' to just two lines. Unfortunately, their reaction to the incomplete key scheme created by the missing music was to join this shortened recitative tonally to the key in which the next scene begins, B flat, which entailed complete rewriting of the remaining part of the monologue, with the result that 'the crucial dramatic moment of Aeneas' decision, on which hangs the outcome of the entire opera, thereby loses all importance in itself and functions simply as a link from one motion (the escape from the storm) to another (preparing of ships)'; Harris, *Henry Purcell's 'Dido and Aeneas'*, p. 145; see also p. 128.

102   The index to the *c.*1771 edition of the music clearly attributes the new and replacement

scale adaptations incorporated into the Academy's score of *Dido* are much more extensive than those in *King Arthur*. However, it is clear that the alterations to both works were designed to achieve the same goal of updating the music stylistically to make it more palatable to eighteenth-century audiences: rhythmic 'irregularities' like Purcell's characteristic Scotch snap are reversed; melismas are shortened, often through extra text repetition; the harmonic language is simplified, dissonance made less harsh and harmonic rhythm decreased; cadences are rewritten and underlay changed so that final syllables occur on the first beat of the bar; and elisions between movements are removed so that groups of pieces are structured more like late eighteenth-century number opera – indeed in the 1774 Academy libretto for *Dido* solo movements are designated respectively as 'recitative' and 'aria'.[103] Further evidence of attempts to divest the operas of their seventeenth-century form can be seen in Arne's drastic reduction of the Act IV passacaglia in *King Arthur* and the removal of its dance element, which Harris suggests demonstrates 'a late eighteenth-century impatience with dance-oriented operatic tableaux built on repeating basses in the style of the great chaconnes of Lully's operas'.[104] Moreover, Higney suggests that the rewriting of 'Come Follow me' as a solo based on Purcell's imitative chorus illustrates the way in which Purcell's old-fashioned style of word painting was now being replaced by the freer expression of Arne's day.[105]

While the eighteenth-century productions of *Dido* and *King Arthur* form the best-known examples of stylistic updating of Purcell's music, it is clear that the pattern can be found in numerous sources of this period, including Boyce's score of the Te Deum, published in 1755, which is greatly expanded in scale,[106] but has been little studied; the Concert of Antient Music's parts for their 1787 performance of *King Arthur* – which, according to Tuppen, were independent of the Arne version, while similar in nature; and the catches and songs included in the Catch Club manuscripts.[107] Arne, of course, famously wished to go much further in his adaptations for *King Arthur* than Garrick would allow, the surviving letter from Arne written during rehearsals for the production indicating both his low opinion of Purcell's musical style, and his frustration that more of the music was not to be replaced:

> All the other Solo Songs of Purcell are infamously bad; so very bad, that they are privately the objects of sneer and ridicule to the musicians, but, I have not meddled with any, that are not to come from the mouths of your principal Performers. I wish you wou'd only give me leave to *Doctor* this performance, I

---

music to Arne: see the reproduction in Higney, 'Henry Purcell: A Reception/ Dissemination Study', p. 174.

103 Harris, *Henry Purcell's 'Dido and Aeneas'*, pp. 130–47 and Harris, *'King Arthur's* Journey', p. 279.

104 Harris, *'King Arthur's* Journey', pp. 273–4.

105 Higney, 'Henry Purcell: A Reception/Dissemination Study', pp. 175 and 189–200; see also Harris, *'King Arthur's* Journey', pp. 269–73.

106 Holman, *Henry Purcell*, p. 143.

107 Tuppen, 'Purcell in the Eighteenth Century'.

would certainly make it pleasing to the Public, which otherwise, may have an obstruction to the success of the Revival.[108]

Arne's implication that adaptation was necessary in order to make the music acceptable to the audience is notable bearing in mind the fact that the production, while not disastrous, did not achieve great acclaim.[109] He was clearly still irritated by Garrick's refusal to give him free rein in a later letter of 1775, and here expressly referred to the flat reception of the performances, which 'fail[ed] in making that impression on the public, which the managers had an undoubted right to expect'.[110] He describes Purcell's music as 'Cathedral, and not to the taste of a modern theatrical audience', and, as Luckett remarks, it is significant that another eighteenth-century commentator used a similar term somewhat earlier: in 1736 Thomas Gray noted in a letter to Horace Walpole about an earlier (unadapted) production of *King Arthur* that, although he liked the Frost Scene, 'the Songs are all Church-Musick'.[111] What 'cathedral' and 'church-musick' clearly meant was 'old-fashioned': once Purcell's music began to sound out of date to audiences, it risked becoming unpalatable to them, even if they did purport to admire 'ancient' music. Musical updating was thus often necessary if the music was to be well received. Recent accounts of such eighteenth-century updating have therefore tended to be more charitable to the adapters than were earlier assessors such as Cummings, who referred to John Stafford Smith's *c.*1790 edition of Purcell's Te Deum as 'one of the most impertinent pieces of vandalism I am acquainted with'.[112] Harris in particular has argued in favour of judging such adaptations on their own terms, as is sometimes the case with literary reworkings.[113] Nevertheless, there are cautionary tales to be told when, for lack of surviving sources from Purcell's own lifetime, eighteenth-century copies have necessarily been adopted as the principal sources of his music: as the recent case of *Come ye Sons of Art* has demonstrated, even now we are still discovering that versions of Purcell's music we thought were more or less 'authentic' in fact have the mark of the eighteenth century heavily stamped upon them.[114] As well as the Academy of Ancient Music's version of *Dido and Aeneas* reproduced in Macfarren's

---

108 Hubert Langley, *Doctor Arne* (Cambridge: Cambridge University Press, 1938), p. 69; quoted in Harris, '*King Arthur*'s Journey', p. 261, and in part in Gilman, 'David Garrick's *Masque of King Arthur*': 141.

109 Harris says of the run of 19 performances that it was 'hardly shameful, but neither was it record-breaking'; '*King Arthur*'s Journey', p. 262 n. 14.

110 Ibid., p. 262; also quoted in part in Luckett, '"Or Rather Our Musical Shakspeare"', p. 69.

111 Thomas Gray, *Collected Correspondence*, eds Paget Toynbee and Leonard Whibley (3 vols, Oxford: Oxford University Press, 1971), vol. 1, p. 37, quoted in Luckett, '"Or Rather Our Musical Shakspeare"', p. 68.

112 William H. Cummings, 'The Mutilation of a Masterpiece', *Proceedings of the Musical Association* 30 (1903–04): 114.

113 Harris, *Henry Purcell's 'Dido and Aeneas'*, p. 146; she makes similar comments in '*King Arthur*'s Journey', pp. 288–9.

114 See my 'Robert Pindar, Thomas Busby, and the Mysterious Scoring of Henry Purcell's "Come ye Sons of Art"', *Music & Letters* 88 (2007): 1–48.

edition and referred to above, another case in point is the setting of 'St George', which was recognized as a likely later addition to *King Arthur* only in Laurie's revised Purcell Society edition of the opera in 1971.[115]

Reception of Purcell's Liturgical Repertory

Although the existing literature on performances of Purcell's music in the theatre and in concerts is sufficiently large for a clear picture to emerge of the fortunes of that part of his output during the eighteenth century, the same cannot be said of research on his less public repertory: virtually the only published comments about the longevity of his church music, for example, occur in a single paragraph in Luckett's essay '"Or Rather Our Musical Shakspeare"'. Here Luckett notes that Purcell's liturgical music continued to be 'customary fare' in English cathedrals and chapels in the eighteenth century, citing the ten anthems Burney claims were still performed at the Chapel Royal in 1789, and the inclusion of Purcell alongside Blow in Boyce's *Cathedral Music* of 1760.[116] There is a simple explanation for this imbalance in the literature: the contrast between the sheer weight of surviving documentation surrounding theatre and concert performances and the fact that Purcell's other music did not attract the same degree of attention in the press or in official records. For some genres – particularly those that were intended predominantly for domestic use, such as the consort music – we are unlikely to be able to recover much detail of performing trends.[117] Nevertheless, Purcell's liturgical music does have a posthumous performance history, for which evidence exists in the part-books and other records surviving for many religious institutions from the eighteenth century onwards. These have the potential to establish whether, for example, performance of his sacred repertory became restricted to a small number of works as in the case of his theatre music and songs, or whether it was influenced by printed editions such as that of Boyce.[118] There is also evidence to suggest that Purcell's sacred music helped to preserve his reputation in the later eighteenth century: in his anonymously published *Remarks on Mr Avison's*

---

115 See Henry Purcell, *King Arthur*, ed. Margaret Laurie, The Works of Henry Purcell, vol. 26 (rev. edn, London: Novello, 1971), p. 205. See also the attribution reproduced in Higney, 'Henry Purcell: A Reception/Dissemination Study', p. 174.

116 Luckett, '"Or Rather Our Musical Shakspeare"', p. 68.

117 The single exception would appear to be the Golden Sonata, as noted in Hawkins's account of Purcell's music; see n. 141 below.

118 Burney's comment that 'many of [Purcell's] numerous compositions for the church, particularly those printed in the second and third volumes of Dr. Boyce's Collection, are still retained in the King's Chapel and in our cathedrals' suggests that this may have been the case; Burney *A General History of Music*, p. 383. James Hume's ongoing PhD dissertation, 'The Chapel-Royal Part-Books in Eighteenth-Century England' (University of Manchester) will go some way towards filling this gap in relation to the complex Chapel-Royal part-books.

Essay on Musical Expression (London, 1753), William Hayes associated the sacred music of the 'great' Purcell and Croft with the towering ancient figures of Gibbons, Morley, Byrd and Tallis, whom he suggested (in a rebuke to Avison) formed an English 'school' of composing;[119] similar comments associating Purcell and Blow with earlier Renaissance composers as 'our English classics in this sacred science' were made by Rev. George Horne in 1784;[120] and, as we shall see, both Burney and Hawkins give surprising emphasis to Purcell's sacred output in their accounts of his music.[121]

Such questions are significant partly because they can help to create a more balanced view of Purcell's reception than we have at present – a portrait that does not derive from the commercial sphere that so heavily influenced the development of his reputation in the century after his death and that correspondingly suggests less prominence in relation to contemporaries such as Blow. There is, moreover, much that could be learned about the role of historical music in eighteenth-century cathedral repertory: it is clear for example that older styles were periodically used as an antidote to the more secular styles of sacred music that prevailed in the period, which were viewed by some reformers as inappropriate for worship. While some writers, such as Arthur Bedford, made unspecific comments about nature of modern church music, which he claimed is 'now chang'd to a Diversion for Atheists & Libertines',[122] Thomas Tudway used the example of Purcell's funeral sentence *Thou knowest, Lord*, which he says was written 'after ye old way', to suggest a model of the style of music appropriate to devotion:

> I appeal to all [tha]t were p[re]sent, as well such as understood Music, as those [tha]t did not, whither, they ever heard any thing, so rapturously fine, & solemn, & so Heavenly, in ye Operation, w[hi]ch drew tears from all; & yet a plain, Natural Composition; w[hi]ch shews ye pow'r of Music, when tis rightly fitted, & Adapted to devotional purposes.[123]

Of course, Purcell's output of symphony anthems contained a good deal of music in the secularized style of which Tudway was so critical, so it is notable that it should have been Purcell's sombre full anthem that he chose as his exemplar, rather than

---

119 See Luckett, '"Or Rather Our Musical Shakspeare"', p. 69.

120 Horne listed Purcell together with Blow, Tallis and Byrd, Gibbons and King, Croft and Clark, Wise and Weldon, Greene and Handel, as guardians of a 'chaste and pure' style of sacred music. See George Horne, *The Antiquity, Use, and Excellence of Church Music, a Sermon Preached at the Opening of a New Organ in the Cathedral Church of Christ, Canterbury, on Thursday, July 8, 1784* (Oxford, 1784), pp. 8–9, quoted in Thomas Charles Day, 'A Renaissance Revival in Eighteenth-Century England', *Musical Quarterly* 57 (1971): 575.

121 Holst's comment cited on p. 350 below, indeed, suggests that this trend continued into the twentieth century.

122 Arthur Bedford, *The Great Abuse of Musick. In Two Parts* (London, 1711), p. 209.

123 Lbl Harleian 7340, fol. 3, quoted in Hogwood, 'Thomas Tudway's History of Music', p. 29.

music by an earlier composer whose style more consistently represented Tudway's professed ideal.[124] Comprehensive investigation of the role Restoration sacred music played in cathedral and chapel repertories in the eighteenth century and beyond is needed, however, before we can develop a deeper understanding of the reception of this part of Purcell's repertory and the influence of his more public image in this aspect of his reputation.

Critical Comment on Purcell in the Late Eighteenth Century

By the last quarter of the eighteenth century the position of Purcell's music within the performing repertory was a complex one: while a fairly small group of pieces from the more public parts of his output continued to be included in concerts and was revived on the stage, and Purcell's name had been evoked alongside members of the literary canon as a British national icon, the sense that his music was outmoded and required updating prevailed, reflecting a conflict between the antiquarian interest some individuals were developing for music and the predominant belief in musical progress that led new works to be valued more highly than old ones. Such contradictions came to the fore in the first published monuments of music history produced in Britain: John Hawkins's *A General History of the Science and Practice of Music* (1776) and Charles Burney's *A General History of Music from the Earliest Ages to the Present Period* (1776–89). Much has been written on the historiographical significance of these two writers, and they are often quoted by scholars seeking opinions on Purcell's music that are lacking for earlier periods. However, Luckett's article remains the only published research to focus specifically on their respective depictions and opinions of Purcell;[125] his relatively short account only encompasses a fraction of the evidence that can be gleaned from the two books about the way in which Burney and Hawkins were influenced both by the afterlife of Purcell's music in the eighteenth century and by prevailing opinions about historical repertory in their time, and about the significance of their opinions to later commentary on Purcell and his contemporaries.

The well-known view of the contrasts between Burney's and Hawkins's approaches to music history – in which Hawkins is depicted as an antiquarian of the Academy of Ancient Music, whose interest was primarily in religious music, and who saw modern music as corrupt, overly virtuosic and in decline, while

---

124 Hogwood points out, however, that Tudway's opinions of this sacred repertory were inconsistent and complex, not least because his aims in copying the Harleian collection changed during its compilation; see ibid.

125 Luckett, '"Or Rather Our Musical Shakspeare"', pp. 70–74. However, Pinnock also gives a brief overview of Burney's account of Purcell in 'The Purcell Phenomenon', pp. 6–7, and Alan Howard also considers aspects of both writers' views of Purcell in his unpublished dissertation. See 'Purcell and the Poetics of Artifice', pp. 21–3, 30–31, 38 and 48–50.

Burney is seen as the popular, fashionable writer with a strong belief in musical progress, and a corresponding hostility towards the music of the past – only partially explains their accounts of Purcell, since there are notable similarities in their coverage.[126] Both, in fact, pick up on the most significant tropes surrounding Purcell that had developed during the eighteenth century: Hawkins states that he 'is chiefly remembered for his vocal compositions' and refers to 'the excellencies of Purcell in vocal composition';[127] Burney singles out for praise the 'exquisite expression of the words' in 'From Rosy Bow'rs', which, he feels, 'render it one of the most affecting compositions extant to *every Englishman* who regards Music not merely as an agreeable arrangement and combination of sounds, but as the vehicle of sentiment, and voice and passion'.[128] Elsewhere he makes more explicit reference to Purcell as a national icon, 'who is as much the pride of an Englishman in Music, as Shakspeare in productions for the stage, Milton in epic poetry, Lock in metaphysics, or Sir Isaac Newton in philosophy and mathematics'.[129] In addition, they each note the tragedy of his early death, which Hawkins simply describes as 'a great affliction to the lovers of his art',[130] but which Burney uses to explain the fact that 'we have no school for composition, no well-digested method of study, nor, indeed, models of our own'.[131] Although neither is apparently aware of it, they also have a tendency to attribute significance to those works of Purcell that had remained popular in their own lifetimes, such as the mad songs, and *King Arthur*, which Hawkins notes 'seems to have been the most admired' of Purcell's theatre works,[132] and which Burney believes includes movements that 'contain not a single passage that the best composers of the present times, if it presented itself to their imagination, would reject'.[133] And both writers place what today would

---

126　For this contrasting view of the two writers, see Weber, *The Rise of Musical Classics*, pp. 205–22. On Burney, see also Kerry S. Grant, *Dr. Burney as Critic and Historian of Music*, Studies in Musicology, vol. 62 (Ann Arbor: UMI Research Press, 1983) and Roger Lonsdale, *Dr Charles Burney: a Literary Biography* (Oxford: Clarendon, 1989; first published 1965); and on Hawkins, see Percy A. Scholes, *The Life and Activities of Sir John Hawkins, Musician, Magistrate and Friend of Johnson* (London: Oxford University Press, 1953).

127　Hawkins, *A General History of the Science and Practice of Music*, pp. 753 and 747. Howard, however, points out that Hawkins did not consider his statement 'worthy of further examination'; Howard, 'Purcell and the Poetics of Artifice', p. 21.

128　Burney, *A General History of Music*, p. 393. Also quoted in Luckett, '"Or Rather Our Musical Shakspeare"', p. 72. See also Howard, 'Purcell and the Poetics of Musical Artifice', p. 22.

129　Burney, *A General History of Music*, p. 380; see also the description used by Luckett as the title for his article, in ibid., p. 396; and Howard, 'Purcell and the Poetics of Musical Artifice', pp. 30–31.

130　Hawkins, *A General History of the Science and Practice of Music*, p. 749.

131　Burney, *A General History of Music*, p. 405.

132　Hawkins, *A General History of the Science and Practice of Music*, p. 753.

133　Burney, *A General History of Music*, p. 392. Burney notes that 'it has been lately revived, well performed, and printed', clearly referring to the Garrick–Arne production of 1770. He seems unaware that Arne's approach to the work did not support his claim about

be regarded as an unusually heavy emphasis on what they regard as Purcell's Italian models, particularly Carissimi and Stradella, to the exclusion of any French influences, which is understandable given the predominance of Italian music in their own times.[134]

Burney's methodology for his *History* seems to have differed most from Hawkins's in the fact that he travelled widely in Europe to acquire materials and information, whereas Hawkins's research seems to have been based in libraries within England, but this disparity would have been largely insignificant to their coverage of English composers like Purcell who were virtually unknown on the continent. In fact their sources of information on Purcell were very similar: they each make reference to *Orpheus Britannicus*, *Ayres for the Theatre*, the score of *Dioclesian*, *Harmonia Sacra*, the 1697 *Te Deum*, the 1683 *Sonnata's* and Playford's *Pleasant Musical Companion*.[135] Burney also evidently did have access to a wide range of manuscript sources – as well as the court financial records, he refers to manuscripts of sacred music at York Minster, together with materials copied at Christ Church by Aldrich, Tudway's collection, and the important Purcell autograph in the Royal Music collection, now Lbl R.M. 20.h.8.[136] Yet, although he lists the works by Purcell in these manuscripts, he in fact refers to them infrequently in his account, so both authors remain largely reliant on their printed sources in describing and analysing Purcell's music. This helps to confirm the impact that printing had on Purcell's posthumous reputation, and Hawkins in particular seems to associate print with success.[137] What is surprising, however, is that their accounts do not really mirror the popular image of Purcell that had grown up in the music printing of the eighteenth century and

---

modern composers' opinions of Purcell's music. He contradicts this view himself in an earlier comment quoted on pp. 333–4 below.

134 See, for instance, Hawkins, *A General History of the Science and Practice of Music*, pp. 744 and 759; Burney, *A General History of Music*, p. 399.

135 In addition, Hawkins used copies of Downes's *Roscius Anglicanus* (1708), the 1684 publication of *Welcome to all the Pleasures*, a copy of the 1697 *Sonatas* and Frances Purcell's *Choice Collection* of 1696, while Burney referred to Boyce's *Cathedral Music* (1760–63), and Wood's *Athenae Oxonienses* (1691–92) as well as *The Theater of Music* (1685), and he appears to have been aware of Purcell's 1692 collection *Some Select Songs ... in the Fairy Queen*, although he misattributes the music to *Oedipus* instead. See Burney, *A General History of Music*, p. 390: 'He published the Music to a masque sung in the tragedy of *Oedipus*, when it was revived in 1692.' This list should not be considered definitive, however, since Hawkins did refer to Boyce, Wood and to the *Theater of Music* elsewhere in his writing about Restoration music, in sections on Blow and Locke. Hawkins, *A General History of the Science and Practice of Music*, pp. 714, 716–17 and 741.

136 In contrast, Hawkins only mentions an autograph of *Blessed are They that Fear the Lord* – presumably the copy now incorporated within Lbl Add. 30931 – together with archive records from Westminster Abbey and the court chequebook.

137 His account begins with what amounts to a description of the publications of which he is aware, and he seems to distinguish between the works surviving in manuscript only and those in print where he lists 'the rest of Purcell's compositions in print', which, he says, are 'proof of Purcell's extensive genius'; Hawkins, *A General History of the Science and Practice of Music*, p. 745.

the posthumous performing history of his music· his theatre music and the *Orpheus Britannicus* songs certainly do receive ample coverage, but Hawkins considers that Purcell's attention was 'equally divided between both the church and the theatre', and both suggest that his music needs to be viewed in terms of his sacred, theatrical and chamber output.[138]

We can probably explain at least some of the similarities in the views expressed by the two writers and the parts of Purcell's output they describe through Burney's reliance in the later volumes of his *General History* on Hawkins's already-published complete work. Nevertheless, their overall opinions of Purcell are quite different and tend to fit the stereotypical images that have been attributed to them by modern commentators. Hawkins, as Luckett notes, generally avoids passing judgement,[139] preferring statements of fact until he comes to discuss Purcell's instrumental pieces, which, he writes, 'fall short of his other works'.[140] Yet even here he is careful not to impart blame on Purcell personally, claiming that instrumental music in general was 'wanting in spirit and force' towards the end of the seventeenth century; it soon becomes clear he means that it lacked the characteristics of Corelli's sonatas, which 'Purcell lived rather too early to profit by'.[141] His reformist opinions of music as a potentially corrupting force also surface in his criticism of Purcell's tavern music, for which, he claims, the composer 'merit[s] censure for having prostituted his invention, by adapting music to some of the most wretched ribaldry that was ever obtruded on the world for humour'.[142]

In contrast, Burney is by no means reluctant to impart his views to the reader, as elsewhere in his *History*. In Purcell's case, however, he seems torn between two mutually exclusive positions, which are described by Luckett: on the one hand, Burney recognizes Purcell's iconic status, and therefore refers repeatedly to his 'genius' as a composer, and to his 'admirable' music;[143] on the other, as a progressive, Burney cannot help but reveal not only that Purcell's music has largely fallen out of favour, but that he himself finds much of it archaic, or 'Gothic', and – in terms of harmony in particular – downright erroneous.[144] Many of his analyses

---

138 Hawkins, *A General History of the Science and Practice of Music*, pp. 744 and 753; Burney, *A General History of Music*, p. 383; this parallel is almost certainly an example of Burney's reliance on Hawkins.

139 Luckett, '"Or Rather Our Musical Shakspeare"', p. 70.

140 Hawkins, *A General History of the Science and Practice of Music*, p. 754.

141 Ibid. Hawkins quotes the whole of the Golden Sonata, which was the only one of Purcell's trio sonatas to gain a lasting reputation in the eighteenth century, and of which he says (ibid., p. 755): 'the reputation is not yet extinct.' On Hawkins's placing of Purcell in relation to his antecedents and successors as an instrumental composer, see Howard, 'Purcell and the Poetics of Artifice', pp. 22–3.

142 Hawkins, *A General History of the Science and Practice of Music*, p. 747.

143 See, for example, Burney, *A General History of Music*, pp. 383, 385, 388 and 389.

144 See his well-known lament that Purcell 'built his fame with such perishable materials, that his worth and works are daily diminishing'; ibid., p. 380; his negative comments on the 'Gothic' practice of writing music above a ground bass in ibid., p. 394; and his criticisms of Purcell's harmonic language in ibid., pp. 384–5. Luckett outlines this two-

of Purcell's music are in fact filled with backhanded compliments, as these extracts demonstrate:

> The first movement of his full anthem in eight parts, 'O Lord God of hosts,' is a noble composition, *alla Palestrina*, in which all the laws of fugue upon two, and sometimes more, subjects, are preserved inviolable; the harmony, though bold, is, in general, chaste, and the effect of the whole spirited and majestic. The second movement is extremely pathetic and expressive; but, both in that and the last movement, he seem trying experiments in harmony; and, in hazarding new combinations, he seems now and then to give the ear more pain than pleasure …
>
> The complete service of Purcell, in B flat, printed by Boyce, is a most agreeable and excellent piece of counterpoint, of which the modulation frequently stimulates attention by unexpected transitions, yet of so sober a kind as never to give the ear the least uneasiness, till we come to be bottom of p. 110, and then the same crudities of the sharp 3d with the flat 6th, and flat 3d, 4th, and 5th, as have been elsewhere censured, occur; which, I hope, in spite of my reverence for Purcell, the organists of our cathedrals scruple not to change for better harmony.[145]

Burney eventually succumbs, at the end of his account of Purcell, to list the composer's 'defects', which include melody that 'wants symmetry and grace', harmony that 'is not always so pure as it ought to be', the excessive repetition of single words, and poor string writing that is 'equally deficient in force, invention, and effect'.[146] It is easy to agree with Luckett's comment that Burney makes positive comments about Purcell 'almost … against his better judgement':[147] fundamentally, the highest praise Burney is able to give Purcell is that he 'revived and invigorated' English music at a time when it 'was manifestly in decline', and thus became England's national composer.[148] Luckett describes Burney's portrayal of Purcell as 'contradictory',[149] but this verdict begins to appear too charitable when one considers the vehemence of Burney's attack on John Blow. Alongside a lengthy list of 'specimens of Dr. Blow's Crudities', Burney describes Blow as 'unequal, and frequently unhappy in his attempts at new harmony and modulation', and 'confused and inaccurate' as a harmonist, with 'crudities … so numerous' in one piece 'as to throw a doubt on

---

sided portrayal of the composer in '"Or Rather Our Musical Shakspeare"', pp. 71–2.

145 Burney, *A General History of Music*, pp. 384 and 385. Burney gives a lengthy footnote at the end of the first-quoted passage explaining the 'harmonical licences' taken by Purcell, since they 'may lead young students into error'.

146 Ibid., pp. 402–3. See also Howard, 'Purcell and the Poetics of Artifice', p. 38; and Higney, 'Henry Purcell: A Reception/Dissemination Study', pp. 184–6, where Burney's apparent criticism of Purcell's mimetic techniques is noted.

147 Luckett, '"Or Rather Our Musical Shakspeare"', p. 73.

148 Burney, *A General History of Music*, p. 404.

149 Luckett, '"Or Rather Our Musical Shakspeare"', p. 71.

his learning, as well as genius'.[150] Burney, indeed, cannot understand why Blow was 'so celebrated and honoured by his cotemporaries' or by Boyce.[151] Yet when we examine the faults he painstakingly exemplifies, it soon becomes clear that most are melodic and harmonic figurations that were in fact characteristic of the Restoration generally, and therefore equally applicable to Purcell's as to Blow's music. Since Burney explicitly claims that 'it does not appear that Purcell, whom he did himself the honour to call his scholar, or Crofts, or Clark, his pupils, ever threw notes about at random, in his manner, or insulted the ear with lawless discords, which no concords can render tolerable',[152] one cannot help but wonder if Blow is in fact being used here as a musical scapegoat to deflect criticism away from Purcell, England's national composer, whose music Burney personally disliked, but could not bring himself wholeheartedly to condemn.[153]

Editions of Purcell's Music

The notable emphasis placed on printed editions of Purcell's music by both Burney and Hawkins serves to highlight the important role such editions played in the development and maintenance of Purcell's posthumous reputation. As mentioned above, this was not just because printed music was more accessible than material surviving only in manuscript, but also because publication came to be associated with status during the course of the eighteenth century. The potential of the printed edition to serve as a monument was also developed in this period and – while at first such editions were primarily associated with recent composers, *Orpheus Britannicus* being an important early example – they took on an increasingly historical character, with two distinct types of emphasis: on the one hand there were editions intended to preserve 'ancient' repertory in specific genres; on the other, we see the first attempts to publish posthumously the complete works of particular 'great' individuals.[154] Purcell's music was associated with both trends,

---

150 Burney, *A General History of Music*, pp. 351–2.

151 Ibid.

152 Ibid., p. 352.

153 Howard also notes that Burney is 'far kinder to Purcell than to almost any of his contemporaries' in his identification of 'crudities' and that 'Blow comes off particularly badly'; Howard, 'Purcell and the Poetics of Artifice', p. 31. Howard has also pointed out (personal correspondence, 6 November 2009) that Burney's disingenuousness is heightened by the fact that he groups Purcell with Croft and Clarke, the next generation of composers, rather than with Blow, a more obvious stylistic partner if one is considering the whole of Purcell's *oeuvre*, including his early works.

154 Lying slightly outside this pattern is John Stafford Smith's important edition *Musica Antiqua: A Selection of Music of this and other Countries from the Commencement of the Twelfth to the Beginning of the Eighteenth Century* (London, c.1812), which has been described by Day as the first 'history of music in examples'. Some Purcell is included here. See Thomas Charles Day, 'Old Music in England, 1790–1820', *Revue Belge de Musicologie*

but unfortunately our knowledge of its role in this history is highly fragmented due to the incomplete nature of research in this field: in addition to King's article on Goodison's edition cited above, the only published work has focused on specific parts of Purcell's output – editions of *Dido and Aeneas* assessed by Harris, of Purcell's keyboard works by Hogwood, and of parts of his sacred output by Fiona Palmer.[155] Thus there is much that remains to be written on the role of the published edition in Purcell's reception, and in particular on the often close links between publication and performance.

Weber notes that the concept of preserving historical repertory was 'rooted in both church music and musical learning',[156] and there are, of course, important antecedents in England to the printed collections of ancient sacred repertory that appeared in the eighteenth century: Barnard's *First Book of Selected Church Musick* (1641), which contained no works by living composers and appears to have been intended for performance; Aldrich's manuscript collection and arrangements; and most significantly Tudway's seven substantial volumes of 'all ye Church Musick, both Ancient and Modern, from Henry ye 8ths time, till now',[157] collected for the Harley family. Publishing seems to have become important to the idea of preserving ancient sacred music in England because of the developing association between print and accuracy. The earliest indications of this perception of the role of print for sacred music occur in Croft's preface to his *Musica Sacra* of 1724 (p. 1), where the composer laments:

> As to what concerns the frequent Transcribing *Church-Musick*, (the only Way hitherto made use of in *Choirs*, to continue the same); 'tis observable, that at this Day it is very difficult to find in the Cathedrals, any one Antient valuable Piece of *Musick*, that does not abound with Faults and Imperfections; The unavoidable Effect of their falling into the Hands of careless and unskilful *Transcribers*; which is an Injury much to be regretted by all who have any Concern or Value those great Authors, or their Works.[158]

When John Alcock, organist of Lichfield Cathedral, proposed an edition of 'the choicest antient and modern Services' in 1752, he did so similarly 'Having observed how incorrect the Services, &c. are at Cathedrals';[159] and in the preface

---

26–7 (1972–73): 34–5.

155 Harris, *Henry Purcell's 'Dido and Aeneas'*, pp. 148–51, 157, 160 and 162–3; Hogwood, 'Creating the Corpus'; Palmer, *Vincent Novello*, pp. 158–67. Palmer gives a detailed account of Novello's production of the Purcell sacred-music series. As noted below, the early editions of the Purcell Society and its committee members are also briefly included in Pinnock and Lingard's unpublished conference paper, 'Seeking the Bubble'.

156 Weber, *The Rise of Musical Classics*, p. 23.

157 Ibid., p. 42. On this topic, see also Weber, 'The Eighteenth-Century Origins of the Musical Canon', *Journal of the Royal Musical Association* 114 (1989): 11–14.

158 William Croft, *Musica Sacra, or, Select Anthems in Score* (London, [1724]), p. 1. I am grateful to Alan Howard for drawing my attention towards this source.

159 Quoted from an advertisement in the *London Evening Post*, 6–8 August 1752, in H. Diack

to his *Cathedral Music* Boyce also noted 'that many gross errors have crept into their productions by the carelessness of copyists'.[160] Such comments indicate that these published collections were intended for use by performers, and Boyce indeed suggests that choirmasters might allow their singers copies of 'these legible score-books to sing from'.[161] However, Johnstone observes that when the imminent arrival of the first volume was announced in April 1760, Boyce specifically proposed that 'all Noblemen and Gentlemen who laudably promote Science, in whatever Branch it appears[,] will not think the above Work unworthy of a Place in their best chosen Libraries',[162] and his preface announces that he wishes to preserve 'these valuable remains of my ingenious countrymen', so there is a clear sense here in which the music is also being preserved as a record and model. In this context, Purcell's role is remarkably small: Boyce included just nine anthems and the B flat service from Purcell's sacred output, marginally fewer than the two services and ten anthems by Blow,[163] so there is little sense here in which his national profile was higher than that of his Restoration contemporaries. It was only in the 1820s, when Vincent Novello published a five-volume collection of Purcell's sacred works, that more of the composer's output in this genre came into print;[164] much work remains to be done to place this edition and Purcell's music more generally within the context of the movement to reform cathedral music and improve standards in this period that led to the revival of other early English composers of sacred repertory.[165]

For Purcell's music, the more important side to the publication of historical repertory lay in its association with national pride.[166] In this respect, it is significant that the earliest attempt to publish Purcell's complete works, begun by Benjamin Goodison in the late 1780s, was almost certainly inspired by Samuel Arnold's Handel edition of 1787–97, which in turn grew out of the great national Handel

---

Johnstone, 'The Genesis of Boyce's "Cathedral Music"', *Music & Letters* 56 (1975): 29. As Johnstone notes, Alcock's plan came to nothing because he withdrew in the light of Maurice Greene's similar intentions; Greene's collection was still unpublished at his death and was completed by his pupil William Boyce as *Cathedral Music*; ibid.: 30.

160 William Boyce, *Cathedral Music: Being a Collection in Score of the Most Valuable and Useful Compositions for that Service, by the Several English Masters of the last Two Hundred Years* (3 vols, London, 1760–63), vol. 2, p. iii. Boyce quotes extensively from Croft in his introduction, so may have followed him in this respect.

161 Ibid.

162 Quoted from an advertisement in *The Public Advertiser*, 29 April 1760, in Johnstone, 'The Genesis of Boyce's "Cathedral Music"': 31. Johnstone notes in ibid.: 32 that Boyce's list of just 112 subscribers consisted principally of professional musicians, however.

163 I am grateful to Alan Howard for these figures.

164 See Palmer, *Vincent Novello*, pp. 158–67.

165 See Suzanne Cole, *Thomas Tallis and his Music in Victorian England*, Music in Britain, 1600–1900 (Woodbridge: Boydell and Brewer, 2008), pp. 33–7; and Palmer, *Vincent Novello*, pp. 139–47.

166 Howard assesses various aspects of Purcell's importance to British nationalism in 'Purcell and the Poetics of Artifice', pp. 27–39.

commemoration of 1784.[167] Goodison, who at first seems to have had ambitions to publish music by Handel as well as Purcell, clearly felt there was a patriotic purpose behind his plan to produce a collected edition of Purcell's works, since he explained that such a project 'seems due to the Memory of our excellent Country Man'; later he was even more explicit, stating that 'some Degree of national Credit may result from their being made generally known'.[168] Such patriotic sentiments came to the fore in the nineteenth century and, as we shall see, Purcell's music was revived in this period as part of the broader nationalistic aims of the figures involved in the English Musical Renaissance. Evidence for this trend is clear in all the major editions of Purcell's music in the period. Novello, for example, began the written volume accompanying his sacred-music edition by quoting Burney's comparison of Purcell with Shakespeare, Milton and Newton (see above p. 331), and the publications produced under the aegis of the Musical Antiquarian Society between 1841 and 1848 – which included four volumes of Purcell's music[169] – were designed to preserve the works of 'early English Composers', according to the society's founding 'laws'.[170] The very title of G.E.P. Arkwright's Old English Edition of 1889–1902 betokens its similar aims, although its inclusion of Purcell's music was limited to songs selected from *Orpheus Britannicus*. Most importantly, while the stated purpose of the Purcell Society was simply one of 'doing justice to the memory of Henry Purcell', William H. Cummings's preface to the first edition produced in the society's projected complete edition in 1878 does not seek to hide its patriotic rhetoric:

> The task of completing the noblest possible monument to our English master – viz. the publication of his Complete Works – is thus … a heavy one. But the Purcell Society enters upon it with a well-founded trust in the sympathy and support of the musical public. For that the Committee now appeal, desiring to enrich the available treasures of English art, and to wipe away a national reproach by doing justice to one of whom the nation has abundant reason to be proud.[171]

Cummings clearly had a sense of regret that a *Gesamtausgabe* for Purcell had not yet been produced and that so few of Purcell's works had been published. He

---

167 On Arnold's edition, see J.M. Coopersmith, 'The First *Gesamtausgabe*: Dr. Arnold's Edition of Handel's Works', *Notes* Series 2/4 (1947): 277–91 and 438–49; and Paul Hirsch, 'Dr. Arnold's Handel Edition (1787–1797)', *Music Review* 8 (1947): 106–16.

168 From the first and fifth printed prospectuses for the edition, reproduced in King, 'Benjamin Goodison and the First "Complete Edition" of Purcell', p. 393.

169 These were *Dido and Aeneas* (1841), *Bonduca* (1842), *King Arthur* (1843), and the 1692 St Cecilia's Day ode *Hail, bright Cecilia* (1848). See Turbet, 'The Musical Antiquarian Society': 17–18 and n. 98 above.

170 See Turbet, 'The Musical Antiquarian Society': 13.

171 Henry Purcell, *The Yorkshire Feast Song*, ed. W.H. Cummings under the Supervision of the Purcell Society, The Works of Henry Purcell, vol. 1 (London: Novello, Ewer and co., 1878), pp. 1–2.

was aware of the practical difficulties that had faced earlier editors who had tried to preserve the composer's music in print: Goodison in particular, he notes, had had 'only about 100 subscribers' – in fact his list amounted to 105 – and had been forced to abandon his edition after producing only a handful of works.[172] While Cummings's explanation for Goodison's failure is simply that 'the time was not ripe for such an enterprise',[173] the evidence suggests that it was in fact symptomatic of a broader problem that was to afflict most of the large-scale publishing enterprises that focused on or included Purcell's output: production of such editions was heavily reliant on a small number of enthusiastic individuals who were unable to muster extensive support for their work. Vincent Novello's sacred-music edition had only 62 subscribers;[174] the Musical Antiquarian Society had a brief period of popularity from its inception in 1840 to 1842, but declined rapidly from that point and produced its last publication in 1848;[175] and the Purcell Society edition itself never gained the momentum it needed – only two volumes were published in its first decade, and the edition was in fact only completed in 1965, by which point a revised version had already begun to be compiled.[176] A handful of musicologists

---

172 Ibid., p. 2. Goodison's edition included *King Arthur, The Indian Queen*, the masque from *Oedipus, Celebrate this Festival, Great Parent, hail!, The Yorkshire Feast Song*, a set of sacred music, and the misattributed music from *The Tempest*. See also Luckett, '"Or Rather Our Musical Shakspeare"', p. 74.

173 Purcell, *The Yorkshire Feast Song*, ed. Cummings, p. 2.

174 Palmer, *Vincent Novello*, p. 166.

175 See Turbet, 'The Musical Antiquarian Society': 14–16; and Turbet, 'Musical Antiquarian Society', in *Grove Music Online,* http://www.oxfordmusiconline.com (accessed 22 September 2009). William Chappell, the founder of the Society, claimed in his article for *Grove's Dictionary* that subscriptions were cancelled by many members because they felt 'the works are more fitted for societies than for private families' and that 'the books occupied too much space' (quoted in Turbet, 'The Musical Antiquarian Society': 16), which suggests a mismatch between the antiquarian aims of the Society's committee and the subscribers' predominant wish to put the music to practical domestic use.

176 Watkins Shaw and Margaret Laurie, 'Purcell Society', in *Grove Music Online,* http:// www.oxfordmusiconline.com (accessed 22 September 2009). The failure to complete the Purcell Society edition within a reasonable time period was clearly a matter of regret amongst those seeking to promote English music at the time. Barclay Squire complained in 1921 that 'a country which owns Purcell and yet has not succeeded in completing the edition of his works begun forty-five years ago cannot be expected to take any interest in the music of its minor composers'; 11 years later A.K. Holland bemoaned the fact that the edition 'is still far short of completion'; and Vaughan Williams was still frustrated by the edition in 1951, writing 'The Purcell Society has, I believe, at last almost completed its labours, carried on by the devotion of a few experts who gave their scanty leisure to the work and were entirely neglected by the State or the public'. See Pinnock, 'The Purcell Phenomenon', p. 9, quoting William Barclay Squire, 'The Music of Shadwell's "Tempest"', *Musical Quarterly* 7 (1921): 572, and Vaughan Williams's foreword to Watkins Shaw (ed.), *Eight Concerts of Henry Purcell's Music … with a foreword by Ralph Vaughan Williams and eight essays* (London: Arts Council, 1951), p. 7; and A.K. Holland, *Henry Purcell: The English Musical Tradition* (2nd edn, London:

undertook the task of making most of the editions – most notably Vincent Novello, George Macfarren, Edward Rimbault, Cummings, J.A. Fuller Maitland, William Barclay Squire and later Edward Dent – and the influence of these figures on broader acceptance and promotion of Purcell's music deserves detailed attention because of the deep connections many of them had in English musical life in the period, their broader importance as antiquarians[177] and the key role most of them played in the English Musical Renaissance more generally.

One part of Purcell's output did become popular outside England: his keyboard music, excerpts from which were published in a number of European editions in the nineteenth and twentieth centuries. Hogwood has demonstrated that the most important of these was Aristide and Louise Farrenc's *Le Trésor des Pianistes* of 1861, in which they included a complete transcription of the 1696 *Choice Collection* that had been published by Frances Purcell, partly on the basis of material provided for them by William Chappell.[178] This was followed by Amédée Méraux's *Les clavecinistes de 1637 à 1790* (Paris, 1867), in which Purcell was described as 'without doubt, the most able and most fertile of all the English composers', a comment that seems to have inspired Cummings to begin the Purcell Society editions, since, he announced, 'when the genius of our countrymen is thus asserted in other lands; when his music, as in the case of M. Méraux's volumes, is printed for the use of foreign connoisseurs, and especially when foreign writers point to the neglect which Purcell suffers, it is time for us to consider what practical measures of appreciation and homage can be taken.'[179] Nevertheless, and despite Cummings's claim that Purcell's fame had 'spread to every country where the art is cherished',[180] it was the twentieth century before even a limited number of Purcell's works became available in editions produced outside Britain.

Penguin, 1948; first published London: Bell, 1932), p. 175.

177   Novello, Rimbault and Cummings were particularly important collectors of early music manuscripts, alongside several other individuals connected with the two societies, including Julian Marshall, whose name appears in the list of the 'Permanent Committee' of the Purcell Society in its first volume of 1878. See A. Hyatt King, *Some British Collectors of Music, c.1600–1960* (Cambridge: Cambridge University Press, 1963); for earlier collectors, see Robert Thompson's chapter in this volume, pp. 13–16 above. Pinnock and Lingard note the importance of editors such as Cummings and Fuller Maitland in producing 'popular' editions of Purcell's music 'hoping that choral societies would adopt them as substitutes for Handel/Haydn/Mendelssohn and buy the vocal scores in bulk'; Pinnock and Lingard, 'Seeking the Bubble'. However, no detailed research has been carried out to relate the sources these figures acquired to their editing activities.

178   Hogwood, 'Creating the Corpus', pp. 68–9. Hogwood notes that the Farrencs were considerably less inclined than most nineteenth-century editors to adapt or add to the notation in their sources.

179   Purcell, *The Yorkshire Feast Song*, ed. Cummings, p. 2.

180   Ibid., p. 1.

Purcell and the English Musical Renaissance

The increase in the number of editions of old English music that began in the 1840s and included the music of Byrd, Tallis, Gibbons and other sixteenth-century figures alongside selected composers from the seventeenth century, can be mapped onto a 'growing desire to preserve and perpetuate whatever is most venerable and beautiful in English art' that began in the early Victorian era.[181] The inclusion of Purcell's works in the ensuing organized attempt to create a sense of English musical tradition and to revitalize national music-making during the nineteenth and early twentieth centuries has been relatively well covered in the literature on the English Musical Renaissance,[182] but the subject has, of course, been approached purely from the perspective of understanding the figures involved in the Renaissance itself; to my knowledge there has been almost no consideration of the impact this had on subsequent views of the music of Purcell himself, and there is certainly nothing equivalent to the detailed study recently carried out by Suzanne Cole on the role of Tallis's music in the revival.[183] This is all the more surprising because Purcell was, as Pinnock notes, 'the only earlier English composer for whose works the entire musical community had assumed a proud, collective responsibility; the only one honoured with a complete edition in progress, until Fellowes set to work on Byrd in the 1930s'.[184] Thus while it is clear who were the key figures involved in promoting Purcell's music in the period – the individuals responsible for producing the editions noted above (particularly Cummings, Fuller Maitland and Barclay Squire), the major English composers of the Renaissance (Parry and more importantly Holst and Vaughan Williams), and other high-profile figures of the musical establishment (such as Stanford, Grove and Boris Ord) – there is much still to be learned about the long-term effects of their nationalistic aims on perceptions and understanding of Purcell's music.

The music editions referred to above were a particularly important means through which the small group of people interested in promoting Purcell as

---

181 Edward Taylor, of the Musical Antiquarian Society, quoted in Cole, *Thomas Tallis and His Music*, p. 35.

182 For example, Meirion Hughes and Robert Stradling mention the lengthy article on Purcell in the first edition of *Grove's Dictionary*, the revival of interest in his operas in the years following the inception of the Purcell Society, the importance of particular individuals, and the overshadowing of Purcell by the Bach revival at the turn of the twentieth century. See *The English Musical Renaissance 1840–1940: Constructing a National Music* (2nd edn, Manchester and New York: Manchester University Press, 2001), pp. 26, 36, 48, 75 and 136. More limited reference to Purcell's importance to Vaughan Williams, Britten and Tippett is made by Michael Trend in *The Music Makers: Heirs and Rebels of the English Musical Renaissance – Edward Elgar to Benjamin Britten* (London: Weidenfeld and Nicolson, 1985), pp. 101, 218, 225 and 239.

183 Cole outlines the broad history of the renewed interest in the past in Victorian England with particular reference to Tallis's music in *Thomas Tallis and his Music*, pp. 33–44.

184 Pinnock, 'The Purcell Phenomenon', p. 11. A similar point is made in Howard, 'Purcell and the Poetics of Artifice', pp. 33–4.

England's national composer in the late nineteenth and early twentieth centuries could make his music more available to the broader public, and they also sought to raise his profile through organizing performances and through their writings about music. Study of these media could reveal a good deal about attitude towards Purcell in the period. The most significant performance events occurred at the time of major anniversaries and were clearly designed to help the process of monumentalizing the composer, gaining maximum publicity and exposure for Purcell's music. Bumpus reports that there was a ceremony held by members of the 'Purcell Club' in 1858 (then considered the bicentenary of the composer's birth) in Westminster Abbey,[185] but the commemoration of 1895 was much grander, and was clearly carefully orchestrated by the proponents of the Purcell revival. Centring around the date of the composer's death on 21 November, there was a series of coordinated events: they began with the fully staged production of *Dido* at the Lyceum Theatre; then there was a commemorative service in Westminster Abbey, which even involved the laying of a wreath by Stainer, Grove, Bridge, Parry, Stanford, Cummings and Barclay Squire; that evening saw the first London performance of Parry's 'Ode in Honour of Purcell'; and then the following day a performance of *Hail, bright Cecilia* was given in the Queen's Hall by the Philharmonic Society.[186] Meanwhile the British Museum mounted a concordant exhibition of portraits and manuscripts, and there were several reflections on Purcell published in the press.[187]

Pinnock and Lingard describe in detail the way in which this celebration was used to concentrate the efforts of the revivalists and became the blueprint for future commemorations at the time of the Festival of Britain in 1951, the tercentenary of Purcell's birth in 1959, and the tercentenary of his death in 1995:[188] each was masterminded by a few influential musical figures (Anthony Lewis, Constant Lambert, Edward Dent, Jack Westrup, Boris Ord, Tippett and Britten in the 1950s, primarily members of the Purcell Society committee headed by Curtis Price in the 1990s); each comprised a small number of high-profile performances; and there was corresponding written commentary in which the same individuals

---

185 John S. Bumpus, *A History of English Cathedral Music, 1549–1889* (1st edn reprinted, Farnborough: Gregg, 1972; first published London: T. Werner Laurie, 1908), p. 156. The commemoration is also described in Pinnock, 'The Purcell Phenomenon', pp. 10–11.

186 Comment on these events was published anonymously in 'The Purcell Bi-Centenary Commemoration', *Musical Times and Singing Class Circular* 36 (1895): 811–13. Pinnock and Lingard also quote from reviews of the commemoration in a short-lived publication called *The Year's Music* in 'Seeking the Bubble'.

187 See, for example, the articles on the composer published together in the October issue of *The Musical Times and Singing Class Circular* 36 (1895): Joseph Bennett, 'Henry Purcell: an Appreciation': 725–30; J. Frederick Bridge, 'Purcell's Birthplace and Residences': 733–5; William H. Cummings, 'A Brief Life of Purcell': 730–33; Cummings, 'Portraits of Purcell': 735–6. See also the excerpts from the *Illustrated London News* and the *Monthly Musical Record* reproduced in Burden, *Purcell Remembered*, pp. 146–7.

188 Pinnock and Lingard, 'Seeking the Bubble'.

extolled the national importance of Purcell.[189] What seems to have changed with the passage of time, however, were the power relationships in these celebrations – from the encouragement of amateur engagement with the music in 1895 to festivals 'effectively controlled by the great and good in English music ... held fatally aloof' in the 1950s, to the dominance of the record industry in the 1990s.[190] Nevertheless, Pinnock and Lingard's survey of the impact these anniversaries have had on perception and understanding of Purcell is necessarily preliminary, and vast amounts of surviving primary evidence could be explored in order to further our knowledge of this aspect of Purcell's reception, as well as to situate it more clearly within the broader context of the performance and recording history of Purcell's music in the twentieth century and beyond, which remains almost entirely overlooked.[191]

The other significantly under-researched area concerns historiographical material relating to Purcell. Again, this is abundantly available, but although writings by the nineteenth-century proponents of the English Musical Renaissance have been brought into the narrative of that era to some extent, as mentioned above, the portrayal of Purcell that emerged in the broader field of musicological literature and the perpetuation of stereotypes that resulted from the interdependence of writers on one another have yet to be investigated in detail.[192] The predominant impression of Purcell seems to have developed via a combination of the aspects of his music that were emphasized by the English revivalists and the long-lasting historiographical tendency, developed in the post-Darwin era, to construct evolutionary historical narratives. Since these sorts of diachronic histories frequently centred on a teleological view of inexorable musical development towards grand opera and the symphony, Purcell was predictably treated as a composer who was

---

189 Ibid.

190 Ibid. See also Pinnock's earlier reflections on the role of the record industry written just prior to the 1995 tercentenary in 'The Purcell Phenomenon', pp. 13–15.

191 Brief reference to a number of early recordings including Purcell is, however, made, in Harry Haskell, *The Early Music Revival: A History* (New York: Dover, 1996; first published London: Thames and Hudson, 1988), pp. 114, 117–18, 129 and 149.

192 The only exceptions are John Higney's brief survey of the evaluation of Purcell published in *The Harmonicon* in July 1823 (a passage demonstrating heavy reliance on Burney, incidentally), and Alan Howard's consideration of the reception of Purcell's consort music. The latter study draws particularly on the important early biographies by Cummings (published in 1881), by Holland (1932) and by Westrup (1937), but also on more specialized articles, in a perceptive analysis of the predominant tropes that can be identified in writings on Purcell's instrumental music. These include its secondary importance as non-vocal music, its conservatism and its position within the context of earlier English consort music on the one hand, and the Italian sonata on the other. See John Higney, '"The Most Perfect Models": Purcell, Handel, Haydn, and Mendelssohn in *The Harmonicon* (1823–1833)' (Unpublished paper presented at conference Purcell, Handel, Haydn, Mendelssohn: Anniversary Reflections, Oxford, 27–29 March 2009); and Howard, 'Purcell and the Poetics of Artifice', pp. 11, 23–6 and 50–66. Howard also touches on a number of broader historiographical topics, as mentioned below.

a misfit, excluded from the primary narrative of Western music history. Nowhere is this clearer than in Parry's description of Purcell from *The Evolution of the Art of Music* (1896):

> Almost completely outside the direct course of musical evolution stands the unique and highly individual genius of Purcell. The sources of his artistic generalisations can be traced, as is inevitable even with the most pre-eminently 'inspired' of composers; but isolation was entailed by the peculiarly characteristic line he adopted, and the fact that almost all the genuine vitality dropped straight out of English art directly he died; while none of his remarkably English achievements penetrated so far afield as to have any sort of influence upon the course of musical progress on the Continent. ... England lay far from the centres of musical activity, and the general course of musical evolution went on in Europe with hardly any reference whatever to his remarkable artistic achievements.[193]

Even a cursory glance at the major music histories published in the twentieth century demonstrates how deeply ingrained this view has been,[194] but there is much research needed if we are to develop a more nuanced understanding of this historiographical perspective and its implications for Purcell's reception.

Within the context of the English Musical Renaissance, the most notable stereotype associated with Purcell was the almost exclusive concentration in accounts of the composer on his vocal output, and particularly his dramatic music. We can, of course, trace this emphasis back as far as *Orpheus Britannicus*, but during the late nineteenth century Purcell's reputation as a vocal composer was appropriated for specific purposes in a manner that was to have a lasting impact on the way in which he was perceived more broadly, as these comments written by Holst in his 1927 essay 'Henry Purcell: the Dramatic Composer of England' demonstrate:

---

193 C. Hubert H. Parry, *The Evolution of the Art of Music*, International Scientific Series, vol. 80 (London: Kegan Paul, 1896; first published as *The Art of Music* (London: Kegan Paul, 1893)), pp. 142–3. This passage does not occur in the first edition of Parry's book, which was published as *The Art of Music* in 1893, and the insertion of which it forms part is worthy of detailed investigation, since it says much about his largely negative views of Purcell's music and the affinity he felt with German music, which he here associates closely with the English tradition. See also the summary of Parry's and Stanford's predominant characterizations of English music given by Hughes and Stradling in *The English Musical Renaissance*, p. 45.

194 See, for example, Alfred Einstein, *A Short History of Music* (London: Dent, 1936), p. 81; Paul Henry Lang, *Music in Western Civilization* (London: Dent, 1942; first published 1941), pp. 417 and 518; and Alec Harman and Anthony Milner, *Late Renaissance and Baroque Music*, Man and his Music, vol. 2 (London: Barrie and Rockliff, 1959; republished as Alec Harman (with Anthony Milner) and Wilfred Mellers, *Man and his Music: The Story of Musical Experience in the West* (London: Barrie and Rockliff, 1964)), p. 437.

[*Dido and Aeneas*] is one of the most original expressions of genius in all opera. Mozart remains the greatest prodigy in musical history, but he was brought up in a fine tradit[i]on – in opera, as well as in other music. In England there was not then, nor has there ever been, any tradition of opera. Purcell was first a choir-boy at the Chapel Royal; then he was organist of Westminster Abbey. Yet at the age of about thirty-one he wrote the only perfect English opera ever written, and the only opera of the seventeenth century, as far as I know, that is performed as a whole nowadays, for the sheer pleasure it gives as opera. Throughout the whole work not a word is spoken. Between the lovely airs and choruses there are dialogues, set to easy, free, and melodious music. Probably the English language has never been set so perfectly, either before or since. Playford said of Purcell: 'He had a peculiar genius to express the energy of English words.' There is no chance for vocal display in the ordinary sense of the term, but there is every chance to display powers of expression simply and beautifully. ...

Having written a perfect opera – the only perfect English opera – Purcell never wrote or even attempted to write another. He never again set the English language to delightful, free, lyrical recitative (except in certain short works), but fell into dull, conventional recitative secco that anybody could have written. Above all, he never wrote another big work with any semblance of dramatic unity. Purcell's 'accommodating disposition' was probably responsible for this. He was at the mercy of his environment.[195]

There are three aspects of Purcell's image that we can see being developed in this representative passage. First, *Dido* seems to have been seized upon as the seed of an English operatic tradition that was stifled by the restrictions of the times but that might otherwise have led to a national operatic form had Purcell only had successors – a form, indeed, that these later composers now sought to create. In his influential biography of Purcell, Jack Westrup took this further, describing *Dido* as 'the prelude to an achievement that was never realized, either by Purcell or by his successors',[196] and the same sentiment was still being expressed in 1959 by Harman and Milner, who claimed that 'judging by the tremendous success of Arne's *Artaxerxes* (1762), it is possible that had Purcell lived another twenty years or so he might well have established a national operatic tradition'.[197] The clearest exposition of this viewpoint, however, was given by Donald Francis Tovey in his essay 'The Main Stream of Music' from 1938:

---

195 Gustav Holst, 'Henry Purcell: The Dramatic Composer of England', in Hubert J. Foss (ed.), *The Heritage of Music* (3 vols, London: Oxford University Press, 1927–51), vol. 1, pp. 47–9 and 51; quoted in Harris, *Henry Purcell's 'Dido and Aeneas'*, pp. 153–4.

196 Jack A. Westrup, *Henry Purcell*, The Master Musicians (2nd edn, London: Dent; New York: Dutton, 1943; first published 1937), p. 125.

197 Harman, with Milner, *Man and his Music*, p. 437.

Our greatest musical genius, Henry Purcell, was born either fifty years too soon or fifty years too late: too late to be a master of the Golden Age, now that instrumental music had flooded out every landmark of Palestrina's art: too early to gain command of the future resources of Bach and Handel. His opera *Dido and Aeneas*, written for the pupils of Mr Josiah Priest's boarding-school, with a libretto by Nahum Tate, of the firm of Tate and Brady, achieves musical coherence and anticipates every quality of the operas in which Gluck reformed dramatic music nearly a century later. If Purcell had been allowed to write more operas on such lines he would have carried a recognizable main stream of music through all the tangle of mountain-torrents and parched arroyos which the musical historian finds so interesting in the eighteenth century. ...

We can hardly doubt that, if the musical resources of Bach and Handel had been at Purcell's command, his genius would have had the power to break through the bonds of the Philistines, and in fact I know no other case where musical genius has come into the world so manifestly at the wrong time and place, without having found the opportunity to develop some other art or science more ready for the work of a great mind.[198]

Although the idea that *Dido and Aeneas* was Purcell's most important work derived originally from Hawkins – who, because he believed erroneously that the opera was composed by Purcell at the age of 19, stated that 'the fame of Dido and Aeneas directed the eyes of the managers [of the public stage] towards Purcell, and Purcell was easily prevailed on ... to enter into their service'[199] – it is important to note that *Dido*'s profile remained low until the very end of the nineteenth century and opinions of the opera's quality were clearly divided at this point: an anonymous review of the 1877 performance given by the newly formed (and little known) Liverpool Sacred Harmonic and Purcell Society described *Dido* as 'one of the finest of Purcell's compositions', and mused 'one can only wonder with amazement that Purcell's music has so long lain dormant and that musical entrepreneurs have not

---

198 Donald Francis Tovey, 'The Main Stream of Music', first published in Tovey, *Essays and Lectures on Music*, ed. Hubert J. Foss (London: Oxford University Press, 1949), pp. 336–7; quoted in Burden, *Purcell Remembered*, pp. 147–9. Tovey blames Dryden for dramatick opera, because he 'proceeded to dam the whole future current of English dramatic music by ordaining that the music of his operas should be confined to characters outside the real action of his plays'.

199 Hawkins, *A General History of the Science and Practice of Music*, p. 745. Hawkins's dating of *Dido* must have derived from his knowledge of the date of Tate's earlier play, *Brutus of Alba* (1678), as Harris explains in *Henry Purcell's 'Dido and Aeneas'*, pp. 4–5. Hawkins's own knowledge of *Dido* came through the posthumous adaptations from which the Academy of Ancient Music score derived. His footnote on p. 745 of *A General History of the Science and Practice of Music* notes the discrepancy of text between 'Ah! Belinda' in *Orpheus Britannicus* and what he describes as 'the original opera', where the words are given as 'Ah! my Anna', thus confirming the link between his account and the Academy manuscripts.

long ago discovered the musical mine of wealth at their command';[200] but another reviewer in *The Musical Times and Singing Class Circular* said of the Bach Choir performance in 1888 that the work sometimes 'becomes dull', and concluded that 'the opera, of course, can never possess more than an antiquarian interest, but even for that alone it deserves an occasional hearing'.[201] *Dido's* reputation was in fact only sealed by Stanford's staged performance for the bicentenary celebrations in 1895. The anonymous reviewer of that event in *The Musical Times* felt 'it was meet that the first English opera [*sic*] should find a place in the scheme in honour of our great national composer',[202] and Harris notes that the production seems to have been the catalyst that led the rising English composers of the new generation, such as Vaughan Williams, 'to champion Purcell's vocal music'.[203]

Second, Purcell was identified by the proponents of the English Musical Renaissance as one of the threads that could link them to their national heritage, specifically through his skills in setting the English language. Holst and Vaughan Williams promoted this view primarily by encouraging broader exposure of Purcell's music, but Britten and Tippett explicitly cited Purcell as an influential force in their own compositional styles and encouraged comparison between their music and his: in an interview with John Amis for the BBC in 1959, for example, Britten was asked what he found 'sympathetic' about Purcell's music and answered 'Above all, I *love* his setting of words: I had never realized before I first met Purcell's music that words could be set with such ingenuity, with such colour';[204] the following year he was even more explicit: 'I have always been interested in the setting of words … and Purcell has shown me how wonderfully dramatic the sung English language can be.'[205]

---

200 'The Purcell Concert', *The Liverpool Mercury*, Saturday 10 March 1877.

201 'The Bach Choir', *Musical Times and Singing Class Circular* 29 (1888): 218, quoted in Harris, *Henry Purcell's 'Dido and Aeneas'*, p. 150.

202 'The Purcell Bi-Centenary Commemoration': 811; another part of this review is quoted in Harris, *Henry Purcell's 'Dido and Aeneas'*, p. 152.

203 Harris, *Henry Purcell's 'Dido and Aeneas'*, p. 152.

204 Quoted in Paul Kildea (ed.), *Britten on Music* (Oxford: Oxford University Press, 2003), 'On Purcell's *Dido and Aeneas* (1959)', pp. 163–5.

205 Ibid., 'On Writing English Opera (1960)', pp. 208–9. For other similar examples from both Britten and Tippett, see the other articles on Purcell in Kildea's collection, particularly '250th Anniversary of the Death of Henry Purcell', p. 52; and *The Rise of English Opera* (1951), pp. 112–13; Tippett's 'Our sense of Continuity in English Drama and Music', in Imogen Holst (ed.), *Henry Purcell (1659–1695): Essays on his Music* (London: Oxford University Press, 1959), pp. 42–51; and the quotations from Britten and Tippett given in Burden, *Purcell Remembered*, pp. 167–70. On Tippett see also Trend, *The Music Makers*, pp. 225–6; and on both composers' affinity with Purcell, see Haskell, *The Early Music Revival*, p. 83. Britten discusses his and Peter Pears's approach to performing Purcell's songs and to continuo realization in 'On Realizing the Continuo in Purcell's Songs', in Imogen Holst (ed.), *Henry Purcell (1659–1695): Essays on his Music* (London: Oxford University Press, 1959), pp. 7–13, and the same realizations are given a surprisingly uncritical review for the time in Eric Roseberry, 'The Purcell Realizations', in Christopher Palmer (ed.), *The Britten Companion* (London and Boston: Faber, 1984),

The third component of the image of Purcell created during the English Musical Renaissance – hinted at in Holst's claim that Purcell 'never wrote another big work with any semblance of dramatic unity' – is the idea that the dramatick operas for which Purcell wrote his music were fundamentally flawed, and, indeed, undramatic. In fact Holst makes this notion clearer elsewhere in his essay, and goes further by stating that they are unperformable in modern times:

> 'The Fairy Queen', 'King Arthur', and 'Dioclesian' offer almost insuperable difficulties. They are too dramatic for the concert platform, too incoherent for the stage. Producers must be prepared to cut, to alter the disposition of some numbers, to make discreet changes in the words of others, and, above all, to toil and struggle for a scheme that will inform the work with a semblance of dramatic unity.[206]

As Burden explains, this negative view of the part-sung, part-spoken dramatick operas derived from 'a complete lack of understanding' of the form, which led to the opinion, as expressed by J.A. Fuller Maitland, that 'The musical numbers are almost entirely incidental, that is, they seldom have anything to say to the main action of the play'.[207] At a time when the only kind of opera was all-sung, neither performers nor critics were able to conceive of a successful dramatic form in which the action took place largely in spoken text and the music was not sung by the main characters. Purcell's reputation as a composer of dramatic music – which had been solidified in the eighteenth century when audiences were still equivocal about the idea of all-sung opera – was sufficiently strong for producers to want to stage the dramas, but the complete operas were considered highly problematical.

Although the historiographical implications of this widely held view have yet to be explored, Michael Burden has made a detailed study of the way in which unsympathetic views of the dramatick opera form influenced performances of Purcell's works in this genre, as producers tried to make them conform more to their own ideas of what opera should be. As we have seen, there was a long-standing tradition of updating and 'improving' old music in the eighteenth and nineteenth centuries, and some of the alterations that were imposed on productions of Purcell's operas in the nineteenth and twentieth centuries belong to that trend: the 1895 production of *Dido* is well known for Charles Wood's reorchestration, for instance – apparently involving new wind, brass and timpani parts on top of Purcell's strings[208] – and further examples from Edward Gordon Craig's 1900 *Dido*

---

pp. 356–66.

206 Holst, 'Henry Purcell: The Dramatic Composer of England', p. 52, quoted in Burden, 'Purcell Debauch'd', p. 152.

207 Henry Purcell, *The Music in Dryden's King Arthur [Edited for the Birmingham Festival 1897]*, ed. J.A. Fuller Maitland (London, [1898]), quoted in Burden, 'Purcell Debauch'd', p. 145. See also similar comments in Tippett, 'Our Sense of Continuity in English Drama and Music'.

208 Harris, *Henry Purcell's 'Dido and Aeneas'*, pp. 156–7 (see also descriptions of other

and from the Covent Garden *Fairy Queen* of 1947 are cited by Burden.[209] However, the major reworkings of the dramatick operas that Burden describes, designed 'in an attempt to make the music more "dramatically relevant"',[210] were of a different order altogether. Some productions retained most of Purcell's music but omitted the text altogether – such as in Holst's *King Arthur* performed at Morley College in 1909 and Benjamin Britten's *Fairy Queen* 'cantata' arranged for the Aldeburgh Festival in 1967.[211] Others replaced the spoken material with another text – a brief resumé spoken by Vaughan Williams in the case of the *Fairy Queen* concert at the Royal Victoria Hall in 1911, a completely new text written for Holst's *Dioclesian* of 1921 and an adaptation of Shakespeare's original play text for the *Fairy Queen* produced by Edward Dent and Clive Carey at the New Theatre in Cambridge in 1920.[212] In these productions the order in which Purcell's music appeared was frequently changed, but in other performances even more drastic rearrangement was carried out: Burden is particularly critical of Cummings's extraction of selected scenes from *King Arthur*, which he believes led to a series of 'operetta'-like arrangements, including one by Colin Graham and Philip Ledger in 1970 in which a third of the original music was removed, most of the rest rearranged into two new 'acts', and substantial insertions were made of music from Purcell's other dramatic works.[213]

In 1973 Roger Savage felt moved to write in defence of the idea that *The Fairy Queen* might be performed fully staged in its original version,[214] and 22 years later Burden reiterated the call to reject the kind of ill-informed, piecemeal adaptations that he criticized in his article.[215] Yet even today it is clear that the nineteenth-century approach to dramatick opera still prevails, for while the 2009 Glyndebourne production of *The Fairy Queen* did at least attempt to recreate

---

similar reorchestrations in productions of *Dido* up to the Second World War in ibid., pp. 157–61, and in Haskell, *The Early Music Revival*, pp. 140–45).

209 Burden, 'Purcell's Operas on Craig's Stage': 448; and Burden, 'Purcell Debauch'd', p. 160. See also Haskell, *The Early Music Revival*, pp. 140–41 and 146. There is some sense, indeed, in which reorchestration took over from harmonic alteration as the acceptable form of adaptation: Burden notes that Stanford's justification of Wood's additional instrumentation for the 1895 *Dido* amounts 'to the claim that if Purcell had been alive he would have written such wind parts', and Constant Lambert was also happy to tell the reader that he 'took Purcell's string parts as a basis, ... but adding certain counterpoints, and in general "livening up" the writing for wind instruments'. However, Lambert was careful to explain that he 'did not use any harmonic padding of the type that so defiles nineteenth-century arrangements of earlier periods'. See 'Purcell Debauch'd', pp. 146–7 and 160.

210 Burden, 'Purcell Debauch'd', p. 146.

211 Ibid., pp. 152–3.

212 Ibid., pp. 153–4. A later adaptation by Denis Arundell of Dent's version of the text was used as the basis for the Covent Garden production of 1947, which Burden describes in detail in '"Gallimaufry at Covent Garden"'.

213 Burden, 'Purcell Debauch'd', pp. 149–52.

214 Roger Savage, 'The Shakespeare-Purcell *Fairy Queen*: A Defence and Recommendation', *Early Music* 1 (1973): 201–21.

215 Burden, 'Purcell Debauch'd', p. 162.

something of the multimedia quality of dramatick opera, director Jonathan Kent still considered the text as something of a necessary evil ('we have to tell the story, so there are pure text scenes which take us through the narrative, but I've tried to keep that as contained as possible'[216]), and restructured the work so that it more closely resembled its original source, Shakespeare's *Midsummer Night's Dream*. Much good could be done by further research designed to reveal the extent to which today's understanding of Purcell's public stage works was constructed in the late nineteenth century by figures in the musical establishment who were using Purcell's music for their own very modern purposes. In turn this would leave the way open for practical exploration along the lines Savage recommended of how the dramatick operas *can* work in a modern context without such bowdlerization.

Conclusions

Although this chapter has touched on many aspects of the reception of Purcell's music, it cannot claim to do more than brush the surface of an aspect of scholarship on the composer that remains in its infancy. Nevertheless, it has demonstrated, to some extent at least, how many of our modern opinions of Purcell and his music have their genesis in ideas about his works that developed some considerable time after his death and that have frequently distorted our understanding of his *oeuvre*. What is perhaps most dangerous about the situation as it stands at present is the fact that the incomplete status of the research inevitably leads to overviews such as this that oversimplify what was almost always a complex set of interrelationships between individuals with their own motivations and agendas, the materials that were available to them, and the audiences at whom they were aiming. Clearly part of the problem is that the work that has been carried out so far has tended to focus predominantly on the very areas of Purcell's output that remained most thoroughly documented after his death, particularly the theatre music. That this is a risky path to follow is demonstrated by the evidence revealed here that hints that it was in fact Purcell's sacred music that was most familiar to many: even in the twentieth century Holst could still comment that 'it is by his church music that Purcell is known to most of his countrymen'.[217] In addition, there has perhaps been a tendency to focus more prominently on tracing performance histories in an essentially descriptive way than on reflecting more deeply on the contexts and ideals that motivated such performances. As Samson warns, 'reception histories should be more than just supposedly neutral opinion collecting',[218] and the particular ontological complications of understanding the reception of a performance form

---

216 Transcribed from interview with Kent at http://www.glyndebourne.com/operas/fairy_ queen/, last accessed 23 September 2009.

217 Holst, 'Henry Purcell: the Dramatic Composer of England', quoted in Burden, *Purcell Remembered*, p. 159.

218 Samson, 'Reception'.

like music have been demonstrated in the best-quality work on other composers to require careful and intricate handling.[219]

It would be unfair to suggest that there are no exceptions to this rule: Weber, after all, seeks to place his study of the development of canon firmly within the context of developing Whig and Tory politics in the eighteenth century, and Higney attempts to read eighteenth-century perceptions of Purcell's music through changing aesthetic approaches to composition in the same period. The nationalistic context of the late nineteenth-century Purcell revival has also been assessed in several accounts of the English Musical Renaissance, and Burden has begun the task of examining critical reception of the performances of Purcell's operas in the twentieth century. Nevertheless, there is a great deal that remains to be understood about the political and musical reasons for Purcell's fortunes, particularly in the nineteenth and twentieth centuries, and reception of the composer's music consequently remains one of the most exciting areas for future Purcell research.

---

219 See, for example, Jim Samson, 'Chopin Reception: Theory, History, Analysis', in John Rink and Jim Samson (eds), *Chopin Studies 2* (Cambridge: Cambridge University Press, 1994), pp. 1–17; James Garratt, 'Performing Renaissance Church Music in Nineteenth-Century Germany: Issues and Challenges in the Study of Performative Reception', *Music & Letters* 83 (2002): 187–236; and Cole's *Thomas Tallis and his Music*. For comment on the methodological issues of studying reception history in music, see Leon Botstein, 'Music in History: the Perils of Method in Reception History', *Musical Quarterly* 89 (2006): 1–16.

Bibliography

Primary Sources (including facsimiles)

Music

Blow, John, *Amphion Anglicus: A Work of Many Compositions, for One, Two, Three and Four Voices* (London, 1700).

Boyce, William, *Cathedral Music: Being a Collection in Score of the Most Valuable and Useful Compositions for that Service, by the Several English Masters of the last Two Hundred Years* (3 vols, London, 1760–63).

Carr, John, *Comes Amoris: Or the Companion of Love … The Second Book* (London, 1688).

——, *Comes Amoris: Or the Companion of Love … The Fourth Book* (London, 1693).

Croft, William, *Musica Sacra, or, Select Anthems in Score* (London, [1724]).

Dieupart, Charles, *Six suittes de clavessin* (Amsterdam, 1701).

Gostling, John, *The Gostling Manuscript*, introduction by Franklin B. Zimmerman (Austin: University of Texas Press, 1977).

Grabu, Lewis, *Albion and Albanius: an Opera. Or, Representation in Musick* (London, 1687).

Great York and Albany: Or, the Loyal Welcome to His Royal Highness on His Return from Scotland. To the Tune of, Hey Boys Up Go We (London, 1682).

H., J., *A Choice Compendium, Or, An Exact Collection of the Newest, and Most Delightful Songs* (London, 1681).

Heptinstall, John, *The Songs in Amphitryon, With the Musick. Composed by Mr. Henry Purcell* (London, 1690).

Hilton, John, *Catch that Catch Can, or a New Collection of Catches, Rounds, and Canons* (London, 1663).

Hudgebutt, John, *Thesaurus Musicus: Being, a Collection of the Newest Songs Performed at His Majesties Theatres … The Fourth Book* (London, 1695).

——, *Thesaurus Musicus: Being, a Collection of the Newest Songs Performed at His Majesties Theatres … The Fifth Book* (London, 1696).

The Indifferent Lover, Or, the Roving Batchelor. To a Pleasant new Tune, Sung in the Last new Comedy, called Amphytrion, or, Fond Boy (London: [c.1690]).

Instrumental Music for London Theatres, 1690–1699: Royal College of Music, London, MS 1172, Introduction by Curtis Price, Music for London Entertainment, Series A/3 (facsimile edition, Withyham: Richard Macnutt, 1987).

Joyful Cuckoldom, or the Love of Gentlemen, and Gentlewomen (supposedly London, 1695).

Lawes, Henry and William Lawes, *Choice Psalmes put into Musick, for Three Voices* (London, 1648).

Manuscrit de Mademoiselle La Pierre: pièces de clavecin c.1680 – facsimilé du ms. de la Bibliothèque nationale, Paris, Rés.Vmd.ms.18, Introduction by Pierre Féruselle (facsimile edition, Geneva: Minkoff, 1983).

A new Song in the Play call'd the Spanish Fryer ... sung by a boy (n.p., c.1694).

Playford, Henry, *Apollo's Banquet: Containing Variety of the Newest Tunes, Ayres, Jiggs and Minuets, for the Treble-Violin ... The Second Book* (London, 1691).

——, *The Banquet of Musick: or, a Collection of the Newest and Best Songs Sung at Court, and at Publick Theatres ... The First Book* (London, 1688).

——, *The Dancing-Master: or, Directions for Dancing Country Dances, with the Tunes to each Dance for the Treble-Violin. The Ninth Edition Corrected* (London, 1695).

——, *The Dancing-Master: or, Directions for Dancing Country Dances, with the Tunes to each Dance for the Treble-Violin. The Tenth Edition* (London, 1698).

——, *Harmonia Sacra: or, Divine Hymns and Dialogues* (London, 1688).

——, *The Second Book of the Pleasant Musical Companion: Being a Choice Collection of Catches, in Three and Four Parts ... The Third Edition* (London, 1695).

——, *The Second Book of the Pleasant Musical Companion: Being a Choice Collection of Catches, for Three and Four Voices ... The Fourth Edition* (London, 1701).

——, *The Second Book of the Pleasant Musical Companion: Being a Choice Collection of Catches, for Three and Four Voices ... The Fifth Edition* (London, 1707).

——, *The Second Part of Musick's Hand-maid* (London, 1689).

——, *The Theater of Music: Or a Choice Collection of the Newest and Best Songs Sung at the Court, and Public Theaters* (2 vols, London, 1685).

——, *Three Elegies upon the Much Lamented Loss of our Late Most Gracious Queen Mary* (London, 1695).

——, *Wit and Mirth. An Antidote against Melancholy ... The Third Edition Enlarged with several New Songs and Catches* (London, 1684).

Playford, John, *Catch that Catch Can: or, the Second Part of the Musical Companion* (London, 1685).

——, *Choice Ayres and Songs to Sing to the Theorbo-lute, or Bass-viol ... The Fourth Book* (London, 1683).

——, *The Second Book of the Pleasant Musical Companion: Being a New Collection of Select Catches, Songs, and Glees for Two and Three Voices* (London, 1686/1687).

Purcell, Henry, *A Choice Collection of Lessons for the Harpsichord or Spinnet* (London, 1696).

——, *A Collection of Ayres, Compos'd for the Theatre* (London, 1697)

——, *The Gresham Autograph*, Introduction by Margaret Laurie and Robert Thompson (facsimile edition, London: Novello, 1995).

——, *The Music in Dryden's King Arthur [Edited for the Birmingham Festival 1897]*, ed. J.A. Fuller Maitland (London, [1898]).

——, *A Musical Entertainment Perform'd on November XXII, 1683* (London, 1684).

——, *Orpheus Britannicus: A Collection of all the Choicest Songs for One, Two, and Three Voices* (London, 1698).

——, *Orpheus Britannicus: A Collection of the Choicest Songs, for One, Two, and Three Voices ... The Second Book* (London, 1702).

——, *Some Select Songs as they are Sung in the Fairy Queen* (London, 1692).

——, *Sonnata's of III Parts: Two Viollins and Basse* (London, 1683).

——, *Sonnata's of III Parts ... First Published 1683*, Introduction by Richard Luckett (facsimile edition, London: Paradine, 1975).

——, *Ten Sonatas in Four Parts* (London, 1697).

——, *The Vocal and Instrumental Musick of The Prophetess, or the History of Dioclesian* (London, 1691).

Purcell, Henry and Arne, Thomas, *The Songs, Airs, Duets & Chorusses in the Masque of King Arthur: as Perform'd at the Theatre Royal in Drury Lane. Compos'd by Purcel & Dr. Arne* ([London], [c.1771]).

Smith, John Stafford (ed.), *Musica Antiqua: A Selection of Music of this and other Countries from the Commencement of the Twelfth to the Beginning of the Eighteenth Century* (London, c.1812).

Walsh, John, *The Catch Club or Merry Companions. A Collection of Favourite Catches for Three and Four Voices Compos'd by Mr Henry Purcell, Dr Blow, and the most Eminent Authors. Book II* (London, 1762).

Music Theory and Discourse

Bacilly, Bénigne de, *Remarques curieuses sur l'art de bien chanter* (Paris, 1668), English translation as *A Commentary upon the Art of Proper Singing*, ed. Austin B. Caswell, Music Theorists in Translation, vol. 7 (New York: Institute of Medieval Music, 1968).

Bedford, Arthur, *The Great Abuse of Musick. In Two Parts* (London, 1711).

The Compleat Flute-Master, or the Whole Art of Playing on ye Rechorder (London, 1695).

Lenton, John, *The Gentleman's Diversion, or the Violin Explained* (London, 1693).

Locke, Matthew, *Melothesia, or, Certain General Rules for playing upon a Continued-Bass* (London, 1673)

——, *The Present Practice of Musick Vindicated against the Exceptions and New Way of Attaining Musick Lately Publish'd by Thomas Salmon, M.A.* (London, 1673).

Mace, Thomas, *Musick's Monument, or a Remembrancer of the Best Practical Musick* (London, 1676).

Playford, John, *A Brief Introduction to the Skill of Musick* (London, 1666).

——, *A Brief Introduction to the Skill of Musick ... The Fourth Edition, much Enlarged* (London, 1664).

——, *An Introduction to the Skill of Musick. In Three Books ... The Twelfth Edition. Corrected and Amended by Mr. Henry Purcell* (London, 1694).

——, *An Introduction to the Skill of Musick: In Three Books ... The Thirteenth Edition* (London, 1697).

Purcell, Henry, 'The Art of Descant', in John Playford, *An Introduction to the Skill of Music. In Three Books ... The Twelfth Edition. Corrected and Amended by Mr. Henry Purcell* (London, 1694), pp. 85–144.

Reggio, Pietro, *The Art of Singing or a Treatise, Wherein is Shown How to Sing Well any Song Whatsoever* (Oxford, 1677).

Robinson, Daniel, *An Essay upon Vocal Musick* (Nottingham, 1715).

Shield, William, *An Introduction to Harmony* (London, 1800).

Simpson, Christopher, *Compendium of Practical Musick in Five Parts* (London, 1667).

——, *A Compendium of Practical Musick in Five Parts ... The Third Editio[n]* (London, 1678; originally published 1667).

Tosi, Pier Francesco, *Opinioni de' cantori antichi e moderni, o sieno osservazioni sopra il canto figurato* (Bologna, 1723). English translation as *Observations on the Florid Song: or, Sentiments on the Ancient and Modern Singers*, ed. John Ernest Galliard (2nd edn, London, 1743).

Play Texts, Song Texts and Other Primarily Literary Publications

Carey, Henry, *Poems on Several Occasions ... The Third Edition, Much Enlarged* (London, 1729).

Dryden, John, *Amphitryon; Or, The Two Socia's* (London, 1690).

D'Urfey, Thomas, *The Comical History of Don Quixote. The Third Part. With the Marriage of Mary the Buxome* (London, 1696).

——, *A Fool's Preferment, or the Three Dukes of Dunstable* (London, 1688).

——, *Love for Money: Or, the Boarding School* (London, 1691).

——, *A New Collection of Songs and Poems. By Thomas D'Urfey* (London, 1683).

——, *A New Opera, Call'd Cinthia and Endimion: Or, the Loves of the Deities* (London, 1697).

——, *New Poems, Consisting of Satyrs, Elegies, and Odes: Together with a Choice Collection of the Newest Court Songs* (London, 1690).

——, *Sir Barnaby Whigg: or, No Wit like a Womans* (London, 1681).

——, *Songs Compleat, Pleasant and Divertive* (5 vols, London, 1719).

——, *A Third Collection of New Songs, Never Printed Before. The Words by Mr D'Urfey* (London, 1685).

——, *Wit and Mirth: or Pills to Purge Melancholy ... The Fourth Edition* (5 vols, London, 1719).

Gildon, Charles, *The Complete Art of Poetry. In Six Parts* (2 vols, London, 1718).

[Gildon, Charles], *Measure for Measure. Or Beauty the Best Advocate. As it is Acted at the Theatre in Lincolns-Inn-Fields* (London, 1700).

Gould, [Robert], *The Rival Sisters: Or, the Violence of Love* (London, 1696).

Lee, Nat[haniel], *Theodosius: Or, The Force of Love* (London, 1680).

A New Song Made in the Praise of the West of England. To the Tune of, The Protestant Prince; or, Up the green Forrest (London, [1688]).

An Opera Perform'd at Mr. Josias Priest's Boarding-School at Chelsey. By Young Gentlewomen (n.p., n.d.).

Perrin, Pierre, *Ariadne, or, the Marriage of Bacchus. An Opera, or a Vocal Representation* (London, 1674).

Poems on Affairs of State from Oliver Cromwell to this Present Time ... Part III (London, 1698).

The Prince of Orange VVelcome to London. To the Tune of, The two English Travellers (London, 1688).

Shadwell, Thomas, *The Tempest, or, The Enchanted Island. A Comedy* (London, 1674).

Tate, N[ahum], *Cuckolds-Haven: or, an Alderman No Conjurer* (London, 1685).

York and Albany's Welcome to England. Or, The Loyal Subjects Joy for his most Miraculous Deliverance. To a New Play-House Tune, Much in Request (London, [1682]).

Other Writings: Seventeenth and Eighteenth Centuries

Astell, Mary, *Some Reflections upon Marriage, Occasion'd by the Duke and Dutchess of Mazarine's Case; Which is also Consider'd* (London, 1700).

Blome, Richard, *Cosmography and Geography: in Two Parts* (London, 1693).

Boyer, Abel, *Characters of the Virtues and Vices of the Age; or Moral Reflections, Maxims, and Thoughts Upon Men and Manners* (London, 1695).

Bright, T[imothy], *A Treatise of Melancholie* (London, 1586).

A Catalogue of the Scarce, Valuable and Curious Collection of Music, Manuscript and Printed, of the Reverend and Learned William Gostling ([London], 1777).

Cavendish, Margaret, *The Worlds Olio* (London, 1655).

Cibber, Colley, *An Apology for the Life of Mr. Colley Cibber, Comedian ...With an Historical View of the Stage During his Own Time* (London, 1740).

Dennis, John, *An Essay upon Publick Spirit; Being a Satyr in Prose upon the Manners of Luxury of the Times* (London, 1711).

Downes, John, *Roscius Anglicanus, or an Historical Review of the Stage* (London, 1708).

Dunton, John, *The Dublin Scuffle: Being a Challenge sent by John Dunton, Citizen of London, to Patrick Campbel, Bookseller in Dublin ... To which is added ... Some Account of his Conversation in Ireland* (London, 1699).

Ferrand, James [Jacques], *Erotomania: Or a Treatise Discoursing of the Essence, Causes, Symptomes, Prognosticks, and Cure of Love or Erotique Melancholy*, trans. Edmund Chilmead (Oxford, 1640).

F[yge], S[arah], *The Female Advocate: or, an Answer to a late Satyr against the Pride, Lust and Inconstancy, &c. of Woman* (London, 1686).

[Gildon, Charles], *The Life of Mr. Thomas Betterton, the Late Eminent Tragedian. Wherein the Action and Utterance of the Stage, Bar, and Pulpit, are distinctly consider'd* (London, 1710).

—— (ed.), *The Lives and Characters of the English Dramatick Poets ... First Begun by Mr. Langbain, Improv'd and Continued Down to the Present Time, by a Careful Hand* (London, 1699).

Glanvill, Joseph, *Saducismus Triumphatus: Or Full and Plain Evidence Concerning Witches and Apparitions* (London, 1681).

Halket, Lady Anne, *Instructions for Youth* (Edinburgh, 1701).

Harvey, Gideon, *Morbus Anglicus: Or, the Anatomy of Consumptions* (London, 1666).

Horne, George, *The Antiquity, Use, and Excellence of Church Music, a Sermon Preached at the Opening of a New Organ in the Cathedral Church of Christ, Canterbury, on Thursday, July 8, 1784* (Oxford, 1784).

[?Jordan, Thomas], *The Lord Mayor's Show: Being a Description of the Solemnity at the Inauguration of the truly Loyal and Right Honourable Sir William Prichard, K^t* (London, 1682).

Jorden, Edward, *A Briefe Discourse of a Disease Called the Suffocation of the Mother* (London, 1603).

King James the First, *Daemonologie* (Edinburgh, 1597).

Langbaine, Gerard, *An Account of the English Dramatick Poets: Or, some Observations and Remarks on the Lives and Writings, of all those that have been Publish'd ... in the English Tongue* (Oxford, 1691).

Laurentius, Andreas, *A Discourse of the Preservation of the Sight; of Melancholike Diseases; of Rheumes, and of Old Age* (London, 1599).

[Macky, John], *A Journey Through England. In Familiar Letters from a Gentleman Here, to his Friend Abroad ... The Second Edition, Considerably Improv'd* (London, 1722).

[Martin, Joseph], *The Contented Subjects; Or, the Citizens Joy* (London, [1682]).

Pietas Universitatis Oxoniensis in Obitum Augustissimae et Desideratissimae Reginae Mariae (Oxford, 1695).

Prynne, William, *Histriomastix: The Player's Scourge, or Actor's Tragedy* (London, 1633).

Ramesey, William, *The Gentlemans Companion: Or, a Character of True Nobility and Gentility* (London, 1672).

Savile, George, Marquis of Halifax, *The Lady's New-Years Gift, or, Advice to a Daughter* (London, 1688).

Scot, Reginald, *Discouerie of Witchcraft* (London, 1584).

T[aubman], M[atthew], *Londons Great Jubilee Restor'd and Perform'd on Tuesday, October the 29th 1689* (London, 1689).

Taubman, M[atthew], *London's Triumph, or the Goldsmiths Jubilee* (London, 1687).

Waldron, Francis (ed.), *Roscius Anglicanus, or an Historical Review of the Stage after it had been Suppress'd by means of the late Unhappy Civil War ... 'till the ... Restoration ... Giving an Account of its Rise Again* (London, 1789).

Waterhouse, Edward, *The Gentlemans Monitor; or, a Sober Inspection into the Vertues, Vices, and Ordinary Means, of the Rise and Decay of Men and Families* (London, 1665).

Wood, Anthony à, *Athenae Oxonienses: An Exact History of all the Writers and Bishops who have had their Education in the most Ancient and Famous University of Oxford* (2 vols, London, 1691–92).

The Words of Such Pieces as are Now Most Usually Performed by the Academy of Ancient Music (London, 1761; 2nd edn, London, 1768).

Other Writings: Nineteenth and Twentieth Centuries

'The Bach Choir', *Musical Times and Singing Class Circular* 29 (1888): 218.

Bennett, Joseph, 'Henry Purcell: an Appreciation', *Musical Times and Singing Class Circular* 36 (1895): 725–30.

Boaden, James, *Memoirs of the Life of John Philip Kemble Esq. Including a History of the Stage from the Time of Garrick to the Present Period* (2 vols, London, 1825).

Bridge, J. Frederick, 'Purcell's Birthplace and Residences', *Musical Times and Singing Class Circular* 36 (1895): 733–5.

Britten, Benjamin, 'On Realizing the Continuo in Purcell's Songs', in Imogen Holst (ed.), *Henry Purcell (1659–95): Essays on his Music* (London: Oxford University Press, 1959), pp. 7–13.

Bumpus, John S., *A History of English Cathedral Music, 1549–1889* (New edn, Farnborough: Gregg, 1972; first published London: T. Werner Laurie, 1908).

Cummings, William H., 'A Brief Life of Purcell', *Musical Times and Singing Class Circular* 36 (1895): 730–33.

——, 'Portraits of Purcell', *Musical Times and Singing Class Circular* 36 (1895): 735–6.

——, 'The Mutilation of a Masterpiece', *Proceedings of the Musical Association* 30 (1903–1904): 113–27.

Einstein, Alfred, *A Short History of Music* (London: Dent, 1936).

Genest, John, *Some Account of the English Stage: from the Restoration in 1660 to 1830* (10 vols, Bath: H.E. Carrington, 1832).

Harman, Alec and Anthony Milner, *Late Renaissance and Baroque Music*, Man and his Music, vol. 2 (London: Barrie and Rockliff, 1959; republished as Alec Harman (with Anthony Milner) and Wilfred Mellers, *Man and his Music: The Story of Musical Experience in the West* (London: Barrie and Rockliff, 1964)).

Holland, A.K., *Henry Purcell: The English Musical Tradition* (2nd edn, London: Penguin, 1948; first published London: Bell, 1932).

Holst, Gustav, 'Henry Purcell: The Dramatic Composer of England', in Hubert J. Foss (ed.), *The Heritage of Music* (3 vols, London: Oxford University Press, 1927–51), vol. 1, pp. 46–52.

Lang, Paul Henry, *Music in Western Civilization* (London: Dent, 1942; first published 1941).

Lowe, Robert W., *Thomas Betterton*, Eminent Actors, vol. 2 (London: Kegan Paul, Trench, Trübner, 1891).

Malone, Edmond (ed.), *The Critical and Miscellaneous Prose Works of John Dryden … With Notes and Illustrations; an Account of the Life and Writings of the Author … and a Collection of his Letters* (4 vols, London, 1800).

Parry, C. Hubert H., *The Evolution of the Art of Music*, International Scientific Series, vol. 80 (London: Kegan Paul, 1896; first published as *The Art of Music* (London: Kegan Paul, 1893)).

'The Purcell Bi-Centenary Commemoration', *Musical Times and Singing Class Circular* 36 (1895): 811–13.

Shaw, Watkins (ed.), *Eight Concerts of Henry Purcell's Music … with a foreword by Ralph Vaughan Williams and eight essays* (London: Arts Council, 1951).

Squire, William Barclay, 'The Music of Shadwell's "Tempest"', *Musical Quarterly* 7 (1921): 565–78.
Tippett, Michael, 'Our sense of Continuity in English Drama and Music', in Imogen Holst (ed.), *Henry Purcell (1659–95): Essays on his Music* (London: Oxford University Press, 1959), pp. 42–51.
Tovey, Donald Francis, *Essays and Lectures on Music*, ed. Hubert J. Foss (London: Oxford University Press, 1949).
Ward, Adolphus William, *A History of English Dramatic Literature to the Death of Queen Anne* (3 vols, 2nd edn, London: Macmillan, 1899).
Westrup, Jack A., *Henry Purcell*, The Master Musicians (2nd edn, London: Dent; New York: Dutton, 1943; first published 1937).

Modern Editions of Primary Texts

Braybrooke, Richard, Lord (ed.), *Memoirs of Samuel Pepys … Comprising his Diary from 1659 to 1669, Deciphered by the Rev. John Smith, A.B., from the Original Shorthand MS. in the Pepysian Library, and a Selection from his Private Correspondence* (2 vols, London: Henry Colburn, 1825).
Burden, Michael (ed.), *Henry Purcell's Operas: The Complete Texts* (Oxford and New York: Oxford University Press, 2000).
Burney, Charles, *A General History of Music from the Earliest Ages to the Present Period*, ed. Frank Mercer (2 vols, New York: Dover, 1957; first published London: Foulis, 1935).
Burton, Robert, *Anatomy of Melancholy*, eds Thomas C. Faulkner, Nicolas K. Kiessling and Rhonda L. Blair (6 vols, Oxford: Clarendon, 1989–2000).
Chan, Mary and Jamie C. Kassler (eds), *Roger North's The Musicall Grammarian 1728*, Cambridge Studies in Music (Cambridge: Cambridge University Press, 1990).
Danchin, Pierre (ed.), *The Prologues and Epilogues of the Restoration, 1660–1700: A Complete Edition* (7 vols, Nancy: Presses Universitaires de Nancy, 1981–88).
The Diary of John Evelyn: Now First Printed in Full from the Manuscripts Belonging to Mr John Evelyn, ed. E.S. De Beer (6 vols, Oxford: Clarendon, 1955).
The Diary of Samuel Pepys: a New and Complete Transcription, eds Robert Latham and William Matthews (11 vols, London: Bell, 1970–83).
Downes, John, *Roscius Anglicanus*, eds Judith Milhous and Robert D. Hume (London: Society for Theatre Research, 1987).
Dryden, John, *Plays: Albion and Albanius, Don Sebastian, Amphitryon*, eds Earl Miner, George R. Guffey and Franklin B. Zimmerman, The Works of John Dryden, vol. 15 (Berkeley, Los Angeles and London: University of California Press, 1976).
——, *Plays: King Arthur, Cleomenes, Love Triumphant, contributions to The Pilgrim*, ed. Vinton A. Dearing, The Works of John Dryden, vol. 16 (Berkeley, Los Angeles and London: University of California Press, 1996).
D'Urfey, Thomas, *The Songs of Thomas D'Urfey*, ed. Cyrus Lawrence Day, Harvard Studies in English, vol. 9 (Cambridge, MA: Harvard University Press, 1933).

Eward, Suzanne (ed.), *Gloucester Cathedral Chapter Act Book, 1616–1687*, Gloucester Record Series, vol. 21 (Bristol: Bristol and Gloucestershire Archaeological Society, 2007).

Gray, Thomas, *Collected Correspondence*, eds Paget Toynbee and Leonard Whibley (3 vols, Oxford: Oxford University Press, 1971).

Hawkins, John, *A General History of the Science and Practice of Music*, reprinted with a new introduction by Charles Cudworth (2 vols, New York: Dover, 1963; first published London: Novello, 1853).

Hobbes, Thomas, *Leviathan (1651)*, ed. Richard Tuck, Cambridge Texts in the History of Political Thought (Cambridge: Cambridge University Press, 1991).

Kildea, Paul (ed.), *Britten on Music* (Oxford: Oxford University Press, 2003).

Langhans, Edward A. (ed.), *Restoration Promptbooks* (Carbondale: Southern Illinois University Press, 1981).

Locke, John, *Two Treatises on Government (1690)*, ed. Peter Laslett, Cambridge Texts in the History of Political Thought (Cambridge, Cambridge University Press, 1988).

Luttrell, Narcissus, *A Brief Historical Relation of State Affairs from September 1678 to April 1714* (6 vols, Oxford, Oxford University Press, 1857).

Macfarlane, Alan (ed.), *The Diary of Ralph Josselin, 1616–1683*, Records of Social and Economic History New Series, vol. 3 (Oxford: Oxford University Press for The British Academy, 1976).

North, Roger, *Notes of Me: the Autobiography of Roger North*, ed. Peter Millard (Toronto: University of Toronto Press, 2000).

Saint-Évremond, C.M. de Saint-Denis, *Letters of Saint-Évremond*, ed. John Hayward (London: Routledge, 1930).

Spencer, Christopher (ed.), *Five Restoration Adaptations of Shakespeare* (Urbana: University of Illinois Press, 1965).

Synopsis of Vocal Musick by A. B. Philo-Mus, ed. Rebecca Herissone, Music Theory in Britain, 1500–1700: Critical Editions (Aldershot; Ashgate, 2006).

Wilson, John (ed.), *Roger North on Music: Being a Selection from his Essays Written during the Years c.1695–1728* (London: Novello, 1959).

Modern Editions of Music

Blow, John, *Jesus Seeing the Multitudes*, ed. Alan Howard, The Web Library of Seventeenth-Century Music, no. 16, http://aaswebsv.aas.duke.edu/wlscm.

——, *Venus and Adonis*, ed. Bruce Wood, The Purcell Society Edition Companion Series, vol. 2 (London: Stainer & Bell, 2008).

Cox, Geoffrey (ed.), *Faber Early Organ Series: European Organ Music of the 16th and 17th Centuries, vol. 3: England 1660–1710* (London: Faber, 1986).

Draghi, Giovanni Battista, *Harpsichord Music*, ed. Robert Klakowich, Recent Researches in the Music of the Baroque Era, vol. 56 (Madison: A-R Editions, 1986).

Grabu, Louis, *Albion and Albanius*, ed. Bryan White, The Purcell Society Edition Companion Series, vol. 1 (London: Stainer and Bell, 2007).

The Harpsichord Master 1697: Containing Instructions for Learners by Henry Purcell, ed. Robert Petre (Wellington: Price Milburn Music; London: Faber, 1980).

Hillier, Paul (ed.), *The Catch Book: 153 Catches, Including the Complete Catches of Henry Purcell* (Oxford: Oxford University Press, 1987).

Locke, Matthew, *Dramatic Music*, ed. Michael Tilmouth, Musica Britannica, vol. 51 (London: Stainer and Bell, 1986).

London, British Library MS Add. 39569: Babell MS, Introduction by Bruce Gustafson, 17th-Century Keyboard Music, vol. 19 (New York: Garland, 1987).

Purcell, Henry, *Birthday Odes for Queen Mary, Part I*, ed. Bruce Wood, The Works of Henry Purcell, vol. 11 (new edn, London: Novello, 1993).

——, *Birthday Odes for Queen Mary, Part II*, ed. Bruce Wood, The Works of Henry Purcell, vol. 24 (new edn, London: Novello, 1998).

——, *Catches*, ed. Ian Spink, The Works of Henry Purcell, vol. 22a (London: Novello, 2000).

——, *Catches, Rounds, Two-Part and Three-Part Songs*, ed. W. Barclay Squire and J.A. Fuller-Maitland, The Works of Henry Purcell, vol. 22 (London: Novello, 1922).

——, *Dido and Aeneas*, ed. Margaret Laurie, The Works of Henry Purcell, vol. 3 (new edn, Sevenoaks: Novello, 1979).

——, *Dido and Aeneas*, ed. Ellen Harris, Oxford Operas (Oxford: Oxford University Press, 1987).

——, *Dido and Aeneas*, ed. Ellen T. Harris, Eulenburg Miniature Scores (London: Eulenburg, 1987).

——, *Dioclesian*, ed. Margaret Laurie, The Works of Henry Purcell, vol. 9 (rev. edn, London: Novello, 1961).

——, *Dramatic Music, Part I*, ed. Margaret Laurie, The Works of Henry Purcell, vol. 16 (new edn, London: Novello, 2007).

——, *Dramatic Music, Part II*, ed. Ian Spink, The Works of Henry Purcell, vol. 20 (new edn, London: Novello, 1998).

——, *Dramatic Music, Part III*, ed. Margaret Laurie, The Works of Henry Purcell, vol. 21 (new edn, London: Stainer and Bell, 2010).

——, *Duets, Dialogues and Trios*, ed. Ian Spink, The Works of Henry Purcell, vol. 22b (London: Novello, 2007).

——, *Eight Suites*, ed. Howard Ferguson, Purcell Complete Keyboard Works, vol. 1 (London: Stainer and Bell, 1964).

——, *The Fairy Queen*, ed. John South Shedlock, The Works of Henry Purcell, vol. 12 (London: Novello; New York: Novello and Ewer, 1903).

——, *The Fairy-Queen: An Opera*, ed. Michael Burden, Eulenburg Miniature Scores (New York and London: Eulenburg, 2009).

——, *The Fairy Queen*, eds Bruce Wood and Andrew Pinnock, The Works of Henry Purcell, vol. 12 (new edn, London: Stainer and Bell, 2009).

——, *Fantazias and Miscellaneous Instrumental Music*, ed. Michael Tilmouth with Alan Browning and Peter Holman, The Works of Henry Purcell, vol. 31 (rev. edn, London and Sevenoaks: Novello, 1990).

——, *The Indian Queen*, eds Margaret Laurie and Andrew Pinnock, The Works of Henry Purcell, vol. 19 (new edn, London: Novello, 1994).

——, *King Arthur*, ed. Margaret Laurie, The Works of Henry Purcell, vol. 26 (rev. edn, London: Novello, 1971).

——, *Miscellaneous Keyboard Pieces*, ed. Howard Ferguson, Purcell Complete Keyboard Works, vol. 2 (London: Stainer and Bell, 1964).

——, *My Beloved Spake*, ed. Vincent Novello, Purcell's Sacred Music, no. 13 (London: Novello, c.1829).

——, *Ode for St Cecilia's Day 1692*, ed. Christopher Hogwood (London: Eulenburg, 2009).

——, *Royal Welcome Songs, Part I*, ed. Bruce Wood, The Works of Henry Purcell, vol. 15 (new edn, London: Novello, 2000).

——, *Royal Welcome Songs, Part II*, ed. Bruce Wood, The Works of Henry Purcell, vol. 18 (new edn, London: Novello, 2005).

——, *Sacred Music, Part I*, ed. G.E.P. Arkwright, The Works of Henry Purcell, vol. 13a (London: Novello, 1921).

——, *Sacred Music, Part I: Nine Anthems with Orchestral Accompaniment*, ed. Peter Dennison, The Works of Henry Purcell, vol. 13 (rev. edn, London: Novello, 1988).

——, *Sacred Music, Part II: Nine Anthems with Strings*, ed. Lionel Pike, The Works of Henry Purcell, vol. 14 (new edn, London: Novello, 2003).

——, *Sacred Music, Part IV: Anthems*, eds Anthony Lewis and Nigel Fortune, The Works of Henry Purcell, vol. 28 (London: Novello, 1959).

——, *Sacred Music, Part V: Anthems*, eds Anthony Lewis and Nigel Fortune, The Works of Henry Purcell, vol. 29 (rev. edn, London: Novello, 1967; new edn first published 1959).

——, *Sacred Music, Part VII: Anthems and Miscellaneous Sacred Music*, eds Anthony Lewis and Nigel Fortune, The Works of Henry Purcell, vol. 32 (London: Novello, 1962).

——, *Secular Songs for Solo Voice*, ed. Margaret Laurie, The Works of Henry Purcell, vol. 25 (new edn, Borough Green: Novello, 1985).

——, *Sonatas of Three Parts*, ed. Roger Fiske (2 vols, London: Eulenburg, 1975).

——, *Symphony Songs*, ed. Bruce Wood, The Works of Henry Purcell, vol. 27 (new edn, London: Stainer and Bell, 2007).

——, *Ten Sonatas of Four Parts*, ed. Christopher Hogwood (2 vols, London: Eulenburg, 1978).

——, *Ten Sonatas of Four Parts*, ed. Michael Tilmouth, The Works of Henry Purcell, vol. 7 (rev. edn, London: Novello, 1981).

——, *Thirty Songs in Two Volumes*, ed. Timothy Roberts (2 vols, Oxford: Oxford University Press, 1995).

——, *Three Odes for St Cecilia's Day*, The Works of Henry Purcell, vol. 10 (new edn, London: Novello, 1990).

——, *Twelve Sonatas of Three Parts*, ed. Michael Tilmouth, The Works of Henry Purcell, vol. 5 (new edn, Borough Green: Novello, 1976).

———, *Twenty Keyboard Pieces; and One by Orlando Gibbons: From Purcell's Autograph Manuscript in the British Library, MS Mus.1.*, ed. Davitt Moroney (London: Associated Board, 1999).

———, *The Yorkshire Feast Song*, ed. W.H. Cummings under the Supervision of the Purcell Society, The Works of Henry Purcell, vol. 1 (London: Novello, Ewer and co., 1878).

Sabol, Andrew J. (ed.), *Four Hundred Songs and Dances from the Stuart Masque* (Providence, RI: Brown University Press, 1978).

Winkler, Amanda Eubanks (ed.), *Music for Macbeth*, Recent Researches in the Music of the Baroque Era, vol. 133 (Middleton: A-R Editions, 2004).

Audio Recordings

A Baroque Celebration: Music by Bach, Handel, Lully, Purcell and Others, New York Kammermusiker, Double Reed Ensemble, dir. Ilonna Pederson (Dorian Sono Luminus DOR-90189, *rec.* 1993).

The Complete Odes and Welcome Songs of Henry Purcell (1659–1695), The King's Consort, dir. Robert King (Hyperion CDS44031–8, *rec.* 1988–92).

The Complete Sacred Music of Henry Purcell, The King's Consort, dir. Robert King (Hyperion CDS44141–51, *rec.* 1991–94).

Folk Songs and Ballads, Alfred Deller, The Complete Vanguard Recordings, Vol. 1 (Musical Concepts MC193, 2008).

Music for the Coronation of James II, 1685, The Choir of the Chapel Royal, The Musicians Extra-Ordinary, dir. Andrew Gant (Signum Classics SIGCD094, *rec.* 2007).

Purcell, Henry, *Ayres for the Theatre*, The Parley of Instruments, dir. Peter Holman (Hyperion CDA66212, *rec.* 1986).

———, *Come Ye Sons of Art, Welcome to All the Pleasures, Funeral Music for Queen Mary, Funeral Sentences*, Taverner Consort, Taverner Choir, Taverner Players, dir. Andrew Parrott (EMI Reflexe CDC 7496352, *rec.* 1988).

———, *Dido and Aeneas*, Taverner Choir and Players, dir. Andrew Parrott (Chandos ABRD 1034, *rec.* 1981).

———, *Dido and Aeneas*, English Concert, dir. Trevor Pinnock (Archiv 289 427 6242 8, *rec.* 1988).

———, *Dido and Aeneas*, Le Concert d'Astrée and European Voices, dir. Emmanuelle Haïm (Virgin Classics 5-45605-2, *rec.* 2003).

———, *Dido and Aeneas*, Ama Deus Baroque Ensemble, dir. Valentin Radu (Lyrichord LEMS 8057, *rec.* 2007).

———, *Dido and Aeneas*, Orchestra of the Age of Enlightenment, dir. Elizabeth Kenny and Steven Devine (Chandos CHAN 0757, *rec.* 2008).

———, *The Fairy Queen*, Les Arts Florissants, dir. William Christie (Harmonia Mundi, HMC 901308.09, *rec.* 1989).

——, *King Arthur*, Les Arts Florissants, dir. William Christie (Erato, 4509-98535-2, *rec.* 1995).

——, *Musique de scène – Airs d'opéras – Odes et Chants sacrés*, Deller Consort dir. Alfred Deller (Harmonia Mundi HMD 218, *rec. c.*1969).

——, *Ode on St Cecilia's Day 1692*, Taverner Choir, Taverner Players, dir. Andrew Parrott (EMI CDC 7474902, *rec.* 1985).

——, *Suites and Transcriptions for Harpsichord*, Terence Charlston (Naxos 8.553982, *rec.* 1997).

——, *Victorious Love*, Carolyn Sampson (BIS-SACD-1536, *rec.* 2006).

Catalogues, Databases and Datasets

Printed Sources

Arnott, James F. and John W. Robinson, *English Theatrical Literature, 1559–1900: A Bibliography* (London: Society for Theatre Research, 1970).

Ashbee, Andrew, *Records of English Court Music, vol. 1: 1660–1685* (Snodland, Kent: Ashbee, 1986).

Ashbee, Andrew, Robert Thompson and Jonathan Wainwright (eds), *The Viola da Gamba Society Index of Manuscripts Containing Consort Music* (2 vols, Aldershot and Burlington: Ashgate, 2001, 2008).

Avery, Emmett L. (ed.), *The London Stage, 1660–1800: A Calendar of Plays, Entertainments and Afterpieces, together with Casts, Box-receipts and Contemporary Comment. Part 2: 1700–1729* (2 vols, Carbondale: Southern Illinois University Press, 1960).

Bickley, Francis et al. (eds), *Calendar of State Papers Preserved in the Public Record Office, Domestic Series, James II* (3 vols, London: Her Majesty's Stationery Office, 1960–72).

Burrows, Donald and Martha J. Ronish, *A Catalogue of Handel's Musical Autographs* (Oxford: Oxford University Press, 1994).

Crosby, Brian, *A Catalogue of Durham Cathedral Music Manuscripts* (Oxford: Oxford University Press, 1986).

Day, Cyrus Lawrence, and Eleanore Boswell Murrie, *English Song-Books, 1651–1702: A Bibliography, With a First-Line Index of Songs* (London: for the Bibliographical Society at Oxford University Press, 1940 (for 1937)).

Fenlon, Iain, *Catalogue of the Printed Music and Music Manuscripts before 1801 in the Music Library of the University of Birmingham, Barber Institute of Fine Arts* (London: Mansell, 1976).

Green, Mary Anne Everett, et al. (eds), *Calendar of State Papers, Domestic Series, of the Reign of Charles II … Preserved in the State Paper Department of Her Majesty's Public Record Office* (28 vols: vols 1–7, London: Longman, Green, Longman and Roberts, 1860–66; vols 8–28, London: Her/His Majesty's Stationery Office, 1893–1939).

Hardy, William John (ed.), *Calendar of State Papers, Domestic Series, of the Reign of William and Mary ... Preserved in the Public Record Office* (6 vols, London: Her/His Majesty's Stationery Office, 1895–1908).

Hogan, Charles Beecher (ed.), *The London Stage, 1660–1800: A Calendar of Plays, Entertainments and Afterpieces, together with Casts, Box-receipts and Contemporary Comment. Part 5: 1776–1800* (3 vols, Carbondale: Southern Illinois University Press, 1968).

Hughes-Hughes, Augustus, *Catalogue of Manuscript Music in the British Museum* (3 vols, London: British Museum, 1906–1909; repr. 1966).

Hunter, David, *Opera and Song Books Published in England, 1703–1726: A Descriptive Bibliography* (London: Bibliographical Society, 1997).

Index to the London Stage, 1660–1800, compiled by Ben Ross Schneider, Jr (Carbondale: Southern Illinois University Press, 1979).

Jackson, Alfred, 'Play Notices from the Burney Newspapers, 1700–1703', *Proceedings of the Modern Language Association* 48 (1933): 815–49.

Lennep, William Van (ed.), with a Critical Introduction by Emmett L. Avery and Arthur H. Scouten, *The London Stage, 1660–1800: A Calendar of Plays, Entertainments and Afterpieces, together with Casts, Box-receipts and Contemporary Comment. Part 1: 1660–1700* (Carbondale: Southern Illinois University Press, 1965).

The London Stage, 1660–1800, ed. William van Lennep, Emmet L. Avery, Arthur H. Scouten, et al. (11 vols, Carbondale: Southern Illinois University Press, 1960–68).

McShane, Angela J., *Political Broadside Ballads of Seventeenth-Century England: A Critical Bibliography* (London: Pickering and Chatto, 2011).

Milhous, Judith and Robert D. Hume (eds), *A Register of English Theatrical Documents, 1660–1737* (2 vols, Carbondale: Southern Illinois University Press, 1991).

Scouten, Arthur H. (ed.), *The London Stage, 1660–1800: A Calendar of Plays, Entertainments and Afterpieces, together with Casts, Box-receipts and Contemporary Comment. Part 3: 1729–1747* (2 vols, Carbondale: Southern Illinois University Press, 1961).

Stone, George Winchester Jr. (ed.), *The London Stage, 1660–1800: A Calendar of Plays, Entertainments and Afterpieces, together with Casts, Box-receipts and Contemporary Comment. Part 4: 1747–1776* (3 vols, Carbondale: Southern Illinois University Press, 1962).

Summers, Montague, *A Bibliography of Restoration Drama* (London: Fortune Press, [1935]).

Tilmouth, Michael, 'A Calendar of References to Music in Newspapers published in London and the Provinces (1660–1719)', *Royal Musical Association Research Chronicle* 1 (1961): ii–vii, 1–107; 2 (1962): 1–15.

White, Eric Walter, 'Early Theatrical Performances of Purcell's Operas, with a Calendar of Recorded Performances, 1690–1710', *Theatre Notebook* 23 (1958–59): 43–65.

The Words of Such Pieces as are Now Most Usually Performed by the Academy of Ancient Music (London: n.p., 1761; 2nd edn, London: Printed by J. Dixwell, 1768).

Online Sources

Gants, David L., *A Digital Catalogue of Watermarks and Type Ornaments Used by William Stansby in the Printing of The Workes of Beniamin Jonson* (London: 1616), http://www2.iath.virginia.edu/gants/.

International Association of Paper Historians, *International Standard for the Registration of Papers*, http://www.paperhistory.org/standard.htm.

Milhous, Judith and Robert D. Hume (eds), *The London Stage 1660–1800: A New Version of Part 2, 1700–1729 … Draft of the Calendar for Volume I, 1700–1711*, http://www.personal.psu.edu/hb1/London%20Stage%202001/.

Milsom, John, *Christ Church Library Music Catalogue*, http://library.chch.ox.ac.uk/music/.

Mosser, Daniel W. and Ernest W. Sullivan II, *The Thomas L. Gravell Watermark Archive*, http://www.gravell.org/.

Secondary Literature

Adams, Martin, *Henry Purcell: The Origins and Development of his Musical Style* (Cambridge: Cambridge University Press, 1995).

——, 'More on Dating *Dido*' (Correspondence), *Early Music* 21 (1993): 510.

——, 'Purcell, Blow and the English Court Ode', in Curtis Price (ed.), *Purcell Studies* (Cambridge: Cambridge University Press, 1995), pp. 172–91.

——, Review of Michael Burden (ed.), *The Purcell Companion* (London: Faber, 1995; Portland, OR: Amadeus Press, 1995), in *Music & Letters* 77 (1996): 264–8.

Alden, John, *The Muses Mourn: A Checklist of Verse Occasioned by the Death of Charles II* (Charlottesville: Bibliographical Society of the University of Virginia, 1958).

Alsop, J.D., 'Macky, John (d. 1726)', in *Oxford Dictionary of National Biography*, http://www.oxforddnb.com.

Álvarez-Recio, Leticia, 'Nahum Tate's *The History of King Richard the Second* (1681): Politics and Censorship during the Exclusion Crisis', *Restoration and Eighteenth-Century Theatre Research* 24/1 (Summer 2009): 17–30.

Apetrei, Sarah, '"Call No Man Master Upon Earth": Mary Astell's Tory Feminism and an Unknown Correspondence', *Eighteenth-Century Studies* 41 (2008): 507–23.

Arkwright, Godfrey E.P., 'Purcell's Church Music', *Musical Antiquary* 1 (1909–10): 63–72, 234–48.

Armistead, J.M., *Nathaniel Lee*, Twayne's English Authors Series, vol. 270 (Boston: Twayne, 1979).

——, 'The Occultism of Dryden's "American" Plays in Context', *Seventeenth Century* 1 (1986): 127–52.

Arnold, F.T., *The Art of Accompaniment from a Thorough-Bass as Practised in the XVIIth and XVIIIth Centuries* (2 vols, New York: Dover, 1965; first published London: Oxford University Press, 1931).

Arundell, Dennis, 'The Gordian Knot Untied', *Times Literary Supplement* 1220 (4 June 1925): 384; see also correspondence, 'The Gordian Knot Untied', *Times Literary Supplement* 1222 (18 June 1925): 416.

Ashley, Maurice, *James II* (Minneapolis: University of Minnesota Press, 1977).

Austern, Linda Phyllis, '"Alluring the Auditorie to Effeminacie": Music and the Idea of the Feminine in Early Modern England', *Music & Letters* 74 (1993): 343–54.

——, '"Art to Enchant": Musical Magic and its Practitioners in English Renaissance Drama', *Journal of the Royal Musical Association* 115 (1990): 191–206.

——, '"For, Love's a Good Musician": Performance, Audition, and Erotic Disorders in Early Modern Europe', *Musical Quarterly* 82 (1998): 614–53.

——, 'Music and Manly Wit in Seventeenth-Century England', in Rebecca Herissone (ed.), *Concepts of Creativity in Seventeenth-Century England* (Woodbridge: Boydell and Brewer, forthcoming).

——, 'Musical Treatments for Lovesickness: The Early Modern Heritage', in Peregrine Horden (ed.), *Music as Medicine: The History of Music Therapy since Antiquity* (Aldershot and Brookfield: Ashgate, 2000), pp. 213–45.

——, '"No Pill's Gonna Cure My Ill": Gender, Erotic Melancholy, and Traditions of Musical Healing in the Modern West', in Penelope M. Gouk (ed.), *Musical Healing in Cultural Context* (Aldershot: Ashgate, 2000), pp. 113–36.

——, '"No Women Are Indeed": The Boy Actor as Vocal Seductress in Late Sixteenth- and Early Seventeenth-Century English Drama', in Leslie C. Dunn and Nancy A. Jones (eds), *Embodied Voices: Representing Female Vocality in Western Culture*, New Perspectives in Music History and Criticism (Cambridge: Cambridge University Press, 1994), pp. 83–102.

Babb, Lawrence, *The Elizabethan Malady: A Study of Melancholia in English Literature from 1580 to 1642* (East Lansing: Michigan State College Press, 1951).

Babinet de Rencogne, Gustave, 'Recueil de documents pour servir à l'histoire de commerce et de l'industrie en Angoumois: Recherches sur l'origine des moulins à papier de l'Angoumois', *Bulletin de la société archéologique et historique de la Charente* Série 5/2 (1878–79): 3–160.

Baldwin, Olive and Thelma Wilson, 'Alfred Deller, John Freeman and Mr Pate', *Music & Letters* 50 (1969): 103–10.

——, 'The Music for Durfey's *Cinthia and Endimion*', *Theatre Notebook* 41 (1987): 70–74.

——, 'A Purcell Problem Solved', *Musical Times* 122 (1981): 445.

——, 'Purcell's Mad Songs in the time of Handel, Haydn and Mendelssohn' (Unpublished paper presented at conference Purcell, Handel, Haydn, Mendelssohn: Anniversary Reflections, Oxford, 27–29 March 2009).

——, 'Purcell's Sopranos', *Musical Times* 123 (1982): 602–9.

——, 'Purcell's Stage Singers', in Michael Burden (ed.), *Performing the Music of Henry Purcell* (Oxford: Clarendon, 1996), pp. 105–29.

——, 'Richard Leveridge, 1670–1758. 1: Purcell and the Dramatic Operas', *Musical Times* 111 (1970): 592–4.

——, '"Who can from Joy Refraine?": Purcell's Birthday Song for the Duke of Gloucester', *Musical Times* 122 (1981): 596–9.

Banks, Chris, 'British Library MS Mus. 1: a Recently Discovered Manuscript of Keyboard Music by Henry Purcell and Giovanni Battista Draghi', *Brio* 32 (1995): 87–93.

Barroll, Leeds, *Anna of Denmark Queen of England: A Cultural Biography* (Philadelphia: University of Pennsylvania Press, 2001).

Battigelli, Anna, *Margaret Cavendish and the Exiles of the Mind* (Lexington: University of Kentucky Press, 1998).

——, 'Political Thought/Political Action: Margaret Cavendish's Hobbesian Dilemma', in Hilda L. Smith (ed.), *Women Writers and the Early Modern British Political Tradition* (Cambridge: Cambridge University Press, 1998), pp. 40–55.

Baynton-Williams, Ashley, 'Richard Blome', http://www.mapforum.com/09/9blome. htm.

Beechey, Gwilym, 'A New Source of Seventeenth-Century Keyboard Music', *Music & Letters* 50 (1969): 278–89.

Bent, Ian, 'The "Compositional Process" in Music Theory 1713–1850', *Music Analysis* 3 (1984): 29–55.

Bent, Margaret, 'The Grammar of Early Music: Preconditions for Analysis', in Cristle Collins Judd (ed.), *Tonal Structures in Early Music* (New York: Garland, 1996), pp. 15–59.

Berg, Willem E.J., *De réfugiés in de Nederlanden na de herroeping van het Edict van Nantes* (Amsterdam: Müller, 1845).

Bicknell, Stephen, *The History of the English Organ* (Cambridge: Cambridge University Press, 1996).

Bjurström, Per, *Giacomo Torelli and Baroque Stage Design*, Figura, New Series, vol. 2 (Stockholm: Nationalmuseum, 1961).

Boal, Ellen T., 'Purcell's Clock Tempos and Fantasias', *Journal of the Viola da Gamba Society of America* 20 (1983): 24–39.

Bohlman, Philip V., 'Ontologies of Music', in Nicholas Cook and Mark Everist (eds), *Rethinking Music* (Oxford and New York: Oxford University Press, 1999), pp. 17–34.

Boorman, Stanley, 'The Musical Text', in Nicholas Cook and Mark Everist (eds), *Rethinking Music* (Oxford and New York: Oxford University Press, 1999), pp. 403–23.

——, Review of Stephen Spector (ed.) *Essays in Paper Analysis* (Washington: Folger Shakespeare Library, 1987), in *Music & Letters* 69 (1988): 495–6.

——, 'Watermarks', in *Grove Music Online*, http://www.oxfordmusiconline.com.

Boorman, Stanley, and Stephen Spector, 'Essays in Paper Analysis', *Music & Letters*, 70 (1989): 599–601.

Bostridge, Ian, *Witchcraft and Its Transformations, c.1650–c.1750* (Oxford: Clarendon, 1997).

Boswell, Eleanore, *The Restoration Court Stage (1660–1702), with a Particular Account of the Production of 'Calisto'* (Cambridge, MA: Harvard University Press; London: Allen and Unwin, 1932).

Botstein, Leon, 'Music in History: the Perils of Method in Reception History', *Musical Quarterly* 89 (2006): 1–16.

Braverman, Richard, 'Libertines and Parasites', *Restoration: Studies in English Literary Culture, 1660–1700* 11 (1987): 73–86.

——, *Plots and Counterplots: Sexual Politics and the Body Politic in English Literature, 1660–1730* (Cambridge: Cambridge University Press, 1993).

Briggs, Robin, '"Many Reasons Why": Witchcraft and the Problem of Multiple Explanation', in Jonathan Barry, Marianne Hester and Gareth Roberts (eds), *Witchcraft in Early Modern Europe: Studies in Culture and Belief* (Cambridge: Cambridge University Press, 1996), pp. 49–63.

Britland, Karen, *Drama at the Courts of Queen Henrietta Maria* (Cambridge and New York: Cambridge University Press, 2006).

Broude, Ronald, 'Le Cerf, Lully, and the Workshop Tradition', in Ronald Broude (ed.), *Studies in the History of Music 3: The Creative Process* (New York: Broude Brothers, 1992), pp. 17–30.

Brown, Clare, and Peter Holman, 'Thomas Busby and his "Fac Similes of Celebrated Composers"', *Early Music Performer* 12 (2003): 3–12.

Brown, Jonathan, *Kings and Connoisseurs: Collecting Art in Seventeenth-Century Europe*, The A.W. Mellon Lectures in the Fine Arts, vol. 43 (New Haven and London: Yale University Press, 1995).

Brown, Pamela Allen, and Peter Parolin (eds), *Women Players in England, 1500–1660: Beyond the All-Male Stage* (Aldershot: Ashgate, 2005).

Browning, Andrew, *Thomas Osborne, Earl of Danby and Duke of Leeds 1632–1712* (3 vols, Glasgow: Jackson, 1944–51).

Brusse, M.J., *Hoe het bosch papier wordt* (Rotterdam: W.L. and J. Brusse, 1917).

Bucholz, R.O., *The Augustan Court: Queen Anne and the Decline of Court Culture* (Stanford: Stanford University Press, 1993).

Burden, Michael, 'Aspects of Purcell's Operas', in Michael Burden (ed.), *Henry Purcell's Operas: The Complete Texts* (Oxford and New York: Oxford University Press, 2000), pp. 3–27.

——, 'Casting Issues in the Original Production of Purcell's Opera "The Fairy-Queen"', *Music & Letters* 84 (2003): 596–607.

——, 'Dancing Monkeys at Dorset Garden', *Theatre Notebook* 57 (2003): 119–35.

——, '"For the Lustre of the Subject": Music for the Lord Mayor's Day in the Restoration', *Early Music* 23 (1995): 585–602.

——, 'Fox and Pitt as Grimbald and Philidel: an 18th-century Political Use for *King Arthur*' (Unpublished paper presented at conference Purcell, Handel, Haydn, Mendelssohn: Anniversary Reflections, Oxford, 27–29 March 2009).

——, '"Gallimaufry at Covent Garden": Purcell's *The Fairy Queen* in 1946', *Early Music* 23 (1995): 268–84.

——, '"Great Minds against Themselves Conspire": Purcell's Dido as a Conspiracy Theorist', in Michael Burden (ed.), *A Woman Scorn'd: Responses to the Dido Myth* (London: Faber, 1998), pp. 227–47.

——, '"He Had the Honour to be Your Master": Lady Rhoda Cavendish's Music Lessons with Henry Purcell', *Music & Letters* 76 (1995): 532–9.

—— (ed.), *Performing the Music of Henry Purcell* (Oxford: Clarendon, 1996).

—— (ed.), *The Purcell Companion* (London: Faber, 1995; Portland, OR: Amadeus Press, 1995).

——, 'Purcell Debauch'd: The Dramatick Operas in Performance', in Michael Burden (ed.) *Performing the Music of Henry Purcell* (Oxford: Clarendon, 1996), pp. 145–62.

——, *Purcell Remembered* (London and Boston: Faber, 1995).

——, 'Purcell's *King Arthur* in the 1730s', *Restoration: Studies in English Literary Culture, 1660–1700* 34 (2010): 117–38.

——, 'Purcell's Operas on Craig's Stage: the Productions of the Purcell Operatic Society', *Early Music* 32 (2004): 443–58.

——, Review of Ellen T. Harris, *Henry Purcell's 'Dido and Aeneas'* (Oxford: Clarendon, 1987), in *Musical Times* 130 (1989): 85–6.

——, 'To Repeat (or Not to Repeat)? Dance Cues in Restoration English Opera', *Early Music* 35 (2007): 397–417.

——, 'Where Did Purcell Keep his Theatre Band?', *Early Music* 37 (2009): 429–43.

—— (ed.), *A Woman Scorn'd: Responses to the Dido Myth* (London: Faber, 1998).

Bush-Bailey, Gilli, *Treading the Bawds: Actresses and Playwrights on the Late-Stuart Stage* (Manchester: Manchester University Press, 2006).

Butler, Martin, 'Politics and the Masque: *The Triumph of Peace*', *The Seventeenth Century* 2 (1987): 117–41.

——, 'Politics and the Masque: *Salmacida Spolia*', in Thomas Healy and Jonathan Sawday (eds), *Literature and the English Civil War* (Cambridge: Cambridge University Press, 1990), pp. 59–74.

Butt, John, *Bach Interpretation: Articulation Marks in Primary Sources of J.S. Bach*, Cambridge Musical Texts and Monographs (Cambridge: Cambridge University Press, 1990).

——, 'The Seventeenth-Century Musical "Work"', in Tim Carter and John Butt (eds), *The Cambridge History of Seventeenth-Century Music* (Cambridge: Cambridge University Press, 2005), pp. 27–54.

Buttrey, John, 'The Dating of *Dido*' (Correspondence), *Early Music* 20 (1992): 703.

——, 'Dating Purcell's Dido and Aeneas', *Proceedings of the Royal Musical Association* 94 (1967–68): 51–62.

——, 'The Evolution of English Opera between 1656 and 1695: A Re-investigation' (PhD dissertation, University of Cambridge, 1967).

——, 'New Light on Robert Cambert in London, and his *Ballet en Musique*', *Early Music* 23 (1995): 198–220.

Byrt, John, 'Writing the Unwritable', *Musical Times* 138 (1997): 18–24.

Bywaters, David, *Dryden in Revolutionary England* (Berkeley: University of California Press, 1991).

Canfield, J. Douglas, *Tricksters and Estates: On the Ideology of Restoration Comedy* (Lexington: University of Kentucky Press, 1997).

Carter, Stephanie, 'Music Publishing and Compositional Activity in Restoration England, 1650–1700' (PhD dissertation, University of Manchester, 2011).

——, 'Published Variants and Creativity: An Overview of John Playford's Role as Editor', in Rebecca Herissone (ed.), *Concepts of Creativity in Seventeenth-Century England* (Woodbridge: Boydell and Brewer, forthcoming).

Chan, Mary, 'A Mid-Seventeenth-Century Music Meeting and Playford's Publishing', in Edward D. Olleson, Susan Wollenberg and John Caldwell (eds), *The Well Enchanting Skill: Music, Poetry and Drama in the Culture of the Renaissance – Essays in Honour of F.W. Sternfeld* (Oxford: Clarendon, 1990), pp. 231–44.

Chapman, Robert William, 'An Inventory of Paper, 1674', *The Library* Series 4/7 (1927): 402–8.

Charteris, Richard, 'A Checklist of the Manuscript Sources of Henry Purcell's Music in the University of California, William Andrews Clark Memorial Library, Los Angeles', *Notes* Series 2/52 (1995–96): 407–21.

——, 'Some Manuscript Discoveries of Henry Purcell and his Contemporaries in the Newberry Library, Chicago', *Notes* 37 (1980–81): 7–13.

Clark, Stuart, *Thinking with Demons: The Idea of Witchcraft in Early Modern Europe* (Oxford: Oxford University Press, 1997).

Cole, Suzanne, *Thomas Tallis and his Music in Victorian England*, Music in Britain, 1600–1900 (Woodbridge: Boydell and Brewer, 2008).

Cook, Nicholas, 'Playing God: Creativity, Analysis, and Aesthetic Inclusion', in Irène Deliège and Geraint A. Wiggins (eds), *Musical Creativity: Multidisciplinary Research in Theory and Practice* (Hove: Psychology Press, 2006), pp. 9–24.

Cooper, Barry, 'Keyboard Music', in Ian Spink (ed.), *The Blackwell History of Music in Britain, vol. 3: The Seventeenth Century* (Oxford: Blackwell, 1992), pp. 341–66.

Coopersmith, J.M., 'The First *Gesamtausgabe*: Dr. Arnold's Edition of Handel's Works', *Notes* Series 2/4 (1947): 277–91 and 438–49.

Cowen, Tyler, *Good and Plenty: The Creative Successes of American Arts Funding* (Princeton: Princeton University Press, 2006).

——, *In Praise of Commercial Culture* (Cambridge, MA and London: Harvard University Press, 1998).

Crawford, Katherine, *European Sexualities, 1400–1800*, eds William Beik, T.C.W. Blanning and Brendan Simms, New Approaches to European History (Cambridge: Cambridge University Press, 2007).

Crawford, Patricia, *Women and Religion in England, 1500–1720* (London: Routledge, 1993).

Cunningham, John, *The Consort Music of William Lawes, 1602–1645* (Woodbridge: Boydell and Brewer, 2010).

Cusick, Suzanne G, '"There Was Not One Lady Who Failed to Shed a Tear": Arianna's Lament and the Construction of Modern Womanhood', *Early Music* 22 (1994): 21–41.

Cyr, Mary, 'On Performing Eighteenth-Century Haute-Contre Roles', *Musical Times* 118 (1977): 291–5.

——, 'Tempo Gradations in Purcell's Sonatas', *Performance Practice Review* 7 (1994): 182–98.

Dadelsen, Georg von, *Beiträge zur Chronologie der Werke Johann Sebastian Bachs*, Tübinger Bach-Studien, vol. 4/5 (Trossingen: Hohner, 1958).

Dahlhaus, Carl, *Foundations of Music History*, trans. J.B. Robinson (Cambridge, London and New York: Cambridge University Press, 1983).

Dart, Thurston, 'Recorder "Gracings" in 1700', *Galpin Society Journal* 12 (1959): 93–4.

——, *The Interpretation of Music*, Hutchinson's University Library, Music Series (4th edn, London: Hutchinson, 1967; first published London: Hutchinson, 1954).

——, 'Purcell and Bull', *Musical Times* 104 (1963): 30–31.

Davies, Horton, *Worship and Theology in England from Andrewes to Baxter and Fox, 1603–1690*, Worship and Theology in England, vol. 2 (Princeton: Princeton University Press; London: Oxford University Press, 1975).

Day, Cyrus Lawrence and Eleanore Boswell Murrie, 'Playford *versus* Pearson', *The Library* Series 4/17 (1937): 427–47.

Day, Thomas Charles, 'Old Music in England, 1790–1820', *Revue Belge de Musicologie* 26–7 (1972–73): 27–37.

——, 'A Renaissance Revival in Eighteenth-Century England', *Musical Quarterly* 57 (1971): 575–92.

De Krey, Gary S., *London and the Restoration, 1659–1683*, Cambridge Studies in Early Modern British History (Cambridge: Cambridge University Press, 2005).

Dent, Edward J., *Foundations of English Opera: A Study of Music Drama in England during the Seventeenth Century* (Cambridge: Cambridge University Press, 1928).

Dessauer, Rolf, 'DYLUX, Thomas L. Gravell, and Watermarks of Stamps and Papers', in Mosser, Daniel W., Michael Saffle and Ernest W. Sullivan (eds), *Puzzles in Paper: Concepts in Historical Watermarks* (New Castle, DE: Oak Knoll Press; London: British Library, 2000), pp. 183–5.

Devine, Patrick F. and Harry M. White (eds), *The Maynooth International Musicological Conference, 1995: Selected Proceedings, II*, Irish Musical Studies, vol. 5 (Dublin: Four Courts, 1996).

Dexter, Keri, *'A Good Quire of Voices': The Provision of Choral Music at St George's Chapel, Windsor Castle, and Eton College, c.1640–1733* (Aldershot and Burlington: Ashgate, 2002).

——, 'The Restoration "Symphony" Anthem in Organ Transcription: Contemporary Techniques and Transmission' (MMus Dissertation, University of Reading, 1996).

Dixon, Laurinda S., Perilous *Chastity: Women and Illness in Pre-Enlightenment Art and Medicine* (Ithaca: Cornell University Press, 1995).

Dolan, Francis E., *Dangerous Familiars: Representations of Domestic Crime in England, 1550–1700* (Ithaca: Cornell University Press, 1994).

Donington, Robert, *A Performer's Guide to Baroque Music* (London: Faber, 1973).

——, 'Performing Purcell's Music Today', in Imogen Holst (ed.), *Henry Purcell 1659–1695: Essays on his Music* (London: Oxford University Press, 1959), pp. 74–102.

——, 'A Problem of Inequality', *Musical Quarterly* 53 (1967): 503–17.

Dreyfus, Laurence, *Bach and the Patterns of Invention* (Cambridge, MA: Harvard University Press, 1996).

——, 'Bachian Invention and its Mechanisms', in John Butt (ed.), *The Cambridge Companion to Bach* (Cambridge: Cambridge University Press, 1997), pp. 171–92.

——, *Bach's Continuo Group: Players and Practices in His Vocal Works*, Studies in the History of Music, vol. 3 (Cambridge, MA and London: Harvard University Press, 1987).

Duffy, Maureen, *Henry Purcell* (London: Fourth Estate, 1994).

Dugaw, Dianne, '"Critical Instants": Theatre Songs in the Age of Dryden and Purcell', *Eighteenth-Century Studies* 23 (1989–90): 157–81.

——, '"The Rationall Spirituall Part": Dryden and Purcell's Baroque *King Arthur*', in Jayne Lewis and Maxmillian E. Novak (eds), *Enchanted Ground: Reimagining John Dryden* (Toronto: University of Toronto Press, 2004), pp. 273–89.

Dürr, Alfred, 'Zur Chronologie der Leipziger Vokalwerke J.S. Bachs', *Bach-Jahrbuch* 44 (1957): 5–162; repr. as book of the same title, Musikwissenschaftliche Arbeiten, vol. 26 (Kassel and London: Bärenreiter, 1976).

——, *Studien über die frühen Kantaten Johann Sebastian Bachs* (rev. edn, Wiesbaden: Breitkopf & Härtel, 1977).

Fabbri, Paolo, 'On the Origins of an Operatic Topos: The Mad-Scene', in Iain Fenlon and Tim Carter (eds), *Con Che Soavità: Studies in Italian Opera, Song, and Dance, 1580–1740* (Oxford: Clarendon, 1995), pp. 157–95.

Ferguson, Howard, *Keyboard Interpretation from the 14th to the 19th Century: an Introduction* (London: Oxford University Press, 1975).

——, 'Purcell's Harpsichord Music', *Proceedings of the Royal Musical Association* 91 (1964–65): 1–9.

Finney, Gretchen Ludke, *Musical Backgrounds for English Literature: 1580–1650* (New Brunswick: Rutgers University Press, 1962).

Firth, C.H., 'Sir William Davenant and the Revival of the Drama during the Protectorate', *English Historical Review* 18 (1903): 319–21.

Fisk, Deborah Payne (ed.), *The Cambridge Companion to English Restoration Theatre* (Cambridge: Cambridge University Press, 2000).

Fletcher, Anthony, *Gender, Sex and Subordination in England, 1500–1800* (New Haven: Yale University Press, 1995).

Ford, Robert, 'Osborn MS 515, A Guardbook of Restoration Instrumental Music', *Fontes Artis Musicae* 30 (1983): 174–84.

——, 'Purcell as his Own Editor: the Funeral Sentences', *Journal of Musicological Research* 7 (1986): 47–67.

——, Review of Franklin B. Zimmerman, *Henry Purcell: A Guide to Research*, Garland Composer Resource Manuals, vol. 18 (New York and London: Garland, 1989), in *Journal of Musicological Research* 10 (1991): 283–5.

——, 'A Sacred Song Not by Purcell', *Musical Times* 125 (1984): 45–7.

Fortune Nigel, 'Purcell: The Domestic Sacred Music', in F.W. Sternfeld, Nigel Fortune and Edward Olleson (eds), *Essays on Opera and English Music in Honour of Sir Jack Westrup* (Oxford: Blackwell, 1975), pp. 62–78.

Fortune, Nigel with Iain Fenlon, 'Music Manuscripts of John Browne (1608–91) and from Stanford Hall, Leicestershire', in Ian Bent (ed.), *Source Materials and the Interpretation of Music: a Memorial Volume to Thurston Dart* (London: Stainer and Bell, 1981), pp. 155–68.

Fortune, Nigel and Franklin B. Zimmerman, 'Purcell's Autographs', in Imogen Holst (ed.), *Henry Purcell 1659–1695: Essays on his Music* (London: Oxford University Press, 1959), pp. 106–21.

Foss, Michael, *Man of Wit to Man of Business: The Arts and Changing Patronage 1660–1750* (Bristol: Bristol Classic Press, 1988; originally published as *The Age of Patronage*, London: Hamish Hamilton, 1971).

Foucault, Michel, *Madness and Civilization: A History of Insanity in the Age of Reason*, trans. Richard Howard (New York: Vintage Books, 1988).

Freeman, Andrew, *Father Smith, otherwise Bernard Schmidt, being an Account of a Seventeenth Century Organ Maker*, edited, annotated and with new material by John Rowntree (Oxford: Positif Press, 1977; first published London: Musical Opinion, 1926).

Freud, Sigmund, *Jokes and Their Relation to the Unconscious*, trans. James Strachey (New York: Norton, 1960).

Gallagher, Catherine, 'Embracing the Absolute: The Politics of the Female Subject in Seventeenth-Century England', *Genders* 1 (1988): 24–39.

Garratt, James, 'Performing Renaissance Church Music in Nineteenth-Century Germany: Issues and Challenges in the Study of Performative Reception', *Music & Letters* 83 (2002): 187–236.

Giles, Peter, *The History and Technique of the Counter-tenor: A Study of the Male High Voice Family* (Aldershot: Scolar, 1994).

Gill, Pat, *Interpreting Ladies: Women, Wit and Morality in the Restoration Comedy of Manners* (Athens: University of Georgia Press, 1994).

Gilman, Todd, 'David Garrick's *Masque of King Arthur* with Thomas Arne's Score (1770)', *Restoration: Studies in English Literary Culture, 1660–1700* 34 (2010): 139–62.

Godt, Irving, 'Purcell and Dido (and Aeneas)', *Studies in the History of Music* 2 (1988): 60–82.

Goetze, Martin, 'Transposing Organs and Pitch in England', *FoMRHI Quarterly* 78 (1995): 61–7.

Goldie, Mark, 'The Earliest Notice of Purcell's *Dido and Aeneas*', *Early Music* 20 (1992): 392–400.

Goodare, Julian (ed.), *The Scottish Witch-Hunt in Context* (Manchester: Manchester University Press, 2002).

Gorce, Jérôme de La, *Berain, dessinateur du Roi Soleil* (Paris: Herscher, 1986).

——, 'Quelques rapports entre les dessins d'opéras français du règne de Louis XIV et l'architecture, la sculpture et la peinture', in Jérôme de La Gorce (ed.), *Iconographie et arts du spectacle: actes du séminaire CNRS (G.D.R. 712), Paris, 1992*, Histoire de l'art et iconographie, vol. 2 (Paris: Klincksieck, 1996), pp. 135–54.

——, 'Some Notes on Lully's Orchestra', in John Hajdu Heyer (ed.), *Jean-Baptiste Lully and the Music of the French Baroque: Essays in Honor of James R. Anthony* (Cambridge: Cambridge University Press, 1989), pp. 99–112.

Gouk, Penelope, 'Music, Melancholy, and Medical Spirits in Early Modern Thought', in Peregrine Horden (ed.), *Music as Medicine: The History of Music Therapy since Antiquity* (Aldershot and Brookfield: Ashgate, 2000), pp. 173–94.

——, *Music, Science and Natural Magic in Seventeenth-Century England* (New Haven: Yale University Press, 1999).

Grampp, William D., *Pricing the Priceless: Art, Artists, and Economics* (New York: Basic Books, 1989).

Grant, Kerry S., *Dr. Burney as Critic and Historian of Music*, Studies in Musicology, vol. 62 (Ann Arbor: UMI Research Press, 1983).

Greenblatt, Stephen, *Shakespearean Negotiations: The Circulation of Social Energy in Renaissance England* (Oxford: Clarendon, 1988).

Grimshaw, Julian, '*Fuga* in Early Byrd', *Early Music* 37 (2009): 251–65.

——, 'Morley's Rule for First-Species Canon', *Early Music* 34 (2006): 661–6.

——, 'Sixteenth-Century English *Fuga*: Sequential and Peak-Note Subjects', *Musical Times* 148 (2007): 61–78.

Gustafson, Bruce, 'Charles Babel', *Die Musik in Geschichte und Gegenwart. Personenteil* (17 vols, Kassel: Bärenreiter, 1999–2007), vol. 1, col. 1250.

Gwynn, Dominic, 'The English Organ in Purcell's Lifetime', in Michael Burden (ed.), *Performing the Music of Henry Purcell* (Oxford: Clarendon, 1996), pp. 20–38.

——, 'Lost Worlds: The English Organ before 1700', in Thomas Donahue (ed.), *Music and its Questions: Essays in Honor of Peter Williams* (Richmond, VA: Organ Historical Society Press, 2007), pp. 23–47.

——, 'Organ Pitch in Seventeenth-Century England', *BIOS Journal* 9 (1985): 65–78.

——, 'Purcell's Organ at Westminster Abbey: A Note on the Cover Illustration', *Early Music* 23 (1995): 550.

Habermas, Jürgen, *The Structural Transformation of the Public Sphere: An Inquiry into a Category of Bourgeois Society*, trans. Thomas Burger with Frederick Lawrence, Studies in Contemporary German Social Thought (Cambridge, MA: MIT Press; Cambridge: Polity, 1989). First published as *Strukturwandel der Öffentlichkeit: Untersuchungen zu einer Kategorie der bürgerlichen Gesellschaft*, Politica, vol. 4 (Neuwied: Luchterhand, 1962).

Hammond, Paul, 'The King's Two Bodies: Representations of Charles II', in Jeremy Black and Jeremy Gregory (eds), *Culture, Politics and Society in Britain, 1660–1800* (Manchester: Manchester University Press, 1991), pp. 13–48.

Handley, Stuart, 'Butler, James, Second Duke of Ormond (1665–1745)', in *Oxford Dictionary of National Biography*, http://www.oxforddnb.com.

Harben, Henry A. *A Dictionary of London: Being Notes Topographical and Historical Relating to the Streets and Principal Buildings in the City of London* (London: Jenkins, 1918).

Harris, Anthony, *Night's Black Agents: Witchcraft and Magic in Seventeenth-Century English Drama* (Manchester: Manchester University Press, 1980).

Harris, Ellen T., *Henry Purcell's 'Dido and Aeneas'* (Oxford: Clarendon, 1987).

——, '*King Arthur*'s Journey into the Eighteenth Century', in Curtis Price (ed.), *Purcell Studies* (Cambridge: Cambridge University Press, 1995), pp. 257–89.

Harris, Tim, 'Scott [Crofts], James, Duke of Monmouth and First Duke of Buccleuch (1649–1685)', in *Oxford Dictionary of National Biography*, http://www.oxforddnb.com.

Haskell, Harry, *The Early Music Revival: A History* (New York: Dover, 1996; first published London: Thames and Hudson, 1988).

Hawes, Clement, *Mania and Literary Style: The Rhetoric of Enthusiasm from the Ranters to Christopher Smart* (Cambridge: Cambridge University Press, 1996).

Haynes, Bruce, *A History of Performing Pitch: The Story of 'A'* (Lanham: Scarecrow, 2002).

Heawood, Edward, *Watermarks, Mainly of the 17th and 18th Centuries*, Monumenta chartae papyraceae historian illustrantia, vol. 1 (2nd rev. edn, Hilversum: Paper Publications Society, 1969).

Hefling, Stephen, *Rhythmic Alteration in Seventeenth- and Eighteenth-Century Music: Notes Inégales and Overdotting* (New York: Schirmer, 1993).

Heighes, Simon, and Peter Ward Jones, 'Hayes: (2) Philip Hayes', in *Grove Music Online*, http://www.oxfordmusiconline.com.

Heller, Wendy, *Emblems of Eloquence: Opera and Women's Voices in Seventeenth-Century Venice* (Berkeley: University of California Press, 2003).

——, '"A Present for the Ladies": Ovid, Montaigne, and the Redemption of Purcell's Dido', *Music & Letters* 84 (2003): 189–208.

Herissone, Rebecca, 'The Compositional Techniques of Henry Purcell as Revealed through Autograph Revisions Made to His Works' (MMus dissertation, King's College, London, 1993).

—— (ed.), *Concepts of Creativity in Seventeenth-Century England* (Woodbridge: Boydell and Brewer, forthcoming).

——, '"Fowle Originalls" and "Fayre Writeing": Reconsidering Purcell's Compositional Process', *Journal of Musicology* 23 (2006): 569–619.

——, *Music Theory in Seventeenth-Century England*, Oxford Monographs on Music (Oxford: Oxford University Press, 2000).

——, *Musical Creativity in Restoration England* (Cambridge: Cambridge University Press, forthcoming).

——, 'Playford, Purcell, and the Functions of Music Publishing in Restoration England', *Journal of the American Musicological Society* 63 (2010): 243–89.

——, 'Purcell's Revisions of his Own Works', in Curtis Price (ed.), *Purcell Studies* (Cambridge: Cambridge University Press, 1995), pp. 51–86.

——, Review of Martin Adams, *Henry Purcell: The Origins and Development of his Musical Style* (Cambridge: Cambridge University Press, 1995), in *Early Music History* 15 (1996): 270–76.

——, 'The Revision Process in William Turner's Anthem "O Praise the Lord"', *Journal of the Royal Musical Association* 123 (1998): 1–38.

——, 'Richard Goodson the Elder's Ode "Janus did ever to thy sight": Evidence of Compositional Procedures in the Early Eighteenth Century', *Music & Letters* 79 (1998): 167–91.

——, 'Robert Pindar, Thomas Busby, and the Mysterious Scoring of Henry Purcell's "Come ye Sons of Art"', *Music & Letters* 88 (2007): 1–48.

——, 'The Theory and Practice of Composition in the English Restoration Period' (PhD dissertation, University of Cambridge, 1996).

——, '"To entitle himself to ye Composition": Investigating Concepts of Authorship and Originality in Seventeenth-Century English Ceremonial Music' (Unpublished paper presented at the Annual Meeting of the Society for Seventeenth-Century Music, Huntington Library, San Marino, 17–19 April 2008).

——, 'To Fill, Forbear, or Adorne': The Organ Accompaniment of Restoration Sacred Music, RMA Monographs, vol. 14 (Aldershot: Ashgate, 2006).

Highfill, Philip H., Kalman A. Burnim and Edward A. Langhans, A Biographical Dictionary of Actors, Actresses, Musicians, Dancers, Managers and Other Stage Personnel in London 1660–1800 (16 vols, Carbondale: Southern Illinois University Press, 1973–93).

Higney, John, 'Henry Purcell: A Reception/Dissemination Study, 1695–1771' (PhD dissertation, University of Western Ontario, 2008).

——, '"The Most Perfect Models": Purcell, Handel, Haydn, and Mendelssohn in The Harmonicon (1823–1833)' (Unpublished paper presented at conference Purcell, Handel, Haydn, Mendelssohn: Anniversary Reflections, Oxford, 27–29 March 2009).

Hirsch, Paul, 'Dr. Arnold's Handel Edition (1787–1797)', Music Review 8 (1947): 106–16.

Hogwood, Christopher, 'Creating the Corpus: The "Complete Keyboard Music" of Henry Purcell', in Christopher Hogwood (ed.), The Keyboard in Baroque Europe (Cambridge and New York: Cambridge University Press, 2003), pp. 67–89.

——, 'A New English Keyboard Manuscript of the Seventeenth Century: Autograph Music by Draghi and Purcell', British Library Journal 21 (1995): 161–75.

——, 'Thomas Tudway's History of Music', in Christopher Hogwood and Richard Luckett (eds), Music in Eighteenth-Century England: Essays in Memory of Charles Cudworth (Cambridge: Cambridge University Press, 1983), pp. 19–48.

Hogwood, Christopher and Richard Luckett (eds), Music in Eighteenth-Century England: Essays in Memory of Charles Cudworth (Cambridge: Cambridge University Press, 1983).

Holman, Peter, 'Bartholomew Isaack and "Mr Isaack" of Eton: a Confusing Tale of Restoration Musicians', Musical Times 128 (1987): 381–5.

——, 'Compositional Choices in Henry Purcell's Three Parts upon a Ground', Early Music 29 (2001): 250–61.

——, Dowland: Lachrimae (1604), Cambridge Music Handbooks (Cambridge: Cambridge University Press, 1999).

——, '"Evenly, Softly and Sweetly Acchording to All": The Organ Accompaniment of English Consort Music', in Andrew Ashbee and Peter Holman (eds), John Jenkins and his Time: Studies in English Consort Music (Oxford: Clarendon, 1996), pp. 353–82.

——, Four and Twenty Fiddlers: The Violin at the English Court 1540–1690, Oxford Monographs on Music (Oxford: Clarendon, 1993).

——, Henry Purcell, Oxford Studies of Composers (Oxford: Oxford University Press, 1994).

——, 'The Italian Connection: Giovanni Battista Draghi and Henry Purcell', *Early Music Performer* 22 (2008): 4–19.

——, 'Original Sets of Parts for Restoration Concerted Music at Oxford', in Michael Burden (ed.), *Performing the Music of Henry Purcell* (Oxford: Clarendon, 1996), pp. 9–19.

—— (ed.), *Purcell*, The Baroque Composers (Farnham: Ashgate, 2010).

——, 'Purcell and Pitch', *Early Music* 24 (1996): 366.

——, 'Purcell and Roseingrave: a New Autograph', in Curtis Price (ed.), *Purcell Studies* (Cambridge: Cambridge University Press, 1995), pp. 94–105.

——, 'Purcell's Orchestra', *Musical Times* 137 (1996): 17–23.

——, 'Reluctant Continuo', *Early Music* 9 (1981): 75–8.

——, Response to Layton Ring, Correspondence, 'Malice Afterthought', *Musical Times* 134 (1993): 615.

——, Review of Henry Purcell, *Dido and Aeneas*, ed. Ellen Harris, Oxford Operas (Oxford: Oxford University Press, 1987), in *Music & Letters* 71 (1990): 617–20.

——, sleeve notes to *Odes on the Death of Henry Purcell*, The Parley of Instruments and Parley of Instruments Choir, dir. Roy Goodman and Peter Holman (Hyperion CDA 66578, *rec.* 1992).

Holman, Peter and Robert Thompson, 'Purcell: (3) Henry Purcell (ii)', in *Grove Music Online*, http://www.oxfordmusiconline.com.

Holst, Imogen (ed.), *Henry Purcell, 1659–1695: Essays on his Music* (London: Oxford University Press, 1959).

Holub, Robert C., *Reception Theory: a Critical Introduction*, New Accents Series (London: Routledge, 2003; first published London: Methuen, 1984).

Hotson, Leslie, *The Commonwealth and Restoration Stage* (Cambridge, MA: Harvard University Press, 1928).

Houck, Stacey, 'John Playford and the English Musical Market', in Jessie Ann Owens (ed.), *'Noyses, Sounds and Sweet Aires': Music in Early Modern England* (Seattle and London: Folger Shakespeare Library, 2006), pp. 48–61.

Howard, Alan, 'Composition as an Act of Performance: Artifice and Expression in Purcell's Sacred Partsong *Since God so tender a regard'*, *Journal of the Royal Musical Association* 132 (2007): 32–59.

——, 'John Blow in Parallel Texts', Review of John Blow, *Venus and Adonis*, ed. Bruce Wood, Purcell Society Companion Series, vol. 2 (London: Stainer & Bell, 2008), in *Early Music* 37 (2009): 318–20.

——, 'Manuscript Publishing in the Commonwealth Period: A Neglected Source of Consort Music by Golding and Locke', *Music & Letters*, 90 (2009): 35–67.

——, 'Purcell and the Poetics of Artifice: Compositional Strategies in the Fantasias and Sonatas' (PhD dissertation, King's College, London, 2006).

Howe, Elizabeth, *The First English Actresses: Women and Drama 1660–1700* (Cambridge: Cambridge University Press, 1992).

Hughes, Derek, *English Drama 1660–1700* (Oxford: Clarendon, 1996).

Hughes, Meirion, and Robert Stradling, *The English Musical Renaissance 1840–1940: Constructing A National Music* (2nd edn, Manchester and New York: Manchester University Press, 2001).

Hughes-Hughes, Augustus, William Barclay Squire and F.M. O'Donoghue, 'The Purcell Exhibits at the British Museum', *Musical Times and Singing Class Circular*, 36 (1895): 797–9.
——, 'Henry Purcell's Handwriting', *Musical Times and Singing Class Circular*, 37 (1896): 81–3.
Hume, Robert D., *The Development of English Drama in the Late Seventeenth Century* (Oxford: Clarendon, 1976).
——, 'The Dorset Garden Theatre: A Review of Facts and Problems', *Theatre Notebook* 33 (1979): 4–17.
——, 'Dryden on Creation: "Imagination" in the Later Criticism', *The Review of English Studies* 21 (1970): 295–314.
——, 'The Economics of Culture in London, 1660–1740', *Huntington Library Quarterly* 69 (2006): 487–533.
—— (ed.), *The London Theatre World 1660–1800* (Carbondale: Southern Illinois University Press, 1980).
——, 'The Nature of the Dorset Garden Theatre', *Theatre Notebook* 36 (1982): 99–109.
——, 'The Politics of Opera in Late Seventeenth-Century London', *Cambridge Opera Journal* 10 (1998): 15–43.
——, 'Theatres and Repertory', in Joseph Donohue (ed.), *The Cambridge History of British Theatre: Vol. 2 – 1660 to 1895* (Cambridge: Cambridge University Press, 2004), pp. 53–70.
——, 'The Uses of Montague Summers: A Pioneer Reconsidered', *Restoration: Studies in English Literary Culture, 1660–1700* 3 (1979): 59–65.
Humphreys, Mark, 'Daniel Purcell: A Biography and Thematic Catalogue', (DPhil dissertation, University of Oxford, 2005).
Hunter, David, 'Music Copyright in Britain to 1800', *Music & Letters* 67 (1986): 269–82.
——, 'Patronizing Handel, Inventing Audiences: The Intersections of Class, Money, Music, and History', *Early Music* 28 (2000): 32–49.
Hurley, David Ross, *Handel's Muse: Patterns of Creation in his Oratorios and Musical Dramas, 1743–1751* (Oxford: Oxford University Press, 2000).
Hutter, Michael and David Throsby (eds), *Beyond Price: Value in Culture, Economics, and the Arts*, Murphy Institute Studies in Political Economy (Cambridge and New York: Cambridge University Press, 2008).
Hutton, Ronald, *Charles the Second: King of England, Scotland and Ireland* (Oxford: Clarendon, 1989).
Jackson, Stanley, *Melancholia and Depression: From Hippocratic Times to Modern Times* (New Haven: Yale University Press, 1986).
Jander, Owen Hughes, 'Staff-Liner Identification: a Technique for the Age of Microfilm', *Journal of the American Musicological Society* 20 (1967): 112–16.
Jeanneret, Christine, *L'oeuvre en filigrane: une étude philologique des manuscrits de musique pour clavier à Rome au XVIIe siècle*, Historiae musicae cultores, vol. 116 (Florence: Olschki, 2009).
Johnson, Douglas, 'Beethoven Scholars and Beethoven's Sketches', *19th-Century Music* 2 (1978): 3–17.

Johnson, Douglas, Alan Tyson and Robert Winter, *The Beethoven Sketchbooks: History, Reconstruction, Inventory* (Oxford: Clarendon, 1985).

Johnson, James, *A Profane Wit: The Life of John Wilmot, Earl of Rochester* (Rochester: University of Rochester Press, 2004).

Johnston, Gregory S., 'Polyphonic Keyboard Accompaniment in the Early Baroque: an Alternative to Basso Continuo', *Early Music* 26 (1998): 51–64.

Johnstone, Andrew, '"As It Was in the Beginning": Organ and Choir Pitch in Early Anglican Church Music', *Early Music* 31 (2003): 506–26.

Johnstone, H. Diack, 'The English Beat', in Robert Judd (ed.), *Aspects of Keyboard Music: Essays in Honour of Susi Jeans on the Occasion of her Seventy-Fifth Birthday* (Oxford: Positif Press, 1992), pp. 34–44.

——, 'The Genesis of Boyce's "Cathedral Music"', *Music & Letters* 56 (1975): 26–40.

——, 'Ornamentation in the Keyboard Music of Henry Purcell and his Contemporaries', in Michael Burden (ed.), *Performing the Music of Henry Purcell* (Oxford: Clarendon, 1996), pp. 82–104.

Jones, Edward Huws, *The Performance of English Song, 1610–1670*, Outstanding Dissertations in Music from British Universities (New York: Garland, 1989).

Kent, Jonathan, Interview on Direction of Glyndebourne production of *The Fairy Queen*, 2009, http://www.glyndebourne.com/operas/fairy_queen/.

Kenyon, Nicholas 'Henry Purcell: Towards a Tercentenary', in Michael Burden (ed.), *Performing the Music of Henry Purcell* (Oxford: Clarendon, 1996), pp. 1–6.

Kephart, Carolyn, 'Thomas Durfey's *Cinthia and Endimion*: A Reconsideration', *Theatre Notebook* 39 (1985): 134–9.

Kerman, Joseph, 'A Glimmer from the Dark Ages', in Curtis Price (ed.), *Purcell: 'Dido and Aeneas' – An Opera*, Norton Critical Score (London: Norton, 1986), pp. 224–8.

——, 'Sketch Studies', in D. Kern Holoman and Claude V. Palisca (eds), *Musicology in the 1980s: Methods, Goals, Opportunities* (New York: Da Capo, 1982), pp. 53–65.

Kidson, Frank, *British Music Publishers, Printers and Engravers: London, Provincial, Scottish, and Irish. From Queen Elizabeth's Reign to George the Fourth's* (London: W.E. Hill, 1900; repr. Benjamin Blom, 1967).

King, Alec Hyatt, 'Benjamin Goodison and the First "Complete Edition" of Purcell', in Richard Baum and Wolfgang Rehm (eds), *Musik und Verlag: Karl Vötterle zum 65. Geburtstag* (Kassel: Barenreiter, 1968), pp. 391–6.

——, *Some British Collectors of Music, c.1600–1960* (Cambridge: Cambridge University Press, 1963).

King, Thomas A., *The Gendering of Men, 1600–1750, vol. 1: The English Phallus* (Madison: University of Wisconsin Press, 2004).

Kingsford, Peter, *Victorian Lives in North Mymms* Ch. 9, 'Change in Bell Barr', http://www.brookmans.com/history/kingsford4/ch9.shtml.

Klakowich, Robert, 'Seventeenth-Century English Keyboard Autographs', *Journal of the Royal Musical Association* 121 (1996): 132–5.

Knights, Mark, *Politics and Opinion in Crisis, 1678–81*, Cambridge Studies in Early Modern British History (Cambridge: Cambridge University Press, 1994).

Kolbrener, William, and Michal Michelson (eds), *Mary Astell: Reason, Gender, Faith* (Aldershot and Burlington: Ashgate, 2007).

Konrad, Ulrich, 'The Use of Watermarks in Musicology', in Daniel W. Mosser, Michael Saffle and Ernest W. Sullivan (eds), *Puzzles in Paper: Concepts in Historical Watermarks* (New Castle, DE: Oak Knoll Press; London: British Library, 2000), pp. 93–106.

Köster, Patricia, 'Purcell's Swan Song: A Long Reverberation in Women's Fiction', in Thomas R. Cleary (ed.), *Time, Literature and the Arts: Essays in Honor of Samuel L. Macey* (Victoria: University of Victoria, 1994), pp. 140–56.

Kristeva, Julia, *Black Sun: Depression and Melancholy*, trans. Leon S. Roudiez (New York: Columbia University Press, 1989).

Krummel, Donald W., *English Music Printing, 1553–1700* (London: Bibliographical Society, 1975).

LaHaye, Laura, 'Mercantilism', in Steven N. Durlauf and Lawrence Blume (eds), *The New Palgrave Dictionary of Economics* (2nd edn, Basingstoke: Palgrave Macmillan, 2008), pp. 568–9.

Lam, Basil, Review of Alfred Dürr, *Studien über die frühen Kantaten Johann Sebastian Bachs* (rev. edn, Wiesbaden: Breitkopf & Härtel, 1977) and *Zur Chronologie der Leipziger Vokalwerke J.S. Bachs* (2nd impression, Kassel and London: Bärenreiter, 1976), in *Music & Letters* 60 (1979): 325–8.

Langley, Hubert, *Doctor Arne* (Cambridge: Cambridge University Press, 1938).

Laqueur, Thomas, *Making Sex: Body and Gender from the Greeks to Freud* (Cambridge, MA: Harvard University Press, 1990).

Larner, Christina, *Witchcraft and Religion: The Politics of Popular Belief* (New York: Blackwell, 1984).

LaRue, Jan, 'Classification of Watermarks for Musicological Purposes', *Fontes Artis Musicae* 13 (1966): 59–63.

———, 'Watermarks and Musicology', *Journal of Musicology* 18 (2001): 313–43 (first published in *Acta Musicologica* 33 (1961): 120–46).

Lasocki, David, 'The *Compleat Flute-Master* Reincarnated', *American Recorder Magazine* 11 (1970): 83–5.

Laurie, Margaret, 'The "Cambury" Purcell Manuscript', in Patrick F. Devine and Harry White (eds), *The Maynooth International Musicological Conference 1995: Selected Proceedings, II*, Irish Musical Studies, vol. 5 (Dublin: Four Courts, 1996), pp. 262–71.

———, 'The Chapel Royal Part-books', in Oliver Neighbour (ed.), *Music and Bibliography: Essays in Honour of Alec Hyatt King* (New York: Saur; London: Bingley, 1980), pp. 28–50.

———, Correspondence, *Musical Times* 105 (1964): 198.

———, 'Continuity and Tempo in Purcell's Vocal Works', in Curtis Price (ed.), *Purcell Studies* (Cambridge: Cambridge University Press, 1995), pp. 192–206.

———, 'Did Purcell set *The Tempest?*', *Proceedings of the Royal Musical Association* 90 (1963–64): 41–57.

———, 'Purcell's Stage Works' (PhD dissertation, University of Cambridge, 1962).

Lawrence, W.J., 'The French Opera in London – A Riddle of 1686', *Times Literary Supplement*, 1782 (28 March 1936): 263.

——, Response to Dennis Arundell, 'The Gordian Knot Untied', *Times Literary Supplement*, 1221 (11 June 1925): 400.

Leacroft, Richard, *The Development of the English Playhouse: an Illustrated Survey of Theatre Building in England from Medieval to Modern Times* (London: Eyre Methuen, 1973).

Lee, Hugh M., 'Purcell's *Dido and Aneas* [*sic*]: Aeneas as Romantic Hero', *Vergilius* 23 (1977): 21–9.

Levack, Brian P., 'The Great Scottish Witch Hunt of 1661–1662', *Journal of British Studies* 20 (1980): 90–108.

Lindley, David (ed.), *The Court Masque*, Revels Plays Companion Library (Manchester: Manchester University Press, 1984).

Lister, Rebecca Crow, '"Wild Thro' the Woods I'le Fly": Female Mad Songs in Seventeenth-Century English Drama' (DMA dissertation, Florida State University, 1997).

Little, Meredith, and Natalie Jenne, *Dance and the Music of J.S. Bach*, Music Scholarship and Performance (Bloomington, IN: Indiana University Press, 1991).

Lockwood, Lewis, 'Beethoven's Sketches for *Sehnsucht* (WoO 146)', in Alan Tyson (ed.), *Beethoven Studies* (New York: Norton, 1974), pp. 97–122.

Long, Kenneth R., *The Music of the English Church* (London: Hodder and Stoughton, 1972).

Lonsdale, Roger, *Dr. Charles Burney: A Literary Biography* (Oxford: Clarendon, 1989; first published 1965).

Love, Harold, *The Culture and Commerce of Texts: Scribal Publication in Seventeenth-Century England* (Amherst: University of Massachusetts Press, 1998; originally published as *Scribal Publication in Seventeenth-Century England* (Oxford: Clarendon, 1993)).

Lowenthal, Cynthia, *Performing Identities on the Restoration Stage* (Carbondale: Southern Illinois Press, 2003).

Lowerre, Kathryn, *Music and Musicians on the London Stage, 1695–1705*, Performance in the Long Eighteenth Century: Studies in Theatre, Music, Dance (Farnham and Burlington: Ashgate, 2009).

Luckett, Richard, 'Exotick but Rational Entertainments: The English Dramatick Operas', in Marie Axton and Raymond Williams (eds), *English Drama: Forms and Development – Essays in Honour of Muriel Clara Bradbrook* (Cambridge, London and New York: Cambridge University Press, 1977), pp. 123–41.

——, 'A New Source for "Venus and Adonis"', *Musical Times* 130 (1989): 76–9.

——, 'The Playfords and the Purcells', in Robin Myers, Michael Harris and Giles Mandelbrote (eds), *Music and the Book Trade: From the Sixteenth to the Twentieth Century* (New Castle, DE: Oak Knoll Press; London: The British Library, 2008), pp. 45–67.

——, '"Or Rather Our Musical Shakspeare": Charles Burney's Purcell', in Christopher Hogwood and Richard Luckett (eds), *Music in Eighteenth-Century England: Essays in Memory of Charles Cudworth* (Cambridge: Cambridge University Press, 1983), pp. 59–77.

Mabbett, Margaret, 'Italian Musicians in Restoration England (1660–1690)', *Music & Letters* 67 (1986): 237–47.

MacCormick, Ian (ed.), *Secret Sexualities: A Sourcebook of Seventeenth- and Eighteenth-Century Writing* (London: Routledge, 1997).

MacDonald, Michael, *Mystical Bedlam: Madness, Anxiety and Healing in Seventeenth-Century England* (Cambridge: Cambridge University Press, 1981).

Macfarlane, Alan, *Witchcraft in Tudor and Stuart England: A Regional and Comparative Study* (London: Routledge and Kegan Paul, 1970).

Mack, Maynard (ed. and trans.), *The Last and Greatest Art: Some Unpublished Poetical Manuscripts of Alexander Pope* (Newark: University of Delaware Press; London and Toronto: Associated University Presses, 1984).

Mack, Phyllis, *Visionary Women: Ecstatic Prophecy in Seventeenth-Century England* (Berkeley: University of California Press, 1992).

MacKinnon, Dolly, '"Poor Senseless Bess, Clothed in Her Rags and Folly": Early Modern Women, Madness, and Song in Seventeenth-Century England', *Parergon* 18 (2001): 119–51.

Mandell, Laura, *Misogynous Economies: The Business of Literature in Eighteenth-Century Britain* (Lexington: University of Kentucky Press, 1999).

Mangsen, Sandra, 'New Sources for Odes by Purcell and Handel from a Collection in London, Ontario', *Music & Letters* 81 (2000): 13–40.

Manning, Robert, Review of Franklin B. Zimmerman, *Henry Purcell: A Guide to Research*, Garland Composer Resource Manuals, vol. 18 (New York and London: Garland, 1989), in *Music & Letters* 71 (1990): 552–4.

Manning, Robert, 'Revisions and Reworkings in Purcell's Anthems', *Soundings* 9 (1982): 29–37.

Marchand, James, 'What Every Medievalist Should Know', 20, http://www.the-orb.net/wemsk/codicologywemsk.html.

Marsden, Jean I., *Fatal Desire: Women, Sexuality, and the English Stage, 1660–1720* (Ithaca: Cornell University Press, 2006).

Marshall, Robert Lewis, *The Compositional Process of J.S. Bach* (2 vols, Princeton: Princeton University Press, 1972).

Marston, Nicholas, 'Sketch', in *Grove Music Online*, http://www.oxfordmusiconline.com.

Maus, Katharine Eisaman, '"Playhouse Flesh and Blood": Sexual Ideology and the Restoration Actress', *ELH: A Journal of English Literary History* 46 (1979): 595–617.

McGuinness, Rosamond, *English Court Odes, 1660–1820*, Oxford Monographs on Music (Oxford: Clarendon, 1971).

——, 'The Ground Bass in the English Court Ode', *Music & Letters* 51 (1970): 118–40 and 265–78.

McKenzie, Donald F., 'Printers of the Mind: Some Notes on Bibliographical Theories and Printing-House Practices', *Studies in Bibliography: Papers of the Bibliographical Society of the University of Virginia* 22 (1969): 1–75.

McLean, Hugh, 'Purcell, and Blow in Japan', *Musical Times* 104 (1963): 702–5.

McManus, Clare, *Women on the Renaissance Stage: Anna of Denmark and Female Masquing in the Stuart Court 1590–1619* (Manchester: Manchester University Press, 2002).

McVeagh, John, *Thomas Durfey and Restoration Drama: The Work of a Forgotten Writer*, Studies in Early Modern English Literature (Aldershot and Burlington: Ashgate, 2000).

Mendel, Arthur, 'Recent Developments in Bach Chronology', *Musical Quarterly*, 46 (1960): 283–300.

Mendelson, Sara and Patricia Crawford, *Women in Early Modern England, 1550–1720* (Oxford: Clarendon, 1998).

Miehling, Klaus, 'Das Tempo bei Henry Purcell', *Basler Jahrbuch für historische Musikpraxis* 15 (1991): 117–47.

Milhous, Judith, 'Betterton, Thomas', in *Oxford Dictionary of National Biography*, http://www.oxforddnb.com (last accessed 1 April 2011).

——, 'The Multimedia Spectacular on the Restoration Stage', in Shirley Strum Kenny (ed.), *British Theatre and the Other Arts, 1660–1800* (Washington DC: Folger Shakespeare Library; London: Associated University Presses, 1984), pp. 41–66.

——, 'Opera Finances in London, 1674–1738', *Journal of the American Musicological Society* 37 (1984): 567–92.

——, *Thomas Betterton and the Management of Lincoln's Inn Fields, 1695–1708* (Carbondale: Southern Illinois University Press, 1979).

Milhous, Judith and Robert D. Hume, 'Dating Play Premières from Publication Data, 1660–1700', *Harvard Library Bulletin* 22 (1974): 374–405.

——, *Vice Chamberlain Coke's Theatrical Papers 1706–1715: Edited from the Manuscripts in the Harvard Theatre Collection and Elsewhere* (Carbondale: Southern Illinois University Press, 1982).

Miller, Anthony, 'The Roman Triumph in Purcell's Odes', *Music & Letters* 83 (2002): 371–82.

Milsom, John, 'Absorbing Lassus', *Early Music* 33 (2005): 305–20.

——, 'Analysing Josquin', in Richard Sherr (ed.), *The Josquin Companion* (Oxford: Oxford University Press, 2000), pp. 431–84.

——, 'Crecquillon, Clemens, and Four-Vice "Fuga"', in Eric Jas (ed.), *Beyond Contemporary Fame: Reassessing the Art of Clemens non Papa and Thomas Crecquillon* (Turnhout: Brepols, 2005), pp. 293–345.

Miserandino-Gaherty, Cathie, 'The Codicology and Rastrology of GB-Ob Mus. Sch. MSS c. 64–9: Manuscripts in Support of Transmission Theory', *Chelys*, 25 (1996–97): 78–87.

Moore, Robert Etheridge, *Henry Purcell and the Restoration Theatre* (Cambridge, MA: Harvard University Press; London: Heinemann, 1961).

Morris, Timothy, 'Voice Ranges, Voice Types, and Pitch in Purcell's Concerted Works', in Michael Burden (ed.), *Performing the Music of Henry Purcell* (Oxford: Clarendon, 1996), pp. 130–42.

Moschini, Daniela (trans. Conor Fahy), 'La Marqua d'Acqua: a System for the Digital recording of Watermarks', in Mosser, Daniel W., Michael Saffle and

Ernest W. Sullivan (eds), *Puzzles in Paper: Concepts in Historical Watermarks* (New Castle, DE: Oak Knoll Press; London: British Library, 2000), pp. 187–92.

Mosser, Daniel W., Michael Saffle and Ernest W. Sullivan (eds), *Puzzles in Paper: Concepts in Historical Watermarks* (New Castle, DE: Oak Knoll Press; London: British Library, 2000).

Mosser, Daniel W. and Ernest W. Sullivan II, 'The Thomas L. Gravell Watermark Archive on the Internet', in Mosser, Daniel W., Michael Saffle and Ernest W. Sullivan (eds), *Puzzles in Paper: Concepts in Historical Watermarks* (New Castle, DE: Oak Knoll Press; London: British Library, 2000), pp. 211–28.

Mullally, Robert, 'A Female Aeneas?' *Musical Times* 130 (1989): 80–82.

Muller, Frans and Julie, 'Completing the Picture: The Importance of Reconstructing Early Opera', *Early Music* 33 (2005): 667–81.

Muller, Julia (ed.), 'Thomas Betterton, *The Prophetess: Or, the History of Dioclesian*', in Michael Burden (ed.) *Henry Purcell's Operas: The Complete Texts* (Oxford: Oxford University Press, 2000), 171–251.

——, *Words and Music in Henry Purcell's First Semi-Opera, Dioclesian: An Approach to Early Music through Early Theatre*, Studies in the History and Interpretation of Music, vol. 28 (Lewiston, Queenston and Lampeter: Edwin Mellen Press, 1990).

Muller, Julia and Frans, 'Purcell's *Dioclesian* on the Dorset Garden Stage', in Michael Burden (ed.), *Performing the Music of Henry Purcell* (Oxford: Oxford University Press, 1996), pp. 232–42.

Murata, Margaret, 'Roman Cantata Scores as Traces of Musical Culture and Signs of its Place in Society', in Angelo Pompilio (ed.), *Atti del XIV congresso della Società internazionale di musicologia, Bologna, 1987: trasmissione e recezione delle forme di cultura musicale* (3 vols, Turin: Edizioni di Torino, 1990), vol. 3, pp. 272–84.

Myers, Robin, Michael Harris and Giles Mandelbrote (eds), *Music and the Book Trade: From the Sixteenth to the Twentieth Century* (New Castle, DE: Oak Knoll Press; London: The British Library, 2008).

Needham, Paul, 'Allan H. Stevenson and the Bibliographical Uses of Paper', *Studies in Bibliography* 47 (1994): 24–65.

Neighbour, Oliver (ed.), *Music and Bibliography: Essays in Honour of Alec Hyatt King* (New York: Saur; London: Bingley, 1980).

Neumann, Frederick, *Ornamentation in Baroque and Post-Baroque Music: with Special Emphasis on J.S. Bach* (Princeton: Princeton University Press, 1978).

Newton, W. Douglas, *Catholic London* (London: Hale, 1950).

Ng, Kah-Ming, 'Ornaments, §6: English Baroque', *Grove Music Online*, http://www.oxfordmusiconline.com.

Nicoll, Allardyce, *The Development of the Theatre: A Study of Theatrical Art from the Beginnings to the Present Day* (5th rev. edn, London: Harrap, 1966).

——, *A History of English Drama 1660–1900: Vol. 1 – A History of Restoration Drama, 1660–1700* (4th edn, Cambridge: Cambridge University Press, 1952).

Notestein, Wallace, *A History of Witchcraft in England from 1558 to 1718* (New York: Russell and Russell, 1965; first published Washington: American Historical Association, 1911).

Noyes, Robert Gale, 'Conventions of Song in Restoration Tragedy', *Proceedings of the Modern Language Association*, 53 (1938): 162–88.

Ogg, David, *Europe in the Seventeenth Century* (9th edn, London: A. and C. Black, 1971).

Oliver, H.J., *Sir Robert Howard, 1626–1698): A Critical Biography* (Durham, NC: Duke University Press, 1963).

Olleson, Edward D., Susan Wollenberg and John Caldwell (eds), *The Well Enchanting Skill: Music, Poetry and Drama in the Culture of the Renaissance – Essays in Honour of F.W. Sternfeld* (Oxford; Clarendon, 1990).

Olmsted, Anthony A., 'The Capitalization of Musical Production: The Conceptual and Spatial Development of London's Public Concerts, 1660–1750', in Regula Burckhardt Qureshi (ed.), *Music and Marx: Ideas, Practice, Politics, Critical and Cultural Musicology* (New York and London: Routledge, 2002), pp. 106–38.

Orgel, Stephen, 'Acting Scripts, Performing Texts', in Randall McLeod (ed.), *Crisis in Editing: Texts of the English Renaissance – Papers given at the Twenty-Fourth Annual Conference on Editorial Problems* (New York: AMS Press, 1994), pp. 251–94.

Orgel, Stephen, *Impersonations: The Performance of Gender in Shakespeare's England* (Cambridge: Cambridge University Press, 1996).

Orgel, Stephen and Roy Strong (eds), *Inigo Jones: The Theatre of the Stuart Court including the Complete Designs for Productions at Court, for the most part in the Collection of the Duke of Devonshire, together with their Texts and Historical Documentation* (2 vols, London: Sotheby Parke Bernet; Berkeley and Los Angeles: University of California Press, 1973).

Orrell, John, *The Theatres of Inigo Jones and John Webb* (Cambridge and New York: Cambridge University Press, 1985).

Owen, Susan J. (ed.), *A Companion to Restoration Drama*, Blackwell Companions to Literature and Culture, vol. 12 (Oxford: Blackwell, 2001).

——, *Restoration Theatre and Crisis* (Oxford: Clarendon, 1996).

Owens, Jessie Ann, *Composers at Work: The Craft of Musical Composition, 1450–1600* (New York and Oxford: Oxford University Press, 1997).

—— (ed.), *'Noyses, Sounds and Sweet Aires': Music in Early Modern England* (Seattle and London: Folger Shakespeare Library, 2006).

Palmer, Fiona M., *Vincent Novello (1781–1861): Music for the Masses*, Music in Nineteenth-Century Britain (Aldershot: Ashgate, 2006).

Parrott, Andrew, *The Essential Bach Choir* (Woodbridge: Boydell and Brewer, 2000).

——, 'Falsetto and the French: "Une toute autre marche"', *Basler Jahrbuch für historische Musikpraxis* 26 (2002): 129–48.

——, 'Performing Purcell', in Michael Burden (ed.), *The Purcell Companion* (London: Faber, 1995; Portland, OR: Amadeus Press, 1995), pp. 387–444.

Paster, Gail Kern, *The Body Embarrassed: Drama and the Disciplines of Shame in Early Modern England* (Ithaca: Cornell University Press, 1993).

Pateman, Carole, *The Sexual Contract: Aspects of Patriarchal Liberalism* (Stanford: Stanford University Press, 1988).

Patterson, Annabel, *Censorship and Interpretation: The Conditions of Writing and Reading in Early Modern England* (rev. edn, Madison and London: University of Wisconsin Press, 1990).

Peacock, John, *The Stage Designs of Inigo Jones: The European Context* (Cambridge: Cambridge University Press, 1995).

Pearson, Jacqueline, *The Prostituted Muse: Images of Women and Women Dramatists, 1642–1737* (New York and London: Harvester-Wheatsheaf, 1988).

Peel, Edgar, and Pat Southern, *The Trials of the Lancashire Witches: A Study of Seventeenth-Century Witchcraft* (New York: Taplinger, 1969).

Peraino, Judith A., 'I am an Opera: Identifying with Henry Purcell's *Dido and Aeneas*', in Corinne E. Blackmer and Patricia Juliana Smith (eds), *En Travesti: Women, Gender Subversion, Opera*, Between Men – Between Women: Lesbian and Gay Studies (New York: Columbia University Press, 1995), pp. 99–131.

Peters, Julie Stone, *Theatre of the Book 1480–1880: Print, Text, and Performance in Europe* (Oxford: Oxford University Press, 2000).

Pick, John and Malcolm Anderton, *Arts Administration* (2nd edn, London and New York: Spon, 1996).

Pickering, Oliver, 'Henry Hall of Hereford's Poetical Tributes to Henry Purcell', *The Library: The Transactions of the Bibliographical Society* 16 (1994): 19–29.

Pike, Lionel, 'Alternative Versions of Purcell's "Praise the Lord, O my soul, O Lord my God"', in Patrick F. Devine and Harry M. White (eds), *The Maynooth International Musicological Conference, 1995: Selected Proceedings, II*, Irish Musical Studies, vol. 5 (Dublin: Four Courts, 1996), pp. 272–80.

——, 'The Ferial Version of Purcell's "I was glad"', *Royal Musical Association Research Chronicle* 35 (2002): 41–59.

——, 'Purcell's "Rejoice in the Lord", All Ways', *Music & Letters* 82 (2001): 391–420.

Pinnock, Andrew, 'Book IV in Plain Brown Wrappers: Translations and Travesties of Dido', in Michael Burden (ed.), *A Woman Scorn'd: Responses to the Dido Myth* (London: Faber, 1998), pp. 249–71.

——, 'A Double Vision of Albion: Allegorical Re-Alignments in the Dryden-Purcell Semi-Opera *King Arthur*', *Restoration: Studies in English Literary Culture, 1660–1700* 34 (2010): 55–81.

——, 'Fairest Isle™——Land of the Scholar-Kings', *Early Music* 23 (1995): 651–65.

——, 'The Purcell Phenomenon', in Michael Burden (ed.), *The Purcell Companion* (London: Faber, 1995; Portland, OR: Amadeus Press, 1995), pp. 3–17.

——, '"From Rosy Bowers": Coming to Purcell the Bibliographical Way', in Michael Burden (ed.), *Henry Purcell's Operas: The Complete Texts* (Oxford and New York: Oxford University Press, 2000), pp. 31–93.

——, '*King Arthur* Expos'd: A Lesson in Anatomy', in Curtis Price (ed.), *Purcell Studies* (Cambridge: Cambridge University Press, 1995), pp. 243–56.

——, 'Play into Opera: Purcell's *The Indian Queen*', *Early Music* 18 (1990): 3–21.

Pinnock, Andrew and Will Lingard, 'Seeking the Bubble: The Economic Basis of Musical Reputation, and the role of the Anniversary as Value Inflator' (Unpublished paper presented at conference Purcell, Handel, Haydn, Mendelssohn: Anniversary Reflections, Oxford, 27–29 March 2009).

Pinnock, Andrew and Bruce Wood, 'Come, Ye Sons of Art – Again: Court Cross-Subsidy for Purcell's Opera Orchestra, 1690–1695', *Early Music* 37 (2009): 445–66.

——, 'A Mangled Chime: The Accidental Death of the Opera Libretto in Civil War England', *Early Music* 36 (2008): 265–84.

Pinto, David, *For the Violls: The Consort and Dance Music of William Lawes* (Richmond: Fretwork, 1995).

——, 'New Lamps for Old: the Versions of the Royall Consort', in Andrew Ashbee (ed.), *William Lawes (1602–1645): Essays on his Life, Times and Work* (Aldershot: Ashgate, 1998), pp. 251–81.

Plank, Steven E., '"And Now About the Cauldron Sing": Music and the Supernatural on the Restoration Stage', *Early Music* 18 (1990): 392–407.

Porter, Roy, *Mind-Forg'd Manacles* (London: Athlone, 1987).

Potter, John, 'The Tenor–Castrato Connection, 1760–1860', *Early Music* 35 (2007): 97–110.

Potter, Lois, *Secret Rites and Secret Writing: Royalist Literature, 1641–1660* (Cambridge: Cambridge University Press, 1989).

Potts, Alistair James, 'The Development of the Playhouse in Seventeenth-Century London' (PhD dissertation, University of Cambridge, 1998), http://playhousehistory.co.uk.

Price, Curtis, Correspondence, *Journal of the American Musicological Society*, 64 (2011): 266–74.

——, 'Dido and Aeneas in Context', in Curtis Price (ed.), *Purcell: 'Dido and Aeneas' – An Opera*, Norton Critical Score (London: Norton, 1986), pp. 3–41.

——, 'Dido and Aeneas: Questions of Style and Evidence', *Early Music* 22 (1994): 115–25.

——, *Henry Purcell and the London Stage* (Cambridge: Cambridge University Press, 1984).

——, 'In Search of Purcell's Character', in Curtis Price (ed.), *Purcell Studies* (Cambridge: Cambridge University Press, 1995), pp. 1–5.

——., *Music in the Restoration Theatre: with a Catalogue of Instrumental Music in the Plays, 1665–1713*, Studies in Musicology, vol. 4 (Ann Arbor: UMI Research Press, 1979).

——, 'New Light on Purcell's Keyboard Music', in Curtis Price (ed.), *Purcell Studies* (Cambridge: Cambridge University Press, 1995), pp. 87–93.

——, 'Newly Discovered Autograph Keyboard Music of Purcell and Draghi', *Journal of the Royal Musical Association* 120 (1995): 77–111.

——, 'Political Allegory in Late-Seventeenth-Century English Opera', in Nigel Fortune (ed.), *Music and Theatre: Essays in Honour of Winton Dean* (Cambridge: Cambridge University Press, 1987), pp. 1–29.

——, 'Preface', in Curtis Price (ed.), *Purcell Studies* (Cambridge; Cambridge University Press, 1995), pp xi–xii.

—— (ed.), *Purcell Studies* (Cambridge: Cambridge University Press, 1995).

——, Review of Franklin B. Zimmerman, *Henry Purcell: A Guide to Research*, Garland Composer Resource Manuals, vol. 18 (New York and London: Garland, 1989), in *Early Music* 17 (1989): 575–7.

——, Review of Henry Purcell, *The Fairy Queen*, Les Arts Florissants, dir. William Christie (Harmonia Mundi, HMC 901308.09, *rec.* 1989), in *Early Music*, 18 (1990): 493–6.

Price, Curtis and Irene Cholij, 'Dido's Bass Sorceress', *Musical Times* 127 (1986): 615–18.

Price, Curtis and Judith Milhous, 'Harpsichords in the London Theatres, 1697–1715', *Early Music* 18 (1990): 38–46.

Purkiss, Diane, 'Desire and Its Deformities: Fantasies of Witchcraft in the English Civil War', *Journal of Medieval and Early Modern Studies* 27 (1997): 103–32.

——, *The Witch in History: Early Modern and Twentieth-Century Representations* (London: Routledge, 1996).

Quinsey, Katherine M. (ed.), *Broken Boundaries: Women and Feminism in Restoration Drama* (Lexington: University of Kentucky Press, 1996).

Radden, Jennifer (ed.), *The Nature of Melancholy: From Aristotle to Kristeva* (New York: Oxford University Press, 2000).

Radice, Mark, Review of Peter Holman, *Henry Purcell*, Oxford Studies of Composers (Oxford: Oxford University Press, 1994), Michael Burden, *Purcell Remembered* (London and Boston: Faber, 1995), and Curtis Price (ed.), *Purcell Studies* (Cambridge: Cambridge University Press, 1995), in *Notes*, Series 2/53 (1996–97): 791–5.

——, 'Theater Architecture at the Time of Purcell and its Influence on his "Dramatick Operas"', *Musical Quarterly* 74 (1990): 98–130.

Ravelhofer, Barbara, *The Early Stuart Masque: Dance, Costume, and Music* (Oxford: Oxford University Press, 2006).

Reimer, Stephen R., 'Manuscript Studies: Medieval and Early Modern', http://www.ualberta.ca/~sreimer/ms-course/course/defintn.htm.

Reyher, Paul, *Les Masques anglais: étude sur les ballets et la vie de cour en Angleterre (1512–1640)* (Paris: Hachette, 1909).

Rifkin, Joshua, 'Miracles, Motivicity, and Mannerism: Adrian Willaert's Videns Dominus flentes sorores Lazari and Some Aspects of Motet Composition in the 1520s', in Dolores Pesce (ed.), *Hearing the Motet: Essays on the Motet of the Middle Ages and Renaissance* (New York and Oxford: Oxford University Press, 1997), pp. 243–64.

Ring, Layton, Correspondence, 'Malice Afterthought', *Musical Times* 134 (1993): 614–15.

Roberts, David, *The Ladies: Female Patronage in Restoration Drama 1660–1700*, Oxford English Monographs (Oxford: Clarendon; New York: Oxford University Press, 1989).

——, *Thomas Betterton: The Greatest Actor of the Restoration Stage* (Cambridge and New York: Cambridge University Press, 2010).

Robins, Brian, *Catch and Glee Culture in Eighteenth-Century England* (Woodbridge: Boydell and Brewer, 2006).

Rogers, John, *The Matter of Revolution: Science, Poetry, and Politics in the Age of Milton* (Ithaca and London: Cornell University Press, 1996).

Rogers, Pat, 'The Breeches Part', in Paul-Gabriel Bouce (ed.), *Sexuality in Eighteenth-Century Britain* (Manchester: Manchester University Press, 1982), pp. 244–58.

Rogers, Vanessa, '"Britons Strike Home": Ballad Opera and the Eighteenth-Century Purcell Revival, 1728–1760' (Unpublished paper presented at conference Purcell, Handel, Haydn, Mendelssohn: Anniversary Reflections, Oxford, 27–29 March 2009).

Rohrer, Katherine T., 'Poetic Metre, Musical Metre, and the Dance in Purcell's Songs', in Curtis Price (ed.), *Purcell Studies* (Cambridge: Cambridge University Press, 1995), pp. 207–42.

Ronen, Ruth-Eva, 'Of Costume and Etiquette: Staging in the Time of Purcell', in Michael Burden (ed.) *Performing the Music of Henry Purcell* (Oxford: Clarendon, 1996), pp. 197–211.

Roper, H.R. Trevor, *Religion, the Reformation and Social Change: The European Witch-Craze of the Sixteenth and Seventeenth Centuries and Other Essays* (New York: Harper, 1969).

Rosand, Ellen, 'The Descending Tetrachord: An Emblem of Lament', *Musical Quarterly* 65 (1979): 346–59.

——, 'Operatic Madness: A Challenge to Convention', in Steven Paul Scher (ed.), *Music and Text: Critical Inquiries* (Cambridge: Cambridge University Press, 1992), pp. 241–87.

Rose, Gloria, 'A New Purcell Source', *Journal of the American Musicological Society* 25 (1972): 230–36.

Rose, Stephen, 'Memory and the Early Musician', *Early Music Performer* 13 (2004): 3–8.

Roseberry, Eric, 'The Purcell Realizations', in Christopher Palmer (ed.), *The Britten Companion* (London and Boston: Faber, 1984), pp. 356–66.

Rosenfeld, Sybil, *Georgian Scene Painters and Scene Painting* (Cambridge: Cambridge University Press, 1981).

——, *A Short History of Scene Design in Great Britain*, Drama and Theatre Studies (Oxford: Blackwell, 1973).

Rubin, Emanuel, *The English Glee in the Reign of George III: Participatory Art Music for an Urban Society* (Warren, MI: Harmonie Park Press, 2003).

Sadler, Graham, 'The Role of the Keyboard Continuo in French Opera, 1673–1776', *Early Music* 8 (1980): 148–57.

——, 'The *Basse Continue* in Lully's Operas: Evidence Old and New', in Jérôme de La Gorce and Herbert Schneider (eds), *Quellenstudien zu Jean-Baptiste Lully/L'oeuvre de Lully: Etudes des Sources – Hommage à Lionel Sawkins*, Musikwissenschaftliche Publikationen, vol. 13 (Hildesheim: Olms, 1999), pp. 382–97.

Sambrook, James, 'Walsh, William (*bap.* 1662, *d.* 1708)', in *Oxford Dictionary of National Biography*, http://www.oxforddnb.com.

Samson, Jim, 'Chopin Reception: Theory, History, Analysis', in John Rink and Jim Samson (eds), *Chopin Studies 2* (Cambridge: Cambridge University Press, 1994), pp. 1–17.

——, 'Reception', in *Grove Music Online*, http://www.oxfordmusiconline.com.

Sanford, Sally A., 'A Comparison of French and Italian Singing in the Seventeenth Century', *Journal of Seventeenth-Century Music* 1/i (1995), http://sscm-jscm.press. illinois.edu/v1/no1/sanford.html.

Sasaki, Tsutomu, 'The Dating of the Aosta Manuscript from Watermarks', *Acta Musicologica* 64 (1992): 1–16.

Saunders, Suparmi Elizabeth, *The Dating of the Trent Codices from their Watermarks: With a Study of the Local Liturgy of Trent in the Fifteenth Century*, Outstanding Dissertations in Music from British Universities (New York and London: Garland, 1989).

Savage, Roger, 'Calling Up Genius: Purcell, Roger North, and Charlotte Butler', in Michael Burden (ed.), *Performing the Music of Henry Purcell* (Oxford: Clarendon, 1996), pp. 212–31.

——, 'Producing *Dido and Aeneas*: An Investigation into Sixteen Problems', in *The Purcell Companion*, ed. Michael Burden (London: Faber, 1995; Portland, OR: Amadeus Press, 1995), pp. 445–68; originally published as 'Producing *Dido and Aeneas*', *Early Music* 4 (1976): 393–404.

——, 'The Shakespeare-Purcell *Fairy Queen*: A Defence and Recommendation', *Early Music* 1 (1973): 201–21.

Sawkins, Lionel, '*Trembleurs* and Cold People: How Should They Shiver?', in Michael Burden (ed.), *Performing the Music of Henry Purcell* (Oxford: Clarendon, 1996), pp. 243–64.

Schab, Alon, 'Distress'd Sources?: A Critical Consideration of the Authority of Purcell's *Ayres for the Theatre*', *Early Music* 37 (2009): 633–45.

——, 'Revisiting the Known and Unknown Misprints in Purcell's "Dioclesian"', *Music & Letters* 91 (2010): 343–56.

Schiebinger, Londa, 'The Philosopher's Beard: Women and Gender in Science', in Roy Porter (ed.), *The Cambridge History of Science, vol. 4: Eighteenth-Century Science* (Cambridge: Cambridge University Press, 2003), pp. 184–211.

Schiesari, Juliana, *The Gendering of Melancholia: Feminism, Psychoanalysis, and the Symbolics of Loss in Renaissance Literature* (Ithaca: Cornell University Press, 1992).

Schmalfeldt, Janet, 'In Search of Dido', *Journal of Musicology* 18 (2001): 584–615.

Scholes, Percy A., *The Life and Activities of Sir John Hawkins, Musician, Magistrate and Friend of Johnson* (London: Oxford University Press, 1953).

Schubert, Peter N., 'Hidden Forms in Palestrina's First Book of Four-Voice Motets', *Journal of the American Musicological Society* 60 (2007): 483–556.

Schulte, Alfred, 'Papiermuhlen- and Wasserzeichenforschung', *Gutenberg Jahrbuch* 9 (1934): 9–27.

Scoville, Warren C., *The Persecution of Huguenots and French Economic Development, 1680–1720* (Berkeley and Los Angeles: University of California Press, 1960).

Searle, Arthur, 'Marshall, Julian', in *Grove Music Online*, http://www. oxfordmusiconline.com.

Sedgwick, Eve, *Between Men: English Literature and Male Homosocial Desire* (New York: Columbia University Press, 1985).

Semmens, Richard, 'Dancing and Dance Music in Purcell's Operas', in Michael Burden (ed.) *Performing the Music of Henry Purcell* (Oxford: Clarendon, 1996), pp. 180–96.

——, Review of Curtis Price (ed.), *Purcell Studies* (Cambridge: Cambridge University Press, 1995), in *Music & Letters*, 78 (1997): 107–10.

Shapiro, Michael, 'The Introduction of Actresses in England: Delay or Defensiveness?', in Viviana Comensoli and Anne Russell (eds), *Enacting Gender on the English Renaissance Stage* (Urbana: University of Illinois Press, 1999), pp. 177–200.

Sharpe, James, *Instruments of Darkness: Witchcraft in England, 1550–1750* (London: Hamish Hamilton, 1996).

Sharpe, Kevin, *Criticism and Compliment: The Politics of Literature in the England of Charles I*, Cambridge Studies in Early Modern British History (Cambridge: Cambridge University Press, 1987).

Shaw, H. Watkins, 'A Cambridge Music Manuscript from the English Chapel Royal', *Music & Letters* 42 (1961): 263–7.

——, 'A Collection of Musical Manuscripts in the Autograph of Henry Purcell and Other English Composers, *c.*1665–85', *The Library: The Transactions of the Bibliographical Society*, Series 5/14 (1959): 126-31.

——, 'A Contemporary Source of English Music of the Purcellian Period', *Acta Musicologica* 31 (1959): 38–44.

——, 'Staggins, Nicholas', in *Grove Music Online*, http://www.oxfordmusiconline. com.

——, *A Study of the Bing-Gostling Part Books in the Library of York Minster together with a Systematic Catalogue* (Oxford: Oxford University Press, 1994).

——, *The Succession of Organists of the Chapel Royal and the Cathedrals of England and Wales from c.1538*, Oxford Studies in British Church Music (Oxford: Clarendon, 1991).

Shaw, H. Watkins and Robert Ford, 'Flackton, William', in *Grove Music Online*, http://www.oxfordmusiconline.com.

Shaw, Watkins, and Margaret Laurie, 'Purcell Society', in *Grove Music Online*, http:// www.oxfordmusiconline.com.

Shay, Robert, 'Bass Parts to an Unknown Purcell Suite at Yale', *Notes* Series 2/57 (2000–01): 819–33.

——, 'Henry Purcell and "Ancient" Music in Restoration England' (PhD dissertation, University of North Carolina at Chapel Hill, 1991).

——, '"Naturalizing" Palestrina and Carissimi in Late Seventeenth-Century Oxford: Henry Aldrich and His Recompositions', *Music & Letters* 77 (1996): 368–400.

——, 'Purcell as Collector of "Ancient" Music: Fitzwilliam MS 88', in Curtis Price (ed.), *Purcell Studies* (Cambridge: Cambridge University Press, 1995), pp. 35–50.

——, 'Purcell's Revisions to the Funeral Sentences Revisited', *Early Music* 26 (1998): 457–67.

——, Review of Michael Burden (ed.), *Performing the Music of Henry Purcell* (Oxford: Clarendon, 1996), in *Journal of Seventeenth-Century Music* 4/i (1998), para. 4.1, http://sscm-jscm.press.illinois.edu/v4/no1/shay.html.

Shay, Robert, Review of Michael Burden (ed.), *The Purcell Companion* (London: Faber, 1995; Portland, OR: Amadeus Press, 1995), in *Notes* Series 2/54 (1997–98): 69–71.

Shay, Robert, and Robert Thompson, *Purcell Manuscripts: The Principal Musical Sources* (Cambridge: Cambridge University Press, 2000).

Shearon, Stephen, 'Watermarks and Rastra in Neapolitan Music Manuscripts, 1700–1815', in Daniel W. Mosser, Michael Saffle and Ernest W. Sullivan (eds), *Puzzles in Paper: Concepts in Historical Watermarks* (New Castle, DE: Oak Knoll Press; London: British Library, 2000), pp. 107–24.

Shorter, Edward, *The Making of the Modern Family* (New York: Basic Books, 1977).

Simpson, Claude M., *The British Broadside Ballad and its Music* (New Brunswick: Rutgers University Press, 1966).

Small, Carol Ann, 'Phosphorescence Watermark Imaging', in Mosser, Daniel W., Michael Saffle and Ernest W. Sullivan (eds), *Puzzles in Paper: Concepts in Historical Watermarks* (New Castle, DE: Oak Knoll Press; London: British Library, 2000), pp. 169–81.

Smith, Bruce R., *The Acoustic World of Early Modern England: Attending to the O-Factor* (Chicago: University of Chicago Press, 1999).

Smith, Jeremy L. 'Watermark Evidence and the Hidden Editions of Thomas East', in Daniel W. Mosser, Michael Saffle and Ernest W. Sullivan (eds), *Puzzles in Paper: Concepts in Historical Watermarks* (New Castle, DE: Oak Knoll Press; London: British Library, 2000), pp. 67–80.

Smith, John Harrington, *The Gay Couple in Restoration Comedy* (New York: Octagon Books, 1971; first published Cambridge, MA: Harvard University Press, 1948).

Solomon, Maynard, 'The Rochlitz Anecdotes: Issues of Authenticity in Early Mozart Biography', in Cliff Eisen (ed.) *Mozart Studies* (Oxford: Clarendon, 1991), pp. 1–59.

Southern, Richard, *Changeable Scenery: Its Origin and Development in the British Theatre* (London: Faber, 1952).

Spector, Stephen (ed.) *Essays in Paper Analysis* (Washington: Folger Shakespeare Library, 1987).

Spencer, Robert, 'Singing Purcell's Songs', *Early Music Performer* 2 (1999): 3–15; 3 (1999): 2–11.

Spink, Ian, 'Purcell's Music for "The Libertine"', *Music & Letters* 81 (2000): 520–31.

——, 'Purcell's Odes: Propaganda and Panegyric', in Curtis Price (ed.), *Purcell Studies* (Cambridge: Cambridge University Press, 1995), pp. 145–71.

——, *Restoration Cathedral Music, 1660–1714*, Oxford Studies in British Church Music (Oxford: Clarendon, 1995).

Spitta, Philipp, *Johann Sebastian Bach* (2 vols, Leipzig: Breitkopf, 1873–80).

Springborg, Patricia, 'Astell, Masham, and Locke: Religion and Politics', in Hilda L. Smith (ed.), *Women Writers and the Early Modern British Political Tradition* (Cambridge: Cambridge University Press, 1998), pp. 105–25.

Squire, W. Barclay, 'Purcell's "Dido and Aeneas"', *Musical Times* 59 (1918): 252–4.

——, 'Purcell's Dramatic Music', *Sammelbände der Internationalen Musikgesellschaft* 5 (1903–04): 489–564.

——, 'An Unknown Autograph of Henry Purcell', *Musical Antiquary* 3 (1911–12): 5–17.

Staves, Susan, *Players' Scepters: Fictions of Authority in the Restoration* (Lincoln: University of Nebraska Press, 1979).

Stevenson, Allan, *The Problem of the Missale Speciale* (London: Bibliographical Society, and Pittsburg: Thomas C. Pears, 1967).

——, 'Watermarks are Twins', *Studies in Bibliography* 4 (1951–52): 57–91.

Straub, Kristina, *Sexual Suspects: Eighteenth-Century Players and Sexual Ideology* (Princeton: Princeton University Press, 1992).

Stone, George Winchester, Jr. (ed.), *The Stage and the Page: London's 'Whole Show' in the Eighteenth-Century Theatre*, Publications from the Clark Library Professorship, UCLA, vol. 6 (Berkeley and London: University of California Press, 1981).

Stone, Lawrence, *The Family, Sex, and Marriage in England 1500–1800* (New York: Harper and Row, 1977).

Stroup, Thomas B., and Arthur L. Cooke, 'Introduction to *Sophonisba*', in *The Works of Nathaniel Lee*, eds Thomas B. Stroup and Arthur L. Cooke, vol. 1 (New Brunswick: Scarecrow Press, 1954), pp. 75–80.

Stuart, David and Greg Skidmore, 'Cavalli's *Erismena*', *Early Music* 38 (2010): 482–3.

Summers, Montague, *The Restoration Theatre* (London: Kegan Paul, Trench and Trübner, 1934).

Tanselle, G. Thomas, 'Textual Instability and Editorial Idealism', *Studies in Bibliography* 49 (1996): 1–61.

Tassel, Eric Van, 'Music for the Church', in Michael Burden (ed.), *The Purcell Companion* (London: Faber, 1994; Portland, OR: Amadeus Press, 1995), pp. 101–99.

Temperley, Nicholas, 'John Playford and the Metrical Psalms', *Journal of the American Musicological Society* 25 (1972): 331–78.

——, 'John Playford and the Stationers' Company', *Music & Letters* 54 (1973): 203–12.

Thomas, Keith, *Religion and the Decline of Magic* (London: Weidenfeld and Nicolson, 1971).

——, 'Women and the Civil War Sects', *Past and Present* 13 (1958): 42–62.

Thompson, Robert, 'Draghi, Giovanni Battista (1640–1708)', in *Oxford Dictionary of National Biography*, http://www.oxforddnb.com.

——, 'English Music Manuscripts and the Fine Paper Trade, 1660–1688' (2 vols, PhD Dissertation, University of London, 1988).

——, 'A further look at the Consort Music Manuscripts in Archbishop Marsh's Library, Dublin', *Chelys* 24 (1995): 3–18.

——, 'George Jeffreys and the "Stile Nuovo" in English Sacred Music: a New Date for his Autograph Score, British Library Add. MS 10338', *Music & Letters* 70 (1989): 317–41.

——, 'Manuscript Music in Purcell's London', *Early Music* 23 (1995): 605–18.

——, 'Purcell's Great Autographs', in Curtis Price (ed.), *Purcell Studies* (Cambridge: Cambridge University Press, 1995), pp. 6–34.

——, 'The Sources of Locke's Consort "For Seaverall Friends"', *Chelys* 19 (1990): 16–44.

——, 'The Sources of Purcell's Fantasias', *Chelys* 25 (1996–97): 88–96.

Tilmouth, Michael, 'Revisions in the Chamber Music of Matthew Locke', *Proceedings of the Royal Musical Association* 98 (1971–72): 89–100.

——, 'The Technique and Forms of Purcell's Sonatas', *Music & Letters* 40 (1959): 109–21.

Tippett, Michael, Obituary of Alfred Deller, in *Early Music* 8 (1980): 43.

Toft, Robert, 'Bartleman, James', in *Grove Music Online*, http://www.oxfordmusiconline.com.

Tomlinson, Gary, *Music in Renaissance Magic: Toward a Historiography of Others* (Chicago: University of Chicago Press, 1993).

Tomlinson, Sophie, *Women on Stage in Stuart Drama* (Cambridge: Cambridge University Press, 2005).

Towne, Gary, 'Music and Liturgy in Sixteenth-Century Italy: The Bergamo Organ Book and its Liturgical Implications', *Journal of Musicology* 6 (1988): 471–509.

Trend, Michael, *The Music Makers: Heirs and Rebels of the English Musical Renaissance – Edward Elgar to Benjamin Britten* (London: Weidenfeld and Nicolson, 1985).

Trumbach, Randolph, *The Rise of the Egalitarian Family* (New York: Academic Press, 1978).

Tuppen, Sandra, 'Purcell in the Eighteenth Century: Music for the "Quality, Gentry, and Others"' (Unpublished paper presented at conference Purcell, Handel, Haydn, Mendelssohn: Anniversary Reflections, Oxford, 27–29 March 2009).

Turbet, Richard, 'Musical Antiquarian Society', in *Grove Music Online*, http://www.oxfordmusiconline.com.

——, 'The Musical Antiquarian Society, 1840–1848', *Brio* 29 (1992): 13–20.

Tyson, Alan, 'Mozart's "Haydn" Quartets: the Contribution of Paper Studies', in Christoph Wolff and Robert Riggs (eds), *The String Quartets of Haydn, Mozart and Beethoven: Studies of the Autograph Manuscripts – A Conference at Isham Memorial Library, March 15–17, 1979*, Isham Library Papers, vol. 3 (Cambridge, MA: Harvard University Press, 1980), pp. 179–90.

——, *Mozart: Studies of the Autograph Scores* (Cambridge, MA and London: Harvard University Press, 1987).

——, 'The Problem of Beethoven's "First" Leonore Overture', *Journal of the American Musicological Society* 28 (1975): 292–334.

Vander Motten, Jean-Pierre, 'Howard, Sir Robert (1626–1698)', in *Oxford Dictionary of National Biography*, http://www.oxforddnb.com.

Varwig, Bettina, '"Mutato Semper Habitu": Heinrich Schütz and the Culture of Rhetoric', *Music & Letters* 90 (2009): 215–39.

——, 'One More Time: J.S. Bach and Seventeenth-Century Traditions of Rhetoric', *Eighteenth-Century Music* 5 (2008): 179–208.

Veevers, Erica, *Images of Love and Religion: Queen Henrietta Maria and Court Entertainments* (Cambridge: Cambridge University Press, 1989).

Veith, Ilza, *Hysteria: The History of a Disease* (Chicago: University of Chicago Press, 1965).

Voorn, Henk, *De papiermolens in de provincie Noord-Holland*, De geschiedenis der Nederlandse papier-industrie, vol. 1 (Haarlem: Papierwereld, 1960).

Wainwright, Jonathan, *Musical Patronage in Seventeenth-Century England: Christopher, First Baron Hatton (1605–1670)* (Aldershot: Scolar Press; Brookfield: Ashgate, 1997).

Walker, D.P., *Spiritual and Demonic Magic: From Ficino to Campanella* (Notre Dame: University of Notre Dame Press, 1975).

Walkling, Andrew R., 'The Apotheosis of Absolutism and the Interrupted Masque: Theater, Music, and Monarchy in Restoration England', in Julia Marciari Alexander and Catharine MacLeod (eds), *Politics, Transgression, and Representation at the Court of Charles II* (New Haven and London: Yale Center for British Art/Yale University Press, 2007), pp. 193–231.

——, '"The Dating of Purcell's *Dido and Aeneas*"?: a reply to Bruce Wood and Andrew Pinnock', *Early Music* 22 (1994): 469–81.

——, 'Masque and Politics at the Restoration Court: John Crowne's *Calisto*', *Early Music* 24 (1996): 27–62.

——, 'The Masque of Actaeon and the Antimasque of Mercury: Dance, Dramatic Structure, and Tragic Exposition in *Dido and Aeneas*', *Journal of the American Musicological Society* 63 (2010): 191–242.

——, 'Performance and Political Allegory in Restoration England: What to Interpret and When', in Michael Burden (ed.), *Performing the Music of Henry Purcell* (Oxford: Clarendon, 1996), pp. 163–79.

——, 'Political Allegory in Purcell's "Dido and Aeneas"', *Music & Letters* 76 (1995): 540–71.

——, 'Politics and the Restoration Masque: The Case of *Dido and Aeneas*', in Gerald MacLean (ed.), *Culture and Society in the Stuart Restoration: Literature, Drama, History* (Cambridge: Cambridge University Press, 1995), pp. 52–69.

——, 'Politics and Theatrical Culture in Restoration England', *History Compass* 5 (2007): 1500–20.

——, Response to Curtis Price, Correspondence, *Journal of the American Musicological Society*, 64 (2011): 266–74.

Walls, Peter, 'The Baroque Era: Strings', in Howard Mayer Brown and Stanley Sadie (eds), *Performance Practice: Music after 1600*, The New Grove Handbooks in Music (Basingstoke: Macmillan, 1989), pp. 44–80.

——, *Music in the English Courtly Masque, 1604–1640*, Oxford Monographs on Music (Oxford: Clarendon, 1996).

Ward, John M., 'And who but Ladie Greensleeues', in Edward D. Olleson, Susan Wollenberg and John Caldwell (eds), *The Well Enchanting Skill: Music, Poetry, and Drama in the Culture of the Renaissance – Essays in Honour of F.W. Sternfeld* (Oxford: Clarendon, 1990), pp. 181–212.

——, 'The British Broadside Ballad and its Music', *Journal of the American Musicological Society* 20 (1967): 28–86.

——, 'The Hunt's Up', *Proceedings of the Royal Musical Association* 106 (1979–80): 1–25.

——, 'The Morris Tune', *Journal of the American Musicological Society* 39 (1986): 294–331.

——, *Music for Elizabethan Lutes: Osborn Commonplace-book Tablatures and Related Sources* (2 vols, Oxford: Oxford University Press, 1992).

Weber, Harold, *The Restoration Rake-Hero: Transformations in Sexual Understanding in Seventeenth-Century England* (Madison: University of Wisconsin Press, 1986).

Weber, William, 'The Eighteenth-Century Origins of the Musical Canon', *Journal of the Royal Musical Association* 114 (1989): 6–17.

——, 'The Intellectual Origins of Musical Canon in Eighteenth-Century England', *Journal of the American Musicological Society* 48 (1994): 488–520.

——, *The Rise of Musical Classics in Eighteenth-Century England: a Study in Canon, Ritual and Ideology* (Oxford: Clarendon, 1992).

Weil, Rachel, *Political Passions: Gender, the Family and Political Argument in England 1680–1714* (Manchester: Manchester University Press, 1999).

Weiss, Wisso and Yoshitake Kobayashi, *Katalog der Wasserzeichen in Bachs Originalhandschriften*, Neue Ausgabe sämtlicher Werke, Johann Sebastian Bach, Serie 9, vol. 1 Addenda (2 vols, Kassel, Basel and London: Bärenreiter, 1985).

Wells, Robin Headlam, 'John Dowland and Elizabethan Melancholy', *Early Music* 13 (1985): 514–28.

Westrup, Jack A., *Purcell*, The Master Musicians (rev. edn, Oxford: Oxford University Press, 1995; originally published London: Dent, 1937).

White, Bryan, 'Letter from Aleppo: Dating the Chelsea School Performance of *Dido and Aeneas*', *Early Music* 37 (2009): 417–28.

——, '"Studying a little of the *French* Air": Louis Grabu's *Albion and Albanius* and the Dramatic Operas of Henry Purcell', in Rachel Cowgill, David Cooper and Clive Brown (eds), *Art and Ideology in European Opera: Essays in Honour of Julian Rushton* (Woodbridge: Boydell and Brewer, 2010), pp. 12–39.

White, Eric Walter, 'New Light on *Dido and Aeneas*', in Imogen Holst (ed.), *Henry Purcell (1659–95): Essays on his Music* (London: Oxford University Press, 1959), pp. 14–34.

Williams, Sarah, '"Now Rise Infernal Tones": Representations of Early Modern English Witchcraft in Sound and Music' (PhD dissertation, Northwestern University, 2006).

Willis, Deborah, *Malevolent Nurture: Witch-Hunting and Maternal Power in Early Modern England* (Ithaca: Cornell University Press, 1995).

Wills, Garry, *Witches and Jesuits: Shakespeare's Macbeth* (New York: Oxford University Press, 1995).

Wilson, Elisa Fraser, 'The Countertenor Voice in the Symphony Anthems of Henry Purcell: A Study of Range and Tessitura' (DMA dissertation, University of Illinois at Urbana-Champaign, 2003).

Wilson, John Harold. *All the King's Ladies: Actresses of the Restoration* (Chicago: University of Chicago Press, 1958).

Winkler, Amanda Eubanks, 'Enthusiasm and Its Discontents: Religion, Prophecy, and Madness in the Music for *Sophonisba* and the *Island Princess*', *Journal of Musicology* 23, (2006): 307–30.

——, 'Gender and Genre: Musical Conventions on the English Stage, 1660–1705' (PhD dissertation, University of Michigan, 2000).

——, *O Let Us Howle Some Heavy Note: Music for Witches, the Melancholic, and the Mad on the Seventeenth-Century English Stage* (Bloomington: Indiana University Press, 2006).

——, 'Sexless Spirits?: Gender Ideology and Dryden's Musical Magic', *Musical Quarterly* 93 (2010): 297–328.

Winn, James Anderson, 'Dryden's Songs', in Jayne Lewis and Maxmillian E. Novak (eds), *Enchanted Ground: Reimagining John Dryden* (Toronto: University of Toronto Press, 2004), pp. 290–317.

——, *John Dryden and His World* (New Haven and London: Yale University Press, 1987).

——, '"A Versifying Maid of Honour": Anne Finch and the Libretto for *Venus and Adonis*', *Review of English Studies*, New Series 59 (2008): 67–85.

——, '*When Beauty Fires the Blood': Love and the Arts in the Age of Dryden* (Ann Arbor: University of Michigan Press, 1992).

Wintle, Christopher, 'Corelli's Tonal Models: The Trio Sonata Op. III, n.1', in Sergio Durante and Pierluigi Petrobelli (eds), *Nuovissimi studi Corelliani: atti del terzo congresso internazionale, Fusignano, 4–7 settembre, 1980*, Quaderni della Rivista italiana di musicologia, vol. 7 (Florence: Olschki, 1982), pp. 29–69.

Wolf, Eugene K., 'The Rediscovered Autograph of Mozart's Fantasy and Sonata in C Minor, K. 475/457', *Journal of Musicology* 10 (1992): 3–47.

Wolf, Eugene K. and Edward H. Roesner (eds), *Studies in Musical Sources and Style: Essays in Honour of Jan LaRue* (Madison: A-R Editions, 1990).

Wolf, Eugene K. and Jean K. Wolf, 'A Newly Identified Complex of Manuscripts from Mannheim', *Journal of the American Musicological Society* 27 (1974): 379–437.

Wolf, Jean K. and Eugene K. Wolf, 'Rastrology and its Use in Eighteenth-Century Manuscript Studies', in Eugene K. Wolf and Edward H. Roesner (eds), *Studies in Musical Sources and Style: Essays in Honour of Jan LaRue* (Madison: A-R Editions, 1990), pp. 237–92.

Wollston, Silas, 'New Light on Purcell's Early Overtures', *Early Music* 37 (2009): 647–55.

Wood, Bruce, 'Blow, John', in *Grove Music Online*, http://www.oxfordmusiconline.com.

——, 'A Coronation Anthem – Lost and Found', *Musical Times* 118 (1977): 466–8.

——, 'The First Performance of Purcell's Funeral Music for Queen Mary', in Michael Burden (ed.), *Performing the Music of Henry Purcell* (Oxford: Clarendon, 1996), pp. 61–81.

——, 'A Newly Identified Purcell Autograph', *Music & Letters* 59 (1978): 329–32.

——, 'A Note on Two Cambridge Manuscripts and their Copyists', *Music & Letters* 56 (1975): 308–12.

——, 'Only Purcell e're shall equal Blow', in Curtis Price (ed.), *Purcell Studies* (Cambridge; Cambridge University Press, 1995), pp. 106–44.

——, *Purcell: An Extraordinary Life* (London: ABRSM Publishing, 2009).

——, 'Purcell's Odes: A Reappraisal', in Michael Burden (ed.), *The Purcell Companion* (London: Faber, 1994; Portland, OR: Amadeus Press, 1995), pp. 200–53.

——, Review of *The Complete Sacred Music of Henry Purcell*, The King's Consort, dir. Robert King, vols 1 and 2 (Hyperion CDA66585 and CDA66609, *rec.* 1991–92, in *Early Music* 20 (1992): 693–4.

——, Review of Henry Purcell, *Come Ye Sons of Art, Welcome to All the Pleasures, Funeral Music for Queen Mary, Funeral Sentences*, Taverner Consort, Taverner Choir, Taverner Players, dir. Andrew Parrott (EMI Reflexe CDC 7496352, *rec.* 1988), in *Early Music* 18 (1990): 496–502.

Wood, Bruce and Andrew Pinnock, 'Not Known at this Address: More on the Dating of *Dido*' (Correspondence), *Early Music* 23 (1995): 188–9.

——, '"Singin' in the Rain": Yet More on Dating *Dido*' (Correspondence), *Early Music* 22 (1994): 365–7.

——, sleeve notes to Purcell, Henry, *Fantazias and In Nomines*, Fretwork (Virgin Veritas, 7243 5 45062 2 2, *rec.* 1995).

——, '"Unscarr'd by Turning Times"? The Dating of Purcell's *Dido and Aeneas*', *Early Music* 20 (1992): 372–90.

Woolley, Andrew, 'English Keyboard Sources and their Contexts, *c.*1660–1720' (PhD dissertation, University of Leeds, 2008).

Wright, Peter A., 'Johannes Wiser's Paper and the Copying of his Manuscripts', in Peter A. Wright (ed.), *I codici musicali trentini: nuove scoperte e nuovi orientamenti della ricerca*, Biblioteca musicale Laurence K.J. Feininger (Trent: Provincia autonoma di Trento, 1996), pp. 31–53.

——, 'Paper Evidence and the Dating of Trent 91', *Music & Letters* 76 (1995): 487–508.

——, *The Related Parts of Trent, Museo Provinciale d'Arte MSS 87 (1374) and 92 (1379): a Paleographical and Text-Critical Study*, Outstanding Dissertations in Music from British Universities (New York and London: Garland, 1989).

Wulstan, David, 'Purcell in Performance', *Leading Notes: Journal of the National Early Music Association* 5 (1995): 10–13; 6 (1996): 20–26.

Zaslaw, Neal, 'The Enigma of the Haute-Contre', *Musical Times* 115 (1974): 939–41.

Zimmerman, Franklin B., 'Anthems of Purcell and Contemporaries in a Newly Rediscovered "Gostling Manuscript"', *Acta Musicologica* 41 (1969): 55–70.

——, *Henry Purcell, 1659–1695: An Analytical Catalogue of his Music* (London: Macmillan; New York: St. Martin's Press, 1963).

——, *Henry Purcell: A Guide to Research*, Garland Composer Resource Manuals, vol. 18 (New York and London: Garland, 1989).

——, *Henry Purcell, 1659–1695. His Life and Times* (2nd edn, Philadelphia: University of Pennsylvania Press, 1983).

——, 'Purcell and Monteverdi', *Musical Times* 99 (1958): 368–9.

——, 'Purcell's Handwriting', in Imogen Holst (ed.), *Henry Purcell (1659–95): Essays on his Music* (London: Oxford University Press, 1959), pp. 103–5.

Zohn, Steven, 'Music Paper at the Dresden Court and the Chronology of Telemann's Instrumental Music', in Daniel W. Mosser, Michael Saffle and Ernest W. Sullivan (eds), *Puzzles in Paper: Concepts in Historical Watermarks* (New Castle, DE: Oak Knoll Press; London: British Library, 2000), pp. 125–68.

Zwicker, Steven N., 'How Many Political Arguments Can Dance on the Head of a Pin?', *Restoration: Studies in English Literary Culture, 1660–1700* 34 (2010): 103–16.

——, *Lines of Authority: Politics and English Literary Culture, 1649–1689* (Ithaca and London: Cornell University Press, 1993).

——, *Politics and Language in Dryden's Poetry: The Arts of Disguise* (Princeton: Princeton University Press, 1984).

Index of Purcell's Works

Catches

'Ape, a Lion, a Fox and an Ass, An' 281
'Come my Hearts, Play your Parts' 231 n. 89,
  232, 238–41
'Down with Bacchus' 230 n. 86, 232
'Glass was just Tim'd to the Critical Hour,
  The' 232
'God Save our Sov'reign Charles' 232
'Is Charleroy's Siege come to?' 203, 232
'Let us Drink to the Blades Intrench'd on
  the Shannon' 232
'Let's Live good honest Lives' 232, 236, 238
  n. 105
'My Lady's Coachman, John' 281–2
'Now England's Great Council's
  assembled' 231 n. 89, 232, 233
'Now we are Met and Humours
  Agree' 231 n. 89, 232, 235, 236 n. 97
'Room for th'Express, at Length here it
  Comes' 232, 233
'Since the Duke is Return'd' 231 n. 89, 232,
  233, 236–8, 257, 258, 281
'Surrender of Lim'rick, The' 232
''Tis Women make us Love' 293
'To this Place We're now Come' 222 n. 51
'True Englishmen, Drink a good
  Health' 230 n. 86, 232, 234–5

Instrumental Ensemble Music

Chacony 79
Fantazias 38, 109, 110, 125, 129, 160, 261–6
  Fantazia 2 82
  Fantazia 6 101 n. 117
  Fantazia 8 103, 104–5, 107

Fantazia on One Note 47
Funeral March 256 n. 163
Sonatas of Four Parts 30, 47, 51 n. 150, 72 n. 28,
  332 n. 135
  Sonata 7 35 n. 92, 47, 82, 91
  Sonata 8 47, 82–3, 91
  Sonata 9 47, 81–3, 328 n. 117, 333 n. 141
Sonatas of Three Parts 52, 54–62, 160–63
  Sonata 1 103, 125
  Sonata 2 125
  Sonata 6 104, 107
  Sonata 7 163
  Sonata 9 60
  Sonata 11 60
Suite in G 79, 258, 259 n. 174, 260

Keyboard Music

Almand in G major (Z662/ii) 152–3
New Ground, A 143, 159
Voluntary for Double Organ 142–3

Odes

Arise, my Muse 213–14
  Overture 256 n. 163
Celebrate this Festival 138, 214 n. 26, 323, 339
  n. 172
  Crown the Altar' 138
  'I Envy not the Pride of May' 257–8
Celestial Music:
  Overture 256 n. 163
Come ye Sons of Art 53, 129, 207, 214 n. 26, 327
  'Sound the Trumpet' 138
Fly, bold Rebellion 213

From Hardy Climes 209 n. 15, 260
From those Serene and Rapturous Joys 210
  'With Trumpets and Shouts' 152
Great Parent, hail! 242–3, 339 n. 172
Hail, bright Cecilia 25, 31, 109, 117, 129, 138,
  156, 157, 338 n. 169, 342
  'Hark each Tree' 138
  Symphony 157
  ''Tis Nature's Voice' 157
Love's Goddess sure was Blind 214 n. 26, 256
  Overture 256 n. 163
Now does the Glorious Day Appear 211–12,
  214 n. 26
Of Old, when Heroes thought it Base 13, 242,
  339 n. 172
Sound the Trumpet, Beat the Drum 137, 256,
  258
  'To Urania and Caesar' 247–8, 255–6
*Summer's Absence Unconcerned we Bear,
  The* 210
Swifter, Isis, Swifter Flow 99 n. 112, 210
  Symphony 35 n. 92
Welcome to All the Pleasures 122–3, 129, 332
  n. 135
  'Here the Deities' 143, 159
  Overture 155
Welcome, Vicegerent of the Mighty King 266
Welcome, welcome, Glorious Morn 214 n. 26
What shall be Done in Behalf of the Man? 202,
  209 n. 15, 236, 260
  'Long live great Charles' 257 n. 168
Who can from Joy Refrain? 25, 30, 36 n. 94,
  40, 46, 209 n. 15
  'The Father's brave' 156
  Symphony 156
Who hath Believed our Report? 90 n. 82
Why are all the Muses Mute? 213 n. 25, 260
Ye Tuneful Muses 137, 258
  'Be Lively, then, and Gay' 258
Yorkshire Feast Song, *see Of Old, when
  Heroes thought it Base*

Sacred Music

Beati omnes qui timent Dominum 259 n. 174
Be Merciful 28 n. 66
Behold now, Praise the Lord 89
Blessed are They that Fear the Lord 29, 218,
  219, 332 n. 136

Blessed is He that Considereth the Poor 46
*Blessed is He whose Unrighteousness is
  Forgiven* 95
Blessed is the Man that Feareth the Lord 45,
  46, 128
Blow up the Trumpet in Sion 220 n. 51
Bow Down thine Ear 79, 219 n. 46
Funeral Sentences 31, 35 n. 92, 73, 76–8, 81,
  84–5, 89, 91, 98
  In the Midst of Life 29, 84
  Thou Knowest, Lord (Z27) 84
  Thou Knowest, Lord (Z58C) 217–18,
    329–30
Hear me, O Lord 35 n. 92, 81
Hear my Prayer, O Lord 218, 219 n. 46
I was Glad (full anthem) 217
I was Glad (Z19) 35, 79, 217 n. 36
I Will Give Thanks unto Thee O Lord 35 n. 92
In Thee O Lord do I put my Trust 29–30, 33,
  219 n. 46
Let mine Eyes Run Down with Tears 30, 33–5,
  74, 81, 107 n. 133
Lord, how Long wilt thou be Angry? 219 n. 46
*Lord is King, and hath put on Glorious Apparel,
  The* 220 n. 50
*Lord is King, be the People never so Impatient,
  The* 200 n. 50
Lord is King, the Earth may be Glad, The 15
Lord is my Light, The 30, 33, 218, 219
My Beloved Spake 15, 35 n. 92, 46, 70–72, 73,
  78–83, 85–91, 93, 94, 98, 105–9
My Heart is Fixed 79
My Heart is Inditing 153–4, 217, 219, 256
  n. 163
My Song shall be Alway 17 n. 22, 36, 51 n. 150,
  119 n. 21, 128, 157, 219
O Consider my Adversity 25
O Give Thanks 36, 37, 44, 151, 219–20
O God, Thou hast Cast me Out 95
O Lord God of Hosts 334
O Lord, Grant the King a Long Life 219
O Lord, Rebuke me Not 45, 220 n. 50
O Lord, thou art my God 219 n. 46
O Sing unto the Lord 219
Out of the Deep 14, 30
Praise the Lord, O Jerusalem 217
*Praise the Lord, O my Soul, and All that is
  within me* 219 n. 46
*Praise the Lord, O my Soul, O Lord my
  God* 219 n. 46

Rejoice in the Lord Alway 39, 79
Save me, O God 95
Service in B♭ 51 n. 150, 334, 337
    Benedicite 35, 81
Sing unto God 17 n. 22, 36, 37
Te Deum and Jubilate 15, 51 n. 150, 61 n. 179,
    109, 316–17, 326, 327, 332
Thy way, O God 128
Turn thou us, O good Lord 220 n. 51
Way of God is an Undefiled Way, The 219

Solo Songs and Duets

Bell Barr, *see* 'I Love and I Must'
Bess of Bedlam, *see* 'From Silent Shades'
'Cease Anxious World' 15
'From Silent Shades' 123, 147–9, 150, 257,
    291–2, 322
'High on a Throne of Glitt'ring Ore' 214–15,
    221
'I Love and I Must' 48
'If Music be the Food of Love' 145–6
'If Pray'rs and Tears' 203, 221
'Incassum, Lesbia, incassum domus' 221
'Lovely Albina's come ashore' 215–16, 221
'O dive custos Auriacae domus' 221
'O Solitude' 31 n. 80, 38, 147, 150
'What a Sad Fate' 35 n. 92

Symphony Song

If ever I more Riches did Desire 124

Theatre Music

Abdelazer:
    Jig 143–4
    'Lucinda is Bewitching Fair' 146–7
    Overture 155
Amphitryon 252–3, 260
    'Fair Iris and her Swain' 253, 322
Bonduca 230 n. 85, 316, 323, 338 n. 169
    Overture 155
    'Britons Strike Home' 254, 322
Cinthia and Endimion 243 n. 118, 254
    'Musing on Cares of Human Fate' 229
Circe 260 n. 179, 297, 301

Magicians' Dance 256 n. 163
Cleomenes, The Spartan Hero:
    'No, no, poor suffering Heart' 244 nn.
    121 and 123
Comical History of Don Quixote, Part I:
    'Let the Dreadful Engines' 291, 322
Comical History of Don Quixote, Part II:
    'Genius of England' 321
Comical History of Don Quixote, Part III:
    'From Rosy Bow'rs' 278–9, 292, 322, 331
Cuckolds-Haven:
    'How Great are the Blessings' 222 n. 55,
    246–8, 255–6, 258
Dido and Aeneas 4, 10, 25, 53, 115, 117, 118,
    124, 150, 155, 157, 159, 174, 192,
    193, 203, 207–8, 222–9, 243 n. 118,
    255, 267, 279–81, 285–6, 287–8, 297,
    300–301, 305, 306, 314, 324–7, 336,
    338 n. 169, 345–7, 348–9
    'Ah! Belinda' 287, 288, 346 n. 199
    Epilogue 222
    'Fear no Danger' 323
    'Harm's our Delight' 124
    'In our Deep-vaulted Cell' 124
    'Our next Motion' 300
    Overture 156
    Prologue 222, 226–7
    'Thanks to these Lonesome Vales' 150
    'Wayward Sisters' 300
    'When I am Laid in Earth' 287, 288
Dioclesian 156, 158, 183, 187 n. 112, 188,
    189, 192, 195, 198, 250–52, 297, 301,
    315, 348
    First Act Tune 219 n. 49
    'Let the Soldiers Rejoice' 249 n. 139, 322
Distress'd Innocence 191–2, 258 n. 172, 260,
    261 n. 181
    Second Act Tune 152–3
English Lawyer, The 230 n. 85
Fairy Queen, The 16, 28, 31, 39, 129–30, 153,
    173, 174, 178, 188, 189, 190, 192, 193,
    198–9, 281, 306, 348, 349–50
    'Come let us leave the town' 130
    'If Love's a sweet Passion' 148, 153
    'Let the Fifes and the Clarions' 130
    Monkeys' Dance 193
    'Now the Night is chas'd away' 153–4
    'O Let me Weep' 287
    'One charming Night' 153
    'Thousand Ways we'll Find, A' 130

'Thus the Gloomy World' 147–8
'When I have often Heard' 145
Fool's Preferment, A 246, 253, 257, 290–91
   'Here's a Health to the King' 222 n. 55,
     246, 253
   'I'll Sail upon the Dog Star' 291
   'I Sigh'd and I Pin'd' 291
   'There's Nothing so Fatal as
     Woman' 291
Gordian Knot Unty'd, The 258 n. 172, 259–61
History of King Richard the Second, The:
   'Retir'd from any Mortal's Sight' 243
     n. 119
Indian Queen, The 183, 190, 192, 316, 323,
     339 n. 172
   'I Attempt from Lovesickness to
     Fly' 293
   Trumpet Overture 101 n. 117
   'Ye twice Ten Hundred Deities' 296
King Arthur 3, 8, 129–30, 187 n. 112, 190, 192,
     195–6, 253–5, 260 n. 179, 306, 314,
     315–16, 323, 325–8, 331, 338 n. 169,
     339 n. 172, 349
   'Come Follow me' 326
   'Come if you Dare' 148
   'Fairest Isle' 130, 148, 152, 321, 322
   First Music 258
   Frost Scene 123, 327
   Overture 256 n. 163
   Passacaglia 326
Knight of Malta, The 230 n. 85
Libertine, The 218 n. 40
   Symphony, Act V 256 n. 163
   'To Arms, heroic Prince' *see Massacre of
     Paris, The*
Married Beau, The:

Slow Aire 256 n. 163
Massacre of Paris, The:
   'Thy Genius, Lo!' 244 n. 120
   'To Arms, heroic Prince' 244 n. 120
Oedipus 316, 323, 332 n. 135, 339 n. 172
   'Music for a While' 136, 159, 296
Regulus:
   'Ah me! To many Deaths Decreed' 133–4,
     135
Richmond Heiress, The 230 n. 85
Rival Sisters, The:
   'Celia has a Thousand Charms' 286–7
   Overture 256 n. 163
Sir Anthony Love 260
Sir Barnaby Whigg:
   'Blow, Boreas, blow' 245, 246 n. 129
Sophonisba:
   'Beneath a Poplar's Shadow' 294–5
Spanish Fryar, The
   'Whilst I with Grief did on you
     Look' 244 n. 122
Theodosius 248–9, 252–3, 266
   'Now the fight's done' 238
Timon of Athens 316
Tyrannick Love:
   'Ah! How Sweet it is to Love' 256 n. 163
Virtuous Wife, The 51, 191–2
   Fourth Act Tune 256 n. 163

Misattributed Music

King Arthur:
   'St George' 328
Macbeth 323
Tempest, The 184 n. 97, 191 n. 133, 305–6,
     323, 339 n. 172

General Index

Abell, John 137
absolutism 178, 204, 272, 273 n. 13, 300
Academy of Ancient Music, The 314,
    323–5, 327, 330, 346 n. 199
Adams, Martin 6 n. 19, 101–2, 227 n. 77
Addison, Joseph 319
advertisements, newspaper 173, 316, 317, 322
Agrippa, Cornelius 294, 295
Ainsley, John-Mark 138
Albrici, Bartolomeo 132
Alcock, John 336
Aldeburgh Festival 349
Aldrich, Henry 51–2, 68, 74, 241 n. 112,
    332, 336
allegory 9–10, 201–4, 208, 215–16, 217–20,
    222, 224–30, 243–55; *see also*
    propaganda
Allestree, Richard:
    The Ladies Calling 274–5
Anne, Queen 215, 236 n. 97
anthem:
    copying of 444
    political connections 207, 216–20
    symphony anthem 38–9, 44–5, 117, 119,
        123, 128, 157, 329
    texts 217–20
    verse anthem 105, 309
    see also sacred music
antiquarianism 7, 13, 14, 29, 51–3, 71, 74,
    318, 321, 323, 330, 339 n. 175, 340
Arkwright, G.E.P. 16, 71–2, 338
Arne, Thomas:
    King Arthur 325–7, 331 n. 133
Arnold, Samuel 306, 337–8
Arnott, James 172–3
Arundell, Dennis 192, 259 n. 175, 349 n. 212
Astell, Mary 272–3

Austern, Linda 281 n. 50, 283, 293, 295
Avery, Emmet L.:
    London Stage ... Part II, The 167–8,
        171–2, 304
Avison, Charles 328–9
Ayliff, Mrs 133–4

Babell, Charles 142–4
Bach, Johann Sebastian 19, 67, 69, 102, 115,
    119, 128, 151, 304, 341 n. 182, 346
Bacilly, Bénigne de 151
Badham, Charles 71, 81, 86, 89–91, 94
Baldwin, Olive 322
ballad 249, 256–61; *see also* opera: ballad
    opera
Banister, John 179, 205
Barker, John 13–14
Barnard, John:
    First Book of Selected Church Musick 336
Bayly, Anselm:
    *Practical Treatise on Singing and
        Playing* 151
Beard, John 322
Bedford, Arthur 329
Beethoven, Ludwig van 66, 74–5, 96, 304
Behn, Aphra 274
Bell Bar 48–9
Berain, Jean 188
Bernhard, Christoph 111
Betterton, Thomas 173, 180–84, 194, 196,
    197, 199, 250–51, 313
Bickley, Francis:
    Calendar of State Papers 170
Billington, Elizabeth 322
binding 21–2, 27–30, 49
Bishops, Seven 234–5
Blome, Richard:

Cosmography and Geography 60–61
Blow, John 127, 165, 205, 221, 241 n. 112,
    332 n. 135
    autographs 14, 29, 31, 37, 38, 39, 41,
       52, 89
    as church composer 311
    as court composer 209–10
    creativity 74, 110
    Go Perjured Man 52
    handwriting 16, 71 n. 23
    Lord, Who shall dwell in Thy
       Tabernacle? 156
    Mark how the Lark and Linnet Sing 139,
       312 n. 35
    O Lord, thou art my God 218
    reception 308, 311, 328, 329, 334–5, 337
    'Rules for Playing of a Thorough-
       Bass' 160
    Service in G 110
    Venus and Adonis 97, 174, 192, 195, 223,
       226, 227 n. 75
    We will Rejoice in thy Salvation 218
    'Whilst on Septimnius's panting
       Breast' 84 n. 68
Boal, Ellen T. 119, 122, 125
Bohlman, Philip 93
Boorman, Stanley 97
Bostridge, Ian 300
Boswell, Eleanore 170–71
Bouchier, Josiah 137, 139
Bowers, Fredson 191
bowing techniques 116, 120
Bowman, Henry 15
Bowman, James 128
Bowman, John 291, 301
Boyce, William 326
    Cathedral Music 71, 328, 332 n. 135, 334,
       335, 337
Bracegirdle, Anne 244 n. 122, 291
Brémond, Sebastien:
    Ballet et musique 227
Bridge, Frederick 15, 192, 342
Briggs, Robin 297
British Broadcasting Corporation 130, 190,
    347
British Museum 15, 342
Britten, Benjamin 341 n. 182, 342, 347, 349
Bull, John 17 n. 22
Burden, Michael 8 n. 21, 47, 158, 174, 187,
      190, 193, 194, 195, 223 n. 58, 226 n. 70,

228 n. 80, 246 n. 133, 280, 287–8, 306–7,
    314, 320 n. 78, 321 n. 80, 348–9, 351
    Performing the Music of Henry Purcell 3,
      115–16
    Purcell Companion, The 3, 4, 5–6
    Purcell Remembered 305, 307 n. 20
    Woman Scorn'd, A 270
Burke, Dorothy 222, 223 n. 58
Burmeister, Joachim 111
Burney, Charles 11, 310, 328, 329
    General History, A 304–5, 330–35, 338
Burnim, Kalman A.:
    Biographical Dictionary, A, see Highfill,
      Philip H.
Burton, Robert:
    Anatomy of Melancholy 283, 284, 288,
      294
Burwell, Mary 151
Butler, James, First Duke of Ormond 242
Butler, James, Second Duke of
    Ormond 242–3
Buttrey, John 189, 205, 224–8
Byrd, William 84, 110, 321, 329, 341
Byrt, John 153
Bywaters, David 253, 254

Caccini, Giulio:
    Le nuove musiche 131–2, 133, 144–5
Cambert, Robert 135, 178, 180
Cambridge 45, 197, 349
Canfield, Douglas:
    Tricksters and Estates 281
canon:
    literary 312–13, 321, 330
    musical 308, 313, 318, 321, 351
Canterbury 14, 29, 36, 37, 45, 70, 117
Carey, Clive 349
Carey, Henry 320
Carissimi, Giacomo 332
Carr, John 27, 265 n. 200
    Comes Amoris … The Fourth Book 145–6
Carter, Stephanie 55
catch 206–8, 230–41, 243, 281–2, 293, 302;
    see also song: drinking song
Catherine of Braganza 132
Causabon, Meric 294
Cavalli, Francesco:
    Erismena 194
Cavendish, Margaret:
    The World's Olio 275

Cavendish (née Cartwright), Rhoda 47
censorship 204, 208
Chan, Mary 54
Chapel Royal 13–14, 36, 37, 39, 44, 117,
    127–8, 136, 138, 180, 186, 216, 219,
    269, 308, 328
Chappell, William 339 n. 175, 340
Charles I, King 220 n. 51, 250 n. 142, 265
    n. 197, 271, 272
Charles II, King 56, 60, 132, 134–5, 137,
    178, 181, 182–3, 200, 203, 210, 211,
    217–19, 224, 230, 234, 239 n. 107, 249,
    254, 257, 263–4, 278 n. 30
Cholij, Irena 280, 300 n. 38
Christ Church, Oxford 51, 74 n. 39, 332
Christie, William 129–30, 137, 151, 153–4
Church, John 37
Cibber, Colley 170
Civil War 175–6, 271, 298–9
Clark, Richard 16
Clark, Stuart 298 n. 129
Clarke, Jeremiah 74, 205, 315, 329 n. 120, 335
    Come, come Along with a Dance and a
        Song 311 n. 34, 312 n. 35
    I will Love thee, O Lord my Strength 218
    Shore's Trumpet Tune 98
clefs, *see* notation
codicology 2, 7, 18, 21–32, 53–63, 93
'Cold and Raw' 256–7
Cole, Suzanne 341
Coleman, Charles 132, 177
collation 25, 27–30, 56–7
Compleat Flute-Master, The 150
Concert of Antient Music, The 314, 323–4,
    326
concert, public 182, 309, 317, 322, 324
Coniack, Madame 134
Connolly, Sarah 150
consort music 156, 160, 328, 333, 343 n. 192;
    see also fantazia
continuo 116, 119, 155–62
    accompaniment styles 159–62
    instrumentation 156–9
Cook, Nicholas 68, 101
Cooke, Henry 14, 132, 145
Cooper, Barry 140
copyists, anonymous 31, 52, 153
    London A 31, 38–9, 89–90
copyright 198, 310
Corelli, Arcangelo 69, 317 n. 60, 321, 333

counterpoint, imitative 102–10, 262–6
countertenor 126, 136–9, 163; *see also*
    singing techniques
Covent Garden 349
Cowen, Tyler 196
Cowley, Abraham 211, 312
Cox, Geoffrey 140
Craig, Edward Gordon 348–9
Cranford, William 236 n. 96
creativity 65–70, 74–6, 91–3, 95–104, 109–13
Croft, William 14, 15, 37, 74, 311 n. 34, 329,
    335
    Musica Sacra 336
Cromwell, Oliver 250 n. 142, 299
Cross, Letitia 278–9, 292
Cross, Thomas 56
Crowe, Lucy 150
Crowne, John:
    Calisto 135, 173, 227, 230
Cummings, William 16, 327, 338–9, 340,
    341, 342, 343 n. 192, 349
Cusick, Suzanne 287
Cyr, Mary 125, 137

Dahlhaus, Carl 303 n. 3
Damascene, Alexander 137
Danchin, Pierre 173
Dart, Thurston 154, 190
Davenant, Alexander 183
Davenant, Charles 180, 183
Davenant, William 176–81, 199
    Circe 301
    Macbeth 179, 299, 300
    Siege of Rhodes, The 177
    Tempest, The 179, 180
Davies, Moll 278 n. 30
Davis, William 15
Day, Cyrus Lawrence 229 n. 83
    English Song Books 190
Deller, Alfred 136
Dennis, John 319
Dennison, Peter 71, 86
Dent, Edward J. 340, 342, 349
    Foundations of English Opera 175, 192
Devine, Steven 155
Dexter, Keri 44
Dieupart, Charles 142
Dolan, Francis 298, 301
Dolle, William 187
Donington, Robert 115, 119, 144, 151

Dove, Henry 265 n. 200
Dowland, John 284
Downes, John:
    Roscius Anglicanus 170, 332 n. 135
Draghi, Giovanni Battista 49–50, 118, 132, 210
    'Where art thou, God of Dreams?' 132
Dreyfus, Laurence 69, 102
Dryden, John, 8, 170, 182, 195–6, 245 n. 126,
        259, 269, 313, 346 n. 198
    Albion and Albanius 182–3, 250–51, 254
    Amphitryon 250, 252–3
    Cleomenes, The Spartan Hero 244
    creativity 111–12
    Don Sebastian 181 n. 86
    Indian Emperour, The 296
    King Arthur 253–5
    Oedipus 279, 296, 300
    Spanish Fryar, The 244 n. 122
Dublin 325 n. 100
Duffy, Maureen 47
Dugaw, Dianne 270 n. 4
Dunton, John 243 n. 117
D'Urfey, Thomas 211 n. 23, 244 n. 122, 279
    Arise my Muse 214–15
    Cinthia and Endimion 229–30
    *Comical History of Don Quixote, The First
        Part* 291, 322
    *Comical History of Don Quixote, The
        Third Part* 278–9, 292, 322
    Epilogue to *Dido and Aeneas* 222, 224,
        227 n. 74
    Fool's Preferment, A 246, 257, 290–91
    Love for Money 279
    Of Old, when Heroes thought it Base 242
    Sir Barnaby Whigg 245–6
    Virtuous Wife, The 51
Durham 45, 51
dynamics 132–4

Eccles, John 74, 195, 205, 291, 301
    'I Burn, I Burn' 244 n. 122
English Musical Renaissance 11, 338, 341–51
erotomania 10, 285–8
d'Este, Maria Beatrice 217, 218, 226–7
Evelyn, John 118, 132, 133, 137
Exclusion Crisis 231, 233 n. 90, 238, 241,
        251, 263–4, 251

Fabbri, Paolo 289–90
fantazia 110, 160, 261–6

Farmer, Thomas 221
Farrenc, Aristide 340
Farrenc, Louise 340
Fede, Innocenzo 132
Fellowes, Edmund 341
feminist studies 168–9
Ferguson, Howard 140–41, 151–3
Ferrand, Jacques:
    Erotomania 284–5, 288
Festival of Britain 342
Ficino, Marsillio 284, 294, 295
Finch, Anne 227 n. 75
Finger, Gottfried 195, 311 n. 34
Fisk, Deborah Payne:
    *Cambridge Companion to English
        Restoration Theatre, The* 270
Fiske, Roger 161
Flackton, William 14–15, 29, 70–71, 81
Flatman, Thomas 211 n. 23
Fletcher, Anthony 273, 274 n. 16
Fletcher, John:
    *The Prophetess, or the History of
        Dioclesian* 250–51
Forcer, Francis 51
Ford, Robert 73, 77–8, 81, 83, 85, 86, 91
Foucault, Michel 289
'Furstenburg, La' 51

Garrick, David 325, 326–7, 331 n. 133
Gates, Bernard 13, 157
Gaultier, Jacques 134
Gay, John:
    Beggar's Opera, The 322
gender distinctions 271–82, 284–7, 290–92,
        295–7
gender studies 271, 279–81, 298
Genest, John:
    Some Account of the English Stage 169–70
Gentleman's Journal, The 145, 221, 257
Gibbons, Christopher 110, 160
Gibbons, Orlando 50, 84, 110, 160, 329, 341
Gildon, Charles 170, 319–20
    Measure for Measure 301, 305
Gill, Pat 281
Gilman, Todd 314
Glanvill, Joseph:
    Saducismus Triumphatus 299–300
Glorious Revolution 209, 224, 231, 234–5,
        249, 251, 257, 259, 260 n. 178, 300,
        308

Gloucester 42, 44
Glyndebourne 349–50
Godt, Irving 287
Goetze, Martin 126
Goldsbrough, Arnold 190
Goodison, Benjamin 71, 306, 307, 337–8, 339
Goodson, Richard 47, 68
Gorce, Jerome de la 187
Gostling, John 41, 45, 46, 130, 218, 219, 220
Gostling, William 36, 218 n. 42
Gouk, Penelope 283, 293, 295
Gould, Robert:
    Rival Sisters, The 286–7
Grabu, Louis:
    Albion and Albanius 138, 158, 182–3, 195,
        227, 250, 252 n. 147
Graham, Colin 349
Gray, Thomas 327
Green, Mary Anne Everett:
    Calendar of State Papers 170
Greene, Maurice 329 n. 120, 336 n. 159
Greg, Walter 191
ground bass 157, 158–9, 211, 287, 288, 296,
    333 n. 144
Grove, George 341, 342
Gwyn, Nell 278 n. 30
Gwynn, Dominic 126–7

Habermas, Jürgen 201 n. 2
Haïm, Emmanuelle 155, 157
Hall, Henry 308, 312
    Yes my Aminta, 'tis too True 312 n. 35
Handel, George Frideric 184, 317–18, 322,
    324, 329 n. 120, 337–8
handwriting studies 21–2, 30–31
Hardy, William John:
    Calendar of State Papers 170
Harley, Edward 52, 94
Harman, Alec 345
Harmonicon, The 343 n. 192
Harpsichord Master, The 141
Harris, Ellen 2–3, 53, 124, 193, 226, 227,
    279, 280, 286 n. 69, 306, 314, 324–6,
    327, 336, 347
Harris, Henry 180, 181
Harrop, Sarah 322
Hart James 265 n. 200
Hawkins, James 29, 45, 74 n. 36
Hawkins, John 11, 144, 150, 310, 314 n. 46,
    328 n. 117, 329, 335, 346

General History, A 174, 304–5, 330–33
Hayes, Philip 13–15, 53, 70–72, 78, 81, 86, 90
Hayes, William 329
Haym, Nicola 156
Haynes, Bruce 126–9
Heller, Wendy 280, 287
Henrietta Maria, Queen 134, 145
Henstridge, Daniel 16, 31, 37, 42–3, 45, 74
    n. 38, 77, 81, 90, 94, 110, 117 n. 13
Heptinstall, John 54, 62, 252 n. 149
Herissone, Rebecca 31–2, 33, 37, 39, 65
    n. 1, 67–8, 74, 75, 78–9, 81–4, 91–6,
    99, 122, 162, 178, 192, 267
'Hey Boys, up go We' 236–7, 257, 258
Highfill, Philip H. 168
    Biographical Dictionary, A 167
Higney, John 307, 312–13, 316, 317, 318,
    326, 343 n. 192, 351
Hillier, Paul 237 n. 101
historiography 343–4, 348
Hobbes, Thomas:
    Leviathan 271–2, 273
Hodge, Robert 47, 51
Hogwood, Christopher 52, 190, 307, 330
    n. 124, 336, 340
Holland, A.K. 339 n. 176, 343 n. 192
Holman, Peter 1, 6, 44, 75 n. 41, 78 n. 57,
    84 n. 68, 101–2, 119, 124, 125, 128,
    157–60, 179, 190, 216 n. 35, 219, 258,
    259 n. 174, 260, 262, 282, 292
    Four and Twenty Fiddlers 115, 176
    Henry Purcell 4
Holst, Gustav 341, 344–5, 347, 348, 349, 350
Hopkins, Paul 223
Horne, George 329
Hotson, Leslie 170–71
Houck, Stacey 54, 206 n. 12
Howard, Alan 102, 104 n. 127, 147, 265–6,
    307, 314 n. 46, 331 n. 127, 335 n. 153,
    343 n. 192
Howard, Annabella (née Dyve) 48–9
Howard, Diana 47
Howard, Robert 47–8
    Indian Queen, The 296
Howe, Elizabeth 281
Howell, John 138
Hudgebutt, John:
    *Thesaurus Musicus … The Fourth
        Book* 147
Hughes, Derek:

English Drama 169
Hughes, Meirion 341 n. 182
Hughes-Hughes, Augustus 15–16, 30
Hull, Edward 52
Hume, Robert D. 170 n. 25, 171, 172, 185,
    189, 190, 196–7, 199, 205, 251 n. 143,
    270 n. 4, 315 n. 50; *see also* Milhous,
    Judith
    London Theatre World, The 166–9, 171,
      172
    Development of English Drama, The 169
Humfrey, Pelham 14, 30, 37, 39, 52, 74
    By the Waters of Babylon 89
humours 283–5, 293
Humphreys, Mark 195
Hurley, David 67

improvisation 75, 100, 118
inequality, *see* rhythmic alteration
instruments:
    bass viol 156
    bass violin 156
    double bass 156–7
    guitar 118, 159
    harpsichord 158, 159
    lute 99 n. 109, 156, 158, 159
    oboe 116, 129
    organ 126–7, 156, 160
    recorder 116, 120 n. 22 126, 127–8, 129,
      150, 154
    symbolic associations of 187
intertextuality 255–61
Isaack, William 15, 40, 46, 71 n. 23, 73 n. 32,
    86, 90–91, 94, 95, 98

Jackson, Edward 42–3, 44
James II, King 132, 200, 210, 213 n. 25, 217,
    224, 226–7, 228, 231, 234–9, 242,
    246–7, 250–51, 258, 260, 264
Jeanneret, Christine 20
Jeffreys, George 27
Jenkins, John 263, 265
Johnstone, H. Diack 141–3, 337
Jones, Edward Huws 131, 149 n. 164
Jones, Inigo 175, 176, 185, 188
Jonson, Ben 176
Jorden, Edward:
    Briefe Discourse of a Disease 285 n. 64
Joyful Cuckoldom 244 n. 123
Jullien, Gilles 142

Kenny, Elizabeth 155
Kent, Jonathan 350
Kenyon, Nicholas 1
Kerman, Joseph 66–7, 72, 73, 76, 82, 85, 90,
    101, 285 n. 68
Kéroualle, Louise de 264
keyboard music 28, 47, 49–50, 99–100, 118,
    307, 336, 340
Killigrew, Charles 180–81
Killigrew, Thomas 132, 179–80, 194, 276
King, Alec Hyatt 306, 336
King, Robert (*c.*1660–1726) 98
King, Robert (1960–) 116, 128, 130, 151,
    153, 156
King, Thomas 282
King, William 42
Klakowich, Robert 140
Köster, Patricia 292
Krummel, Donald 54

Lambert, Constant 342, 349 n. 209
Lander, Thomas 130
Langbaine, Gerard 170
Langhans, Edward A. 168, 172, 185–6
    Biographical Dictionary, see Highfill,
      Philip H.
lament, *see* song
Laqueur, Thomas 269, 272 n. 10
Laurie, Margaret 3, 120–21, 122, 123, 146,
    159, 189, 190, 191–3, 224, 305, 328
Lawes, Henry 132, 177
Lawes, William 68, 265, 312 n. 37
Leacroft, Richard:
    *The Development of the English
      Playhouse* 184–5
Ledger, Philip 349
Lee, Nathaniel:
    Massacre of Paris, The 243–4
    Oedipus, see Dryden, John
    Sophonisba 294–5
    Theodosius 248–9
Lennep, William Van:
    London Stage … Part I, The 167–8, 171–2,
      190, 304
Lenton, John:
    The Gentleman's Diversion 116, 121, 146
Leveridge, Richard 301, 315
Lewis, Anthony 190, 342
Licensing Act 204 n. 5
'Liliburlero' 260–61

Limerick, Fall of 232, 233 n. 91, 234
Lincoln 45
Lindley, David:
    The Court Masque 176
Lingard, Will 340 n. 177, 342–3
Linley, Elizabeth 322
Lister, Rebecca 290
Liverpool Sacred Harmonic and Purcell
    Society 346
Locke, John:
    Two Treatises on Government 272, 273
Locke, Matthew 39, 136, 205, 221, 265, 332
    n. 135
    Consort of Four Parts 262–3
    creativity 72–3, 74, 75–6, 104–5, 107,
        110
    manuscript sources 68, 77 n. 52, 160
    Melothesia 141
    Psyche 8 n. 21, 180, 245, 316
    as theatre composer 177, 179
    theoretical writings 141
Lockwood, Lewis 66, 75 n. 41
Loftis, John 168
Lord Chamberlain 179, 181, 184
Lord Mayor's Show 246–7
Louis XIV, King 134, 137
Love, Harold 96, 98
Lowe, Edward 68, 75–6
Lowerre, Kathryn:
    *Music and Musicians on the London
        Stage* 195
Luckett, Richard 8 n. 21, 54, 223, 305–6,
    312, 314, 317, 318, 327, 328, 330,
    333–4
Lully, Jean-Baptiste 78 n. 57, 116, 134, 155,
    158, 180, 187, 198, 326
    Cadmus et Hermione 135

MacDonald, Michael:
    Mystical Bedlam 289
Mace, Thomas:
    Musick's Monument 75–6, 112, 265
Macfarren, G. Alexander 324–5, 327, 340
McGuinness, Rosamond 211
Mack, Maynard 112
Mack, Phyllis 295
MacKinnon, Dolly 292
Macky, John 318
madness 10, 196, 284, 285, 289–95; *see also*
    song: mad song

Maidwell, Lewis 241
Maitland, J.A. Fuller 340, 341, 348
Malcolm, Alexander 129
Manning, Robert 73, 76–7, 81, 83
manuscript function:
    antiquarianism 51–3, 94
    archiving 38–42, 94
    composition 32–5, 94–5
    education 47–51
    performance 35–8, 94, 99
    transmission 42–7, 94
manuscripts:
    B-Bc V.14.981 56
    Bu 5001 13–14, 17 n. 20, 30, 33, 37
    CA Mus. 10, 11 37, 45
    Cfm 88 13, 28, 30, 38, 39–40, 46, 78, 89,
        93, 95
    Cfm 117 15, 16, 17 n. 24, 46, 71, 81, 83,
        85–90, 94, 217 n. 36
    Cfm 152 14, 17 n. 20, 36–7
    Cfm 653 51
    Cfm 683 25
    Cfm 684 40, 46
    Cjc T.2–4, T.6–8 45
    Ckc Rowe 22 17 n. 24
    Ctc RISM 2, 4 45
    Cu EDC 10/7/6 29, 45
    DRc Mus. C34 28 n. 66
    En Inglis 94 MS 3343 17 n. 20
    F-Pn Res. Vmd. 18 50
    H 30.b.10 46
    J-Tn N5/10 17 n. 22, 36
    KNt MR 2–5.3 53
    KNt MR 2–5.4 15, 72, 81, 86, 88–90
    Lam 3 16, 28, 39, 147–9, 153
    Lam 24 52
    Lbl Add. 10338 27
    Lbl Add. 15979 324 n. 98
    Lbl Add. 17801 263
    Lbl Add. 17820 81, 86 n. 78
    Lbl Add. 24889 244 n. 121
    Lbl Add. 29397 147–8
    Lbl Add. 30303 215 n. 29
    Lbl Add. 30930 13, 16, 25, 27, 28, 30, 31,
        38, 46–7, 82, 89, 91, 93, 258, 262–3,
        265 n. 201, 266 n. 204
    Lbl Add. 30931 14, 29, 78, 89, 218 n. 42,
        332 n. 136
    Lbl Add. 30932 71, 73, 78, 79, 81, 82, 83,
        85, 86, 89–90, 94, 107 n. 133

Lbl Add. 30933 74 n. 38, 110
Lbl Add. 30931–3 14, 70, 81, 91, 94
Lbl Add. 30934 13, 30, 311 n. 34
Lbl Add. 31435 263 n. 188
Lbl Add. 31445 45
Lbl Add. 31446 51
Lbl Add. 31450 324
Lbl Add. 33234 27
Lbl Add. 33240 16
Lbl Add. 34695 51
Lbl Add. 39569 50, 142–3
Lbl Add. 40139 148
Lbl Add. 47845 25
Lbl Add. 50860 90, 94
Lbl Egerton 2956 13
Lbl Harleian 7337–42 52, 90 n. 84, 94, 336
Lbl Mus. 1 3, 20, 28, 47, 49–51
Lbl R.M. 20.h.8 13, 16, 28, 30, 38–9, 89,
    93, 95, 99 n. 112, 124, 152, 210, 219,
    332
Lbl R.M. 24.e.7 247 n. 135
Lbl R.M. 24.e.9 157
Lbl R.M 27.a.1–3, 5, 6, 8 17 n. 20, 37
Lam 25 A, 25 D 324 n. 98
Lcm 993 53
Lcm 1061 41
Lcm 1172 51 n. 148
Lcm 2011 16
Lg Safe 3 16, 28, 47, 49, 99, 145, 146–7
Ll Mus. 2–4 45
Mp BRm 370 Bp35 29, 41, 42, 45, 46
Ob Mus.a.1 17 n. 20, 33, 35
Ob Mus.c.26 13, 25, 30, 31, 33–4, 74
Ob Mus.c.27 157
Ob Mus.c.27* 40, 46
Ob Mus.c.28 38
Ob Mus.Sch.c.138 104–5
Ob Mus.Sch.e.399 51
Ob Mus.Sch.e.426 50
Ob Tenbury 785 25, 152
Ob Tenbury 789 45
Ob Tenbury 1031 71, 81, 85, 86, 88–91,
    94
Ob Tenbury 1176–82 41, 45, 46
Ob Tenbury 1266 53, 124, 306 n. 13, 324
Ob Tenbury 1309 117 n. 13
Ob Tenbury 1505 41, 46
Och Mus. 3 47
Och Mus. 38 51 n. 150
Och Mus. 39 52

Och Mus. 620 47
Och Mus. 628 89
Och Mus. 766 51 n. 150
Och Mus. 787 51 n. 150
Och Mus. 824–7 51 n. 150
Och Mus. 828–31 51 n. 150
Och Mus. 1177 50, 152
Och Mus. 1188–9 17 n. 22, 36, 119 n.
    21, 128
Och Mus. 1215 44
Ooc Ua 34–7 52
US-AUS HRC [formerly Pre-1700]
    85 45, 46, 218
US-LAuc fC6966/M4/A627/1700 31, 45
    n. 123, 77–8
US-LAuc fP985/M4/C697 159
US-NH Filmer 7 259 n. 174
US-NH Osborn 9 148–9
US-NHub 9 17 n. 20
US-NHub Osborn 515 36
US-NYp Drexel 5061 262 n. 187
US-R M2040/A628/Folio 16, 89
US-Ws F 770 324 n. 98
WO A.3.4 37
Y M1 (1–8)S 41, 42
Y M12(S) 236
Marlborough, Lady 48–9
marriage 273–4, 277
Marshall, Julian 15, 72 n. 27, 340 n. 177
Marshall, Robert 67
Marston, Nicholas 67
Mary II, Queen 200, 207, 210–15, 217, 218
    n. 40, 221, 224–6, 242, 246 n. 133,
    251, 256–7, 308
Mary of Modena 132
masque, court 175–7, 188, 207, 212–13, 222,
    225
Massinger, Philip:
    The Prophetess, or the History of
        Dioclesian, see Fletcher, John
Matteis, Nicola 116
melancholia 282–8, 299
Méraux, Amédée 340
metre 3, 120–22
Miehling, Klaus 122
Milhous, Judith 159, 168, 170 n. 25, 171,
    182, 189, 190, 197, 270 n. 4; *see also*
    Hume, Robert D.
Milner, Anthony 345
Milsom, John 68–9, 104

Milton, John 272–3, 321, 331, 338
Miner, Earl 242 n. 147
Monteverdi, Claudio 17 n. 21
More, Henry 294
Morgan, Charles 27
Morley College 349
Morley, Thomas 329
Moroney, Davitt 140
Morris, Timothy 130, 138
Motteux, Peter 133
    Arsinoë 188
    Island Princess, The 187, 315, 316
Mountfort, William 290
Mullally, Robert 279
Muller, Frans 181, 186, 188–9
Muller, Julia 181, 186, 188–9, 250 n. 142
Murata, Margaret 62
Murrie, Eleanore Boswell:
    English Song Books, see Day, Cyrus
        Lawrence
Musical Antiquarian Society 324, 338, 339,
    341 n. 181

nationalism 321–2, 338, 339 n. 176, 340,
    341–2, 351
Neoplatonism 284, 294, 295–6
Neumann, Frederick 115, 154
Newmarket 210
Newton, Isaac 331, 338
Nicoll, Allardyce 171
    History of Restoration Drama, A 169, 190
Nine Years' War 24, 62
Nivers, Guillaume 142
Noblemen and Gentlemen's Catch Club,
    The 323
North, Francis 156
North, Roger 61, 112–13, 118, 125, 129,
    139–40, 151, 156, 181, 262, 304, 314
    n. 46, 318
    The Musicall Grammarian 8 n. 21,
        149–50, 155
notation 97–100, 116, 118–19, 120–25,
    138–9, 160, 162
notes inégales, see rhythmic alteration
Nottebohm, Gustav 66
Novello, Vincent 71, 72 n. 27, 86, 90 n. 84,
    337, 338, 339, 340
Noyes, Robert 293

Oates, Titus 241

ode 206, 207, 208, 209–11, 241–2, 256–60,
    310
    creativity 95
    performance practice 122–3, 129, 130,
        136, 137–8, 157, 160
    sources 38–9, 52, 119, 157
    texts 211–16, 242–3, 247
one-sex theory 269, 274–5
opera:
    all-sung 177, 179, 183, 222–9, 279,
        345–6, 348, 351
    ballad opera 322
    dramatick opera 8 n. 21, 159, 160, 172,
        181, 191, 194, 198–9, 250–51, 253–5,
        279, 307, 315, 319–20, 346 n. 198,
        348–40, 351
    Italian 316, 317–21, 322
Ord, Boris 341, 342
Orgel, Stephen 176, 191
ornamentation 100, 139–40
    keyboard 140–44
    vocal 116, 119–20, 132–4, 144–50
Osborne, Thomas 242
overdotting, *see* rhythmic alteration
overture 154–5
Owen, Susan J. 204
    Companion to Restoration Drama, A 166,
        168–9
Owens, Jessie Ann 67
Oxford 51, 76, 119, 120, 157, 221

Paisible, James 129, 252 n. 146
Palmer, Fiona 324 n. 98, 336
paper studies 18–19, 21–6, 27, 28, 29–30,
    34, 49, 56–62
Parliament 210, 231, 233 n. 90, 263–4, 273,
    300
Parrott, Andrew 3, 115–16, 120, 129, 130,
    136–7, 138, 139, 156
Parry, Charles Hubert Hastings 341, 342
    Evolution of the Art of Music, The 344
Parthenia 50
Paster, Gail Kern 298
Pate, John 281
Pateman, Carole 272 n. 11
patronage 178, 196, 201, 207, 309, 311
Patterson, Annabel 204, 228
Peacock, John 188
Pears, Peter 347 n. 205
Pearson, Jacqueline 281

Pepys, Samuel 118, 133, 145, 170
Peraino, Judith 279–80
Perrin, Pierre:
    Ariane 134, 178, 188, 194, 227
Peterborough 45
Philips, Ambrose 321 n. 80
Pickering, Oliver 308 n. 24
Pigott, Francis 31
Pike, Lionel 162
Pinnock, Andrew 4, 9, 190–91, 192, 224 n.
        66, 227, 256–7, 264 n. 196, 280–81,
        307, 340 n. 177, 341, 342–3
Pinnock, Trevor 155
Pinto, David 265
pitch standards 116, 126–30, 136–7, 163
Plank, Steven 296–7, 300
play texts:
    dating of 171–2
    epilogues 173
    as evidence for staging 184, 187
    as evidence for theatre music 191
    medical disorders referred to in 284–95
    political references in 205–6, 207–8,
        243–55
    prologues 173
    publication of 172
    witchcraft referred to in 295–7
Playford family 24, 27, 28
Playford, Henry 26
    Apollo's Banquet ... The Second Book 152
    Harmonia Sacra 54, 332
    Orpheus Britannicus 312, 313, 319
    Pleasant Musical Companion, The 332
    Second Part of Musick's Hand-maid, The 143
    Theater of Music, The 84 n. 68, 229, 332
        n. 135
    *Three Elegies upon the Much Lamented
        Loss* 221
Playford, John 54, 56, 221, 236 n. 96, 312
        n. 37
    *Brief Introduction to the Skill of Musick
        ... The Fourth Edition, A* 131–2, 133,
        144
    *Introduction to the Skill of Musick ... The
        Thirteenth Edition, An* 145, 150
    *Introduction to the Skill of Musick ... The
        Twelfth Edition, An* 105, 121–2
    Catch that Catch Can 231
    *Choice Ayres and Songs ... The Fourth
        Book* 123, 148

Pointer, John 192
political symbolism, *see* allegory *and*
        propaganda
Pope, Alexander 112, 259
Porter, Roy:
    Mind-Forg'd Manacles 289
Potter, Lois 204
Potts, Alistair 186
Prelleur, Peter 129
Price, Curtis 49–50, 154, 159, 186, 224, 225,
        226, 227, 244 n. 121, 245 n. 127, 250,
        254 n. 157, 257, 261 n. 181, 280, 285
        n. 68, 286 n. 69, 288, 291 n. 92, 293,
        300 n. 138, 342
    Henry Purcell and the London Stage 189,
        192–3, 205, 255
    Music in the Restoration Theatre 189–90
    Purcell Studies 2, 20–21, 78, 81, 91, 306
Priest, Josias 223, 279, 280
printing of music 27, 53–62, 148
Pritchard, William 237–8
prompt books 172, 184
propaganda 202–3, 206, 211–16, 230–38,
        242–3, 258; *see also* allegory
publication of music:
    for amateur market 148, 198–9, 309, 310
    associated with accuracy 336–7
    modern editions 337–42
    as monument 178, 335–9, 341
    for performance use 337, 339 n. 175
    in playbooks 249, 252–3
    posthumous 311–12, 314, 316
    as source for antiquarians 332, 335
    by subscription 339
Prynne, William:
    Histriomastix 279
Purcell Club 342
Purcell, Daniel 195, 205, 312 n. 35, 315
Purcell, Frances 48, 49, 61, 311–12, 316, 340
Purcell, Henry:
    anniversary commemorations 1–2, 3, 4,
        15, 16, 17, 195, 342–3, 347
    autograph manuscripts 13–18, 32–40,
        70–72, 73, 74
    Choice Collection of Lessons, A 121, 141,
        143, 152, 332 n. 135, 340
    *Collection of Ayres, Compos'd for the
        Theatre, A* 51, 152–3, 159, 190, 256 n.
        163, 332
    as court composer 209, 219, 256–9, 269

creativity 2–3, 8, 32–5, 39–40, 73–83,
   85–91, 94–5, 99, 102–10, 241, 258, 259
   n. 174, 263, 265–7
death 215–16, 311–12, 331
as entrepreneur 165, 308–9, 311, 314
handwriting 14–16, 30–31, 34, 36, 49
*Musical Entertainment Perform'd on
   November XII 1683, A* 51 n. 150, 332
   n. 135
as national icon 319–21, 330–31, 334–5,
   337–8, 341–3, 345–7
Orpheus Britannicus 48, 49, 152, 155,
   294, 306 n. 13, 308, 312, 313, 332, 333,
   335, 338, 344, 346 n. 199
performance history 10–11, 306,
   314–18, 321–8, 348–50
political views 200–201, 208–9, 234–5,
   254–5, 266–7
reception 3, 10–11, 52–3, 165–6, 194,
   310–14, 317–21, 326–35, 337–51
religious beliefs 200
as self-publisher 160, 198–9
*Some Select Songs as they are Sung in the
   Fairy Queen* 198–9, 332 n. 135
Sonnata's of III Parts 24, 52, 54, 55–62,
   125, 160, 162, 332
Te Deum and Jubilate 51 n. 150, 332
as teacher 47–50
Ten Sonatas in Four Parts 47, 51 n. 150,
   82–3, 332 n. 135
text setting 313–14, 319–20, 331, 344–5,
   347
as theatre composer 165, 183–4, 191–2,
   228–30, 248–9, 251–5, 269, 279,
   291–2, 296, 302, 309, 315, 344–5
theoretical writings 105, 121–2, 141
*Vocal and Instrumental Musick of The
   Prophetess, The* 51 n. 150, 54, 55,
   61–2, 198, 332
Purcell Society 71–2, 97, 121, 159, 162, 163,
   190–93, 194, 252 n. 148, 328, 338–40,
   341 n. 182, 342
Purkiss, Dianne 298–9

Quarles, Francis 312

Radu, Valentin 157
rastrology 21, 26–7, 29, 34
Ravelhofer, Barbara:
   The Early Stuart Masque 176

Ravenscroft, Edward:
   The English Lawyer 243
reception studies 303–7
Reggio, Pietro 132
   'Arise ye Subterranean Winds' 133, 147
   Art of Singing, The 120, 131, 132–4, 144,
      145–6, 150
   Songs 150 n. 167
   'Underneath this Myrtle Shade' 133
religious enthusiasm 293–5
Reyher, Paul:
   Les Masques anglais 175–6
rhetoric 111, 203, 206, 207, 211, 212–13, 214,
   225, 227 n. 75, 228–9, 233, 246, 258,
   275, 294, 300, 312 n. 37, 321 n. 80, 338
rhythmic alteration 116, 119–20, 150–55
Rich, Christopher 183, 315
Rimbault, Edward 244 n. 123, 340
Robert, David:
   Thomas Betterton 182
Robins, Brian:
   Catch and Glee Culture 282
Robinson, Daniel:
   Essay upon Vocal Musick 122
Robinson, John 172–3
Roche, Anne de la:
   Rare en tout 227
Rochester 43–4, 81, 90
Rogers, Vanessa 322
Rohrer, Katherine 2, 102
Roman Catholicism 201, 218, 228, 231, 238
   n. 105, 239 n. 107, 244 n. 122, 245,
   264, 296–7, 300, 301
Rosand, Ellen 287, 289–90
Roseingrave, Daniel 17 n. 23, 44
Rosenfeld, Sybil 187
Royal Society 269
Rye House Plot 219

Sabol, Andrew:
   Four Hundred Songs and Dances 176
sacred music 95, 126–9, 136, 160, 162, 310,
   328–30, 333, 336–8, 350; *see also*
      anthem
Sadler, Graham 158
St Paul's Cathedral 41, 91, 316
Sampson, Carolyn 150
Samson, Jim 303, 350
Savage, Roger 8 n. 21, 188, 280, 349
Sawkins, Lionel 123

Schab, Alon 55, 256 n. 163
Schiesari, Julia 284
Schmalfeldt, Janet 280, 287
Scot, Reginald:
    Discouerie of Witchcraft 299
Scotch snap 153, 155, 326
Scott, James, Duke of Monmouth 250, 264
Sebenico, Giovanni 132
Sedgewick, Eve Kosofsky 282
Sedley, Charles 211 n. 23, 214 n. 26
Settle, Elkanah:
    Empress of Morocco, The 187
    Virgin Prophetess, The 195
sexuality studies 279–81
Shadwell, Thomas 211–12
    Lancashire Witches, The 245
    Libertine, The 218 n. 40
    Psyche 180, 187, 188
    Tempest, The 157–8, 186, 187
Shakespeare, William 175, 176, 320–21, 338
    As You Like It 284
    Hamlet 292
    Macbeth 296 n. 118, 299, 300–301
    Midsummer Night's Dream, A 349, 350
    Richard II 243 n. 119
    Tempest, The 295
Shaw, Harold Watkins 3, 41
Shay, Robert 2, 3, 4, 7, 21, 40, 84, 259 n. 174
    Purcell Manuscripts 2, 21, 30, 31, 38,
        71–2, 93, 218, 220 n. 51, 257 n. 165
Shedlock, J.S. 16
Shield, William 66
Siege of Limerick 219
Simpson, Christopher:
    Compendium of Practical Musick 103–4,
        105 n. 131, 110, 124
singing techniques 116, 120, 131–6; see also
    countertenor
Skipwith, Thomas 183
Smith, Bernard 127
Smith, John Harrington 281
Smith, John Stafford 327
    Musica Antiqua 335 n. 154
song:
    drinking song 221, 222 n. 55, 239, 246,
        281–2, 333; see also catch
    lament 286–7, 302
    mad song 10, 290–92, 294–5, 302, 322,
        331
    sacred partsong 265–6

solo song 28, 38–9, 47, 102, 156, 160,
    221–2, 310, 333
symphony song 38–9, 130, 207, 216 n.
    35
Sons of the Clergy, Festival of the 316, 317
Southern, Richard:
    Changeable Scenery 185
Spectator, The 319
Spink, Ian 191, 210, 211, 222 n. 55, 233
    n. 90, 234 n. 92, 236 n. 96, 237 nn.
    101–2, 238 n. 105, 241 n. 112
Spitta, Philipp 19
Squire, William Barclay 16, 47, 223, 339 n.
    176, 340, 341, 342
Staggins, Nicholas 165, 197, 210
Stainer, John 342
Stanford, Charles Villiers 341, 342, 347, 349
    n. 209
Staves, Susan 273
Steele, Richard 319
Stevenson, Allan 19
Stradella, Alessandro 332
Stradling, Robert 341 n. 182
Strong, Roy 176
Summers, Montague 171
    Bibliography of Restoration Drama 190
    Restoration Theatre, The 166
Synopsis of Vocal Musick 145

Tallis, Thomas 84, 329, 341
Tate, Nahum 203, 211 n. 23, 242, 312 nn. 35
    and 37
    Brutus of Alba 346 n. 199
    Cuckolds-Haven 246–7
    Dido and Aeneas 222–3, 226, 227–8,
        282–3, 285, 288, 301
    History of King Richard the Second,
        The 208, 243
temperament, keyboard 120, 129
Temperley, Nicholas 54
tempo 116, 119, 120–25
Test Act 239 n. 107
theatre, London 9, 159
    actors 169, 179, 183–4, 269, 271, 279,
        300–301, 302
    actresses 168–9, 269, 276–9
    architecture 184–7
    child performers 174, 198, 276, 286
    competition in 171, 178, 182
    costumes 188

economics of 178–9, 183–4, 196–8, 199
 machinery in 180, 184–6
 management of 172, 183–4
 marketing of 197–9
 musicians in 186–7, 279
 scenery in 175, 176–7, 181, 184–6
theatre companies:
 Duke's 176, 180–81
 King's 179, 243 n. 119, 180–81, 276
 Patent 315, 316
 United 181, 182–4, 186, 315
theatre music 10, 52, 119–20, 129–30, 157–9,
   160, 189–93, 222–30, 243–61, 279,
   281, 286–7, 290, 291–4, 310, 314–18,
   321–6, 333, 350
theatres:
 Cockpit 177
 Dorset Garden 180, 181, 183, 184–6,
   191, 194, 198
 Hall Theatre, Whitehall 173
 Lincoln's Inn Fields 117, 184, 280, 313,
   315
 Theatre Royal, Drury Lane 28, 134, 179,
   181, 184–6, 188, 191, 194, 198, 229,
   315, 316
Thompson, Robert 2, 3, 7, 20, 91, 146, 262,
   263 nn. 189 and 190
 Purcell Manuscripts, *see* Shay, Robert
Thornhill, James 188
thoroughbass, *see* continuo
Three Choirs Festival 316
Tilmouth, Michael 60, 72–3, 82, 162, 304
time signatures 120–25
Tippett, Michael 66, 136, 341 n. 182, 342,
   347, 348 n. 207
Tomkins, Thomas 265 n. 197
Tomlinson, Gary 295–6
Torelli, Giacomo 188
Tosi, Pier Francesco 134, 139, 145, 149
Tovey, Donald Francis 345–6
Tucker, William 90, 94
Tudway, Thomas 52, 90 n. 84, 94, 304, 317,
   329–30, 332, 336
Tuppen, Sandra 192, 314, 323, 324 n. 95, 326
Turner, William 68, 138, 210
Twenty-Four Violins 130, 179, 186, 265 n.
   200
Tyson, Alan 19, 66

Underwood, David:

'The Poor Endymion Lov'd too
   Well' 229 n. 83
Universal Journal, The 320, 321 n. 80
updating, musical 325–8, 348–9

Van Tassel, Eric 219
Vigarani, Carlo 188
Virgil:
 Aeneid, The 222, 227, 280, 285, 288

Wainwright, Jonathan 20
Walker, D.P. 295–6
Walkling, Andrew 196, 228
Walls, Peter:
 Music in the English Courtly Masque 176
Walsh, John 61
Walsh, William 259
Walter, John 15, 38, 40, 46, 51 n. 150
watermarks 16, 19, 23–6, 29, 56–61
Webb, John 175, 177, 185
Weber, Harold:
 Restoration Rake-Hero, The 281
Weber, William 307, 313 n. 43, 314, 317,
   318, 319, 321 n. 80, 322, 324 n. 95,
   336, 351
Weil, Rachel 272 n. 11
welcome songs, *see* odes
Weldon, John 329 n. 120
Welstead, Leonard 321 n. 80
Westminster Abbey 48, 126–7, 332 n. 136,
   342, 345
Westrup, Jack A. 82 n. 65, 175, 184 n. 97,
   215, 300, 342, 343 n. 192, 345
White, Bryan 174, 195, 223–4, 279 n. 37
White, Eric Walter 305
William III, King 200, 210, 214–15, 217, 218,
   219, 224–7, 231, 234–6, 238 n. 105,
   241, 242–3, 246 n. 133, 251, 253, 260,
   308
Williams, Ralph Vaughan 1, 339 n. 176,
   341, 347, 349
Willis, Deborah 298
Wilson, Thelma 322
Wilson, Timothy 138
Winchester 44, 210, 311 n. 34
Windsor 37, 40, 46, 71 n. 23, 91, 128, 210,
   215, 219, 249, 256, 264 n. 196
Winn, James 182, 189, 215, 216 n. 32, 227
   n. 75, 254 n. 157, 255 n. 160, 270 n. 4,
   296 n. 118

Wintle, Christopher 69
Wise, Michael 241 n. 112, 329 n. 120
witchcraft 10, 196, 295–301
Wood, Anthony à:
    Athenae Oxonienses 332 n. 135
Wood, Bruce 2, 3, 4, 31 n. 80, 36, 97,
    120–21, 122, 123–4, 138, 144, 186,
    190–91, 192, 195, 210, 211, 214 n. 27,
    217, 224 n. 66, 227, 256–7, 264 n. 196,
    308 n. 24
Wood, Charles 348, 349 n. 209
women, *see* feminist studies *and* gender
    distinctions
Woolley, Andrew 32, 98–9
Worcester Cathedral 37, 128
Wren, Charles 43–4

Wren, Christopher 185
Wren, Robert 36
Wynn, Watkin Williams 323

York 242, 332

Zaslaw, Neil 137
Zimmerman, Franklin B. 15 n. 11, 215 n. 29,
    217 n. 36, 219, 220 n. 51, 234 n. 92,
    236, 237–8, 257 n. 168
    Henry Purcell: A Guide to Research 5
    Henry Purcell (1659–1695): An Analytical
    Catalogue 5, 17, 190, 217 n. 39, 230 n.
    85, 246 n. 131, 257 n. 165, 259 n. 174,
    262 n. 186
Zwicker, Steven 189, 196, 204, 208 n. 14